International Studies of the

Committee on International Relations

University of Notre Dame

American Diplomacy
in
a New Era

Hans J. Morgenthau Bernhard G. Bechhoefer L. P. Bloomfield
J. Gus Liebenow Robert H. Ferrell John C. Campbell
Fred Greene William Gerber Harold B. Hoskins

American Diplomacy in a New Era

Edited by STEPHEN D. KERTESZ

Arthur P. Whitaker *Myron Weiner* *Chitoshi Yanaga*

J. B. Duroselle *Lindsay Rogers* *Ernest Griffith*

Robert E. Elder *H. R. Ludden* *Philip E. Mosely*

UNIVERSITY OF NOTRE DAME PRESS 1961

Notre Dame, Indiana

Library of Congress Catalog Card Number: 61-8466
Manufactured in the United States

PREFACE

The Committee on International Relations decided some years ago to sponsor conferences and publish a symposium on the general role of diplomacy in the mid-20th century. *Diplomacy in a Changing World,* published in 1959, was the outcome of this effort. When the project was nearing completion it became clear that problems of American diplomacy since the Second World War have been so complex that there should be a second volume dealing specifically with them.

The present volume is, then, a modest endeavor to clarify the course of American diplomacy since 1945—its major objectives, and problems of formulating and implementing them. Part One examines major foreign policy issues, together with diplomacy involving specific areas. Part Two deals with policy-making and organizational problems. Part Three offers thoughts about the future. All the contributors to this volume are American scholars with the exception of Professor J. B. Duroselle, who appraises the virtues and shortcomings of American diplomacy through the eyes of a Frenchman.

While this second volume gathers important material and analyzes some crucial problems of American diplomacy, it is not all-inclusive. Other aspects of American foreign policy and diplomacy will appear in monographs to be published by the Committee.

The editorial task was greatly facilitated by the exemplary cooperation of all contributors. In the early stage of the volume I benefited from the wise counsel of Professor M. A. Fitzsimons of the University of Notre Dame, but to my sorrow he was unable to participate in the editorial work for reasons of health. Special thanks go to my friend of many years, Professor Robert H. Ferrell of Indiana University, who acted as editorial consultant. He read all the manuscripts and his comments and suggestions were most helpful for the solution of problems inherent in a collective work. I am grateful to my research assistants, and particularly to John Crutcher who participated in the editorial work with zeal and deep curiosity. Bernard

Browne and Peter Sampo prepared the index of names. May I also express my gratitude to the Guggenheim Foundation which made possible for me a recent trip to Western European countries for the study of NATO diplomacy.

S. D. K.

CONTENTS

1: A NEW ERA

Stephen D. Kertesz

Statesmen today have a difficult task indeed. International relations and conflicts present entirely different alternatives from those in the past. With the advent of atomic and thermonuclear weapons the character, means and ends of warfare have undergone a fundamental change. From the stone age to our time the destruction caused by war has been restricted in space, and most of the time wars were fought for limited objectives. At the time of the establishment of the modern state system war was considered a legally authorized and regulated contest of state armies. In the words of Albericus Gentilis: *Bellum est publicorum armorum justa contentio.* It is true that during two world wars the belligerents violated many rules of warfare which had been generally accepted in some earlier periods of history, but the fundamental purpose remained unchanged—to impose the victor's will on an overpowered enemy.

In the second half of the twentieth century a major war would no longer be a continuation of diplomacy by other means. After the Napoleonic era, Karl von Clausewitz, in writing his famous book on war, could have had no idea of the destructive capability of contemporary military weapons. Now it is doubtful whether in a serious armed conflict between leading powers the victor would enjoy the fruits of victory. In such cases war would not only defeat the purposes of diplomacy but would become a threat to civilization, if not to the human race. It is unlikely that statesmen of democratic countries today would deliberately resort to war as a means of resolving their differences. The prospect of an atomic holocaust makes the role of diplomacy in the peaceful solution of conflicts more important than ever before.

Meanwhile, diplomacy itself has undergone fundamental changes and today differs greatly from the diplomacy of previous eras, for a multiplicity of new factors has complicated the conduct of international affairs. Modern means of communication, personal diplomacy of leading statesmen, the increased role of specialists, and the important function of international organizations have downgraded the regular diplomatic representatives and the traditional diplomatic methods. Above all, major changes in the society of states have influenced the nature and scope of diplomatic activities and have made questionable, in many ways, the value of traditional diplomatic concepts.

Traditional diplomatic practices are not effective between communist and noncommunist states. Diplomacy in the past has operated most successfully in a state system characterized by a measure of intellectual unity that limited the ambitions of states, established a diplomatic framework, and made possible the acceptance of some general rules of conduct. The situation changed when in the 20th century an ideological conflict between the Soviet Union and the Western democracies overturned many of the principles of generations. Possessing incompatible ideologies, the two power blocs of the present century face each other under conditions that differ radically from those of previous times. There have been somewhat similar historical eras—the Muslim expansions and crusades, religious conflicts in Europe in the 16th and 17th centuries, and intense political clashes during the era of the French revolution. But those times of trouble were nothing compared to the grave split, the almost irreparable division, between the two major power blocs of today. The situation has been aggravated by the fact that the leading states in both blocs possess weapons of unprecedented power.

Still, the expansive and subversive nature of Soviet power is not the only challenge to present-day Western diplomacy. Under the impact of Western political thought, in particular the ideas of the American and French revolutions, and of modern industrial and technological advance, the whole of human society in recent years has been undergoing a momentous transformation. Western political mistakes frequently have originated in a lack of understanding of the strength and vitality of the new political and social forces in this changing world. The temptation is for Western, particularly American, political leaders to blame communist machinations for Western failures. Such attitudes attribute to communism greater strength than it has, and picture its leaders as shrewder than they really are. Because of the communist threat, adherents of some schools of thought have viewed the contemporary world crisis almost exclusively as a struggle between the communist and noncommunist worlds. This perspective is too narrow; it omits the fact of nationalism which is rampant everywhere, and also the many new social forces reshaping the images men have of themselves in newly established countries.

If communism were to disappear overnight, the international problems of the contemporary world would remain baffling. The numbers and dimensions of complicating factors in international affairs have increased and are now truly staggering. Among them are the spread of the industrial revolution and the idea of nationalism; the population explosion; new political and social revolutions and the awareness of millions throughout the world of the possibility of a better economic future; the increasing influence of ideological factors in world politics; the effect of the atomic age; the emergence of the superpowers; Europe's changed power position; the multiplication of members in the society of states; the proliferation of global, functional, and regional international organizations; and now, competition for leadership in outer space.

Then there is a special and subtle aspect of contemporary diplomacy, incapable of easy statement, which deserves some explanation. Here I refer to a misunderstanding of the distinction between diplomacy and foreign policy. Although diplomacy in a strict sense means the execution of foreign policy decisions through government channels, this volume uses the word *diplomacy* in a broad sense. Pedantic distinctions are not helpful. It is, indeed, impossible to evaluate diplomatic methods and techniques and organizational problems without considering the basic issues of foreign policy. The traditional distinction between foreign policy and diplomacy has often been blurred. Diplomatic methods and procedures may on occasion be as important as a basic policy. But—and this is the point—in the conduct of world affairs in recent years this blurring has gone too far. At conferences and summit meetings heads of government and foreign ministers decide policies, make agreements and accept obligations. Frequently they are both policy makers and negotiators. New methods used increasingly in the policy-making process and in the field of diplomacy often make it difficult if not impossible to establish a clear distinction between the flaws of diplomacy and the shortcomings of policy. Debacles in foreign affairs may come from wrong diplomatic methods as well as shortsighted policies, and often they are caused by the interaction of both. Fumbling in policies sometimes involves the choice of wrong diplomatic procedure—for example, summit meetings before the establishment of a basis of possible agreement through diplomatic channels. In such premature meetings leading statesmen face unpleasant alternatives. They may have to choose between avowal of failure, acceptance of meaningless declarations, or the making of imprudent concessions. A variety of the latter case is the conclusion of unclear agreements which the contracting parties can interpret differently. Often agreements in principle only disguise disagreements in practice. Such agreements and high-level declarations are time bombs in international politics, because the same issues will arise again and usually under worsening conditions. The Teheran, Yalta, and Potsdam agreements, the summit meeting in 1955, and the Camp David talks in 1959, are cases in point.

I have mentioned some of the new diplomatic problems of our day. It is clear that in the rapidly changing and expanding political world, diplomatic methods and procedures have become greatly diversified. The scope of diplomacy has broadened; its methods have extended into new areas in the changed political climate of world affairs. Channels and types of contemporary diplomacy may therefore be grouped conveniently into the following categories:

1. Contacts and negotiations through the usual bilateral diplomatic channels.

2. A great variety of *ad hoc* international conferences, whether of a technical nature or so-called summit meetings—political gatherings of the highest representatives of leading powers.

3. Consultative diplomacy of permanent collective bodies, such as NATO and other regional and functional organizations.

4. Open diplomacy by conference as introduced by the League of Nations and further developed after the Second World War by the United Nations. This variation of an old art has appropriately been called parliamentary diplomacy.

5. Apart from parliamentary diplomacy practiced in the UN and its organs, the diplomacy of parliamentarians has developed in the following international assemblies: (1), the Consultative Assembly of the Council of Europe; (2), the Nordic Council; (3), the Common Assembly of the European Coal and Steel Community, the European Economic Community and the European Community for Atomic Energy; (4), the Assembly of the Western European Union; (5), the Conference of NATO Parliamentarians; (6), the Benelux Parliamentary Council. Although their nature, composition, and functions differ greatly, all these international assemblies are responses to a new need in Western Europe and the North Atlantic area.

6. Cultural diplomacy and informational activities.

7. Economic diplomacy, that is, economic activities encompassing economic aid, loans, investments, and trade agreements.

8. Diplomacy through technical assistance.

9. Subsidiary but important arenas of diplomacy are the activities of nongovernmental organizations on the basis of article 71 of the Charter of the UN, and other actions of private groups and individuals in international affairs.

Some of these methods and procedures were inherited from traditional diplomacy, such as bilateral negotiations through diplomatic channels or multilateral negotiations at international conferences. Most of them are the result of recent developments. The various diplomatic methods, however, do not exclude each other; they often overlap and can be used almost simultaneously in many combinations. Thus, contemporary diplomacy is not unlike an orchestra. A band of performers and a great many instruments are present. The success of the concert greatly depends on the talent, alertness, and spirit of the conductor. If he gives the right signs, instruments will be played on time in an appropriate way. But it is easier to satisfy the orchestra members and the audience in Carnegie Hall than that enormous audience in the realm of international politics where nations with varying cultural backgrounds and often conflicting national interests react differently to the same "symphony."

These changes in diplomatic techniques and problems are naturally of great importance to the United States. While mankind has tottered between a promising future and a dead end, American foreign policy has been initiating new departures in co-operation with other nations, endeavors that have brought tremendous successes and some dismal failures. The challenges of the contemporary world have been generally recognized. Responses to them—plans for specific co-operative actions—have proved more difficult. Even so, American foreign political achievements seem almost miraculous if we take into consideration domestic and global political difficulties. A genuine world community in which all nations and people would co-operate on a friendly basis and compete only in achievements is today more of an aspiration than a reality. International life is still similar to a jungle in which reason and good will are not sufficient for survival. Where propagandists displace the diplomats, their devious campaigns make true communication between nations impossible. Traditional methods of Western diplomacy do not seem effective against communist diplomacy which operates without moral restraint and in a different system of logic. How far can American diplomacy go in the struggle against this new evil without jeopardizing the fundamental principles and values of democracy itself?

Nonetheless Americans have inherited and employed the Western methods of diplomacy and have somehow managed to maintain not merely their own freedom but that of a large part of the world. (One should perhaps add that in the new and dangerous diplomacy of the mid-20th century the United States has had no equal partners. Despite the American co-operative spirit, on important occasions a superpower is necessarily in a lonely position. Of course, former world powers may have had more experience and can boast more professional skill in diplomacy, but their historical traditions and the rigid concepts inherent therein are not always assets in a quickly changing situation.)

At the outset of the period under consideration in the present volume, roughly the years 1945-1960, the United States suffered from too optimistic a view of world affairs—one of the recurring defects of America's virtues. This was a serious handicap. A consequence of the essentially optimistic outlook of the average American is confidence in one's fellow man in foreign affairs as well as at home. This feature of American thinking explains in some measure the confidence placed in communist leaders during the Second World War. When it became obvious later that Stalin did not reciprocate American good will, choosing as he did to impose communism on nations occupied or threatened by the Red Army, the United States, through a radical reversal of traditional American policies, engaged in a policy of alliances and undertook to support Western Europe and other "freedom-loving" nations against communist expansion and subversion. If Soviet diplomacy had continued to simulate co-operation in the postwar period, the USSR probably could have obtained gigantic economic help from the United States, which stood ready to rehabilitate the entire devastated world, and first of all the Allied nations. The Marshall Plan was open to the Soviet Union, but Stalin decided against Russian and satellite participation. It was a lucky turn of affairs, for the Russians might have wrecked the Marshall Plan. The awakening of the West after 1945 was slow. The Soviet Union had a free hand during a decisive period and the United States in 1947 had to initiate the policy of containment from a very unfavorable position.

Eventually the Russians exhausted American trust and good will; the Americans thereupon rose manfully to the challenge. Events since 1947 have proved that the United States was able to face up to major Soviet challenges. Whatever the difficulties and imperfections of the American political system, repeated shocks caused by Soviet violations of agreements, communist aggression, and the vituperative attacks and twisted statements of Andrei Vyshinsky and other Soviet representatives in the meetings of the United Nations enraged even the most isolationist congressmen. Communist aggression in Greece, seizure of power in the East Central European countries, the blockade of Berlin, and aggression in Korea changed complacent American policies, provoked counter-measures and created a bond of co-operation in the free world.

There followed a series of memorable measures. The Truman Doctrine, the Marshall Plan and consequent spectacular rehabilitation of the European economy, establishment of NATO, support of integration movements in Europe, mutual security and defense agreements, and economic aid agreements were characteristic features of the new American foreign policy that began in 1947. The United States now has many well-defined obligations through NATO and the OAS in the North Atlantic and Western Hemisphere areas. In the Far East, Southern Asia, the Middle East and Africa, the United States has assumed manifold political, military and economic responsibilities, the nature and extent of which vary from country to country. The United States, as a principle of foreign policy, supports the forces fighting misery, ignorance, foreign encroachment, and subversion. A rising living standard in underdeveloped countries is one of the major political objectives of American foreign policy. These goals are in harmony with the general aspirations and interests of mankind. Popular manifestations during President Eisenhower's trip in Asian, African and Latin-American countries suggested that uncounted millions of people are aware of America's generous and peaceful policy.

Yet, a series of challenges have remained unanswered, some were met only haltingly, and new challenges have appeared on the scene. The Hungarian revolution of 1956 exposed the weakness of the American policy of liberation. It demonstrated dramatically that the West was unable to liberate the nations held in Soviet captivity. Then there have been new problems connected with economic aid. Since Europe has lost power and authority in many regions, people of underdeveloped areas look to the United States for economic help. The practice of helping one's fellow men is an American tradition; whereas development of military strength has been a reaction to Soviet policy, the idea of economic aid and technical assistance originates in deeper springs of the American conscience. But the nature and extent of economic aid is a delicate issue for which there is no readily applicable general rule. There is no substitute for wisdom and good political judgment in dealing with varying problems in specific cases. Not all underdeveloped nations can be helped equally—the needs of some are less urgent than others—and national policy has to play a decisive role in determining allocation of foreign aid. Americans have forced themselves to balance the demands of their conscience with the capabilities of their national economy. There are difficult problems here. Western diplomacy has never been confronted with issues of such complexity and magnitude.

Above all the difficulties of America and the West has loomed the problem of world communism. Communist imperialism, led by two powerful states, China and the Soviet Union, has been the chief danger of the contemporary world. Between the communist and noncommunist states the methods of diplomacy will doubtless remain crude, and the balance of power will prove precarious for the foreseeable future. At present, negotiations between free nations have an entirely different character and meaning than those with the Soviet Union and China. The application of Leninism to international relations is the fundamental cause of the cold war, for Leninist philosophy rejects the moral principles necessary for a cooperative society of states. Rules of diplomacy accepted for orderly international intercourse cannot operate between communist and noncommunist states. Diplomats representing such different state systems speak different languages—and not only linguistically. Differences in semantics have been manifestations of basic disagreements on human ends and the means to achieve them.

In relations between communist and noncommunist states, strength has proved to be the cardinal condition of effective diplomacy and for this reason the United States has sought to maintain and develop its military forces. Never before has Frederick the Great's dictum, diplomacy without armaments is like music without instruments, proved so correct. A Soviet break-through in the field of long-range missiles or other weapons development could have fatal consequences for the democracies; totalitarian leaders have little moral restraint, are not under the control of their societies, and might be tempted to deliver a knockout blow in the belief that it would make American retaliation impossible or ineffective. The deterrent to such a temptation is American control of strategic naval and air bases and superiority in weapons and means of delivery, to a degree that would make aggression unpromising.

One cannot emphasize enough that in view of the communist ideology and approach to international problems, Western strength has proved the only serious inducement for negotiation. Without deterrent power, the West is not in a negotiating position and cannot contain communist expansion. Military superiority and preparedness, however, cannot be achieved and maintained in the missile age without willingness of citizens to make sacrifices. In our time the huge costs of armaments are increased by complex modern weapons that rapidly become obsolete. The danger exists that the American society, amidst enjoyment of the highest living standard on the globe, might refuse sacrifices that threaten comfort. Such a state of mind was the overture to doom for several empires in the past, and similar attitudes weakened French and British power in the 1930s. A balanced budget is a desirable objective under normal circumstances, but overriding commitment to it can be a source of catastrophe in a situation where national existence is at stake amidst world revolutionary upheavals.

And will the American taxpayer support not merely strong military forces, but also pay willingly for economic assistance to the underdeveloped countries? Containment of communism has become more difficult in recent years because the increasing economic and industrial strength of the Soviet Union supports Premier Nikita Khrushchev's new and dynamic brand of diplomacy. Until about 1955 only the United States and other Western countries gave substantial aid to underdeveloped countries. The situation has now changed. Soviet bloc countries have developed intensive trade relations in Asia, Africa, and Latin America, and are giving substantial technical assistance and other aid to some strategically important underdeveloped states. The political implications of Soviet economic penetration appeared most clearly in the case of Cuba, for the extension of Soviet influence into the Caribbean has created an open challenge to American diplomacy.

Yet another question arises. There are some important structural shortcomings in the foreign-policy machinery of the United States that adversely affect the making and executing of American policy: Will these shortcomings be faced quickly enough? In the past, casual arrangements between branches of the American government shaped the foreign political activities of the United States. This method was satisfactory as long as a few well-informed people made the decisions in foreign affairs and as long as the United States was not a leading world power. But there has not been enough effort to meet the structural requirements of the new situation. No simple solution will suffice. Multiplication of government agencies and research organizations does not solve the problem. And although specialization is necessary in our time, debates about the relative importance of specialists and "generalists" in diplomacy do not clarify basic issues.

This problem of inefficient foreign-policy machinery is a serious matter. There are many causes of inefficiency in the machinery of contemporary American foreign relations. The sheer bigness of American diplomatic establishments abroad creates organizational and security problems. Questions connected with centralization and decentralization require solution, particularly in the case of the multiple embassies and missions in such areas as Paris. And on the domestic scene the tactical mistakes in the course of the U-2 affair in 1960 revealed and demonstrated *ad oculos* serious weaknesses in American government machinery. Lack of co-ordination of top-level government operations showed the need for organizational reform on the highest plane. It has been clear for some time that one of the pitfalls for American diplomacy is the fragmentation of the conduct and execution of American foreign policy into many separate agencies and services, both in Washington and abroad. This writer agrees wholeheartedly with Secretary Christian A. Herter that "the Secretary of State should, under the President, have in his relations with other Departments, a clear primacy in foreign relations and in all matters with a substantial effect upon foreign relations." *

There have been inadequacies in the administrative structure of American foreign relations for a long time. Since the era of Theodore Roosevelt, State Department and Foreign Service reforms have been carried out, but they have usually lagged behind requirements. The

* Secretary Herter's testimony on June 10, 1960, before the Subcommittee on National Policy Machinery of the Senate Committee on Government Operations. *Foreign Service Journal*, XXXVII (August, 1960), 21-24.

Foreign Service Act of 1946 was probably the first adequate legislative measure. Not until then did the salary level of the chiefs of American diplomatic missions change from that established in 1855. The State Department's functional difficulties have persisted to the present day. The Act of 1946 and even more recent organizational reforms have not been effectively implemented, partly because of lack of appropriations. The budget of the State Department is a convenient target for economy drives. For such reasons and many more, the State Department has seldom had an opportunity to accomplish its tasks under satisfactory conditions. Sometimes its handicaps have been overwhelming.

The unfavorable position of American diplomacy on the domestic political scene impairs its effectiveness in international politics and hinders the development of a self-assertive foreign service. There is no constituency or pressure group behind the Department of State, and the authority of American diplomats is not sufficiently recognized at home. Because of this anomalous situation, vocal amateurs often have great influence in making and executing American foreign policy. The public usually blames the State Department for policy failures and credits political leaders for success, although the truth lies many times in the opposite direction. It would be a tragedy for the American people, and the noncommunist world as well, if the United States were not to fulfill its mission in this crucial period of history and were to fail to act properly because of internal political inadequacies. Much more can be done within the limits of the existing constitutional framework to improve the handling of foreign policy, and one of the conditions for improvement is a Department of State and a Foreign Service domestically recognized as above party politics. American diplomats would thus represent to foreign nations the essential continuity of American foreign policy. Recent organizational reforms have strengthened the structure and efficiency of the American Foreign Service, yet no organizational reform can be meaningful without considerable improvement in public attitudes and Congressional actions.

There is, indeed, a brighter side to this picture. In recent years the Senate Committee on Foreign Relations has handled problems pertaining to appointments and general foreign policy questions in a nonpartisan spirit. Excellent studies on problems of American foreign policy have been prepared by American scholarly institutions in response to the request of the committee's chairman, Senator J. William Fulbright.* These are indications of a constructive Congressional role in foreign affairs.

The problems of American diplomacy remain. To embody the ideas and ideals of the Declaration of Independence in international relations is the enormous task of our time. It is both an intellectual and practical challenge. American strength is a basic necessity, but military and economic strength is not enough in the world battle of ideas. Many people look to the United States for leadership and consider America a nation of destiny. They have faith in American ability to provide a better future for mankind. If people did not have faith in Western ways of solving their problems, American diplomacy could not win the competition for men's minds. Although Americans have been primarily preoccupied with domestic affairs since the establishment of the Republic, a powerful tradition, extending from 1776 to our own time, has proclaimed political affirmations of universal validity. Americans believe in the fundamental rights and liberties of all men, and in equality of opportunity for all men. They believe in the world-wide value of democracy, in the principle that people can rule themselves. As Abraham Lincoln once said: "Our Declaration of Independence meant liberty not alone for the people of this country but hope for all the world for all future time. It means in due course the weight should be lifted from the shoulders of all men."

This creed, however, is not self-applying. Leadership in ideas and the creation of harmony in this divided and confused world is a very difficult task. We should remember the Red Queen's warning to Alice, that "it takes all the running you can do to keep in the same place." Since in our era the pace of history itself is constantly accelerating, we have to run much faster than was necessary in the past in order to make any progress. Moreover, mere running is not sufficient. Summit meetings, high-level contacts, and tours in foreign countries are no substitute for policy. To find the right direction and determine the proper pace of running—this is the difficult but essential art of American statesmanship on which the fate of mankind depends.

* For these studies see 86th Cong., 2d Sess., US Senate Committee on Foreign Relations, *United States Foreign Policy: Compilation of Studies* (2 vols., Washington, 1960).

This revolutionary epoch of our present day is a time of rising expectations and intellectual confusion, of universal social and political upheaval. Its diplomatic problems are bewildering. The authors of this volume deal in detail with these problems. American diplomacy, let us hope, will continue to operate with success according to Western traditions, endeavoring to create a measure of order out of the chaos.

PART ONE

FOREIGN POLICY ISSUES AND AREA DIPLOMACY

2: FROM WARTIME CO-OPERATION TO NATO

Stephen D. Kertesz

The United States came to world power some sixty-odd years ago in the very last years of the 19th century. Its emergence in 1898 was spectacularly sudden, and it was only natural that the American government and people would be unsure of themselves and pursue an erratic policy for some years, even decades, thereafter. In the past, great powers usually accumulated strength and acquired skill in foreign affairs through the course of many centuries. Such a gradual development had no opportunity to take place in the case of the United States. There followed a considerable uncertainty for almost a half century. Theodore Roosevelt participated with gusto in international politics, and Woodrow Wilson's wartime policy and pronouncements apparently meant the end of isolationism and the beginning of American leadership in world affairs. After the First World War, however, an isolationist attitude appeared in the 1920s which culminated in the neutrality legislation of the late 1930s. At the outbreak of the Second World War, the United States was still bound by its neutrality legislation. The subsequent cash-and-carry policy, the destroyer-bases deal, later lend-lease, and the patrolling of the Atlantic sea lanes, indicated a renewal of responsibility in American foreign policy. But the final irrevocable acceptance of leadership by the United States in the 20th century did not come until December 7, 1941. It was later characterized by Senator Arthur Vandenberg, a one-time leader of American isolationism, in the following words: "In my own mind, my convictions regarding international cooperation and collective security for peace took firm form on the afternoon of the Pearl Harbor attack. That day ended isolationism for any realist." [1]

Senator Vandenberg's recognition of America's new position in world affairs was realistic, but it did not change the fact that the

[1] Arthur H. Vandenberg, Jr., ed., *The Private Papers of Senator Vandenberg* (Boston, Mass., 1952), p. 1.

German and Japanese aggressions in 1939 and 1941 had found the United States militarily weak and psychologically unprepared. The nation was stunned by the sudden onslaught of its enemies; it had failed to understand that good intentions were of small value in a world of malevolent dictators.

In the following months the country moved to secure itself and to fight back with as many allies as possible. At the same time it sought to understand its new position in the world. The Nazi attack on Russia, and the subsequent Japanese aggression, had almost automatically established a military alliance between the Western democracies and the Soviet Union, a strange but necessary combination of powers. Success in the war, although the United States did not immediately realize it, required waging the fight against Germany and Japan in such a way that the democratic nations not only would defeat the enemy but keep a potentially dangerous ally, the USSR, from expanding territorially. The West failed to achieve this objective partly because of military weakness, partly because of political mistakes, but more particularly because of a misconception about the possibilities of postwar co-operation with Stalin. Even so, a politically and militarily unprepared United States, thrust into the war against its will, sought manfully to learn its lessons about the duties of a great power. When the war was over the lessons were not altogether learned. The nation, contrary to its frequent behavior before the crucial year 1941, this time kept trying. Finally, with the signing of the North Atlantic Treaty in 1949 the giant of the New World came politically of age. Its political awareness at last had caught up with its physical strength. The education of the North American Republic had proved a harrowing, but by 1949, a largely successful affair.

WARTIME POLICY AND ITS AFTERMATH

It is often said that during the war the Western leaders considered all issues from the point of view of military victory and did not give much thought to postwar problems. There is some truth in this allegation. The military unpreparedness of the Western democracies on the eve of the Second World War, and their consequent weakness in the first years of the war, almost obsessed the British and American leaders with the idea of military victory. This attitude was not unnatural. In an all-out struggle political ideas usually do not prevail without military victory, regardless of their intrinsic value. But surely it is not accurate to state that in the minds of the American and British leaders military considerations alone had a place during the war. In the first period of the war, the English-speaking powers, and especially the United States, had some fundamental ideas as to the future peace settlement. Some of their ideas pertained to the realm of principle, others belonged to the sphere of practical politics. The United States Government repeatedly expressed its determination not to recognize territorial changes that took place during the war and not to make final territorial agreements before the peace conference. Secretary of State Cordell Hull energetically upheld this policy during the early period of the war when the English-speaking powers were militarily weak. On his insistence the Russo-British alliance treaty, signed on May 26, 1942, omitted territorial clauses.[2]

President Roosevelt discussed in his message to Congress in January, 1941, the four essential human freedoms that were to be the foundation of the forthcoming world order, and there was considerable indication that these principles would find their way into practice. The Atlantic Charter and the United Nations declaration described these ideas in more detail, and Soviet Russia adhered to them without reservation. The acceptance by the Soviet Union of a series of interallied agreements, the dissolution of the Comintern, the nominal re-establishment in Russia of the Orthodox Church, and the emphasis on the Russian patriotic character of the war—all these factors created the impression abroad, and to some extent even in the minds of the Russian people, that serious changes had taken place in Stalin's empire.

In harmony with this belief and expectation, the Western hopes for future peace were therefore based on a new security organization to bring about world-wide co-operation. The USSR was considered one of the pillars of the forthcoming democratic world order. President Roosevelt in particular entertained optimistic hopes that he could bring the Soviet Union into a democratic world community as a genuine partner if the West only treated the Russians with patience and generosity. The prospective establishment of the UN

[2] For the background of pertinent negotiations see Winston S. Churchill, *The Grand Alliance* (Boston, 1950), pp. 628-30; *The Memoirs of Cordell Hull* (New York, 1948), II, 1165-77; Sumner Welles, *Seven Decisions that Shaped History* (New York, 1951), pp. 126-27, 134-35.

was probably the major reason why concrete plans for the reorganization of Europe were not considered during the period of wartime co-operation.

Co-operation with the Soviet Union was undoubtedly necessary while the war was going on in Europe, and Russian military intervention was thought necessary in the Far East, but President Roosevelt's ideas of Soviet-Western co-operation went far beyond immediate military considerations. He intended to develop an intimate friendship with the Russians and then solve all postwar problems in close collaboration with the Soviet Union within the framework of a general security organization.

Other factors strengthened this approach. General Charles de Gaulle's attitude did not help him make friends in London and Washington, and France did not appear to be a potentially strong power in postwar Europe. Moreover, in some important American quarters traditional suspicion against British imperialism persisted, despite the difficulties that John Bull was having in keeping his head above water. The most important factor, however, was the nature and actions of the Third Reich. Hitler's aggressions and the brutalities of the Nazi regime had provoked strong anti-German feelings in the United States, particularly in leading political circles, and during the war had created an atmosphere which prevented clear thinking on the political problems of postwar Europe. Although the Allied countries gradually accepted the idea of a punitive peace, they thought the United Nations could handle major political problems and Allied differences over the future of the defeated countries.

A punitive peace involved the destruction of German and Japanese power which, in turn, created power vacuums on each side of the Soviet Union, a nation with a strong propensity toward expansion by virtue of both its communist doctrine and the Russian imperialistic tradition. An emotional state of mind, understandable in wartime, created the atmosphere wherein the unrealistic principle of unconditional surrender, the various plans for the partition of Germany, and the Morgenthau Plan found acceptance. Such policies and the psychological reaction to strategic bombing played into Goebbels' hands, and late in 1944 an infuriated Hitler concentrated and used his remaining strategic reserves in an offensive against the Anglo-American forces in the last stage of the war. Meanwhile, the postwar position of the major victorious powers was greatly influenced by the zones of occupation, plans for which were worked out in 1943 and approved at Quebec in September, 1944, and at Yalta.

Simultaneously with these developments, lend-lease material continued to flow to the Soviet Union at an increasing rate, even after the Soviet victory at Stalingrad. Guns and other war materials were mainly produced in the USSR, but the more than 400,000 American and Canadian trucks and other lend-lease equipment increased the mobility of the Red Army when the tide of the war had turned, and greatly facilitated its rapid advance towards the heart of Europe and its occupation of East Central Europe. Without these accelerated lend-lease shipments the Russians might have reached the end of hostilities fighting on their own soil. Such a situation would have improved chances for a reasonable European settlement much more than any previous agreements, commitments, or declarations of principle accepted by the Soviet leaders.

During the war the United States tried to avoid agreements which could lead to lasting American involvement in Europe. In harmony with this traditional attitude, American political and military leaders did not want to participate in the occupation and administration of Europe outside of Italy and the American zone of Germany. In the autumn of 1943 the joint chiefs of staff decided that the United States should take no responsibilities "in the area of the Balkans including Austria." They maintained this position until John G. Winant, United States representative on the European Advisory Commission, had personally intervened, proposing to President Roosevelt that the United States participate in the Control Commission for Austria. After the renewed efforts of Winant, the joint chiefs of staff had agreed by December, 1944, that the American army would occupy and administer a zone in Austria,[3] but an extended stay of American troops in Europe was not even considered. When Stalin asked Roosevelt at Yalta to express an opinion as to how long the United States would be willing to keep occupation forces in Germany, the president replied: "I can get the people and Congress to co-operate fully for peace, but not to keep an army in Europe for a long time. Two years would be the limit." [4]

[3] See Philip E. Mosely, "Hopes and Failures: American Policy Toward East Central Europe, 1941-1947" in Stephen D. Kertesz ed., *The Fate of East Central Europe* (Notre Dame, 1956), pp. 62-63.

[4] Edward R. Stettinius, Jr., *Roosevelt and the Russians: The Yalta Conference* (Garden City, N.Y., 1949), p. 127.

The Soviet approach to postwar problems was entirely different than most Western political leaders, including those making United States policy, expected. Although Stalin did not hesitate to sign declarations of principle, his strategic planning and thinking were concentrated on specific issues, and he asked for the recognition of Soviet territorial claims as early as December, 1941, at his first meeting with Anthony Eden. In the last stage of the war the Soviet army occupied strategically important areas in the heart of Europe. In these regions the activities of the Red Army, Soviet diplomatic pressure, and internal subversion by communist agents received careful co-ordination. As a result the power situation underwent fundamental transformations in East Central Europe. Establishment of communist-dominated governments began even before the end of hostilities. Vyshinsky's visit to Rumania and his ultimatum to King Michael less than three weeks after the signing of the Yalta Agreement is a case in point.

A few days after the German surrender, Churchill expressed strong misgivings in a dramatic message to President Truman. He called the president's attention on May 12, 1945, to the Iron Curtain that had been drawn around the territories occupied by Russian troops.[5] On June 4, 1945, he suggested that the American army postpone its retreat from the central sector in Germany until "the settlement of many great things which would be the true foundation of world peace."[6] Truman, however, did not want to violate the agreement about the occupation of Germany approved by President Roosevelt, and he thought it "impossible to delay the withdrawal of American troops from the Soviet Zone in order to press the settlement of other problems."[7] At Potsdam, President Truman still "hoped that Stalin was a man who would keep his agreements";[8] and in December, 1945, his secretary of state, James F. Byrnes, still hoped that the Soviet Union and the United States had a "common purpose."[9] Conferences of American and British statesmen with Stalin clearly showed the difficulties involved in the personal diplomacy of statesmen whenever they have greatly differing backgrounds, different

[5] Winston S. Churchill, *Triumph and Tragedy* (Boston, 1953), p. 573.

[6] *Ibid.*, p. 603.

[7] *Ibid.*, p. 604.

[8] Harry S. Truman, *Year of Decisions* (Garden City, N.Y., 1955), p. 350.

[9] James F. Byrnes, *Speaking Frankly* (New York, 1947), p. 255.

views on the nature of world politics, and mutually exclusive aims and expectations for the future of mankind.

Soviet expansionist intentions had become obvious as early as 1944. The actions of the Red Army in Poland, particularly during the Warsaw revolt, and of the Russian representatives at Dumbarton Oaks and at the armistice negotiations with Bulgaria, Rumania, and Hungary, were a clear indication of Soviet policies. Consequently, in September, 1944, Secretary Hull had begun to wonder "whether Stalin and the Kremlin had determined to reverse their policy decided upon at Moscow and Tehran and to pursue a contrary course." He asked the American ambassador in Moscow, Averell Harriman, the reason for the new trend of Soviet foreign policy, and the ambassador reported: "When the Russians saw victory in sight they began to put into practice the policies they intended to follow in peace." [10]

Despite the hardly disguised Soviet policy of conquest by arms, terrorism, and subversion, the Western powers continued the policy of co-operation with the USSR even after the end of hostilities, until there was utterly no chance of co-operating further. In this period of psychological letdown the European state system had ceased to operate, the countries of Western Europe were in a condition of extreme weakness, and the American people were preparing wholeheartedly for peace. In harmony with overwhelming Congressional and popular opinion, the American army demobilized with great rapidity, despite the unsettled condition of world affairs. Moreover, Washington offered the Baruch Plan of atomic control which combined the prohibition of mass-destruction weapons with effective international inspection. In this psychological climate the Western governments and their peoples were not prepared to consider the threat or use of force, and the Soviet Union had practically a free hand to consolidate its position in the subjugated East Central European countries, and could encourage and support the Chinese communist army in China's key area, Manchuria. If Soviet diplomacy had continued to simulate co-operation in the postwar years, the USSR could have obtained gigantic economic help from the United States, which was ready to rehabilitate the devastated world, and primarily the Allied nations. Despite deteriorating relations, the United States invited the Soviet Union and the satellite states in

[10] *The Memoirs of Cordell Hull,* II, 1459-60.

June, 1947, to participate in the Marshall Plan. The Kremlin's negative attitude made such participation impossible. Europe's division into two camps thus became a reality.

THE UN AND THE BEGINNING OF THE COLD WAR

At the outset of the postwar years American foreign policy did not permit pressure on the Soviet Union because the two countries had fought together against the Nazi foe and American diplomacy in 1945 restricted itself to an attempt at persuasion and tried to continue a policy of co-operation regardless of certain aspects of American national interest. President Truman used strong words when Molotov visited him in Washington prior to the San Francisco Conference,[11] and he energetically raised issues at Potsdam, but the fact remained that tough language around the conference table did not impress the shrewd power politicians of the Kremlin because the gradually hardening Western attitude occurred after the demobilization of the American army. Diplomats who diligently drafted notes of protest against Soviet violations of agreements could hardly influence the course of events.

Only once in this period did the Americans perhaps use diplomatically their strength deriving from possession of the atomic bomb. In general this special ace in the hole remained obscurely in the background. Secretary Byrnes has written in his memoirs that a threatening Soviet attitude in northern Iran, and Stalin's speech on February 9, 1946, in which the Russian dictator announced the new Five Year Plan "with its emphasis on rearmament instead of the production of consumer goods," [12] opened the eyes of American policy makers. When Stalin received a stern warning from President Truman to evacuate Azerbaijan "or the United States would move in," [13] he understood the meaning of the message and moved out. Subsequent Soviet behavior in the Iranian conflict showed that the Kremlin was aware of the implication of the American atomic monopoly. It is unlikely that United Nations pressure alone could have forced the Soviet army to evacuate this area which has been coveted by Russia for a long time. This appears to have been the

[11] Harry S. Truman, *op. cit.*, pp. 79-82.

[12] Byrnes, *op. cit.*, p. 255.

[13] Letter of President Truman to the author, March 13, 1959, confirming this point made by him in several public statements.

only instance when the military potential inherent in the American atomic monopoly may have provided a means of diplomatic pressure —although an indirect effect of American atomic monopoly might have been the general reluctance of the Soviets in 1945-1949 to commit open military aggression outside their military sphere established during the Second World War. Churchill was probably right when he claimed that in the immediate postwar years American atomic power saved Western Europe from Soviet domination.

Meanwhile the United States put its hopes in the UN. In harmony with the declarations of principle promulgated by President Roosevelt during the war and accepted by Congress, a serious attempt was made at San Francisco to establish an effective universal organization. Unlike the Covenant of the League of Nations, the Charter of the United Nations made clear the division of power between Security Council and General Assembly. The Security Council was supposed to fulfill some major functions of an international government. To realize these functions, continued co-operation of the five permanent members would have been essential. As for the Assembly, it was to be the symbol and beginning of a world parliament. These expectations never materialized. The ultimate cause of their failure has been the division of the world by differing concepts of human ends and the ways of achieving them; the General Assembly has only reflected the existing rift between nations. Another important cause has been the lack of stability in the world setting: social, national, and political revolutionary movements further complicated the world scene. And, while the Covenant of the League was part of the peace treaties that established a new order after the First World War, the drafting of the Charter and the making of peace were two separate procedures during and after the Second World War. For many reasons, the kind of international order to be maintained by the UN was never established.

One cannot overemphasize the great political difference between the League of Nations and the United Nations. It lies not so much in the different legal structures of the Covenant and the Charter but rather in the changed nature of the world setting and in the practices of the two world organizations. Memberships in the League and in the UN reflect greatly different worlds. In the pre-1914 era, relations between the great powers in Europe decided the major issues in international politics, and as a rule the great powers did not consult the rest of the world. This situation did not change essentially under the League system. When the Soviet Union became a member during the declining period of the League, Litvinov appeared as an apostle of collective security and co-operated with the Western democracies most of the time. Russia's "record in the Council and the Assembly, and her conduct toward the aggressive powers, were more consistent with the Covenant than those of any great power." [14] But extra-European countries did not have much influence at Geneva. The smaller European nations usually had influence only when their policies were in harmony with those of the great powers.

The United Nations reflects the picture of a different world. Its organs deal with the staggering international problems of the atomic age. Since the UN is primarily a political and not a legal organization, its potentialities are limited by the facts of contemporary world politics. One of the most important factors is the role of Soviet diplomacy, which is fundamentally different than it was in Litvinov's time. In the UN the Soviet Union is not only the fighting leader of the communist camp, but an eager protector of all nationalist movements that it can use to weaken the Western countries. "National liberation" is considered but the first step toward a communist system. Nikita Khrushchev expressed this old communist precept quite bluntly during the revolutionary events of 1958 in Iraq.[15] While the Kremlin has established in East Central Europe a new brand of colonialism, Soviet delegates in the UN support all anticolonial movements. Delegates of the communist puppet regimes speak and vote as one man, following the lead of the Soviet delegate in support of "anti-imperialist" policies.[16] Communist unwillingness to cooperate in the UN for the establishment of world order and security, and particularly Soviet abuses of the veto power, acted as the most

[14] F. P. Walters, *A History of the League of Nations*, 2 vols. (Oxford, 1952), II, 585.

[15] "The Arabs are not Marxists," Khrushchev said. "They are fighting under another flag—under the flag of nationalism. We hail them. National liberation is the first step." *New York Times*, July 23, 1958.

[16] A universal world organization offers many possibilities for abuses, but at the same time it is a convenient forum for the exposure of double-talk and violations of international obligations. Besides Soviet aggressiveness and violation of agreements, intemperate and false statements by Vyshinsky and other Soviet representatives at meetings of the UN revealed the true character of Soviet policy and enraged even the most isolationist congressmen, thus facilitating the development of American participation and leadership in a constructive Western policy.

important eye opener in many countries. Since it became clear that a permanent member of the Security Council was able to obstruct all collective measures for the maintenance of peace and for the suppression of acts of aggression, a great number of states have tried to obtain military, political, and economic security through more specific agreements. The United States played a leading role in this "within the Charter but outside the veto" policy. The UN hence has been a much different organization than the League of Nations.

Only gradually did the Western nations rise to the challenge of postwar realities. The awakening of the West was slow, and many accomplished facts, especially in East Central Europe and in China, could not have been changed without the use of force. The Western governments and peoples in 1945-1947 were unwilling to take such action. The Soviet Union had a free hand during a decisive period, and American diplomacy, operating in 1947 and thereafter within the framework of a policy of containment, had to initiate defensive moves from very unfavorable positions. Still, the West did move forward. Despite long-standing isolationist traditions and some other handicaps of the American political system, the United States has proved able to answer new challenges effectively, though sometimes haltingly. The Truman Doctrine saved Greece and Turkey from communist subversion and Soviet domination. Through expanded application of this doctrine the United States accepted world-wide responsibility, becoming an almost universal guarantor against aggression. Mutual assistance and economic aid programs, bilateral treaties, and regional agencies such as the Colombo Plan and SEATO have created forums of co-operation between the United States and many nations.

In the rehabilitation of Europe, economic measures came first. The almost hopeless economic situation that existed in Europe in the postwar years was changed by the Marshall Plan—an unprecedented venture in American and European politics—which demonstrated the political maturity of the North Atlantic nations. One of the consequences of the ensuing European Recovery Program was the establishment in 1948 of the Organization for European Economic Co-operation (OEEC), which has continued to be the center of constructive economic endeavors. The OEEC distributed American aid to European countries and established the European Payments Union and the European Productivity Agency. The result of these activities was large-scale liberalization of European trade, substantial re-establishment of the convertibility of European currencies, and a spectacular rehabilitation of European productivity.[17]

Then came political measures. The Senate's acceptance of the Vandenberg Resolution in June, 1948, by the overwhelming vote of 64 to 4, showed that this body, strongly isolationist on the eve of the Second World War, recognized the new American responsibilities in world affairs and was willing to act in a flexible way and in a spirit that disregarded old political traditions. The resolution recommended the association of the United States with regional or other arrangements for individual and collective self-defense under Article 51 of the United Nations Charter. The American foreign policy thus launched resulted in the conclusion of the North Atlantic Treaty and other multilateral and bilateral defensive agreements.

In Western Europe a feeling of much greater security appeared after the establishment of the North Atlantic Treaty Organization. NATO's protective shield and retaliatory capacity greatly improved the political and psychological climate, and brought a measure of stability to Europe. This stability made possible the spectacular rehabilitation of Western Europe, followed by unprecedented economic growth and the beginning of a new era of co-operation and some integration in the North Atlantic area.

NATO—A NEW DEPARTURE

The North Atlantic Treaty Organization is a *sui generis* regional organization that defies simple definition. It bases itself on intergovernment co-operation. Having no supranational character, all its decisions must be unanimous. Nevertheless, under the influence of world events and through organic growth, NATO has become much more than a simple alliance. The functions of the North Atlantic Council and its subordinate organs, and the position of the secretary general, are without precedent in the history of international organizations. NATO is unprecedented even as a military alliance. Within its framework a chain of unified military commands, composed of representatives from member countries, was established during a

[17] Appraisal of these achievements and of the operational methods of the OEEC, which served as a model to several international agencies, is outside of the scope of this essay. But one fact is relevant and deserves emphasis: since political, military, and economic security interact, progress in the economic field could not have been lasting in an atmosphere of insecurity and fear.

period of peace. Integration of armies and armaments necessarily creates an interdependence that has important political consequences.

Before NATO reached its present stage of development, it went through several transformations, the systematic discussion of which is outside the scope of this essay. Its forerunner in Western Europe was the Brussels Treaty of March, 1948, signed by France, the United Kingdom, and the three Benelux countries. The North Atlantic Treaty, consisting of 14 concise articles, was signed in Washington on April 4, 1949, by the United States, Canada, Denmark, Iceland, Italy, Norway, Portugal and the five signatories of the Brussels Treaty. Soviet actions in East Central Europe, particularly the communist seizure of power in Prague in February, 1948, and the Berlin blockade in 1948-1949, gave an impetus to these developments. Less than six months after the establishment of NATO, the explosion of an atomic bomb in the Soviet Union had a further effect on Western military considerations although the actual change in the balance of power occurred later when Soviet operational capabilities in the atomic field became evident. NATO's ability to evolve and carry out a new Western strategy became enormously important when the Anglo-American atomic monopoly ceased to exist, resulting in a radical change in the world balance of military power.

The treaty established a defensive alliance which operates, on the basis of Article 51 of the Charter, within the framework of the United Nations. Although an armed attack against any one of the contracting parties is considered "an attack against them all," NATO's purpose is broader than the military defense of the geographic area defined in Article 6 of the treaty. The members have determined "to safeguard the freedom, common heritage and civilization of their peoples, founded on the principles of democracy, individual liberty and the rule of law." These all-embracing objectives have followed from recognition that Soviet Russian imperialism does not restrict itself to any particular area and does not use only military means for expansion. Thus military defense alone is not sufficient against the global communist threat. The awareness of the need for consultation in global affairs and for NATO co-operation in non-military fields greatly increased later.

Although NATO is primarily a military alliance, it was destined from the outset to be much more than a strictly military alliance. NATO inherited the best practices of traditional diplomacy and adapted them to the new requirements of contemporary politics. The chain of integrated military commands has been paralleled by the machinery of a permanent diplomatic organization.

The communist threat naturally was the reason for this diplomatic organization. The dynamic communist movement, the direction and character of which often changes, threatens the values and way of life usually associated with Western civilization. NATO's policy for the defense of these values can cope with threats on all fronts on the basis of the flexible provisions of Article 2, in which the contracting parties pledged that they will contribute toward the further development of "peaceful and friendly international relations by strengthening their free institutions, by bringing about a better understanding of the principles upon which these institutions are founded, and by promoting conditions of stability and well-being."

NATO is not a new Concert of Europe. Though most of its members belong culturally to the same Western European family of nations, NATO is nevertheless an entirely different political entity. It operates in a changed world setting and its primary goal is defense against the strongest military power on the European continent, a power that is at the same time the center of a world-wide subversive movement.

Moreover, NATO has extra-European ties. Its most powerful member, the United States, has global interests, participates in other regional organizations and has concluded bilateral treaties of mutual assistance with the Philippine Islands, Japan, Korea, the Republic of China, and other countries. The interlocking membership of several NATO members in regional organizations symbolizes the extension of free-world defense to major areas of the globe. Secretary Dulles even proposed at the NATO Council meeting in Paris on December 16, 1957, that the secretary general of NATO "should explore developing closer ties between the various collective-defense organizations, if this is agreeable to all concerned." [18] Although this proposal

[18] The final Declaration issued by the NATO Council on December 19, 1957, stated: "To the many nations which have gained their independence since the end of the Second World War and to all other peoples, who like ourselves, are dedicated to freedom in peace, we offer our co-operation on a basis of complete equality and in a spirit of fraternity." *North Atlantic Treaty Organization Meeting of Heads of Government, Paris, December 1957* (Washington, 1958), p. 104.

The NATO and specifically the American attitude in this respect was characterized by Secretary Dulles in his report of December 23, 1957. He recalled suggested only an exchange of experience and information, not a merger of existing organizations or extension of the NATO area, several members of the OAS manifested a reserved attitude toward an OAS link with NATO. Establishment of a consultative relationship between different kinds of organizations would probably be a difficult task remaining in the exploratory stage for some time.

Certainly the organizational divisions of NATO sound altogether unlike a new Concert of Europe. NATO has gone much farther than the loose association of states of Europe in the nineteenth century. Before the communist aggression in Korea, the North Atlantic Council had met three times and concentrated on the establishment of various military and civilian bodies. The highest military organ became the *Military Committee,* consisting of the chiefs of staff of the member countries. The *Standing Group* is the executive agency of the military committee: its members are the representatives of France, the United Kingdom, and the United States. The *Regional Planning Groups* prepare regional defense plans. The economic and financial aspect of the common defense effort made necessary the establishment of the *Defense Financial and Economic Board* and the *Military Production and Supply Board.* Finally, the Council, meeting

the terms of the unanimous report of the Foreign Relations Committee which submitted the NATO Treaty for ratification to the United States Senate: "It would be particularly unfortunate if our Government took part in 'exclusive' consultations with Atlantic Pact members over situations of deep concern to friendly states in Asia, Africa, Latin America, or the Middle East." Then Dulles continued: "That principle is as sound today as it ever was. It would be disruptive of the unity which is essential within the free world, if free-world countries who are not members of NATO felt that their fate was being determined by members of the NATO Council in their absence.

"That, it can be said with absolute confidence, is not going to happen. There was no evidence of desire on the part of the NATO Council or any of the members to attempt to set itself up as supreme over other free-world countries or other free-world organizations.

"One evidence of that fact—concrete evidence—is that NATO now has the desire to explore on a basis of mutuality a possibility of liaison with other collective-defense organizations of a regional character, such as the Organization of American States, the Southeast Asia Treaty Organization, and the Baghdad Pact.

"The fact is that the peace of any part of the world can be put in jeopardy by what goes on in another part of the world. So it is in the common interest that there should be efforts to create a sense of cohesion and of confident interdependence as between the free-world nations everywhere." *The NATO Conference in Paris:* Report by President Eisenhower and Secretary of State Dulles, December 23, 1957 (Washington, 1958), p. 7.

in May, 1950, set up a permanent body, the *Council of Deputies* of the Foreign Ministers, for co-ordination and for regular political exchanges between member governments. In harmony with the non-military objectives of the treaty, the Council resolved "to secure the economic progress and prosperity of the peoples of their countries, and to promote the economic and social development of other peoples of the free world."

The United States has, of course, been the major provider of military equipment for the NATO allies. Development of NATO's military strength was greatly helped by the enactment of the Mutual Defense Act, signed by President Truman in October, 1949. Of the $1,450 million appropriated for military aid throughout the world in 1950, $1,000 million were earmarked for the NATO countries. In January, 1950, the United States signed bilateral agreements with eight European NATO countries that requested military and financial aid. At the same time President Truman approved the "integrated defense plan" for the North Atlantic area.

Then, shortly after the Mutual Defense Assistance Program was initiated, the Korean War broke out, greatly affecting the fortunes of NATO. In June, 1950, the members of NATO realized that what had happened in Korea could happen in Germany as well, and the Council in its session of September, 1950, adopted a "forward strategy." This strategy meant resistance to Soviet aggression as far to the east as possible, that is, at least along the Rhine River. But the 14 Western divisions, faced by 175 Soviet divisions, could hardly have been adequate for the task. In addition to satellite divisions of doubtful value, the Soviet Union had 125 divisions in immediate reserve. There was general agreement in the Council that it was necessary to create "an integrated force under a centralized command, adequate to deter aggression and to ensure the defense of Western Europe."

This exigency raised the question of German membership in NATO. At the Council meeting of September, 1950, Secretary Acheson argued in support of German participation in Europe's defense, but France opposed the plan.[19] The principle of German participation in the common defense, however, was accepted at the Council meeting the following December. The French government worked out a plan for "a European Army linked to the political

[19] France followed a strong anti-German policy in the early postwar years. *Cf.* Alexander Werth, *France 1940-1955* (New York, 1956), pp. 305-16.

institutions of a united Europe," and Premier René Pleven submitted it to the French Assembly on October 24, 1950. The Pleven Plan provided for a European Minister of Defense responsible to a European Assembly and "a complete fusion of all the human and material elements" of the proposed army. The European Defense Community (EDC) Treaty met defeat in the French Parliament in August, 1954,[20] and the German Federal Republic did not enter NATO until May, 1955. Meanwhile, the defense of NATO's eastern flank was secured when, following the invitation of the Council, Greece and Turkey joined NATO in February, 1952. Extension of NATO's responsibilities to the Eastern Mediterranean and the Black Sea was not favored by the Scandinavian countries, but they yielded to the wishes of the majority. The case of Denmark is a good example of how persuasion was used to convince even the most reluctant Scandinavian member of the necessity of Greek and Turkish participation in NATO.[21]

The Council appointed General Dwight D. Eisenhower as Supreme Commander of the Allied Forces in Europe (SACEUR) in December, 1950. He established the Supreme Headquarters Allied Powers, Europe (SHAPE) near Paris and began to organize an integrated NATO army for defense of the NATO land area in Europe. This work has been continued by his successors, the American Generals Matthew B. Ridgway, Alfred M. Gruenther, and Lauris Norstad.

The NATO area is divided among three Commands and a Regional Planning Group. *Allied Command Europe* extends from the North Cape to North Africa and from the Atlantic to the eastern border of Turkey, but the United Kingdom, Portugal, and Algeria are excluded. Their defense remains a national responsibility. The Supreme Allied Commander Europe has four subordinate commands —one each in the northern, central, and southern parts of Europe, and one in the Mediterranean area.[22] The Atlantic Ocean Command (SACLANT) extends from the North Pole to the Tropic of Cancer

[20] See Herbert Luethy, *France Against Herself* (New York, 1955); Raymond Aron and Daniel Lerner, *France Defeats EDC* (New York, 1957); Edgar S. Furniss, Jr., *France, Troubled Ally* (New York, 1960).

[21] See Joe R. Williams, "Denmark and NATO: The Problem of a Small State in a Collective Security System," *International Organization*, X (1956), 390-401.

[22] See Colonel Andrew J. Goodpaster, "The Development of SHAPE: 1950-1953," *International Organization*, IX (1955), 257-62.

and from the coastal waters of North America to those of Europe and Africa, including Portuguese waters and the islands in the area, such as Iceland and the Azores, but excluding the British Isles and the Channel. *The Channel Committee* and *The Channel Command* cover the English Channel and the southern part of the North Sea. Strategy for the defense of North America is prepared by *The Canada-United States Regional Planning Group.* The national forces of member countries fall into three categories: forces assigned in peacetime to NATO commands, forces earmarked for these commands in the event of mobilization or war, and forces remaining under national control. The NATO commanders prepare defense plans for their respective areas, determine the force requirements, and deploy and exercise the forces under their command. SACLANT does not have assigned forces but some naval contingents are earmarked for its use in the event of war. Allied naval forces in the Mediterranean (with the exception of French forces) are assigned or earmarked for SACEUR. The Sixth Fleet is earmarked for assignment to SACEUR if war breaks out.

The fact that a communist aggression in the Western Pacific triggered important developments within NATO clearly demonstrated the global character of the Soviet threat and the consequent political interdependence of NATO with regions situated outside its geographically-limited defense commitments.

The process of strengthening the Atlantic security system proved a task of great magnitude, and it necessitated almost continuous negotiations among the members of NATO. Although the Marshall Plan made possible the re-establishment of the economic strength of Europe, the cost of modern armaments has been prohibitive for most of the NATO members. The purpose of the organization would be undermined if the military expenditures of its member nations were to cause an economic setback. Therefore, the question of the limit of each member's contribution to the maintenance of military readiness and the measure and form of American aid to members of NATO became highly controversial.[23] These problems came under discussion at the Ottawa meeting of the Council in September, 1951, when for the first time member states were represented by their foreign ministers, defense ministers, and economic or finance minis-

[23] For the politico-economic implications of NATO, see Lincoln Gordon, "Economic Aspects of Coalition Diplomacy—the NATO Experience," *International Organization,* X (1956), 529-43.

ters. This meeting appointed a Temporary Council Committee (TCC) consisting of the "three wise men"—Averell Harriman from the United States, Jean Monnet from France, and Sir Edwin Plowden from the United Kingdom—"to survey urgently the requirements of external security, and particularly of fulfilling a militarily acceptable NATO plan for the defense of Western Europe, and the realistic political-economic capabilities of the member countries." The TCC prepared in three months "the first comprehensive review of how the resources of the member countries under peacetime conditions can best be employed in the interest of common security."

The Ministerial Council, meeting at Lisbon in February, 1952, accepted the recommendations of the report, including a build-up of NATO military forces by the end of 1952 to a total of about 50 combat-ready divisions in Central Europe and some 4,000 aircraft, and approved the report of the Atlantic Community Committee which advocated the expansion and liberalization of trade, strengthening the social and economic structure of states, and close collaboration of NATO with the OEEC and other international bodies. The Lisbon meeting was a milestone in NATO's institutional development as well. The North Atlantic Council was to function thenceforth as a permanent body so that it could make decisions promptly. The *Palais de Chaillot* in Paris became the provisional headquarters of an international staff and secretariat headed by a new high official of NATO, the secretary general, who was to preside over the Council's permanent sessions. The secretariat incorporated several boards that until that time had functioned separately. The NATO headquarters moved to the *Place du Maréchal de Lattre de Tassigny* in early 1960.

Important duties of the secretariat include the annual review and planning, in the form of an annual report similar to the one submitted by the TCC. The contribution of each member to defense expenditure has remained a major issue.

In April, 1952, Lord Ismay was appointed vice chairman of the Council and secretary general of NATO. He was succeeded in the spring of 1957 by one of the most dynamic statesmen of our time, Paul-Henri Spaak of Belgium. Ministerial Council sessions, usually two a year, were until 1957 under a chairmanship rotating among the foreign ministers of member countries. In accord with the Council's decision in December, 1956, the secretary general has become the presiding officer at all Council meetings, including ministerial sessions, and the rotating chairmanship of the foreign minister has served mainly for ceremonial functions. The secretary general, his deputy, and other high officials of the secretariat play a more important political role than international civil servants usually do in international organizations.

All member states have appointed representatives to NATO. These representatives form a special diplomatic body in Paris, an addition to the group of diplomats accredited to the French government and to the OEEC. The intimate relationship between the permanent staff and diplomats accredited to NATO demonstrates a trend toward the closer collaboration of representatives of the member states.[24]

DEVELOPMENT OF THE ALLIANCE

One of NATO's most difficult problems arose when the French National Assembly rejected EDC in August, 1954, but this setback was soon countered by the London and Paris Conferences, and the Ministerial Meeting of the North Atlantic Council held on October 22. Signing of the Paris agreements on the following day solved the difficulties connected with Germany's participation in the defense of Europe. In virtue of these agreements, France, the United Kingdom, and the United States terminated the occupation regime in the

[24] A systematic discussion of NATO's organizational development is outside the scope of this paper. For the pertinent data see *The NATO Handbook* (Paris, 1959), and *Facts about NATO* published by NATO's Information Service. For more detailed discussion see Lord Ismay, *NATO, the First Five Years,* 1949-1954, and his "Report to the Ministerial Meeting of the North Atlantic Council at Bonn, May 1957," *NATO Letter,* V (June, 1957). Ben T. Moore's book, *NATO and the Future of Europe* (New York, 1958) contains a comprehensive bibliographic note. For the various phases and aspects of NATO's development, *see* the symposia published by *The Annals of the American Academy of Political and Social Science:* "NATO and World Peace" (July, 1953); "The Future of the Western Alliance" (July, 1957); Norman J. Padelford, "Political Cooperation in the North Atlantic Community," *International Organization,* IX (1955), 353-65; "A Selected Bibliography on Regionalism and Regional Arrangements," *International Organization,* X (1956), 575-603; Gardner Patterson and Edgar S. Furniss, Jr., *NATO, A Critical Appraisal* (Princeton, 1957); Ruth C. Lawson, "Concerting Policies in the North Atlantic Community," *International Organization,* XII (1958), 163-79; Klaus Knorr, ed., *NATO and American Security* (Princeton, 1959); M. Margaret Ball, *NATO and the European Union Movement* (London, 1959), Alastair Buchan, *NATO in the 1960's—The Implications of Interdependence* (New York, 1960).

Federal Republic of Germany and, with some restrictions, recognized it as a sovereign state. The Brussels Treaty Organization transformed itself into the Western European Union (WEU), and the German Federal Republic and Italy joined this new regional organization. The British pledge to continued maintenance of the United Kingdom forces on the Continent assigned to SACEUR greatly contributed to the consolidation of the new arrangement. Although this British undertaking was subject to escape clauses, it was a new turn in British foreign policy that evoked general optimism for the success of the new political arrangements in Western Europe. Functions of the WEU include control of armaments, and this new regional organization has supplemented NATO's activities in Western Europe in some important military matters.

In March, 1955, the United States gave a pledge to maintain American forces on the Continent of Europe as long as necessary. Since NATO's strategy is based on the "shield and sword" concept, stationing of American and British troops on the mainland of Europe is of the greatest importance for European security. In a major conflict, the shield forces would resist Soviet aggression on the mainland of Europe, while the United States and British strategic air forces would throw their retaliatory power against the Soviet Union.

Following an invitation of the Council, the Federal Republic of Germany joined NATO in May, 1955. The Federal Republic will eventually contribute 12 army divisions, more than 1,000 ground-based aircraft, 48 naval aircraft, and 90 naval units to NATO's defense system. Today Germany has more divisions under NATO command than any other member state, although these German divisions are far from full strength.

Since the number of combat-ready NATO divisions remained far behind the goals set in 1951, it became necessary to rely on tactical atomic weapons to balance the numerical strength of the Soviet army. Therefore, the Ministerial Council, meeting in the fall of 1954, reduced the Lisbon target to 30 divisions equipped with tactical atomic weapons.[25] The 30 division goal pertains to Allied Forces,

[25] General Norstad pointed out in an interview, which appeared in *US News and World Report*, November 30, 1956, that in 1951 NATO was required to plan primarily on the basis of conventional weapons. "To defend the central region, between the Baltic and the Alps, our 1951 plans, based upon absolute military requirements, called for about 65 divisions. In fact, some of the earlier studies suggested that more than 90 divisions would be required." *NATO Letter*, IV (December, 1956), 36.

Central Europe, and not to Allied Command Europe as a whole. Although this goal has not been reached, modernization of NATO forces and the build-up of military installations has continued.

The strengthening of the North Atlantic Security system could have been reversed by the *détente* engineered by Stalin's successors which culminated in the Geneva "meeting at the summit" in July, 1955. On this occasion the chief Soviet delegates appeared ready to negotiate seriously with the West on disarmament, unification of Germany, and other major problems. But the subsequent meeting of the French, British, and United States foreign ministers with Molotov revealed once more the unreliability of Soviet promises and declarations of intention. The Ministerial Council, meeting in December, 1955, expressed the desire of seeing the Atlantic forces equipped with the most modern weapons. A firm attitude towards improvement of NATO's defense posture was proven necessary by the subsequent Soviet penetration of the Middle East, the intervention in Poland, and the brutal suppression of the Hungarian Revolution. In 1957, the USSR on several occasions rejected disarmament proposals that were approved by the overwhelming majority of the General Assembly of the UN.[26] Thus Stalin's successors demonstrated that only the rigidity of Soviet policy had changed, not the threat. The hardly disguised expansionist intentions of the Soviet regime remained a permanent factor, fully justifying endeavors for strengthening NATO's forces.

Today the NATO forces comprise nearly 100 active and reserve divisions, more than 1,000 combat vessels, and about 5,000 tactical aircraft. The power of these forces has been increased by modern equipment and nuclear capability. In the last two years modern tactical weapons systems such as the Honest John and Matador missiles have been increasingly introduced, which means that NATO divisions are equipped with ground-to-ground and ground-to-air missiles.

Since 1950 NATO's military strength has risen in many other ways. Many military installations such as air and naval bases and pipelines support the organization and operation of NATO armies. For example, NATO now has 150 airfields suitable for jet aircraft, as compared to less than 20 in 1950. It is difficult to present the progress statistically, but it has been estimated that in wartime the numerical strength of NATO forces would be four or five times

[26] See below, pp. 83ff.

greater than it was in 1950. Moreover, the NATO nations have worked out joint strategic plans under which all these forces would operate in wartime. The objective of a chain of integrated commands and a well-established communication system is to secure co-operation in war along a 4,000-mile front, from the north of Norway to the east of Turkey.

This somewhat optimistic picture is darkened by the lack of conventional strength in the critical central area of the Continent where the shield consists of only slightly over twenty-one combat-ready divisions (five US, three UK, seven German, two French, two Belgian, two Dutch, and a Canadian brigade), some of which are understrength.[27] This force faces about 90 Soviet divisions based in the captive countries and the Western part of the USSR, together with more than 20 satellite divisions. Thus, despite many encouraging results, NATO's efforts cannot be considered satisfactory. The percentage of gross national product devoted to NATO forces by each of the allies does not approach the level devoted to the opposing forces by the USSR, although the defense expenditures of NATO countries increased considerably after 1949.[28]

The disproportion in conventional armaments is great, and it is even greater in sheer military manpower. While the United States has developed strong thermonuclear striking power, the conventional forces built up during the Korean war and military expenditures in the budget have been considerably reduced since 1954. Britain announced a cut in her manpower contribution to NATO's forces in December, 1956,[29] and France transferred to Algeria about two divisions from the French forces assigned to NATO.

Although both NATO and Soviet forces rely increasingly on tactical nuclear weapons, conventional forces remain important. Therefore, the reluctance of some European states to strengthen their ground forces is a serious problem. Lack of military manpower is

[27] In the North, the Danish commitment to NATO is slightly more than one division and Norway provides one division. To the South, Italy provides seven divisions, Greece five and Turkey twelve divisions. For the comparative military strength of the Soviet Union and the NATO powers see *NATO Letter*, VII (December, 1959), 22-27.

[28] For the total defense expenditures of NATO countries in the years 1949 to 1960, see *NATO Letter*, IX (January, 1961), 14.

[29] The Defense White Paper of 1957 provided for the abolition of conscription by 1962 and the likelihood exists that British contributions to NATO forces on the Continent will be further reduced.

probably the greatest weakness of NATO, for even in the nuclear age man remains the ultimate force. In addition to relevant psychological and political factors, new Soviet strategic concepts rely on ground forces, particularly after the first phase of a nuclear war when there is mutual exhaustion of nuclear striking capability.[30] Strong NATO ground forces might become decisive in this "broken-back" period of a war. It is not of less importance that in time of peace such NATO forces can also deter Soviet probing actions in Europe. The Soviet Union might, under favorable international circumstances, attempt limited aggressions that either could not be resisted or—if the West did not have the alternative of fighting a conventional war—could trigger off a total nuclear war. Strength of the shield is of great importance because effective resistance against a local aggression gives time to consider the alternatives before the beginning of an all-out nuclear conflict.

Although the great Soviet superiority in ground forces has been a matter of public knowledge, there was bewilderment in Europe when President Eisenhower on March 11, 1959, bluntly stated: "We are certainly not going to fight a ground war in Europe."[31] Because of the apprehension created by this statement, Defense Secretary Neil H. McElroy affirmed to the House Foreign Affairs Committee that the United States would fight with everything it had, including ground troops, if war broke out in Europe.[32] If it were not for NATO ground forces, a huge Soviet army could march to the English Channel by sheer weight, even without using atomic weapons. In such a situation it would be necessary for the United States to make the decision to fight a nuclear war that could also devastate North

[30] See Raymond L. Garthoff, *Soviet Strategy in the Nuclear Age* (New York, 1958); H. S. Dinerstein, *War and the Soviet Union: Nuclear Weapons and the Revolution in Soviet Military and Political Thinking* (New York, 1959). William W. Kaufmann, "The Crisis in Military Affairs," *World Politics,* X (1958), 579-603. George W. Rathjens, Jr. "NATO Strategy: Total War" in *NATO and American Security,* ed. by Klaus Knorr (Princeton, 1959), pp. 67-68. For a critical analysis of why the European nations are reluctant to contribute more divisions to NATO forces, see Arnold Wolfers, "Europe and the NATO Shield," *International Organization,* XII (1958), 425-39. For American strategy and NATO, see Henry A. Kissinger, *Nuclear Weapons and Foreign Policy* (New York, 1957), pp. 269-315; Roger Hilsman, "On NATO Strategy" in *Alliance Policy in the Cold War,* ed. by Arnold Wolfers (Baltimore, 1959), pp. 146-83; Oskar Morgenstern, *The Question of National Defense* (New York, 1959).

[31] *New York Times,* March 12, 1959.

[32] *Ibid.,* March 22, 1959.

America. The policy of massive retaliation, promulgated by Secretary Dulles in January, 1954, would work both ways today and would invite a "retaliation for retaliation" to American shores.

Despite this unpleasant prospect NATO would be obligated to use nuclear weapons in any major war. This is the only way the West can offset the communist numerical superiority in troops, whether armed with conventional or atomic weapons. While circumstances have been changing, the meaning of the "shield and sword" concept in NATO strategy has remained essentially the same. The British and American strategic air forces are not under NATO command, yet only the British and American forces have been armed with nuclear weapons, which creates an imbalance in NATO and restricts the retaliatory "sword" role to American and British forces.

As long as there existed a decisive American superiority in atomic weapons, the imbalance between NATO and Soviet ground forces was not of particular concern, but this situation has changed gradually. The change was spectacularly demonstrated in the fall of 1957 when the two Sputniks made only too obvious the Soviet capabilities in the field of ballistic missiles. Consequently, in December, 1957, the NATO heads of government decided "to establish stocks of nuclear warheads, which will be readily available for the defense of the Alliance in case of need." The same meeting decided "that intermediate range ballistic missiles will have to be put at the disposal of the Supreme Allied Commander Europe." [33] Use of missiles in a particular country would be decided on a bilateral basis, but atomic warheads would remain under American control until the last moment.

In accord with the decision of December, 1957, the United States concluded agreements with seven NATO countries (Britain, France, Canada, West Germany, Greece, Turkey, and the Netherlands) for transfer of nuclear-weapons information and military equipment which will enable them to train their forces in the use of nuclear weapons and to develop nuclear defense plans. Nuclear armament components, including nuclear warheads, will remain in American hands until a time of emergency; and there will be no transfer of either information or equipment that could help a receiving nation "to design, develop, or fabricate its own nuclear weapon." Only the United Kingdom will receive such help, for the Atomic Energy Act

[33] *North Atlantic Treaty Organization Meeting of Heads of Government, Paris, December 1957, Texts of Statements* (Washington, 1958), p. 108.

of 1958 provided that secrets of atomic weapons design could be given only to a nation that had made substantial progress in producing atomic weapons. This provision excluded France, a country that entered the "nuclear club" in 1960 and desires a position comparable to that of Britain in sharing United States nuclear weapon secrets.

Because of Britain's atomic capabilities, there is a marked difference between the American treatment of France as compared to that of Britain. One of the sources of French dissatisfaction with NATO originates in the fact that from the point of view of nuclear weapons there are two categories of states in NATO, and France does not belong to the privileged group. The atomic agreement concluded with France is of a limited nature.[34] The United States-British agreement is much different. It gives custody of the Thor intermediate ballistic missiles to the Royal Air Force. Although the nuclear warheads remain in the hands of US Strategic Air Command, the operational employment of Thor assigned to the RAF in Britain is a matter for joint decision by both governments. In April, 1960, the British government decided, because of the high expenditures involved, to abandon the project for the Blue Streak missile, which was to have a range of 2,800 miles. Instead they will rely for the present on the British V-bomber force. Meanwhile, the government is considering the purchase from the United States of missiles like the Polaris or the projected Skybolt air-to-ground missile (when they are ready) for use with the V-bomber force and a British-manufactured nuclear warhead. Thus Britain abandoned her own long-range missile program and will rely on the United States for such weapons.

Since the United States has denied France a position similar to Britain's, President de Gaulle turned to countermeasures. For example, he withheld permission for the installation on French territory of NATO missile bases and atomic arsenals under United States con-

[34] The agreement with France provides only for the transfer of enriched uranium to be used by France in the development of a land-based prototype of a submarine nuclear power plant.

The agreement with Britain provides for the transfer of secret design information for the building of nuclear weapons and an atomic submarine power plant. It also permits the exchange of materials used in the manufacture of weapons.

The agreements with the five other NATO allies provide for the exchange of information for the training of troops in the use of nuclear weapons and the transfer of non-nuclear parts of devices for launching atomic weapons. The agreement with Canada also provides for co-operation in the development of military reactors.

trol. This French policy forced General Norstad in August, 1959, to order the transfer to Britain and Germany of over 200 American fighter-bombers based in France. In Britain and Germany these bombers would have access to nuclear bombs in an emergency. Though circumstances required this transfer, it meant abandonment of a tactical deployment of combat aircraft units that the air force had labored to achieve.

Meanwhile in the cases of both Britain and France, there has been an unfortunate duplication in research in atomic weapons. Before the aforementioned liberalization of the Atomic Energy Act, Britain had to spend many millions of pounds to discover what the United States already knew in the thermonuclear field. Similarly, France had to spend billions of francs for the production of atomic bombs. Since it was foreseen that France would become a nuclear power, it now appears that the United States policy that excluded French participation in the privileges accorded to the British in the nuclear field has not been wise.[35] Of course, Britain's special position in the McMahon Act was one of the consequences of the British breakthrough in the atomic field. Repercussions in international politics because of the rise of a fourth country with atomic power have also influenced American policy makers, and there were the uncertainties of French politics, especially with regard to the Algerian problem and the French attitude towards NATO.

There were additional difficulties inherent in the attempt to reconcile United States policy with the realities of French politics. They point up the desirability of greater political integration within the Alliance, without which it will be impossible to achieve genuine military co-operation and unity. President de Gaulle supports intergovernment co-operation, but he opposes integration of national armies. Because of his opposition, the North Atlantic Council, meeting in December, 1959, could not find a formula for an integrated continental air defense, without which Europe's air defense will remain in a precarious condition. President de Gaulle knows, of course, that missiles as well as airplanes can cross frontiers in a few minutes,

[35] Paul-Henri Spaak pointed out in an article that France "is doing all over again in the atomic field, alone or almost alone, what has already been done by the United States and the United Kingdom. France is spending and is being obliged to spend billions of francs and a wealth of intellectual energy on the task of discovering for itself what its allies already know." "New Tests for NATO," *Foreign Affairs*, XXXVII (1959), 365.

but his opposition to integrated command is connected with his general philosophy in foreign political matters.

The spread of nuclear information remains a serious problem. The Soviet government strongly protested the agreements between the United States and seven NATO countries for transfer of nuclear weapons information. Many American citizens and pacifist organizations expressed concern. But Soviet policies almost forced the United States to conclude these agreements, which went into effect in July and August of 1959. It should be emphasized again that the information transferred under the agreements is to help train Allied forces in the use of nuclear weapons, now in the NATO atomic stockpile, with the delivery systems in their hands, but these agreements do not provide for the transfer of any information which would assist in the design or manufacture of nuclear weapons.

As long as the Kremlin is building the Red Army's atomic capabilities and preventing any progress toward a genuine disarmament combined with effective international inspection, NATO has no choice but to strengthen its military capabilities with atomic weapons. Otherwise, the members of the Alliance would not have the strength and confidence necessary to reject Soviet threats. A NATO army that would deliberately limit itself to an inferior weapons system in the face of ruthless and aggressive Soviet power would have little chance in the event of conflict, and NATO members would have to yield to Soviet atomic missile blackmail. As long as NATO is required to use nuclear weapons as the only effective defense against Soviet aggression, it is in the general Western interest that several European NATO members should have forces with atomic delivery capability in the form of trained units and equipment for use of atomic weapons. Intermediate-range missile bases have been installed in Great Britain, Italy, and Turkey; but in the last two countries the Jupiter missiles are not yet operational, even though arrangements for their deployment have been completed. The sharing of nuclear capability is an important step towards development of self-confidence in European NATO members. On the other hand, long-range missiles and nuclear warheads on the mainland of Europe must, for obvious reasons, remain under an ironclad NATO chain of command. Any other situation would impair NATO's military effectiveness and unity.

While co-operation and unity are highly desirable objectives, the great disparity between the power of the United States and that of other NATO members is a fact that cannot be eliminated through a fiction of equality. Most NATO members recognize and even expect American leadership, but in concrete cases some members resent its display or even discreet exercise. Although a democratic alliance depends on the voluntary co-operation of its members, NATO co-operation cannot become in all respects a two-way street because of the disproportion in power. This disequilibrium along with the ensuing frictions constitute all the more serious a problem because the NATO forces face a monolithic power. On the other side of the curtain, members of the Warsaw Pact, the so-called Eastern NATO, are in no position to question the Kremlin on military matters; the huge communist forces operate under a unified command.

The situation is similar in the political field: while the Soviet satellites and the USSR operate as a unit in international relations, co-ordination of NATO actions must come in each instance through diplomatic negotiations. The Council is a permanent diplomatic conference. Its members have the spirit of co-operation, but they have no supranational power and they have to follow the instructions of their governments. Although NATO's integrated military commands have some supranational characteristics, in the absence of a NATO government the military chiefs receive orders from their national authorities. Since the problem remains that of who will command the generals under whom NATO forces would operate in a conflict, NATO's diplomatic machinery is the cornerstone of the Western alliance. General Norstad has formulated the problem in the following way:

> Our present strategy, influenced as it must be by the hopes and the needs of 15 nations, is inevitably one of compromise. This has certainly given us a useful start. But for the Alliance to have continuing life and meaning, it needs an increasing authority. Action to pass to the Alliance greater control over atomic weapons and subjecting their use more directly to the collective will, if politically feasible, could be a great new step.[36]

General Norstad further developed these ideas in a speech delivered at the Sixth Annual Conference of the NATO Parliamentarians Conference in November, 1960. He proposed to make NATO a fourth atomic power with its own nuclear striking force. Since all member nations would have an essentially equal voice in the control

[36] *NATO Letter*, VIII (January, 1960), 10.

of both land- and sea-based mid-range ballistic missiles, NATO would have a "sword" of its own. Moreover, the "shield" would be greatly strengthened with tactical atomic weapons. The resolution accepted by the Conference took notice of the Norstad Plan, and called on the Council of NATO to develop methods to establish the Alliance's political authority over the delivery system for and use of nuclear weapons.

But even the strongest NATO arsenal would be of doubtful value if the policy-making process could not be brought into harmony with contemporary requirements. In view of the political nature of the NATO Alliance, the ultimate responsibility for decision and action rests on national governments, and thus the efficiency of inter-allied diplomacy is of the utmost importance.

CONSULTATIVE DIPLOMACY IN NATO

Although traditional diplomacy is still of primary importance in bilateral contacts, there has developed in contemporary international politics a superstructure of new methods in the form of collective diplomacy. One of the most important developments in NATO is the institutionalization of consultation in the Council, where international political problems receive discussion collectively on a regular basis.

Article 4 of the North Atlantic Treaty provided for consultation of the member states "whenever, in the opinion of any of them, the territorial integrity, political independence or security of any of the Parties is threatened." Consultation, however, was used only sporadically during the first five years of NATO's existence. Events in 1955, and particularly the Suez crisis in 1956, gave impetus to the development of consultation. In 1955, the Berlin Conference and both Geneva conferences followed preparatory meetings of the North Atlantic Council at which delegates of the fifteen NATO members discussed acute problems of international politics relevant to negotiations with the Soviet Union. Since France, England, and the United States had no mandate to negotiate and conclude agreements with the USSR in the name of the other NATO countries, they consulted them before negotiating with the Russians. From that time on, the NATO Council has been an instrument for continuous consultation.[37] Consultation has become an accepted process in which the skill of individual diplomats sometimes is more important than the power position of their respective countries. This is one of the reasons why many states have been represented in the Council by outstanding plenipotentiaries.

The quality of representation has assured high standards in NATO discussions, and Council members have been able to transmit and interpret NATO policies for their governments clearly and directly. If unity of purpose exists, an exchange of information and opinions by experienced representatives may help even the strongest power. This method is more practical than consultation through bilateral channels. Discussions in NATO often illuminate new aspects of events and constitute a mutual educative process of the highest order. It is a measure of NATO's success that sometimes unity of view is achieved only after lively debates.

The new technique of multilateral diplomacy has amalgamated the conference method with the advantages of traditional diplomacy. The European Alliance after 1815 and the Concert of Europe were historical precedents for the kind of collective consultation which NATO has developed, although there were no permanent organs or any such organization like NATO. Sometimes, however, NATO consultation is at variance with the traditional procedures of diplomacy. Then tension may develop between practitioners of the two different methods. In the case of Cyprus, negotiations were conducted through regular diplomatic channels and consultation took place in the Council. On occasion representatives of the same country have disagreed among themselves as to the respective utility of consultation and the traditional diplomatic methods to expedite solution of a conflict.

The procedure of the Council is well established. As a rule it meets once a week, at which time the secretary general submits topics for discussion. The following week, representatives of the fifteen member governments may take positions on the basis of instructions from their governments. The Political Affairs Division of the Secretariat sometimes prepares, on the Council's instructions, background papers on political problems to be discussed in the Council. These papers

[37] There is a sharp difference between the procedure and attitudes in the process of consultation, on the one hand, and those in formal negotiations aiming at the conclusion of specific agreements, on the other.

go to the delegations of member countries and to the Committee of Political Advisors in which deputy heads usually represent the delegations. This Committee also performs important tasks in connection with the exchange of information and views in NATO and in the process of harmonizing and co-ordinating NATO policies; quite often the NATO Council instructs the Political Committee to discuss pertinent problems with a view to achieve such harmonization or coordination. Preparatory work by the Political Affairs Division of the Secretariat and by the NATO Committe of Political Advisors is of great importance because it is desirable that the outline of the position acceptable to fifteen member countries be worked out even before the Council meetings. Careful preparation greatly facilitates the task of the Council, which becomes an instrument for the formulation and expression of unity. In particular it is an organ for consultation in the following categories:

First—The relations between the NATO area and the Soviet Union. The Soviet threat to all NATO members is the primary *casus foederis* and remains the source of common danger.

Second—Advancement of the ends of NATO. This category pertains, for example, to peaceful settlement of any international dispute involving NATO members (Art. 1) and particularly to the application of Article 2 which provides for "the further development of peaceful and friendly international relations by strengthening their free institutions, by bringing about a better understanding of the principles upon which these institutions are founded, and by promoting conditions of stability and well-being."

Major examples of conflicts arising between member states are the Icelandic territorial sea and fishery controversy and the case of Cyprus. The Cyprus settlement was not negotiated in NATO but was greatly facilitated by various NATO efforts to bring about conciliation. Even during the most violent periods of the civil war in Cyprus, representatives of Greece and Turkey remained on speaking terms in the Council and, with the help of the secretary general, were constantly working for a settlement. In such delicate matters, the Council through consultation is often able to explore cautiously the possibility of settlement without fomenting hostile feelings.

The conflict between Britain and Iceland displayed the weakness of NATO diplomacy whenever member states involved in a dispute are unwilling to accept reasonable suggestions for a settlement. Eventually the United Kingdom was willing to accept a solution worked out by NATO in 1958. This settlement would have satisfied materially all legitimate Icelandic interests, but the Icelandic government could not accept a compromise because of the Icelandic internal political situation; it demanded the *de jure* recognition of the twelve-mile limit. Eventually, in an agreement signed in February, 1961, Britain conceded to Iceland almost all she has demanded.

In both cases NATO exercised an important restraining influence. If NATO had not existed, Greco-Turkish relations might have deteriorated beyond repair, and the British could have applied stronger measures against Iceland. In the latter case the Icelandic government could have asked for Russian support. This possibility, of course, was highly unlikely in view of the defense agreement between the United States and Iceland. The Icelandic government might have appealed to the United States for support, with rather damaging effects upon the United States defense structure if the American efforts to restrain the United Kingdom had been unsuccessful. Be that as it may, Iceland's defiance of a powerful ally and rejection of NATO's recommendation shows her independence. A similar incident would be unthinkable in the Soviet orbit.

When emotions dominate a situation, consultation or any other reasonable procedure is difficult. The problem of Cyprus, and the conflict between Great Britain and Iceland, are outstanding examples of this kind of situation. But even in delicate cases the process of confidential consultation clarifies the political atmosphere and makes possible the discovery of a basis of agreement or disagreement, whichever the case may be. In the upshot, it is rather reassuring to see that in NATO's history, consultation concerning disputes between members has consumed relatively little energy and time and has not become a major activity of the Council.

Third—While consultation is extremely valuable for the advancement of NATO's purposes within its own sphere, it has also an increasing importance in areas outside NATO's jurisdiction. Since the Soviet threat has assumed a global character, it is difficult to draw a line between the areas within and outside NATO's jurisdiction. Several NATO members have interests in the Far East, Middle East, Africa and other areas beyond NATO's original jurisdiction, and a growing category of consultations insofar as volume and importance are concerned, relates to exchange of information and views on developments outside of the NATO area. A common policy for dealing with conflicts in such areas can be worked out through consultation.

Paul-Henri Spaak, commenting on Article 4 even before the NATO Treaty was signed, explained that consultation between the signatories could also take place in the case of an incident occurring outside the geographical area of the pact if one of the parties considered its security involved.[38] But experience showed that the attitude of members in such cases may vary according to the particulars of each situation. There are, moreover, problems of global character, such as economic aid and disarmament. In these fields co-operation of NATO members is most desirable. Since the important international political problems mutually interact, a narrow interpretation of NATO's sphere and purposes would not be wise.

Consultation has been used most successfully in working out a united Western proposal in the field of disarmament. Indeed, the question of disarmament might almost be considered within NATO's sphere and purposes, because it is so intimately connected with the whole defense strategy and strategic position with respect to the USSR. Throughout the London negotiations between the USSR and the Western Four in the summer of 1957, an informal liaison was systematically maintained with the NATO Council in Paris. Simultaneous negotiations in London and Paris made possible the working-out of the united Western proposal presented at the Disarmament Conference in London on August 29. This united Western position was supported not only by Western European countries, but in the 12th General Assembly of the UN by twenty-four nations which sponsored a resolution endorsing the principles of the Western proposals. In the final vote 57 states accepted the resolution, with only the Soviet bloc voting against it.[39] The achievement of a common policy in such a complicated field as disarmament is a striking example of successful co-operation of NATO powers through consultation.

Favorable trends in NATO consultation have been occasionally balanced by serious setbacks. The system of consultation was in full operation in 1956 when the second half of the year witnessed a hardening of the cold war, the outbreak of the Polish and Hungarian revolutions, and the secretly prepared Anglo-French action in Suez. The Suez affair was certainly a case which should have been a direct concern of NATO, but there was no consultation. This lack of co-operation was the result of a series of political mistakes and of a

[38] *New York Times,* March 19, 1949.

[39] *Disarmament: The Intensified Effort* (Washington, 1958), p. 57.

mutual lack of confidence. *Peccatur intra muros et extra muros.* This incident was a blow to the system of consultation and could have threatened the very existence of NATO. But nothing better proved the vitality of NATO than the fact that the Suez crisis eventually strengthened rather than weakened the organization. An important psychological result of the unilateral Anglo-French action and the American response to it, and of the Soviet intervention in Hungary, was general realization of the need for Western unity. After this critical period England and the continental European countries showed remarkable solidarity, although most European countries were not sympathetic with the British and French action at Suez.

Amidst the dramatic events in 1956, NATO further strengthened its technique of multilateral diplomacy. The Committee of Three on Non-Military Co-operation in NATO was set up in May "to advise the Council on ways and means to improve and extend NATO co-operation in non-military fields and to develop greater unity within the Atlantic Community." The committee, consisting of three foreign ministers—Lester B. Pearson of Canada, Gaetano Martino of Italy, and Halvard Lange of Norway—sent out a questionnaire to the government of each NATO member. Analysis and examination of the replies was followed by individual consultation with representatives of member states. The draft of the report made up by the committee was re-examined in November, 1956, in the light of the preceding events. The final text was approved at the Ministerial Council Meeting in December, 1956. The report is an all-embracing program both for co-operation in the political, economic, cultural, and information fields and for the organization and function of NATO. It stated that: "An Alliance in which the members ignore each other's interests or engage in political or economic conflict, or harbor suspicions of each other, cannot be effective either for deterrence or defense. Recent experience makes this clearer than ever before."

The chapter on political co-operation in the report restated some passages from the 1952 report of the "three wise men" concerning the role of consultation in political co-operation, and made some further suggestions.[40] It emphasized that there was "a pressing requirement for all members to make consultation in NATO an integral part of the making of national policy." In order to have effective political consultation about actions to be taken, members "should inform the Council of any development which significantly affects

[40] See above, p. 35.

the Alliance." At their annual spring meeting the NATO foreign ministers "should make an appraisal of the political progress of the Alliance and consider the lines along which it should advance." The secretary general should submit an annual report that would serve as a basis for the discussion of the foreign ministers. The peaceful settlement of intermember disputes within the NATO framework before resorting to any other international agency was recommended; and the secretary general was empowered "to offer his good offices informally at any time to the parties in dispute, and with their consent to initiate or facilitate procedures of inquiry, mediation, conciliation, or arbitration."

Although the procedure of consultation is not new, governments have never before used it so extensively and systematically. Views are exchanged on such important matters as the Berlin crisis and the reunification of Germany, negotiations at the summit, suspension of nuclear tests, and establishment of zones of inspection to prevent surprise attack. In harmony with this spirit of co-operation, the United States in the spring of 1958 disclosed to the Council its policies concerning Formosa and the Chinese offshore islands. In a similar way, Britain and the United States discussed the 1958 Middle Eastern situation in the Council and made clear that under certain circumstances they would respond with military assistance to the request of friendly governments endangered by subversion and aggression. At that time the United States had received a request from President Camille Chamoun of Lebanon who, explaining that his regime was threatened by external aggression, asked for support. The American delegate pointed out in the NATO Council that the United States would like to avoid military intervention in Lebanon but that events might make it necessary. When the coup took place in Iraq, there was no time for another consultation, and President Eisenhower simply ordered the Marines to land in Lebanon as requested by Chamoun. Despite the correctness of the procedure, leading political circles in some NATO countries, France and Turkey in particular, resented that a second consultation did not take place before military intervention, although this point of view was not expressed in the NATO Council. According to French opinion, American policy did not take into account France's centuries-old connection in Lebanon. France thought she should have participated in the intervention or at least have been consulted before the landing. The Turks were resentful that Turkey was not consulted before a military action, which seriously affected the Middle Eastern situation, was undertaken in her neighborhood.[41]

This incident illustrates one of the characteristics of NATO diplomacy, namely, that in a concrete case consultation might mean different things for different nations. Generally speaking, consultation to Americans means both exchange of information and exchange of views concerning the attitude or action to be taken in connection with a political problem. The purpose of an exchange of views can be either to inform the member countries of national policy in connection with a certain area or development or to harmonize the policy of member governments or again to achieve co-ordinated policy. According to more restrictive interpretations, however, NATO consultation in most cases is not consultation in the sense the Americans use the word, but only exchange of information. In reality, bilateral diplomacy between friendly states, and consultation in a collective body, have the same object: exchange of ideas to promote understanding and agreement. Senator Theodore F. Green said at the NATO Parliamentarians' Conference on November 18, 1958, that NATO is not ready to be transformed into a political union, and he defined the role of consultation in the following way:

> The North Atlantic Council can be a useful forum for greater political consultation, but it is unrealistic and even undesirable to expect to develop a common NATO foreign policy. What should be sought instead is a greater coordination of the foreign policies of NATO members, or at the very least a thorough exchange of views, so that members acquire a greater understanding of each other's problems, and so that no member feels it is being left out of decisions which affect it.

The Report of the Committee of Three on Non-Military Co-operation in NATO defines correctly the meaning and importance of consultation:

> Consultation within an alliance means more than an exchange of information, though that is necessary. It means more than letting the NATO Council know about national decisions that have already been taken; or trying to enlist support for those decisions. It means the discussion of problems collectively, in the early stages of policy formation, and before national positions

[41] For the international legal aspects of the case, see Quincy Wright, "United States Intervention in the Lebanon," *American Journal of International Law*, LIII (1959), 112-25. For the difficulties connected with the American landing in Lebanon, see Charles W. Thayer, *Diplomat* (New York, 1959), pp. 1-37.

become fixed. At best, this will result in collective decisions on matters of common interest affecting the Alliance. At the least, it will ensure that no action is taken by one member without a knowledge of the views of the others.

From the point of view of results, the following can be said about NATO consultations:

First—A consultation is successful when a meeting of minds is possible and there is agreement on policies.

Second—It may well be that after consultation some NATO members decide to follow different courses, and thus consultation would be unsuccessful even though it would at least clarify attitudes. An unsuccessful consultation took place in July, 1958, when the United States and Britain accepted and France opposed a summit meeting within the framework of the UN Security Council. The NATO Council failed to reconcile the differing Allied views, and President de Gaulle in his separate letter to Khrushchev stated that he preferred a summit conference at Geneva rather than a special session of the UN on the Middle East crisis.[42] Difference of policy, however, is not necessarily harmful, and there are areas in which the unity of NATO members is not essential. It would not be wise for NATO states to form a bloc in the UN. It would not even be practical to co-ordinate Western policies for UN matters in Paris. New problems may arise every day in the UN, and necessary co-ordination should be done in New York by Western delegations to the UN. Of course, it may be a matter of controversy whether in some cases a uniform NATO policy is desirable or whether the member states should have a free hand. It has been assumed that the common spirit resulting from an exchange of ideas in the NATO Council promotes common policies even without binding agreements.

Third—The consultation is most unsatisfactory when some member states announce their intended policies in the Council and a number of representatives do not react at all. This was the case in the summer of 1958 when Britain and the United States declared their intentions concerning the Middle and Far East. The small powers have a reasonable explanation for their reserved attitude. Parliaments and the public in some small countries are not always interested in the solution of a conflict outside NATO's jurisdiction. And most of them are unwilling to take a position in cases outside NATO's jurisdiction. They have little information through their own channels

[42] *New York Times*, July 11, 21, 23, 25, 26, 31, and August 1, 1958.

on Far Eastern and other non-NATO problems and they usually are little interested in them. They are reluctant to express even an opinion. Some high NATO officials and those great powers which announce their policies to the NATO Council resent such an attitude in the belief that each member state has the responsibility to express at least an opinion. Since there is a high degree of interdependence in our shrinking world, this thesis is not without validity. Some small states argue that the squirrels do not even know the weapons of the elephants, so how could they have a well-considered opinion concerning strategy or even tactics for a struggle when some basic factors of the situation are not within their grasp. They do not have sufficient information concerning American global capabilities and know even less the strength of the opposing forces in a particular area. The inequality of military strength between the members of the nuclear club, on the one hand, and the remaining states on the other, has become added reason for a reserved attitude even within the Alliance.

Although United States policy in the Formosa Straits, or Anglo-American intervention in the Middle East, could have led to general conflict, some small NATO members thought that their silence during consultation was the better course. In such cases silence should not be understood as implying either consent or indifference. Here silence is a consequence of weakness and lack of direct interest in, and possibly of information on, distant areas. Thus these small states accept information given them in distant conflicts with a feeling of fatalism, for they do not want to take a position on every world issue brought before the Council.

Secretary General Spaak took a different position on the responsibilities of small NATO states in matters outside NATO's immediate sphere. Pointing out in a speech before the Conference of NATO Parliamentarians in November, 1958, that several countries remained silent regarding the Anglo-American statement of policy in Middle Eastern affairs, he gave the following interpretation of consultation:

> From the moment when we claim that we can be consulted because we know that a conflict breaking out in the Middle East could have direct repercussions on our own situation, we are committed; from the moment when we call for consultations and still more take part in them, that is, give our views, then our responsibility begins.[43]

[43] *NATO Letter*, VI (December, 1958), 9.

This far-reaching interpretation of "responsibility through consultation" is not accepted by the majority of small powers. Even Spaak pointed out that he did not know whether diplomatic silence in the Council meant yes or no.

Of course, "silence" is only one of the manifestations of the major problem which has presented itself, namely, as to whether NATO can achieve a common or co-ordinated policy in matters lying outside the NATO area. That smaller countries prefer not to say anything in the discussion of such problems is due not only to the fact that they either do not have the necessary information or else have no opinion as to the question of how far NATO action in third areas should go. Underlying their attitude is a reluctance to extend even by implication the NATO commitment outside of the treaty area. This is one of the important problems of the Alliance at the present time and there is no indication as yet of what the future trend will be.

Since NATO consultation is a new method of collective diplomacy, it is not surprising that many aspects of it are unclarified. When great powers such as the United States and Great Britain submit important diplomatic notes to the NATO Council and discuss their foreign political problems there with representatives of small powers, it is a revolution in diplomacy. Thus Spaak has commented:

> The only word I can find to describe this new picture is "moving," when we see . . . that President Eisenhower does not write to M. Bulganin or to M. Khrushchev without making sure that his letter is approved by the head of the Government or by the Foreign Minister of the smallest country in the Alliance.
>
> Public opinion must be made aware that something entirely new has happened and that diplomatic traditions and customs have been turned upside down. . . . these consultations have not been a matter of pure form. Many of the drafts submitted to the Atlantic Council have been not only discussed, but also commented on and criticized and . . . in nearly all cases I think, the large countries which have submitted the text of their letters or notes have taken the remarks made into account.[44]

It is true that the disparity in economic and military power, and in world responsibilities, is a source of difficulty in consultation. There are, moreover, special difficulties in the case of the United States. The position of a superpower is characterized by a certain loneliness. The United States, as the richest and strongest member of the coalition,

[44] *Ibid.*, pp. 7-8.

necessarily acts as banker, and the other NATO countries as receivers. They expect American support for their defense plans. Moreover, the strongest power in NATO has global problems of a different nature from those of the small European states with their limited interest. The possession or lack of power contributes to the formation of different points of view. In addition, the American political system has what is probably the most complicated machinery for the formulation of foreign policy. The presentation by the United States of problems for NATO consultation before American policy has been sufficiently clarified in Washington could open a Pandora's box.

NATO consultation is a new and almost revolutionary method of diplomacy, but not a panacea for international ills. It may facilitate the solution of conflicts, but it cannot eliminate the substantial differences that originate in varying conceptions of the Soviet threat and of the best Western response to it. Domestic political considerations, national interests, and diverse approaches to political problems may cause friction, but considering these and many other difficulties the success of consultation has been impressive.

Although there is a clear legal obligation to consult only in cases when "the territorial integrity, political independence or security of the member states is threatened," there is some evidence that NATO has created a common spirit and habit of co-operation that is effective even in domestic politics and in areas outside NATO's functions. On occasion some governments have been able to neutralize domestic opposition to an unpopular action because they could present it as the desire of a group of countries belonging to NATO, whereas they might not have been successful if that desire had been the result only of bilateral negotiations or some domestic political considerations. Consequently, the political climate created by NATO consultation may be conducive to co-operation even in issues not directly related to NATO, and perhaps even in unpopular ones.

Despite the natural difficulties and ups and downs of international politics, the process of multilateral consultation has been making steady progress within NATO. It has become one of the important sources of a more co-operative attitude. Its systematic application will greatly influence the habits of governments and will have a considerable effect on individual representatives. A habit of co-operation develops in NATO bodies, and it continues to influence representatives even after they return home and act in different capacities and circumstances.

TOWARDS AN ATLANTIC COMMUNITY

If countries in the North Atlantic area could co-operate effectively, they would become easily the strongest power center in the world. But fifteen governments control the resources of NATO and their affirmative decisions are necessary for action. This politically unintegrated NATO structure confronts the monolithic Soviet empire in which decisions are made most of the time at a single center, the Kremlin. Since free nations cannot be forced to co-operate by methods contrary to Western principles, a united policy can emerge only through consultation.

The habit of consultation is not only necessary in the day-to-day decision-making process but has potentialities for furthering a community spirit on the shores of the North Atlantic. A growing sense of community would create a congenial political atmosphere in which NATO could be of more use for a variety of purposes. The democratic character of the leading NATO countries is a cardinal factor in this process.

The development of a habit of co-operation is all the more important because the favorable disposition of governments toward consultation should be only the first step toward further integration in the North Atlantic area. Support of national parliaments, public opinion, and the entire bureaucratic apparatus of the member states will be necessary for strengthening unity within NATO through consultation. It is difficult to change old social attitudes and phobias, and consequently the growth of a habit of co-operation must be gradual. European history does not offer many encouraging examples in this respect. On the other hand, the English and American inclination to compromise is a favorable influence that will foster co-operation. Traditions and practices developed in the Pan American Conferences and the British Commonwealth are useful; they constitute the major American and British contributions to the creation of a community feeling within NATO.

The important thing is that, in the light of events of the last few years, members of NATO more fully realize how related their freedom and security are. A NATO that would be merely a strict military alliance, exposed to transformations in military technology and the uncertainties of power politics, could not fulfill its promise. Therefore, it should grow from a military alliance into a permanent international organization of a general character in the North Atlantic area.

The road ahead will not be easy. Although close co-operation in the North Atlantic area has proved its value, there are obstacles to further development along this line. We have, in fact, witnessed glaring failures. Space does not permit fuller discussion of political mistakes made by members of the Alliance and of desirable reforms for NATO. The rapidly changing political scene, both outside and inside the Western coalition, will always present new problems. Secretary Spaak pointed out at the Fourth Annual Assembly of the Atlantic Treaty Association at Boston in September, 1958, that in 1949 the communist threat was essentially European and military, while in 1958 it had become more Asian and African, and more economic and social than military. He asked: "Is it sufficient, at the present time to construct a solid military barrier along the Elbe, on the eastern frontier of the free world if the free world is to be outflanked politically, militarily and economically in the Middle East and Africa?" He stated that the idea of a military Atlantic Alliance restricted to a geographic area was no longer adequate in 1958, and suggested:

> A common policy, probably of world-wide scope, must be added to it . . . Another thing which should be done as quickly as possible is the organization of scientific cooperation, and even economic and social action should be harmonized. In a word, the Atlantic Alliance should become the Atlantic Community.[45]

Although controversies within NATO on important policy questions and military defense weaken the West, the differences are not basic from the long-range point of view, and they are often exaggerated by public discussion which, though the natural corollary of a democratic political system in both domestic and international relations, is nevertheless sometimes prejudicial to the attainment of a common understanding. Public support for NATO remains necessary, because NATO operates within democratic societies. There is something to be gained by public discussion, although it often magnifies differences to Western disadvantage. This has been particularly true in connection with the problem raised by President de Gaulle over leadership of the Alliance and France's role in it. The public controversy inside and outside the Alliance over Germany's bid for military supply depots and air training facilities in Spain is another example.

International conditions make imperative a closer economic co-

[45] *Ibid.*, VI (September-October, 1958), 21-22.

operation in NATO. One of the most important Western tasks is the organization of technical assistance and economic aid on a global scale. But it is even more important that the economic diplomacy of the NATO countries should become part of an over-all NATO policy. Otherwise the West cannot compete successfully with the centrally directed communist economic diplomacy. Although communist foreign aid, trade, loans, and investments are still small compared to similar Western activities, they are concentrated on strategically important countries and in some cases are carried out without regard to cost.

It should be noted, however, that economic questions, particularly questions of trade and development assistance, are matters of great interest to a number of countries that are not members of NATO. These countries also have a great deal to contribute to the general economic growth and to the assistance of developing countries. It was with this situation in mind that Undersecretary Dillon made his proposals at the meeting of the Special Economic Committee in Paris, January 12-14, 1960, for a reorganization of the OEEC into the OECD (Organization for Economic Cooperation and Development), aiming at closer co-ordination of economic policies, at trade and technical assistance, and at full membership in the new organization for the United States and Canada. The supreme objective of the OECD should be the planning and organization of a global Marshall Plan in harmony with similar activities of the United Nations. A preliminary condition of such a grandiose scheme is the avoidance of a trade war between the European Economic Community and the European Free Trade Association, and the establishment of co-operation, if not of some kind of union, between them. Of course, NATO's primary objectives are military and political, but the economic problem today is part of the political problem, and NATO's leadership should have considerable influence on the conduct of Western economic diplomacy.[46]

[46] Representatives of twenty nations signed the OECD treaty in Paris on December 14, 1960. The target date is September 30, 1961, when the OECD will begin to function and replace the OEEC if by this date fifteen of the signatory powers ratify the treaty.

The new organization will have the United States and Canada as full members in addition to Austria, Belgium, Britain, Denmark, France, West Germany, Greece, Iceland, Ireland, Italy, Luxembourg, The Netherlands, Norway, Portugal, Spain, Sweden, Switzerland and Turkey. Major goals of the OECD are: to achieve rates of economic growth and levels of employment in member states

One cannot emphasize enough the need for more co-operation in the cultural field. The existence of a North Atlantic civilization has been generally recognized, but a new Erasmus is needed to express meaningfully and to formulate definitively the idea of a Euro-American cultural community. This community presents a plurality of cultures, but there can be unity in diversity. Fundamental ideas associated with Western civilization are basic to NATO countries. Co-ordination within NATO on the cultural front, especially co-operation in scientific achievements, may be more important than the present co-ordination of defense expenditures, however necessary and important the latter may be. A common understanding of the basic conditions of life is a prerequisite for common survival. In this and many other respects, the contributions of conferences of NATO parliamentarians are important. They are symbols of solidarity among NATO nations. Organized contact and co-operation of American congressmen with members of Canadian and European parliaments should be developed more systematically.

Despite some serious crises on the world scene and within NATO, there has been progress in Atlantic co-operation since 1949. The two secretary generals of NATO strengthened not only the structure of the Alliance but strongly supported co-operative policies in the North Atlantic area. This trend has not changed with the resignation of Secretary Spaak on January 31, 1961. Although fear was expressed that the new administration might change American policy toward the Atlantic nations, President Kennedy in his message to NATO, February 15, 1961, not only pledged the United States to maintain its full military commitments to the Atlantic Alliance but in some respects went further than the previous administration. In particular, he stressed the importance of achieving common Atlantic policies in nonmilitary fields and emphasized that the interest of the Atlantic Community transgresses the military sphere:

> The dangers to our security and the challenges of our enterprise take many forms—economic, ideological and political. Through its various instruments, the Atlantic Community must equip itself to respond with speed and unity of purpose on every front—by improving our processes of consultation, by expanding the area of

---

as high as possible, to contribute to sound economic development in underdeveloped areas as well as in the treaty family, and to work for an expansion of world trade on a multilateral and nondiscriminatory basis. No member will be obligated to undertake any action unless it specifically approves.

> our co-operation to include common problems of trade and money, and by uniting in the effort to construct a sound, growing economy for the entire noncommunist world.

After having dealt with economic problems and the role to be played by the OECD, the President returned to the heart of the contemporary political challenge:

> Although the technical task here is economic, our ultimate purpose transcends material considerations. The challenge is to create a new partnership between the old nations in the north and the new nations to the south. In the end, we must build that partnership not merely on a common interest in economic growth, but on a common commitment to the principles of political freedom.

Strengthening NATO is not only a Western interest; it is important for the whole noncommunist world and the future of mankind. The security community in the North Atlantic area should be the powerhouse of the world, the beacon of freedom pointing toward happier developments for the human race. Integration in the North Atlantic area does not imply antagonism toward other regions. It can foster freedom everywhere. Without a strong NATO it would be difficult for countries in Africa and Asia to follow a neutralist policy. More integration of the North Atlantic area would make possible closer co-operation with the rest of the noncommunist world, and continuation of that Western civilization which has made possible the progress of all mankind.

3: THE CONTAINMENT POLICY AND THE RATIONALE OF THE ALLIANCE SYSTEM

Hans J. Morgenthau

In order to understand the rationale of the policies of containment and alliances that the United States has pursued since 1947, it is necessary to connect these policies with the traditional American attitude towards foreign policy. This attitude was committed to two major tenets: to limit the permanent American involvement in foreign policy to the Western Hemisphere and, insofar as the rest of the world was concerned, to assist it in ridding itself of the evils of power politics. During the concluding phase of the Second World War the United States took upon itself the task of reconstruction by reviving the traditional conception of a world free of power politics. Emerging from the war as the most powerful nation on earth, without whose global involvement the political world could not be reconstructed nor its national interests safeguarded, the United States now faced the traditional dilemma of trying to reform a world which refused to be reformed, without the benefit of the isolationist escape. On the one hand, it was committed by its tradition to limiting its continuous involvement in international affairs to the Western Hemisphere, whose peaceful and harmonious state in the shadow of American hegemony was contrasted with the rivalries and wars, in short, the power politics, of the rest of the world. On the other hand, with only two power centers left in the world, of which the other happened to be the Soviet Union, the choice of 1920 was no longer open to the United States; that choice would now have meant anarchy in Europe and Asia to be followed by the establishment of order under the auspices of communism. How, then, could the United States combine its tradition of steering clear of power politics outside the Western Hemisphere with its inevitable involvement in the affairs of the world?

If the United States could no longer isolate itself from a world infected with what it chose to call power politics, it had to decontaminate the world from that infection in order to make it safe for the United States to get permanently involved with it. Thus the leaders of the United States anticipated a postwar world and prepared for its coming where, in the words of Secretary of State Cordell Hull, "there will no longer be need for spheres of influence, for alliances, for balance of power, or any other of the special arrangements through which, in the unhappy past, the nations strove to safeguard their security or promote their interests." [1] These expectations, voiced in 1943 after Great Britain, the Soviet Union, and the United States had agreed upon the establishment of the United Nations, moved President Roosevelt on March 1, 1945, in his report to Congress on the Yalta Conference, to declare:

> The Crimean Conference . . . spells the end of the system of unilateral action and exclusive alliances and spheres of influence and balances of power and all the other expedients which have been tried for centuries—and have failed.
>
> We propose to substitute for all these a universal organization in which all peace-loving nations will finally have a chance to join.[2]

When Wilson prepared for the postwar world with similar expectations, his contemporaries could still try to restore the traditional hemispheric limitations of the American purpose by returning to isolationism. They simply disavowed him by turning their backs on America's involvement in the affairs of the world. No such disavowal of Roosevelt's and Hull's expectations was necessary, and no such return to isolationism was possible, when the American people faced the world at the end of the Second World War. There was a moment in the immediate aftermath of that war when the United States appeared to yield to the temptation of doing what it had done after the First World War: dismantle the power with which it had won the war and act as though the potential for that power did not exist. This was the moment when it disbanded its armed forces and abruptly cancelled Lend-Lease. Yet at the very moment it was thus tempted, the threat of Russian power destroyed the attractiveness of the temptation.

The Soviet Union's interpretation of the Yalta agreements in terms

[1] Report to Congress on Moscow Conference, *New York Times*, November 19, 1943.

[2] *Nothing to Fear:* The Selected Addresses of Franklin Delano Roosevelt 1932-1945 (Cambridge, 1946), p. 453.

of the expansion of Russian power and not of international co-operation revealed the utopian character of Roosevelt's and Hull's expectations and threatened the European balance of power and, through it, the vital interests of the United States. It made obvious that for the United States the fruit of victory was to be neither a minimal normalcy without power politics nor the safety of hemispheric isolation. Thus the expansion of Russian power, threatening the security of the United States, by virtue of the selfsame Yalta agreements upon which we had pinned the expectations of an "American" world without power politics, ushered in the most formidable of all the crises of American foreign policy.

That crisis proceeded in two stages. The first stage was a period of adaptation, of restoration, of re-creation culminating in the "fifteen weeks" of 1947 during which a whole new system of American foreign policy was devised, derived from a radically new concept of American foreign policy. When toward the close of the Second World War the emerging postwar world refused to respond to the traditional expectations of the American leaders, the United States, morally outraged and intellectually stunned, was for some fateful months incapable of translating the shock of disappointment into coherent understanding and consistent action. The political world had finally caught up with the American fugitives from politics. They had again stepped beyond the continental limits in order to rid the world of a source of trouble, expecting to return to the normal peace of the hemisphere after the performance of the task. Yet before that task was fully completed, the United States found itself already in the throes of new trouble, less tractable than any it had ever faced before and less likely to yield to the drastic remedy of total war. The traditional purpose was now clearly beyond attainment, and no new purpose had yet emerged to take its place. An aimless and inconsistent foreign policy reflected that lack of purpose. In the words of Sir Winston Churchill:

> We can now see the deadly hiatus which existed between the fading of President Roosevelt's strength and the growth of President Truman's grip of the vast world problem. In this melancholy void one President could not act and the other could not know. Neither the military chiefs nor the State Department received the guidance they required. The former confined themselves to their professional sphere; the latter did not comprehend the issues involved. The indispensable political direction was lacking at the moment when it was most needed. The United States stood on

the scene of victory, master of world fortunes, but without a true and coherent design.[3]

That lack of design was most clearly revealed and had the most grievous consequences for the United States in Central Europe and China. In Central Europe, the lack of design consisted in the divorcement of military operations from political objectives. Or, to put it more precisely, military operations remained tied to political assumptions which, in the spring of 1945, had become obsolete. These assumptions were the Wilsonian expectations of the American leaders. It was on the basis of these assumptions that the West agreed to have its armies stop at a certain line in Central Europe and pull them back to that line if they should have gone beyond it. And it was on the basis of the same assumptions that the American generals refused to march straight east and take Berlin and instead followed a course of action that might have been sounder from a strictly military point of view but proved to be unrewarding politically.

Yet if these assumptions were wrong—as they obviously were—and if the postwar world was still a world of power politics, of balance of power, alliances, and spheres of influence, then these military measures were politically pernicious and laid the ground for the political and military predicament that we have had to struggle with ever since. Had the United States been aware of the nature of the political world that it was to enter at the end of the Second World War, it would have bent every effort, consistent with the overwhelming goal of winning the war, to keep the Red Army as far east as possible. Had it followed this course, today West Berlin would not be an island in a red sea, Czechoslovakia would not be a Russian satellite, and the Red Army would not stand 100 miles east of the Rhine. The United States did not follow this course because it was so anxious to continue to live in a political environment of security and reasonable harmony—although that environment was now no longer hemispheric but had become world-wide—that it took the expectation for the fact and understood the political world in terms not of its intrinsic political nature but of its own apolitical expectations. In one word, the United States attempted to continue pursuing its traditional foreign policy by assuming that the world was as conducive to this achievement as the Western Hemisphere had been. The assumption being erroneous, the attempt was bound to fail.

[3] Winston Churchill, *Triumph and Tragedy* (Boston, 1953), pp. 455-56.

It is a tribute to the pragmatic genius of America, which is capable of meeting a practical problem on its own merits in a matter-of-fact way and without the hindrance of traditional though obsolete patterns of thought and action, that the "deadly hiatus," filled with such erroneous thinking, inarticulate action, and untoward results, was relatively brief and was followed by a radically new departure in thought and action. By 1947 a new pattern of American foreign policy was set. It manifested itself in four political innovations: containment, the Truman doctrine, the Marshall Plan, and the American alliance system. They have in common the permanent assumption by the United States of responsibilities beyond the limits of the Western Hemisphere. We have learned to take these responsibilities for granted and have thus tended to forget how complete and unprecedented a departure from the American tradition the permanent assumption of these responsibilities constitutes.

The American tradition limited the continuous activities of the United States in foreign affairs to the Western Hemisphere. The great reversal of 1947 extended the permanent military commitment of the United States immediately beyond the Rhine and potentially to any region anywhere threatened by communist aggression or subversion. It further committed the economic resources of the United States directly to the support of the nations of Western Europe, of Greece and Turkey, and potentially of any nation anywhere which needed them to preserve its freedom. It had become the policy of the United States, in the words of the Truman Doctrine, "to support free peoples who are resisting attempted subjugation by armed minorities, or by outside pressures." Since peoples throughout the world—in Europe, Africa, Asia, and Latin America—are resisting such subjugation, the commitments of the United States have, by virtue of the Truman Doctrine, become world-wide, unlimited geographically and limited only by a lack of need for support or unwillingness to accept it.

Of the traditional foreign policy of the United States, this revolution in America's relations to the outside world has made short shrift. Nothing is left of it but a memory of, and, in some, a vain desire to return to an age when the United States was committed to defend only its own territory and not the nations of Western Europe, Berlin, Pakistan, Thailand, Australia, New Zealand, South Viet Nam, Korea, and Taiwan, and when the United States endeavored to transform the world by its own example rather than by intervening, assisting, and advising throughout the world.

What accounts for this radical transformation, which, in view of the issues solved, constitutes also a magnificent achievement? Why is it that in 1947 America found within itself the resources to combat, with such magnificent assurance, the threat of Russian power? The threat of Russian power is different in magnitude but not in kind from the threats that America had to deal and did deal with successfully in the 18th and 19th centuries at its western and southern frontiers, and in the two world wars in Europe. The redskins, it is true, threatened the United States more directly than did the Red Army. Yet the threat to the European balance of power, of which the Red Army is the instrument as were the German armies of the two world wars, is merely a more insidious and more deadly threat to American security than were the Indian forays, and it was so understood by America. After an initial period of intellectual doubt and vacillation, the United States reacted to the successive threats to the balance of power in Europe as it had reacted to the threats to its territorial integrity in America: by appropriate acts of self-defense. The threat of Russian power, then, fitted into the American experience of external threats, and the answer to it was to be found among the traditional weapons of American self-defense, adapted to the exigencies of a novel situation.

More particularly, the kind of answer required was traditional in two respects. The quality of the answer depended upon American decision alone, and the answer was consummated in one unequivocal action. The United States could take the place of Great Britain as the champion of Greece and Turkey or it could refrain from doing so. The implementation of the decision to take Britain's place through economic and military assistance followed with virtual inevitability from the decision itself. This was the kind of decision and these were the policies to which the United States was conditioned by the experiences of its history. As the threat of Russian power was not in essence different from the threats which America had faced throughout its history, so the decisions and policies designed to meet that threat did not differ essentially in their unilateral and unambiguous nature from the policies through which the United States had defended and promoted its interests in the past. In one word, the policy of containment was an adequate response to the threat of Russian power and eminently successful in that it achieved what it set out to achieve: the containment of Russian military power within the limits it had reached at the end of the Second World War.

However, the policy of containment was less obviously successful in the measure that it had to be more than a simple military response to a military threat. The United States was conditioned by its historic experience to consider the issues of foreign policy primarily in military terms. Thus it tended to interpret threats to its interests that could somehow be traced to the Soviet Union in military terms, and tried to counter them by military means. Both the conduct of the Korean War and the policy of alliances, conceived as a universal response to the communist threat, demonstrate the limitations of the policy of containment.

The Korean War started as an outright military aggression that confronted the United States with the traditional choice of opposing or not opposing it with military means. The American response, in its swiftness, its purposeful determination and its effectiveness, was in the best tradition of American responses to military threats. Yet it lost its traditional qualities as soon as the threat lost its purely military character and transformed itself into a complex political issue in which the Korean War appeared a mere manifestation of Russian and Chinese power and communist expansionism.

From the outset, the Korean War was interpreted, and in all likelihood misinterpreted, as the opening shot, which the Soviet Union had fired by proxy, in a military campaign to conquer the world. The Korean War was seen in the context of the communist goal of world conquest, as an initial limited and probing operation pursuant to a master plan that envisaged the military conquest of the world. There is no empirical evidence to support this interpretation of the Korean War, and what empirical evidence there is points to a different interpretation. It is much more likely that in 1950 the North Korean government was as eager to unite the country by marching south as the South Korean government was eager to unite it by marching north. While the United States was willing and able to restrain the South Koreans, the Soviet Union seems to have given the North Koreans a free hand, after having been assured that there was no risk of American intervention. When events proved this assurance to be fallacious, the general who had been the Russian proconsul in North Korea was dismissed and reappeared from oblivion only in the late 1950s. Within the over-all context of Soviet foreign policy, the Korean War is likely to have been an accident, the unintended result of an isolated miscalculation rather than part of a grand design for world conquest.

While the Korean War was thus falsely connected with Russian power and communist expansionism, it was mistakenly divorced from the national interest of China. For due to its geographic location in the proximity of China, Korea has existed as an autonomous state for most of its long history by virtue of the control or intervention of its powerful neighbor. Whenever the power of China was not sufficient to protect the autonomy of Korea, another nation, generally Japan, would try to gain a foothold on the Korean peninsula. Since the first century B.C. the international status of Korea has by and large been determined either by the supremacy of Chinese power or by the rivalry between China and Japan over control of the Korean peninsula.

From these two fallacious assumptions, the United States tried to develop the purpose of the Korean War. In view of what it thought was Russian involvement, the United States was anxious to limit the war to the Korean peninsula. In view of what it thought was Chinese detachment, the United States did not hesitate to advance to the Yalu River. And Chinese intervention only strengthened American anxiety to limit the Korean War. While the United States started to fight the war with the purpose of resisting the North Korean aggression, it expanded this strictly military purpose to the political one of uniting Korea by force of arms, a campaign to be limited—in view of Russian, and regardless of Chinese, power—to the peninsula. Yet the intervention of Chinese power compelled the United States to limit its purpose to the restoration of the status quo at the 38th parallel. Thus the intrusion of the political factor into what seemed to be at the outset a strictly military emergency to be met by military means called for political calculations of a much higher order of subtlety and complexity. The United States, unprepared by its historic experience for such a task, was not equal to it.

America, once its policy of containment had met successfully the Russian military threat to the noncommunist world's survival, had to achieve three different tasks. First of all, it had to create out of the makeshift arrangements aimed at meeting the Russian military threat a viable international order which would translate common interests into a common purpose, fuse the power of individual nations, and assign to them responsibilities commensurate with their interests and power. Second, it had to create a relationship with the uncommitted new nations of Africa and Asia, which would further a new domestic and international stability of peace and freedom in the image of the stability achieved by the United States. Third, it had to establish a relationship conducive both to peace and freedom with those nations who were unwilling objects of communist domination, such as the nations of Eastern Europe.

How did the United States endeavor to meet these tasks? The answer to this question is simple and the very simplicity of the answer is the measure of America's failure. The United States conceived of these tasks primarily in military terms, that is, in terms of actual or potential alliances.

The relationships within an alliance are determined by two fundamental factors: the interests and the power of its members. The interests which tie the United States to its European allies are more profound, more comprehensive, and more stable than are the interests that alliances have traditionally been based upon. Far from concerning nothing more than a limited territorial advantage against a temporary enemy, these interests enclose the national identity of all its members within a common civilization, threatened by an alien and oppressive social system. Thus this alliance was not formed, as alliances typically are, through a process of haggling and horse-trading among suspicious temporary associates, looking already for more advantageous associations elsewhere. Rather this alliance sprang naturally and almost inevitably from a common concern with a common heritage that had a chance to survive only through common support. The members of the alliance had to choose between the alliance and the loss of their national identity and cultural heritage; that is to say, they had no choice at all.

The cement that kept that alliance together was the paramount power of the United States. While in past alliances power had been unequally distributed with one ally being predominant, rarely had there been such a concentration of paramount power in one ally, with all the other allies, even collectively, being in a subordinate position. And rarely had there been so all-persuasive a paramount power which was at the same time coterminous with the concerns of the alliance. For the United States was not only paramount in the military and economic fields, but also in the intangible sphere of the values of Western civilization. In one word, the United States had become in every respect the predominant power of the alliance.

Had the institutions and operations of the alliance been commensurate with the comprehensiveness and intensity of the interests underlying it, and had the influence exerted by the United States been commensurate with its power, the alliance would have fallen very little short of, if it had not amounted to, a confederation of states, merging their most vital activities in the fields of foreign policy, defense, finance, and economics. Nothing of the kind occurred. For the United States proved to be incapable of playing the role it ought to have played as the paramount member of the Western alliance. Three inherited patterns of thought and action prevented it from playing that role: the limitation of the direct exercise of American power to the Western Hemisphere, the principle of equality, and the military approach to foreign policy.

The two previous occasions which carried American power beyond the limits of the Western Hemisphere were peculiar in that they allowed American power to retreat into its traditional limits after it had failed to establish itself firmly beyond them. The liquidation of the conquests of the Spanish-American War, in view of the accidental and peripheral connection with the American purpose, could begin virtually as soon as the conquests had been made. The failure of Wilson's attempt to make the world safe for democracy rendered pointless the presence of American power in Europe. The nature of the Russian threat after the Second World War left the United States no rational choice but to establish its power in permanence at the circumference of the Russian empire. But on what terms was that power to be established? Should it be the supremacy of American power, which in its consistent application would reduce America's allies to the status of satellites, or was it to be the equality of all members of the alliance, which, in its ideal realization, would issue in the harmonious co-operation of like-minded nations? These alternatives confronted the United States with a dilemma which could not be solved through the consistent realization of either alternative without denying one or the other essential of American policy.

American power had to operate not in conquered territory where the conqueror could rule as he saw fit, but in the territory of friendly nations, whose consent, if not desire, provided the only title for the American presence. The purpose of the presence was the defense of the freedom and territorial integrity of the allies. Thus the United States, in the measure that it would have reduced its allies to the status of satellites, would have defeated the very purpose for which the European nations had become its allies. On the other hand, the establishment of the alliance on the basis of complete equality was feasible only on the assumption that the identity of interests among the allies and their awareness of it was so complete that they would be capable of pursuing common ends with common measures through free and equal co-operation. In the degree that this co-operation would fall short of the ideal expectation, the purpose of the alliance as a co-operative effort on behalf of the common interests would be defeated.

The United States refused to bring its superior power to bear on the alliance on behalf of common interests, naturally inchoate and competing with divergent ones. Thus it forewent the creation of a common framework of permanent and organic co-operation among allies unequal in power and responsibility; yet it safeguarded the essential freedoms which the sacrifice of equal status would have brought. When the United States left the Western Hemisphere, it carried with it only its military and economic power, but not its creative imagination and its constructive will. Significantly enough, this imagination and will came to play—and rather abortively at that—in that one sphere which is closest to the American tradition in foreign affairs, that is, in the military sphere; and NATO is presently its rather forlorn and brittle monument.

The United States emerged from the Second World War as the most powerful nation on earth by chance and not by design, and it assumed the leadership of the coalition of free nations by virtue of necessity and not of choice. In consequence, its will and mind were not equal to its power, responsibility, and opportunity. Had these attributes of America been the result of conscious choice and deliberate aspiration, America would have been intellectually and morally prepared when what it had chosen and aspired to had come to pass. Since it was not so prepared, it approached the tasks incumbent upon the paramount power of the Western alliance with unbecoming humility and unwarranted self-restraint. The political predominance required by the paramountcy of its power was incompatible with its anti-imperialist tradition, which is the manifestation abroad of the principle of equality. Confronted with the choice between assuming the position of leadership commensurate with its power and treating its allies as equals, the United States chose the latter alternative. Accustomed to expand its rule into political empty spaces but not to impose it, however gently and beneficially, upon existing political entities, it endeavored to establish within the Western alliance the same kind of consensus with the same methods of rational persuasion and economic inducements as those by which the American commonwealth had been created, maintained, and developed.

Yet the application of the equalitarian principle of the democratic consensus to the relations among allies resulted in disintegration and anarchy. For as the integrating effects of the domestic equalitarian consensus depends upon a pre-established hierarchical relationship in the form of a sovereign central government, so must whatever equality there can be among allies, drastically differing in power and responsibility, be subordinated to a hierarchical relationship between the paramount power and the others. This hierarchical relationship has been lacking between the United States and its allies. Two kinds of consequences have flown from this lack. Either the alliance has been incapable of pursuing new, positive policies in common, or else the most determined ally has been able to impose its will upon the United States.

Of the former consequence, NATO is the outstanding example. The principle of equality among its fifteen members, applied to the political operations and over-all military planning of the alliance, put a virtually insurmountable obstacle in the way of new policies to be pursued by the fifteen allies in response to new opportunities or new threats. The principle of equality would have been compatible with new departures in policy only on the unattainable conditions that all members of the alliance had an equal interest in such departures, were equally aware of these interests, and agreed completely on the means to be used in support of these interests. Short of an open threat of military conquest or revolution, such as confronted the members of NATO in the late 1940s, these conditions cannot be expected to be present at the same time. In the absence of one or the other of them, the best an alliance, thus constituted, can achieve is the translation of the lowest common denominator of agreed interests into common action. That denominator is likely to tend toward that irreducible minimum of common policies without which the alliance itself would cease to exist as an operating agency. Thus while the objective conditions under which the fifteen allies live require a degree of unity in purpose and action far transcending that of a traditional alliance, and while NATO was designed at its inception to be the instrument of that kind of unity, in actual performance

NATO has become more and more undistinguishable from a traditional alliance, and rather loosely knit and stagnating at that.

The other consequence of the equalitarian approach to alliances has been most marked in the bilateral relations between the United States and its allies. Governments that govern only because the United States maintains them, such as the government of Formosa, and governments that have no alternative to American association, such as the government of Spain, have been able to play a winning game in which the United States holds all the trumps. The United States has not been disposed to play these trumps for two reasons. On the one hand, its commitment to the principle of equality made it impossible for it to bring its superior power to bear upon a weak ally on behalf of its interests. On the other hand, these interests were conceived in terms of what I have suggested elsewhere might be called the collector's approach to alliances. That is to say, the United States has been primarily interested in the conclusion of alliances per se, regardless of the specific and concrete interests these alliances were supposed to serve. An alliance thus conceived is a standing invitation, readily accepted, for a weak ally to make the alliance serve its specific and concrete interests. Thus the United States has paid for the willingness of weak and even unviable nations to become its allies by underwriting the interests of these nations, regardless of whether these interests coincide with, or even run counter, to its own.

This relationship, unhealthy even by the standards of traditional foreign policy, is a far cry from the new order through which the United States was called upon to realize the common purpose of the nations of Western civilization in the atomic age. The factors which brought that relationship about are also responsible for the American failure to project the American purpose into the areas of the world that are either uncommitted or unwillingly committed to communism. The United States was not able to free itself from the pattern of thought and action established by both its tradition and its successful reaction to the threat of Russian power in the aftermath of the Second World War, that is, to conceive of its relations to the outside world primarily in military terms. Thus it saw itself surrounded by allies, by uncommitted nations which thus far had refused to become allies, and by satellites which Russian power had thus far prevented from becoming allies. From this picture of the world, three militarily-oriented policies ensued. The allies had to be kept in the American orbit, the uncommitted nations had to be drawn into it, and the satellites had to be liberated in order to enable them to join it. The Baghdad Pact, SEATO, and the Eisenhower Doctrine were open-ended—and largely unsuccessful—invitations to the uncommitted nations of Asia and the Middle East to become allies of the United States or at least to accept military assistance from it.

These policies were by and large unsuccessful because the picture of the world from which they derived was at odds with both the facts of experience and the interests of the United States. What the United States had to cope with outside Europe was not the threat of Russian military power but the promise of the new order of communism. A policy of military alliances was irrelevant to the problems raised by that promise. It was also counter-productive; for by strengthening more often than not the forces of the status quo and the military establishments in the allied nations, it tended to identify the United States with those forces and with preparations for war and, in turn, gave communism the opportunity to identify itself with the forces of progress and peace.

The policy of foreign aid, considered the main instrument for strengthening the uncommitted nations in their uncommitted position, has similarly suffered from this predominantly military orientation. But it has also suffered from two other handicaps.

The American theory and practice of foreign aid derives by and large from certain unexamined assumptions that are part of the American folklore of politics. The popular mind has established a number of simple and highly doubtful correlations between foreign aid, on the one hand, and a rising standard of living, social and political stability, democratic institutions and practices, and a peaceful foreign policy, on the other. The simplicity of these correlations is so reassuring and so reminiscent of the Wilsonian correlation between democratic institutions and domestic and international order and peace that the general philosophic proposition is hardly ever questioned, however much the contrary empirical evidence in specific cases forces drastic adaptations in practice.

Thus fundamental questions like the following, concerning the technological results of foreign aid, are hardly ever asked explicitly: what are the probable social, political, and moral effects of foreign aid under different circumstances? Does successful foreign aid require a particular intellectual, political, and moral climate, or will the injection of economic capital and technological capability from the outside create this climate? To what extent and under what conditions is it possible for one nation to transform through outside intervention the economic and technological life of another nation? More specifically, in terms of the political objective of keeping the uncommitted nations uncommitted, how is one to create that positive relationship in the mind of the recipient between the aid and its beneficial results, on the one hand, and the political philosophy, system, and objectives of the giver, on the other? As long as the recipient disapproves of the politics of the giver, despite the aid he has received, the political effects of the aid are lost. These effects are similarly lost as long as the recipient remains unconvinced that the aid received is but a natural, if not inevitable, manifestation of the politics of the giver. Foreign aid, then, remains politically ineffective as long as the recipient says either that "aid is good, but the politics of the giver is bad" or, "aid is good, but the politics of the giver—good, bad, or indifferent—have nothing to do with it."

Questions such as these require for answers policies of extraordinary subtlety and intricacy. The simple correlation underlying American policy between foreign aid and what the United States desires in the uncommitted nations could not provide them. That correlation is a projection of the domestic experience of America onto the international scene. Capital formation and investment and technological innovation created the wealth and prosperity of America, and, so it was assumed, the export of American capital and technology into the underdeveloped nations would bring forth similar results there. The similarity between this and the Wilsonian expectation is striking. Wilson wanted to bring the peace and order of America to the rest of the world by exporting the democratic institutions of America. His contemporary heirs want to bring the wealth and prosperity of America to the rest of the world through the export of American capital and technology. Yet while the failure of the Wilsonian experiment was quickly and drastically revealed, the failure of foreign aid, simplistically conceived, has been less obvious, albeit no less drastic.

However, even if the United States had developed a well thought-out philosophy of foreign aid, its application in practice would have come up against the same equalitarian principle that, as we have seen, has frustrated the alliance policy of the United States. Yet while the application of this principle to our alliance policy was rather unwarranted by the objective situation, foreign aid has confronted the United States with a real dilemma. For if you apply the equalitarian principle, expressed in the slogan "no strings attached," to foreign aid, you put yourself at the mercy of unenlightened or corrupt governments that might misuse foreign aid through incompetence or by design. If, on the other hand, you assume responsibility for the way your aid is used, you feed the nationalistic suspicion of "imperialist" motives. By choosing the former horn of the dilemma, the United States has given the recipient governments at least a potential leverage against itself, similar to that its allies enjoy. This leverage is increased by the competitive participation of the Soviet Union in foreign aid, which allows the recipient governments to play one superpower against the other. However, the Soviet Union uses foreign aid as an integral part of its political policy, seeking the expansion of its influence either directly or through communist movements, while the United States has been incapable of serving consistently either its own purpose or the purpose of the underdeveloped nations.

The insufficiency of America's endeavors to realize its purpose in its relations with the outside world has come to a head in the failure of its policies towards the satellites of the Soviet Union. The total and obvious character of that failure suggests, as we shall see, the nature of the remedy. The inspiration from which the policies towards the satellites are derived is within the tradition of the American purpose of expanding the area of freedom. As a particular manifestation of that purpose, these policies continue the anti-imperialistic tradition of America, yet with one significant difference. The anti-imperialistic tradition of America has operated on two levels, the general one of revulsion against the normal practices of European power politics and the specific one of revulsion against a particular case of oppression of one nation by another. The political consequences of the first type stemmed from the abstention and isolationism of Washington's Farewell Address. The second type had by and large no political consequence at all, but only led to an emotional commitment to what appeared to be the cause of freedom and to humanitarian assistance for its suffering supporters. Thus the American anti-imperialism of the 19th century supported the national movements of Europe against their monarchical enemies and opposed certain colonial ventures of European nations, and the American anti-imperialism of the early 20th century took its stand against Imperial and Nazi Germany and against Tsarist and Soviet Russia. The America of both periods received the fighters in the lost causes of freedom as citizens.

The new anti-imperialism, aimed at the conquests of the Soviet Union, obviously partakes of these characteristics, but it possessses a quality which its predecessors lacked. It has become an integral and crucial part of the foreign policy of the United States. The traditional anti-imperialism of America was without a political objective either by virtue of its very nature or else because the radius of an active American foreign policy was limited to the Western Hemisphere. The new anti-imperialism can no longer afford to condemn the suppression of liberty from afar and limit its tribute to freedom to charitable deeds. Committed to the containment of communism, that is, to the preservation of national freedom threatened by Soviet imperialism throughout the world, the United States can reconcile itself to the loss of national freedom on the other side of the line of containment only if it ceases being anti-imperialistic altogether. If it wants to remain faithful to its anti-imperialist tradition, it must embark upon positive political and military policies on behalf not only of the preservation but also the expansion of national freedom. Yet at this point, when it came to adapting the traditional attitude of America to the opportunities and limitations of the contemporary world, the crisis of perplexity of the American purpose was most strikingly revealed.

The American purpose of expanding the area of freedom encountered in its new connection with the foreign policy of the United States a new opportunity and a new limitation. It did not come to terms with either. Of this failure, the policy of liberation and the explicit inaction on the occasion of the Hungarian revolution of 1956 have been the outward manifestations. The policy of liberation manifested unconcern with the limitations; inaction on the occasion of the Hungarian revolution demonstrated unawareness of the opportunities.

The policy of liberation must be seen both as a logical extension of the policy of containment and as the positive implementation of the American refusal to recognize the legitimacy of the European conquests of the Soviet Union. Both Stalin and his successors attempted to liquidate the cold war by concluding with the United States an agreement dividing Europe, if not the world, into two spheres of influence, with the European conquests of the Soviet

Union being recognized as definite and legitimate. The United States has consistently refused to consider even the possibility of such an agreement. The United States could let it go at that, satisfied with containing Russian power within the limits reached in 1945, and that is essentially what it did up to the beginning of 1953. The impulse to go beyond this negative policy of containment and non-recognition and to give that policy a positive implementation stems of course from the traditional purpose of America. But once America yielded to that impulse, it was up against the problem as to what kind of positive policy to pursue.

Consistent with its general conception of foreign policy, the United States conceived of liberation essentially in military terms, that is, as the evacuation of Eastern Europe by the Red Army. Such an evacuation could only be brought about through military pressure carrying the risk of war. As the London *Economist* put it on August 30, 1952, when the policy of liberation was first proclaimed: —"Unhappily 'liberation' applied to Eastern Europe—and Asia—means either the risk of war or it means nothing. . . . 'Liberation' entails no risk of war only when it means nothing." Since, according to repeated official statements, liberation was to be achieved without resort to war, it was, as conceived by American policy, incapable of achievement.

Thus what pretended to be a new dynamic policy in harmony with the purpose of America turned out to be no policy at all, nothing more than a verbal pronouncement, incapable of implementation by action. However, that commitment was understood by the Soviet Union as a threat and by the satellites as a promise. As such, far from contributing anything to the liberation of the satellites, it served, on the one hand, as a pretext for the Soviet Union to maintain its military rule of Eastern Europe and, on the other, as an incentive for the satellites to entertain illusions about what the United States might do, and to be disillusioned with American policy and reconciled to their fate when no action was forthcoming. Therefore, the policy of liberation not only did not liberate, but actually strengthened the forces opposed and detrimental to liberty.

Of this self-defeating unreality of the policy of liberation, the Hungarian revolution of 1956 provided the ultimate test. For here the United States was faced not with the impossible task of liberating without resort to war but with the opportunity to support a liberation already achieved. If it remained inactive under these most favorable circumstances, it would demonstrate that there was no such thing as a policy of liberation but only verbal pronouncements designed to give the appearance that there was one. This is indeed what happened. The United States declared from the outset through its most authoritative spokesman, the president, that it would abstain from active interference. While it is a moot question as to how much the United States could have done, there can be no doubt, especially in view of the dissension within the Soviet government over the use of force, in the meantime revealed by Khrushchev, that it could have done more than nothing.

The United States failed utterly to relate the American purpose of extending the area of freedom to the political situations within which it was called upon to act. But that failure revealed both the nature and the innate strength of its purpose. In spite of what it said and did, the facts of its life, past and present, spoke louder than its purposeful words and deeds. The words and deeds had by and large been ineffectual and even counter-productive. Yet they were overshadowed and in rare moments obliterated by the universal awareness that equality in freedom had still a home in America. As the Hungarian revolution illuminated like a stroke of lightning the nature of man, showing the urge for freedom as elemental a human quality as the lust for power or the desire for wealth, so did the awareness of the freedom achieved within the American borders act as a corrective for words and deeds seemingly oblivious of the American purpose.

Thus when the vice president of the United States visited Poland in the spring of 1959 and when the president in the fall of that year visited India, the major uncommitted nation, they were greeted with a popular enthusiasm that was meant not for their persons but for the nation they represented. They were greeted, as Woodrow Wilson and Franklin Delano Roosevelt had been before them, as living symbols of what the nation was thought to stand for, and the enthusiasm the nation evoked in the person of its representatives was due, it is safe to assume, not to its wealth and power but to its purpose, which sets it apart from all other nations and makes it a model for other nations to emulate. When these living symbols of America ventured abroad they carried with them, as it were, the American purpose of expanding the area of freedom. They came not only as a symbol of what America has achieved at home, but also of what it was to achieve abroad.

Thus an ironic twist of historic development made the outside world appear to understand the American purpose better than did America itself, and through a paradoxical reversal of roles the outside world had to recall the American message to an America incapable of making clear to the world what it was about. America, in ineffectual perplexity, tried to give the world its message, relating its traditional purpose to the contemporary world. Yet what it could not do for itself through the conscious effort of words and deeds, its very existence did for it. The living presence of its achievements carried the promise of further achievements to the world, and the hope of the world carried that message back to America.

4: AMERICAN POLICIES AND DISARMAMENT

Bernhard G. Bechhoefer

Probably never before has the public clamor for at least some progress on the road to disarmament been so widespread and so passionate as it is today. Yet at the same time, the US Government is under unusually severe pressure to provide the country with the great and costly military power needed to assure its national survival and that of its friends. This creates a dilemma for our government. One possible solution would be an international agreement on the reduction and control of some or all forms of armaments. Unfortunately, this solution has not come within sight despite a dozen years of almost incessant negotiations. Therefore, it is logical to inquire whether progress on the road to disarmament is possible under existing world conditions without jeopardizing our national security. It is logical to inquire whether within the existing foreign policy framework of the US and indeed of the entire free world some alternative road might be preferable in seeking a relaxation of world tensions.

The objective of any essay such as this is to evaluate disarmament negotiations within the framework of our national policy and to estimate their usefulness. A *sine qua non* of any such evaluation is a review of the disarmament policies and actions of the major governments since the Second World War in the broadest possible perspective. The disarmament negotiations should not be isolated and insulated from other aspects of international relations. Nor should the present be divorced from the past to which it is so closely and firmly linked. Only in this perspective do the disarmament negotiations lose their atmosphere of unreality and become something more than academic debates contributing nothing to the international realities of the era.

It is apparent that, during the period since the end of the Second World War, there has been a vast volume of discussion within the United Nations on the problem of disarmament. The subject has appeared every year on the agenda of the General Assembly. Linked to the direct discussions within the United Nations are collateral discussions, both within and outside the United Nations. Within the United Nations these include such matters as the attempts to develop United Nations armed forces to maintain world peace, the establishment of the International Atomic Energy Agency under the aegis of the United Nations, the broad Soviet proposals for lessening world tensions, which appear every year without fail at every session of the United Nations General Assembly, and the efforts to set aside funds to assist underdeveloped areas, such funds to be taken from the savings realized through an agreed disarmament program.

Developments outside the United Nations, which are related to the disarmament program, include several vast propaganda efforts of the Soviet Union, such as the Stockholm Appeal, the appeal of scientists for immediate elimination of nuclear weapons testing, and the accusations that the United States waged bacteriological warfare in Korea. Likewise, the Summit Conference in Geneva in 1955 and the lengthy correspondence between President Eisenhower and Mr. Bulganin were directly related to disarmament. Then, many policies pursued by all the major powers have implications in the field of disarmament.

This total of developments in the international scene since the Second World War creates a vast amorphous mass which is extremely confusing and difficult to interpret. The volume of material is so vast that it is difficult to separate the essential from the nonessential. This confusion is increased by the Soviet approach, which during all this period was dominantly propagandistic, punctuated with occasional suggestions that opened surprisingly attractive vistas for genuine negotiations and ultimate agreement. Likewise the Western approach, especially during the period of woeful conventional military weakness prior to 1951, could not be entirely forthright, because it was necessary to avoid a situation in which Soviet distortions of the Western position might destroy the program for strengthening the military posture of the West.

All this has resulted in creating a situation in which it has been difficult for all but a small core of specialists to keep abreast of these developments, much less to understand them.

The confusion of the disarmament debate eliminates the possibility of a narrative which is strictly chronological. To bring some order out of the chaos, it becomes necessary to divide the negotiations somewhat arbitrarily into periods and to paint with a broad sweep their outlines and general importance rather than the details of the proposals both of the free world and the Soviet Union, which in many instances appear regularly like leitmotifs throughout the negotiations. The periods which I have chosen are:

1. The wartime period of great power negotiations leading to the formation of the United Nations at Dumbarton Oaks and San Francisco. While the formal disarmament negotiations did not commence until the first meeting of the United Nations in January 1946, the terms of reference for the negotiations—both procedurally and substantively—emerged earlier, and in part at least were incorporated into the United Nations Charter.

2. The period from the first General Assembly of the United Nations in 1946 until the creation of the United Nations Disarmament Commission in the fall of 1951.

3. The period of maximum Soviet intransigence from the fall of 1952 until the General Assembly of 1954.

4. The period from 1954 until the refusal of the Soviet Union in December, 1957, to participate further in the Disarmament Commission.

A new phase of the negotiations commenced in the summer of 1958.

The initial terms of reference for postwar negotiations on the regulation of armaments developed during the wartime partnership of the great powers in the Second World War, and were ultimately incorporated into the Charter of the United Nations. The leaders of the principal powers engaged in the struggle against Germany had witnessed the terrible effects of the rapid demobilization of the Western powers at the end of the First World War and the resulting military weakness which permitted the rise of Hitler. They were determined to prevent a recurrence. The Atlantic Charter of 1941 and the Declaration of Four Nations on General Security of 1943 envisaged the demilitarization of the enemy, but not of the principal allies.

Paragraph eight of the Atlantic Charter, drawn up by President Roosevelt and Mr. Churchill on August 11, 1941, stated: "Since no future peace can be maintained if land, sea, or air armaments continue to be employed by nations which threaten, or may threaten, aggression outside their frontiers, they believe, pending the establishment of a wider and permanent system of general security, that the disarmament of such nations is essential. They will likewise aid and encourage all other practicable measures which will lighten for peace-loving peoples the crushing burden of armaments."[1]

Churchill reported to his home Cabinet that this provision was "most remarkable for its realism. The president undoubtedly contemplates the disarmament of the guilty nations, coupled with the maintenance of strong united British and American armaments both by sea and air for a long indefinite period."[2] And in the course of Anglo-American discussions in Washington in the spring of 1943 on the organization of the United Nations after the war, the president made clear his own conviction that while a United Nations, world-wide in scope with advisory regional councils, could have powers to recommend policy, "the real decisions should be made by the United States, Great Britain, Russia and China, who would be the powers for many years to come that would have to police the world."[3]

The Declaration of Four Nations on General Security, signed in Moscow on October 30, 1943, recorded the adherence of the Soviet Union and China to these ideas of the Atlantic Charter, and confirmed the intent of the principal powers to maintain peace by "joint action" when necessary. The Declaration stated in a provision which later found its way verbatim into the United Nations Charter (Article 106), "That for the purpose of maintaining international peace and security pending the re-establishment of law and order and the inauguration of a system of general security, they will consult with one another and as occasion requires with other members of the United Nations with a view to joint action on behalf of the community of nations."[4]

Thus the famous doctrine of the "Four Policemen" continued to govern the thinking of the great powers at least until the first session of the General Assembly of the United Nations in January, 1946.

[1] Text in US Department of State, *Cooperative War Effort* (Washington, 1942), p. 4; reproduced in Ruth Russell, A *History of the United Nations Charter* (Washington, 1958), Appendix B, p. 975. See pp. 37-38 in Russell, *op. cit.*, for brief drafting history of this provision.

[2] Winston Churchill, *The Grand Alliance*, p. 441; quoted in Russell, *op. cit.*, p. 38.

[3] At a meeting on March 27, 1943, attended by Roosevelt, Eden, Hull, Welles, Halifax, William Strang, and Hopkins, as reported by Hopkins. Robert E. Sherwood, *Roosevelt and Hopkins* (New York, 1948), p. 717.

[4] Text in US Department of State, *Toward the Peace:* Documents (Washington, 1945), p. 6; reproduced in Russell, *op. cit.*, p. 977.

The doctrine, stated in blunt terms, had two facets:

1. The negative side of the doctrine was that the four great powers should forcibly disarm Germany and Japan and also assure that no other states developed sufficient armaments to threaten world peace.
2. The second and positive facet, implicit in the Atlantic Charter and explicit in the later Declaration of the Four Nations, was that the Four Nations after the war must remain militarily strong. The Four Powers would police the world until the establishment of an international system of security which would take over the task. The Soviet Union gave its full endorsement to this doctrine.

It was inevitable that the doctrine of the Four Policemen should receive considerable modification before it reached the light of day in formal proposals for a United Nations. The doctrine ran roughshod over the role of smaller states in international deliberations. It excluded France from the great powers.

Therefore, as the proposals for the United Nations gradually evolved from the original planning documents, while the ideas of the underlying Atlantic Charter remained, they were couched in more diplomatic terms.

The United Nations, rather than the Four Policemen, could be responsible for the decisions concerning the levels of armaments of the smaller states. Likewise the international police force would be an instrument of the United Nations rather than of the Four Powers. The Four Powers would act only until the United Nations Police Force could be established.

Within the United Nations, however, the organ which was to carry out these powers not only in the interim but also for the long-term maintenance of peace, was the Security Council, in which the Four Powers—US, UK, USSR, and China—and France held the permanent seats; and a military staff committee consisting of "the Chiefs of Staff of the permanent members of the Security Council" was given responsibility for the "strategic direction of any armed forces placed at the disposal of the Security Council." [5]

[5] Relevant provisions of the United Nations Charter are as follows:

Article 11 permitted the General Assembly to "consider the general principles of cooperation in the maintenance of international peace and security, including the principles governing disarmament and the regulation of armaments, and [allowed the Assembly to] make recommendations with regard to such principles to the Members or to the Security Council or to both."

Under Article 26, the Security Council was made responsible for "formulat-

The basic concept remained, as conceived by President Roosevelt and Mr. Churchill, that the United States and the United Kingdom after the Second World War would remain strong and would not repeat the headlong demobilization and disarmament which had permitted the rise of Hitler.

The United Nations was not intended to repeat the fruitless debates on disarmament which occupied the League of Nations during almost the entire period between the First and Second World Wars. It was no accident that in the Charter of the United Nations the word "disarmament" appears only twice: in Article 11, permitting the General Assembly to "consider . . . the principles governing disarmament and the regulation of armaments," and in Article 47, authorizing the Military Staff Committee to advise the Security Council on "the regulation of armaments and *possible* disarmament" (italics added).

The General Assembly, as a long-range planning organization making recommendations but taking no action, was authorized only to consider the principles of disarmament. The Security Council, with its responsibility for world peace, was concerned not with "disarmament" but with "regulation of armaments." [6] The immediate task for the Security Council was to create an international armed force capable of maintaining world peace, to disarm the Axis nations, and to regulate the armaments of all except the great powers so that no state could disturb the peace.

---

ing" plans for "establishment of a system for the regulation of armaments."

Article 43 stipulated that armed forces which the members agreed to make available to the Security Council were to be provided under agreements concluded "between the Security Council and Members or—groups of Members"; and

Article 45 enjoined the Members to "hold immediately available national air-force contingents for combined international enforcement action." Provisions for the Military Staff Committee are outlined in Article 47.

Four-Power authority to act in the interim was provided in Article 106 and Article 107, which together comprise ch. 17, "Transitional Security Arrangements."

[6] See Article 26. An official Soviet comment on Article 26 was as follows: "One cannot fail to note that this refers to regulation of armaments, which of course includes their possible reduction. On the other hand, it is plain that the limit of such reduction is represented by the contingents necessary for collective action prescribed by the Security Council." S. B. Krylov, *Materials for the History of the United Nations,* Academy of Sciences of the USSR (1949), unpublished.

This wartime thinking on the subject of regulation of armaments persisted for many years in the peacetime negotiations under the United Nations and is a factor in placing in perspective the later proposals both of the Soviet Union and of the West.

The San Francisco Conference approved the Charter of the United Nations on June 26, 1945, subject to ratification by the states participating in the Conference. The first session of the General Assembly was convoked in January, 1946.

As we have seen, in the field of regulation of armaments the anticipation was that the initial activities of the United Nations would be confined to disarming the enemy states and creating a security force under direction of the United Nations. A second and distinctly lower priority would be regulation of the armaments of states other than great powers, "in order to permit the establishment and maintenance of international peace and security with the least diversion for armaments of the world's human and economic resources." Determination of "the principles governing disarmament" by the UN General Assembly had a lower priority, and development of any detailed program for disarmament was never mentioned in the Charter.

Immediately after the signing of the Charter in August 1945, the explosion of the atomic bomb over Hiroshima introduced a challenge which altered the thinking of all countries and completely changed the terms of reference of the disarmament problem in the United Nations. This frightening magnification of destructive capability brought to the fore the problem of regulation of armaments. The United States took the initiative in urging international control of atomic energy. Negotiations to establish this international control would proceed simultaneously with negotiations for an international security force under direction of the United Nations. The United States at this time, however, did not contemplate any United Nations consideration of regulating and reducing conventional armaments.

Since the United States initiative in international control of atomic energy represented a departure from the previously agreed programs of the great powers in the field of international security, the program was submitted to the great powers prior to any action in the United Nations. President Truman met in Washington with the prime ministers of the United Kingdom and Canada in November, 1945, in conversations which resulted in a declaration calling for international action under auspices of the United Nations. The secretary of state and the foreign ministers of the United Kingdom and the Soviet Union met at Moscow in December, 1945, and the Soviet Union agreed to sponsor, along with Canada, China, France, the United Kingdom, and the United States, a resolution establishing the United Nations Atomic Energy Commission. This move was approved by the General Assembly in its first session in London of January, 1946, and the United States in that year made the specific proposals usually described as the Baruch Plan.[7]

Even at this early stage, another event transpired which affected all the negotiations for regulation of armaments. This event was the rapid demobilization of the armed forces of the Western powers immediately after the Second World War. The Western powers had made the same mistake as after the First World War, resulting in military weakness which was fully exploited by Russia.

It is not here possible to go into a detailed discussion of plans presented to the United Nations Atomic Energy Commission or of negotiations in that body. It suffices to point out that the so-called Baruch Plan submitted by the US provided for international control of the entire process of producing atomic weapons, from the uranium mines to the completed weapons. Between 1946 and 1948 serious negotiation, much of it secret, took place in the Security Council of the United Nations, in the United Nations Atomic Energy Commission, and in the committees and subcommittees of the United Nations Atomic Energy Commission. The Baruch proposals received elaboration during these studies. The Soviet Union submitted counterproposals. The best way of analyzing the proposals and negotiations is through concentrating on the most important divergences between the Soviet position and that of the United States. These divergences are set forth in some detail in the three reports of the United Nations Atomic Energy Commission to the United Nations Security Council, and particularly in the second report.[8] When

[7] Text published as Annex 1 in UN Document AEC/18/Rev. 1, *The First Report of the Atomic Energy Commission to the Security Council*, December 31, 1946.

[8] UN Document AEC/18/Rev. 1, *The First Report of the United Nations Atomic Energy Commission to the Security Council*, December 31, 1946; UN Document AEC/26, *The Second Report of the United Nations Atomic Energy Commission to the Security Council*, September 11, 1947 (see part III, pp. 74-88 for detail on major divergences); UN Document AEC/31/Rev. 1, *The Third Report of the Atomic Energy Commission to the Security Council*, May 17, 1948.

viewed in perspective it seems clear that the divergences which attracted greatest attention during the negotiations were of less importance than more technical differences which received little publicity.

The feature of the Baruch Plan which unquestionably attracted most attention when the plan was presented was its insistence on international ownership of materials and facilities concerned with nuclear fission. The Soviet Union rejected this idea and advocated a system of inspection. Actually, the positions of the United States and the Soviet Union were far closer than was apparent during the negotiations. Much later, in 1952, without any change in US policy, Ambassador Benjamin Cohen in the UN Disarmament Commission restated the Baruch proposals without reference to the idea of ownership.[9] Part of this restatement follows almost verbatim the section of the second report of the Atomic Energy Commission to the Security Council dealing with ownership, the only changes being substitution of words such as "authority over" and "control" for the word "ownership." [10]

Many years later, when secrecy had been lifted from problems associated with fission, differences were further narrowed. Most of the instrumentation and automation associated with safeguards to prevent diversion of fissionable materials from peaceful purposes were also essential to operation of nuclear facilities.[11] Therefore, unless there was to be duplication of staffs, the individuals responsible for inspection would also have functions in connection with the operation of the installations. Thus divergences between the two views in fact went no further than a second divergence which received less publicity—the question of whether permanent inspectors should be stationed at nuclear facilities or whether inspections should be periodic. Western proposals insisted upon permanent inspectors. The Soviet Union until much later would agree only upon periodic inspection.

Another divergence which attracted public notice during the negotiations also proved less important over the perspective of the years

[9] On May 14, 1952, in Committee One of the UN Disarmament Commission. Text in US Mission to the United Nations, press release no. 1472.

[10] Compare with pp. 18-21 of UN Document AEC/26, *The Second Report of UNAEC to the Security Council.*

[11] See statement of Richard I. Kirk, May 14, 1957, to Committee on Foreign Relations and Senate members of Joint Committee on Atomic Energy, *Hearings on the Statute of the* IAEA, Committee Print., GPO Publication 92318, p. 93.

than was thought at the time. This was the problem of the great power veto in the international control organ responsible for regulation of atomic energy. Baruch had originally insisted with vehemence that no state should have the right to a veto in the control organization. Ultimately the Soviet Union accepted this idea but insisted that in event of any violation of the convention concerning atomic energy, the control organization could go little further than to determine the violation and notify the UN Security Council. Any steps to punish the violator would have to be taken by the Security Council, using the procedures provided by the United Nations Charter in the event of a threat to the peace.[12] The Security Council under these circumstances could not act without the concurrence of its five permanent members including the Soviet Union, and thus a veto would in fact exist.

Here again, the difference between the Soviet and US positions was far less in substance than in appearance. The United States always recognized that a major violation of the atomic energy convention by a great power such as the Soviet Union would mean a world war. Under such circumstances, it would make little difference whether the United Nations Security Council acted or failed to act because of the great power veto. The burden of punishing the aggressor could not conceivably be placed upon the United Nations, which lacked military strength to deal with a major power. Thus the divergence between the two positions on the veto was not large. The United States wished to give the control organ, where no veto existed, powers to punish minor violations, such as stopping the flow of fissionable materials to the violators. The Soviet Union disagreed.

Major differences between the Soviet and US positions, which never were bridged during the negotiations, attracted far less public attention.

The United States insisted that the international inspectors should have authority to go anywhere in any country to locate clandestine facilities. The Soviet Union insisted that the inspectors should have this right only where a violation was proved, and that in exercise of this right the control authority should not interfere with the sovereign rights of states. The Soviet Union never presented any feasible procedures to deal with the problem of clandestine facilities or indeed with any facilities other than so-called "declared facilities"

[12] UN Document AEC/26, *The Second Report of the UNAEC to the Security Council*, pp. 77, 82, 85, 95, 163-65, 171-78, 183-84.

—facilities which each state would disclose to the control authority.[13]

The greatest difference between the Western viewpoint and that of the Soviet Union was on the timing of the prohibition of nuclear warfare and the installation of the control system. The position for which the Soviet Union contended during most of the discussions was that there should be two conventions on atomic energy, the first prohibiting production and use of nuclear weapons and requiring destruction of stockpiles, and the second providing for a control system—with the first convention preceding the second. This position was unacceptable to the United States, since the United States would have no assurance that after the first convention the Soviet Union would ever permit installation of controls which would breach the iron curtain.

In later stages of the negotiations the Soviet Union suggested that the two conventions come into effect simultaneously.[14] This likewise was no solution since the prohibition of nuclear weapons is a single act and installation of a control system a long series of acts. Until many years later, it was never possible to pin down the Soviet Union to any position on whether prohibition of nuclear weapons should take place during the early or the late stages of installation of the control system.

While the Soviet Union was thus taking positions which made impossible any serious agreement, it should be pointed out that the Baruch Plan contained nothing to indicate the stages when nuclear weapons and nuclear warfare would, in fact, be prohibited and when stockpiles of fissionable material would be devoted to peaceful use. The Soviet representatives assumed that prohibition of atomic weapons under the Baruch Plan would not take place until the final stage of the plan after the control authority had established itself in all areas of the world. Any thorough system of inspection such as that of the Baruch Plan would in its initial stages benefit the United States and the Western powers more than the Soviet Union. Since we have no iron curtain in the West, the Soviet Union had little to gain from an inspection system established in the West, while the

[13] *Ibid.* See pp. 58-70 for the specific proposals for inspection of declared facilities and detection of clandestine activities endorsed by the majority of the commission. See pp. 93-95 for a summary of the Soviet position on this point as given in Mr. Gromyko's answers, on September 5, 1947, to the Cadogan questionnaire of August 11, 1947.

[14] UN Document A/C.1/310, *USSR: Draft Resolution,* October 2, 1948.

West had much to gain from penetration of the iron curtain. If nothing would be done to restrict production or use of atomic weapons until the entire process of international control had been established, the Soviet Union would be called upon to make huge concessions which would strategically benefit the West prior to any concessions by the West. The most serious and detailed discussions of the Baruch Plan related to this precise point and the final Soviet rejection did not take place until it became apparent that the United States had at that time no proposals on the timing of the program.

The third report of the United Nations Atomic Energy Commission to the Security Council, dated May 17, 1948, repeated the divergences and "recommends that, until such time as the General Assembly finds that this situation no longer exists, or until such time as the sponsors of the General Assembly resolution of 24 January 1946, who are the permanent members of the Atomic Energy Commission, find, through prior consultation, that there exists a basis for agreement on the initial control of atomic energy, negotiations in the Atomic Energy Commission be suspended." [15] The General Assembly failed to keep the negotiations alive.

Thus May, 1948, marked the end of the first major effort after the Second World War to secure some agreement to limit armaments. The pattern developed in the early part of these negotiations, of serious and detailed discussions comparatively free of propaganda and invective, was not again duplicated until the spring of 1957.

In October, 1946, at the opening of the UN General Assembly, Vyacheslav Molotov, the Soviet foreign minister, introduced in the General Assembly a resolution advocating a general reduction of armaments, with prohibition of the production and use of atomic energy for military purposes.[16] As a result of this Soviet initiative, the United Nations in its first year had before it the entire problem of disarmament and it has remained before the United Nations ever since. As pointed out, this development was contrary to expectations of the great powers when they were formulating proposals for a United Nations. This action of the Soviet Union in one respect differed from the action of the United States in bringing before the United Nations the problem of the control of atomic energy. The

[15] UN Document AEC/31/Rev. 1, United Nations Atomic Energy Commission, *Third Report to the Security Council,* May 17, 1948, p. 5.

[16] UN Document A/Bur/42, *USSR: Draft Proposal,* October 29, 1946.

United States had recognized that the proposals for control of atomic energy represented a change from positions previously agreed upon by the great powers. Therefore, the United States' initial approach had used the mechanism of the great power consultation, and no action was taken in the United Nations until agreement on procedures had been reached among the great powers, including the USSR. The Soviet Union, on the other hand, made its proposal in the United Nations without consultation with the other great powers.

After considerable negotiation the Soviet proposal resulted in a resolution which led to the United Nations Commission for Conventional Armaments. The resolution made clear that the UN Atomic Energy Commission was to continue to have jurisdiction over control of atomic energy and other weapons of mass destruction.

The United Nations at this time recognized that a third and related problem was creation of an international security system under the United Nations, and accordingly requested the United Nations Military Staff Committee to submit to it, as a matter of urgency, recommendations concerning such an armed force.

Unlike the debate in the UN Atomic Energy Commission, discussions in the Commission for Conventional Armaments never passed the stage of propaganda. In 1947 and 1948 a large proportion of the time of the Commission was devoted to purely procedural discussions of the plan of work and of the jurisdictional limits of the Commission.

The main Soviet proposals were prohibition of nuclear weapons (which was outside the jurisdiction of the Commission) and a general one-third reduction in all armaments and armed forces.[17] This was clearly propaganda since the Soviet Union resisted efforts to establish the figures from which the one-third reduction would take place or to verify that reductions had taken place. Furthermore, in view of the admitted superiority of the Soviet bloc in conventional armaments, such reduction, even if faithfully observed, would have widened the strategic imbalance already favoring the Soviet Union.

[17] UN Documents A/658, *USSR: Proposal for Strengthening the Cause of Peace and Removing the Menace of a New War*, September 25, 1948; A/723, *USSR: Draft Resolution on Prohibition of the Atomic Weapon and Reduction by One-Third of the Armaments and Armed Forces of the Permanent Members of the Security Council*, November 17, 1948. These proposals were repeated in 1949, 1950, 1952 and 1953.

In addition, the Soviet Union introduced proposals which had been previously submitted to the United Nations General Assembly, that members of the United Nations should submit information on armed forces in the territory of other members and in former enemy states, and on the location and personnel of air and naval bases similarly maintained. Again this move was apparently pure propaganda to create pressures on the United States and the Western powers to speed demobilization.

The United States and other Western powers did not advance any serious program for conventional disarmament until much later. As pointed out, the Western powers had not contemplated disarmament discussions in the United Nations until after development of a United Nations security force. It was therefore not surprising that the Western powers had no immediate disarmament program. In general, in the early discussions of the Commission the Western powers confined their proposals to procedural matters, to the relation of political settlements to disarmament, and to certain general principles. On the problem of the relation of disarmament to political matters, the United States took the position that regulation of armaments depends on international peace. The Soviet Union claimed that the first step toward world confidence was immediate reduction of armaments. Debates in the Commission on this problem were in the main characterized by Soviet propaganda broadsides. By the summer of 1948, the Commission had gone no further than to adopt a resolution, with the Soviet Union dissenting, that disarmament could only be put into effect in an atmosphere of international confidence and security and that examples of conditions essential to such confidence and security were the establishment of an United Nations armed force, international control of atomic energy, and conclusion of peace settlements with Germany and Japan.[18]

As to other principles which might govern disarmament, the Commission listed, in broad terms, certain obvious ideas: the convention should provide for adherence of all states, the system for regulation and reduction of armaments should provide for the least possible diversion for armaments of the world's human and economic resources, and the disarmament system must include safeguards.[19]

In the General Assembly of 1948 the French proposed as a first step in a program for reduction of armaments a census of all armed

[18] Text in UN Document S/C.3/25, August 12, 1948.
[19] *Ibid.*

forces and armaments with provisions for verification of the census. The Soviet Union opposed this French proposal. After the Commission for Conventional Armaments had approved a French paper describing the methods to be followed in collecting and verifying data, the Soviet Union vetoed a resolution of the United States in the Security Council to approve the French proposals.[20]

The General Assembly in the fall of 1949 went no further than to endorse the French proposals for an arms census, note the inability of the major powers to reach agreement, and request the Commission to continue its work.[21] The Soviet Union withdrew from the Conventional Arms Commission in April, 1950, at its first meeting after the adjournment of the General Assembly, because of failure to seat the representative of the Chinese communists.

In the summer of 1950 the United States, perhaps taking advantage of the absence of the Soviet Union from the meetings, introduced into the Commission for Conventional Armaments preliminary studies made within the United States Government on phases of disarmament.[22] These studies, as well as the French proposal for census and verification, were of some use later when the Western powers developed their comprehensive disarmament proposals. At best they represented an extremely preliminary and tentative approach. The census and verification proposal provided merely for a one-time operation. The US paper on industrial safeguards was only a half-page in length.

[20] See UN Document A/1361, *Report of the Security Council to the General Assembly Covering the Period from 16 July 1949 to 15 July 1950*, pp. 35-42; and A/1873, *Report of the Security Council to the General Assembly Covering the Period from 16 July 1950 to 15 July 1951*, pp. 85-86 for summary of the debate during 1949 and 1950. Text of the French proposals is in UN Document S/C.3/40, adopted by the commission on August 1, 1949, by a vote of 8-3. Reproduced on pp. 274-79 of *Disarmament and Security: A Collection of Documents 1919-1955*, compiled by Senate subcommittee on disarmament, US GPO Publication 73652 (1956) (hereafter cited: *Senate Collection*).

[21] UN General Assembly Resolution 300 (IV), December 5, 1949.

[22] UN Document S/C.3/SC.3/23, *United States: General Views on Item 3 —"Safeguards"—of the Plan of Work adopted by the Commission for Conventional Armaments*, tabled May 18, 1950; UN Document S/C.3/SC.3/25, *United States: General Views on the Nature and Scope of "Military Safeguards"—Information on Military and Para-Military Establishments to be Reported, Inspected and Verified*, circulated on July 13, 1950; UN Document S/C.3/SC.3/26, *United States: General Views on the Nature and Scope of "Industrial Safeguards"—Safeguards through Industrial Information*, circulated July 13, 1950. Texts reproduced in *Senate Collection*, pp. 279-86.

Negotiations in the United Nations Military Staff Committee to establish a United Nations military force to maintain world peace, as required by the United Nations Charter, were equally futile. After two years of failure to agree, the Committe ground slowly to a halt. The only unique feature of these negotiations concerned the size of the proposed United Nations forces; the US stood alone in advocating large forces, with the United Kingdom, France, and China joining the USSR in opposition.

Thus from 1948 to 1951 there was a stalemate in all UN negotiations on armaments.

During this period the important developments were outside the United Nations. In October, 1948, the Soviet Union exploded an atomic device, ending the atomic monopoly of the United States. In the winter and spring of 1950, the Soviet Union withdrew from all organs of the United Nations because of failure of the United Nations to seat the representative of Communist China. On June 21, 1950, the North Korean communists launched their attack on South Korea. The Security Council, with the Soviet Union absent, was in a position to find a breach of peace and recommend that members of the United Nations assist the South Koreans in resisting the communist aggression. The Security Council approved a United Nations command to direct the contingents made available by UN members for the Korean warfare. In August, 1950, the Soviet Union returned to the Security Council and later to other organs of the United Nations and embarked upon a program of verbal attacks upon the West of greater intensity than before.

This Soviet pattern, first of boycotting the United Nations and later of intensifying use of the United Nations for propaganda, had its reflection in disarmament. It was at this time that the Soviet Union commenced two efforts in the field of propaganda which were to dominate its speeches for several years thereafter. The first of these was the so-called Stockholm Appeal—a petition circulated all over the world and securing ostensibly millions of signatures, the message of which can be summarized in the three words, "Ban the Bomb." [23] The second was the campaign to prove that United States troops had used bacteriological warfare in Korea.

While propaganda aspects of the charges of bacteriological warfare were simple and obvious, their relation to disarmament was legalistic.

[23] Appeal of the World Peace Council, World Congress of Defenders of Peace, Stockholm, March 19, 1950.

The United States during the period between the First and Second World Wars had signed the Geneva conventions outlawing chemical and bacteriological warfare, but the Senate had never ratified the conventions. As a result the United States and a few other states including Japan were the only other states not bound by such conventions. One apparent objective of the Soviet Union in raising the bacteriological warfare charges was to secure a General Assembly recommendation that all states ratify the Geneva convention prohibiting bacteriological and chemical warfare. This convention contained no safeguards. A General Assembly recommendation for a convention prohibiting bacteriological and chemical warfare without safeguards would furnish a precedent for a similar recommendation in connection with atomic warfare.[24]

While the climax of both of these propaganda campaigns came later, the campaigns commenced in 1950.

In analyzing this period of complete frustration, it is possible to contend that the Soviet initiative in placing the disarmament problem before the United Nations in 1946 was based upon a desire to broaden the UN discussions, which prior to that time had been confined to atomic energy. The Soviet Union may even have realized at this early stage more clearly than the United States that agreement on control of nuclear weapons was unlikely in absence of some agreement concerning conventional armaments. The United States and the West were unlikely to give up the sole weapon where they had superiority in absence of Soviet concessions in conventional armaments where the Russians had superiority. In the absence of some agreement on conventional weapons, it was inevitable that Western proposals on atomic energy must provide for deep penetration of the Iron Curtain prior to any agreements to outlaw nuclear weapons.

Regardless of Soviet intentions in 1946, it became increasingly clear that the object of the Soviet Union in the negotiations was to secure, if possible, the unilateral disarmament of the West. The United Nations would be a propaganda vehicle to hasten that object. Apparently the Soviet rulers had concluded that as a result of the rapid demobilization at the end of the Second World War, a power vacuum might again be created such as had existed after the First

[24] For discussion see *US Participation in the UN: Report by the President to the Congress for the Year 1952*, US Department of State publication 5034 (August, 1953), pp. 49-54.

World War and which had permitted German rearmament. The chief indications that this was the true Soviet view are:

1. The Soviet initiative in disarmament was linked to the line of the communist parties directed at US armed forces throughout the world "to bring the boys home." Indeed the initial Soviet disarmament proposal in the United Nations—for a disclosure of armed forces abroad—was directly calculated to advance this propaganda line.

2. Soviet propaganda for reduction of armed forces and armaments was accompanied by aggressive efforts to extend the Iron Curtain to Hungary, Czechoslovakia, Greece, Berlin and, at a somewhat later time, South Korea. These aggressive Soviet policies had to be based upon vast Soviet superiority in military strength.

3. Soviet proposals in the Commission for Conventional Armaments never went into detail but were slogans capable of superficial propaganda treatment.

4. All Soviet proposals had one thing in common. Even if the Soviet Union carried out to the letter its obligations, the proposals would weaken the West militarily far more than they would weaken the Soviet Union.

5. The "Ban the Bomb" and bacteriological warfare propaganda campaigns furnish evidence that the objective of the Soviet Union in disarmament during this period was to secure unilateral disarmament of the West. The propaganda campaign within the United Nations having proved ineffective, the Soviet Union intensified its efforts outside.

While the Soviet Union was using disarmament negotiations as a propaganda vehicle, the Western powers—except for the Baruch Plan to control atomic energy—had no program at all. The West found itself in the propaganda position of saying no to Soviet suggestions and offering nothing in their place. This was the situation when the General Assembly convened in 1951.

Despite this frustration, the majority of the United Nations demanded negotiations and in each session of the General Assembly overwhelmingly adopted suggestions which would leave open an avenue of negotiations or a ray of hope.

President Truman had suggested to the United Nations General Assembly in 1950 that it might be useful to consolidate the work of the Atomic Energy Commission and the Commission for Conventional Armaments and create a single disarmament commission.[25] While this suggestion was procedural, it was the first sign of a drastic change in the character of disarmament negotiations.

The time was at hand for such a change. With the Soviet Union in possession of nuclear weapons, the possibility no longer existed that she might accept an international control system permitting penetration of the Iron Curtain prior to commitments to outlaw nuclear weapons. It was inconceivable that the United States would prohibit nuclear weapons, where it had superiority, without some action to correct the strategic imbalance favoring the Soviet Union in conventional weapons. The only possible road for further negotiation involved action in both the nuclear and non-nuclear areas.

The General Assembly resolution of January 11, 1952, created the Disarmament Commission to deal with the disarmament problem and outlined its functions and program.[26] The procedure for negotiations established by this resolution continued until the end of 1957.

While the resolution of January 11, 1952, is in its terms largely procedural, its importance goes far beyond procedure. Western support for merger of the Conventional Arms Commission necessarily brought with it shifts in Western policy.

In the first place, when the President of the United States in the autumn of 1950 had suggested a single Disarmament Commission, he emphasized that disarmament must include all kinds of weapons.[27] This was the final US departure from the position that regulation of armaments could be solved solely through the Baruch Plan.

In the same speech the president had abandoned the earlier condition of the United States that disarmament negotiations could not go forward until an improvement in the general political situation. President Truman recognized that agreement in disarmament would lead to reduction of tension and therefore that discussion of disarma-

[25] "A New Page in History," address by the president of the United States (Mr. Truman) before the United Nations General Assembly, October 24, 1950; text in *Senate Collection*, pp. 985-90.

[26] United Nations General Assembly Resolution 502 (VI) of January 11, 1952. Text reproduced as Annex I in UN Document DC/20, *Second Report of the Disarmament Commission*, June, 1953, pp. 158-60.

[27] "First, the plan must include all kinds of weapons. Outlawing any particular kind of weapon is not enough. The conflict in Korea bears tragic witness to the fact that aggression, whatever the weapons used, brings frightful destruction." *Senate Collection*, p. 988.

ment could go forward simultaneously with attempts to solve other international political problems.

The General Assembly resolution of January 11, 1952, set forth as the aim of the Disarmament Commission a draft treaty calling for:

1. Regulation and balanced reduction of all armed forces and all armaments.
2. Elimination of weapons of mass destruction.
3. Effective international control of atomic energy.
4. Safeguards.

This became the framework for proposals until 1956.

The resolution showed that the United States was willing to reconsider the Baruch Plan. Instead of endorsing the plan, the resolution that stated "unless a better or no less effective system is devised, the United Nation Plan for the international control of atomic energy and the prohibition of atomic weapons should continue to serve as the basis for the international control of atomic energy to insure the prohibition of atomic weapons and the use of atomic energy for peaceful purposes only."

Discussions in the General Assembly again emphasized the overwhelming desire of smaller states for continued negotiations and for some great power agreement in this field.

Despite Soviet objections to reference in the resolution to the Baruch Plan, the United States and the Western powers had sufficiently changed their approach to the problem of disarmament to create the hope, if not expectation, that the Soviet Union would negotiate in the Disarmament Commission. Benjamin V. Cohen was named as the United States representative in the Disarmament Commission, which had its first important meeting on March 14, 1952. At that time Ambassador Cohen, after introducing a short draft plan of work, made an appeal with almost religious fervor for progress as rapidly as possible to the goal of a world where national armaments would be reduced drastically and where mass armies and other instruments of mass destruction would be eliminated so that no state need fear aggression from another state.[28]

In reply, the Soviets accused the United States of bacteriological warfare in North Korea and Communist China. Agreement on a work plan permitting discussions to advance was finally secured in

[28] Text in US Mission to the United Nations, press release no. 1442, March 14, 1952.

April. On April 5 the United States submitted the first of a series of working papers which ultimately dealt with all phases of regulation, limitation, and balanced reduction of all armaments and armed forces—the object of the work of the Disarmament Commission.

This first paper was entitled "Proposals for Progressive and Continuing Disclosure and Verification of Armed Forces and Armaments." [29] It was the first US paper of consequence since the Baruch proposals and showed a change in US positions. The most important ideas in this proposal were:

1. The United States recognized that in the existing state of international tension it was impossible to suggest immediate disclosure by all states of their military secrets. Therefore the disclosure and verification would take place in five stages proceeding from the less secret areas, which would be disclosed and verified in the early stages, to the more secret areas.

2. The United States recognized that disclosures of atomic weapons must parallel disclosures of armed forces and conventional weapons and for the first time suggested a specific timetable for disclosing atomic secrets.

3. The United States for the first time took into consideration that it was desirable to arrange the inspection system in such a manner "that verification can take place with the minimum of interference in the internal life of the respective countries." This was the earliest recognition that the limitations and reductions of armaments might have to be tailored to the inspection system and could take place only to the extent that a universally acceptable inspection system could be devised.

4. By implication, at least, the paper recognized the impossibility of any agreements between the Soviet Union and the West which would upset the strategic balance.

The general approach of the disclosure and verification paper was realistic and fair, but such an appraisal certainly would not extend to the details of stages of disclosure and verification as set forth in the annexes. While information to be disclosed in the early stages would, from the standpoint of the United States, probably be that which was least sensitive, this fact would not hold true from the standpoint of the Soviet Union. It can be conceded that a literal implementation of the program contained in this paper would have resulted in the

[29] UN Document DC/C.2/1; text in DC/20, pp. 23-30, and in *Senate Collection,* p. 318.

early stages in strategic benefits to the United States and the West and in a strategic loss to the Soviet Union. In presenting the proposals, however, Benjamin Cohen specifically stated, "these proposals are intended only to provide a basis for discussion. They are not intended to express definitive or inflexible positions of my government and my government itself may wish to suggest changes and revisions as our discussions proceed. We welcome suggestions and constructive criticism. The United States does not commit itself or ask others to commit themselves to the working paper as it is submitted. It is intended only to provide a basis on which we can intelligently undertake an exchange of views on the procedures necessary to provide progressive disclosure and effective verification of our armed strength." [30]

This was the general line pursued by Cohen and later by Morehead Patterson during this phase of the negotiations. Indeed it was the only possible line in a serious negotiation. It would have been completely unrealistic in a negotiation with the Soviet Union for the West to confront the Soviets with a final position from which they could not make concessions.

Soviet reaction to the disclosure and verification papers was one of unmitigated rage. In all future negotiations the Soviet Union attacked this paper with invective comparable only to the attacks on the Baruch Plan. Perhaps the key to Soviet wrath lay in the extremely favorable reception which this paper received from other governments. It was no longer possible for the Soviet Union to contend that the West had no disarmament program outside the field of atomic energy. Factors which made the plan in its original form unacceptable to the Soviet Union and which unquestionably would have been altered in any serious discussions were not suitable to glib propaganda attack. In short, the intense Soviet opposition to the paper may have stemmed from its propaganda value to the West, a value which derived from the paper's realistic and reasonable approach.

The disclosure and verification paper was far the most important of the papers introduced to the Disarmament Commission at this session, since it suggested for the first time the step-by-step approach both in the field of reduction of armaments and in machinery to insure observance of commitments, which soon thereafter, with the

[30] Text in United States Mission to the United Nations, press release no. 1459, April 5, 1952.

dawn of the thermonuclear age, was adopted by both the USSR and the West.

The second paper submitted by the United States on April 24, 1952, was entitled "Essential Principles for a Disarmament Program." [31] This extremely brief paper, in its essentials, set forth the philosophy of a comprehensive disarmament program. It paralleled views expressed by the United States representatives in the United Nations on previous occasions—for example, in the address of Secretary of State Acheson in the General Assembly on November 8, 1951.

The goal of disarmament was not to regulate but to prevent war. To achieve this goal, all states must co-operate to establish an open and substantially disarmed world in which armed forces and armaments would be so reduced that no state would be in condition to start a war and "in which no State will be in a position to undertake preparations for war without other States having knowledge of such preparation long before an offending State could start a war." This idea foreshadowed the "open skies" doctrine.

The paper in effect described the Fourth Freedom—freedom from fear—in the famous Four Freedoms speech of President Roosevelt during the Second World War, one of the sources of the disarmament provisions of the United Nations Charter.[32]

The Soviet representative attacked even this paper with broad diatribes.

On May 28, 1952, France, the United Kingdom, and the United States placed before the Disarmament Commission proposals for limiting armed forces; on August 12, the same governments submitted a supplement to the earlier paper dealing with the approach towards limiting armaments as well as forces.[33] These papers were

[31] UN Document DC/C.1/1; text in DC/20, pp. 63-64, and in *Senate Collection,* p. 86.

[32] Compare "The fourth is freedom from fear—which, translated into world terms, means a world-wide reduction of armaments to such a point and in such a thorough fashion that no nation will be in a position to commit an act of physical aggression against any neighbor—anywhere in the World." State of the Union message by the president (Mr. Roosevelt), January, 1941; quoted in Russell, *op. cit.,* p. 29.

[33] UN Document DC/10, *Working Paper Setting forth Proposals for Fixing Numerical Limitation of all Armed Forces,* submitted by the UK, US, and France, text in DC/20, pp. 100-102; *Supplement to Tripartite Working Paper Setting Forth Proposals for Fixing Numerical Limitation of all Armed Forces,* text in DC/20, pp. 130-31.

the answer of the West to the Soviet proposals for a one-third reduction of forces and armaments. In essence, they proposed ceilings of between 1,000,000 and 1,500,000 for the Soviet Union, the United States and China, and between 700,000 and 800,000 for the United Kingdom and France. In addition, ceilings should be worked out for other states having substantial forces, with these ceilings to be relative to those for the five powers.

Arms would be limited to such as were necessary and appropriate to maintain the ceilings proposed for the armed forces.

Reflecting and reinstating the premise of maintained great power strength, one of the most important features of these papers was their emphasis that the ceilings for armed forces and armaments should be worked out in a manner to "avoid a disequilibrium of power dangerous to international peace and security."[34]

Cohen made it clear, however, that the figures were tentative. He said that "we do not believe that agreed ceilings should necessarily be fixed indefinitely. One of the errors which the United States, the United Kingdom and France wished to avoid is the error of assuming that the status quo should be permanent. Changing factors may require changed maximum ceilings."[35]

Cohen in his presentation also made it clear that in fixing the ceilings it would be necessary to go into the problem of types of armed forces permitted. This problem would arise through consideration of the armaments required for such armed forces.

While the Soviet Union attacked these papers with almost as much vehemence as the disclosure and verification paper, this general American approach reappeared during 1956 and 1957 and received the support of the Soviet Union.

On control of atomic energy, the United States position remained as it had been since 1949. The United States supported the Baruch Plan until a better plan was devised. Even so, two developments in the negotiations made clear that the United States was far less rigid than several years earlier.

1. The disclosure and verification paper provided for some disclosures in the field of atomic energy from the beginning of a disarmament program, and therefore constituted modification of the Baruch Plan.

[34] DC/20, *op. cit.*, p. 100.

[35] Text in US Mission to the United Nations, press release no. 1483, May 28, 1952.

2. On May 14, 1952, Cohen restated the Baruch Plan without once using the term "ownership" in connection with nuclear facilities.[36] This restatement was less a modification of the Baruch Plan than a clarification of the confusion which had arisen because of the different implications in Russian and English of the term "ownership." Although this restatement did not change the Baruch Plan, it should have eliminated one of the misunderstandings which, during 1946 and 1947, had caused the greatest controversy. This development was probably a surprise to the Soviet Union, and it would have been unrealistic to anticipate any reaction during the 1952 discussions.

During the disarmament discussions in 1952, the Soviet Union made no substantive proposals. The only Soviet written paper was a plan of work for the Disarmament Commission which would have predetermined the outcome of the discussions.[37] Its first item was "Adoption of a decision on the unconditional prohibition of atomic weapons and all other kinds of weapons of mass destruction and on the establishment of strict international control over the observance of such prohibition, it being understood that prohibition of atomic weapons and international control shall be put into effect simultaneously." This plan of work did not state the subject for discussion, but the conclusion which must result from the discussion. If this plan had been adopted, the Disarmament Commission would have committed itself to the Soviet position in advance of any discussion.

The Disarmament Commission completed its discussions for the year early in September, 1952. This session of the General Assembly took place during the presidential campaign in the United States, and its progress was slowed down by that campaign. It would have been difficult for the United States representative to express any government view on disarmament until after the election and until there was some indication of the attitude of the new administration. The disarmament discussions did not resume until March 18, 1953. By that time, President Eisenhower in his inaugural address had stated clearly his support of the approach of the previous administration: "We stand ready to engage with any and all others in joint effort to remove the causes of mutual fear and distrust among nations so as to make possible drastic reduction of armaments. The sole requisites for undertaking such effort are that—in their purpose—

[36] See note 9 above.

[37] UN Document DC/4/ Rev. 1, March 19, 1952; text in DC/20, pp. 6-7.

they be aimed logically and honestly toward securing peace for all; and that—in their results—they provide methods by which every participating nation will prove good faith in carrying out its pledge." [38]

Despite this presidential endorsement of the disarmament efforts, the next development did not arise until the General Assembly discussions in 1953. At that time representatives of some of the smaller powers proposed that "the representatives of the principal powers involved should seek in private an acceptable solution and report to the Disarmament Commission." [39] The comparative freedom from propaganda of certain informal discussions in the 1951 General Assembly gave hope that private meetings of representatives of a few states might result in progress. The Disarmament Commission met on April 19, 1954, and immediately established a subcommittee consisting of representatives of Canada, France, the Soviet Union, the United Kingdom and the United States, with the suggestion that the subcommittee meet immediately. The substantive discussions commenced in London in May, with Morehead Patterson, a prominent industrial leader, representing the US.

Perhaps the unique feature of this first session of the subcommittee was its informality and secrecy. During the meetings from May 13 until the end of June, none of the representatives gave press handouts. Indeed, the British magazine *Punch* in a humorous article referred to this series of meetings as a session so secret that everyone forgot about it.[40] Likewise, for the first time in disarmament negotiations since the first year of the Baruch talks, social relations were established with the Soviet staff.

In substance, the meetings of the subcommittee were a continuation of the 1952 discussions of the Disarmament Commission. In 1952 the Western governments had gone a great distance towards presenting the outlines of a complete program for comprehensive and drastic disarmament both in the nuclear and conventional fields.

There were two gaps in the program. The disclosure and verification paper which was the only one dealing with safeguards did not consider the international control authority required to enforce the

[38] January 20, 1953, GPO publication 26011.

[39] UN General Assembly Resolution 715 (VIII), November 28, 1953; text in A/2630, *Resolutions Adopted by the General Assembly at its Eighth Session during the Period from 15 September to 9 December 1953*, pp. 3-4.

[40] *Punch* article, June, 1954.

program. An even more important gap was the problem of the timing of reductions of armed forces and conventional weapons, prohibition of atomic weapons, and installation of controls. On this subject, the Soviet Union had a consistent position—reductions and prohibitions came first. The West had proposed that installation of controls take place by stages and likewise, prohibitions and reductions. There were no proposals from the West concerning the time between phasing of the prohibitions and reductions and installation of controls. During the 1954 subcommitee meetings in London, the Western powers moved to remedy these omissions with two new papers.

The earlier of the two papers was the United States working paper on establishment of an international control organ.[41] This paper went into more detail than any previous papers or proposals. Emphasis was on the type of problem that would have to be solved, rather than any specific solution. The United States in presenting this paper stressed that it was not putting forward a rigid position with the thought that other states "should either take it or leave it." "Let us think of this paper merely as one approach in an attempt to come to grips with basic issues of substance. From the discussions of specific problems raised, we hope to narrow the differences among us and perhaps to arrive at a position which all of us can approach." [42] This approach was consistent with the course which the West pursued during these negotiations. The control organ paper, while useful, did not bring into the negotiations any highly original ideas.

The United Kingdom on May 17, 1954, and again on May 26 had similarly attempted to make discussions more specific through questions submitted to the Soviet representative. In the main these efforts failed. The Soviet representative refused discussion of details of the control machinery or of safeguards until after a decision either outlawing nuclear weapons altogether or outlawing their use.

The other paper introduced by the Western powers represented a large forward step in elaboration of the Western position. This was

[41] UN Document DC/SC.1/5, May 25, 1954, *United States: Working Paper on Methods of Implementing and Enforcing Disarmament Programmes: the Establishment of International Control Organs with Appropriate Rights and Powers*; text in *Senate Collection*, pp. 325-32.

[42] UN Document DC/SC.1/PV.9, May 25, 1954; quoted in *The Record on Disarmament*, report of US Deputy Representative, Morehead Patterson, Department of State publication 5581, September 13, 1954, p. 6.

the British-French memorandum of June 11, 1954, on timing the elements of a disarmament program.[43] In this memorandum for the first time during the disarmament negotiations the Western powers made proposals as to how and when elimination of nuclear weapons and reduction of armed forces and conventional weapons would take place. A control organ should be constituted. Prohibitions and reductions should take place as soon as the control organ would report itself able to fulfill its functions. This position followed from the proposal in the "Disclosure and Verification paper" submitted by the United States, that disclosure and verification should take place in stages. The earlier paper had stopped short of stating that when disclosure and verification resulted in a situation where some prohibitions and reductions might take place with a reasonable assurance that the commitments would be observed, then the prohibitions and reductions should actually take place at that time and not be delayed until the end of the program.

The second important feature of the Anglo-French memorandum was the proposal for three stages. The first stage would be, in effect, a freeze of military manpower and military expenditure. The second covered half of the agreed reductions of conventional armaments and armed forces and cessation of manufacture of nuclear weapons. In the third stage the remaining half of reductions of armed forces and conventional armaments would take place, accompanied by elimination of nuclear weapons.

The United States gave general support to the British-French memorandum, explaining that support did not necessarily include endorsement of every detail. The United States anticipated that when the states got down to drawing up a treaty, the manner of carrying out the treaty would be more complicated than was indicated in the British-French memorandum.[44] This foreshadowed the reappraisal of all positions which became essential as a result of the development of thermonuclear weapons.

During the subcommittee meetings the Soviet Union rejected the British-French proposals as decisively as it had rejected the control organ paper, and on the same general ground. The Soviet Union insisted that the first step in any discussion must be an unconditional prohibition of nuclear weapons or at least of their use. The first

[43] UN Document DC/SC.1/10, *France and the United Kingdom: Memorandum of June 11, 1954;* text in *Senate Collection,* pp. 332-33.

[44] *The Record on Disarmament, op. cit.,* p. 9.

paragraph of the British-French memorandum contained the following language: "The States Members of the Subcommittee regard themselves prohibited in accordance with the terms of the Charter of the United Nations from the use of nuclear weapons except in defense against aggression." The Soviet representative claimed that this was a conditional rather than unconditional prohibition of use of nuclear weapons. By some sort of scholastic reasoning, he contended that such a statement was, in effect, legalization of nuclear weapons. Therefore, in his discussions of the British-French memorandum he was unwilling to go beyond the first paragraph.

While there were no new proposals on control of atomic energy, the United States representative in forceful language emphasized that if the United States were not ready and willing to consider proposals for control of atomic energy in addition to those contained in the Baruch Plan, he would not be present at the sessions.[45]

The Soviet position during the discussions showed some evolution. At the opening of the meetings the Soviet Union went no further than to table, before the subcommittee, the exact proposals which it had made to the General Assembly the previous autumn and which that body had rejected.[46] Submission of such a proposal ran counter to the hopes of the General Assembly in suggesting private discussions for development of new approaches.

Approximately midway in the negotiations, on June 1, 1954, the Soviet Union submitted a second proposal calling for prohibition of the use of atomic weapons and other weapons of mass destruction as *a first step* towards a complete disarmament program.[47] The Soviet Union on several occasions had proposed prohibition of use of nuclear weapons and indeed this was the specific proposal of the greatest Soviet propaganda campaign of this period—the Stockholm Appeal. The novel feature of this suggestion was that it preceded a general disarmament program. Here was the first indication of an alternative to a general program of comprehensive disarmament. It showed that the Soviet Union might support partial measures of disarmament which would reduce tensions in advance of a general and drastic disarmament program.

Towards the end of the discussions the Soviet Union added to its previous proposals suggestions for an international control organ,

[45] Philip Noel-Baker, *The Arms Race* (London, 1958), pp. 207, 225-26.
[46] UN Document DC/SC.1/1, May 14, 1954, USSR: *Draft Resolution.*
[47] UN Document DC/SC.1/7, June 1, 1954, USSR: *Draft Resolution.*

which proved to be identical with the suggestion which the Soviet Union had made in the United Nations Atomic Energy Commission in 1947 and which the General Assembly had rejected as inadequate.[48] While this Soviet proposal, therefore, did nothing to advance the discussions, it was important in two ways. First, during all the years after 1948 the Soviet Union had moved away from detailed proposals in the direction of propaganda slogans. This 1954 proposal, in going back to 1947, may have foreshadowed the relaxation of positions which materialized the next fall.

The second importance of this proposal was that it showed in a dramatic way that the so-called Soviet concessions since 1947 were merely academic propaganda exercises with little substance. In 1952 Vyshinsky had made a proposal which he labeled a great concession to the West, but which he had refused to explain.[49] This proposal was that the Soviet Union was willing to accept "inspection on a continuing basis" at certain installations instead of insisting on "periodic inspections." When, for the first time in May, 1954, the Soviet Union got around to defining "inspection on a continuing basis," the language was identical with that made in 1947 for "periodic inspection." [50]

The French-British proposals of June 11, 1954, came far too late in the discussions to permit Soviet response during these meetings. The meetings adjourned on June 25 with a noncommittal report to the Disarmament Commission but with informal though brief discussions of the future in which the Soviets substituted smiles for scowls.

In the Disarmament Commission discussion of the report of the first session of the subcommittee, neither the West nor the Soviet Union went further than to restate their positions with unaccustomed brevity. At the opening of the General Assembly, however, on September 30, 1954, the Soviet representative introduced a proposal, the most important feature of which was to suggest that the British-French memorandum be used as a basis for an international disarma-

[48] UN Document DC/SC.1/9, June 11, 1954, *USSR: Proposal.*

[49] UN Document A/C.1/698, January 12, 1952, *USSR: Draft Resolution,* para. 6. See also the statement by the Soviet representatives made at the 487th meeting of Committee One, January 12, 1952.

[50] See UN Documents DC/SC.1/PU.4, *Verbatim Record of the Fourth Meeting,* May 17, 1957, and DC/SC.1/PV.5, *Verbatim Record of the Fifth Meeting,* May 20, 1954, for the statement by the Soviet representative (Mr. Malik) and discussion on this point.

ment treaty.[51] The Soviet representative, Vyshinsky, set forth his proposal in such a manner as to create the impression that the Soviet Union had accepted practically the entire Western position and that with little difficulty it would be possible to reach agreement between the Soviet Union and the West. As a result of detailed discussions, which were far more precise than any disarmament discussions since rejection of the Baruch Plan in 1948, it became clear that differences between the Soviet Union and the West had narrowed, but not to the extent claimed by Vyshinsky. In the field of conventional armaments the Soviet Union was accepting the Western position that the approach should be through establishing ceilings for the armed forces and reducing armed forces to those ceilings. Likewise, the Soviet Union accepted the Western position that reductions should take place in stages rather than all at one time.

On the fundamental problem of the relation in time between prohibition of atomic weapons and installation of controls to insure observance of the prohibition, the Soviet Union at least indicated willingness to negotiate. The traditional Soviet line had been that prohibition of atomic weapons and institution of controls should be simultaneous. As the US representative, Ambassador Wadsworth, pointed out, " 'Simultaneous' is a pretty word, but . . . in this context, it is literally meaningless. The prohibition of controls is a long series of acts. The real question is this: At what point during the development of the control organ would prohibition of atomic weapons take place?" [52]

Vyshinsky, in this General Assembly, stated that the Soviet Union was at least willing to negotiate on a basis where the "prohibition of nuclear weapons and the institution of international controls must be completed within the same period." [53] This might be interpreted as acceptance in principle of the most fundamental idea in the British-French memorandum—that the prohibitions and reductions should not take place until a control organ was in a position to insure observance of commitments.

All of this was unquestionably a change in the Soviet position, but far short of Soviet agreement to the Western positions.

[51] UN Document A/2742, September 30, 1954, *USSR: Draft Resolution*, para. 1.

[52] Text in US Mission to the United Nations, press release no. 1973, October 12, 1954, p. 5.

[53] Statement in Committee One, October 11, 1954.

The Soviet Union still confined itself to a discussion of general principles. On many previous occasions, the Soviet concessions proved to be non-existent when attempts were made to translate general principles into specific provisions.

The chief import of the new Soviet approach was that it opened a vast area for future discussion. Both Vyshinsky and Ambassador Wadsworth recognized that the General Assembly was not an appropriate organ for such discussion. Since the 1954 meetings of the subcommittee had succeeded in narrowing differences between the West and the Soviet Union, the General Assembly unanimously and enthusiastically welcomed further sessions of the subcommittee.[54]

The General Assembly of 1954 is a convenient terminal point for the phase of disarmament negotiations which commenced with establishment of the Disarmament Commission by the General Assembly of 1951. It is true that in 1955 the British and French sought to elaborate and improve their earlier proposals, thus focusing on the past. Still, the reappraisal of earlier positions which was taking place simultaneously in the United States and the USSR and which foreshadowed changes for the future completely eclipsed this tactic. It is also true that the chief circumstances leading to the reappraisal of positions—development of thermonuclear weapons, and the death of Stalin—had taken place before 1954. In the main these events were not reflected in the disarmament negotiations until after the 1954 General Assembly. It is therefore convenient at this point to summarize and appraise the 1951-1954 period.

The achievement of the West during this period was to outline a program for comprehensive and drastic disarmament, both in the nuclear and conventional fields, with adequate safeguards. The West had moved from its earlier preoccupation with control of atomic energy. Indeed with Soviet development of nuclear weapons it was no longer possible to think in terms of Western monopoly of such weapons. With the partial rearmament of the West as a result of Korea, the West again had strength in conventional armaments so that it could afford to suggest reductions.

The West during this period showed flexibility. Western representatives stressed that the specific proposals were "working papers" to encourage genuine negotiation, and not rigid positions. This flexi-

[54] UN General Assembly Resolution 808 (IX), November 4, 1954; text in A/2890, *Resolutions Adopted by the General Assembly during its Ninth Session from 21 September to 17 December 1954*, p. 3.

ble attitude extended to the earlier Baruch proposals which became a starting point for discussion rather than an international edict.

The Western position, in addition, recognized that a disarmament agreement should not result in a strategic advantage to either side.

As a result of this moderation, the Western positions evoked genuine enthusiasm in the United Nations. The unanimous support —except for USSR and its satellites—of the Western proposals reflected both the universal desire for lessening of international tensions and a conviction that the West was moving to accomplish this object.

The adamant Soviet opposition to all Western proposals and the repetition of propaganda diatribes is more difficult to explain.

In earlier years, it seems probable that the Soviet Union hoped to use the disarmament negotiations to secure the unilateral disarmament of the West. By 1952, it should logically have been evident to the Soviet Union that intransigent Soviet stands produced alarm and rearmament rather than disarmament.

It is probable that the Soviet Union never took the Western proposals seriously. It was general knowledge that the US representatives, Cohen and Patterson, never had easy access to the White House or even to the secretary of state. Gromyko at one time remarked that Cohen was a genuine believer in disarmament but that he had no influence in his government. The US advisers were invariably outranked by their counterparts in other delegations. It was obvious that the staff engaged in disarmament work was too small to convert the outlines of the program into a detailed international agreement.

It is difficult, however, to relate this Soviet suspicion of the US position to the Soviet tactics. If the Soviet representatives believed that the US was insincere, the logical tactic would have been to negotiate intensively in order to demonstrate US insincerity.

It seems probable that Soviet intransigence was part of the rigidity which pervaded all phases of Soviet life during the last years of Stalin. Stalin had counselled his military leaders to study the lessons of the Second World War and apply them to the future.

The military leadership of the USSR, in public at least, followed one fixed idea. Stalin was the greatest military genius of all time and was the source of all policy.[55] The disarmament negotiations were

[55] For brief discussion on "Stalinist" military doctrine up to 1955, see Raymond L. Garthoff, *Soviet Strategy in the Nuclear Age* (New York, 1958), pp. 6-12, 61-63.

part of the military policy. Following this advice, presumably the Soviet leadership continued to hope for unilateral disarmament of the West even after events in Korea made this improbable. Even in 1952 the Soviet leadership relied on propaganda, violence, and invective to force Western disarmament, though the tactic had proved unproductive.

Stalin was dead in 1954, but the old policy continued. An interesting appraisal of Soviet policy during this period—perhaps true—has come from Khrushchev himself: "Dulles once claimed that the Soviet had tried for months to torpedo the disarmament talks. Unfortunately this imperialist statesman was practically right. Only it was not the Soviet which tried to torpedo the talks, but Molotov, Kaganovitch and Shepilov." [56]

Development of thermonuclear weapons by both the US and the USSR in 1953-1954 precipitated reappraisal of the entire political and military policies of both nations. Reappraisal of disarmament policies was merely one important facet of a far broader review.

Events which forced this reappraisal were:

1. The US detonation of the first hydrogen bomb at Eniwetok on November 1, 1952.

2. The first Soviet test of a thermonuclear device on August 12, 1953.

3. The far more powerful US thermonuclear test at Bikini on March 1, 1954, with the consequent radiation exposure of the Japanese fishermen on the *Fortunate Dragon* nearly one hundred miles downwind.

Churchill has vividly described these events as follows:

> We must realize that the gulf between the conventional high explosive bomb in use at the end of the war with Germany on the one hand, and the atomic bomb as used against Japan on the other, is smaller than the gulf developing between that bomb and the hydrogen bomb.[57]

And a year later:

> The atomic bomb with all its terror, did not carry us outside the scope of human control or manageable events in thought or action,

[56] As quoted by David Price, MP, *Hansard*, July 23, 1957, col. 307; cited in Noel-Baker, *op. cit.*, p. 226.

[57] April 5, 1954, in the House of Commons; text in *British Information Services*, T.12, April 5, 1954.

> in peace or war . . . [But with] the first comprehensive review of the hydrogen bomb, the entire foundation of human affairs was revolutionized and mankind placed in a situation both measureless and laden with doom.
>
> It is now the fact that a quantity of plutonium, probably less than would fill this box on the table—it is quite a safe thing to store—would suffice to produce weapons which would give indisputable world domination to any great power which was the only one to have it. There is no absolute defense against the hydrogen bomb, nor is any method in sight by which any nation or any country can be completely guaranteed against the devastating injury which even a score of them might inflict on wide regions.[58]

The US had pointed out in earlier disarmament discussions that it was becoming increasingly more difficult to account accurately for past production of fissionable materials, and thus to ensure their use for purposes of peace. Each year the margin of error in accounting would increase the risk to national security in any program to eliminate nuclear weapons. Development of a thermonuclear weapon such as that at Bikini, which could be produced with relative ease, multiplied by many times the risk of concealment from international inspection of stockpiles of fissionable materials. A quantity of concealed nuclear materials so small that it would almost certainly escape detection would suffice to destroy a nation.

While in retrospect the general lines of a reappraisal of disarmament policy seem fairly obvious, the bureaucratic processes leading to reappraisal both in the US and in the Soviet Union were slow and circuitous. The new policies emerged in segments and until November, 1956, it was not possible to fit the pieces together.

A period of intensive studies in the US Government started in March, 1955, with appointment of Governor Harold Stassen to the newly created position of Special Assistant to the President on Disarmament—a position with Cabinet rank. For the first time since the disbanding of Baruch's team, the US representative on disarmament had easy access to the White House, and had staff and other support to work out a detailed program.

The first indication of a new approach actually had appeared long before Stassen's appointment and creation of the machinery to carry out the approach. On December 8, 1953, President Eisenhower in his address to the United Nations General Assembly spoke of the

[58] March 1, 1955, in the House of Commons; text in *British Information Services*, T.6, March 2, 1955.

awful arithmetic of the atomic bomb, "the probability of civilization destroyed . . . the annihilation of the irreplaceable heritage of mankind." One of the objectives of his proposal to create an International Atomic Energy Agency to develop the peaceful uses of the atom was to "open up a new channel for peaceful discussion, and initiate at least a new approach to the many difficult problems that must be solved in both private and public if the world is to shake off the inertia imposed by fear and is to make positive progress toward peace." [59]

This was the beginning of the search for confidence-building measures to reduce the danger of war—which in the thermonuclear age must precede any comprehensive disarmament program. It took time to develop the US position sufficiently to suggest specific measures.

Negotiation on the one measure suggested in the president's December 8 address—the IAEA—did not commence until January, 1955, partly because of Soviet-created obstacles.

Emergence of similar measures in the field of disarmament took much longer. The doctrine of massive retaliation had become the major tenet of US strategic policy. The strength of the massive retaliation deterrent lay in convincing aggressors that invasion, even if confined to conventional weapons, would be met by nuclear attack. After Bikini the effect of massive retaliation as a deterrent was undermined, since the retaliator himself could be destroyed by the forces which he had unloosed.

The later US disarmament proposals sought not only to lessen the chances of local wars, but also, and equally important, to prevent local wars from turning into all-out wars. This latter aim ran counter to massive retaliation, although it depended upon a theory of deterrence, now revised to incorporate "selective retaliation" and "tactical atomic weapons" for "limited" war.

The best statement of this change in strategic doctrine is found in the late Secretary Dulles's article in *Foreign Affairs* of October, 1957, entitled "Challenge and Response in US Policy":

> In the future it may thus be feasible to place less reliance upon deterrence of vast retaliatory power. It may be possible to defend countries by nuclear weapons so mobile, or so placed, as to make

[59] "Atomic Power for Peace," address by the president (Mr. Eisenhower) before the United Nations General Assembly, December 8, 1953; text in *Senate Collection*, pp. 995-1001.

> military invasion with conventional forces a hazardous attempt. For example, terrain is often such that invasion routes can be decisively dominated by nuclear artillery. Thus, in contrast to the 1950 decade, it may be that by the 1960 decade the nations which are around the Sino-Soviet perimeter can possess an effective defense against full-scale conventional attack and thus confront any aggressor with the choice between failing or himself initiating nuclear war against the defending country. Thus the tables may be turned, in the sense that instead of those who are non-aggressive having to rely upon all-out nuclear retaliatory power for their protection, would-be aggressors will be unable to count on a successful conventional aggression, but must themselves weigh the consequences of invoking nuclear war.[60]

The change took place some time between March, 1954, when Dulles on two occasions enunciated the old doctrine, and December, 1955, when he first restated—but less precisely than in 1957—the US policy. The specific US decisions on the new disarmament program were made in November, 1956—almost a year later. Thus US disarmament policy in 1955 and 1956 had to be conducted within limits imposed by the H-bomb's drastic impairment of the theory of deterrence. Until reinstatement of a new theory of deterrence, serious negotiations both political and technical could not resume.

While it is always difficult to determine what happens in the Kremlin, the evidence is convincing that a reappraisal of disarmament policy was taking place in the USSR almost simultaneously with the US reappraisal, and that the development of thermonuclear weapons triggered the Soviet reappraisal.

In early 1954 the Soviet disarmament representative, Jacob Malik, when confronted with the terrible arithmetic of nuclear explosives, took the same line that all Soviet representatives had taken in the past: a nuclear holocaust would destroy decadent capitalism but communism would survive. In the next two years the Soviet leaders not only conceded that nuclear warfare would destroy both sides but, more important, brought this message to the Soviet people.

In January, 1956, Bulganin, in one of the letters to President Eisenhower, stated that the "newest implements of war . . . place the

[60] Text also issued in Department of State, press release no. 528, September 18, 1957.

peoples in all countries in an equally dangerous situation in the event that international power is disturbed." [61]

In February, 1956, Khrushchev told the Congress of the Communist Party that, "The principle of peaceful coexistence is gaining increasingly wider international recognition. And this is logical since there is no other way out in the present situation. Indeed, there are only two ways: either peaceful coexistence or the most devastating war in history." [62]

In April, 1956, Khrushchev stated during his visit to London: "Today as a result of the development of techniques, war would be of benefit neither to one side nor to the other. It can only bring colossal destruction." [63]

These are three of a host of similar statements. At the same time the Soviet line on the surface became less menacing.

Emphasis on peaceful coexistence increased, accompanied by such events as the Austrian Peace Treaty of 1955, establishment of the IAEA, and closing of the Soviet bases at Porkkala and Port Arthur. Another symptom of this change was the increase in cultural contacts between East and West. It is, of course, beyond the scope of this article to measure the changes in international temperature following, for example, the Hungarian rebellion of 1956 or preceding the Berlin difficulties of 1958-1959.

In 1954, it was generally impossible to get Soviet disarmament representatives to concede that the Soviet Union would use the atom bomb even if attacked. Soviet statements on nuclear warfare remained identified with the "Ban the Bomb" propaganda. Beginning in November, 1955, the Soviet leaders began to proclaim their own theory of deterrence through threat of nuclear retaliation. Following the announcement of a new Soviet thermonuclear explosion on November 26, 1955, Khrushchev, then on tour in India, declared: "I want to tell you, my friends, that never shall the Soviet Union misuse this weapon, and we shall be happy if these bombs lie and get on the nerves of those who would like to start a war. Let them

[61] Letter from Premier Bulganin to President Eisenhower, January 23, 1956; text in *Eisenhower-Bulganin Correspondence*, White House Disarmament Staff, Secretariat Note 157, April 1, 1957.

[62] Statement by USSR Communist Party First Secretary Khrushchev, before the Twentieth Congress of the Soviet Communist Party, February 14, 1956. *New York Times*, February 15, 1956.

[63] Statement at a luncheon given by Mr. Malik, April 19, 1956. *Soviet News*, no. 3375 (April 20, 1956), p. 2.

know that war cannot be started, for if you start it you will be answered in kind."[64] Statements like this were accompanied by Soviet versions of selective retaliation and limited war which form an interesting, though not identical, parallel with US statements.[65]

It should be emphasized that this kind of reappraisal could never have taken place until the death of Stalin loosened the extreme rigidities of Soviet policy. As a result of the reappraisal, the Soviet Union had inevitably developed a theory of deterrence not too different from the US theory.

The background of the virtually simultaneous reappraisal of policy in both the US and the USSR is essential to an understanding of the highly technical and often confusing positions taken in the disarmament negotiations during 1955 and 1956. During this period there was one important proposal, the Soviet proposal of May 10, 1955, which requires full analysis. The remaining moves by both the Soviet Union and the West could broadly be described as interim sparring, preceding the decisions on new positions.

On May 10, 1955, the Soviet Union submitted to the subcommittee of the Disarmament Commission a proposal which showed clearly the changes in Soviet position.[66] The leading features of this proposal were:

1. The USSR admitted that past nuclear production was outside the reach of a control system and proposed nuclear reductions and prohibitions in stages, with discontinuance of nuclear tests "as one of the first measures."

2. The Soviet Union went a long distance towards accepting the Western proposals for reduction of armed forces and conventional armaments.

3. The Soviet Union suggested far more detailed and precise safeguards than ever before, and specifically agreed that the International Control Organ should "have permanently in all States . . . its own staff of inspectors having within the bounds of the control functions they exercise, unimpeded access at all times to all objects of control."

[64] Statement made at a public rally in Bangalore, November 26, 1955. *Soviet News*, Press Department of Soviet Embassy in London (Nov. 30, 1955).

[65] See Garthoff, *op. cit.*, chs. 4 and 5, for a detailed discussion of this point; also Henry A. Kissinger, *Nuclear Weapons and Foreign Policy* (New York, 1957), ch. 11, especially pp. 381-97.

[66] UN Document No. DC/SC.1/26/Rev. 2, Annex 15 of DC171, *Second Report of the Sub-Committee of the Disarmament Commission*, October 7, 1955.

The important Soviet change of position was recognition that it was no longer possible to account for past nuclear production, and therefore that nuclear disarmament must take place in stages. The Soviet position had moved some distance towards realistic consideration of the dangers of the existing international picture.

The Soviet Union was now suggesting immediately attainable goals for the first stage of a disarmament agreement, rather than concentrating on the ultimate objectives of a disarmament program. The Soviet concessions to the Western position on reduction of armed forces and conventional armaments and on safeguards measurably narrowed the differences between the Soviet Union and the West on the first stages.

Reappraisal of US positions had not gone far enough by May 10, 1955, to permit the type of negotiation required to secure an agreement. Western proposals during all of 1955, and indeed during 1956, were frankly stopgap measures while reappraisal and government debate were brought to a decision. On May 10, 1955, Stassen had occupied his position as Special Assistant to the President on Disarmament for less than two months. Not until August was he appointed to act as the US deputy representative on the subcommittee of the Disarmament Commission and thus given responsibility for negotiations with the Soviet Union. The task forces which Stassen later established to undertake technical studies in the field of disarmament—studies which should have been undertaken many years before—had not yet been appointed.

One of Stassen's first acts as deputy representative on the Disarmament Commission subcommittee was to place a reservation on all of the US "pre-Geneva substantive positions" pending reappraisal of the US position.[67] While this reservation of positions was understandable and possibly was technically correct, politically it must be acknowledged to have been a tactical error. The US might well have stressed its continuous adherence to the long-range objectives of comprehensive disarmament as set forth in the paper, "General Principles of a Disarmament Program," submitted to the Disarmament Commission in 1952. At the same time the United States could have pointed out that technical developments required changes in measures for reaching that goal. This would have accomplished the purpose of the reservation of positions without exposing the

[67] Statement before the UNDC subcommittee, September 6, 1955, UN Document DC/SC.1/PU.55, p. 26.

United States to the charge of repudiating its proposals as soon as the Soviet Union showed interest in them. A more limited reservation of positions would also have been much closer to President Eisenhower's declaration of policy in his December 8, 1953, address to the United Nations. This unnecessarily sweeping reservation of positions not only gave the Soviet Union a propaganda advantage, but probably hindered negotiations. After September, 1955, the Soviet Union waited two years before submitting proposals opening the road to genuine negotiation.

In a broad way, the remaining proposals of the Soviet Union and all proposals of the West during 1955 and 1956 may be described as interim sparring, pending reappraisal of positions. The first of the US separable first-step, confidence-building proposals was made by the president at Geneva in the summer of 1955. He suggested what has come to be known as the "open skies" plan, mutual exchange of blueprints "of our military establishments . . . from one end of our countries to the other" and verification of these through reciprocal aerial inspection. Emphasis on this proposal as a safeguard against surprise attack has obscured the "confidence-building" function which was to be its prime contribution. The "open skies" proposal, standing by itself, would clearly benefit the West more than the Soviet Union, since the West would learn far more from aerial reconnaissance than would the Soviet Union. The "open skies" plan could not become a negotiable part of a disarmament program except as one item of a package which would not materially affect the strategic balance between East and West. In 1957, but not until then, this proposal did become part of such a package.

In 1956, as the appraisal of US positions progressed, the United States took several steps which foreshadowed the 1957 negotiations for confidence-building measures. The United States suggested demonstration test areas of roughly 30,000 square miles for testing and refining aerial inspection and ground techniques, and technical exchange measures among the five subcommittee nations to study methods of control, inspection, and reporting.[68] The United States also suggested the tentative subjects for a first-stage package of "first steps." [69]

[68] Tabled in the UNDC subcommittee on March 21, 1956. UN Documents DC/SC.1/39 and DC/SC.1/40, Annexes 3 and 4 to DC/83, *Third Report of the Sub-Committee of the Disarmament Commission*, May 4, 1956.

[69] See UN Document DC/SC.1/45 (Annex 9 of DC/83), "United States of America: Summary Memorandum," tabled May 3, 1956.

The British and French, during 1955 and 1956, made modifications of their paper of June 11, 1954, in an attempt to improve it and conform it to the changed frame of reference of the negotiations.[70] These proposals looked to the past rather than to the future, and accomplished little towards narrowing the differences between the Soviet Union and the West.

During 1955 and 1956 it became clear that the Soviet Union had shifted from its advocacy of a complete disarmament program to a partial first-step approach. As a matter of fact, the Soviet Union threw into the hopper no less than six separate first-step proposals: renunciation of "first use" of nuclear weapons; freeze on foreign troops in Europe; a zone of limitation and joint inspection of armaments in Central Europe; ban on atomic weapons in armament of troops in Germany; reduction of military budgets by 15 per cent; cessation of H-bomb tests.[71]

The USSR made one other interesting proposal in March, 1956, to undertake reductions in conventional armaments independently of nuclear provisions.[72] Prior thereto the Soviet Union had insisted that reduction in conventional armaments—where the Soviet Union had superiority—could take place only as part of a program for eliminating nuclear weapons (where presumably the West had superiority). The shift probably reflected the increased nuclear power of the Soviet Union and the diminished importance of conventional armaments as a result of the development of thermonuclear weapons.

[70] See the following: UN Document DC/SC.1/32, "France: Working Paper, Proposals concerning the Structure of the International Disarmament Organization," September 2, 1955; DC/SC.1/33, "France: Working Paper, Proposals concerning the Powers of the Control Administration," September 2, 1955; DC/SC.1/34, "United Kingdom: Memorandum. The Control Organ: Methods, Objects and Rights of Inspection and Supervision," September 13, 1955; DC/SC.1/35, "France: Working Paper, Proposal concerning the Objects which should be Subject to Control," Oct. 6, 1955; DC/SC.1/38, "France and the United Kingdom: Working Document: Proposed Synthesis," March 19, 1956; DC/SC.1/44, "France and the United Kingdom: Working Paper on Control," May 3, 1956.

[71] See UN Document DC/SC.1/12/Rev. 1, February 25, 1955, and DC/SC.1/19/Rev. 1, March 18, 1955, Soviet proposals tabled in the subcommittee in 1955; DC/SC.1/41, March 27, 1956, proposals tabled in the subcommittee in 1956; conference document CF/DOC/6, July 20, 1955, and CF/DOC/11, July 21, 1955, proposals made at heads of government conference, texts in Department of State publication 6046, pp. 48-50, 55-56.

[72] UN Document DC/SC.1/41, March 27, 1956.

It may seem cavalier to treat two full years of meetings—at the summit, the foreign ministers' meeting, subcommittee, Disarmament Commission, and General Assembly, plus an unprecedented flood of public diplomatic correspondence—as sparring. The fact remains that until decisions on the US reappraisal, such meetings no matter how numerous could only be debates even as among our allies, not true negotiation.

This situation changed in mid-November, 1956, when the first US decisions based on the reappraisal at last were made.

The US decisions made in November, 1956, were outlined by Ambassador Lodge before the General Assembly on January 14, 1957. They were introduced into the subcommittee by Governor Stassen at its second meeting on March 19, 1957.[73] The session of the subcommittee which commenced on March 18 lasted until September 6 and was properly described by our Department of State as "the intensified effort." [74] During this period there were seventy-one meetings of the subcommittee and a far greater number of informal discussions among all or some of the five members of the subcommittee.

During these discussions two techniques developed which facilitated negotiation. The first of these was adoption of a separable item-by-item agenda as the basis for subcommittee discussion, an approach urged by the French representative, Jules Moch, in April, 1956, but only now adopted as an agreed technique: to consider component elements in an agreement "point-by-point rather than plan-against-plan." [75]

This approach had advantages. It permitted singling out of areas of agreement and in so doing facilitated the serious and open exchange of views needed for further changes. Moreover it gave time for frequent referral of new ideas to home governments without interrupting negotiation. The philosophy of this approach was expressed by Stassen: "We are more likely to move towards agreement if we start with areas of agreement and then gradually and carefully expand them to move by move, point by point." [76]

[73] UN Document DC/SC.1/PU.88, pp. 21-30.

[74] *Disarmament: The Intensified Effort 1955-1958*, Department of State publication 6676 (July, 1958); see chs. 5-7.

[75] Statement by Moch before the UNDC subcommittee, March 18, 1957, DC/SC.1/PV 87, p. 49. His earlier proposal was on April 9, 1956; see DC/SC.1/PV78, pp. 9-10.

[76] UN Document DC/SC.1/PV. 88, p. 17.

The second innovation was the regular cultivation of informal sessions among the Western Four and with the USSR. These served to reinstate the purpose envisaged by the subcommittee—private informal consultations among the principal powers.

Although the subcommittee sessions were secret, the formal verbatim recording of all that was said inhibited free and frank interchange, and the knowledge that at the end of the session all the "secret" verbatims would be released to the public largely negated their private character.

These disadvantages were overcome during the 1957 London negotiations by deliberate cultivation of a complementary channel of communication with the Soviet Union frequent enough to permit the fullest exchange of news. There was no effort to press the Soviets for a quick response. On the contrary, the US delegate urged the Soviet delegate to take time to refer to his government if necessary. Possibly reflecting the new approach not only in substance but in negotiating techniques, for six months the discussions in the subcommittee were moderate in tone with absence of the propaganda statements which had characterized previous sessions. This serious and moderate approach did not correspond with the climate of East-West relations which otherwise prevailed. The Soviet repression of Hungary's revolution in the autumn of 1956, and the simultaneous Suez episode, had reversed the trend towards relaxation of tensions symbolized by the 1955 Geneva summit meeting. Moderation shown by the Soviet Union during 1957 in the disarmament discussions seemed to show the concern of the Soviet Union over this issue.

Prior to the meetings, the West had indicated, as we have seen, that its approach toward negotiation would be to develop confidence-building measures which would lessen the danger of war and be a prelude towards further moves towards disarmament. The Soviet Union, early in the discussions, indicated willingness to go along with this approach and suggested measures to accomplish this object.

Specific measures brought forward in the negotiations were highly technical, with political and strategic innuendoes going far beyond the specific texts. The following discussion on the substance of the 1957 negotiations outlines in broad terms the suggestions of the Soviet Union and the West concerning the main points under discussion, to show how the differences in view narrowed during negotiation.

The agenda adopted for discussion contained the following points:

nuclear test explosions, conventional disarmament, nuclear disarmament, international control organ, missiles and rockets, zones of limitation and inspection, and "other proposals."

Nuclear Test Explosions

The item of nuclear test explosions stood first upon the agenda, partly because of the importance which the General Assembly attached to this problem. An additional reason, however, was that the safeguards to insure observance of commitments were far simpler for this than for most of the other subjects. In general, the problem on which disarmament negotiations have invariably broken down has been safeguards.

Prior to November, 1956, the United States had taken the position that cessation of tests of weapons must come in the later stages of a disarmament agreement, and subsequent to agreement that all new production of fissionable materials should be for peaceful purposes (the "cut-off"). The November, 1956, decisions permitted such a step to follow installation of machinery to insure the cut-off. During the 1957 negotiations new US decisions in May and August permitted temporary suspension of tests to be moved forward in the timetable, so as to become literally the first step in an agreed series of first-stage partial measures.

On May 6, 1957, the United Kingdom tabled in the subcommittee a memorandum which, among other things, requested a committee of technical experts to consider methods of limitation and control of tests.[77] On June 14, the Soviet representative announced that his government was willing to recognize the Western contention that tests should be subject to control. Furthermore the Soviet Union would accept—in lieu of cessation of tests—a two- or three-year moratorium, under supervision of an international commission with control posts in the territories of the United States, the United Kingdom, the Soviet Union, and in the Pacific area.[78]

This was recognized immediately as a move toward the Western position. On July 2, in a four-power statement, the Western nations welcomed this move and noted that Soviet acceptance of control posts "now brings within the realm of possibility a temporary sus-

[77] Text in UN Document DC/SC.1/56, "United Kingdom: Memorandum on Nuclear Test Explosions," May 6, 1957.

[78] Text in UN Document DC/SC.1/60, "USSR: Proposal on the Cessation of Atomic and Hydrogen Weapons Tests," June 14, 1957.

pension of nuclear testing as part of an agreement for a first step in disarmament."[79] The US representative stated that the United States was willing to have suspension of testing begin with ratification of a first-step treaty even prior to installation of inspection posts to verify the suspension. Test suspension would thus become the first operative clause of the agreement. The United States at that time proposed ten months as adequate for installation of testing inspection posts and adherence of other states. If this move were successful, the United States would consider extending the temporary cessation for a longer period. Agreement on suspension of testing "would be singled out as the first measure that would be effective under a treaty, but the treaty would include also the related and desirable provisions" such as the cut-off.[80] The cut-off, however, in contrast to arrangements on test cessation, was to take place only after "installation of an inspection system adequate to verify compliance."

On August 21 the United States made a further important move to reach agreement by extending the suspension period from ten to twelve months and by adding a second temporary suspension period of a full year conditional only on "satisfactory progress" in preparing an inspection system to supervise the nuclear production cut-off. If the cut-off inspection system were not actually installed at the end of the two years, testing might be resumed at the discretion of each party.[81]

The Western powers and the Soviet Union had thus reached agreement in principle on this item. Failure to turn this agreement in principle into a working agreement then arose from Western insistence that this subject be linked to other parts of the treaty.

Nuclear Disarmament

The third item on the 1957 London agenda was nuclear disarmament. We shall deal with this item prior to the second item because

[79] UN Document DC/SC.1/59, "Joint Statement of Canada, France, the United Kingdom and the United States on the Temporary Suspension of Nuclear Test Explosions," July 2, 1957.

[80] UN Document DC/SC.1/PV. 128, p. 40. The new US position on testing and related nuclear provisions was presented in detail at three meetings, July 2 (*ibid.*, pp. 28-45), July 3 (DC/SC.1/PV. 129, pp. 2-14), and July 5 (DC/SC.1/PV. 130, pp. 2-14).

[81] Statement by Mr. Stassen on behalf of the Four Powers, UN Document DC/SC.1/PV. 149, pp. 21-22.

of its close connection to test explosions. As we have seen, the United States in 1956 had taken the position that it was no longer possible to account for past production of fissionable materials and therefore an agreement for elimination of nuclear weapons could not be effective. It was, however, possible to establish a safeguard system which would insure that new production of nuclear weapons would be devoted to peaceful purposes. The Western powers insisted during the 1957 discussions that the first-stage agreement should include agreement on a cut-off, and that the second period of one year for suspension of tests should depend upon progress in preparing an inspection system to supervise the cut-off.

This Western position reflected the view that cessation of tests, standing alone, would not diminish the threat of nuclear warfare. It would, of course, hinder states, other than the three already possessing them, in developing nuclear weapons. It would do nothing to stop the nuclear race between the United States and the Soviet Union. Furthermore, this agreement might create an unwarranted complacency among other countries that at last the threat of nuclear warfare had diminished.

During the discussions the United States took one step towards elimination of nuclear weapons by proposing that "the parties which are producers of fissionable materials for weapons purposes . . . undertake to provide under international supervision for equitable transfers, in successive increments of fissionable materials from previous production, to non-weapons purposes." [82] This process, if carried out, might ultimately eliminate the stockpiles of fissionable materials available for weapons. However, this elimination could be accomplished only after many years.

The proposals for a cut-off were never accepted by the Soviet Union. The Soviet Union was willing either to proceed with an agreement on cessation or suspension of tests independently of other provisions in the nuclear field, or include in the agreement provisions for elimination of nuclear weapons—which, of course, could not be enforced.[83]

[82] Mr. Stassen discussed transfers from past nuclear production on March 20, March 28, April 12, April 15, and July 5, 1957. The main elaboration was on July 5; see DC/SC.1/PV. 130, pp. 2-6.

[83] A major statement of Soviet policy on nuclear provisions was made by Mr. Zorin on July 8, 1957. For elaboration of the Soviet position on a cut-off see the verbatim record, DC/SC.1/PV. 132, pp. 7-11, 23-24.

Soviet refusal to consider a cut-off in the absence of a totally unenforceable agreement to eliminate nuclear weapons may reflect the Soviet devotion, in previous years, to the propaganda theme of "Ban the Bomb." This was one of two differences in view which apparently caused the breakdown of the 1957 negotiations.

Conventional Disarmament

Substantial agreement on conventional disarmament was attained for a first-stage partial agreement. On April 30, the USSR reiterated its acceptance of the Western proposals that force levels for the first step be set at 2,500,000 each for the US and USSR and 750,000 each for the UK and France. This was conditional upon agreement to a second-stage ceiling of 1,500,000 each for US and USSR and 650,000 each for UK and France.[84] In June the US suggested levels for the second stage of 2,100,000 each for US and USSR and 700,000 each for UK and France. In a third stage, force levels would be further reduced to 1,700,000 each for the US and USSR and 650,000 each for UK and France.[85] (These provisions were reiterated in the four-power working paper of August 29, 1957.) In July the Soviet representative stated that the Soviet government would accept these second- and third-stage levels provided the reductions "were in fact effected under the partial agreement and were not made contingent upon the settlement of political and other issues." [86]

On the subject of reduction in armaments, the US representative on June 26 said that if the USSR would submit a list of the arms which it would dispose of under the reductions contemplated in the Soviet proposals of April 30, the US was prepared to "present in return a proposed list of armaments reductions which it would be prepared to make, likewise substantial in amount and citing specific quantities of identified types of armaments, significant in kind and of post-Second World War manufactures and in the case of naval vessels, of types in active service, which the US is prepared to have

[84] The USSR had first announced this conditional "agreement" to Western force levels at a meeting of the Disarmament Commission on July 12, 1956, repeating the provisions in the proposals of November 17, 1956, March 18, 1957, and April 30, 1957. Text of the April 30, 1957, proposals in DC/SC.1/55 (Annex 1 of DC/112, *Fourth Report of the Subcommittee*), pp. 2-3.

[85] Statements made by the US, French, and UK representatives on June 25, 1957, UN Document DC/SC.1/PV. 124, pp. 2, 6, 9.

[86] Statement by Mr. Zorin on July 19, 1957, UN Document DC/SC.1/PV. 138, p. 10.

considered in relation to its proposed first stage reductions to 2.5 million men."[87] Once both lists were agreed upon, the items listed for reduction could be placed in disarmament depots under international supervision during the first year of first-stage reductions. Their ultimate disposal would be agreed to in later negotiations.

The USSR agreed in principle to this idea.

International Control Organ

The 1957 negotiations contained little on the subject of an international control organ. When the item first arose, Mr. Zorin remarked: "I am reminded of the course discussions of the disarmament question have taken throughout the period it has been under examination, both in the Sub-Committee and, before its establishment, in the United Nations. Let me remind you that, as soon as a rapprochement seemed imminent and there was any possibility of agreement on the substance of any question, the issue of control was almost invariably raised and became an obstacle to the conclusion of any agreement."[88]

Actually, the Soviet Union in its May 10, 1955, proposals had accepted most of the general principles for which the West was contending: installation of controls in stages, presence permanently in all states of international inspectors with access to objects of control, installation of adequate controls to ensure the prohibitions and reductions. Therefore it was possible to concentrate the 1957 discussions on the commitments which would be subject to control rather than on the details of the systems.

The general Western suggestions concerning an International Control Organization—paragraph VIII of the four-power August 29 proposals—were noncontroversial. Complications arose in 1958 and 1959 when technical discussion attempted to spell out the control systems.

Missiles and Rockets

The Western powers proposed first on July 25 and then formally on August 29 "the establishment of a technical committee to study the design of an inspection system which would make it possible to assure that the sending of objects through outer space will be exclu-

[87] UN Document DC/SC.1/PV. 125, p. 5.
[88] UN Document DC/SC.1/PV. 112, May 8, 1957, p. 35.

sively for peaceful and scientific purposes."[89] This inoffensive suggestion produced no discussion, possibly because of imminence of the launching of the first Sputnik.

Zones of Limitation and Inspection

The final item of the agenda (excepting "other proposals"), "zones of limitation and inspection," resulted in more discussion than any other item, although much of this took place in the informal consultations which are not part of the public record.

As noted earlier, the original US "open skies" proposal could not result in genuine negotiation since it would clearly benefit the West more than the Soviet Union. In 1957, however, the proposals were presented in terms which were negotiable.[90]

Proposals for inspection zones were so complicated that even the experts had difficulty in following the details, but adjustment of opposing positions was evident. The first move toward accommodation came at the end of 1956:

1. The USSR on November 17, 1956, accepted the idea of aerial photography, "for the purpose of facilitating the quickest achievement of agreement." Bulganin's letter of that date to President Eisenhower suggested a zone in Europe where reciprocal aerial inspection would be permitted.

2. The US November, 1956, decisions, announced in January, 1957, abandoned the idea of unlimited world-wide "open skies" as a condition to agreement, and proposed "progressive installation" of aerial and ground inspection as a safeguard against great surprise attack, and to verify agreed reductions in force levels and armament.

The stage was set for discussion of the size and location of the beginning zones and the extent both of aerial inspection and ground inspection within the zones.

This negotiation was much more difficult than the others, since it involved not only all five members of the subcommittee, part of whose territories were within the inspection zones, but many other states,

[89] See para. 6 of DC/SC.1/66, "Canada, France, the United Kingdom and the United States of America, Working Paper: Proposals for Partial Measures of Disarmament" (Annex 5, DC/113, *Fifth Report of the Subcommittee*). See verbatim records of July 25 and July 26 for desultory discussion.

[90] See pp. 43-46 of *Disarmament: The Intensified Effort* for a more detailed account of the 1957 negotiations on this subject.

specifically Germany. Many knotty problems arose during the negotiation. For example, a European zone permitting both aerial overflight and ground inspection might, in effect, disarm and neutralize Germany. Likewise an inspection zone in Europe with zones extending approximately equal distances on either side of the iron curtain could perpetuate the unnatural division of Germany. Also, any proposals for an East-West inspection zone of approximately equal size on either side of the iron curtain would fail to take into consideration that the areas in Europe west of the iron curtain are a fraction of the areas to the east.

The complexities required intensive negotiation in the North Atlantic Council during June and July. On July 22, in an address on disarmament, Secretary of State Dulles outlined the US position on zones, and immediately flew to London where, on August 2, he presented the positions to the subcommittee on behalf of the four powers, "with the concurrence in principle of their European allies and in continuing consultation with them." [91] In general the proposals included either a broad zone including all of the United States and the Soviet Union, or a narrow zone including certain territories within the Arctic circle. If either of these zones was acceptable to the Soviet Union, the four powers proposed a broad zone in Europe or in the alternative a more limited zone which would include a part of the territory of the Soviet Union. The Soviet Union rejected the polar zone and was unwilling to discuss either of these possibilities for a European zone.

Other Proposals

Under the heading of "other proposals," the Soviet Union continued to advance its demands for liquidation of foreign bases in Europe. But instead of insisting upon their complete elimination, the Soviet Union suggested agreement in the first instance "as to which of those bases can be liquidated during a period of one or two years."

Likewise the Soviet Union continued to call for reduction of one-third of the foreign troops in Germany and a substantial reduction

[91] UN Document DC/SC.1/62/Rev. 1, "Delegations of Canada, France, the United Kingdom and the United States: Working Paper on Systems of Inspection to Safeguard against the Possibility of Surprise Attack," August 2, 1957, Annex 1 of DC/113, *Fifth Report of the Subcommittee*, p. 2.

of the armed forces of the US, the UK, and France in the territory of NATO countries.[92] The Soviet Union did not say that such reductions were a *sine qua non* for agreement.

By the middle of August, 1957, when the four Western powers completed presentation of their position, it was apparent that positions of the Soviet Union and the West were close on the subjects of nuclear testing, limitation and reduction of armed forces and armaments, and the general approach towards safeguards and international control. The divergences related to control of fissionable material and zones where aerial inspection and ground posts should be established to insure against the possibility of surprise attack.

By that time, however, the Western powers had already taken the position which became paragraph eleven of the August 29 proposals. This paragraph read as follows: "This working paper is offered for negotiation on the understanding that its provisions are inseparable. Failure to fulfill any of the provisions of the conventions would create a situation calling for examination at the request of any party." This provision eliminated the possibility of any agreement in 1957.

On August 27, Zorin broke the spirit of quiet negotiation which had prevailed throughout the conference with an unexpected and violent ninety-minute attack on the West—"the aggressive North Atlantic bloc . . . the fruitless disarmament talks . . . ruling circles . . . double game"—and accused the United States of designing its inspection proposals "to contribute to the preparation of aggressive war." [93]

President Eisenhower voiced the shock and disappointment of the free world in a statement the following day:

> It is deeply disappointing to all true lovers of peace that the Soviet Union should have already attacked, with such scornful words, the proposals which Canada, France, the United Kingdom and the United States are putting forward at the United Nations Disarmament Subcommittee in London. It is noteworthy that this attack coincides with the boastful statement by the Soviet Union that they have made advances in the development of means for bringing mass destruction to any part of the world. . . .

[92] See UN Document DC/SC.1/55, "Proposals on the Implementation of Partial Disarmament Measures submitted by the USSR," April 30, 1957, Annex 7 of DC/112, *Fourth Report of the Subcommittee,* pp. 4-6.

[93] UN Document DC/SC.1/65/Rev. 1, "Statement of the Soviet Government with reference to the Disarmament Talks," August 27, 1957, Annex 4 of DC/113, *Fifth Report.*

> It would be tragic if these important first-stage proposals, fraught with such significance for the peace of the world, were rejected by the Soviet Union even before they could have been seriously studied and before the Western presentation is complete. Such a Soviet attitude would condemn humanity to an indefinite future of immeasurable danger.[94]

The rejection was abruptly confirmed on August 29 when without the courtesy of even perfunctory reference to a referral to his home government Zorin declared the Western proposals entirely unacceptable.

On September 6 after 157 meetings, the subcommittee recessed sine die.

The United Nations Twelfth General Assembly which convened in the fall of 1957 was quickly termed the "Disarmament General Assembly." At no time in recent years had foreign ministers and other heads of delegations given such prominence to disarmament in their opening remarks during the general debate, nor had proposals received such world-wide review. This reflected the desire to keep negotiation alive to avoid a nuclear holocaust.

The one important step taken by this General Assembly was to pass, over Soviet objection, a twenty-four-nation resolution endorsing in substance the August 29 proposals of the Western powers.[95] This was the first occasion since 1948 when the Western powers sought a substantive resolution of the General Assembly approving their positions over Soviet objection.

On November 4, ten days before the final vote on the General Assembly resolution endorsing the four-power proposals, the Soviet Union declared that it would not participate in the Disarmament Commission and its subcommittee in their existing composition. The Soviet Union proposed in place of the Disarmament Commission a committee of the whole consisting of all members of the United Nations. Obviously such a committee would be too unwieldy to permit negotiation.

The Western powers sought to go part way towards meeting the Soviet objections through enlargement of the Disarmament Commission. However, the Soviet Union refused all suggestions for a

[94] White House press release, statement by the president, August 28, 1957.

[95] UN General Assembly Resolution No. 1148 (XII), November 14, 1957; text in A/3805, *Resolutions adopted by the General Assembly during its Twelfth Session from 17 September to 14 December 1957*, p. 3.

commission smaller than the total membership of the General Assembly, except an Albanian suggestion for a commission in which the Soviet Union and its satellites would constitute half the membership of the commission. The General Assembly, in fact, expanded the membership of the commission to twenty-five members but the Soviet Union declined to participate.[96] Thus the long negotiations within the framework of the United Nations came to a new turn. The technical committees which resumed negotiations in the summer of 1958 arose from direct negotiations between the Soviet Union and the Western powers outside the United Nations.

It was difficult to appraise the sudden Soviet change in attitude commencing on August 27, 1957. After six months of harmonious negotiation which greatly narrowed the gap between the Soviet Union and the West, and which seemed to be leading towards at least a partial agreement, the Soviet Union drastically changed its attitude. It resumed denunciation of the West, and its propaganda blasts broke up the entire structure of disarmament negotiations. Several factors may have entered into this change:

1. The Soviet Union has at all times in the disarmament negotiations shown fear of the rearmament of Germany. When it became apparent that the Western position concerning inspection zones was being modified, partly because of the opposition of Germany, the Soviet Union hardened its position. The pending German elections certainly influenced such a change, since it seems reasonably clear that, rightly or wrongly, the Soviet Union believed that failure to secure agreement in disarmament would diminish the chances of Chancellor Adenauer for re-election.

2. In the first week of July, 1957, Khrushchev emerged the victor in a political clash within the Kremlin, and we now know that the majority of the Presidium had opposed Khrushchev's position. It is entirely possible that Khrushchev secured his majority of the Central Committee of the Communist Party, which overruled the Presidium, by concession in the field of disarmament to the more rigid views of the opposition.

3. Soviet refusal to continue discussions in the subcommittee of the Disarmament Commission or in the Disarmament Commission itself was easier to explain than its change in policy. The initial purpose of the subcommittee was to create a small organization which could operate effectively and in which the Western position could

[96] UN General Assembly Resolution No. 1150 (XII), *loc. cit.*, p. 4.

be quickly formulated and expressed. When, in June of 1957, the Western members of the subcommittee decided that no positions would be advanced in the subcommittee without first being referred to NATO, the entire objective of the subcommittee had disappeared. By the month of July, 1957, it became apparent that NATO concurrence was extremely slow and difficult to obtain.

Likewise, the Soviet refusal to go forward in the Disarmament Commission is understandable. In 1948, the General Assembly had approved Western proposals for control of atomic energy based upon the Baruch Plan despite Soviet opposition. This was a futile act since no system could possibly be implemented without the Soviet Union. From 1948 until the autumn of 1957, the Western powers had consequently never requested the General Assembly to endorse their proposals in the absence of Soviet agreement. In 1957 the Western powers departed from this precedent and, for reasons difficult to understand, once again secured the General Assembly endorsement of the August 29, 1957, proposals. The only apparent benefit which the West could receive from such endorsement would be in the field of propaganda. Therefore the Soviet refusal to continue negotiations in the Disarmament Commission could be explained as an effort to prevent further propaganda "victories" for the West through majorities which the Soviet representative described as "automatic."

4. The simplest and most usual explanation of the Soviet change has been that with the scientific triumphs in the development of outer space missiles—the ICBM on August 26, 1957, and the first satellite on October 2—the Soviet Union had no further interest in disarmament and was reverting to its previous policy of using the disarmament negotiations to weaken the West. While such a motive probably never has been absent from Soviet calculations, developments after 1957 seem clearly to rule out this motive as the primary motive of Soviet policy. If such had been the case, it seems unlikely that the technical discussions of 1958 and 1959 would ever have been undertaken. Nor would Khrushchev in his September, 1959, speech to the United Nations have opened the door to new negotiations for partial disarmament.

5. It is possible that one of the chief motives of the Soviet Union in breaking off negotiation in the Disarmament Commission was to shift the level of negotiation to the summit. As pointed out, it seems clear that during the period from 1948, after resignation of Baruch, at

least until 1955, the Soviet Union had the impression that the United States attached little importance to disarmament. Appointment of Stassen in 1955 with Cabinet rank must have created an impression that at long last the US was giving attention to disarmament proposals and the US representative could speak with authority for his government. In the late spring of 1957 it became obvious to the Soviet Union that Stassen had reached the limit of his negotiating authority. It was logical to conclude that further disarmament negotiations could take place only at the summit. This was the position taken by Khrushchev when the Soviet Union refused to proceed further in the Disarmament Commission. Negotiations at the foreign ministers level undoubtedly seemed illogical from the Soviet viewpoint, partly because of the well-known Soviet antipathy to the late Secretary of State Dulles and partly because the Soviet foreign minister plays a far less important role in his country than does his equivalent in Western countries.

It seems probable that the revived Soviet intransigence arose not from a change in position but from belief that the procedures and methods of the period from 1952 to 1957 were no longer useful. While occasionally the Soviet representatives have reverted to the old Soviet line that a nuclear struggle would result merely in destruction of Western capitalism and that the Soviet Union would escape unscathed, nevertheless the Soviet Union continues to stress even to its own people the threat of nuclear destruction.

This interpretation is strengthened by the fact that when disarmament negotiations resumed, the technical groups conducting negotiations started where the subcommittee of the Disarmament Commission had left off in August, 1957. A measure of agreement had already been reached on cessation of nuclear tests and also on the necessity of guarding against surprise attack. Two technical groups, half of the membership of which consisted of the Soviet Union and its satellites, commenced in the fall of 1958 to study the safeguards required in these fields.

In the meantime, the United States and other Western powers had dropped their requirement set forth in the August 29 proposals that the provisions of the package were inseparable. Technical discussions of safeguards to prevent surprise attack bogged down early in 1958 and were adjourned indefinitely. The negotiations for a system to detect nuclear explosions continued despite intransigence and uncompromising positions taken by the Soviet government.

The possibilities of disarmament change with rapidity as the months and years of our hectic postwar era pass by, and so a new phase of disarmament began in the summer of 1958. The present essay was completed in July, 1960. Meanwhile developments have taken place which probably have not changed greatly either the groundwork or the pattern of negotiations.

The conference in Geneva to secure discontinuance of nuclear tests has continued almost without interruption. Differences between the Soviet Union and the West have narrowed to a point where small additional concessions could result in an accord. Such concessions might have come from the summit meeting if there had been one. After the debacle at the summit the negotiations resumed with no noticeable stiffening of the Soviet position. In the US a large and vocal sector of public opinion favors resumption of nuclear tests as essential to US security. Further Soviet concessions resulting in an accord seem unlikely until the Soviet Union has some assurance that an accord would have support of the next US administration. Problems of the test cessation conference fulfill the prediction so often expressed by John Foster Dulles that the greatest difficulties with the Russians arise after agreement in principle, when negotiators sit down to draw up the detailed annexes to implement the agreement.

An important recent development was the explosion in 1960 of nuclear devices in the Sahara desert by the French. While this event established that France has the potential of becoming a fourth nuclear power, realization of this potential is probably years away. France has not become a party to the test cessation conference.

A renewed effort to negotiate on the general subject of disarmament ended in an impasse. On September 18, 1959, Khrushchev appeared before the General Assembly of the United Nations and delivered a long address calling for "general and complete world disarmament" in four years.[97] In his address he quoted almost literally, but without attribution, language used in previous negotiations by Benjamin V. Cohen and Jules Moch. While in the existing state of world tensions a proposal for complete disarmament cannot be taken seriously, Khrushchev nevertheless opened the door to nego-

[97] *New York Times*, Sept. 19, 1959. It is a hopeful sign that Khrushchev in February, 1960, in a major address in Moscow, contended that the vastness of destruction that would result from a nuclear war prevents the US from starting one.

tiations through his statement that if "the Western powers do not manifest their readiness to embark on general and complete disarmament, then the Soviet government is ready to come to an agreement with other states on the appropriate partial steps of disarmament and the strengthening of security." [98] The Western powers favored renewal of the discussions and agreed with the Soviet Union to set up a ten-nation disarmament commission to meet in Geneva in the middle of March, 1960. The president appointed as the US representative Frederick Eaton, one of America's outstanding attorneys.

When the commission met, the Soviet Union resubmitted the proposals for general and complete disarmament which Khrushchev had made to the United Nations. However, all efforts of the Western delegates to direct the discussion to partial steps of disarmament or even to the initial steps in a program of general disarmament failed completely. The Western governments on March 15, 1960, submitted a proposal calling ultimately for as drastic a program as the Soviet proposals.[99] In addition the Western proposal detailed measures and procedures which would come into effect in the first stage. Practically none of the first-stage measures dealt with subjects which Khrushchev had indicated in his General Assembly speech. Furthermore, the Western position was in the main further away from known Soviet positions than the 1957 Western proposals which the Soviet Union had rejected.

After failure of the summit conference the Soviet representative submitted on June 2, 1960, revised proposals which did elaborate on the first-stage proposals and moved closer to views expressed in the meetings by the Western delegates and in particular by France.[100] Western delegates found this new approach encouraging and determined to revise their March 15 proposals. On June 27 before they could submit their revised proposals, all of the Soviet bloc quit the session and announced their intention to submit their proposals to the General Assembly.[101]

The Western June 27 proposals, with possibly one exception, do not appear to have narrowed the differences between the Soviet and Western positions.

[98] *Loc. cit.*
[99] See Department of State press release No. 120, Mar. 14, 1960.
[100] United Nations General Assembly Document A 4374, June 2, 1960.
[101] For text of revised proposals, see *New York Times,* June 28, 1960, page 10.

The most obvious conclusion that could be drawn from the postwar years of complicated and confusing disarmament negotiations is that no glib formula will suffice to explain them. Nevertheless such explanations are frequently advanced. For example, it is contended that the Soviet position in disarmament negotiations rests solely on propaganda. While there is a modicum of truth in this statement, particularly for the period prior to 1955, it certainly does not completely explain Soviet positions.

Similarly, critics of the Western position frequently contend that the Western powers have never taken disarmament seriously. To these critics, the Western proposals were of such a nature that the West knew that they would be unacceptable to the Soviet Union and whenever the Soviet Union showed some inclination to agree, the Western powers withdrew the proposals. There is a scintilla of evidence to support such a view, but it is so slight in relation to the total negotiations that it is of little consequence.

While no simple formula can act as the key to the negotiations, some generalization is possible—generalization which receives overwhelming support from the record:

First, both the Soviet Union and the West, throughout the period, made proposals which would, if accepted, have destroyed the strategic balance in favor of the proponent of the proposals. The Baruch Plan came under this head, as well as all Soviet proposals prior to May 10, 1955. Commencing with 1952, however, Western proposals became more flexible. Although in their initial form they would unquestionably have secured strategic advantages for the West, they could be modified in such manner as to permit agreement maintaining the strategic balance. The sole important exceptions were the US proposals on aerial overflight during 1955 and 1956 (but not 1957). Commencing in 1955, the Soviet Union likewise began to make proposals which could be negotiated without creating a strategic imbalance. This trend furnishes a gauge of the seriousness of negotiations.

Second, over the years it became apparent that the chief obstacle to agreement was the problem of safeguards. Any system of inspection in its early stages would of necessity result in strategic advantages to the West through a breach of the iron curtain. Therefore any agreement must, of necessity, provide compensation to the Soviet Union. It has become increasingly clear that the most fruitful course of negotiation is to single out an area where safeguards will result in a minimum breach of the Iron Curtain. Technical discussion can then go forward to devise the system of safeguards with some possibility of success. This is the approach taken in discussions on nuclear testing, progressing in 1960 at Geneva, and in the suspended technical negotiations on surprise attack.

Third, it has likewise become apparent that the Soviet Union, even when making serious proposals, focuses on the propaganda aspects of those proposals. When the Western powers have made proposals which expose them to Soviet propaganda, the Soviet Union has rarely hesitated to interrupt any negotiation, no matter how serious, to secure a cheap propaganda advantage. Therefore, genuine negotiation is aided when the Western proposals are not only sound but attractive and thus do not lend themselves to propaganda attack.

Fourth, a close relation exists between the seriousness of Soviet negotiating efforts and the detail in which proposals are submitted. When the Soviet Union has no intention of negotiating, its proposals are usually confined to one or two sentences which are little more than propaganda slogans, such as "Ban the Bomb." In the Disarmament Commission subcommittee discussions of 1957, and in the technical discussions of 1958 and 1959, the Soviet Union has gone into considerable detail.

Fifth, there is some relation between the military strength of the West and the willingness of the Soviet Union to negotiate. Unquestionably, the Soviet Union became much more serious about disarmament after the Western rearmament following Korea. Probably the most important factor in the Soviet reappraisal of policy which took place in 1954 and 1955, was development of thermonuclear weapons, resulting in the Soviet leaders' conceding that a nuclear war would destroy the Soviet Union as well as the West. It follows that a strong Western military posture increases the possibilities of a disarmament agreement which will enhance the security of both East and West.

Sixth, the temperature of the disarmament negotiations tends to parallel the temperature of general political differences between the Soviet Union and the West. Since 1955 the Soviet Union, however, has taken more moderate positions in disarmament than on other political subjects. This was particularly true in 1957, when the disarmament negotiations moved in an atmosphere of good will despite the deterioration in political relations resulting from the Hungarian revolution.

Seventh, it is fundamental that the West should be in a position to take advantage of negotiating opportunities arising from so-called Soviet concessions. This requires that the West have a flexible policy which can be easily applied to the infinite number of situations that may arise during negotiations. It is also fundamental that the West —and in particular the United States, because of its military strength —have immediately available adequate staff to turn an agreement in principle into a treaty or convention that is technically sound and that protects the West. Secretary of State Dulles frequently pointed out that the crucial test of any disarmament agreement would not be the initial agreement but the accompanying annexes. In the past, the United States on several occasions found itself in a position where it lacked the organization—and for that matter, the policy—to produce the detailed annexes.

All of these guideposts point to the close relation of the disarmament negotiations to general East-West problems in the postwar period, a relationship which becomes closer rather than more distant as both the Soviet Union and the West become aware that some solution of the arms race, diminishing the possibility of a nuclear holocaust, is essential to the survival of civilization.

5: UNITED STATES POLICY IN THE WESTERN HEMISPHERE

Arthur P. Whitaker

The policy of the United States in relation to the Western Hemisphere at the present time is little more than the sum of its policies towards the three political entities that share the New World with it: Latin America, Canada, and the remaining European possessions. Only one important policy, that of Hemisphere defense, is addressed to the Western Hemisphere as a whole, and in operation even this repeats the threefold pattern, for it is implemented by separate arrangements with Latin America and Canada, with the European possessions in America occupying a special status apart from both arrangements. This threefold division is therefore the basis of the organization of the present essay.

The policy of the United States is still marked by some survivals from the long period before the Second World War when it was powerfully influenced by a concept of the Western Hemisphere as a whole. These survivals are most numerous in its Latin-American policy, for it was in relation to that area that the concept first took shape and had its fullest development. It emerged early in the 19th century at the beginning of Latin-American independence in the form of what the present writer has called the Western Hemisphere idea, that is, the idea that the peoples of the New World formed a distinct and coherent group, united with one another by geographical propinquity, history, and common ideals and interests, and set apart from the wicked Old World (*i.e.*, Europe) by superior virtues as well as by the wide Atlantic. Shared by many Latin Americans, this idea enjoyed a long vogue in the United States, where it found policy expression in a variety of ways that included both the unilateral Monroe Doctrine and multilateral Pan Americanism. Its influence on policy alternately waxed and waned with the vicissitudes of American and world affairs for more than a century until in the 1930s it was raised to its all-time high by the threat from the Axis and Japan. But during these years it became identified with isolationism in the minds of many, and it has never recovered from the reaction against isolationism that followed the attack on Pearl Harbor in 1941; though in any case its strength would have been sapped by the necessity of coping with the world-wide problems that have faced the United States since that time. How far the United States has moved away from the concept of a Pan American community set apart from the Old World is most vividly illustrated by the fact that it alone of the Pan American states has become a member of NATO, a military alliance all but two of whose members are Old World states.

What, then, is the basic concept of United States policy towards the other parts of the Western Hemisphere today? In a broad sense it may be described as functionalism, in contradistinction to the doctrinaire quality of the Western Hemisphere idea. That is, instead of deriving policy from the presuppositions of that idea, the United States now adapts policy to the requirements of its national and international interests and obligations as a world power. Even from this point of view, however, its Hemisphere neighbors are important objects of United States foreign policy despite the fact that none of them occupies a front-line position in the cold war, which has been the major policy determinant of the period since 1946. For example, aside from the claims of propinquity and surviving Hemisphere sentiment, Latin America and Canada bulk very large in the foreign trade and investments of the United States, possess considerable influence in international organizations of which the United States is a member, and could be of great value to it in case the cold war should turn hot.

The application of the functional principle is necessarily shaped to a large extent by the material and psychological factors peculiar to each area of the world. The fact that each of the other three divisions of the Western Hemisphere is a distinct area in these respects largely explains the threefold pattern of policy reflected in the following pages. Latin America will be discussed first and most fully, since it is the largest, most populous, and most complex of the three, and the one which has been the chief object of policy discussions in the United States most of the time from the early 19th century to the present.

LATIN AMERICA

Why a Latin-American Policy?

The historical fact just mentioned provides the answer to the otherwise puzzling question: Why does the United States have a Latin American policy? If this term means anything at all, it means that the United States has a policy which is essentially uniform for all the countries of that area, and significantly different from its policies towards other areas of the world. The puzzling thing is that there are so many obvious reasons why Latin America should not be treated as a unit in United States policy.[1] Though the twenty independent countries that compose it have some common bonds, they are highly diversified in area, population, power, economic and political development, and racial origins; and they have no linguistic unity, for French is the official language of Haiti, Portuguese of Brazil, and Spanish of the other countries, which also contain millions of people whose first or only language is an Indian one. Spread over a vast area, cut up by mountains, jungles, and deserts, most of them have little direct communication with the rest, and 90 per cent of their foreign trade, which provides a large proportion of their national income, is carried on with other parts of the world, mainly the United States and Europe.

In these circumstances it might seem more natural for any departures from the general foreign policy of the United States to reflect this diversity in one way or another, for example, by varying from one part of Latin America to another according to the special requirements of each of the five or six regions into which the area is divided. There have in fact been some tentative developments in

[1] Compare Secretary of State Dean Acheson's vigorous statement of January 12, 1950, on the parallel question of an Asian policy: ". . . I am frequently asked: Has the State Department got an Asian policy? And it seems to me that that discloses such a depth of ignorance that it is very hard to begin to deal with it. The peoples of Asia are so incredibly diverse and their problems are so incredibly diverse that how could anyone, even the most utter charlatan believe that he had a uniform policy which would deal with all of them. On the other hand there are very important similarities in ideas and in problems among the peoples of Asia and so what we come to . . . is the fact that there must be certain similarities of approach, and there must be very great dissimilarities in action." Quoted in Ruhl Bartlett (ed.), *The Record of American Diplomacy*, 3d ed. (New York, 1954), pp. 760-61, from *Bulletin*, 22 (January 23, 1950), 111.

this direction at various times. The leading example is the special Caribbean or Panama Canal policy which was followed during the first third of this century, until its most distinctive features were first blurred and then erased by the new Pan Americanism that took shape after 1933. In this case, as in all the others, the traditional approach finally prevailed. This approach was represented first by the Monroe Doctrine of 1823 and later by the Pan American movement launched in 1889; it was based on the assumption, which was a corollary of the Western Hemisphere idea, that there is a fundamental unity among the Latin-American states, and this assumption led to the conclusion that there should accordingly be a basic uniformity in United States dealings with them. Confirmed and greatly strengthened in the Franklin Roosevelt era, this tradition now has a hold which, despite Fidel Castro's current attack on it, is not likely to be broken for many years to come so far as most of the people of America are concerned.[2]

History also helps to explain the ambiguity which has been the distinctive characteristic of United States policy toward Latin America in recent years and which became clearly apparent for the first time shortly after the Second World War. On the one hand, the functional approach mentioned above has led to the loss of the preferential position that Latin America had held in United States policy, and most conspicuously during the heyday of the Good Neighbor Policy in the middle and later 1930s. One illustration of the change is provided by the case of the Pan American system, now called the Organization of American States (OAS). For many years it was the only regional association of which the United States was a member. Now it is only one of several such associations and it is overshadowed by one of them, NATO. Another sign is the infrequency with which recent secretaries of state have visited Latin America as compared with other areas, particularly Europe. The

[2] A striking illustration of this tradition's vitality was very recently provided by the Argentine government's appeal to "the Pan-American feeling of the Cuban government" to "express disapproval of any statement which may be construed as intereference by an extra-continental power in American hemispheric affairs" (*New York Times*, July 15, 1960, report from Havana by Tad Szulc). The reference was, of course, to Soviet Premier Khrushchev's interference in the controversy between Cuba and the United States. This illustration is all the more striking because, until recently, Argentina was one of the American countries in which the tradition of Pan American solidarity was weakest. Cuba promptly rejected Argentina's request.

most striking evidence of the change, however, is the relatively small share of United States foreign aid that has gone to the Latin-American countries since the Second World War. A leading authority in this field, J. Fred Rippy, has made a careful study of this question in which he stresses comparisons with Asian and African countries, mainly on the basis of population, and on this basis he concludes that at any rate in the most recent years covered (1956-1957) the Latin Americans received "about as much as they deserved."[3] His conclusion is sound if the same criteria are applied to all countries, but that is what the Latin Americans do not like. As Good Neighbors and members of the Pan American family they feel entitled to preferential treatment.

Instead of accepting this criterion, however, the United States has measured its aid to the Latin Americans by the yardstick that it has used for other parts of the world and has justified the low level of its aid to them mainly on two grounds: first, that they were not devastated during the Second World War; and second, that they are not a critical area in the cold war. Some of the main results have been that Latin America received no Marshall Plan aid or anything like it; that it has been allotted a microscopic share of military aid and defense support aid (*i.e.*, economic aid related to defense), and a relatively large share of technical co-operation funds, which share, however, has been small in absolute amount (about $26 million in 1956 and $29 million in 1958, for all twenty Latin-American countries); and that, with only two significant exceptions, it has received no direct grant aid. The two exceptions are Bolivia and Guatemala; in both cases the grants were made to meet threats of communist penetration in revolutionary situations. The point to be stressed here is not whether the application of these criteria to Latin America was just or wise, but rather that this application amounted to a denial of the Latin Americans' appeal to the traditional concept of a special relationship with the United States, though the latter nation recognizes and acts on that concept in other cases.

Herein lies a major source of the ambiguity of the United States policy toward Latin America. The classic instance of its application of the "special relationship" concept in recent years was provided by the crisis of 1954 over the communist-infected regime of President Jacobo Arbenz Guzmán in Guatemala. On that occasion, Secretary

[3] J. Fred Rippy, *Globe and Hemisphere: Latin America's Place in Postwar Foreign Relations of the United States* (Chicago, 1958), p. 233.

of State John Foster Dulles threatened to invoke the Monroe Doctrine if the other American governments failed to take action through OAS channels, and through Dulles the United States made a unilateral effort (unsuccessful, to be sure) to prevent the shipment of arms to Arbenz by the exercise of the right of visit and search. This was an expression of the old special-relationship idea in the hegemonic terms long objected to by Latin Americans. It has also been expressed on many occasions in terms more welcome to them, but in any case, the point is that United States spokesmen have continued to talk in Hemispheric terms of the prewar period despite the fact that in some important respects the policy actually followed does not accord with these terms.

The existence of this ambiguous quality need not be attributed to insincerity, for the policy makers of this period may have been, and doubtless were, quite sincere. The explanation is probably to be found rather in the force of traditional habit, the attraction of clichés of well-established serviceability, and the disinclination of United States policy makers, especially in the Latin-American field, to analyze the theoretical bases of policy. This disinclination was particularly marked in Cordell Hull, the last American secretary of state to take a deep personal interest in his government's Latin-American policy. Since his time this policy has been left largely to assistant secretaries of state, who have not had the authority, even when they had the inclination, to address themselves publicly to such an analysis; and one must admit that it might not have been in the public interest for them to do so, in view of what they would have had to report. No prudent government advertises facts about its policies that would be unwelcome to governments and peoples whose co-operation and good will it would like to have.

Organization of American States

Let us repeat and emphasize that, though its scope and significance have been greatly reduced in the past two decades, there still exists a special relationship between the United States and Latin America, for it is necessarily a major factor in the Latin-American policy of the United States. The relationship is best represented by the OAS, which grew out of the movement initiated by the First Pan American Conference, held at Washington in 1889-1890, and is therefore the oldest regional organization in the world today. It did not assume its present name and form, however, until 1948, when the Conference of Bogotá gave the Pan American system its first constitution or fundamental statute, the Charter of Bogotá, which went into effect at once. The conference also co-ordinated existing inter-American agreements for the peaceful settlement of disputes in the Pact of Bogotá, which remains incompletely ratified,[4] though most of its constituent parts are in effect as among most of the member states.

The third chief foundation of the OAS is the Inter-American Treaty of Reciprocal Assistance, commonly called the Rio Defense Treaty, which had already been adopted by a special conference at Rio de Janeiro and Petropolis, Brazil, in 1947. This treaty illustrates some important points in the relationship between the United States and Latin America. To begin with, it marked the culmination of an effort begun in 1936 to set up a regional security system. The leadership in that direction has always come mainly from the United States, whereas the Latin Americans have generally stressed inter-American co-operation for peaceful purposes, particularly economic co-operation, which usually means United States aid to Latin America. In this instance, warm support was given by most Latin Americans in the hope—largely unfulfilled—that by entering into a security arrangement with the United States they might be able to reduce their own military expenditures. Even in this case, however, the initiative came mainly from the United States, for, like the subsequent North Atlantic Defense Treaty, for which it helped pave the way, the Rio Defense Treaty was in part a product of United States reaction to the cold war and the failure of the United Nations Security Council to function as expected. Both instruments set up regional arrangements under the United Nations Charter to help fill the gap created by this failure.

The two regional arrangements are therefore alike in some respects, but there are also important differences; and one of these illustrates another salient aspect of relations between the United States and Latin America. This is the fact that the inter-American arrangement is much more loose-jointed than the other, since it has no close counterpart to NATO, no permanent military forces whatever like those of NATO, and hence no high command like SHAPE. At the Bogotá Conference in 1948 the United States tried hard to

[4] The following are the countries that had deposited instruments of ratification of the Pact of Bogotá up to June 1, 1960: Costa Rica, El Salvador, Haiti, Honduras, Mexico, Nicaragua, Panama, Dominican Republic and Uruguay.

get a permanent Defense Council set up, but even this effort was blocked by Latin-American insistence upon developing the pacific rather than military aspects of the OAS. Our third and last illustration of the difference is provided by the fact that the Rio Defense Treaty provides for defense against aggression from within the system as well as from outside it, whereas the North Atlantic Treaty does not. There were several reasons for this feature of the Rio Treaty, but one of the most important appears to have been the Latin-American desire to impose a multilateral curb upon a type of action which it was believed the United States might take unilaterally in an emergency, as it was prepared to do in 1944 when the military dictatorship in Argentina threatened to invade democratic Uruguay.

In connection with the Rio Defense Treaty, attention should be called to one of the most significant facts about the OAS and therefore about the relations between the United States and Latin America: the OAS is an association in which one member is a superpower and all the rest are small powers—a situation which cannot be matched in any other international association in the world, outside the Soviet sphere of influence. To be sure, there are wide differences in power, as in population and wealth, among the Latin-American states themselves, but not one of them has risen even to the rank of a "middle" power such as the Netherlands and Canada. The disparity between the United States and Latin America in this respect is therefore very great, and it has gone on increasing throughout the present century, first with the mechanization of war and now with the development of nuclear weapons.

There is a similar disparity between the United States and Latin America in wealth, and this too has grown steadily throughout the present century. Only in population has the story been different. Smaller than that of the United States by a substantial margin in 1900, the combined population of the Latin-American countries has now forged ahead and continues to grow so rapidly that, according to present indications, it will be twice as large as that of the United States by the end of the century. Whatever the ultimate effect of this population explosion may be, its immediate effect has been to increase the difficulty of raising Latin-American living standards and in general of satisfying the rising expectations which are a source of grave unrest in that area as well as in other parts of the world. This ferment may be as highly desirable as one pleases from certain points of view, but it has the unfortunate further effect of producing domestic and international tensions which impair the ability of Latin America to contribute to the security system set up by the Rio Defense Treaty.

A basic principle of inter-American relations, enshrined in the OAS Charter after having been recognized on many occasions, is the juridical equality of states, large and small alike. This has long been a principle of general international law, but the Latin-American states have insisted upon it with a special pertinacity that is best explained by their interpretation of it, which makes it an absolute bar to intervention by one state in the affairs of another. This interpretation was not a generally accepted rule of international law, nor was it recognized by the United States, when Latin-American views on this subject took shape in the late 19th and early 20th centuries, during which time several interventions were carried out in Latin America by European powers, mainly for the collection of debts. Consequently, while not relaxing their insistence upon juridical equality, the Latin Americans sought to bring about the adoption of a specific, absolute, unconditional, and permanent ban on intervention. This ban they finally persuaded the United States to agree to in the Buenos Aires Inter-American Conference of 1936, at the height of the Good Neighbor era. The ban took the form of a protocol which had the force of a treaty and was ratified by the US Senate in 1937. The protocol could be interpreted as prohibiting only unilateral, not multilateral, intervention; but that door was finally closed in 1948 by the Bogotá Conference in the OAS Charter. A similar article had already been incorporated in the United Nations Charter, so that the long Latin-American campaign against intervention seemed to have been crowned with complete success.

Nevertheless, it is now clear that the last word on this subject has not yet been spoken. Indeed, that should have been apparent in 1948, for at the very time that the Bogotá Conference closed the door to multilateral as well as unilateral intervention, it reopened the door to a particular kind of multilateral action under another name, that of enforcement action. The reference here is to the declaration of the Bogotá Conference that enforcement action taken under the Rio Defense Treaty should not be construed as constituting intervention. That this is a striking proposition can be seen from the fact that, under the Rio Treaty, enforcement action can be taken against an American as well as a non-American state, and that it includes measures ranging from diplomatic sanctions through economic sanctions to the use of armed force. Also, the scope of the exception was further widened by the Anti-Communist Declaration of the Caracas Inter-American Conference in 1954, which authorized the invocation of the Rio Treaty to prevent "international communism" from controlling any American government. To be sure, the exception was made for a most worthy purpose—to curb aggression and communism in the Americas; but the fact that an exception had been made was not admitted by either conference. On the contrary, they reinforced the fiction that the rule of nonintervention was absolute, and continued to do lip service to the doctrine that all interventions without exception are bad, regardless of purpose, method, or other circumstances. The failure of these conferences to face the facts left the issue clouded and sowed the seeds of future controversy.

The issue remains clouded today, and the seeds have sprouted. The chief sufferer is the United States and the main source of trouble is the lack of any clear-cut definition of intervention, with the result that the field is left wide open to interested interpretation. As the strongest American power, the United States naturally interprets intervention narrowly, mainly in terms of armed intervention. Just as naturally the relatively weak Latin Americans interpret it broadly, to include not only armed but also diplomatic, economic, and intellectual intervention; indeed, it would hardly be an exaggeration to say that they apply the term to almost anything the United States does that affects them unpleasantly. In view of the muddled state of the question, this application is hardly surprising, but it is regrettable, for the situation seems made to order for breeding Yankeephobia. So many Latin Americans are now affected by what the United States does, or does not do, and the Latin Americans are so deeply divided among themselves, that hardly a month passes without the cry of "Yankee intervention" arising from one quarter or another, and not infrequently from the quarter opposite to the one that raised it the day before, so that by the year's end the cry has become well-nigh universal. It was this sort of thing that set the stage for the disgraceful demonstrations against Vice President Richard M. Nixon and his wife on their South American tour in May, 1958—demonstrations which were carried out by small minorities, to be sure, but which the authorities seemed extraordinarily impotent to control.

Intervention, therefore, still remains a problem in the relations of the United States with Latin America. (It is also still a problem in the relations of the Latin-American states with one another, but that lies outside the scope of this essay.) It will be difficult to solve for several reasons: because of the prevalence of the mistaken belief that it has already been solved by adopting the rule of absolute nonintervention; because of the emotional attachment to this rule, which is especially strong among Latin Americans, above all in their relations with the United States; and because any solution would require a meeting of minds among twenty-one states, the difficulty of which is greatly augmented in this case by the wide differences in the definition of intervention prevailing in the United States on the one hand and Latin America on the other.

A drastic remedy was proposed several years ago by a group of policy planners in the United States, including Assistant Secretary of State Spruille Braden. In their view, nonintervention was a practical impossibility in the relations of this country with the Latin-American states, since the United States affects them so vitally in so many ways that whatever it does or refuses to do about them amounts in effect to intervention. On this assumption it was proposed that the United States should abandon the fiction of nonintervention and deliberately use its influence in Latin America to promote the development of democratic, progressive, co-operative regimes in that area. The assumption was valid, but the proposal did not solve the problem before us, but rather evaded it, for it failed to come to grips with the very core of the problem, which is that, however unrealistic nonintervention may be, the United States is committed to it by permanent international agreements which cannot be altered without the consent of the other parties, the Latin-American states, and that this consent is not at all likely to be forthcoming. Yet no better way out of the impasse has been found, and the dual problem of intervention-nonintervention remains to haunt the United States and the Latin-American states in their relations with one another.

Bilateral Relations

So much has been said above about the relations of the United States with Latin America through the multilateral agency of the OAS that in order to maintain the proper perspective the reader should be reminded of the great continuing importance of the older bilateral, government-to-government channels. Indeed, it is through the latter that some of the most important multilateral policies and principles are given effect, with the inevitable result that the product usually bears a strong imprint of United States national policy. A prime instance is provided by the Hemisphere defense system. This was set up by a multilateral agreement, the Rio Defense Treaty; but the strengthening of Hemisphere defenses contemplated by that agreement has been achieved mainly through the series of bilateral military pacts negotiated with each of a dozen Latin-American governments by the United States in pursuance of the Rio Treaty.

Likewise, in the economic field there is a series of inter-American declarations of principles, the first of which was adopted by the Montevideo Conference more than a quarter of a century ago; but these are conceived in such general terms and have so little binding effect that the actual terms of economic relations among the American nations are determined in most instances either by bilateral agreements between pairs of governments or by the unilateral action of a single government. In fact, this is the field in which the inter-American controls over national policies are weakest. The United States has steadily resisted Latin-American efforts to make the controls more effective, for the very good reason that it finds itself faced by a solid phalanx of Latin-American opposition on many important economic questions. This opposition is not likely to relax for a long time to come, since it is due to a situation which shows no signs of changing greatly in the near future, that is, the contrast between the highly developed economy of the United States and the relatively underdeveloped economies of even the most advanced Latin-American countries. Specific policy problems that face the United States in this connection will be noted below.

Some Policy Problems

In view of the fact that the United States is a world power in an increasingly interdependent world, the first problem that should be considered in connection with its relations with Latin America is what the policy for that area ought to be in the context of world affairs. One such problem, which arose during the gestation and birth of the United Nations, 1943-1945, was whether the Inter-American System should become an effective regional system, in accordance with the trend of the past dozen years, or whether it should be cut back to its very modest proportions of the preceding period, on the theory that regionalism would hamstring the United

Nations. The answer finally given by the United States for itself was in favor of effective regionalism, and the United Nations Conference of 1945 gave substantially the same answer, though in terms of world-wide applicability, with the result that Article 51 of the completed United Nations Charter has made possible not only the Rio Defense Treaty but similar regional security arrangements, such as NATO and SEATO, affecting other parts of the world.[5]

Since then the United States has been faced by another major problem of the same type. What should its policy towards Latin America be in the context of the cold war? Should that policy be developed in accordance with the general policy of the United States in the cold war? An emphatically negative answer has very recently been given to this question by W. S. Woytinsky in a pamphlet entitled "The United States and Latin America's Economy." [6] After stating that the remoteness of Latin America from the centers of global strategy "makes the objectives of United States policy in Latin America radically different from those in Europe, Africa or Asia," he continues: "The main source of vacillation and apparent contradictions in our policy toward the South [Latin America] is the fact that this policy is considered a part of our global strategy, which it is not" (p. 43).

This is a very questionable proposition. It is of course true that Latin America, like every other region of the world, presents the United States with certain special problems that require special treatment, but it is equally true that the cold war is being waged in every region of the world, including Latin America. Though the latter's involvement has been less deep than the others', it has nevertheless been unmistakable. For example, in the United Nations Assembly, where many actions of the cold war have been fought,

[5] Latin America played an important part at the San Francisco Conference in bringing about the modification of the Dumbarton Oaks proposals of 1944 so as to permit regional security action under the United Nations Charter. See Arthur P. Whitaker, "Development of American Regionalism: The Organization of American States," *International Conciliation*, No. 469 (March, 1951), pp. 129-31.

[6] Described on the cover as "A Tamiment Institute Public Service Pamphlet." No date or place of publication. Originally published in *The New Leader*, November 24, 1958. In "Auge y miseria en Latinoamérica," *Cuadernos* (Paris), No. 34 (January-February, 1959), p. 42, the same author concluded that the "primordial problem" of Latin America lies not in lack of investment capital but in the psychology of its people and in its political and social institutions.

Latin America's twenty votes (one fourth of the present total) have played a significant role; and it might be added that they have almost invariably been cast on the side of the United States on cold war issues, though not when other issues have been involved.[7] Also, Latin America has been a target of the Soviet Union's typical cold war tactics of political and economic penetration. Despite distance and other handicaps, these have occasionally met with conspicuous success, as in the communist infiltration of the governments of Guatemala, 1951-1954, and Cuba since 1959, and in the anti-Nixon outbursts in South America in 1958.

In April, 1959, the General Secretary of ORIT (Organización Interamericana del Trabajo), the Inter-American branch of the International Confederation of Free Trade Unions, warned that the Soviet Union was intensifying efforts of this kind in the Americas as well as in Asia, Africa, the Middle East, and certain countries of Western Europe. He charged that in Latin America these efforts took form in a conspiracy launched in Santiago, Chile, in February, 1959 and from there extended first to Mexico and then to other Latin-American countries, and that one of its major objectives was to discredit the free trade union movement. "Anti-economic strikes," he asserted, "are organized on the fringe of responsible free trade jurisdiction. Attempts are made at preventing the establishment of true democracy in countries such as Colombia, Peru, Chile and Argentina. Artificial conflicts are created in Venezuela in order to harry the activities of a constitutional government . . . Caracas has been chosen as the center for these maneuvers . . . [which are] covered by the liberties that now exist in [Venezuela]." [8]

The threat of communist penetration soon shifted to Cuba. By early 1960 the danger became acute as the leaders of the new Fidel Castro regime tried to pick a quarrel with the United States while welcoming the advances of the Soviet Union and denouncing anti-communism as counter-revolutionary. Nevertheless, Washington adhered to a policy of patience and forbearance. Its course was widely criticized in the United States, but under the circumstances respect for the rule of nonintervention and for Latin-American opinion left

[7] For the most recent analysis of the Latin-American group in the United Nations, see Thomas Hovet, Jr., *Bloc Politics in the United Nations* (Cambridge, 1960), pp. 65-69.

[8] *Inter-American Labor Bulletin,* June 1959, p. 2; article reprinted from the Mexico City daily, *Novedades,* of April 23, 1959.

it little choice in the matter. Until proof not merely of communist influence but of communist control in Cuba could be established, the Caracas Anti-Communist Declaration of 1954 would not apply and sanctions under the Rio Defense Treaty could not be invoked. Moreover, only a two-thirds vote of all the American states could invoke them, and Latin-American opinion, though increasingly critical of the Castro regime, was not prepared for such drastic action.

Respect for Latin-American opinion deterred the United States for nearly a year from adopting any of the unilateral reprisals open to it lest it again incur the charge of intervention, as in the somewhat similar case of Guatemala in 1954. At last, in early July, 1960, finding Castro's conduct intolerable, the United States Government cut Cuba's sugar quota. Castro, charging economic aggression, took his case to the United Nations Security Council. Premier Khrushchev came to his support with the assertion that the Monroe Doctrine is dead and with the threat of a rocket attack on the United States if it intervened in Cuba. The United States replied with a reassertion of the Monroe Doctrine, and Peru called for a meeting of American ministers of foreign affairs to consider "the defense of the [American] regional system." [9] On the initiative of its Latin-American members, Argentina and Ecuador, the Security Council referred Cuba's complaint to the OAS, which was expected to consider it, along with a controversy between Venezuela and the Dominican Republic, at a foreign ministers' meeting in late August or September.

Towards a New Policy

Since the cold war is being waged in Latin America, the United States has been quite right in shaping its policy there in accordance with its cold war strategy. Indeed, aside from the defects in that strategy which have marked it everywhere, the chief trouble with United States policy towards Latin America was that it did not give sufficient weight to the communist threat in that area until 1958. In the official policy glosses of the preceding decade one encounters again and again explanations to the effect that Latin America was not a critical area in the cold war. Such statements were true only in the sense that the Soviet Union lacked contiguous territory on which to base a military or political campaign, but experience has shown that that was a very limited sense. And the worst of it was

[9] For Argentina's reaction to Khrushchev's interposition in the Cuban case, see above, note 2.

that Washington's top policy makers acted as if Latin America could be kept on ice indefinitely without any deterioration of the good will built up in the Roosevelt-Hull-Welles era of the Good Neighbor policy while the United States concentrated its attention and funds on other areas, some of which had recently been its enemies while others were currently neutral if not antagonistic. Though warning voices were raised from time to time at lower levels, they were not heeded at the top until May, 1958, when the near-tragedy of the Nixon tour brought a rude awakening from this pipe dream.

With a magnanimity that does him credit, Vice President Nixon laid a large measure of the responsibility for the Latin-American hostility from which he had suffered on the mistaken policy of the government of which he himself was a part. His view gained general acceptance in Washington and it was accordingly announced that great improvements were going to be made in that policy. Proposals to this end were brought together in a report, dated December 27, 1958, by Milton S. Eisenhower,[10] the president's brother. Some of these were adopted and others appeared to be in the making.

The remedial measures have ranged all the way from President Eisenhower's good-will visit to South America early in 1960 to the provision of more money on new grounds. Except for a large increase in the funds available for cultural relations, including the exchange of students, teachers, technicians, and others, most of the innovations lie in the economic field and involve concessions to Latin America on some of the disputed issues referred to earlier in this essay.

The chief concession to date has been the agreement of the United States to join in setting up an Inter-American Development Bank. The bank held its first meeting in El Salvador in February, 1960. Of its capital of $1,000 million, $450 million was provided by the United States. This is a measure long desired by Latin Americans to aid in their economic development, but long opposed by the United States on the ground that ample funds were already available for sound public projects in this field through institutions such as the World Bank and the Export-Import Bank (a United States institution), and that private enterprise should rely for its financing on private capital, such as United States investors could supply.

[10] Milton S. Eisenhower, *United States-Latin American Relations, 1953-1958. Report to the President, December 28, 1958* (Washington, 1959). Reprinted from *Bulletin*, 40 (January 19, 1959).

It has repeatedly been pointed out that large amounts of United States private capital were already invested in Latin America ($9,000 million at the end of 1959) and that more would certainly be available for sound projects. Latin Americans, however, have always been cool to this advice, partly through fear of large-scale foreign capital investments as an instrument of foreign economic penetration, and partly because of their growing faith in the thesis that wealthy nations (*e.g.*, the United States) are under an obligation to aid poorer nations (*e.g.*, those in Latin America) through government channels. As a further concession President Eisenhower announced at a press conference on July 11, 1960, in the midst of the deepening crisis in relations with Cuba, that additional assistance would probably be provided for Latin America. A few days later it was reported that this would take the form of a $500 million addition to the Development Loan Fund, established in 1957 to make "soft" loans.

The issue of public loans versus private investments is also involved in another policy innovation which is apparently in the making, though it has not yet been authoritatively announced. This innovation is the financing of Latin-American government-controlled petroleum entities, such as Petrobrás of Brazil, Pemex of Mexico, Y.P.F. of Argentina, and Y.P.F.B. of Bolivia, by either the new Inter-American Development Bank or the Export-Import Bank or both. In the first of these institutions the United States will have a strong voice, and the second it owns. That it should let them lend financial assistance to agencies of this type was a decided innovation, for it had always denied them help, in pursuance of its general rule that United States Government funds must not be made available to foreign government agencies operating in fields appropriate to private enterprise. According to Washington, the petroleum industry was such a field. The Latin-American governments in question thought otherwise and resented what they regarded as intervention in their domestic affairs.

The issue has been particularly important in the cases of Argentina and Brazil, for both countries face a grave balance-of-payments problem because of their heavy purchases of foreign oil to meet the evergrowing domestic demand, and both hope to solve the problem through the development by Y.P.F. and Petrobrás, respectively, of their own petroleum resources, which are known to be extensive in Argentina and believed to be so in Brazil. Also, in both countries the situation is aggravated by deep political unrest over this and other issues, and small but substantial communist groups are helping to trouble the waters. All this has been known for several years, but only now is the United States beginning to yield on the crucial issue of loans to the government petroleum entities in question. While the change may have been due largely to the lessons learned from the anti-Nixon outbursts in 1958, another factor was the realization that rehabilitated Europe was now able and willing to finance these governmental entities and that if it did so, the business of supplying them with new equipment would probably go to firms in Europe, not the United States.

An even more important innovation, but one which appears less certain at the present writing, is the conclusion of an inter-American agreement on the stabilization of commodity prices, with Latin America as the beneficiary and the United States footing the bill. This is another measure which has long been urged by Latin Americans and opposed by the United States. The latter is now reported to have agreed to it in principle. What will come of it in practice it would be rash to predict. The economic and political issues involved in the proposal are so complex, and the specific application of it might assume so many different forms, that about all one can say with confidence at this stage is that it will probably take a good deal of time and hard bargaining to conclude any significant agreement of this kind, for it would touch the pocketbooks of many producers all over Latin America and virtually all consumers and taxpayers in the United States.

The current revision of the Latin-American policy of the United States raises other important economic questions that merit attention, but space permits us to consider only one of them here. This is a question that possesses exceptional interest because it raises again the issue of the rival claims of regionalism and universalism and because it involves a critical situation in the largest Latin-American country, Brazil, and United States policy in relation to one of the chief world organizations, the International Monetary Fund (IMF). Briefly, the situation is this: in dire need of funds, the government of Brazil recently turned to the IMF for help; the latter, following its usual procedures, first made a careful study of the situation and then offered a substantial loan but attached as a condition a program of austerity, which was rejected by the Brazilian government on the ground that it would provoke violent opposition among the people of that country. The Rio government then turned to Washington for the desired loan, without any such strings attached, though it had hitherto been Washington's rule to support the policies of the IMF by refusing to make loans to countries that have been turned down by the IMF.

The issue seemed to be clear-cut: which would the United States support, Brazil or the IMF? If the former, it would undermine an important world organization which it has helped greatly to found, finance, and operate. On the other hand, if it supported the IMF either by refusing the loan or by attaching substantially the IMF's conditions, the result might be a political upheaval in Brazil, which, as we have noted above in another connection, has recently been made a prime target of the communists in an effort to exploit its already unstable political situation. Yet, despite the fact that the issue appeared to be quite clear, Washington found a solution which it was hoped would help Brazil without letting the IMF down. Announced on June 20, 1959, the decision was to deny Brazil the new loan (thus supporting the IMF) but to help Brazil by postponing the payment of its existing debts. Whether this action would solve the problem, or only delay and perhaps prejudice the solution, remains to be seen.

The last feature of Washington's revised Latin-American policy that we shall take note of is the new attitude which, we are told, it is going to take towards Latin-American dictators, whom it had been charged for some time past with supporting. The rule of nonintervention must be respected, it was explained; but within the limits imposed by this rule the United States would go as far as it could in demonstrating its disapproval of dictatorship. The new attitude was described in a phrase more meaningful to Latin Americans than to North Americans: "For dictators, a formal handshake; for democrats, an *abrazo* [embrace]."

Just how this approach will work out remains to be seen. The late John Foster Dulles said it would not work out at all when a formula of the same kind was proposed to him in 1957. Perhaps he was wrong, but if it is to be effective the discrimination will have to be carried far beyond the amenities of greeting, and it is not easy to see how that could be done without departing from the rule of nonintervention. That something can be done was shown when the United States refused Cuban dictator Batista's request for arms in the last months before his fall. Such simple situations are rare, however, for the problem is fraught with difficulties, beginning in some cases with that of obtaining general agreement as to whether a regime is or is not a dictatorship. It would be unwise for the United States to talk itself into even an appearance of accepting any special responsibilities for this tangled problem of dictatorships in Latin America, when it has no special powers to deal with them. Rather, it should insist that the problem be dealt with multilaterally, as has been done in the case of comunism through the Caracas Declaration of 1954, so that enforcement action, if any, would be taken by the OAS and not unilaterally by the United States.

One may of course hope that this problem will disappear through the continuation of the current trend towards the liquidation of Latin-American dictatorships that began with the Argentine Juan D. Perón's fall in 1955, but it would be rash to count upon this eventuality as a foregone conclusion. Authoritarian governments have been a frequently recurring phenomenon in Latin America throughout the century and a half since the beginning of its independence. Democratic trends have appeared there before, only to be reversed within ten or twenty years, as has happened in this century in Argentina, Brazil, and Colombia, to mention only three of the largest countries in that area.

Perhaps Latin America stands at the end of that era and on the threshold of a new one which will be quite different; but not all the auguries are against the continuation of the authoritarian pattern. On the contrary, one powerful new factor may work in favor of it. Latin Americans, like many other peoples, have recently become obsessed with the desire for rapid economic development; the only two ways of achieving it unaided are either through large-scale investments of private capital, which Latin Americans cannot provide, or through forced savings under an authoritarian government, on the model set by the Soviet Union; and Latin America's deep-rooted tradition of statism combines with other factors to make the adoption of the latter solution a plausible contingency. If the Latin Americans do not insist upon conducting this development at breakneck speed, a third way could be provided by a combination of foreign government loans, private investments, and improvement in the Latin-American terms of trade. This seems to be the solution at which the revised Latin-American policy of the United States is aimed. If so, the United States is at last coming to grips with the chief long-range problem in its relations with Latin America.

As we have noted above, however, there are also political problems that urgently require attention. In addition to those already mentioned, three relating to the armed forces of Latin America have been highlighted by recent developments in that area. One has been raised by Chilean President Jorge Alessandri's proposal for a sweeping reduction of Latin-American armaments. The merits of the proposal are obvious, for such a reduction would release much-needed funds for productive purposes. Yet it is no less obvious that Latin-American disarmament is difficult to separate from general disarmament, and that even in so good a cause the United States should not again assume the role of policeman of the Western Hemisphere, as in Theodore Roosevelt's time. Another problem is the control of arms traffic. For example, the United States has shut off its arms shipments to the turbulent Caribbean area, but mutually hostile Cuba and the Dominican Republic have continued to arm themselves from other sources, such as Belgium and Spain. Third and finally, there is the question whether the United States military assistance program in Latin America should be cut back, increased, or continued on its present scale. The answer depends largely on one's opinion of the political role of the military in Latin America, and opinions on this question differ widely. A decade ago the military was generally identified with dictatorships and oligarchy, but today, in several countries, it is supporting relatively democratic regimes, and some observers regard it as one of the best defenses against communism.

In the important area of cultural relations the United States is just beginning to address itself seriously to a task that it undertook nearly a quarter of a century ago but has performed rather absent-mindedly except when under the pressure of emergency during the Second World War. In this and other respects, in so far as Washington's new Latin-American policy has been revealed, it seems to be moving generally along the right lines, but much remains to be done.

CANADA

"Free but Dependent"

In the last two decades Canada has greatly strengthened and broadened its economy by the addition of large-scale industrial and mineral production to the original agricultural base, and in wealth and power now stands far ahead of the richest and strongest Latin-American states. For this and other reasons it possesses outstanding importance among the nations of the New World from the point of view of United States foreign policy. Nevertheless, its role will be discussed here much more briefly than that of Latin America for it presents a far less complicated group of problems.

This is not by any means to imply that all is sweetness and light between the United States and its northern neighbor. The two countries have always had their differences and difficulties and in the past two or three years these have provoked in Canada a mounting irritation and an anti-Americanism or Yankeephobia very much like the Latin-American variety, except that it has not been marked by physical violence against representatives of the United States and cannot be attributed in any significant degree to communist influence.

The relative simplicity of Canada's case is explained rather by the facts that one state presents a less complicated problem than a group of twenty and that, since Canada is a relatively young state, its relations with the United States are free from most of those complications of tradition which we have noted as a source of ambiguity and misunderstanding in the case of Latin America. Most important of all, Canada, though the largest country in the Western Hemisphere, has always been outside the operational scope of the Western Hemisphere idea. Its own attitude is shown by the fact that it has never taken part in the Pan American movement.[11] There was a prospect that it might do so for a brief time after Hitler's conquest of France, the Low Countries, and Norway in 1940, when Britain, too, was threatened with invasion; but the prospect vanished with the threat. Canada has not availed itself of the opportunity to join the OAS that was offered it by the Charter adopted at Bogotá in 1948, and seems unlikely to do so in the future. The attitude of the United States is shown by the fact that its government did not extend the Monroe Doctrine to Canada until the eve of the Second World War, and by that time the basic conception of Canada's international role was already firmly fixed both at home and abroad: Canada was not to be a member of the Pan American family but to serve as a linchpin between the United States and Great Britain, while the United States performed the same functions between Canada and Latin America.

[11] Early in 1960 Canada joined the Pan American Institute of Geography and History, a specialized organization of the OAS; and on June 16, 1960, Canada's foreign minister, Howard Green, stated that Canada ought to join the OAS for both political and commercial reasons.

This idea of course presupposed the maintenance of satisfactory or at least tolerable relations between the two North American neighbors, which most Canadians have come to regard, whether with or without pleasure, as the most important problem in the whole range of their external relations. In addition, Canada, like Latin America, is joined with the United States in multilateral relationships which include not only the United Nations and its specialized organizations but also an important regional association—in this case, NATO.

"Free but dependent" is the way a journalist described Canada's international role a few years ago.[12] The reference was to its dependence upon the United States. To the great annoyance of many Canadians it began to increase by leaps and bounds at the very time when Canada was establishing its political independence of Great Britain by a gradual, peaceful process, unmarked by any formal declaration of independence by Canada. This independence started with Canada's admission to the League of Nations in 1919, and was unmistakably signalized by the Canadian Parliament's separate declaration of war in 1939, a week after the British declaration.

During this period rapid progress was made towards the present dependence of Canada upon the United States in two major fields, economic and military. The economic came first, for in the 1920s United States investments poured into Canada on an unprecedentedly large scale and laid the groundwork for present-day control of a great part of the economic life of that country by its southern neighbor. In the same decade the United States consolidated its position as one of the world's two greatest naval powers—Britain was the other—and thus started on the course that has made it today by far the greatest of all; and Canada's large overseas trade makes it dependent upon sea power. Moreover, at the close of the 1930s the Axis threat stimulated an upsurge of United States power on land and in the air as well and brought the two neighbors into a close military co-operation, which began with the establishment of joint defense arrangements under the Ogdensburg Agreement of August

[12] John A. Stevenson, "Canada, Free but Dependent," *Foreign Affairs,* 29 (April, 1951), 456-67. The author was the *Manchester Guardian's* Ottawa correspondent. For a more recent discussion, in a broad setting, of Canada's dependence on the United States, see R. St. John Macdonald, "Fundamentals of Canadian Foreign Policy," in London Institute of World Affairs, *The Year Book of World Affairs 1958* (London, 1958), pp. 170-73.

18, 1940. This co-operation has been not only continued but greatly expanded, for in this air and missile age, when the chief antagonists are the United States and the Soviet Union and the next war may be fought across the North Pole, Canada has acquired a strategic importance, vulnerability, and defense value to the United States that it never had before.

In any close association between two states of widely unequal strength, such as the United States and Canada, the weaker must in some degree become dependent upon the stronger, no matter how earnestly both may strive to remain upon a footing of equality. Such an effort has been made in this case and will doubtless continue to be made, but it was bound from the start to fail, for as the Spanish proverb has it, "When two men ride a donkey, one of them must ride behind." That Canada occupies this position in both its military and economic relations with the United States is distasteful to its people, but most of them seem to understand that refusal to ride the donkey of co-operation with the United States would not help but rather hurt. It would not help, because Canada's dependence is a result not of such co-operation but of the fact that it is contiguous to the United States on a frontier some four thousand miles long and is far weaker than the United States in every index of power.

To take only one such index, Canada's population is less than one tenth as large as the United States', and the great majority of its people live within two hundred miles of the United States in a thin band stretching along the whole frontier from the Atlantic to the Pacific. Much has been made, on both sides, of the fact that this frontier is unfortified, but the fact is that it would be useless for Canada, as it is needless for the United States, to fortify it. Canada's best defense is to co-operate. This does not mean submission, but working together, which gives Canadian leaders the best opportunity they could have to speak their minds to their co-workers freely and with maximum effectiveness. To put an end to co-operation would be to cut off a fruitful dialogue without in the least altering the facts of power.

Anti-Americanism in Canada

Canadians have not failed to hold up their end of this dialogue vigorously with advice, remonstrances, and warnings to Washington. With a restraint becoming to diplomacy, though not often practiced since Soviet diplomats set a new style, Canada's official spokesmen have more than once during the cold war publicly laid a restraining hand on Uncle Sam's coattails. In the campaign preceding one of the country's recent national elections the winning party concentrated its fire on the United States to a degree that made one wonder at times whether another cold war front was not being opened.

The official line became less fierce after the election was won, but private citizens of Canada have continued to give full vent to the anti-Americanism built up in that country in recent years. Smoldering resentment burst into flame when, on December 24, 1957, President Eisenhower issued an order placing restrictions on oil imports into the United States. Canada was the chief sufferer and its reaction was "prompt and forceful." According to Bruce Hutchinson, Canadian correspondent of the *Christian Science Monitor*, writing on January 10, 1958, "no recent event has so gravely damaged good American-Canadian relations." [13] Even so temperate a critic and so good a friend of the United States as Lester B. Pearson, Canada's former secretary of state for external affairs, declared that the president's justification of his order in terms of United States national defense was nonsense and that the order was inconsistent with principles to which the United States was committed, not only with the broad principle of collective security, but also with the specific doctrine of economic co-operation incorporated in the NATO treaty.[14]

On May 15, 1958, Pearson returned to the charge in an address in which he warned an audience at Williamsburg, Virginia, of the mounting irritation in his country. In matters of military defense, he said, the United States insisted upon Canada's co-operation in the name of continental solidarity, whereas in the economic field it applied "the old rules of national interest and trade protection," to Canada's great disadvantage, and in both fields took decisions of vital importance to the latter without consulting it. "We are determined," he declared, "to do what we can to preserve and strengthen to the maximum possible extent our distinct identity—politically, economically and culturally." [15]

Another fair example of Canadian grievances was provided by Ian F. McRea, president of the Canadian Manufacturers Association,

[13] Quoted in Percy Bidwell, *Raw Materials: A Study of American Policy* (New York, 1958), p. 321.

[14] *Ibid.*, pp. 340-41.

[15] *New York Times*, May 16, 1958.

at the annual Congress of American Industry in New York City on December 4, 1958. He protested vigorously against Washington's economic policies in general, but particularly against its "contemptuous disregard of our [Canadian] sovereignty" in matters involving United States companies and their Canadian subsidiaries. Such phrases as "flagrant dictation" and "blatant move to throttle the autonomy of these Canadian-based companies" gave added spice to the speech; and in the course of it he entered a more general complaint against the "invasion" of Canada by United States capital, and the virtual exclusion of Canadian products such as oil, other raw materials, and manufactured goods from the American market by high tariffs. Interestingly enough, on this same occasion two Latin-American speakers voiced complaints from that area in the same sense, but theirs were much milder than the Canadian's and related mainly to investments. On other recent occasions Canadians as well as Latin Americans have made much of another grievance: the adverse effects on their national economies of the United States program for the disposal of its surplus agricultural commodities, such as wheat and cotton.

In spite of all these irritations, it seems quite unlikely that there will be any substantial change in the foreseeable future in the nature of the relationship between Canada and the United States that has grown up in the past quarter century. This is fundamentally a cooperative relationship based on common interests and ideals and its value to both parties has grown rather than diminished since the Second World War. Its growth has doubtless been nourished by the cold war climate, but it would probably have taken place in any case since it is a natural growth. In the perspective of Canadian history, Yankeephobia is nothing new, and the present wave of it may be expected to subside if Canadian protests are duly heeded across the border. In that case they will have served a useful purpose by cautioning the United States about two common faults in its treatment of smaller nations: its frequent failure to consider or consult them in matters of importance to them, and its propensity for preaching internationalism to others while pursuing its own national interests. In any case, an even broader purpose will have been served, for the close resemblance between Canadian and Latin-American criticism of the United States will surely lead the latter to appraise Latin-American complaints more seriously and more accurately than in the past. From this point of view it is regrettable that the Canadian wave of protest did not mount five or ten years ago, for if it had done so it might not have required the spectacular anti-Nixon demonstrations of 1958 to win tardy recognition among the top officials in Washington of the gravity of the situation in Latin America.

EUROPEAN POSSESSIONS

In the perspective of this essay the remaining European possessions in America need not detain us long, for, subject to some minor qualifications, United States policy with regard to them can be summed up in two words: "hands off." This policy dates back to the Monroe Doctrine of 1823, which declared: "With the existing colonies of Europe in this hemisphere we have not interfered and shall not interfere." Despite deviations in 1898, when the United States wrested Cuba and Puerto Rico from Spain, and in 1940 when it joined with Latin America to prevent Hitler from seizing them (a contingency which never occurred), it has followed substantially the same policy ever since. Since the Second World War this policy has doubtless been reinforced by the fact that all three of the European owners of these possessions—Great Britain, France, and the Netherlands—have been allies of the United States in the cold war and its partners in NATO. But the reinforcement has been reciprocal, for the anti-colonialism of the United States has been decidedly less pronounced as regards colonies in the New World than in the Old, and the difference is explained largely by the traditional commitment of the Monroe Doctrine not to interfere with European possessions in America.

Three qualifications, all minor, should be noted. In the chronological order of their appearance in history, these are represented by the Caribbean Commission, the United Nations Charter, and the Rio Defense Treaty.

The Caribbean Commission emerged during the Second World War, originally as a bilateral arrangement between the United States and Great Britain, to which France and the Netherlands were soon added. Its initial purpose was to provide for co-operation in dealing with such wartime problems as shipping, commerce, and food supply among their possessions in the Caribbean area. The scope of action was broadened somewhat after the war, but remains confined to the same general type of action and does not give the United States any voice in the political or defense arrangements in or relating to the European possessions involved. The only bases the United States has in any European possessions in the New World are those which it leased from Great Britain under the destroyer-bases agreement of 1940.

Under the United Nations Charter all members are committed to the preparation of colonial possessions for ultimate independence, and the United States has the same right and duty as all other members to see that it is done. But while the United States has complied with this obligation to the extent of raising its own possession, Puerto Rico, to the status of an autonomous "commonwealth" (*Estado Libre*, in Spanish), it has not pressed the European powers to follow suit.[16] Not only has it been less urgently anti-colonial in the New World than in the Old, as noted above, but it has actually resisted an effort, strongly supported in Latin America in the early postwar years, to use the Organization of American States as an instrument for forcing the early liquidation of the last European holdings in America.[17] The United States takes the position that since the problem is not an exclusively American one, it lies outside the jurisdiction of the OAS and should be handled through the United Nations. Brazil shared this view from the outset and other Latin-American governments seem to have come around to it; at any rate the issue has not been brought to the fore again in recent years.

Finally, the Rio Defense Treaty provides for defense against aggression anywhere in the Western Hemisphere, and therefore applies to the European possessions in America. As not only a party to that treaty but also presumably the chief agent in any enforcement measures taken under it, the United States might in certain situations become involved in important measures relating to these possessions. Hitherto, however, no such situation has arisen and none is now visible

[16] Although the European governments' treatment of their American possessions lies outside the scope of this paper, mention should be made of the recent establishment of the Federation of the British West Indies, which, if and when it becomes independent, will presumably join the OAS.

[17] Arthur P. Whitaker, "Development of American Regionalism: The Organization of American States," *International Conciliation*, No. 469 (March, 1951), pp. 151-52.

on the horizon. So far as the United States is concerned, the European possessors will continue to manage their American dominions in their own way, subject to the no-transfer principle which has been a part of the Monroe Doctrine since 1871, and will not be forced, either unilaterally by the United States or by the OAS, to accelerate the pace of emancipation. Nor has there been any sign so far that the United States would support any such action through the United Nations.

6: UNITED STATES POLICY IN SOUTH AND SOUTHEAST ASIA

Myron Weiner

American policy toward South and Southeast Asia has been directed at achieving the maximum security of the area with a minimum of American commitments.

That the United States, since the close of the Second World War, should want to minimize its commitments in this area is quite understandable. While the countries of Southeast Asia, from Burma to the Indonesian archipelago, are rich in tin, oil, tungsten, rubber, and other resources of importance to the United States, the wartime loss of these areas to Japan clearly demonstrated that this region was not vital to America's security. Oil and tin can be obtained elsewhere. For rubber and many other resources there are improved synthetics. Stockpiles in some commodities increasingly make the United States less dependent, particularly on the assumption that any war of a global character is likely to be a quick one. And although India is one of the larger industrial powers in the world, its present production is low compared with that of Western Europe and the United States and the Western powers are in no way dependent upon India's goods. Neither South nor Southeast Asia is, therefore, essential to America's resource or military requirements. If anything, much of Southern Asia is a military liability. Southeast Asia is, as the French discovered in Indochina, indefensible. Guerrilla warfare in the jungles of Malaya, Indochina, and Burma has been difficult to overcome even by the most modern military technology.

The question which confronts us is not why American commitments in South and Southeast Asia are so small, but rather why they exist at all? The answer lies in two realms—in the changes which have occurred in the power balance of the Far East, and in the changes which have occurred within South and Southeast Asia since the war.

Changing International Relations in the Far East

Since Hay's formulation of the Open Door policy in the Far East, American policy in Asia has been predicated on the assumption that our interests could best be served through the creation of a strong and independent China, free of Western, Russian, and Japanese domination. It was on this assumption that the United States gave moral and material support to the Chinese in their war against Japan and, Pearl Harbor notwithstanding, the United States agreed to enter the Far Eastern war.[1] On the assumption too that a free and independent China supported by the United States would be a powerful force for peace and security in Asia, this country urged the other major powers to include China among the United Nations Big Five.

The defeat of the Kuomintang by the communists and the establishment of a strong, independent, but anti-Western regime on the mainland completely shattered the basic assumption upon which American policy was built. This defeat had profound effects upon American policy toward all of Asia. Instead of being able to support and in turn depend upon a free and sympathetic China, the United States now directed its attention toward building countervailing forces in Asia. How to cope with this new and possibly expanding power on the Asian mainland became a fundamental problem. The United States chose to rebuild Japan. The occupation was soon changed from an emphasis upon rehabilitation, demilitarization, and democratization to rearmament. The Korean War and, to a lesser extent, the Indochinese War, hastened American military involvement, for these wars convinced American policy makers that the Soviet Union and China would not confine their expansion to economic and political penetration and subversion, but would resort to military force across international boundaries. The application of the principle of collective security in Asia became a cornerstone of American policy. The related notions of containment, situations of strength, and deterrence, notions which had been developed to cope with expanding Soviet power, were now applied to Asia to cope with expanding Chinese power. But while these principles could be applied

[1] American interest in South and Southeast Asia grew at this time since the Japanese conquest of Southeast Asia raised the problem of how to maintain open supply lines to Chinese forces which had been pushed into southern China. The Burma road operations and flying the "hump" from India were directed at opening supply lines.

with some success to Western Europe where the Soviet threat was perceived by the European powers in much the same way as the United States perceived that threat, where great military and industrial potential existed, and where the United States was willing to commit its total power, they were far less effective in South and Southeast Asia.

The Emergence of the New States

Until the close of the Second World War, all the countries of South and Southeast Asia, with the exception of Thailand, were under colonial rule. For over four hundred years, the Western powers had been active in the Indian Ocean. One by one, the countries of Southern Asia had fallen under Western rule. British, French, Dutch, and American power dominated the area. But the major responsibility for the security of Southern Asia had been in the hands of the British. The Indian Ocean had virtually become a British lake. India and Ceylon guarded the western shores, Malaya and Singapore guarded the east. Access into the Indian Ocean from Europe was protected by British forces at Suez and Aden and a Commonwealth country at the Cape of Good Hope. Further to the east, watching over the Pacific approaches, lay Australia and New Zealand. Until 1942, when the Japanese army swept into Southeast Asia and the Japanese navy took possession of Singapore and the surrounding sea lanes, British power was paramount. The land routes into Southern Asia were never seriously threatened throughout the era of Western rule. The Hindu Kush mountain range in the northwestern part of India (now Pakistan) had been the historic entry point into the subcontinent prior to the Western sea invasions, but throughout the 19th and early 20th centuries the British army carefully protected the northwest frontier against possible Russian intrusion. Iran did become a target of Russian penetration, both for its oil and for its access into the Arabian Sea, but the Russian effort was halted. China was not considered a threat. Throughout the 19th century and until the mid-20th century China was badly divided and incapable of any military expansion. No effort was made, therefore, by the Western powers, to build up security forces in northern Burma, Assam, northern Thailand, northern Indochina, and other points of possible Chinese access.

After 1945 a revolution occurred in Southern Asia comparable to the European events of 1789, 1848, and 1917. The rising strength of nationalist movements, combined with the increasing weakness of the colonial powers as a result of their wars with Germany and Japan, culminated in the creation of ten independent sovereign states where four powers once existed. India, Pakistan, Ceylon, Burma, and later Malaya were freed from British rule; Laos, Cambodia, and Viet Nam from French rule; Indonesia, after a painful struggle, from Dutch rule; and the Philippines from American rule.

The emergence of ten new states with a combined population of over 600 million people was accompanied by the need for establishing a new pattern of relations between these states and the West, an adjustment which would have been necessary even if the cold war had not developed. Even without the cold war, the United States would have been under pressure from these new countries for assistance in their economic development. The United States was, after all, the largest source of capital in the world and just as the United States, Australia, Canada, New Zealand, and many other countries in the 19th century turned toward Great Britain for development assistance, the new states were now likely to turn toward the United States. The difference, however, lay in the fact that during the 19th century it was for the most part private developers who turned to private sources in Britain, while after the Second World War the countries of Southern Asia, with their emphasis on state planning, turned as governments toward the American government. Relations between governments had, in the 20th century, replaced the 19th-century relationship between private entrepreneurs.

The Cold War in Southern Asia

Many of the new states, particularly India, Burma, Ceylon, and Indonesia, did not perceive any external communist threat. For them a corrupt and unpopular Kuomintang government had been replaced by an energetic, popular communist regime faced with problems not unlike their own. Furthermore, these countries perceived their task as one of creating unified national states out of divided pluralistic societies, developing their economies, raising low living standards, eliminating both colonial and feudal vestiges, and establishing and strengthening the institutions of representative government. While the Indians, Burmese, and Indonesians were indeed faced with the threat of communism, these threats appeared largely internal. Not massive military establishments, but forceful police measures as well as programs of land reform and industrial development were seen as requirements.

The leaders of Southern Asia experienced no disenchantment with the Soviet Union as had so many Western intellectuals and political leaders. They had not been closely associated with the Soviet Union during the war, and the period of great disillusionment between 1945 and 1948 was an era in which the new states were first establishing their independence and were preoccupied largely with domestic matters or relations with the former colonial power. Then too, the Soviet threat was in Europe and in no way presented an external military threat to southern Asia.

In each instance of Chinese expansion the new states found what to them was an acceptable justification. India, for example, condemned North Korea in the United Nations for her invasion of South Korea, but warned that the movement of United Nations troops beyond the Yalu would result in defensive activities by the Chinese who feared encroachments into their territory. The Indians and other neutralists were thus critical of the United Nations' forces for moving toward the Chinese border and were sympathetic to the Chinese response. Likewise, Chinese communist threats against Formosa and the offshore islands were interpreted as a legitimate expression of Chinese aspirations for completing the revolution and reuniting all of China. In Indochina, neutralist powers had no sympathy for the French-supported Bao Dai regime and looked upon the Chinese-supported Ho Chi-Minh regime as a manifestation of nationalist sentiment. Finally, while Indians were unhappy about the movement of Chinese troops into Tibet in 1950 in the midst of negotiations, they did agree that Tibet was an integral part of China. Not until 1959 when Tibetans revolted against Chinese domination did the neutralist powers express any sympathy for the Tibetan struggle for autonomy, or did doubt enter their minds as to Communist China's peaceful intentions.

So long, then, as the neutralist powers rejected the American assumption that communism in general and Communist China in particular is a militarily aggressive force, American efforts to win support for principles of collective security were bound to fail.

American Policy and the SEATO Powers

A few countries of Southern Asia were concerned with the possibilities of Communist China's external expansion, but the United States soon found that there were difficulties in applying the concepts of collective security, containment, situations of strength, and massive retaliation. The most pressing threat was in Indochina where a regime sponsored by Communist China, the Viet Minh, led by Ho Chi-Minh, was attacking the French-sponsored Bao Dai regime in the South. Here, where the containment policy would seem to have had its natural application, American policy makers refrained from action. The United States, in pursuit of its long tradition of supporting the abolition of colonialism, felt that any attempt to contain the communist regime by supporting what was virtually a French puppet government would turn all genuinely nationalist sympathies in Indochina towards Viet Minh. On the other hand, the United States hesitated to urge the French to withdraw (although American financial support for the French both at home and in Indochina gave leverage if Washington chose to exercise it) because the withdrawal of the French military forces clearly meant the victory of Ho Chi-Minh. The conflict was thus not between America's anti-colonialism and the need for maintaining strong ties with European allies, but between the principle of anti-colonialism and the principle of containment. Not until political changes occurred within Viet Nam when a genuinely nationalist government under Ngo Dinh Diem emerged, was the conflict resolved. At this point the United States, which had been paralyzed into inaction at the Geneva conference, chose to support Diem over French opposition. The United States thus demonstrated that it was prepared to break with a European ally if choices were available which would permit the United States to take both an anti-colonial and anticommunist position. The rise of an indigenous anticommunist nationalist regime in Indochina resulted in the United States adopting such a position. After the Geneva conference the United States undertook a program of massive economic and military aid to Indochina, providing a billion dollars in 1954 and $1,133,000,000 in 1955.

Several nations of Southern Asia were willing to accept the principle of collective security against communist aggression. In particular, Thailand, the Philippines, and Pakistan were prepared to receive American military assistance and participate in mutual defense arrangements. But the United States soon realized that acceptance of the principle of collective security was not a sufficient requisite for its application.

The principle of collective security is based upon the assumption that noncommunist nations working together could build up sufficient military strength to deter communist aggression. The Vietnamese and their Laotian neighbors feared attacks from Viet Minh or China to the north. The Thais expressed their concern when a Free Thailand Committee was created by a Thai insurgent in China. Pakistan borders on a hostile Afghanistan, in which Soviet influence was increasing. But the United States found that while there was a willingness to participate in mutual security alliances, it would not be feasible to increase the military capabilities of these countries to the same degree the United States had aided the countries of Western Europe. While it might be possible to arm the NATO powers sufficiently to deter Soviet aggression, the countries of South and Southeast Asia were far too small and Communist China far too big to attempt any kind of military balance. Furthermore, the United States was unwilling to commit its own forces as it had in Western Europe. American military men were horrified at the possibilities of committing the American army to fight on the land mass of Asia against superior numbers, particularly in jungle terrain. And finally, while Western Europe needed to be rehabilitated, the countries of Southern Asia first had to be developed. American financial and military assistance could be effectively provided to European powers on a vast scale because the skills and organization existed to permit the use of such aid, while the absorptive capacity of the underdeveloped Asian countries was small. It would take many decades before their economies were developed to such a level that effective modern armies could be maintained.

Although deterrence through the strength of local powers would not be sufficient, and although the United States was unwilling to commit its own forces, the United States still hoped to apply the containment principles. SEATO was to be the answer. The Southeast Asia Defense Treaty brought together, on the one hand, those countries of the area which accepted the premise that communism was militarily expansive, and, on the other, those outside of the area which had an interest in South and Southeast Asia. Pakistan, Thailand, and the Philippines were joined by Australia, New Zealand, Great Britain, and the United States. The SEATO powers agreed to provide mutual economic assistance, but Article 4 was the touchstone of the treaty. First, it provided that in the event of aggression by means of armed attack against any of the signatories in the treaty area or Laos, Cambodia, or Viet Nam, each party would act "to meet the common danger in accordance with its constitutional processes." Second, it noted that if a threat to territorial integrity or political independence arises from something other than an armed attack (*i.e.*, subversion), the parties would be obligated to "consult" with each other on the measures which should be taken for the common defense.

In several crucial ways, the United States had apparently limited its commitments in SEATO. The Southeast Asia Treaty did not predicate anything resembling a joint military force with joint headquarters as did the North Atlantic Treaty Organization. While NATO was clearly designed to build up a defensive force on the continent of Europe which itself would be sufficient to resist and, therefore, deter attack by communist armies, SEATO was built upon an alternative deterrence strategy. This strategy was designated by Secretary Dulles as one of "mobile striking power." The United States thus avoided committing itself either to a massive program of military assistance to the participant powers or to a program committing American forces to fight in the jungles of Southeast Asia. Dulles explained that a mobile striking force would strike at the source of aggression, Communist China, rather than try to fight a ground war. Since an attack upon Communist China obviously meant a large-scale global war, the effect of the new Dulles doctrine was to rule out the SEATO area as a region in which the United States and its allies were prepared to engage in any "limited" warfare comparable to the limited war of Korea. The American experience in Korea and the French experience in Indochina was clearly responsible for this change in emphasis.

In one sense, therefore, the United States had made a turnabout. What began as a relatively low pressure area in which the United States had limited commitments had now become an area which the United States was willing to defend even if it meant a global war. On the other hand, however, the United States was not ruling out the possibility of a limited war but was setting the conditions under which such a war would be permitted. The United States warned that an attack upon a country in the treaty area would be followed by an American attack upon the source of aggression. As long, therefore, as Communist China limited its own engagements, allowing aggression only by the satellite armies of Viet Minh and Pathet Laos, the United States might tolerate a limited war. It was, presumably, upon this assumption that the United States rearmed Viet Nam to cope with any limited attacks by non-Chinese forces. But if Communist China entered the war, obviously Viet Nam could not withstand an attack and American forces would strike directly at Peking. The United States thus ruled out the possibilities of another Korea. In the event that the Chinese communists were unprepared to sit by in any future Indochinese war, the United States had, through the SEATO treaty and the Dulles concept of mobile striking force, committed itself to a global war.

This extension—one might say overextension—of American commitments grew out of applying the concept of collective security to South and Southeast Asia. Under the umbrella of collective security the United States sought to ally itself in mutual security treaties with whatever countries in the world were prepared to participate in such arrangements. One by one the United States signed bilateral or multilateral treaties with countries in the area, prior to the establishment of SEATO. In August, 1951, the United States and Philippine Mutual Defense Treaty was signed. Almost immediately, in September, the United States signed a Mutual Defense Treaty (the ANZUS Pact) with New Zealand and Australia. In the spring of 1953 the United States negotiated a mutual security agreement with Pakistan. Finally in September, 1954, the Southeast Asia Collective Defense Treaty (Manila Pact) was signed.

While Secretary Dulles made clear that the United States did not intend to arm these nations with which it had mutual security agreements, in practice the United States did provide limited military assistance.[2] The effect of this aid, if any, upon deterring communist aggression, is difficult to measure, but its effect upon neighboring countries not participating in mutual security arrangements was immediately apparent.

The recent crisis in Laos called attention to the limitations of existing American instruments and policies for Southeast Asia. The

[2] Between 1950 and 1960 the following military assistance grants were made to countries in South and Southeast Asia as reported in *The Washington Post*, March 6, 1960, from a statement by Defense Secretary Thomas S. Gates, Jr. before the House Foreign Affairs Committee. Figures for Pakistan and Laos have not been released.

Cambodia	$ 74,612,000
Indochina (Laos, Cambodia and Viet Nam before 1954)	716,014,000
Philippines	257,218,000
Thailand	329,500,000
Viet Nam	541,381,000

initial reports from Laos of Chinese penetration (a report which the government of Laos later retracted) caused a stir in Washington, but clearly the United States would not risk total war through the use of its mobile striking power at the "source" of aggression. In February, 1961, the new administration, in recognition of the limits to which nuclear capabilities could be put, moved to provide training in guerilla warfare for American military personnel who might in turn train the military personnel of threatened countries prepared to accept military advice. Disputes within the SEATO powers over whether the neutralist government of Prime Minister Souvanna Phouma should be supported (the British and French position) or that of pro-Western General Phoumi Nosavan, the son-in-law of the Thai Prime Minister (supported by Thailand and Viet Nam), made it difficult for that organization to act in concert. American recognition of the latter was soon followed by Soviet support for Souvanna, and the possibilities of Laos becoming another Korea loomed large. The Laotian situation demonstrated that the instrumentalities erected for our policies in Southeast Asia were inappropriate to our goals of preventing communist penetration without large-scale war: the notion of collective security through SEATO, the military doctrine of mobile striking power, and our reluctance to tender more positive support to neutralist regimes.

The United States and the Neutralist States

The neutralist powers of Asia not only rejected the American principle of collective security but they resented its application to neighboring states on the grounds that it brought the cold war into the area and intensified conflicts between states within Southern Asia. India, in particular, reacted violently to the US-Pakistan Pact and the announcement that the United States would supply arms to Pakistan. India questioned whether Pakistan considered such aid essential to its security against communist aggression or was using its new alliance to strengthen its bargaining position with India in the Kashmir and canal water disputes. The United States attempted to forestall such an interpretation by a clause in the Southeast Asia Collective Defense Treaty which specified that the treaty would apply only to communist aggression. Subsequent joint statements by the Pakistanis and Americans referred to aggression in general and while the United States reiterated that the term aggression was still confined to the communists, the Pakistanis chose to give to such statements and agreements the broadest interpretation possible.

Had the United States been able to demonstrate that the application of the collective security principle to Pakistan was essential for concrete strategic reasons, the reaction to SEATO and similar mutual security arrangements might not have been so hostile. But neither the United States nor Pakistan could demonstrate that any aggression was likely from either China or the Soviet Union. To India it appeared as if the United States had indiscriminately applied collective security principles developed in Western Europe to deal with an area where the possibilities of aggression were remote, and that some of the Asian powers were participating in SEATO for other than the stated reasons.

The United States military aid program did in fact have effects other than those intended. For one, the aid program worsened relations between India and Pakistan. Until the United States and Pakistan began negotiating a mutual security arrangement in 1953 it appeared that the possibilities for a settlement between India and Pakistan were improving. After 1953, both India and Pakistan became more inflexible on the Kashmir dispute. India argued that American military aid to Pakistan had so upset the power balance that she no longer considered a plebiscite feasible. Whether the Kashmir dispute would have been settled had there been no US-Pakistan Pact is of course impossible to say, but the alliance did further strain relations between India and Pakistan, reduce the chances of a settlement, and increase Indian military expenditures. In view of the efforts by the Indian government to cope with the enormous task of economic development, these increased military expenditures represent a severe drain on the country's limited resources.

Moreover, the military aid program had great effect upon the internal politics of the recipient nations. While the Western European governments receiving military aid had strong civil governments, the recipient countries of Asia did not. Thus, military aid strengthened the political position of the military establishment, especially in Thailand and Pakistan. In Pakistan, politicians increasingly turned toward the military as a source of authority and stability when representative institutions failed to function. In late 1958, an army greatly strengthened by American military assistance assumed power, abolished the constitution and representative institutions, and outlawed political parties.

It is true that without American assistance the military had risen to prominence in both Burma and Indonesia, so that in the case of Pakistan the military aid program may have been a negligible factor. Nonetheless it made the United States appear as a participant in the internal political changes in Pakistan. Were other political groups in Pakistan to rise to power such a close relationship with a single political force within the country might result in fundamental changes in US-Pakistan relations.

Finally, as a result of applying the collective security principle to Southern Asia the relations of the United States with the neutralist powers were badly strained. At the close of the war the United States was, along with the Soviet Union, the only major non-Asian power with an anti-imperialist record. During the war the United States actively encouraged the British to hasten Indian independence, and in the postwar struggle between the Dutch and Indonesians the United States backed Indonesia. But after 1947 the warm feeling which many Asians felt toward the United States cooled rapidly.

This cooling occurred in spite of Point Four, development assistance, and the United States information program. Many Americans, particularly the popular press, blamed this growing anti-Americanism on Soviet propaganda, the inadequacies of the United States Information Agency, or upon real or imagined defects in economic aid programs. Asians were accused of ingratitude and the United States Government of being a "sucker."

The attitudes of South and Southeast Asians were shaped more by American diplomatic activities than by economic and information programs. The unwillingness of the United States to recognize the government of Communist China—another Asian nation—was resented by neutral nations. Mutual security treaties were seen as injecting the cold war into the region and as threatening relations among the countries of the area. And in 1955 the United States further alienated India when Secretary Dulles issued a joint statement with the Portuguese foreign minister declaring that the "whole world" (meaning the West) viewed Goa as a province of Portugal. The Indians, who had been pressing the Portuguese to vacate this small colonial pocket on the west coast of India, interpreted the Dulles statement as an endorsement of the Portuguese position.

Southern Asians were again annoyed when the United States, along with France, Great Britain, Russia, and mainland China, met at Geneva to settle the fate of Indochina without consulting any of the countries of South and Southeast Asia. The participants at the Colombo Conference in December, 1953—India, Pakistan, Burma, Indonesia, and Ceylon—felt that the affairs of Asians were again being decided primarily by non-Asians. At least Prime Minister Sir Anthony Eden took the initiative at Geneva to postpone discussions pending an announcement of the recommendations of the Colombo powers, but the United States took no such steps and was in fact clearly unfriendly to India's participation in the United Nations Commission for Indochina. Likewise, the Asian powers which participated in the Bandung Conference of Afro-Asian nations in 1955[3] knew that United States officials were unsympathetic to the holding of such a conference.

The United States and Economic Development

Since the close of the Second World War the United States has spent about $4 billion in nonmilitary assistance in the countries of South and Southeast Asia.

Unfortunately, American economic assistance to the new states became deeply involved with the issues of the cold war. While some American policy makers viewed the technical assistance program and the development assistance program of the International Cooperation Administration as part of the new pattern of relations between the new states and the United States, others viewed these new programs as part of the cold war. Appropriation requests to Congress, for example, have largely been justified by the administration on the ground that technical assistance and development funds were necessary to prevent these new states from succumbing to communism. No wonder that the new states interpreted the aid programs as an instrument of the cold war.

Had all the countries of Southern Asia accepted the American assumptions concerning communist aggression, the requirements of these areas for external assistance and the American emphasis on containment would have been easily reconciled in the aid programs. As it was, the neutralist nations resented American reiteration of the relationship between its aid and the cold war and, in turn, American congressmen resented the continued neutralism of many of these new states. This conflict took many forms. In 1951 Congress let precious

[3] Twelve of the participating nations were from South and Southeast Asia—Burma, Cambodia, Ceylon, India, Indonesia, Laos, Nepal, Pakistan, the Philippines, Thailand, North Viet Nam, and South Viet Nam.

weeks pass when India urgently needed a wheat loan to ease its famine. While congressmen debated whether a neutralist power should be given assistance, the Soviets rushed in shipments of wheat, and America lost the good political effect which might have resulted from a quick humanitarian gesture. Then too, many American congressmen and much of the American public looked upon the aid programs solely as devices whereby the United States sought to improve relations with these areas, and interpreted neutralist and often anti-American attitudes as ingratitude and as indications of the failure of the programs. Congressmen criticized the Indian government for not giving more publicity to the assistance of the United States to the community development program for India's villages. State Department officials pointed out that the United States sought to give Indians a feeling that they were running their own development programs with their own resources. Psychologically, Indians and other Asians had to feel that development was occurring from within, rather than imposed from without, and that it was not dependent upon external assistance. And in fact, the magnitude of America's aid program was infinitesimal compared with what Indians and other Asians were investing in their own development. One could also argue that the American problem was less one of increasing warm feeling toward the United States as a result of aid, but rather one of how to minimize harsh feelings. The giver, especially when assistance is in the form of gifts rather than loans, is rarely well liked. Certainly, American feeling toward Britain in the 19th century was something short of intimacy.

As mentioned, many Asians were wary of the United States precisely because the program was advertised as an instrument of the cold war. Ceylon was denied American aid because of her shipments of rubber to Communist China in violation of the Battle Act (which provides for cutting off assistance to those nations which send strategic goods to enemy nations). At one point neutralist Burma requested that the United States terminate its government aid program, and in Indonesia the Sukiman Cabinet fell in 1952 because it favored a mutual security agreement with the United States.

State Department policy makers have sought to divorce the aid programs from the cold war, but pressures from non-neutralist Asian powers as well as American congressmen have almost totally frustrated such efforts. The non-neutralist powers, such as Pakistan and Thailand, have argued that little advantage would be gained and some internal political disadvantages might result if they allied themselves with the West, unless their alliance brought in more assistance than was granted to Asian neutrals.[4] In addition, many congressmen have operated within a narrowly conceived notion of America's national interest, and an equally narrow conception of America's role and purpose in international affairs.

American Interest in Southern Asia

A postwar American passion for defining the national interest, and for "hardheaded" as distinguished from moralistic and legalistic assessments of power realities, has resulted in a peculiar inability to express America's national purpose in ways which are appealing to other states. That the United States must be concerned with its military security, that communist expansion represents a threat to that security, and that appropriate measures must be taken to meet that threat hardly needs to be reiterated.

American policy makers have been guided by security considerations in shaping policy in Southern Asia. Attempts to justify assistance on the grounds of building democracies is often considered to smack of softheadedness and humanitarianism. The defenders of a broader conception of the national interest are almost forced to argue that the United States cannot be secure unless the new states develop their economies, build unified national states, and avoid totalitarian or authoritarian rule. In one sense the argument is self-defeating. As the United States increases its missile capabilities, as overseas bases become less necessary, and as new synthetics are developed, most of Asia and Africa becomes less important to American security. The time may arrive when the Western Hemisphere could, if necessary, survive as an island in a hostile world. But it is precisely because survival is not the only national purpose and because other values are so important to Americans that such a condition would be intolerable.

Many policy makers have reacted so strongly against prewar moralistic and legalistic attitudes and lack of security-mindedness that every effort has been made to eliminate non-security considerations in the formulation of policy. "Strategy" and "security" have become key

[4] The figures on foreign grants and credits (non-military) do not clearly indicate the differences in allocations to neutralist and non-neutralist states since for security reasons the amount of military aid to specific countries is not made public. Much of this military aid consists of "defense support," such as roads, railroads, etc., which in fact are a disguised form of development assistance.

words in foreign policy analysis. We have seen that South Asians view American policy, even assistance programs, as part of America's concern for security, and there is truth to the charge. Ironically, so long as the United States continues to stress security considerations, neutralist hostility increases, mutual security allies assume a bargaining posture, political and international tensions within the area rise, and security is thereby reduced.

Were the cold war, by some miracle, to disappear, the United States would still have to establish a pattern of relations with the new states of Southern Asia. Over 600 million people living in societies undergoing rapid change, in many cases attempting to adopt democratic institutions, cannot be ignored. The application of collective security principles to Southern Asia has neither made the area secure against communist attack nor led to a satisfactory pattern of relations with the United States. Perhaps it is only when Americans come to accept and make explicit a larger conception of national purpose, one which includes but goes beyond security considerations, and adopt policies consonant with such purposes, will it be possible for the United States to develop a durable pattern of relations with the new states of Southern Asia.

7: UNITED STATES POLICY TOWARDS JAPAN

Chitoshi Yanaga

American policy toward Japan since the end of the Second World War has passed through three distinct stages. In the immediate post-surrender period, from September, 1945 to the end of 1947, it was one of carrying out the declared intentions of the Cairo Declaration, the Yalta Agreement, the Potsdam Proclamation, and the terms of the instrument of surrender. Despite serious differences of opinion regarding procedure in the Council of Foreign Ministers, the United States was able to lead the Allies in implementing the postwar policy which included liquidation of the war and Japan's war-making potential, military, economic and political, and punishment of war criminals, the exaction of war reparations payments, and the encouragement of democratic developments.

The second phase, from the beginning of 1948 to the signing of the San Francisco Peace Treaty in September, 1951, was a period of rapid deterioration of Soviet-American relations culminating in a cold war and the collapse of Nationalist China's power, resulting in the communist takeover of the China mainland. It was characterized by America's decision to build Japan's strength in the face of Soviet obstruction and opposition. Reconstruction and rehabilitation of Japan's national economy along with the building of defense capabilities became overriding considerations of American policy. This was in fact a reversal of the initial post-surrender policy which envisaged a weak and powerless, if not helpless, Japan, incapable not only of attacking any nation but also of defending itself. American policy toward Japan became part of the cold war within the larger policy of meeting the forces of communist expansion in Europe as well as in Asia.

The third phase which began in April, 1952, represents the policy of encouraging and aiding Japan as an independent and sovereign nation allied in the joint defense and preservation of the free world against the encroachments of international communism. Japanese problems have become American problems in a real sense since

Japan's weakness directly affects the security of the United States. Co-operation and collaboration for mutual security based on equality, common objectives, and need for each other have become the foundation of American policy.

INITIAL POST-SURRENDER POLICY

American policy toward Japan since 1945 harks back to the Cairo Declaration of December 1, 1943,[1] in which Roosevelt, Churchill and Chiang Kai-shek made a solemn statement that the three great Allies were fighting the war "to restrain and punish the aggression of Japan" and that "Japan shall be stripped of all the islands in the Pacific which she has seized or occupied since the beginning of World War I and that all the territories Japan has stolen from the Chinese, such as Manchuria, Formosa, and the Pescadores shall be restored to China." It was further agreed that "Japan will also be expelled from all other territories which she has taken by violence and greed" and that the Allies will "procure the unconditional Surrender of Japan."[2] The Cairo Conference made a number of concessions to Chiang's wishes. At the same time, it reflected Roosevelt's hope, if not expectation, that postwar Nationalist China would play a major role on the side of the Western democracies. It was a prelude to assigning great power status to Nationalist China.

The Yalta Conference held in the Crimea in February, 1945, shaped Allied policy toward Japan as well as the Far East. Unaware of Stalin's secret designs and desires, Roosevelt and Churchill acceded readily to his demands. As a price for Soviet participation in the war against Japan, they assented to practically all of Stalin's wishes and demands and offered little resistance to the extensions of Soviet power and influence in the Far East.[3] Apparently Roosevelt and Churchill were too preoccupied with the immediate problem of

[1] Supreme Commander for the Allied Powers (hereafter: SCAP), *Political Reorientation of Japan*, p. 411.

[2] Unconditional surrender was first formulated and enunciated by Roosevelt at a press conference in January, 1943, during the Casablanca Conference and was not part of original State Department thinking. See: *The Memoirs of Cordell Hull* (New York, 1948), II, 1571.

[3] The Allied demand for unconditional surrender stiffened the Japanese attitude, especially that of the military who balked at the idea. This resulted in heated discussions and a considerable delay in acceptance of the demand to surrender. See: Yanaga, *Japan Since Perry*, pp. 618-19.

victory to perceive the basic and long-term implications of Soviet policy.

The Soviet Union agreed on February 11 to enter the war on the side of the Allies, two or three months after Germany's surrender and the end of the war in Europe, on the following conditions:

1. Preservation of the status quo in Outer Mongolia;
2. Restoration of the former rights of Russia which were violated by the treacherous attack of Japan in 1904 in the following manner:
   (a) return of South Sakhalin and all adjacent islands,
   (b) internationalization of the commercial port of Dairen, safeguarding of Russia's pre-eminent interests in Dairen, and the restoration of the lease of Port Arthur as a naval base,
   (c) joint operation of the Chinese Eastern and the South Manchurian railways by the establishment of a joint Soviet-Chinese company;
3. Kurile Islands to be handed over to the Soviet Union.[4]

In order to wring concessions from Roosevelt and Churchill, Stalin successfully feigned reluctance to violate the Soviet-Japanese Neutrality Pact of July, 1941, to enter the war against Japan.

The Potsdam Conference of July, 1945, was also a distinct victory for the Soviets. Britain was represented in the early stages by Prime Minister Churchill and Foreign Secretary Eden, and later by Attlee and Bevin who came into office as a result of the Labour victory in the British elections. The United States was represented by Harry S. Truman who had just recently come into the presidency and had little experience with international problems. Comparatively inexperienced, the British and American representatives were at a disadvantage vis-a-vis Stalin. Secretary of State Byrnes would have been satisfied had the Russians decided not to enter the war against Japan since he was afraid what might happen when the Soviet army entered Manchuria.[5]

American policy had to be formulated and executed within the framework of the Potsdam Proclamation of July 26. The first step in the implementation of the Potsdam Proclamation came even before Japan's notification of surrender. President Truman on August 13, with approval of the United Kingdom, USSR, and China, appointed General Douglas MacArthur as Supreme Commander for

[4] James F. Byrnes, *Speaking Frankly* (New York, 1947), p. 43.
[5] *Ibid.*, p. 208.

the Allied Powers (SCAP). Immediately following the signing of the instrument of surrender on September 2 the initial post-surrender policy for Japan was put into force. From September 2, 1945, to June 19, 1947, when it was reaffirmed by the Far Eastern Commission as its basic post-surrender policy, the occupation was based on the expressed views of the United States which formulated and applied it unilaterally.

Although it was an Allied commitment, the military occupation of Japan was essentially an American undertaking. The Allies took only a limited and minor part in its execution and had hardly any voice in the implementation of its policies. Nationalist China was unable to participate in the occupation because of its preoccupation with the civil war. The Soviet Union did not send any troops, as the United States made it clear that they would be accepted only as part of the occupation forces under SCAP. Moscow had hoped to occupy the northernmost island of Hokkaido, but its plans were frustrated. The dominant position of the Supreme Commander who was an American and appointed by the president of the United States symbolized the role the United States was to play in shaping the policy in and for Japan. Needless to say, this was not in accordance with the wishes and plans of some of the Allies and only after a long diplomatic struggle and jockeying did the Allies finally concede to the United States its dominant position. This was a natural move on the part of the United States because of its distrust of Soviet aims and methods with respect to the control of Japan.

Of decisive importance in securing this position of dominance was the fact that the predominant role of the United States in the Pacific war made it possible to avoid in Japan the creation of separate zones of Allied control as in the case of Germany. American troops entered Japan first and the Soviets were not given the chance to employ obstructionist tactics of the sort that bedeviled the occupation of Germany and Austria. The obstructionist and disruptive tactics employed by the Soviet representative on the Allied Council for Japan in Tokyo were ineffectual. The United States managed to keep the control of Japan in its own hands for it reserved to itself the power to decide and implement policy.

The smooth functioning of military occupation was assured at the outset by a number of wise basic decisions made by the United States without any Soviet interference. One of these was retention of the Emperor, who, had he not made the decision to surrender nor issued the command to the Japanese troops to lay down their arms peaceably, would have contributed to heavy American casualties in an invasion. Equally wise was the decision to keep the existing administrative machinery and use it, thereby facilitating the task of the occupation authorities who could remain inconspicuously in the background. Unlike the situation in Germany, all that had to be done was to issue directives to the Japanese government and they were promptly carried out. The unified command under an American Supreme Commander insured effective control of occupation activities, precluding any possibility of their disruption and of antagonizing the populace.

At the Moscow Conference of Foreign Ministers of December 16-26, 1945, machinery for the occupation of Japan was set up by the United States, United Kingdom, and USSR, with the concurrence of China. The newly-created Far Eastern Commission (FEC), made up of representatives of eleven nations,[6] was vested with power to formulate policies, principles, and standards for enforcement of Japan's obligations under terms of the surrender, to review at the request of any members any directive to the SCAP or any action taken by the SCAP involving policy decisions within the jurisdiction of the FEC, and to consider other matters. In theory the commission's powers were impressive. But it was the United States that was vested with decisive powers. It was empowered to prepare directives in accord with the decisions of the FEC and transmit them through the appropriate government agency to SCAP for implementation. More important was the fact that the United States Government had the power to issue interim directives to the Supreme Commander pending action by the FEC whenever urgent matters came up that were not covered by policies already formulated by the Far Eastern Commission.

The only other machinery created by the foreign ministers at Moscow was the Allied Council for Japan in Tokyo. Constituted by the representatives of the United States, Soviet Union, China and the United Kingdom, its function was to consult with and advise SCAP. Its chairman, General MacArthur, was authorized to issue all orders for the surrender, occupation, and control of Japan. The

[6] The eleven member nations of the FEC were the United States, United Kingdom, USSR, China, France, the Netherlands, Canada, Australia, New Zealand, India, and the Philippine Commonwealth. Its headquarters was in Washington, D.C.

Supreme Commander was the sole executive authority for the Allied Powers in Japan and action in all cases had to be carried out under and through him and his decisions were to be controlling and final. He was to consult and advise with the council in advance of the issuance of orders on matters of substance, provided the exigencies of the situation permitted. The Allied Council was never more than a sounding board and lacked any real power.

United States ocupation policy was a blend of harshness and idealism, implemented by punitive, constructive, corrective and developmental measures. Firm but conflicting measures were put into effect, especially during the initial period. Demilitarization, which was first on the list of priorities, was to be carried far beyond the demobilization of the military forces. It was to be effected economically through destruction of economic bases of military strength and prevention of their revival, and politically through elimination of all military and para-military organizations and all militarist and ultranationalist emphasis from the educational system. The trial and punishment of war criminals and the purge of those responsible for aggression were part of the demilitarization program. Destruction of arms and elimination of the authority of the military were carried out with such speed and thoroughness that it was regretted later when the rebuilding of Japan's defensive forces became necessary. The Japanese accepted complete demilitarization by incorporating a provision in the Constitution outlawing war as an instrument of national policy.[7]

Following the demilitarization program came liberation of political prisoners on October 4, 1945, resulting in release of members of the formerly outlawed communist party. For the first time in Japanese history, the communist party gained legal recognition alongside the other political parties which reemerged. The status of legitimacy acquired by the Japanese communist party added greatly to the difficulties of the occupation. Encouragement of labor unions by the occupation gave labor the right to bargain collectively as well as a political role which it had not previously enjoyed. Aided and abetted,

[7] Article IX of the Constitution reads:

"Aspiring sincerely to an international peace based on justice and order, the Japanese people forever renounce war as a sovereign right of the nation and the threat or use of force as a means of settling international disputes.

"In order to accomplish the aim of the preceding paragraph, land, sea, and air forces as well as other war potential will never be maintained. The right of belligerency of the state will not be recognized."

if not infiltrated and controlled, by the communists, many labor unions hampered the activities of the occupation at every turn. The Supreme Commander was forced to intervene in February, 1947, to prevent a general strike which would have paralyzed the nation.

Undoubtedly one of the most noteworthy achievements of American policy during the occupation was land reform. The Rural Land Reform Directive of December 9, 1945, was issued "to ensure to those who till the soil of Japan the enjoyment of the fruits of their labor." [8] Land ownership was transferred from the landlords to the tenants by the government, a move which made it possible for tenant farmers to purchase land on easy terms, bringing absentee landlordism and tenancy problems to an end. By 1950 more than 3,000,000 farmers had become owners of the land they cultivated. This meant that 89 per cent of the nation's arable land became owner-operated. This was in sharp contrast to the situation at the time of surrender in September, 1945, when only 54 per cent was owner-operated. The reform was to increase agricultural production as well as to lay a firm groundwork for democracy. By eliminating tenancy, a source of friction, it deprived the communists of the most promising avenue for an attack on the Japanese system and frustrated communist plans to subvert the occupation.

Economic Policy and Developments

On the assumption that Japan's military strength and capabilities for war were based upon a high concentration of economic power, the occupation adopted the policy of breaking up the combines. The Holding Company Liquidation Law of November, 1945, the purge of leaders in business and industry, the Anti-Monopoly Law of April, 1946, and the Economic Deconcentration Law of December, 1947, were all measures adopted for this purpose.[9]

By the beginning of 1948, the inadequacy, if not the error, of this approach had become clear,[10] since almost two and a half years after the war's end the revival of industrial production was woefully retarded with only 45 per cent of the 1930-1934 average. Exports were a mere 10 per cent and imports only 30 per cent of the 1930-1934 level. The comfortable assumption that Japanese industry and foreign

[8] SCAP, *op. cit.*, pp. 575 77.
[9] *Ibid.*, pp. 565-74.
[10] Robert A. Fearey, *The Occupation of Japan, the Second Phase, 1948-1950* (New York, 1950) p. 123.

trade would revive automatically in the anticipated trend of Far Eastern and world revival had been completely upset. Moreover, the prospect for an early Japanese peace treaty had vanished with Soviet rejection of the American proposal of July, 1947, for a peace conference. The original estimate that the occupation would last for two years at the most had proved optimistic and unrealistic and had to be revised. The attitude that the Japanese had better solve the problems they had brought upon themselves and that the Allies need not undertake the burden of repairing the damage had to be abandoned. Late in 1947 there arose concern in American business and Congressional circles that the deconcentration program was being carried to lengths which might impair Japan's recovery and obstruct legitimate foreign business activity in Japan. A change in thinking was reflected in the United States Government statement to the Far Eastern Commission and its press release of January 21, 1948,[11] which pointed out that Japan's disarmament had been completed, and exceptional progress had been made in reform of political and economic institutions, and that more emphasis should now be placed on a recovery program. It urged that the Japanese government and people, the Far Eastern Commission and its member states, and SCAP, should take all possible and necessary steps to bring about early revival of the Japanese economy on a peaceful, self-supporting basis. The United States suspended its participation in discussions of the detailed policy proposals known as FEC 230, and a Deconcentration Review Board made up of five leading experts in the anti-trust field was sent to Tokyo by SCAP in May to undertake a study of the situation.

Reparations

There was nothing in American policy toward Japan that approached or even resembled the degree of harshness, if not the vindictiveness, of the Morgenthau plan for Germany which would have taken away all the heavy industries of the Ruhr and partitioned and pastoralized the country.[12] But there was an element of punitive severity reflected along with a somewhat vindictive attitude in the

[11] In his speech at San Francisco on January 7, 1948, Secretary of the Army Kenneth Royall stated that the "aim of American policy was to develop a self-sufficient democratic Japan, able to stand as a deterrent to any future totalitarian war threats." *New York Times,* January 7, 1948.

[12] Henry Morgenthau, Jr., *Germany is Our Problem* (New York, 1945), pp. 16-20.

Pauley Report as well as in the preliminary statement of United States reparation policy for Japan of October 31, 1945, which emphasized that Japan should have the last priority in getting back on the road to political stability and peaceful progress.[13] The task of determining Japan's ability to pay reparations was assigned to Edwin W. Pauley, the United States representative on the Allied Reparations Commission. After spending several weeks in Japan, a visit to Manila, and a meeting with Generalissimo Chiang, Pauley submitted a report in April, 1946.[14] The Pauley Report, which described the industrial combines as "the greatest war potential which made possible Japan's conquests and aggressions," recommended heavy interim reparation payments through a transfer of Japanese property, goods, capital equipment, and industrial plants. The recommendations were based on the assumption that Japan possesses "more industrial capacity than she needs or has ever used for her civilian economy" and that the people were not starving.[15] Pauley believed that the "Allied Powers should take no action to assist Japan in maintaining a standard of living higher than that of neighboring Asiatic countries injured by Japanese aggression," and that "in the over-all comparison of needs, Japan should have the last priority." That the Pauley recommendations were deemed much too drastic, if not unrealistic, appeared when the Army Department sent Clifford S. Strike to Japan in February, 1947, to reappraise Japanese property in connection with the reparations program.[16] In July he urged the immediate repeal of the Pauley Plan, which would have impaired Japan's essential peacetime industrial capacity. Since the Pauley Plan was actuated by desire to end Japan's industrial supremacy in the Far East, SCAP had disapproved it from the outset as tantamount to economic strangulation of Japan.[17]

[13] It stated that "we, as a nation, are concerned to see that Japan is not pauperized but neither is Japan to be allowed to rehabilitate her economic life in a form which will allow her to gain control, or to secure an advantage, over her neighbors."

[14] Edwin W. Pauley, *Report on Japanese Reparations to the President of the United States*, November 1945 to April 1946 (Washington, 1948).

[15] In his letter of transmittal to the president, dated December 18, 1945, Pauley states that this is Japanese propaganda without any foundation.

[16] *New York Times*, February 23, 1947. For the outline of his report see *New York Times*, February 19, 1947.

[17] Royal Institute of International Affairs, *Survey of International Affairs, 1947-48* (London and New York, 1952), p. 336.

War Crimes Trial

One of the main objectives of the occupation was to "insure that Japan will not again become a menace to the United States or to the peace and security of the World." This called for destruction of military power and punishment of the military and government leaders charged with conspiring, planning, preparing, initiating, or waging aggressive war. Accordingly, on December 2 fifty-nine persons suspected of war crimes were arrested. In January, 1946, General MacArthur authorized the Charter of the International Military Tribunal for the Far East,[18] and on February 15 appointed the judges. Although the president of the tribunal, Sir William F. Webb of Australia, expressed his conviction that the emperor was just as guilty as the twenty-five defendants who stood trial, majority opinion prevailed and the tribunal did not place responsibility on the emperor.[19]

On November 12, 1948, six generals including General Hideki Tojo, and one civilian, former Prime Minister Hirota, were sentenced to death by hanging. Execution was deferred pending decision of the Supreme Court of the United States. On December 20 the Supreme Court declared that it lacked jurisdiction to entertain motions for leave to file petitions for writs of *habeas corpus* by five of the condemned prisoners and dismissed all the motions. Execution of the seven death sentences was carried out on December 23, 1948, at a time when American policy had undergone a reversal as new conflicts and new problems had arisen and new alignments had developed among the victors. The impact of the judgment of the International Military Tribunal for the Far East was vitiated also by the fact that the decision was by no means unanimous. Justice Pal of India disagreed with all the findings of the Tribunal on the ground that no conspiracy had been proved.[20] Justice Bernard of France also disagreed with the

[18] General Orders No. 1, General Headquarters, Supreme Commander for the Allied Powers, January 19, 1946. Department of State Publication 2675, pp. 5-10. The Tribunal convened formally on May 3 when twenty-eight persons were indicted as Class A war criminals although trial did not actually begin until June 13. As in the case of the Nuremberg Trial, it was meant to be a deterrent and to vindicate justice, and not vengeance or reprisal. It was given jurisdiction over crimes against peace, conventional war crimes, and crimes against humanity.

[19] Fearey, *op. cit.*, p. 18.

[20] Solis Horwitz, *The Tokyo Trial* (New York, 1950) pp. 562-63.

majority on the basis of the procedure employed in the trial. The two dissenting judges would have acquitted all the defendants of all charges.[21]

The Purge

The basic premise of the Potsdam Proclamation was "that a new order of peace, security and justice will be impossible until irresponsible militarism is driven from the world" and that "the authority and influence of those who have deceived and misled the people of Japan into embarking on world conquest must be eliminated for all time." [22] The purge was designed, therefore, "to eliminate the alliance of military force, feudal privilege, concentrated economic power, and government-controlled priestcraft that ruled Japan." Persons who had been active exponents of militarism and militant nationalism were to be removed and excluded from public office and from any other position of public or substantial private responsibility. The joint chiefs of staff directive[23] to SCAP made it clear that "all persons who have been active exponents of military nationalism and aggression, who have been influential members of any Japanese ultranationalistic, terroristic or secret patriotic society, agencies or affiliates" should be purged. In the absence of evidence to the contrary, it was assumed that any persons who had held key positions of high responsibility since 1937 in industry, finance, commerce, or agriculture had been active exponents of militant nationalism and aggression.[24] This resulted in removal and replacement of practically the entire leadership in government, politics, business, and industry, with the new personnel consequently suffering from lack of experience.

Removal of militarists and ultranationalists from power and influence in government was completed by the summer of 1946, as approximately one thousand persons, both incumbents of and candidates for important positions in the national government, had been removed. This involved screening of all Diet candidates in the April, 1946, election, and the final screening of successful candidates. In

[21] *Ibid.*, pp. 565-67.

[22] SCAP, *op. cit.*, p. 413.

[23] Joint Chiefs of Staff Directive 1380/15, November 3, 1945.

[24] The burden of proof was on the suspects, who were deemed guilty until proved innocent. At the same time they were not given opportunity to prove their innocence.

May the Purge Committee was set up, and screening began, but the scope of the purge was extended considerably in January, 1947.[25] The total number removed and excluded from office reached 210,287 or 0.29 per cent of the population, out of 2,308,806 or 3.2 per cent of the population who were screened. The procedure usually involved no hearings, public or private, no witnesses, no findings of guilt, and no machinery for either prosecution or defense.[26]

In the eyes of SCAP a specific and carefully aimed purge of business and industrial leadership was to be a feature of the economic reforms in Japan. It was felt that even if it were disruptive of the nation's economic development, it was nonetheless necessary in the interest of peace.[27] American policy regarding the purge was modified later, as it became apparent that strengthening Japan's national economy and political stability had acquired special urgency in the face of the rapidly changing and deteriorating international situation. On March 7, 1950, SCAP established a parole board to make recommendations on prisoners' applications for parole. The Soviet Union, however, vigorously protested that SCAP had no authority to parole major war criminals. The Department of State rejected the Soviet protest on the ground that SCAP was the sole executive authority for the Allied powers in Japan. The occupation was impelled to restore those purged to their former positions of leadership and influence. It became apparent that an economic purge, either as a just punitive measure against reactionary leadership in business and industry or as a means of improving the political and social views and attitudes of Japan's managerial class, had failed to achieve the goals hoped for by the occupation authorities.[28]

From a practical point of view, the removal of businessmen and industrialists from their positions as penalty for their political shortcomings was questionable. The purge failed to reduce their political influence, because the hidden connection between business and government continued uninterrupted and undiminished, while it only tended to arouse the antagonism of business and industry toward the

[25] Added were 26 special industries in which the government had controlling interest, approximately 1,000 companies which had been specifically designated by law as essential to the national economy, 78 enterprises which had been established under government subsidy or law, and 278 influential private companies.

[26] John D. Montgomery, *Forced to be Free* (Chicago, 1957), p. 26.

[27] SCAP, *op. cit.*, pp. 99, 549.

[28] Montgomery, *op. cit.*, pp. 124-25.

occupation. So far as the public at large was concerned, there was no swelling tide of resentment against the leaders, in support of the purge or in favor of democratizing the country.

Democratization

The first positive step[29] in the democratization of Japan was promulgation of an electoral law which for the first time gave suffrage to women. In the first postwar general election, which was held in April, 1946, voters sent thirty-nine women to the National Diet. The emperor in his New Year's Day message to the Japanese people on January 1, 1946, disavowed the divinity attributed to him. If the emperor's disavowal seemed unnecessary to many people, the intention of the occupation authorities was clear. What followed in its wake had far-reaching consequences. For the first time in history, the emperor "came down from the clouds," appeared informally in public, mingled and talked with the people as he visited the mines, farms and factories, traveled in airplanes and attended movies, baseball games, and wrestling tournaments. The "humanizing" of the emperor brought the people closer to him, and affection for him intensified although under the new Constitution he had become merely a symbol of the state and the unity of the people. It greatly enhanced rather than detracted from his moral position.

American policy stipulated educational reform as a requisite to democratization. The initial task of the occupation in the field of education was completed in 1946 and 1947. Much of this was negative and preparatory, liquidating the militarist and ultranationalist elements in the system, and included abolition of military training, ban on propagation of State Shinto, removal of teachers with undesirable backgrounds, and elimination of undesirable textbooks. The constructive aspect involved conversion of the educational system into a democratically oriented and operated one. The United States Education Mission, a group of educators and educational administrators invited by SCAP in March, 1946, to survey Japan's educational conditions and needs, submitted its report recommending the broad-

[29] In September, 1945, SCAP issued a directive to the Japanese government ordering the establishment of freedom of speech, and before the end of the month all wartime restrictions on freedom of speech had been removed. On October 4, all restrictions on political, civil and religious liberties were abolished, along with the Special Higher Police (Thought Police) of the Home Ministry. This was followed by repeal of the Peace Preservation Law.

ening of educational opportunities by extending compulsory education to nine years, simplification and standardization through adoption of the 6-3-3-4 system, decentralization of educational control through local school boards and parent-teacher associations, and coeducation. A year later the Diet enacted legislation for a new educational system on the American model, which went into effect on April 1, 1947, with nine years of compulsory education as well as coeducation from kindergarten through the university. Higher education was reorganized along American lines, but standardization was carried to excess particularly at the graduate school level. The educational reform produced a rush to set up colleges where neither need nor financial ability existed. This resulted in the upgrading of normal schools and higher schools into second-rate colleges with the inevitable upgrading of ill-equipped faculty members who lacked training, background and experience for college teaching. Expansion at the college level was unprecedented, as every prefecture established a college or a university. In 1950 there were 400,000 college and university students, while there had been only 72,000 just eleven years earlier in 1939. Education commissions and school boards were set up to decentralize education and educational policy, while parent-teacher associations began functioning everywhere for the first time.

It appears that the occupation authorities tended to regard decentralization per se, a desideratum, if not indispensable for democratic development. This led to decentralization not only in education and economy but in other fields. When the Home Ministry which controlled the centralized police was abolished, a decentralized police system was established in its place. Simultaneously the National Rural Police was created to assume jurisdiction over those sections of the country which did not come under the local police. The new system of local responsibility in police matters was not only expensive but difficult to administer. Gradually cities gave up their police in favor of a central system, which was re-established, and the occupation-inspired reform abandoned.

The New Constitution

No thought had been given to constitutional revision by the Shidehara Cabinet which was formed on October 9, 1945, although only five days earlier a SCAP directive had ordered the rescinding of all restrictions on civil, political, and religious liberties. On the occasion of his visit with General MacArthur on October 11, Prime Minister Shidehara was informed of the urgency of changes in the traditional social order that would require liberalization of the Constitution. The Supreme Commander indicated that among other things, these reforms were necessary: (a) emancipation of women through suffrage; (b) encouragement of the unionization of labor as a safeguard against exploitation and abuse of the working man as a means of raising his standard of living; (c) opening of schools to more liberal education; (d) abolition of systems which through secret inquisition and abuse had held the people in constant fear; and (e) democratization of economic institutions to insure a wide distribution of income and ownership of the means of production and trade.[30]

The prevailing view among Japanese leaders at the time was that obligations under the Potsdam Proclamation could be discharged under the existing Constitution, and revision was not necessary. But on October 13 the Cabinet announced that it had decided to undertake the study of the problem of constitutional revision, and appointed Dr. Joji Matsumoto, Minister without Portfolio, as chairman of the Constitution Problem Investigation Committee.[31] The committee made rapid progress in its draft on a revised constitution. Simultaneously all the political parties busied themselves in the preparation of drafts. On February 1, 1946, General Courtney Whitney, chief of the Government Section, addressed a memorandum to the Supreme Commander informing him that he had unrestricted authority to take any action deemed proper in effecting changes in the Japanese constitutional structure.[32]

Suddenly, without warning, on March 6, the day after a cabinet meeting, the "Draft Outline of Revised Constitution" was made public by the government. This was not the draft prepared by the Matsumoto Committee but rather a separate draft prepared by the Government Section of SCAP and was regarded by the Japanese as more radical than any of the drafts except that of the communist

[30] "Statement to the Japanese Government Concerning Required Reforms," SCAP, *op. cit.*, p. 740.

[31] For an account of drafting the Constitution, by one of the members of the Matsumoto Committee, see Tatsuo Sato, "The Origin and the Development of the Draft Constitution of Japan," *Contemporary Japan*, XXIV (1956-1957), 175-87, 371-87.

[32] "Memorandum for the Supreme Commander on Constitutional Reform," SCAP, *op. cit.*, pp. 622-23.

party.[33] General MacArthur expressed deep satisfaction at the "decision of the Emperor and Government of Japan to submit to the Japanese people a new and enlightened constitution which has my full approval." [34] He added that the document "had been drafted after painstaking investigation and frequent conference between the members of the Japanese government and this headquarters following my initial direction to the cabinet." [35] The SCAP draft which was submitted in early February proved to be "more than a little shock" to Dr. Matsumoto and others in the cabinet because its approach was regarded as "too direct, too drastic, and not suited to the Japanese." [36]

The Diet deliberated on the draft of the new Constitution and made some minor changes. It was promulgated on November 3, 1946, and went into force six months later on May 3, 1947. To provide a basis for a democratic political system, it vested sovereignty in the people and made the emperor "the symbol of the State and of the unity of the people." The principle of legislative supremacy was adopted, making the Diet "the highest organ of state power." Furthermore, the Diet was given the power to designate the prime minister from among its membership. Separation of powers and a system of checks and balances were introduced. The doctrine of judicial review, adopted for the first time, gave the supreme court the power to determine the constitutionality of legislation and administrative acts.

Undoubtedly the most unique feature of the Constitution was the renunciation of war as an instrument of national policy, and the denial of the right to maintain land, sea, and air forces as well as other armaments. A new feature was the comprehensive Bill of Rights, consisting of thirty-one articles and forming the longest chapter in the document, guaranteeing individual rights and freedom while emphasizing the dignity of the individual, the obligation to work together, with liability to taxation, and equal opportunities in education. The preamble had a distinctively American flavor, combining the ideas as well as language of the Declaration of Independence, the preamble to the Constitution of the United States, Lin-

[33] Matsumoto draft of January 4, 1946. SCAP, *op. cit.*, pp. 605-10.

[34] SCAP, *op. cit.*, p. 657.

[35] Premier Yoshida reported that the government reluctantly adopted the occupation-drafted constitution. *New York Times*, December 12, 1957.

[36] Shirasu's letter to General Whitney, February 15, 1946. SCAP, *op. cit.*, p. 624.

coln's Gettysburg Address, and the Atlantic Charter, all of which were obviously much in the minds of the American drafters of the Constitution. To preclude participation of the Japan communist party in the drafting process, the occupation rushed the work to completion in record time, in a matter of a few weeks.[37]

Beginning of a Shift in American Policy

After eighteen months of occupation, General MacArthur declared on March 17, 1947, at a news conference that the occupation had virtually attained Allied objectives, except in the matter of economic recovery which could best be achieved by an independent Japan.[38] The Department of State and the Army disclosed a week later that preparations were being made to open negotiations for a Japanese peace treaty. This gave hope that 1947 might be the year of "peace for Japan."

Meanwhile, after nearly seven weeks, the Moscow Conference of Big Four Foreign Ministers ended in deadlock on April 15 without agreement on German peace and other important problems.[39] This meant the further widening of the breach between the Soviet Union and the West, and the threat of communist imperialism led to far-reaching commitments by the United States in Europe. Impelled by aggressive Soviet policy in the Middle East, President Truman in his historic message to Congress on March 12, 1947, advocated strong American support for free peoples resisting subjugation by armed minorities or external forces. The Truman Doctrine[40] marked a turning point in American policy toward Europe and Asia. Less than two months later came Acheson's Cleveland, Mississippi, address[41] of May 8 in which he attributed failure to revive the workshops of Germany and Japan to the impasse in discussion of German peace, and strongly urged that reconstruction of both Germany and Japan be vigorously pushed to speed recovery of the two continents. In the thinking and planning of the State Department, Asia and Europe were now joined. Acheson emphasized that "the United States is

[37] Montgomery, *op. cit.*, p. 5.

[38] Unofficial estimates of planners in Washington at the time of the surrender put the duration of the occupation at approximately two years. Fearey, *op. cit.*, p. 182.

[39] Royal Institute, *op. cit.*, p. 278.

[40] *Congressional Record*, March 12, 1947, pp. 1980-81.

[41] *Bulletin*, 4 (May 18, 1941), 991-94.

prepared to take up the reconstruction of Japan and Germany independently without waiting for an agreement of the Great Powers."

Secretary of State Marshall on June 5, 1947, made the momentous announcement which envisaged rehabilitation of Europe, seriously and needlessly retarded by failure to reach a peace settlement with Germany and conclusion of a treaty with Austria. The implications were clear. The blame was being placed squarely on the Soviet Union for its policy of holding back European recovery. The United States was apprehensive for deterioration of economic, social, and political conditions in Europe. Under the Marshall Plan the United States would aid in the return of economic health in the world. The goal of American policy was the revival of a working world economy, which would help reenforce political and social conditions in which free institutions could exist.

While Soviet intransigence was making itself felt over a wide front, the United States on July 11, 1947, proposed to the other Far Eastern Commission governments that a conference be held in August to draft a peace treaty for Japan. The Soviet Union registered opposition to any conference of the eleven Far Eastern Commission members on the Japanese peace treaty.[42] Washington responded in August by informing Moscow bluntly that it would insist on an eleven-nation conference to avoid the sort of deadlock that had stymied the German peace settlement. Moscow insisted on preliminary talks by the Big Four Foreign Ministers. Washington was in no way deterred, nor did it modify its stand. Instead it proceeded with preparations for an eleven-nation conference. Before the end of August private commercial relations with Japan were restored, as promised in the formal Allied announcement of June, and four hundred private representatives entered Japan as the first step in resumption of foreign trade.

Determined to set up roadblocks at every turn, the Soviet Union in October, 1947, attacked American policy at the United Nations, asserting that restoration of the industrial power of Japan was contrary to the aims and objectives of the Potsdam Declaration. Much to the surprise of the Allied powers, Nationalist China supported the Soviets in opposing the American policy of fostering Japan's strength. Thus American efforts to begin negotiation by the Far Eastern Commission nations were blocked by Soviet opposition.

[42] The Soviets insisted that peace negotiations be carried on by representatives of the four powers. Fearey, *op. cit.*, p. 183.

After 1947 tension increased between the United States and the Soviet Union, forcing Washington to reappraise thoroughly the Far Eastern situation. During, as well as at the end of the war, American policy was based on the assumption that postwar Nationalist China would become the stable and leading power in the Far East.[43] As a matter of fact President Roosevelt had assigned great power status to China in hope that a unified, stable, and friendly China would act with the United States in the event of conflict in the area. This expectation, based on wishful thinking, was not being fulfilled at all in 1947.[44] The Chinese civil war was going against the Nationalists who had been weakened by division, inefficiency, and corruption. It became clear by 1948 that at the best China would remain a problem, and could not possibly be relied upon to maintain peace and order in the Far East. The exigencies of the situation forced a drastic revision of the United States initial post-surrender policy of perpetuating Japan's military and economic weakness. American policy had been so preoccupied with erecting safeguards against possible future military aggression that it had not seriously examined the possibility that aggression might not come from the former enemy but from a former ally.

REVERSAL OF AMERICAN POLICY, 1948-1951

American policy underwent almost a complete reversal in 1948. Japan was no longer regarded as a onetime enemy; a new role was assigned her as a valuable ally. The unexpectedly compliant and co-operative attitude of the Japanese toward the occupation and its personnel, as well as the orderly and efficient manner in which the occupation policies were carried out by the Japanese government, softened the Americans.[45] Japanese appreciation of the techniques and scientific methods of the West, and eagerness to adopt American ways, helped to create an image of Japan as a country to be trusted and assisted. Fundamentally, however, the reversal in American policy was necessitated by a shift in power alignments.

[43] Harold M. Vinacke, *The United States and the Far East, 1945-1951* (Stanford, 1952), p. 77.

[44] George F. Kennan believed that "We deluded ourselves into the hope that the defeat of Japan and the evacuation of Japanese forces from China would mean a united, free and democratic China." "Current Problems in the Conduct of Foreign Policy," *Bulletin*, 22 (May 15, 1950), 750.

[45] Vinacke, *op. cit.*, p. 77.

Early in 1948 the United States made it clear to the Far Eastern Commission that it had reached the conclusion that more direct and vigorous measures were required for the economic recovery of Japan. Under the new policy of rehabilitating and reviving Japan's industrial production to prewar level, the Pauley reparations policy was a serious deterrent. In the summer of 1947, the Overseas Consultants, Inc., a group of engineers, was sent to Japan by the Department of the Army. In its report of March, 1948,[46] it emphasized that Japan could not pay the large quantities of capital reparations, as had been previously believed by the United States, without seriously impairing its capacity to meet essential peacetime requirements. The experts unequivocally stated that "in our opinion a strong industrial Japan would be less dangerous to the peace and prosperity of the Far East than a continuance of the present state of instability and economic maladjustment in this vast and populous region." It argued against the destruction of Japan's productive facilities, since it would prevent Japan's becoming self-supporting and would be expensive to the American taxpayer, and it urged the scrapping of the existing reparations policy.[47]

In April, Percy H. Johnston, Chairman of the Chemical Bank and Trust Co., undertook a careful survey of economic conditions and took an even more limited view of Japan's capacity to pay reparations than did the Overseas Consultants, Inc. The Johnston group believed that Japan, stripped of its empire but possessing a large and rapidly increasing population, would need all of its resources and more to achieve a self-supporting status at decent standards of living. The Johnston Report,[48] released in May, pointed out that an industrial Japan was of economic, political, and strategic interest to the United States, and that an economically independent Japan would relieve the United States of an annual burden of approximately half a billion dollars, while as the workshop of Asia she could be instrumental in improving Asia's standard of living.[49] Recommendations of the Overseas Consultants and of the Johnston Report were adopted by the United States, and the new policy of giving Japan primacy in indus-

[46] Overseas Consultants, Inc., *Report on Industrial Reparations Survey of Japan to the United States of America* (New York, 1948).

[47] *New York Times,* March 10, 1948.

[48] Department of the Army Press Release, May 19, 1948. *Documents on American Foreign Relations,* 1948 (Princeton, 1950), pp. 160-62.

[49] Royal Institute, *op. cit.,* pp. 337-38.

trial production in the Far East now had the blessings of Washington.

Also in the month of May, 1948, General MacArthur invited five leading experts on antitrust legislation, headed by Ralph A. Young of the Federal Reserve Board, to study Japanese economic and financial conditions. The mission submitted its recommendations in June, calling for immediate institution of a comprehensive economic stabilization program which stressed stabilization of wages, prices, and credit, raw materials allocation controls, efficient tax collection, reduction of government deficit spending, and establishment of a single rate of exchange for the yen.[50]

Meanwhile, efforts were redoubled to build Japan's economic strength. On December 9, 1948, Major General Frank R. McCoy, US representative on the Far Eastern Commission, explained the reasons for the government's suspension of its participation in discussions of FEC 230 which had for its object the dissolution of certain Japanese combines and the widening of income and ownership of Japanese industry and trade. The policy, he stated, had become outmoded and was no longer useful since it had been overtaken by events.[51] Throughout 1948 and 1949 American efforts were directed mainly toward trade revival, which was hampered by the unwillingness of many of Japan's former enemies to admit Japanese traders to their territories, to permit even limited consular and trade offices, to extend most-favored-nation treatment, or to admit Japan to international trade agreements and economic conferences.

Serious doubt had arisen in the minds of American leaders as to China's worth as an ally and the free world's advance base in the Far East. The Nationalist Government, completely shot through with internal cleavage and corruption, was much too weak to eliminate the communists by its own strength.[52] Secretary of State Marshall was reluctant to follow General Wedemeyer's recommendation to give more assistance to Chiang's Nationalist regime. With communist triumphs, the West's position deteriorated rapidly in 1948. By October, Secretary Marshall had come to the conclusion that the Chinese government was incapable of saving itself and could not be saved by

[50] Fearey, *op. cit.*, pp. 124-25; Royal Institute, *op. cit.*, p. 343.

[51] *Documents on American Foreign Relations*, 1948, pp. 163-65.

[52] Kenneth S. Latourette, *The American Record in the Far East*, 1945-1951 (New York, 1952), p. 113.

anything short of armed intervention.[53] Early in 1949, long before collapse of the Nationalist Government on the China mainland,[54] the United States had come to the conclusion that retention and strengthening of Japan as a bulwark in the defense of the Pacific was imperative.

An unfortunate reaction was produced on the occasion of Secretary of the Army Kenneth C. Royall's visit to Japan in February, 1949. At an unofficial news conference he expressed an off-the-record opinion that American troops had better be withdrawn since Japan would have to be written off in event of war with Russia. The statement shocked the Japanese and generated distrust of American policy. President Truman promptly reassured the Japanese that American policy remained unchanged.[55] In spite of official denials, Japanese distrust, fear, anxiety, dismay and resentment could not be easily dispelled. Why should the Japanese co-operate with the United States, some argued, if they are going to be abandoned? Others thought perhaps it would be better to explore the possibility of working out some kind of a deal with the Soviets.

Joseph M. Dodge, a Detroit banker who had played an important role in the German currency reform, was sent by President Truman as financial adviser to the Supreme Commander. His recommendations were adopted by the Japanese government in April, 1949, and, as a result, for the fiscal year 1949-1950 a balanced budget was achieved for the first time in eighteen years.[56] In May, General McCoy issued a statement before the Far Eastern Commission announcing the United States decision to terminate the interim program of reparations deliveries because removal of further reparations from Japan would detract seriously from the occupation objective of stabilizing the Japanese economy and permitting it to move toward self-support. Japan, he said, had already paid substantial reparations

[53] Department of State, *United States Relations with China* (Washington, 1949), pp. 280-82.

[54] Tientsin fell to the communists in January, Nanking in April, Shanghai and Hankow in May, and Canton in October; the Nationalist cause was lost.

[55] Denials came from the army secretary's deputy, William J. Draper, the Supreme Commander, Army Chief of Staff Omar N. Bradley, and several others.

[56] *New York Times*, April 16, 1949. The balanced budget was achieved by the adoption of sound fiscal policies which included elimination of uneconomic and wasteful items, cancellation of extravagant investment projects, more effective collection of taxes, discharge of surplus government workers, and a gradual retirement of the national debt.

through expropriation of her former overseas assets and under the advance transfer program.[57] He declared that the American government was impelled to rescind its interim directive of April 4, 1947. Washington made it clear that it would oppose further industrial reparations from Japan either during the occupation or at the peace settlement. Japanese business now could rehabilitate plants without fear of being stripped for reparations. Japan was given a green light to go ahead and develop its industries without limit.

In accord with the American policy of accelerating trade revival, the Ministry of International Trade and Industry was created. This represented a shift from general industrial production to production geared to the export trade. A tax mission headed by Professor Carl R. Shoup of Columbia University was sent in the spring of 1949 to advise SCAP on reform of the Japanese budgetary and revenue system. Recommendations for a thorough revision of the national, prefectural, and local tax structure were put into effect by the Japanese government.

By the end of 1949 the economic picture was much improved, with the inflationary spiral checked. Industrial production had reached approximately 80 per cent of the 1932-1936 average. As part of the program of encouraging Japanese industrial development, the United States Atomic Energy Commission in November approved Japan's participation in the program for the foreign distribution of radio isotopes.[58] Japan became the first occupied country to receive isotopes from the United States. During 1950 American economic policies concentrated on establishment of Japan's international trade pattern, stimulation of domestic activities, and reinvesting control over economic activity in the Japanese government.

The prominent role assigned to Japan in America's security planning after 1949 was disclosed in the speech of Secretary of State Acheson at the National Press Club on January 12, 1950. In stating that "the Japanese islands lie within the American defense perimeter extending from the Aleutians to Japan and thence to the Ryukyus and to the Philippine Islands," he indicated Japan's role. Shortly thereafter, in February, 1950, the United States joint chiefs of staff on their inspection tour of the Far East noted in Japan that "the former enemy appeared to be not only the strongest bastion but just

[57] Department of State Press Release, May 12, 1949, *New York Times*, May 13, 1949.

[58] *Bulletin*, 21 (November 28, 1949), 834.

about the only tangible thing left of the fruits of victory in the Pacific." By comparison with any other Asian country, they observed, Japan was a miracle of political stability and economic progress.[59]

More than any other event which forced the United States and the West to realize that Japan must be built into a bastion against communism was the outbreak of the Korean War on June 25, 1950. Throughout the fighting, Japan was an effective base of operations for the United Nations forces on land, sea, and in the air. The task of the United Nations would have been immeasurably more difficult if not well nigh impossible without Japan. The war left no doubt that communism's objective was not Korea but Japan, whose industrial complex and increasing productive capacity would be invaluable to the communist world and could tip the scale in its favor. The Soviet Union regarded Japan as a primary target of international communism in Asia, for with Japan in their grasp the rest of Asia would be easy prey.

After the invasion of South Korea by the communist-trained and supported North Korean troops, the SCAP policy of strengthening Japan's defenses was implemented by creation of the National Police Reserve, for the transfer of American troops to the Korean front left Japan utterly defenseless, even against internal subversion. The right of self-defense, which the Supreme Commander had declared almost prophetically in his 1950 New Year message to the Japanese people, was thus translated into reality by the setting up of an internal security force.[60]

The San Francisco Peace Treaty, 1951

The Korean War pointed up the urgency of a Japanese peace treaty. When the United States in July, 1947, first proposed a meeting of the eleven member-nations of the Far Eastern Commission to open negotiations for a peace settlement, the Soviet Union promptly opposed.[61] When relations among the former Allies deteriorated to a point where a conference became impossible, the United States concentrated on economic rehabilitation and reconstruction. Prospects

[59] *New York Times,* February 7, 1950.

[60] General MacArthur declared that Japan had not renounced the right of self-defense against unprovoked attack. *New York Times,* January 1, 1950.

[61] Royal Institute of International Affairs, *Documents on International Affairs 1947-1948,* pp. 716-17, 719-20.

for a peace did not improve at all during 1948. If anything they became worse. The Berlin Blockade imposed by the Soviet Union in June kept the Allies and especially the United States occupied with the crisis. Meanwhile, the mounting communist offensive put the Nationalist Government in an extremely precarious position. In the United States the opening of the presidential campaign in the summer forced peace talks into the background.

Soviet obstruction continued unabated in 1948 and 1949. On November 18, 1948, Foreign Minister Molotov proposed that the Big Four Foreign Ministers' Conference meet in a special conference, preferably in China, to prepare a draft for the Japanese peace treaty. This time, however, the Nationalist Government was less than eager to please the Soviets and declined the invitation. Heavy fighting broke out in North China and Chiang Kai-shek, needing American assistance more than ever, could not afford to antagonize Washington. At the Paris Conference of the Big Four Foreign Ministers, Vyshinsky submitted on May 23, 1949, a completely unexpected proposal for a Japanese peace treaty which included Nationalist China's participation. The United States saw no point in holding a conference since the Soviet Union would never consent to allowing American forces to remain in Japan. It was clear that withdrawal of American troops from Japan would create a power vacuum which the Soviets would lose no time in filling. Secretary Royall's views, expressed in February, that the United States should withdraw troops from Japan, no longer had any support in Washington. It became apparent that Soviet expansionist policies were at the root of the difficulties which held up the Japanese peace.[62]

Toward the end of June, 1949, Secretary of State Acheson announced that the United States was going ahead with preparations for the Japanese peace treaty, to be drafted by all eleven nations of the Far Eastern Commission. On August 18 the State Department issued a statement underscoring the Supreme Commander's authority to encourage Japan to re-enter the stream of international affairs.[63] On November 5 an Associated Press dispatch from Manila carried General MacArthur's view that a Japanese peace treaty should be concluded as soon as possible, and that Nationalist China and the Soviet Union could attend the conference provided they agreed to

[62] Fearey, *op. cit.*, p. 182.

[63] *Bulletin*, 21 (August 29, 1949), 307.

American and British plans.[64] The Department of State immediately endorsed the Manila dispatch, and issued two days later a seven-point peace proposal which made the Japanese peace treaty one of the most important issues in international politics.[65]

In a move to circumvent the obstructionist tactics of the Soviet Union, the United States adopted an ingenious method of bringing about a peace treaty piecemeal, beginning in October, 1948, when the Departments of State and the Army adopted a new policy to relieve the American taxpayer of the financial burden of occupation. Without restoring sovereignty, the United States gradually gave back to Japan practically all the rights and privileges of an independent nation. This began when the United States on January 27, 1950, issued an invitation to the Japanese government to set up overseas offices in the United States for the purpose of undertaking trade promotion activities and consular functions. Then on February 21 it issued an interim directive to SCAP permitting Japan to participate with other nations or groups of nations in such international arrangements and conferences of a technical nature as she might be invited to enter into, accede to, or attend.[66] At the same time American diplomatic missions with the co-operation of SCAP explored possibilities for expanding Japanese trade in South and Southeast Asia.

At the time of outbreak of the Korean War in June, 1950, conversations were in progress in Tokyo between Ambassador John Foster Dulles and General MacArthur in connection with the former's forthcoming assignment to negotiate the Japanese peace. Washington saw that the North Korean attack had "as its ultimate objective the encirclement of Japan by Soviet power and an increased opportunity to subject Japan to its domination and eventual exploitation for aggression." [67] Strong apprehension was felt in Washington that the Soviet Union might seize the initiative for peace, in which event the position of the United States might become irretrievable.

Decision was reached in 1950 by the United States to abandon entirely the conference method of peacemaking since it afforded too many opportunities for obstruction, and, instead, to adopt separate

[64] *New York Times,* November 5, 1949.

[65] J. Lewe Van Aduard, *Japan from Surrender to Peace* (The Hague, 1953), pp. 121-23.

[66] US Department of State, *American Foreign Policy; Basic Documents,* 1950-1955 (Washington, 1957), p. 2405; *Bulletin,* 22 (March 13, 1950), 414.

[67] US Senate, Exec. Documents A, B, C, & D, 82nd Cong., 2d Sess., pp. 17-22.

diplomatic negotiations which no single nation could possibly thwart. On April 19, 1950, Dulles was appointed consultant to the secretary of state to head a presidential mission to visit the capitals of ten nations especially concerned and exchange views regarding the Japanese peace treaty.[68] President Truman on January 10, 1951, appointed Dulles as his special representative to conduct negotiations leading to a peace settlement with Japan and related security arrangements with Japan and other Pacific countries.[69] There was urgent need not only to end the state of war promptly and establish a just peace but also, in MacArthur's words, "to gain an indispensable initiative" by making Japan a vigorous and contributing member of the free world and at the same time strengthen America's security in the Pacific.

The Dulles mission arrived in Tokyo on January 25, 1951, and spent four weeks in Japan.[70] The twofold aim in the Japanese peace settlement was to liquidate the war with Japan which occupied a key position in free Asia and build a strong bulwark against communist aggression in Asia by turning a former enemy into a friend and ally.[71] The objectives of the peace treaty were the restoration of Japan as an equal in the society of nations, offering a chance to Japan to earn her way in the world by becoming self-supporting, promotion of cultural relations between Japan and the West, and assurance to Japan of a reasonable degree of security. The treaty was a recognition on the part of the West and particularly the United States of the danger to the West's security arising from Soviet determination to dominate Japan. China had fallen into the communist orbit, and unless the United States acted, it appeared that Japan too might go the way of China. The United States determined not to let Stalin's boast that "with Japan the Soviets would be invincible" come to pass.

[68] The scope of the mission was announced by President Truman on September 15. *Bulletin,* 23 (September 25, 1950), 513.

[69] *Ibid.*, 24 (January 29, 1951), 185.

[70] Dulles was accompanied by John M. Allison and Robert A. Fearey of the State Department, Assistant Secretary of the Army Earl D. Johnson, Major General Carter B. Magruder, and Colonel C. Stanton Babcock of the Department of Defense, and John D. Rockefeller III in the capacity of educational and cultural adviser.

[71] See Dulles's "Report on the Work of the Presidential Mission to Japan," *Bulletin,* 24 (March 12, 1951), 403; and also his address at Whittier College on March 31, "Progress Report on the Peace in the Pacific," *New York Times,* April 1, 1951.

Dulles reminded Americans that in the Pacific War Japan was formidable when she fought alone against us in Asia.[72]

Of special significance was the novel procedure used in the peace negotiations, which represented a radical departure from the traditional pattern of peacemaking. This was a tactical triumph of American diplomacy which precluded the possibility of a breakdown caused by an intransigent power. Dulles visited Japan not once but three times, June, 1950, January-February, 1951, and April, 1951, to exchange views with Japanese officials, party leaders, and business and labor leaders, as well as occupation officials. Thus, the views of the defeated were taken into consideration by the victors in arriving at the peace settlement. The United States assumed initiative in the negotiations, since the Allied powers had given her the chief responsibility in carrying out the occupation. After eleven months of negotiations[73] the most broadly-based peace treaty in all history was completed. On August 15, 1951, announcement was made of the San Francisco Conference on the Proposed Japanese Peace Treaty.[74]

The conference opened in the San Francisco Opera House on September 4, 1951, and four days later it finished its work with the signing of the treaty by forty-eight nations and Japan, making it the shortest peace conference of recent times.[75] The San Francisco Peace Treaty was not an instrument of vengeance imposed upon the de-

[72] John Foster Dulles, "Japanese Peace Treaty Viewed as Positive Step in Free World's March Toward Peace," *Bulletin*, 25 (October 15, 1951), 616-17.

[73] In March, 1951, the United States circulated its draft, and shortly thereafter the United Kingdom produced a draft of its own. The American draft was revised after being subjected to intensive study and scrutiny by twenty countries. In June the United States and the United Kingdom jointly drafted a text to reflect more adequately the views that had emerged in the meantime. On July 20 announcement was made that the governments of the United States and Great Britain had circulated copies of the draft treaty to fifty-one of the nations which had declared war upon Japan and had asked for comments. The United States at the same time invited them to attend a peace treaty conference to be opened in San Francisco on September 4. *Bulletin*, 25 (July 30, 1951), 186-87.

[74] *Bulletin*, 25 (August 27, 1951), 346-47.

[75] Nationalist China was not represented at the conference because the United States and Great Britain could not agree on which China to invite while Burma and India declined the invitation. The Soviet Union and its satellites were present but did not sign the treaty. The Soviet Union took the opportunity to make nine different charges against the treaty. Japan concluded a separate treaty with Nationalist China on April 28, 1952, the day on which the San Francisco Peace Treaty took effect.

feated. Rather it was a peace which reflected self-restraint, good will and good judgment; it recognized Japan's great culture and tradition while respecting Japanese dignity and giving her opportunity to achieve peace and freedom.[76] It was a treaty of reconciliation which looked to the future and especially to the role Japan was expected to play. American policy was not merely an act of generosity toward a defeated foe; it was an act of enlightened self-interest. It was exceedingly liberal in that it ruled out heavy reparations, indemnities, or restrictions on trade or rearmament. The United States was resolved not to let the Japanese peace negotiations founder on other Asian issues. The treaty took effect on April 28, 1952, and Japan at that moment regained her independence and sovereignty and assumed her rightful place in the community of nations.[77] President Truman observed this occasion by promising that the people of the United States would continue to work with the Japanese people to promote peace and security in accord with the Charter of the United Nations. Prime Minister Yoshida sent a message expressing gratitude for the "enlightened and magnanimous statesmanship of Japan's former enemies" and declaring that "In making our new start today, our people know that no nation can live unto itself, that no nation can draw dividends unless it contributes to a common world effort and invests in the common welfare of humanity." [78]

The Japanese Peace Treaty was the product of American bipartisan foreign policy at its best. It was a superb example of peacemaking. John Foster Dulles, a Republican and the chief architect, was backed by a Democratic president and secretary of state and encouraged and supported by General MacArthur even after the latter had been removed from his post as Supreme Commander. Every step of the negotiations was carried on in closest consultation with the Congressional leaders of both parties. It was a marvelous demonstration of how co-operation between the executive and legislative branches as well as between the two parties can be carried out in American diplomacy.

[76] Report of the Senate Committee on Foreign Relations, February 14, 1952. Department of State, *American Foreign Policy; Basic Documents 1950-1955* (Washington, 1957), p. 466.

[77] President Truman on this date issued a proclamation terminating the state of war with Japan. US Department of State, *American Foreign Policy; Basic Documents*, 1950-1955 (Washington, 1957), pp. 2425-27.

[78] *Bulletin*, 26 (May 5, 1952), 689.

SINCE THE SAN FRANCISCO PEACE TREATY, 1952-1959

American policy since Japan's regaining of independence has been one of acceleration and intensification of changes instituted in 1948-1949. The six and one-half years of occupation convinced the United States of the gravity of economic problems confronting Japan. These were the same economic problems which the world had shrugged off in the 1930s as the exaggerated propaganda rantings of the militarists to justify their aggressions in Asia. Japan's serious economic difficulties were aggravated by rising population as well as paucity of natural resources and industrial raw materials. Before the war, with the resources of the empire to draw upon, Japan was able to maintain a volume of production and overseas trade sufficient to meet the requirements of a population of not more than 70,000,000 people. But stripped of 45 per cent of the land area as a consequence of defeat, and with a population of 85,000,000 which was increasing at an annual rate of 1,500,000, the economic picture was anything but bright.

Prospects for Japan improved appreciably with resumption by the United States of commercial relations on a normal basis on September 30, 1953. Henceforth America's concern for security in the Pacific was reflected continuously in its solicitude for Japan's economic and political well-being. Secretary Dulles repeatedly gave expression to this concern. Speaking on American security, he declared:

> Japan must trade to live and if the free nations fail to make it possible for Japan to earn its way, then inevitably, though reluctantly, her people would turn elsewhere. This would be stupid from an economic point and folly from a political standpoint . . . From a political standpoint it requires little imagination to visualize what would happen if Russia, China and Japan became a united hostile group in the Pacific. It was difficult enough for the United States to defeat Japan when she fought alone in the Pacific with China its enemy and Russia neutral. The free world must shun economic policies which would drive Japan into the Communist bloc.[79]

President Eisenhower, on June 22, 1954, in his address before the National Editorial Association, stressed in similar vein the impor-

[79] "Security in the Pacific," a speech before the Los Angeles World Affairs Council, June 11, 1954. *Bulletin*, 30 (June 28, 1954), 972.

tance of trade with Japan to prevent her from being drawn into the communist orbit.

In July, 1954, the Foreign Operations Administration study group spent some time on a close look at Japan's economic situation to find ways and means of assistance. In Washington, the Departments of State, Defense, Treasury, Commerce, and the Foreign Operations Administration as well as the Council of Economic Advisers, were told at the two cabinet meetings of July 24 and August 6 to find means of increasing Japanese trade with the West so that Japan would not be forced into promoting a greater exchange of goods with Communist China and the Soviet Union. In August, 1954, Secretary Dulles reasserted emphatically that the "United States recognized that one of the major postwar problems is the problem of finding opportunities whereby Japan with its large and industrious population can find a way to earn a useful and profitable living in the world." [80]

Japan was admitted to the Colombo Plan with the support of the United States, as one of the six donor nations, the only Asian nation to be assigned the role of donor, and this admission and recognition gave her a new impetus and opportunity. By bringing Japan into a working relationship with the Commonwealth nations, the United States paved the way for closer co-operation and mutual understanding, enabling Japan to give assistance to underdeveloped countries, thereby rendering communist penetration of these areas more difficult.

Prime Minister Yoshida's visit to the United States in November, 1954, marked the beginning of Japan's personal diplomacy which became increasingly popular in the Eisenhower administration. Addressing the National Press Club in Washington on November 8, 1954, Yoshida made a strong plea for a Marshall Plan for Asia whereby the United States would pour in approximately $4 billion a year to aid underdeveloped countries. The plan was envisioned as a combination of American capital and Japanese technical know-how for the benefit of Asia and the security of the free world. Nothing came of this proposal, but two days later a joint Eisenhower-Yoshida statement declared that the two governments, in co-operation with the free nations of Asia, would continue their united efforts to main-

[80] Press Release 435, August 10, 1954. *Bulletin,* 31 (August 23, 1954), 26.

tain and promote peace and prosperity in Asia. The United States pledged co-operation in Japan's trade expansion and assistance in launching a productivity program. The latter was implemented by the Technical Co-operation Agreement[81] of April 6, 1955, which aimed at strengthening the Japanese economy. A Productivity Center was set up by the Foreign Operations Administration to increase efficiency in industry, agriculture, and commerce. American experts were sent out to work with the Japanese while their industrialists and technicians were brought over to study American methods.

American assistance was stepped up in every possible way during 1955, but there was no assurance that Japan could or would always oblige the United States in her policy decisions. Undersecretary of State Herbert Hoover, Jr., cautioned Americans that the Japanese "will be sensitive for a long time to any semblance of United States interference. There can be no guarantee," he warned, "that Japan's decisions . . . will always be those we would like to see." [82] It was natural that Japan's increasing ability to support herself economically and protect herself militarily should lead to greater freedom of action in international affairs. The United States was confident that Japan could become a source of strength to the free nations in the Far East by becoming strong, independent, and self-respecting, sure of its ability to manage its economic and political problems.

Negotiation first begun by the United States at Geneva on February 21, 1952, to bring Japan into the General Agreement on Tariffs and Trade (GATT) finally saw fruition in 1955. This came only after persistent efforts to overcome the hostility and resistance of some of the countries that refused to give Japan a chance to compete in their markets. On September 10, 1955, Japan was officially admitted to membership as a contracting party but without full benefit of the most-favored-nation treatment, since fourteen nations of Europe withheld it from her. Japan's admission to GATT was one of the outstanding accomplishments of American policy in 1955 and signalized Japan's reintegration in the world trading community.[83]

In a tariff agreement on April 12, 1956, the United States effected a 15 per cent reduction of tariff on Japan's exports during the next three years. America's policy of encouraging Japan's foreign trade in

[81] *Bulletin,* 32 (April 25, 1955), 702-3.

[82] *Ibid.* (June 20, 1955), 1001.

[83] President's First Annual Report on the Operation of Trade Agreements Program to Congress. *Bulletin,* 36 (March 4, 1957), 363-71.

some instances met with the opposition of American manufacturers, notably in cotton goods. Sharp increases in the export of cotton goods to the United States in 1955 alarmed American manufacturers so greatly that the Japanese government announced in December a program of voluntary control of exports of cotton goods for the year 1956. In spite of control, there was widespread outcry against the so-called Japanese invasion of the American market. South Carolina and some other states enacted state laws against Japanese textiles.[84] In September, 1956, the Japanese government adopted a program for control of cotton exports to the United States which for a five-year period beginning on January 1, 1957, imposed an over-all ceiling of 235,000,000 square yards per year on export of all types of cotton cloth and cotton manufactures.[85]

An American trade mission headed by Eugene Broderman, Director of the Far East Division of the Bureau of Foreign Commerce, spent six weeks in Japan in the spring of 1956 and found that the "forward looking policies of the United States toward Japan including the extension of considerable amounts of aid in the postwar years, stand out among our most important accomplishments in Asia." The Broderman mission was convinced that "the maintenance and continued development of Japan as a prosperous and dependable member of the democratic free world is important to the security of the United States." [86]

In Japan's road to recovery, 1956-1957 stood out as a turning point. American policy of rehabilitating Japan bore fruit, and tremendous improvements were noted in virtually every sphere of economic activity. Production exceeded expectations as well as the 1930-1934 level, and people virtually wallowed in prosperity as newspapers hailed the achievement as the biggest boom since the beginning of history. In 1956 Japan overtook Great Britain to become the world's leading shipbuilder, and the following year built a total of 2,424,433 gross tons including an 85,000-ton oil tanker, the largest ever launched in any shipyard. In 1958 Japan launched a 105,000-ton oil tanker, the largest ever built, completing it in a record time of five months. Economic recovery in some fields now seemed complete.

[84] *Bulletin*, 34 (April 30, 1956), 728.

[85] This included 113 million sq. yds. of cotton cloth as against the 150 million sq. yds. in 1956, 83 million sq. yds. of woven and knit apparel, and 39 million sq. yds. of household goods. *Bulletin*, 36 (February 11, 1957), 218-19.

[86] *Bulletin*, 34 (June 11, 1956), 794.

The year 1958, however, brought recession and gloom in the wake of prosperity. Trade deficit in Japan's relations with the United States became the major headache during the year, for she was selling only one half as much as she was buying. The secretary of state in explaining American policy toward Japan told the House Ways and Means Committee on February 24 that "surely our trade policies ought to help make it possible for Japan to gain a livelihood within the free world." [87] The State Department continued its efforts to make the American public and especially business see that national security was closely, if not inseparably, tied to the problem of giving Japan greater access to the American market. Undersecretary of State Christian Herter pointed out that Japan must trade to live and that if the West closed the trade door in Japan's face, she would be forced to turn to the communist bloc.[88] The need to give Japan access to the American market was underscored also by the Assistant Secretary of State for Far Eastern Affairs when he pointed out to the Senate Foreign Relations Committee in May, 1958, that strategically, Japan constituted one of the world's four major industrial complexes which the communist bloc dearly wanted, and emphasized the necessity of keeping her as our ally because she was politically a leader in Asia and was playing an increasing role in economic development of that area.[89]

In addition to the problem of rebuilding Japan's economy, American policy was concerned with the strengthening of defense. As part of the peace settlement at San Francisco, the two nations concluded a security pact which gave the United States the right to station land, sea, and air forces in or about Japan to maintain international security in the Far East and protect Japan against attack from both within and without. Japan agreed not to grant to any third power, without prior consent of the United States, any bases or rights in or relating to bases or right of garrison, maneuver, or transit of troops. The disposition of troops was determined subsequently by an administrative agreement.[90]

[87] *Ibid.*, 38 (March 17, 1958), 435.

[88] "International Trade and Our National Security," an address at the Seventh Annual Washington State International Trade Fair, April 11, 1958. *Bulletin*, 38 (May 5, 1958), 734.

[89] Walter S. Robertson, "United States Policies in the Far East," May 2, 1958. *Bulletin*, 38 (June 2, 1958), 917.

[90] The US–Japan Security Treaty, signed on September 8, 1951, took effect April 28, 1952, simultaneously with the Peace Treaty. It was preceded by the US–Philippine Mutual Defense Treaty of August 30 and the Australia–New Zealand–United States Treaty of September 1.

Japan's Five Year Defense Plan outlined by the National Security Board went into effect in September, 1953.[91] Considerable prodding by the United States was required to push her rearmament program, chiefly because of lack of public support. Secretary Dulles in September, 1953, made a strong plea to the Japanese government to build up its military strength, for he felt that efforts at rearming were lagging visibly. Subsequently, when Finance Minister Ikeda and Assistant Secretary of State Robertson conferred in Washington, they agreed wholeheartedly that Japan's self-defense forces needed strengthening.[92] Vice President Nixon, while on his round-the-world tour in Japan, expressed his views that it was a mistake for the United States to disarm Japan.[93]

American policy to make Japan a more active partner in the Pacific security system was finally realized when the Mutual Defense Agreement went into effect on May 1, 1954. The treaty recognized that Japan as a sovereign nation possessed the right of individual or collective self-defense. In planning the mutual assistance program for Japan, the United States recognized economic stability as an indispensable condition for development of defense capabilities. Needless to say, Japan could contribute only to the extent permitted by her general economic conditions and capacities.[94] In the treaty the two governments agreed to make available equipment, materials, services, and other assistance to one another and to other governments agreed upon. The Japanese government agreed to facilitate production and transfer to the United States needed raw materials, and semiprocessed materials, receive United States government personnel in Japan, grant exemption from duties and taxes to the United States, and act to eliminate international tension and fulfill military obligations. Each government would take security measures regarding articles, services, or information, and consult with each other. As part

[91] On October 15, 1952, the National Security Board was established and the National Police Reserve was converted into the National Security Force of 110,000 men.

[92] Secretary Dulles's anxiety over Japan's security was of long standing. He was worried that the Soviet Union was seeking to subjugate Japan. *New York Times*, January 28, 1953.

[93] *New York Times*, November 19, 1953. General Eichelberger was one of the first Americans publicly to express the view that it was a mistake to disarm Japan.

[94] US Department of State, *American Foreign Policy; Basic Documents, 1950-1955* (Washington, 1947), pp. 2437-41.

of the agreement the United States furnished a Military Assistance Advisory Group to help train Japanese forces.

On June 2 the House of Councillors, in passing the two bills approved by the Lower House for establishment of land, sea, and air self-defense forces, attached a rider that "the dispatch of troops abroad may not be permitted in the light of the provision in the Constitution and the peace loving spirit of the people." On July 1 the new defense establishment came into being under the National Defense Board, with its land, sea, and air-defense forces and joint chiefs of staff. The National Defense Council was established to advise the cabinet in the formulation of national defense policy. At the same time a National Defense College was set up to train officers, and the National Defense Secret Protection Law took effect.

American-Japanese amity suffered a setback in 1954 as a result of the unfortunate accident which overtook the Japanese fishing boat, *Fukuryu Maru*, on March 1. Although the fishing vessel was in a safe area at the time of the Bikini nuclear test, the twenty-three fishermen aboard were exposed to radioactive fallout and the entire catch of tuna fish had to be condemned by Japanese authorities as unsafe. In the summer of 1954 a nationwide movement to ban atomic and hydrogen bombs was launched by Tokyo housewives, and in a matter of twelve months they obtained more than 35 million signatures for a petition. On September 23 the radio operator, Aikichi Kuboyama, one of the fallout victims, died. The United States on January 4, 1955, presented to the Japanese government without reference to the question of legal liability a sum of money as compensation for injuries or damages sustained as the result of nuclear tests in the Marshall Islands in 1954. The Japanese government accepted the compensation, and the incident was closed, though unfortunately not before leftist agitators had exploited the fallout accident to stir up anti-American sentiment.

The Atoms for Peace Exhibition which was opened in Tokyo on November 1, 1955, under joint auspices of the United States Information Service and the *Yomiuri Shimbun*, a Tokyo daily, was a tremendous success with a record attendance. More significant was the fact that it was instrumental in reversing public opinion from adamant opposition against nuclear fission to enthusiastic acceptance and support of "atoms for peace." On November 14 the Atomic Energy Agreement was signed and the Japan Atomic Energy Research Institute established as a central organization for research and development.[95] The Diet on December 23, 1955, authorized creation of the Atomic Energy Commission and in August of the following year the Atomic Energy Fuel Corporation was established to accelerate development and utilization of atomic energy by prospecting and mining with Japan for ores containing uranium and other fissionable materials.[96]

American efforts to assist Japan in developing peaceful uses of atomic energy have taken various forms. In September, 1956, a group of Japanese including Diet members, government officials, and electric power company executives, was brought to the United States to study and observe the industrial use of atomic energy with emphasis on power development. On November 2 the US Atomic Energy Commission authorized the export of a nuclear reactor to Japan. Issuance of the export license to Atomic International of Canoga Park, California, marked the first commercial transaction in the American atomic energy industry.

Japan's Re-entry into World Affairs

Less than two months after regaining independence, on June 23, 1952, Japan formally applied for membership in the United Nations. The United States sponsored in the Security Council Japan's bid for membership, but the Soviet Union used the veto to block admission and frustrate American efforts and continued to do so for the next four years. Meanwhile, on December 24, 1953, the United States relinquished control of the Amami Oshima group, the northernmost islands of the Ryukyu chain, restoring it to Japanese sovereignty. This was America's way of showing confidence in Japan while at the same time supporting her in the policy of regaining some of her lost territory. This further strengthened ties between the United States and Japan.

Japan participated in the Bandung Conference, April 18-24, 1954, which was the first nonwhite international conference involving two continents, Asia and Africa. Although the official attitude of the

[95] Reorganized into a special corporation supported jointly by the government and private interests in June, 1956, the Institute set up on a ninety-acre site at Tokai village, about eighty miles northeast of Tokyo, reactors and laboratories to carry on basic studies on atomic energy and its application, design, construction and operation of reactors, importation, production, and distribution of radioactive isotopes, and training of nuclear scientists and engineers.

[96] Uranium deposits have been found in Tottori prefecture at Ningyo Pass and a refining plant was built at Tokai village in 1958.

United States at the outset was ambiguous and noncommittal, if not indifferent and less than enthusiastic, the Japanese government decided to send a delegation. Participation in the conference brought Japan into the fold of the Afro-Asian bloc, more than two years in advance of her admission to the United Nations, and gave her stature. While this action was obviously an independent one, and if it seemed like a disregard if not defiance of American wishes, it turned out to the advantage of the free world to have Japan as a member of the Afro-Asian bloc and to have her serve as a voice of moderation in the midst of the newly independent and intensely nationalistic countries of Asia.

Months before Japan's admission to the United Nations, the Western nations began to perceive a clearer image of Japan's future role in international affairs in a world of two opposing power blocs. In June, 1956, Justice William O. Douglas of the US Supreme Court included Japan among the six nations of the world expected to dominate the rest of the 20th century.[97] At the Commonwealth Prime Ministers' Conference in London in July, 1956, New Zealand's Prime Minister Holland[98] made a plea for greater Commonwealth support of Japan.

On September 7, 1956, the United States after careful examination of the historical facts reached the conclusion that the islands of Etorofu and Kunashiri, along with the Habomai and Shikotan which are a part of Hokkaido, have always been part of Japan proper and should in justice be acknowledged as under Japanese sovereignty. The United States indicated that it would regard Soviet agreement in this effect a positive contribution to the reduction of tension in the Far East.[99] Surprisingly enough, in October the Soviet Union agreed to cede Habomai and Shikotan after the signing of a peace treaty with Japan.[100]

The most significant achievement of American policy since conclusion of the San Francisco Peace Treaty was admission of Japan as the eightieth member of the United Nations. Beginning in June, 1952, when Japan first made a bid for membership, the United States consistently espoused Japan's cause in the face of the Soviet Union's repeated veto. Four and a half years of persistent efforts were re-

[97] *New York Times,* June 17, 1956.
[98] *Ibid.,* July 5, 1956.
[99] *Bulletin,* 35 (September 24, 1956), 484.
[100] *New York Times,* October 20, 1956.

warded. Finally on December 18, acting on the unanimous recommendation of the Security Council, the General Assembly formally approved Japan's admission by a unanimous vote of 77 to 0. President Eisenhower in congratulating the new member remarked that admission of Japan made the concept and role of the United Nations more meaningful than ever before. "The American people," he said, "rejoice in the action of the General Assembly today and welcome Japan as a new and worthy associate in the world's struggle for peace." Secretary Dulles expressed confidence that the United States had gained a supporter when he said that "we look forward to the exertion of Japan's prestige and influence within the United Nations forum in the vigorous defense of freedom." Foreign Minister Shigemitsu issued a friendly admonition to his Asian and African colleagues when he said that "Arab and Asian nations might well beware of excesses or extreme nationalism." In October of the following year Japan was elected to the Security Council as a nonpermanent member.

The year 1957 got off to an inauspicious start for the United States, for the Girard case stirred up anti-American feeling. The fatal shooting of a Japanese woman at the United States firing range at Somagahara by an army enlisted man, William S. Girard, became the subject of wide and heated discussion in the Diet and in the press of the nation.[101] What was involved was the question of jurisdiction. After the Japan-United States Committee entrusted with decisions on jurisdictional cases conceded Japan's right to try the soldier under the status of forces agreement, the United States Far East Command turned him over to the Japanese authorities.[102] In Washington, both Secretary of State Dulles and Secretary of Defense Wilson, holding that Girard's action was not authorized and therefore not in line of duty, concluded that he was subject to the status of forces agreement. Some members of Congress, however, were ruffled over the decision.[103] At a press conference President Eisenhower expressed confidence that Girard would get a fair trial from the Japanese. But opposition in Congress mounted.[104] The jurisdictional question was settled when on July 11 the United States Supreme Court by a vote of 8 to 0 upheld the government's decision to surrender Girard to the

[101] *Ibid.*, May 17, 1957.
[102] *Ibid.*, May 21, 1957.
[103] *Ibid.*, June 5, 1957.
[104] *Ibid.*, June 6, 1957.

Japanese authorities for trial, holding that it could find no constitutional or statutory barrier. Yet Congressional reaction remained largely critical.[105] Once the jurisdictional issue was settled to the satisfaction of the Japanese authorities, the trial proceeded smoothly and without inordinate publicity or sensationalism. Girard was found guilty but he received a three-year suspended sentence and the case was closed since neither side appealed.[106]

In spite of the unfortunate repercussions of the Girard case on both sides of the Pacific, a new spirit of co-operation based firmly on mutual need was injected into American-Japanese relations.[107] This new era was highlighted by the visit of Prime Minister Kishi to the United States in June of 1957. The prime minister not only conferred with high officials in Washington but played a round of golf with the president, introducing a new twist to personal diplomacy. Although Kishi was the second Japanese premier to pay an official visit, he was the first to be accorded the honor of addressing Congress. In his appearance before Congress on June 20, 1957, he conveyed the deep gratitude of his nation to the United States for the generous aid which had helped to restore Japan's shattered economy, and stressed that association with the United States was most important in Japan's foreign relations.[108] He also pointed out that Japan, as the most advanced industrial nation in Asia, had already demonstrated that economic and social progress could be achieved without use of the communist short cut and that "Japan as a faithful member of the free world has a useful and constructive role to play, particularly in Asia where the free world faces the challenge of international communism." The following day a joint communiqué was issued by the president and the prime minister reiterating that relations between the two countries were based on equality, mutual interest, and mutual benefit, and that efforts must be strengthened to foster conditions necessary for economic and social progress and for strengthening freedom in Asia and throughout the world. They emphasized that high-level world trade beneficial to the free nations, and orderly trade between the two nations, without unnecessary and arbitrary restrictions, was desirable.[109]

[105] *Ibid.*, July 12, 1957.
[106] *Ibid.*, November 19, 1957.
[107] *Bulletin*, 37 (July 15, 1957), 96-97.
[108] *Congressional Record*, June 20, 1957, pp. 8764, 8821.
[109] *Bulletin*, 37 (July 8, 1957), 51-54.

During 1957 security in the Pacific had become in principle, if not completely in fact, a joint undertaking of partners on equal footing actuated by common interests. "Because Japan and the United States are the two largest free nations bordering the Pacific," the Deputy Assistant Secretary of State for Far Eastern Affairs told a San Diego audience, "they must necessarily bear a proportionately large share of the responsibility for promoting peace and welfare in the Far East. It goes without saying that they must work in unison." [110]

Japan's deep concern for world peace was reflected in United Nations deliberations on the Middle East crisis in the summer of 1958. On July 21, Japan introduced a resolution in the Security Council calling for strengthening of the United Nations observation group to enable withdrawal of American forces from Lebanon only to be vetoed by the Soviet Union. Japan's sympathy for the Arab nations was apparent at the third emergency session of the General Assembly, where on August 15, Foreign Minister Fujiyama characterized the rise of nationalism in the Middle East as "an inevitable development in the march of history" and called on world opinion "to respect the reasonable aspirations of the Arab nations to consolidate their independence and preserve their territorial integrity."

Working vigorously toward establishment of a peaceful world within the framework of the United Nations, Foreign Minister Fujiyama on September 18, 1958, called on the General Assembly for unification of Germany, Korea, and Viet Nam, suspension of nuclear tests, settlement of the Indonesia-Netherlands dispute, rectification of the problem of Hungary, and solution of the world population problem. Promising wholehearted co-operation of the Japanese delegation, he strongly urged a more active and serious study of general disarmament, establishment of world economic stability through mutual co-operation, liberalization of trade and assistance to underdeveloped countries, and resolution of the conflict between the free world and the communist world.

Signing of a reparations agreement with South Viet Nam on May 13, 1959, which came after six years of negotiation, represented the fourth and last settlement and removed the last obstacle to

[110] *Ibid.* (November 27, 1957), 840. American economic aid to Japan from the beginning of the occupation through December 31, 1957, had reached the total of $2,400,000,000. This compares with $2,000,000,000 to South Korea, $1,400,000,000 to Taiwan (Formosa) $900,000,000 to the Philippines and $1,700,000,000 to other countries of the Far East.

Japan's normal, friendly relations with all the countries of Southeast Asia. The first of these reparations settlements was with Burma on April 16, 1955, followed by the Philippines on May 9, 1956, and Indonesia on March 1, 1958. According to the agreement signed in Saigon, Japan promised to pay in direct reparations $39 million over a period of five years in goods and services including construction of a hydroelectric power plant, and to make available an additional $16.6 million in loans and credits for the purchase of Japanese products and services and for construction of a chemical plant. The direct method of reparations payments enabled the government of the claimant country to procure reparations goods directly from Japanese manufacturers without going through government channels. With each reparations settlement was signed simultaneously an agreement on economic co-operation between Japan and the claimant country. As a result, reparations agreements have contributed directly to general economic co-operation as well as trade relations.

As an active participant in the United Nations Technical Assistance Program, the Colombo Plan, the United Nations Economic Commission for Asia and the Far East, and the General Agreement on Tariffs and Trade, Japan is giving technical assistance to virtually every Asian country except Communist China and Korea. Japan's program of technical co-operation is being developed on three levels, namely technical co-operation, capital investment in joint stock companies, and participation in development projects. In exchange for exports and services Japan obtains desperately needed industrial raw materials. Her activities, however, are not confined to South and Southeast Asia; they are being extended to the Middle East, Africa, and Latin America.

During 1959 Japan made a bid for Sumatra oil through a program of rehabilitating and expanding petroleum production with a $50 million private loan to Permina, the Indonesian government-owned oil company.[111] The project was conceived by Japanese businessmen as part of the government's over-all policy of maintaining national prosperity by keeping the Asian economy revolving with Japan as its hub. In Alaska, a Japanese company was operating a pulp mill at Sitka, while another concern and the Jewel Ridge Company of Virginia were planning to mine a 15,000-acre deposit of low grade coal on the Bering River under a trade agreement with the United

[111] *New York Times*, August 16, 1959.

States which permitted exploration of Alaska's resources.[112] In Africa a Japanese firm, Shimura Kako Chemical Products Company, together with Anglovaal, the owner of a nickel mine in Southern Rhodesia, signed an agreement to build as a joint enterprise a million-pound-sterling nickel smelting and refining plant at Bindura, the entire output of which is to be exported to Japan. In October representatives of the Nippon Mining Company arrived to study Rhodesia's copper industry with a possible view to Japanese investment.

Japan can never again aspire to the position of the world's third greatest naval power. But 1959 found her well on her way to regaining the position of the world's third maritime power. While the spectacular economic recovery of 1956-1957 was marred by the recession that followed in 1958, prosperity again returned the following year as production reached a new high, and sights were raised so that Japan hoped to be the world's third-ranking producer of steel in a matter of a few years. The trade balance for 1959 was favorable, and for the first time trade with the United States showed a favorable balance for Japan, but this was due to Japan's import restrictions. The result of this prosperity was a foreign exchange balance of $1,250,000,000 at the end of the third quarter of 1959.[113]

In his policy address at the reopening of the Diet in late January, Foreign Minister Fujiyama reiterated his hope that world trade would be liberalized by removal of trade barriers and discriminatory practices. While strongly asserting that Japan could never tolerate infiltration of international communism, he stated that she did not want to ignore or neglect friendly relations with communist countries. In his view there should naturally be such trade between Communist China and Japan as would be mutually beneficial and could be carried on despite absence of formal diplomatic relations. Japan therefore would maintain and promote peaceful relations with the communist nations in hope that this would contribute toward easing of East-West tensions.

The United States from the beginning had strongly opposed any Japanese effort to develop unrestricted trade with Communist China. While the Soviet Union and Red China waged economic offensives not so much for economic gains as for political advantage, there was no way to ascertain in advance to what extent Japan could trade with-

[112] *Ibid.*, August 21, 1959.
[113] *Ibid.*, October 18, 1959.

out gravely jeopardizing her own as well as American political, economic, and security interests. Pronouncements of Japanese leaders have at times appeared to be both contradictory and ambivalent in their attitude toward relations with China. Diplomatically, they have not shown great eagerness to establish formal relations, perhaps out of deference to American policy. In the matter of trade relations, however, Japanese businessmen have shown a keen interest in increasing the volume of trade. Japan's trade with Communist China is one of the difficult problems of American-Japanese relations, which will require a thorough airing and exchange of views and a careful weighing of advantages and disadvantages as well as risks involved before a mutually satisfactory decision can be reached.

The main preoccupation of American policy in 1959 was with the problem of security with special reference to Japan's economic well-being. In this effort to integrate defensive strength with economic development, the governments of the United States and Japan were harassed continuously by the persistent and vigorous propaganda of the Soviet Union and Communist China. No sooner had the year 1959 opened than the United States announced a reduction in Japan's share of the cost of maintaining forces during the fiscal year of 1959.[114] Shortly thereafter, in a move to place mutual defense activities on a basis of partnership, the United States naval base at Yokosuka was opened for joint use by the Maritime Defense Force. After several years of encouragement as well as prodding on the part of the United States, Japan's defense spending for fiscal 1959 reached a total of $426,850,000, which was equivalent to 10 per cent of the national budget and 1.7 per cent of the national income. The total expenditure remained considerably below what the United States would like to see; yet it represented the largest defense outlay since the peace treaty.[115]

An unusually high degree of collaboration had been achieved by spring, as could be seen in the foreign minister's reply to the Soviet warning that presence of American troops in Japan was an open invitation to a nuclear attack. Fujiyama bluntly stated that any attack on American troops would be regarded as an attack on Japan.[116]

Prime Minister Khrushchev in April, 1959, urged Japan to stop

[114] *Ibid.*, January 1, 1959.
[115] *Ibid.*, February 11, 1959.
[116] *Ibid.*, March 5, 1959.

being a "military springboard" for the United States and adopt a neutralist policy.[117] Less than two weeks later, the Soviet Union again called on Japan to take a neutral stand, and warned her against permitting nuclear bases to the United States. It offered as an alternative to the security treaty under discussion its own version of a "collective security" which would include the Soviet Union, Communist China, the United States, Japan, and other Asian nations.[118] It was quite evident that this move was to drive a wedge between the United States and Japan in an effort to wreck the existing security treaty. The Cabinet promptly rejected the Soviet demand for neutrality and repudiation of the security treaty and charged the Soviets with meddling in Japan's internal affairs.[119]

What had upset Washington policy makers in March was the decision of the Tokyo District Court that the presence of American troops and bases in Japan was a violation of Article 9 of the Constitution.[120] This court ruling, which was hailed by the Soviet ambassador as well as the Socialists, was reviewed by the Supreme Court beginning in early September. On December 16, 1959, it reversed the lower court decision, ruling unanimously that the Constitution permitted military forces for self-defense and that the presence of American troops in no way violated the Constitution.[121]

Negotiations for a new security treaty, which were begun in 1958, were carried on during most of 1959. Japan naturally wanted a larger voice in deciding mutual defense matters and the United States acceded to most of her wishes. In October, 1959, Chou En-lai declared that the American-Japanese Security Treaty was a threat to Communist China.[122] Concerted efforts of the Soviet Union and Communist China to disrupt negotiations, however, came to naught. In December, Washington disclosed that a new security treaty, the result of a new look at American-Japanese relations from the point of view of two equals and friends, was ready and would be signed in January, 1960.[123] The treaty was signed in Washington on January 19.

[117] *Ibid.*, April 21, 1959.
[118] *Ibid.*, May 5, 1959.
[119] *Ibid.*, May 16, 1959.
[120] *Ibid.*, March 30, 1959.
[121] *Ibid.*, December 17, 1959.
[122] *Ibid.*, October 6, 1959.
[123] *Ibid.*, December 11, 1959, and January 20, 1960.

Nothing since their admission to the United Nations heartened the Japanese people more than the selection of Tokyo, in August, 1959, as the site of the 1964 World Olympic Games, especially since this would be the first time that the games would be held in Asia. This decision was viewed as an expression of the confidence in Japan's new role in the postwar world. This symbolized to the Japanese the final emergence from the disaster of war to a well-earned and honored place among the world's respected nations and as a recognized leader in Asia. It gave the Japanese a heightened sense of belonging in the world community.

American policy toward Japan, as in other parts of Asia, one may conclude, is a segment of the over-all policy of protecting and promoting the welfare of the American people.[124] As such, its objective is to counter the communist plan for dominating and controlling Asia as a prelude to world domination. To achieve this, the United States must not merely offset the effects of the communist economic and propaganda offensive but seize the initiative and take steps to win over the peoples of free Asia. The United States and the free world can win out in the end only by helping develop the resources and raising the standard of living in Asia to such a level that the Asians will have something worth defending. Washington is aware that such a program cannot possibly succeed without the active participation of Japan.

As a result of long experience of over a century, Japan is in a uniquely advantageous position to introduce Western ideas and techniques to Asian countries. She is the only Asian country which has actually looked to the West for ideas and techniques to improve herself and which voluntarily undertook a carefully planned program of modernization. Japan is also the only Asian nation which has not been subjected to Western colonialism. Consequently she has not developed any deep-rooted antipathy toward the West as in the case of most of the newly independent nations of Asia. She is so Westernized, especially in terms of industrial achievements, that she must be grouped with the economically advanced nations of the West and not with Asian nations. Yet her traditional way of life and system of values make her unmistakably Oriental and more sym-

[124] Robert D. Murphy, "Our Policies in Asia," address before the Foreign Policy Association of Pittsburgh, May 5, 1955. *Bulletin*, 32 (May 23, 1955), 835-40.

pathetic toward other Asians and their problems. Japan is thus in a position to serve as link between the Orient and Occident and even as an intermediary.

In the years immediately ahead, American policy toward Japan faces a test. The years since the Second World War have been on balance very successful for the United States. Even though the ambitious program to democratize Japan was not given a full opportunity, many of the innovations introduced by the United States have helped Japan's domestic and international development. In the broad area of international economic co-operation, however, American policy toward Japan will soon face its most severe test, and its success will be determined largely by adjustments in economic thinking and planning at home.

8: UNITED STATES POLICY IN AFRICA SOUTH OF THE SAHARA

J. Gus Liebenow

For students of American foreign policy the vast region of Africa which lies south of the Sahara Desert remains largely the "Dark Continent." As recently as 1956 a survey by three competent scholars of the first postwar decade of American diplomacy dismissed this area in several sentences and a solitary footnote. A more charitable study issued two years earlier made the point that with most of Africa "still firmly under European colonial rule, the United States has few direct responsibilities there, nor is the region one of rapidly developing crises." [1] One might well have challenged this appraisal of the tranquility in Africa and the stability of colonial rule, particularly in view of the then current Mau Mau emergency in Kenya and the growing success of the nationalist movement in Ghana. Nevertheless, the statement does provide us with a fairly accurate assessment of the importance American officials attached to events in sub-Saharan Africa during the years immediately following the Second World War. This was a region relatively marginal to our over-all global strategy. It appeared to be an island of calm in a sea of troubles. It was a calm, however, that was to be rudely broken in the next few years. By 1960 the American government found itself compelled to tread unfamiliar ways and to be actively and directly concerned with the everyday affairs of a continent that had so long been regarded as remote and mysterious.

[1] William Reitzel, Morton A. Kaplan, and Constance G. Coblenz, *United States Foreign Policy, 1945-1955* (Washington, 1956); Brookings Institution, *Major Problems of United States Foreign Policy, 1954* (Washington, 1954), p. 289.

THE ROOTS OF AFRICAN-AMERICAN RELATIONS

SLAVERY, THE SLAVE TRADE, AND ITS AFTERMATH

During the first seven decades of our existence as a nation, and indeed during practically the whole of the colonial period, American relations with sub-Saharan Africa were dominated by the institution of slavery and its consequences. It was during this long period that the ancestors of more than a tenth of our present citizenry participated in one of the least romanticized waves of immigration adding to the American melting pot. Starting with a small boatload of slaves arriving the year before the *Mayflower*, the traffic increased steadily. By the last half of the 18th century it attained an estimated annual rate of 100,000 persons. Private fortunes were built and even great institutions of learning founded upon the profits from this trade in human cargo.

Official involvement of either the state or federal governments in foreign affairs as a consequence of the slave trade was minimal prior to 1807. It was that year which saw both the United States and Great Britain declaring the traffic illegal. The former, however, refused to make common cause with the British in suppressing this trade. On the contrary, the American government lodged numerous protests against the British practice of search and seizure of American vessels suspected of transporting slaves from West Africa to Cuba, Brazil, and even to the United States itself. It was not until the Civil War, when British sympathies for the Northern cause were being sought, that the Federal Government agreed to co-operate with Her Majesty's Government in suppressing slavery at its source.[2]

Slavery and the West African slave trade did provide the American government with one very direct and sustained relationship with the African continent proper. This came through the establishment of the colony of Liberia as a refuge for more than 15,000 freed American slaves and over 5,000 Africans who had been taken from American slaving ships intercepted in transit. Although private groups such as the American Colonization Society were primarily responsible for most of the problems of resettlement, the United States government and prominent American officials—President Monroe, for example—helped the ex-slaves establish a government modeled along American

[2] Richard W. Van Alstyne, *American Diplomacy in Action* (Stanford, 1944), pp. 438-48.

lines. On various occasions during the century from 1819 to 1919 American military forces defended the "Americo-Liberians" against attack from the Kru and other indigenous tribal groups of that area. Despite the delay from 1847 to 1862 in granting official recognition to the Liberian Republic, we had stated on a number of occasions both during and after this period that we were opposed to the partition of Liberia by the European colonial powers. More recently we indicated that our objections extended equally to Liberia's being placed under the League of Nations mandates system. The United States Government, both directly and through encouragement given to private American bankers, the Firestone Company, and others, found itself involved in assisting the Liberian government in maintaining its financial stability and implementing programs of economic development.[3]

Perhaps an even more obvious foreign policy implication of the slave trade was that it left the American nation with a multiracial complexion. The effects of this situation, however, were long in being realized. Unlike other immigrants, the American Negro during the period of slavery and during most of the era since emancipation found himself incapable of, or uninterested in, influencing United States foreign policy with respect to his country of origin. Until quite recently many middle-class American Negroes regarded the emphasis upon their African heritage as a badge of inferiority. It was partly for this reason that the "back to Africa" movement sponsored by Marcus Garvey during the present century failed so markedly in its objectives.[4]

It has been largely since the Second World War that our multiracial composition has been a significant factor in American diplomacy. One notable exception can be found in the fact that many American Negro colleges and universities were prepared to open their doors to African students. Lincoln, Howard, and other institutions have a remarkable share of alumni among Africa's current crop of political leaders. Moreover, these institutions kept alive the scholarly interest in African affairs during the long period of general disinterest on the part of other academic institutions. Since the war the positive aspect of our multiracial heritage has been manifest in

[3] Raymond L. Buell, *Liberia: A Century of Survival, 1847-1947* (Philadelphia, 1947), pp. 20-47.

[4] E. Franklin Frazier, *Race and Culture Contacts in the Modern World* (New York, 1957), pp. 299-300.

the recognition by both the Truman and Eisenhower administrations that Negro Americans can serve as "bridges of understanding" between the United States and the increasingly race-conscious peoples of Africa. The role played by Dr. Ralph Bunche in the United Nations, the presence of Congressman Diggs at the Ghana independence festivities, and the recent appointment of John Howard Morrow as ambassador to Guinea may be cited as evidence here. There is also the negative side of our multiracial heritage as it bears upon American diplomacy. It is difficult to estimate the actual effect abroad of interracial strife in America; nevertheless, it is evident that major as well as insignificant incidents are given full coverage in the press of Ghana, Guinea, and even the dependent territories of Africa. Our domestic situation has often made it difficult for our officials to take a forthright stand in the United Nations General Assembly on such issues as *apartheid* in the Union of South Africa. It has also made it politically embarrassing for some African nationalist leaders to espouse openly their friendship for the United States.

Anti-Colonialism

While the West Coast slave trade dominated African-American relations during the first half of the 19th century, it was concern with the Arab slave caravans in central and eastern Africa that found the United States Government temporarily abandoning its traditional hemispheric isolation during the latter half of that century. President Arthur's Secretary of State, Frederick T. Frelinghuysen, committed the United States to participation in the Berlin Conference of 1885, which had been called to deal with various problems in the Congo Basin. American interests were partly humanitarian, partly commercial, and partly based upon our long-standing opposition to colonialism. The influence of the American delegation is registered in the acceptance by the European powers of provisions for the outlawing of slavery and the slave trade, the maintenance of the open door principle with respect to economic relations, the observance of freedom of religion, and the recognition of international responsibilities by the colonial government, which in this case was King Leopold II's International Association of the Congo. Although the United States delegation signed the General Act, domestic press reaction to our participation in the conference was hostile. Arthur's successor, Grover Cleveland, did not even bother to submit the treaty to the Senate for ratification. Secretary of State Bayard stated that the United

States declined "to join in the responsible political engagements in so remote and undefined a region as that of the Congo Basin." [5]

The principles that the Americans insisted upon at Berlin in 1885 became the substance of our program when once more the United States found itself in a position of "disposing" with respect to dependent Africa. The popularity of Woodrow Wilson's Fourteen Points was partly based upon the provision against outright annexation of colonies. Wilson's statement, consequently, forced the British, French, Belgians, and South Africans to modify the character of their claims to the former German colonies of Tanganyika, Togo, Cameroons, Ruanda-Urundi, and Southwest Africa. The establishment of a mandates system under the League of Nations, with its provision for the open door and limited machinery for international accountability and control, was the price Wilson insisted upon prior to the division of the colonial spoils.[6] Repeating the pattern of the Berlin Conference, however, the United States not only rejected the notion of accepting direct responsibility for the administration of the Cameroons or any other mandate territory, but the Senate rejected the Treaty of Versailles itself. Thus the government of the United States divested itself of any responsibility for supervising the operation of the mandates system.

The fragility of our traditional anti-colonialism when applied to sub-Saharan Africa was even more effectively demonstrated in the Italo-Ethiopian crisis of May, 1935. Hoping to wash our hands of any attempts to forestall or reverse the Italian invasion, Congress in August of 1935 hurriedly passed a neutrality act. The Act provided that the sale or transporting of arms to *either* of the belligerents would be unlawful whenever the president issued a proclamation establishing the existence of war in any part of the globe.[7]

By 1941 the government of the United States had once more shifted to the principles of Frelinghuysen and Wilson. At the famous Atlantic Charter meeting of Roosevelt and Churchill, the American government again went on record in support of self-determination of all peoples. This decision was given concrete form in our support

[5] Philip Marshall Brown, "Frederick T. Frelinghuysen," in Samuel Flagg Bemis, ed., *The American Secretaries of State and Their Diplomacy*, 10 vols. (New York, 1928), VIII, 32-34.

[6] Quincy Wright, *Mandates under the League of Nations* (Chicago, 1930), pp. 24-64.

[7] Elizabeth P. MacCallum, *Rivalries in Ethiopia* (Boston, 1935), pp. 56-58.

of the establishment of the United Nations Trusteeship System and through our insistence at San Francisco in 1945 that the Charter's provisions be applied broadly to all non-self-governing territories.

ECONOMIC INTERESTS

With the exception of the slave trade, American commercial interests in Africa south of the Sahara were both limited and sporadic during the first century and a half of our national existence. One interesting and often neglected chapter in our history, however, is the thriving trade in ivory, hides, and other products that New England merchants did with the Arabs of Zanzibar during the zenith of the Yankee clipper ships. The United States secured a consular agreement with the sultan of Zanzibar in 1833—two decades before the British were able to do the same. As late as 1850 half of the ships calling at the port of Zanzibar were under the American flag, and over a million dollars of Massachusetts sheeting was sold annually.[8] So popular was this trade that the word "amerikani" has been absorbed into the Swahili language as the term for the cheaper grade of calico. There were other cases of African-American trading relations in this early period, but they were an insignificant factor in our total world trade picture. On the eve of the Second World War our total direct annual imports from all Africa were around $50 million, which was approximately two per cent of our total. Even adding the indirect imports of African commodities which had been processed in Europe, the total was still less than four per cent. American exports to Africa in that period only slightly exceeded $100 million in value.

A similar situation prevailed with respect to American investments in Africa prior to the Second World War. It constituted not only an inconsequential fragment of our total investment picture, but it accounted for less than three per cent of the $6 billion of all foreign investment in sub-Saharan Africa.[9] The bulk of America's $160 million share in investment was concentrated upon the mining industries of the Union of South Africa and the various operations of the Firestone Company in Liberia. Firestone has been concerned not only with rubber production. It has also developed roads, com-

[8] Raymond L. Buell, *Native Problem in Africa*, 2 vols. (New York, 1928), I, 260.

[9] Andrew M. Kamarck, "The African Economy and International Trade," in American Assembly, *The United States and Africa* (New York, 1958), pp. 17-18.

munications, and auxiliary industries in that country. The company has been sharply criticized for its wage policies, its undue influence over the Bank of Monrovia in the past, and its land acquisitions. It must also be recognized, however, that Firestone has done much by way of providing employment for Liberians, stimulating the growth of small businesses, and providing revenues for the Liberian government's education, health, and development programs.[10] Outside of Liberia and the Union of South Africa, American investors found the lack of facilities, health problems, and the hostility of colonial governments constituting barriers to attractive investment possibilities.

Humanitarian and Philanthropic Interests

Christian missionaries, both Protestant and Roman Catholic, have been engaged in religious and humanitarian endeavors in Africa since the early years of the 19th century. Inevitably, the greatest concentration of effort was in Liberia, where the American official contact has been most direct. Americans were active in other areas, and their efforts were particularly significant in the Union, Nigeria, and German East Africa. There were some instances of official resistance to American—and particularly Protestant—missionary efforts in the Belgian Congo and parts of French Africa, but only the Portuguese seem to have been successful in effectively limiting their activities. Few of the American mission groups devoted themselves strictly to evangelism. Either as a means to conversion or in recognition of the fact that Christianity was a way of life that was displacing the tribal cultures, Christian missionaries have undertaken to provide schooling, medical care, new forms of economic activity, and other social and economic services. Until the Second World War and the various development schemes of the colonial governments the missionaries of all nationalities and faiths provided the lion's share of these services to Africans.

Secular societies and foundations in America were also concerned with educational and humanitarian problems in Africa. A commission operating under the auspices of the Phelps-Stokes Fund carried out a study of African education in the early 1920s.[11] Although the recom-

[10] Wayne C. Taylor, "The Firestone Operations in Liberia," in National Planning Association, *United States Business Performance Abroad, Case Study No. 5* (Washington, 1956), pp. 89-107.

[11] See T. Jesse Jones, *Education in Africa* (New York, 1922).

mendations were given little attention by the Belgian, Portuguese, or Liberian governments, they had a considerable effect upon British educational policies in Africa. Other organizations, such as the Rockefeller Foundation and the Carnegie Corporation, since the early 1930s have been sponsoring social research in the Union, French West Africa, the Congo, and most of the British dependencies. Moreover, the contribution made by the Rockefeller Foundation to the eradication and control of yellow fever and other tropical diseases has been of lasting value.[12]

Strategic Interest In Sub-Saharan Africa

The strategic significance of sub-Saharan Africa to the United States did not become apparent until the Second World War, and for the most part its value even then was only indirectly experienced. The fighting between the British and Italian forces in Ethiopia, Eritrea, and Somaliland, and the skirmishes between the Vichy and Free French forces in Equatorial and West Africa, were matters of history by the time the United States actively entered the war. But well before Pearl Harbor the ports on the Red Sea, the South African coast, and in West Africa were useful in the American effort to assist Britain and her allies short of war. Later, the American-constructed air bases at Dakar in French West Africa, Roberts Field in Liberia, and elsewhere, figured prominently in the Allied operations in North Africa, the Middle East, and Southeast Asia. Once again, our greatest attention was directed to Liberia, which President Franklin Roosevelt visited in 1943. There the United States trained and armed Liberian troops, built roads, helped finance and construct a modern port, and began to assist the government of that nation in tackling some of its more pressing problems of health and economic development. The strategic meaning of Liberia to the United Nations is revealed in the fact that it and Ceylon were the only two major suppliers of natural rubber after the fall of Southeast Asia to the Japanese. It was during this period as well that the strategic value of the Belgian Congo, the Rhodesias, Southwest Africa, and other mineral-producing areas became apparent to American officials.

[12] Lord Hailey, *An African Survey*, rev. 1956 (London, 1957), pp. 64, 1132, 288.

THE GROWTH IN UNOFFICIAL INTERESTS AND CONTACTS SINCE 1945

The Popularization of Africa

The growth of unofficial American concern with Africa south of the Sahara as well as the intensification of contacts between private citizens of both areas far outshadows developments at the official level in the postwar period. To Americans in 1945 Africa was still the land of Stanley and Livingstone, the Kimberly diamond mines, Kilimanjaro, and Frank Buck. The enlightened public was limited for the most part to the returned missionary, the serviceman who had been stationed in Accra or who had witnessed the courage of Nigerian troops in Burma, the official of the Firestone Company, the New York cocoa importer, and the rare scholar such as Raymond Buell, Melville Herskovits, or Rayford Logan, who examined African affairs with a more critical eye. There were, of course, other Americans who had learned of Africa through their conversations with that small but highly select group of young Africans who came to study in the United States. It was a group whose ranks included Nkrumah of Ghana, Hastings Banda of Nyasaland, Azikiwe of Nigeria, Peter Koinange of Kenya, and Kalibala of Uganda.

The expansion of popular American concern since the Second World War has been evidenced in many ways. The general public has truly become Africa-conscious as a result of the increased attention by the daily press to such varied events as nationalist riots in Leopoldville, the construction of Kariba Dam in the Rhodesias, the work of Albert Schweitzer in Lambaréné, and the visit to Chicago of barechested dancers from Guinea. Television, too, has brought the daily life of Africa into the American living room. Whole issues of *Atlantic Monthly*, *Life*, and *Holiday* have gone beyond mere travelogue and attempted to deal seriously with African politics, literature, art, and archaeology. Book clubs, the cinema, and the legitimate stage have each found a wide popular appeal in African themes and settings during the past two decades.

Often this popular enthusiasm is superficial, and its rapid dissipation means that it has little direct bearing upon the formulation of American policies with respect to Africa. Nor does it affect African policies with respect to us. We must recognize, however, that this diffuse enthusiasm does establish a climate wherein the American official finds a more receptive—and perhaps a more enlightened—audience for his policies and programs. Increasingly, too, this enthusiasm is being channeled into activity that genuinely enhances American understanding of African problems and African-American relations. Examples of this activity can be found in the growing number of African lecture and discussion series conducted by church groups, the League of Women Voters, the Council of World Affairs, the Kiwanis clubs, and other civic and philanthropic groups. Among these discussion series have been regional, state, and local gatherings of scholars, missionaries, businessmen, and officials, sponsored by the American Assembly following its initial conference at Arden House in 1958.

This popular enthusiasm also finds positive expression in devices for increasing contacts between Americans and Africans. The Rotary International, for example, has established a program of exchange visits between African and American youths. Educational summer tours of Africa have been conducted during the past few years by Dr. Gwendolen Carter and other specialists in African affairs. And certainly not to be overlooked are the ties being established between American and African labor union leaders. One of the most outstanding events in this regard was the $35,000 given by the AFL-CIO to assist Tom Mboya in the construction of a trade union headquarters in Nairobi.

Missionary Interests

Perhaps the most explicit as well as the most persistent unofficial American interest in Africa has been that of the Christian missionaries. Their endeavors in the fields of education, health, and economic development have intensified since the Second World War despite the fact that colonial and nationalist governments have been assuming an increasingly larger proportion of the burden. The American missionary effort in sub-Saharan Africa has more of a Protestant than a Roman Catholic complexion. Roughly 80 per cent of the estimated $30 million spent through American mission channels and the same percentage of the Americans engaged in missionary activity in 1958 were Protestant. The high value the latter group places upon this region is evidenced in the fact that 30 per cent of its world missionary effort is directed to Africa.

In terms of "national credit," it is difficult to evaluate the effect upon African-American relations of American priests and Sisters, working in behalf of the universal Church. National identity is subordinated, and in any case the Americans account for less than two per cent of the Catholic missionary contingent in Africa. Although American Protestants constitute a larger proportion among their co-religionists (18 per cent), they are distributed among 29 denominations.[13] Inasmuch as each of these denominations differs with respect to creed and also social, economic, and political doctrine, the Protestants present a highly diverse—and often contradictory—picture of America. In many instances, moreover, the high material standard of living enjoyed by certain American Protestant missionaries alienates them from the very people they are sent out to serve.

Educational and Scholarly Interests

The most remarkable expansion in African-American contacts has come through the exchange of students, teachers, and research scholars between the two continents. From a mere handful of African students in America before the war, the number rose steadily, reaching a figure in excess of 1,100 in 1959. African students can be found in both small colleges and large universities, in widely dispersed geographic areas, and involved in studying engineering, agriculture, political science, library administration, and a host of other subjects. The African students still constitute only slightly more than two per cent of all foreign students in America, and they come largely from Liberia and British Commonwealth states or dependencies.[14] Rapidly, however, their numbers and geographic diversity appear to be increasing. In some instances the expenses of these students have been paid by the American government under Fulbright, ICA, and other assistance programs. The majority have been subsidized in one way or another by churches and other private groups such as the Carnegie Corporation, the African-American Institute, and the African-American Student Foundation. The last named is an organization formed by a group of American Negro entertainers who have become interested in African affairs. This is but one of many signs that American

[13] Rupert Emerson, "The Character of American Interests in Africa," in American Assembly, *op. cit.*, p. 21; US Senate, Committee on Foreign Relations, 86th Cong., 1st Sess., *United States Foreign Policy Study,* No. 4: Africa (October 23, 1959), pp. 43-44.

[14] US Senate, Committee on Foreign Relations, *op. cit.*, p. 46.

Negroes are more and more becoming involved in promoting African-American relations.

The reverse tide, namely American students going to Africa, has been limited largely to graduate and post-graduate research, although some undergraduates have gone to the Union of South Africa for study under the Fulbright Program. Private agencies such as the Ford Foundation, the Social Science Research Council, and the Carnegie Corporation have been among supporters of advanced studies. Excluding persons sent to sub-Saharan Africa under ICA or other governmental programs having only incidental educational or training aspects for the American participants, the number of American students or research scholars who have gone to that area since 1945 probably does not exceed a thousand. Our scholar exchange has also been limited geographically. By virtue of language facility and the absence of political and social restrictions upon American students, our greatest contacts have been with Liberia and other English-speaking areas.[15]

Direct American assistance to educational endeavors in Africa has also been on the rise. Reference has already been made to the increase in staff of missionary schools during the postwar period. Recently a highly promising program was launched by the African-American Institute to recruit American teachers for employment in secondary schools in Ghana, Nigeria, and other parts of Africa. A number of American universities, moreover, have now "extended their campuses" to Africa as a result of their participation in ICA and other United States government programs. Among the earliest efforts in this regard have been the assistance provided by Oklahoma State (Stillwater) to the Imperial Ethiopian College of Agricultural and Mechanical Arts, and the co-operation of the Prairie View branch of Texas A. and M. with the Liberian government in establishing the Booker T. Washington Institute.[16] More recently inaugurated programs have been those of Michigan State University and Indiana University in Nigeria and of Earlham College in Kenya. In this same vein, mention should be made of the grants totalling $433 million made by the Ford Foundation in 1959 to Makerere University (Uganda), University College of Ibadan (Nigeria), the University College of Rhodesia and Nyasaland, and to the Government of North-

[15] *Ibid.*, pp. 65-66.

[16] *Bulletin*, 32 (February 28, 1955), 350; and 34 (April 9, 1956), 597.

ern Nigeria. In the same year various American business interests agreed to spend at least $1 million on preliminary work towards establishing a University of West Africa in Liberia.[17]

The interest of American scholars and American universities in African affairs has been reflected in other ways as well during the postwar period. The sporadic flowering of courses of African ethnology, politics, and geography in colleges throughout the country has its more systematic counterpart in the establishment of foundation-supported programs in African studies at such universities as Northwestern, Howard, Boston, Roosevelt, Johns Hopkins, Yale, Duquesne, California, and Columbia. The increase in scholarly attention given to African affairs is further reflected in the creation of an African Studies unit in the Library of Congress, and in the establishment in 1957 of the African Studies Association. The Association in 1960 had a membership of 236 academic fellows and 395 nonacademic and student associate members.[18]

Private Economic Interests

Compared to other private groups, American commercial and investment interests have been slower in responding to the new enthusiasm for Africa. In the long run, however, involvement of these interests may have the most important effect upon African-American relations. As far as trade is concerned American imports of diamonds, copper, coffee, cocoa, rubber, sisal, and other bulk commodities had risen in value to $585 million in 1955, which represented a tenfold increase over the prewar situation. Exports, on the other hand, of machinery, automobiles, textiles, chemicals, grain, and other commodities (valued at $507 million) increased only five times over the prewar situation.[19] The increase in commercial activity could be measured in relative as well as absolute terms, for Africa in 1955 accounted for five per cent of our total world trade picture. There has been a steady growth since 1945 in the number of firms in this country concerned with processing African raw materials and of United States shipping lines paying regular calls at African ports. With the easing of dollar restrictions after 1955, American auto-

[17] *African Studies Bulletin,* II (December, 1959), 43-44; and *Africa Special Report,* IV (May, 1959), 15.

[18] *African Studies Bulletin,* I (April, 1958), 1-20; III (March, 1960), 1-3, 28-40.

[19] Kamarck, *op. cit.,* pp. 118, 121.

mobile, tractor, and machinery companies began to find it profitable to establish agencies in Africa and compete with European sellers for the continent's markets.

A similar absolute and relative increase took place in the field of American private investment in Africa. By 1955 the figure had exceeded $1 billion, which represented a fivefold increase over 1939 and advanced Africa's share of total United States private overseas investment from 1 to 2.5 per cent. The bulk of this investment was still directed towards the extractive industries in two countries, the Union of South Africa and Liberia. In 1957 Liberia replaced the Union in order of importance to American investors. There was, however, some diversification of investment since the war. In Liberia, for example, the company launched by the late Secretary of State Stettinius began to develop iron deposits and agricultural commodities other than rubber, thereby diminishing Liberia's dependence upon a single crop. Geographic diversification was also evidenced in Henry J. Kaiser Industries' participation in the Volta River hydroelectric project in Ghana, Olin Mathieson Chemical Corporation's development of bauxite in Guinea, Bethlehem Steel Company's activities in the iron ore areas of Gabon, and the development of the petroleum deposits in the latter country by Socony Mobil.[20]

The increase in private American investment is the result of a complex of factors. In part it can be attributed to a better publicizing of opportunities by African governments and by groups in this country such as the Stanford Research Institute. Undoubtedly, too, the development of transportation, communication, marketing facilities, and labor skills have also to be taken into account. In certain areas companies have been encouraged by the American government to make investments. There are still many obstacles to massive injections of American capital. The possible instability of both colonial and nationalist regimes and the fear of nationalization of industries or manipulation of currency have certainly been barriers. Moreover, Canada, Europe, and Latin America are still regarded as more attractive areas for American investment.[21]

[20] *Foreign Policy Reports*, XXV (June, 1949), 70-71; and *Africa Special Report*, IV (March, 1959), 13; (April, 1959), 11; and (May, 1959), 10.

[21] Emerson, *op. cit.*, p. 18; and Bernard Blankenheimer, "Private Enterprise in Africa," in C. Grove Haines, ed., *Africa Today* (Baltimore, 1955) pp. 453-68.

THE GROWTH IN OFFICIAL CONTACTS AND INTERESTS SINCE 1945

In contrast to the growth in private American interests in Africa since the war, the government of the United States appeared to be less responsive to the dramatic changes taking place in sub-Saharan Africa. At the beginning of the postwar period this great region occupied only a marginal and vaguely defined position in our global strategy. When policies were developed concerning African areas or situations, we appeared to be regarding Africa as but one angle in a triangular and even rectangular relationship. We did not regard the situation as being important in itself or important because of its bearing on peculiarly American interests and problems. It was important, rather, because of its relationship to American military, political, or economic strategy in other quarters of the globe. Moreover, even in these limited spheres of concern, the United States attempted to achieve its objectives through intermediaries rather than by accepting direct responsibility for the formulation and execution of policies.

It is impossible to note the date at which American policies and programs with respect to Africa south of the Sahara underwent a change; nevertheless, the achievement of independence by Ghana in 1957 does serve as a convenient landmark in the gradual reorientation of our diplomacy in Africa. Probably no other event was quite as effective in communicating to American officials the fact that the tide of nationalism was about to sweep the continent of Africa. Moreover, the presence of Soviet officials at the independence celebrations in Accra provided the United States with a grim reminder that the failure of America to respond positively to African nationalist aspirations would encourage others to fill the vacuum. The message was received in 1957, but it was not until 1960 that it was clearly evident that the twin forces of nationalism and international communism had compelled the American government to discard its position of aloofness and to become more actively and directly concerned in developing relations with Africa.

This gradual alteration in the character of our concern with events in sub-Saharan Africa is clearly manifest in the various postwar reorganizations of the Department of State and in the multiplication of federal agencies concerned with affairs in that region. Prior to 1939 practically all problems relating to sub-Saharan Africa (with the exception of Liberia) were dealt with by the Bureau of European

Affairs. This applied even to our interests in the Union of South Africa. The growth of American involvement in the non-Western world during the war and the apparent gap in our knowledge with respect to Africa in particular prompted Secretary of State Cordell Hull to initiate some changes. In 1943 a separate Office of African Affairs was established and placed with the Bureau of Near Eastern, South Asian, and African Affairs. At the end of the war a further organizational improvement took place with the establishment of the Division of Research for Near East and Africa.[22]

It was not until 1956, however, that the growing importance of Africa was once more reflected in changes in the Department of State. That year saw the creation of the post of deputy assistant secretary of state for African Affairs within the Bureau of Near East, South Asian and African Affairs. At the same time recognition of the distinct character of problems and events north and south of the Sahara was evidenced in the division of the Office of African Affairs into two separate branches. Two years later, in 1958, Africa came fully into its own as far as geographic organization of the Department of State is concerned with the appointment of an assistant secretary of state for African Affairs. The bureau under his jurisdiction was divided into an Office of North African Affairs and a separate Office of Middle and Southern African Affairs.[23]

The Bureau of African Affairs has not been the only unit in the Department of State concerned with African problems in recent years. Other units include the Bureau of European Affairs, the Bureau of International Organization Affairs, the Bureau of Intelligence and Research, and the International Education Exchange Service of the Bureau of Public Affairs. Moreover, other agencies in Washington, such as the International Cooperation Agency (heir of ECA, MSA, TCA, and FOA), the United States Information Agency, the Department of Defense, the Department of Agriculture, and the Department of Health, Education and Welfare are concerned with African-American relations and the solution of African problems.[24]

[22] *Bulletin,* 16 (March 23, 1947), 556-59; and 39 (September 22, 1958), 475-76. South Africa continued to be the concern of the European Affairs desk until 1955.

[23] *Bulletin,* 35 (September 24, 1956), 497; and 39 (September 22, 1958), 475-76.

[24] Vernon McKay, "The African Operations of the United States Government Agencies," in American Assembly, *op. cit.*, p. 193.

American official representation in Africa has also undergone both quantitative and qualitative changes during the past two decades. Inasmuch as most of Africa has been under dependency rule, political relations of the United States with African territories have been conducted through the European capitals of the colonial authorities. Even with respect to the independent states, the minimal character of our political concern was measured by the fact that Pretoria, Monrovia, and Addis Ababa were not to be graced with anything higher than an American legation until several years after the war. In terms of official representation our greatest concerns seemed to be directed toward the safeguarding of interests of American nationals, reporting on commercial opportunities, and maintaining United States treaty rights in Africa. From 1939 to 1945 the number of consulates general, consulates, and agencies had grown from 9 to 16, and three fourths of these were in the dependent territories. Staff at the consular level had been increased from 17 to 43 during the same period. Counting diplomatic personnel, consular staff, and military attachés our total representation in sub-Saharan Africa in 1945 numbered less than 75, and this is a region having a population equal to that of the United States and over twice the land mass.

The overseas representation of the United States in sub-Saharan Africa has increased severalfold since 1945. By 1952 our three legations in independent states had been raised to embassy status, and by the end of 1959 the number of embassies had been increased to six, with every prospect that we will establish an embassy in each territory as it achieves its independence. Similarly our consular establishments by 1952 had grown to 17 and by the end of 1959 to 23, of which 18 were in dependent territories. The United States Information Agency, moreover, has maintained offices and libraries in 15 major African cities, and the ICA and the Foreign Agricultural Service of the Department of Agriculture each had seven contract operations in a total of 13 states or territories. The Department of Defense posted military attachés in the capitals of three countries. In terms of total diplomatic, consular, and military attaché personnel our representation had grown from 75 in 1945 to 118 in 1952, and to 262 in 1959. The last figure does not include the 297 employees of ICA working on contracts in Africa.[25]

The attempt of the American government to improve its sub-

[25] US Department of State, *Foreign Service List*, July 1, 1939; October 1, 1945; October 1, 1952; October, 1959.

Saharan representation in qualitative terms has also been evident. It has named to its highest African posts in the Department of State such men as Joseph Palmer II, William Rountree, and others who have had long diplomatic experience in dealing with the problems of that region. Even before Vice President Nixon's implied criticism of some of our diplomatic and consular personnel during his visit to Africa in 1957, the Department of State began to improve its recruitment policies and to take steps to make our representatives more effective.[26] In this regard frequent regional meetings of the heads of American missions are held in Africa to keep our diplomatic and consular staff better informed regarding the total context of African developments and of American foreign policy in that continent. Moreover, foreign service personnel are being urged to establish wider associations with African trade union officials, party leaders, editors, and other elements in the population not normally encountered in official circles. The Department of State is now taking advantage of the area studies and language programs of American universities to prepare foreign service personnel for their assignments in Africa.

Official contacts between Americans and the leaders of African states and territories have intensified in still another way that shows every sign of expanding geometrically in this age of personal diplomacy. Reference here is made to the growth in exchange of official visits. Beginning with the wartime call of President Roosevelt to Monrovia and the return visit by President Barclay to the United States, both Washington and the capital cities of Africa have been putting out the flags for exchange visitors. The most publicized of American official and semiofficial tours of Africa have been those of Secretary of State Stettinius, Vice President Nixon, and Governor Adlai Stevenson. Even Nixon's most partisan critics acknowledge that his visit in 1957 was highly successful in terms of bringing the image of emergent Africa into sharp focus for Americans in the postwar period.

The roster of African visitors to Washington is more extensive and includes President Tubman of Liberia, Emperor Haile Selassie of Ethiopia, Prime Minister Nkrumah of Ghana, President Sékou Touré of Guinea, Sir Roy Welensky of the Federation of Rhodesia and Nyasaland, and Dr. Nnamdi Azikiwe of Eastern Nigeria. The list also includes a number of highly influential unofficial guests such

[26] *Bulletin*, 36 (April 22, 1957), 636-39.

as Tom Mboya of Kenya. The immediate results of these visits are not always evident. They are important sometimes in securing American financial backing for development projects in Africa, establishing exchange scholarship programs, or simply clarifying divergent national points of view. On occasion, they may have adverse results with respect to African-American relations. This almost was the case in 1957 when the refusal of a Delaware restaurant operator to serve a glass of orange juice to the finance minister of Ghana developed into an international incident.

Another way in which official African-American contacts have expanded is through our participation in international conferences and less formal conclaves. Inasmuch as the United States is not an African power and does not have dependencies there, we prefer—and are sometimes compelled—to limit our delegations to observers. This vague status does not prevent Americans from providing invaluable advice and assistance to the official delegates. Such was the case at the Conference on Central and Southern African Transport held at Johannesburg in 1950 and at the Brussels Meeting of the International Scientific Committee for Trypanosomiasis Research in 1958. Our reluctance to collaborate too closely with the colonial powers even on scientific matters is perhaps justified in view of the adverse publicity which greeted the formation of an Anglo-American research team several years ago. On the other hand, we have also been cautious—even to the point of being misunderstood by all parties—when it comes to our participation in such gatherings as the All-African Peoples Conference at Accra in 1958.

It has been in the United Nations, of course, that we have had the most intensive and sustained of these multilateral contacts with African and European leaders. Although issues relating to African dependencies or states have seldom been raised in the Security Council, the United States is required to cope with African problems in a very specific way as a result of its membership on the Trusteeship Council and in a more comprehensive manner as a consequence of its participation in the General Assembly, the Economic and Social Council, and the United Nations specialized agencies. Not only have we thus intensified our contacts with Africans and our concern with African situations, but we are required from time to time to take a public stand on issues we would rather see "brushed under the carpet." The policy of abstaining on key votes, we have come to realize, has not won us friends in either the colonial or anti-colonial camp.

Strategic Interests of the United States in Africa

With the exception of earlier activities in connection with the founding of Liberia, Allied military operations in sub-Saharan Africa during the Second World War provided the United States Government with its first experience of direct and sustained contact with the region. Military considerations, moreover, seemed to enjoy a higher priority than economic and political matters in our official thinking with respect to Africa immediately after the war. Nevertheless, even in this limited sphere of active interest the United States once more manifested that relatively indirect concern and minimal contact with African territories referred to previously.

During the struggle with the Axis powers the defense of Africa was a secondary consideration for the United States. The primary objective of American military forces stationed in Dakar, Khartoum, and other African bases was the maintenance of supply lines to Allied forces operating in Europe, North Africa, and Southeast Asia. Similarly, as the postwar conflict between the Soviet Union and the Western powers developed, the United States tended to evaluate the strategic location of Africa, the presence of natural resources, and other military factors in terms of their relevance to the defense and strengthening of our allies in Western Europe. Characteristically, too, the North Atlantic Treaty of 1949 exempted the United States from direct responsibilities for the defense of sub-Saharan Africa. Only in Liberia and Ethiopia did we assume direct responsibility in 1946 and 1951 respectively, for such matters as the training of troops or the construction of installations that might be used in case of war.[27] The indirect character of American strategic relations with Africa was dramatically underscored in 1951. In that year American, Ethiopian, and South African forces co-operated in the only military venture involving troops from both continents since the end of the Second World War, and this co-operation took place in South Korea—thousands of miles from either Africa or the United States!

The Suez crisis of 1956 once more demonstrated the relativity of

[27] *Bulletin*, 15 (September 29, 1946), 582-83; 24 (May 14, 1951), 151, 778; 27 (July 21, 1952), 105; 28 (June 1, 1953), 785; and 29 (October 17, 1955), 617.

our strategic interests in southern Africa. Our primary considerations were to keep the oil flowing to Western Europe and to restrict Soviet influence in the Middle East. The diplomatic bankruptcy, however, of our two principal NATO allies, Britain and France, compelled the United States to play a more direct role in military matters in northeastern Africa. Although the roving Ambassador, James P. Richards, largely failed in his efforts in 1957 to get the Sudanese and Ethiopian governments to subscribe to the Eisenhower Doctrine, the attempt did constitute a departure from our previous position of aloofness. There are indications, moreover, that as the European colonial powers withdraw or are ejected, the United States may be called upon to play a more direct role in the military affairs of sub-Saharan Africa as a whole. The case of Czechoslovakia supplying arms to Guinea in 1959 quite clearly demonstrates that if we fail to respond to an appeal for arms, the Soviet Union or one of its satellites will not be equally hesitant. It almost seems to be regarded as an affront to African leaders for the United States to question the uses to which these weapons will be put. The efforts of the American government in April, 1960, to keep Africa out of the arms race may well be resented as an attempt to limit African states to minor power status.

The one strategic factor that has consistently figured prominently in America's postwar plans has been the position of sub-Saharan Africa as a supplier of natural resources. Although lagging behind South America, this region has now replaced Southeast Asia as the second most important source of raw materials for American military and industrial needs. In the production of some commodities, such as industrial diamonds and cobalt, Africa enjoys a near monopoly. The Congo, Nigeria, and Southwest Africa provide the Western powers with most of their needs for uranium, germanium, vanadium, columbium, and other minerals so essential to the "jet" and "atomic" ages. Close to one fourth of the gold, manganese, phosphate, chromium, antimony, and platinum used in the United States and Western Europe is supplied through African production. Although the copper, tin, zinc, lead, oil, coal, iron, and asbestos industries are still in the developmental stage, they already serve as invaluable secondary sources to the NATO powers when war, industrial strife, political upheaval, and other crises sever contacts with the normal suppliers. Aside from strategic minerals, sub-Saharan Africa is a major producer of natural rubber, sisal, copra, pyrethrum, and other essential agricultural commodities. While it is true that many of these items can be substituted in an emergency or produced synthetically, they currently occupy an important role in the economic and social life of the United States and Western Europe.

The importance the American government attaches to the physical resources of Africa is revealed in such events as the joint American-British underwriting of the uranium industry in the Union of South Africa; the use of Economic Cooperation Administration funds to develop the cobalt industry in Northern Rhodesia and the Kyanite mines in Kenya; and the encouragement given to private American firms to develop the iron mines at Bomi Hill in Liberia.[28] The remarkable thing about Africa today is that it is still the "dark continent" insofar as concerns knowledge of its resources. As the potential becomes reality, America's concern will become all the greater. For there is not only the interest in seeing that the resources of Africa help fill American needs; the United States also hopes to see that these do not come under the control of those whom we regard as our adversaries.

Economic Interests of the American Government in Africa

The paucity of private commercial and investment interests of the United States in sub-Saharan Africa has been described. Apart from the securing of strategic resources, official American interests in the economic development of this region have been characterized by the same slight concern. During the period from 1945 to 1956 colonial and independent African governments received close to $72 million from the United States in the form of grants not requiring repayment. Although this is a considerable sum, it constituted less than 0.15 per cent of all such grants to foreign governments during the same decade. Similarly, the $343 million received by African territories and states in the form of loans from the Export-Import Bank and other overseas lending agencies of the federal government during the first ten years of the postwar period amounted to only 2.12 per cent of all foreign loans.[29]

In addition to American aid being relatively small, it was also concentrated largely upon the Union of South Africa and the Federation of Rhodesia and Nyasaland. These two units, together with Liberia and Ethiopia, were the only ones prepared to solicit United States aid

[28] *Bulletin*, 22 (June 19, 1950), 1002; and 24 (January 1, 1951), 28.
[29] Emerson, *op. cit.*, p. 17.

on a direct basis. Concentration upon the Union and the Rhodesias was perhaps natural in view of the relatively advanced level of industrial development in those countries. It had the undesired consequence, however, of making it appear that the United States was giving support to regimes advocating white supremacy. American aid, moreover, was regarded as a contribution to the technical superiority of European minorities, thereby delaying the achievement of nationalist objectives by the African majorities.

Direct American aid to dependent areas was much slower in developing. This stemmed largely from American officials taking into account the fears of our NATO allies that American technicians and other personnel might give uncritical and indiscriminate assistance to nationalist movements. There were suspicions, too, that American technicians might attempt to introduce advanced technological programs that would be too disruptive of African economic and social systems. Consequently, where assistance was provided under Economic Cooperation Administration, Point Four, or stockpiling program funds, it was agreed that the United States would, in the words of Assistant Secretary of State George McGhee in 1950, play "only a cooperative role with the administering powers" in developing the economic, social, and political status of Africans.[30]

While the United States *has* channeled aid to African dependencies indirectly through the colonial powers, it is possible that we have avoided identifying ourselves with British and French efforts to maintain their empires. In the process, however, we laid ourselves open to the charge of permitting the giving of higher priorities to the objectives of European reconstruction and Western defense than to the welfare of Africans and the development of viable economies in African territories. One cannot dispute the fact that the immediate postwar development of Africa did provide Western European states with the raw materials necessary for their industrial recovery. It was fiscally advantageous, too, in that it provided the colonial powers with dollar-earning exports while at the same time reducing their dependence upon purchases from the United States, Canada, and other dollar countries. Indeed, the dramatic recovery of Belgium after the war would stand as testimony to the truth of this statement. Similarly, much of our more recent aid under Mutual Security and International Cooperation Agency programs has been justified to both Congress and the American people on the grounds that it aids the short and

[30] *Bulletin*, 22 (June 19, 1950), 999-1003.

long run military objectives of the West. Thus, the construction of roads in Tanganyika, airfields in Ethiopia, and railroads in Mozambique facilitates the development and export of African strategic resources, and these installations may have future military importance to the United States.

While the charge can be substantiated that American economic interests in Africa are relevant largely to the achievement of political or military objectives elsewhere, the case can be overstated. It is true that the development of hydroelectric plants, roads, and telecommunication systems has provided more immediate benefits to European colonial officials and settlers. The long run achievement, however, of higher standards of living, better jobs, and other advantages to Africans should not be ignored. Moreover, in the case of numerous ICA projects, the immediate benefits received by Africans are more significant than the long run and often remote advantages to be realized by either the Europeans or the American government. In this category would belong the construction of a health clinic and medical training center in Ethiopia, the supplying of 2,000 volumes to the Kumasi Technical Institute in Ghana, the instruction provided to African peasant farmers by American advisers in Somalia and Kenya, and the encouragement given everywhere to the expansion of small retail and wholesale businesses, service trades, and raw-material processing industries.[31] Admittedly, the American government does hope that these smaller projects, as well as the more ambitious ones, will lead to the establishment of more diversified and stable economies, the growth of African middle classes, expansion of the notion of free enterprise and private ownership, and other developments that may serve as future bulwarks against the expansion of communism in sub-Saharan Africa.

In assessing the scope of American contributions to postwar African development, one should not leave out of consideration United States aid that has been channeled through the United Nations. The International Bank for Reconstruction and Development extended loans amounting to $548 million from 1950 to 1958 and over $100 million for the year 1958 alone.[32] Since the United States has subscribed to 40 per cent of the bank's shares (compared to an absence

[31] *Bulletin*, 24 (January 1, 1951), 27; 32 (February 7, 1955), 232; 32 (February 28, 1955), 350; 37 (July 15, 1957), 111; 37 (December 30, 1957), 1047; 39 (July 14, 1958), 86.

[32] *Africa Special Report*, III (July, 1958), 8-9.

of interest on the part of the Soviet Union), this contribution must be recognized as a further instrument in the achievement of United States economic objectives in Africa. United Nations development loans, technical assistance programs, and similar projects are financed to a considerable extent by the American government. Assistance through the United Nations results in the accomplishment of American objectives while at the same time avoiding the impression that we were attempting to re-establish Western imperialism under a new label. This auxiliary channel has permitted the United States to provide indirect aid to nations in cases where either they or we might be politically embarrassed by more direct transactions. We have not been prepared, however, to sacrifice the possible political advantages which might come through more direct bilateral agreements.

Political Interests: Anti-Colonialism

The equivocation that had been characteristic of our earlier stands on colonialism in Africa was again manifested in the period following the Second World War. During the military phase of the struggle we went on record against colonialism in such pronouncements as the Atlantic Charter and the Yalta Declaration. Then at the San Francisco Conference of 1945 the United States was one of the prime advocates of the Trusteeship System as an alternative to traditional colonial exploitation. We even gave support to the efforts of the Asian, Latin-American, and other delegations to broaden the language of the United Nations Charter to cover all non-self-governing territories. The zenith, however, of American anti-colonialism with respect to Africa came during the initial meetings of the Council of Foreign Ministers following the war. There we urged that the former Italian colonies of Eritrea, Somaliland, and Libya be placed under direct United Nations trusteeship administration rather than under single-power control.[33]

The credit that had been earned in the bank of anti-colonialism was quickly dissipated once the issues of the cold war began to take precedence over all other considerations. An early indicator of this trend came in 1948 during the communist bid for an electoral victory over the pro-Western government of Alcide de Gasperi. In anticipation of Soviet support for Italian colonial claims, the United States abandoned its earlier stand of opposition to the re-establishment of

[33] Vernon McKay, "International Trusteeship—Role of the United Nations in the Colonial World," *Foreign Policy Reports,* XXII (May 15, 1946), 65.

Italian authority in Somaliland. From this point onward, in the words of one critic, the United States, in formulating policy with respect to Africa,

> tended to opt in virtually all respects for the policies of the metropolitan powers, however modified and qualified in detail, and . . . subordinated its long-range interest in the autonomous development of the native population to short-range considerations of strategy and expediency.[34]

One reason the United States Government supported European colonial rule in Africa was that it kept this vast region out of the main stream of world politics. As Assistant Secretary of State George McGhee stated in 1950:

> In the light of the many critical problems which confront us . . . it is gratifying to be able to single out a region of 10 million square miles in which no significant inroads have been made by Communism, and to be able to characterize the area as relatively stable and secure.[35]

With this area thus insulated against crisis, American officials were left free to concentrate upon the more pressing problems of the cold war. We seemed convinced, moreover, that the level of military, political, and economic development in African dependencies made them woefully unprepared for self-government or independence. Hence the only real alternatives to colonial rule, so Secretary of State John Foster Dulles argued, were either exploitation by indigenous demagogues or a "captivity far worse than present dependence," *i.e.*, Soviet imperialism.[36] Inevitably a gain for the Soviet camp was a loss for the West in strategic terms if in no other. More positive grounds for American support of colonial rule were also presented. We made it clear that we regarded the postwar economic development of Africa as vital to European recovery and to the defense of Europe against Soviet aggression or subversion. So essential did we regard the European-African relationship that even where we eventually supported the achievement of self-government by an African territory, we urged that it keep its "traditional" ties with its former colonial masters.[37] We would thus seem to deny them the freedom of choice we our-

[34] Hans J. Morgenthau, "United States Policy toward Africa," in C. W. Stillman, ed., *Africa in the Modern World* (Chicago, 1955), p. 321.

[35] *Bulletin*, 22 (June 19, 1950), 999-1000.

[36] *Ibid.*, 25 (July 16, 1951), 97-101; 30 (February 8, 1954), 212.

[37] *Ibid.*, 37 (December 9, 1957), 931.

selves exercised after the American Revolution. Finally, very practical reasons could be found for this radical departure of the United States from its historic position of anti-colonialism. A muted voice on this issue was the price the senior partner in the NATO alliance had to pay for the co-operation of Britain, France, and Belgium in achieving more immediate objectives in the struggles with the communist states.

In view of the above, it should be no surprise to find recent secretaries of state and other high officials of the American government cautioning Africans not to regard immediate independence as a panacea for the ills of dependent peoples. The phraseology of American policy became one of support for "orderly transition from colonial to self-governing status," "eventual self-determination," and "evolutionary, but not revolutionary efforts on the part of African leaders." Instead of harsh criticism, the colonial powers were to be accorded "patient understanding" for their efforts in training African technicians and civil servants, establishing viable economies, providing social welfare benefits, and introducing stable political institutions prior to the granting of independence.[38]

Although the record reveals that the United States was in greater agreement with the anti-colonial states than with the colonial powers in the United Nations, nevertheless greater attention has been given to the instances in which we seemed to defer to the interests and policies of our NATO allies.[39] The Afro-Asian states emphasized such matters as our votes in the Trusteeship Council on the matter of establishing timetables for the independence of Tanganyika and on the question of the adequacy of French efforts in Cameroon. They pointed also to the various abstentions in the past on such racial issues as the question of *apartheid* and the treatment of Indians in the Union of South Africa. Less attention has been paid to the votes on the Southwest Africa mandate issue, on the elections in Togoland, and other matters where we cast our lot with the African, Asian, and other anti-colonial states in the United Nations.

This deference to the wishes of the colonial powers apparently extended not only to existing dependencies but to former colonial territories as well. British sensitivities with respect to Ghana appear

[38] *Ibid.*, 25 (July 16, 1951), 97-101; 29 (November 16, 1953), 655-65; 30 (February 8, 1954), 212; 34 (April 30, 1956), 717; 37 (December 9, 1957), 931; 39 (October 27, 1958), 642.

[39] US Senate, Committee on Foreign Relations, *op. cit.*, pp. 73-77.

to have been one of the factors that impeded the rapid development of direct economic and other ties between the United States and the former Gold Coast territory. Even more obvious was the month-long delay in our recognition of the Republic of Guinea following the severance of its political ties with the French Community in November, 1958. It was seven months from the latter date before we appointed an ambassador to this state, and a full ten months elapsed before we risked offending De Gaulle by discussing financial aid with President Sékou Touré. In the meantime, the Soviet government had provided assistance and dispatched large diplomatic and technical missions to Guinea.[40]

By 1959 it had become obvious that the United States could no longer adhere to a policy of implied, let alone explicit, support of European colonial rule. African nationalism had become a force with which we had to reckon. The fire of nationalism had been kindled long ago as a result of the activities of Christian missionaries, Western education, the introduction of new forms of economic enterprise, urbanization, and colonial rule itself. More fuel had been added as a result of the experiences of the Second World War, the colonial welfare and development schemes, and the constant assaults on colonialism made in the United Nations, the Afro-Asian Conference at Bandung in 1955, the All-African Peoples Conference at Accra in 1958, and the Monrovia Conference of Independent States in 1959. Perhaps the most important factors, however, were the initial concessions made to nationalism by the granting of independence to the Sudan (1956), Ghana (1957), and Guinea (1958).

To the surprise of American officials, colonial administrators, and African nationalists themselves, the smoldering embers of nationalist aspirations burst suddenly into a bright flame. During the 14 years following the defeat of the Axis, only the Sudan, Ghana, and Guinea had entered the ranks of new African states. The year 1960 alone is to witness the granting of independence to Cameroon, Togo, Somalia, Mali, Nigeria, the Malagasy Republic, Sierra Leone and most surprising of all—the former Belgian Congo. Immediate independence for any member of the French Community can be achieved by unilateral action of the state concerned. Difficult problems still must be resolved in the multiracial areas of Kenya and the Federation of the Rhodesias and Nyasaland. It seems apparent that African nationalism will triumph there in time. Even the Union of South Africa in the

[40] *Africa Special Report,* IV (May, 1959), 4; IV (October, 1959), 13, 16.

critical year of 1960 saw bloodshed as the white minority attempted to stem the "winds of change," to which Prime Minister Harold Macmillan so eloquently referred in his speech before the South African Parliament. Only Portuguese Guinea, Mozambique, and Angola appear to be insulated from the force of African nationalism. One would be rash, however, to predict that the insulation is anything more than temporary in character.

The emergence of a series of new African states has compelled the United States to re-evaluate all of its strategic, economic, and political policies and programs with respect to this continent. Obviously we have had to discard military planning based upon the assumptions of firm colonial power control and of passivity of African peoples toward the use of their territory and resources. We have had to be prepared to establish diplomatic and consular relations, negotiate trade and investment agreements, sign technical assistance or military assistance pacts, and engage in a host of other bilateral and multilateral transactions with the new nations of Africa. We have had to be prepared to speak out on the problems of racial discrimination in Kenya and elsewhere. In view of our previous history of minimal and indirect concern with sub-Saharan Africa, to do something we will in many cases have to act largely in ignorance or on the basis of fragmentary knowledge. If we are not willing to respond in some fashion, however, it is clear that the Soviet Union, India, and the United Arab Republic are willing to do so. It was with this thought that the Department of State broke with long-standing practice in March, 1960, and criticized the methods employed by South African police in suppressing demonstrations by African nationalists.[41]

In evaluating the significance of the new Africa in international politics, there is a tendency to overemphasize the many racial, tribal, linguistic, and religious differences that divide the 180 million people of the vast subcontinent. It is easy, too, to note that efforts at economic and political union of the new states—such as that proposed between Liberia, Ghana, and Guinea—have not moved much beyond the blueprint stage.[42] Anti-colonialism may well be the rather weak glue which binds these states together. Nevertheless, the African nations have indicated that they are prepared to make their way in the world, singly or in concert. Ties with former colonial authorities will remain or be severed, depending upon their convenience to the

[41] *New York Times*, March 23, 1960.

[42] *Ghana Today*, III (August 5, 1959), 1-2.

emergent state. There is a decided fascination with the neutralist philosophy of Nehru and Sukarno. Neutralism, however, does not mean isolationism, as it did in the American experience prior to the Second World War. The new African states have eagerly sought membership in the United Nations and have participated actively in the affairs of its principal organs and agencies. Indeed, the African Caucusing Group (which includes states both north and south of the Sahara) is already rivaling Latin America as the second largest block in the General Assembly. The group evidences a high degree of cohesion on colonial questions, human rights, economic co-operation, and other key issues.[43] The internationalist character of the African states is further evidenced by the looser associations established with Asian, Latin-American, and other states outside the framework of the United Nations. Neutralism does not apparently preclude Guinea, Ghana, and other African states from injecting themselves directly into the center of the East-West struggle by way of seeking economic, cultural, or military assistance from either of the great power camps.

Political Interests: Anti-communism

Nationalism has not been the only ideology which has forced the United States to re-evaluate its African policies. The abrupt termination of colonial rule has increased the prospects of another ideology, international communism, capitalizing upon the instability which comes as the emergent nations adjust to independence. In the estimation of Vice President Nixon, tropical Africa today occupies the same position in communist strategy that China occupied 25 years ago.[44]

Under colonial rule official contacts between Russian and African leaders were much more limited than those between Americans and Africans. The Soviet Union had no consulates in any of the dependent territories. Their diplomatic relations with the independent states were equally restricted. Liberia has long been reluctant to exchange diplomatic personnel with the Soviet Union, and the Soviet embassy in the Union of South Africa enjoyed only a short life in the immediate postwar period. Only Ethiopia had official Russian representation prior to achievement of independence by the Sudan, Ghana, and

[43] US Senate, Committee on Foreign Relations, *op. cit.*, pp. 76-77; *Africa Special Report*, IV (June, 1959), 13-14.

[44] *Bulletin*, 36 (April 22, 1957), 638.

Guinea. It might also be noted that although the USSR is a member of the United Nations Trusteeship Council, neither Russian nor other Eastern European officials have ever been selected as members of the visiting missions that make triennial tours of inspection in Tanganyika, Ruanda-Urundi, and other trust territories.

Unofficial communist or Soviet contacts with African leaders have been more numerous throughout the postwar period. Whether successful in their endeavors or not, British and French communists have been persistent in currying the favor of African students in London, Paris, and Cairo and have arranged lavish all-expense-paid trips to Russia for them. In 1957 over 550 African youths were brought to the World Youth Festival in Moscow.[45] Communists have infiltrated the ranks of African political parties in dependencies where such organizations are legal. The *Rassemblement Démocratique Africaine* in the Ivory Coast, for example, had a decided communist orientation during its formative years. Apparently there is still communist control of the *Parti de Union Camerounaise,* which has employed violence in turn against the French and the present African government.[46] In areas where manifestly political groups were banned, trade union organizations have served as convenient surrogates for spreading communist influence. In the Anglo-Egyptian Sudan the communists dominated the Sudan Workers Trade Union Federation and united peasants and workers into an effective nationalist group.[47]

In the Union of South Africa the extent of communist successes in winning adherents among African nationalists is difficult to assess. Unfortunately the situation is considerably clouded by the fact that the Suppression of Communism Act of 1950 is not directed strictly against members of the Communist Party or even Soviet sympathizers. It takes into its broad net leaders of any political, economic, or social movement that threatens to undermine the policies of *apartheid*.[48]

At an equal pace with the development of unofficial contacts between communists and colonial Africans, the Soviet Union has

[45] McKay, "The African Operations . . . ," in American Assembly, *op. cit.*, p. 75; *Bulletin*, 39 (October 27, 1958), 645.

[46] US Senate, Committee on Foreign Relations, *op. cit.*, pp. 29-30.

[47] Robert D. Baum, "Commentary" in Haines, ed., *op. cit.*, pp. 284-85.

[48] For a keen analysis of the operations of the Act, see Leo Kuper, *Passive Resistance in South Africa* (New Haven, 1957), especially pp. 47-71.

attempted to parade itself as the leading champion of colonial peoples in the postwar period. It has approached its role seriously, as the intensification of Soviet scholarly interests in African ethnography, economics, language, and other matters would seem to indicate.[49] The Soviet government has used its membership in the General Assembly and Trusteeship Council of the United Nations to full advantage in challenging the colonial powers' sins of omission and commission. The vigor of its attack contrasts sharply with the muted anti-colonialism adopted by the American government, which has avoided offending its NATO allies. Moreover, when convenient the USSR emphasizes its Asian heritage. It attempts to serve for African leaders as a model of a "non-Western" state that rose from the ranks of the "backward" nations to the councils of the mighty in a matter of decades. For a similar reason, African leaders do not share America's fervent distrust of Communist China. Events in Hungary, Tibet, and elsewhere have blurred the image of communism as the antithesis of colonialism, but the Soviet Union still enjoys a propaganda advantage over the United States.

As independence is achieved by the African states, the alliances struck between African nationalists and communists may be revealed as primarily marriages of convenience. In the Sudan, Communist Party control over the vital Sudan Railway Workers Union after independence ultimately resulted in a clash between it and the nationalist government of General Ibrahim Abboud. The conflict was resolved in 1958 with the jailing of the communist leaders and the banning of all trade union activities.[50] Dr. Nkrumah, during his trial in 1948, was charged by his British prosecutors with having had communist affiliations. There is no evidence, however, that communists have made important inroads in independent Ghana, despite the fact that Ghana carries on diplomatic relations with the Soviet Union. On the contrary, the prime minister has supported the International Confederation of Free Trade Unions as a counter movement to the communist-oriented World Federation of Trade Unions.

While the United States must avoid being complacent about the admitted designs of international communism, it should also avoid being alarmist. It must not regard every accrediting of diplomatic personnel, every signing of a trade or technical assistance agreement, and each negotiation leading to cultural and student exchange pro-

[49] *Africa Special Report,* II (October, 1957), 6-7; II (November, 1957), 11-12.
[50] *Ibid.,* IV (January, 1959), 12, 16; IV (February, 1959), 13.

grams between the USSR and an African state as a victory for communism and a defeat for the West. The American government was distressed by the announcement of a long-term credit agreement between Ethiopia and the Soviet Union following Emperor Haile Selassie's visit to Moscow in 1959. The loan of $100 million for industrialization far outstripped American investment efforts in that country.[51] The agreement is placed in proper perspective when it is noted that Ethiopia, since its liberation from Italian rule, has followed a complicated but rational policy of not letting any single power or bloc enjoy a preferred position in the development of its resources. A similar policy of diversification of foreign investment has been adopted by Ghana and Liberia. Even in the case of Guinea, where the Russian, Czech, and even Red Chinese have extensive economic interests and large technical missions, neither American nor other noncommunist investors have at this writing been excluded from the country. It is well to remember that the communist advances came largely after the French, American, and other Western governments had failed to respond in more positive terms to Sékou Touré's appeals for aid. The United States is learning that it must meet the Soviet challenge. This realization is evidenced by such things as the dramatic recommendation that $20 million of ICA funds be spent during 1960-1961 in improving education and training programs in African countries. On the other hand, one can point to the fact that under the Development Loan Fund, the $16 million recommended for all of tropical Africa in 1960 was approximately half the figure suggested for the island of Formosa alone.[52]

From the foregoing analysis it can be seen that the awareness of sub-Saharan Africa which has become evident in both official and private circles in America during the postwar period stands in sharp contrast to the lowly position which that region occupied in our thoughts and foreign policy planning during the first century and a half of our national existence. From a situation in which the interests of the United States in Africa were minimal, contingent upon events in other more important areas, and often handled by representatives of third parties, our concern today with the internal affairs of Africa has become immediate and daily growing in significance. There is

[51] *Ibid.*, IV (July, 1959), 6; IV (September, 1959), 10.

[52] US House of Representatives, 86th Cong., 2nd Sess., Committee on Foreign Affairs, Hearings, Mutual Security Act of 1960 (March 1-3, 1960), pp. 205-206, 276.

little reason, moreover, for anticipating that our concern will become less rather than more. The dynamics of African nationalism, the still unresolved problems of colonialism and multiracial conflict, the pressure of communist activities in that area, the numerical strength of the African bloc in the General Assembly, and the continued economic and strategic importance of Africa to the West make it highly improbable that this region will ever again become isolated from the main stream of world politics. In this light, the need for enlightened and imaginative American foreign policies and diplomatic activity becomes ever more manifest. Advances in this direction have, as we have indicated above, already been made. Much more, however, needs to be done. Without neglecting other areas and problems, the affairs of Africa must be given the attention they deserve and evaluated in terms of their direct impact upon African-American relations. It would seem to be evident, too, that the tendency of the past to rely on Britain, France, and others to do our bidding in Africa is not only a luxury we can ill afford; it constitutes in many instances a positive danger to the accomplishment of our national objectives. Finally, it would seem that only a concerted collaborative effort on the part of public and private agencies and individuals in America can close the chasm of ignorance which now separates us from the knowledge and understanding so essential to the formulation of effective foreign policies and programs.

Editor's note. Since the author of this essay left in June, 1960, for an extended study trip to Africa, a growth of US interests in African affairs has become manifest. The gaining of independence by the African members of the French Community was followed by the rapid increase in the number of US diplomatic posts and information centers in Africa. As of April, 1961, there were 25 US Embassies, 20 Consulate Generals and Consulates, and more than 40 USIA missions and other posts in African countries. President Eisenhower personally took the initiative in the General Assembly in September, 1960, when he proposed multilateral aid to Africa through the UN. Visits of leading American statesmen and officials to Africa, and US efforts in Africa through UNESCO and support for the UN Congo operations are signs of expanding American commitments to Africa. In March, 1961, Ambassador Adlai Stevenson put the US on record in the Security Council as being in favor of UN investigations of Portuguese rule in Angola. In similar cases in the past, the US has abstained from voting, choosing not to irritate a NATO ally.

9: UNITED STATES POLICY IN THE MIDDLE EAST

Robert H. Ferrell

It is still difficult today, in the 1960s, to realize that the Middle East should have any large meaning for American diplomacy, for until the end of the Second World War the relations of the United States with that area of the world did not amount to much. Trade by the United States with the lands around the Eastern Mediterranean and eastward to Iran, from Syria south to Saudi Arabia, has always been small. Emigration to America was virtually nonexistent, except for some Lebanese who for religious and economic reasons made the long journey to the United States. American visitors from time to time went to Palestine or Egypt, from piety or curiosity, but they were almost the only travelers save for a trickle of missionaries and educators. Many individuals in the United States learned about the Holy Land from their Bibles, scanning the strange pictures of oddly square houses set down on rounded hills. But beyond Biblical study, beyond contacts of tourists, missionaries, and teachers, American knowledge or concern did not go.

The Second World War brought the United States out of its hemispheric isolation, and in other dramatic ways changed the pattern of world affairs. The war was a catalyst in the Middle East; out of it came the present-day situation. Large reserves of oil went into production. There also flowered an ardent Arab nationalism similar to that which was developing in the Far East and Africa. The State of Israel appeared on the Middle Eastern scene. During and after the war France and Britain lost their influence in the area. In the 1950s Russia and America maneuvered there for diplomatic and strategic advantage. The United States found itself deeply involved. After the war Americans began to hear about Middle East crises, as they heard of crises in Europe and the Far East.

To say all these things about American involvement in the Middle East is not, of course, to say anything especially new. There is wide realization today that the United States has entered Middle Eastern affairs in earnest, regardless of how slight American contacts previously had been. American and Russian interests clashed on a worldwide scale after 1945, and it was natural that difficulties would appear in the Middle East.

The only special observation which one should make about American diplomacy in the Middle East, before looking in detail into some of the post-1945 developments in the area, is that this part of the world, despite its Suez Canal and oil resources and disquieting Arab-Israeli antagonism, probably is only indirectly vital to the United States. With construction of pipelines and large tankers, the importance of the Suez Canal for oil transport appears to be on the wane. The oil of the Middle East, so important to Europe, can (though far from easily) find replacement from elsewhere, North or South America, or even from new production in Algeria or Libya. The Arab-Israeli entanglement, however large it seems to the United States, is small if viewed against the larger clashes of people the world over. To be sure, no one would wish the Middle East to go, in whole or part, under Russian influence, its resources working for the benefit of the Soviet Union. Every diplomatic effort should be made to prevent such a result. But only if the Russians moved in physically, only if Soviet troops entered the area, would the United States and its allies have reason to react with force. The Middle East is a place most useful to the nations of the free world, and where naturally one would also wish its forty or fifty million inhabitants to live in peace and security; but the liberties and living standards of its inhabitants, even the resources of the area, are not vital to American security. Only because the Middle East offers to Russian troops a bridge into three continents does it possess vital importance to the United States. Any well-directed diplomacy in the region would have to keep that fact in mind.

The complications of American diplomacy in the Middle East date almost entirely from the end of the fighting in Europe and Asia in 1945, and yet it is impossible to ignore the earlier diplomatic history of the area.

Western influence first entered with the crusades and the caravan trade of the Middle Ages. Napoleon tried to establish French influence in the area, but it was not until the 19th century that Britain and France went into the Middle East in force—while the United States was looking in an entirely different direction. America then was expanding across the North American subcontinent, fighting the war with Mexico, preserving itself as one nation in the Civil War. In the early 19th century the French established their influence as protectors of the Christians in Lebanon against the Turks. During the American Civil War an international company under Ferdinand de Lesseps was digging the Suez Canal. The British meanwhile had been championing the Sultan of Turkey against Russia—the Eastern Question, as this involvement became known. They fought the Crimean War of 1854-1856 to preserve Constantinople and the Straits from Russian imperialism. Then came the avowedly temporary occupation of Egypt; Disraeli bought the Khedive Ismail's canal stock in 1875, at a moment when the Khedive was short of funds, and seven years later in 1882 the British bombarded Alexandria and subdued Egypt in an occupation that lasted until the final departure of British troops from the Suez Canal area in 1956.

The Middle East—and one must pass hurriedly over these well-known facts—continued under governance of the Turks until the First World War. When during that conflict the Turks sided with the Central Powers, the British eliminated the nominal Turkish suzerainty over Egypt and aroused the Arabs to eject the Turks from the entire area. There were some famous agreements and understandings, mostly British, during the First World War. In a series of exchanges between July, 1915, and February, 1916, the British high commissioner in Egypt, Sir Henry McMahon, promised the Grand Sherif of Mecca, Hussein ibn Ali, some measure (not too carefully defined) of independence, and the Arab Revolt began on June 5, 1916. The British gave the Arabs other assurances of independence. Together with the Russians, the British and French then undertook, despite their pledges to Hussein, to carve up the area in the Sykes-Picot Agreement concluded between April 26 and October 23, 1916; Russia obtained concessions in Turkey, soon lost because of the Bolshevik revolution, but the agreement otherwise divided the Middle East into roughly its postwar apportionment.[1] And as if one confusion were not enough, the British government in the person of Lord Arthur Balfour gave a letter to Lord Rothschild in November, 1917, which promised the Jews a national home in Palestine, in a vague and uncertain way (no one knew exactly what a national home was; nor where the boundaries of Palestine lay). The First World

[1] A postwar modification in September, 1919, gave the British northern Iraq, where they expected to find oil; and the French took all of Syria.

War ended with these three contradictory plans for the Middle East.

It was impossible to harmonize these promises.[2] The strongest parties, the British and French, came off best. The Jews managed to work quietly to expand the population of their national home, looking toward statehood. The Arabs came off worst, for they were disorganized and often disputing among themselves. Only a few of them were able to present their case in an impressive way to either the British or the French. Arab independence did not emerge from the First World War, but instead a congeries of unstable new protectorates—Iraq, Transjordan, Syria and Lebanon, Palestine. The French and British mandatories, while allowing nominal Arab participation in government, failed to give much authority, at least in the early years. Two sons of the Grand Sherif Hussein, the Emirs Abdullah and Feisal, became rulers respectively of Transjordan and Iraq. Their thrones were fragile; it was the British resident Sir Alec Kirkbride who virtually governed through a British subsidy in Transjordan, and the British minister in Baghdad who presided over the successive Iraqi ministries. Someone noticed at Feisal's inauguration in 1921 that his throne was, literally, made in England. The French under League mandate governed tightly in Syria and Lebanon. The British ruled under League mandate in Palestine. In Egypt the British kept most of the government in their hands until promulgation of a new Anglo-Egyptian treaty in 1936. It was all a far cry from the hopes of the Arabs during the Revolt of 1916-1918.

During the interwar years the sources of power were indeed thinly veiled. On occasion the French and British showed their authority in ways that anyone could understand. The Emir Feisal, for example, was thrown out of Damascus without ceremony in 1920, in such an undignified way that the British, perhaps, were moved to award him the throne in Iraq. "I have the honor to communicate to Your Royal Highness," said the official French letter of July 27, 1920, "a decision of the French Government requesting you to leave Damascus as soon as possible. A special train will be at the disposal of Your Royal Highness and suite. This train will leave the Hejaz Station at 0500 hours tomorrow, July 28, 1920."[3] In Egypt in 1924 the British be-

[2] Former Prime Minister Clement Attlee, under whose government Britain abandoned the Palestine mandate, has admitted frankly that Britain gave "incompatible assurances" to the Arabs and Jews. *As It Happened* (New York, 1954), p. 245.

[3] James Morris, *The Hashemite Kings* (New York, 1959), p. 51.

came incensed naturally when some young nationalists murdered the commander of the Egyptian and Sudanese army, Sir Lee Stack. The British high commissioner, General Sir Edmund Allenby, accompanied by a regiment of British troops on parade from the nearby Kasr-el-Nil Barracks, went to the house of the Egyptian prime minister, Saad Zaghlul Pasha, and presented a note of such severity that it reminded one of Clive in India a century and a half before. As late as 1942, when Britain's fortunes were at low point and Rommel was threatening to break into Alexandria and Cairo, the British ambassador in Egypt did not hesitate to throw tanks around King Farouk's Abdin Palace and force the Egyptian monarch, who was nominally independent because of the treaty of 1936, to appoint a cabinet favorable to the Allies.

In such manner were the Middle Eastern pawns maneuvered on the Anglo-French chessboard, and such was roughly the apparent state of affairs at the end of the Second World War when the United States and Britain stood victorious and when the United States began to find itself involved in the Middle East. There was one change, but it was minor. The British had forced the French out of Syria and Lebanon in 1941, incidental to eliminating Vichy French interests in the Eastern Mediterranean. British diplomacy with American support forestalled a Gaullist return to the Middle East in 1945. But elimination of one of the interwar powers did not mean, so the British believed, that there would be any especially new pattern of power in the area—rather, that Britain had assumed French prerogatives. Few individuals in 1945 foresaw the rapid decline of Britain's empire. Few people outside the Middle East would have predicted the postwar enthusiasms and excesses of Arab nationalism. It would have seemed unlikely that a state named Israel would arise within three years. There were some few Russian efforts to participate along with Britain and the United States in Middle Eastern affairs, although only in peripheral ways, such as demand for trusteeship over Italian Libya, or requests for concessions and a special position along the Turkish Straits, or the prolonged effort by the Russians in 1945-1946 to foster a separatist movement in northern Iran. Few Western statesmen realized that the old 19th-century Eastern Question, the aspiration of Russia for concessions from the Ottoman empire, was to revive in the mid-20th century in the guise of support for the Arab nationalists—and even, to a degree, for the Israeli nationalists—with the purpose of eliminating Britain and America from the area and making Russian interests supreme.

To set down the situation of 1945 in the above explanation of politics and diplomacy is not to see it in its entirety. There were important economic and social developments which must at least be touched upon.

Economically, the major development in the Middle East since the First World War, especially since 1945, has been extraction of oil. Western Europe by the mid-1950s was drawing most of its oil from the Middle East. In the crisis year 1956 Europe was importing about 2,100,000 barrels per day from the Middle East.[4] Crude oil production in Western Europe came to a bare 200,000 barrels, with about 700,000 in crude and product imports from the Western Hemisphere. Oil accounted for almost 20 per cent of the Continent's energy requirements. To be sure, the relative importance of oil as a source of energy varied from country to country. In the United Kingdom, with relatively high coal production, oil met only 13 per cent of energy needs, whereas Sweden used oil for about 45 per cent of its needs. But if oil accounted generally for 20 per cent of Europe's energy requirements, each 5 per cent decrease in oil (70 per cent of which came from the Middle East) meant a 1 per cent decline in total energy available and, therefore, of productivity, unless alternate oil sources or fuels appeared. The oil consumption of Europe was rising rapidly after the Second World War; between 1948 and 1956 it increased 100 per cent. Europe had predicated its economic growth upon a vast expansion in energy. It counted on oil to provide for more than half of that expansion.

In the drilling and extracting of oil American companies were dominating the Middle East. The Arabian-American Oil Company (Aramco) which operated in Saudi Arabia was the greatest single private American investment overseas. The Kuwait fields, the largest single producer in the Middle East, operated on a joint British-American basis. The much smaller Bahrain oil fields, though in

[4] The following account is based on the figures in Walter J. Levy, "Issues in International Oil Policy," *Foreign Affairs*, vol. 35 (1956-57), 454-69. See also Benjamin Shwadran, *The Middle East, Oil and the Great Powers* (New York, 1959); George Lenczowski, *Oil and State in the Middle East* (Ithaca, N.Y., 1960).

British-supervised territory, were American-exploited. The Americans had a substantial cut in the Iraqi, Persian, and Qatari fields (Qatar was a tiny territory on the eastern fringe of Arabia; like Kuwait and Bahrain it was British-ruled, through a native potentate). The American share in Middle East oil production had been 13 per cent in 1939, and the British 60 per cent—the balance going mostly to French and Dutch companies. By 1956 the American share was 65 per cent, and the British 30 per cent.

Much of the oil revenues—by the mid-1950s the average figure was a flat 50 per cent of total profits—went to the local rulers or governments, and in some countries there frequently was scandalous misuse of these huge funds. Despite the poverty of their subjects the rulers of Saudi Arabia, Abdel Aziz ibn Saud and after his death his son Saud ibn Abdel Aziz, lived in absurd pleasure. The younger Saud maintained twenty-four palaces in different parts of his kingdom. By the end of the 1950s he was tearing down an oldish but undeniably handsome palace at Riyadh and putting up the world's most king-sized palace, nearly a square mile in area, at a cost of at least fifty million dollars. The palace would contain schools for his many sons, together with a zoo, a private mosque, a hospital, and quarters for his concubines who numbered perhaps a hundred. It was a far cry from the pre-oil austerities of the Grand Sherif Hussein, the old Hashemite of the First World War whom the elder Saud had expelled from Arabia to a refuge in Cyprus. Hussein's fortunes had never been high. The sherif, among other activities devoted to sustenance of the royal exchequer, had maintained in Mecca a monopoly over the sale of dried lizards to pilgrims, the lizards being supposed to contain holy, tonic properties.[5]

In the glorious post-1945 era of oil the absurdities of the Saudis were perhaps about to be outdone by the riches of the Sheikh of Kuwait, who prior to the Second World War had been on British bounty. In an unbelievably short time the sheikh became the richest man in the world. His income in 1957 was $280,000,000. About one third of this income he invested in London, and the $90,000,000 or so involved represented about ten per cent of the ready money available for investment in the entire sterling area. The sheikh did undertake many projects for the social welfare of his subjects. Still he had plenty of money left over. When he paid a visit to Paris he could dispense his largesse with abandon. A story has it that when he

[5] James Morris, *The Hashemite Kings*, p. 54.

departed from Paris after a recent trip he left his two new Cadillacs to his French chauffeur.[6]

Despite the discovery of oil, there remained the enormous extremes of wealth and position in the region, extremes which probably were not to be found anywhere else in the world. They raised questions as to the stability of so unbalanced a social structure. Estimates of the average annual income of the fellahin of Egypt ranged from $75 to $90, not far from Indian and Chinese levels. Today the per capita income in Egypt is $134, which is $1 less than in 1949. The social contrasts of the area were obvious to all visitors. The late Khalil Totah, a Palestinian Arab who emigrated to the United States, found upon a trip to the Middle East in the early 1950s that "The economic and social chasm between the masses and the thin layer of upper crust is too deep and wide to be trifled with. The situation calls for something drastic and immediate. The pashas who whiz by in their Packards and Cadillacs on the streets of Cairo are bound to arouse the anger and hate of those who go barefooted on the hot sidewalks." [7]

A recent writer, S. A. Morrison, believes that the Western nations must accept a good deal of responsibility for the present-day socio-economic plight of the Middle East. He maintains that, quite apart from exploiting Middle Eastern oil, they have changed the economy of the area—in such places as Egypt, Syria, and Iraq—from subsistence agriculture to exporting agriculture, making the Middle East susceptible to the gyrations of international trade. By also dividing the area politically after the First World War, they made economic rationalization more difficult. By relying, inadvertently or purposely, on the wealthier Middle East citizens, the West accentuated the differences in economic status between rich and poor. And the introduction of Western sartorial fashions and social practices made the gulf between privileged and underprivileged more obvious.[8]

It does seem clear that if the Western nations, now led by the United States, wish to preserve influence in the Middle East, they will have to make the acquaintance and cultivate not the princes and sheikhs on whose good will they have so long relied but "the rising

[6] James Morris, *Islam Inflamed: A Middle East Picture* (New York, 1957), p. 238.

[7] Khalil Totah, *Dynamite in the Middle East* (New York, 1955), p. 49.

[8] *Middle East Tensions: Political, Social and Religious* (New York, 1954), pp. 77-78.

middle classes, the Socialists, the intelligentsia, the radical would-be politicians, the Western-trained economists and technicians, who tend to become, for lack of opportunities in the economic or political life of their own countries, either cynical business men or else the angry young men of the Arab world." [9] The new order of affairs appears clearly behind the leadership of Gamal Abdel Nasser of Egypt, who came from the lower-middle stratum of Egyptian society and has displayed a sensitive social consciousness, championing the grievances of oppressed groups in all the Arab countries against the excesses of the ruling groups. In past years the British and French relied on the pashas and sheikhs, ruling through them, and these classes extracted a price for their co-operation. The Americans coming into the area dealt with the powers at hand; Nuri as Said in Iraq, Hussein in Jordan, the Saudi family in Arabia. American opposition to Nasser in recent years has laid the United States open to accusation of similar partiality in Egypt, of liking only for the venal politicians and profiteers who had flourished during the reign of Farouk. When the United States championed the causes of President Camille Chamoun in Lebanon and King Hussein in Jordan, many Middle Easterners again thought that they saw the leading Western power siding with privilege and aristocracy against the more numerous elements of the area's populations who were denied political power.

Here, to be sure, there entered the machinations of the Soviet Union, whose diplomats in the postwar years have carefully fostered the belief that the USSR stood for social and economic progress. Russian diplomats have displayed a good deal of the common touch in their behavior in the area, and not infrequently a surprising ability with the language of the Arabs.

Hence when the United States entered the Middle East politically after the war there was a one-sided economic progress in the oil-rich countries—Saudi Arabia, Kuwait, Bahrain, Qatar, Iraq, and Iran—accompanied by a potentially explosive social situation in all the area's countries, with the Soviet Union standing by, waiting for the first sure signs of trouble.

Initial Russian pressures in Turkey and Iran and over Libyan trusteeship resulted in nothing, but shortly there came a development from which the Middle East has not yet recovered and which could

[9] Michael Adams, *Suez and After: Year of Crisis* (Boston, 1958), p. 217.

not have been more inconvenient to Western diplomacy, especially American diplomacy which found itself in the middle of the whole affair. This was the achievement of Israeli independence in May, 1948. No single event proved so disruptive to the already precarious Middle Eastern social and political structure, and bade fair to so endanger Western economic interests—the Suez Canal and the extraction of oil.

The American government played a major part in creating Israel. Even now, years after the event, it is curious to recall the way that politics in the United States moved out over the water's edge, oblivious of any larger effects that might result for the nation's diplomacy and foreign policy.

There had been some rumblings of pro-Zionist sentiment in the American government prior to the end of the war, but the beginning of peace in 1945 had seen little more than campaign promises by the two major American political parties. In the presidential campaign of 1944 the Democratic platform spoke of "a free and democratic Jewish commonwealth in Palestine," while the Republican platform used only the phrase "a free and democratic commonwealth," which presumably could have been Arab-Jewish. Governor Thomas E. Dewey during his unsuccessful campaign had attempted to make the Republican position more obvious by showing that his party too envisioned a Jewish commonwealth.

President Roosevelt in his last weeks of life in early 1945 made a mild attempt to solve the Palestine question. His effort probably added more to the confusion of Allied purposes in the Middle East than to their clarification. At Malta, Roosevelt confided to Churchill that after the Yalta Conference he was going to see Ibn Saud and discuss Palestine. He wanted, he said, to bring about peace between the Arabs and the Jews. Churchill, so James F. Byrnes was to recall, "wished him good luck but didn't seem very hopeful that the President would meet with success. He didn't." [10] The president later told Byrnes that "I had an exceedingly pleasant meeting with Ibn Saud and we agreed about everything until I mentioned Palestine. That was the end of the pleasant conversation." [11] Roosevelt prom-

[10] James F. Byrnes, *Speaking Frankly* (New York, 1947), p. 22.

[11] James F. Byrnes, *All in One Lifetime* (New York, 1958), p. 242. FDR seems to have told Bernard Baruch that of all the men he had talked to in his life, he had obtained least satisfaction from Ibn Saud. Elliott Roosevelt, *As He Saw It* (New York, 1946), p. 245. See also William A. Eddy, *F.D.R. Meets*

ised Ibn Saud that he personally, as president, would make no move hostile to the Arab people, and that the American government would make no change in its basic policy in Palestine without full and prior consultation with both Arabs and Jews. A week before his death—that is, on April 5—FDR signed a letter to Ibn Saud in which he repeated the assurances he had made during the meeting on Great Bitter Lake in the Suez.

Roosevelt's successor, Truman, thus inherited the Palestine problem. Truman appears to have surveyed it partly in terms of humanitarianism, the need to find homes for the surviving Jewish residents of concentration camps; partly as an opportunity to "make the desert bloom" (the new president had visions of a Middle Eastern TVA which could support from twenty to thirty million more people in the area); partly as a redemption of promises made during the First World War, for "promises made by responsible, civilized governments should be kept";[12] partly in terms of political advantage in the United States, although this latter consideration found no expression in Truman's two volumes of memoirs, three chapters of which dealt with the problem of Palestine. The motive of politics nonetheless appears to have carried considerable weight. "I'm sorry, gentlemen," the president told a delegation of American diplomats accredited to the Middle East, "but I have to answer to hundreds of thousands who are anxious for the success of Zionism; I do not have hundreds of thousands of Arabs among my constituents." [13]

Ibn Saud (New York, 1954), pp. 34-36; Ross T. McIntire, *White House Physician* (New York, 1946), pp. 228-31; Eleanor Roosevelt, *This I Remember* (New York, 1949), pp. 341-42.

[12] Harry S. Truman, *Memoirs* (2 vols., 1955-56), II, 132.

[13] William A. Eddy, *F.D.R. Meets Ibn Saud*, p. 37. Colonel Eddy before the war had been a Professor of English at the American University at Cairo, Professor of English at Dartmouth, and President of Hobart and William Smith Colleges. In 1946 he was serving as American minister to Saudi Arabia. Together with the American ministers in Egypt, Lebanon and Syria (a joint appointment), and the consul general to mandated Palestine he had arrived in Washington in the first week in October, 1946, for a White House appointment scheduled for about October 10. The group was kept idle for a month because White House advisers, including David K. Niles, persuaded Truman it would not be politic to have the meeting before the November, 1946, Congressional elections. Afterward the director of the Near East office of the State Department brought the four to a private conference with the president. The spokesman for the group, George Wadsworth, "presented orally an agreed statement in about twenty minutes. There was little discussion and the President asked few questions in the meeting whose Minutes have been carefully guarded in the Depart-

There was perhaps another element in the president's thinking, namely, that in the Palestine question he seems to have been antagonized by advice from the State Department. When coming into office Truman felt keenly his lack of knowledge on many of the great questions of government, and with admirable candor he had solicited help. The office of president, however, has its dignities, and there may have been too much advice from the State Department, the preserve of the "striped-pants boys." [14] Acting Secretary of State Joseph C. Grew presented the president a memorandum dated June 16, 1945, advising a noncommittal attitude toward Palestine, suggesting that "It does not seem, therefore, that you need to go any further, unless you care to do so, than to thank the Zionist leaders for any materials which they may give you and to assure them their views will be given your careful consideration." [15] Truman's temper seems to have risen over this suggestion.

Whatever the inspiration, the president soon moved. He came out in favor of immediate admission to Palestine by the British of 100,000 Jews. A British White Paper in 1939 had set a limited number of certificates of immigration to Palestine, and with the end of fighting the demand for certificates increased and was going to reach the limit in the early autumn of 1945. At that time there were approximately 100,000 Jewish refugees in the American and British zones of Germany. The president wished them admitted to Palestine.

The result of this pronouncement, most unfavorably received by the British and especially by Foreign Secretary Ernest Bevin, was appointment of a commission of inquiry of twelve representative citizens, six American and six British. The commission was to take a "fresh and unbiased approach" to the Palestine issue. For that reason its members were almost totally ignorant of the Middle East.[16] Un-

---

ment of State. Finally, Mr. Truman summed up his position with the utmost candor . . ." *Loc. cit.*

[14] Harry S. Truman, *Memoirs*, I, 69. See also II, 164-65, for three or four acid paragraphs about career men versus elected officials, about how he had decided "to prevent career men from circumventing presidential policy."

[15] Harry S. Truman, *Memoirs*, II, 134.

[16] According to one of the American members, the distinguished former Undersecretary of State William Phillips, "I knew very little about the Middle East, that is why I, indeed why all the members of our committee were chosen." *Ventures in Diplomacy* (Boston, 1952), p. 421. "How were we Neophytes to decide questions upon which experts, who had lived in the country for many years, were unable to agree? I realized that we were afloat in turbulent waters." *Ibid.*, p. 425.

daunted, it set to work, and in April, 1946, brought in a report which recommended admission of 100,000 immigrants but also concluded that relations of Jews and Arabs in Palestine were at the moment so strained that any attempt to establish independence or statehood for the Palestinian Jews would only bring civil strife. It recommended continuation of the British mandate, and eventual trusteeship over the area by the United Nations. President Truman in announcing the results of the commission mentioned only the admission of 100,000 immigrants, and gave the impression that the commission favored the Jews. There followed a considerable public discussion, with the commission's findings pleasing no one. Nothing came from its labors. As one of its American members later wrote, "All that remains is an interesting little volume published by the Government Printing Office." [17]

The president in the summer of 1946 appointed a special cabinet committee on Palestine, with deputies to go to London and work out some solution with the British. The so-called Grady Committee, named after its chairman Henry F. Grady, a San Francisco businessman with State Department experience, produced a detailed plan in July, 1946, providing for Arab and Jewish autonomous communities in Palestine under a central government. Again, no one was pleased. Although the president seems to have appointed the cabinet committee in an effort to get rid of the political provisions of the previous Anglo-American commission's report, the Grady Committee produced a document less agreeable to Truman than that of the commission, for the Grady group after meeting with the British and agreeing on 100,000 certificates for Palestine stipulated that admission of this sizable group of Jewish immigrants would depend on Arab approval, an impossible condition.

Truman repeated his desire for 100,000 certificates in a statement on Yom Kippur, October 4, 1946. Governor Dewey said a few days later that several hundred thousand certificates would be a more likely number. Meanwhile Jewish extremists in Palestine had been wrecking bridges and other edifices, and audaciously blew up a wing of the King David Hotel in Jerusalem, headquarters of the British mandate secretariat. Between 120 and 125 people were killed. Foreign Secretary Bevin said angrily in the House of Commons that Truman had made his statement on Yom Kippur so as to forestall a pronouncement by Dewey. Truman has written in his memoirs that

[17] *Ibid.*, pp. 453-54.

"This was a very undiplomatic—almost hostile—statement for the Foreign Secretary of the British government to make about the President of the United States." Outraged, the president barely managed to contain himself.[18]

But in such manner the Truman administration committed itself to Jewish immigration to Palestine, despite the wishes of the British government, during a time when British forces in Palestine numbering nearly 60,000 troops were finding it impossible to keep the tiny country in order. The appalling atrocities of Hitler's Germany, the extermination of six million Jews, had so increased the demand for a Zionist state in Palestine that Britain found itself, or believed it found itself, helpless to prevent establishment of such a state, regardless of what this novel political entity promised to do to the Western powers' Middle Eastern diplomacy. Jewish extremists in Palestine pressed the British government beyond endurance. The Palestine extremists hesitated at nothing, even the most shameful acts such as garrotting and hanging two British sergeants at Nathanya in 1947, to harass the British out of the country.[19] Having poured far more expenditure into the Holy Land than anyone ever anticipated in 1920 when the British government took up the Palestine mandate, the Attlee cabinet voted early in 1947 to disentangle itself. The decision came at the very same time when Britain for financial reasons felt compelled to turn over its interests in Greece and Turkey to American sponsorship. Simultaneously the British were leaving India. Britain gave the Palestine problem to the United Nations in a request of April 2, 1947. The UN voted a special committee on Palestine (UNSCOP), in which none of the great powers received representation; a majority of the committee recommended termination of the mandate and creation of two separate states, Jewish and Arab, tied in economic union, with the city of Jerusalem under direct UN trusteeship. The Jews were mildly favorable, the Arabs hostile. The Truman administration supported the partition plan. So did the Soviet Union. On November 29, 1947, the General Assembly voted 33 to 13, with 10 abstentions, to partition Palestine. The British

[18] Harry S. Truman, *Memoirs*, II, 154.

[19] After Israel achieved independence the commander of the terrorist organization Irgun Zvai Leumi, Menachem Begin, publicly claimed credit for many of these deeds, and received election to the Knesset, along with Nathan Friedman Yellin, leader of the Stern Gang. Alfred M. Lilienthal, *What Price Israel* (Chicago, 1953), pp. 103ff.

thereupon announced their decision to relinquish the mandate on May 15, 1948.[20]

The problem became one of enforcing the UN decision, and it was here that the UN decision, fair though it probably was, played into the hands of the Zionists; for the United States was in no position to enforce partition, and no one else was either, and the issue was left to the Zionists and Arabs fighting it out in Palestine, with victory within the grasp of the proponents of a fully independent State of Israel. There was some canvassing of American military capabilities during the crucial months between the UN decision of November, 1947, and departure of the British the following May. There were hardly any American troops available for dispatch to Palestine. The president moreover was unwilling to send them, if they were available. When the United States in March, 1948, shifted its policy to advocacy of an Anglo-French-American trusteeship of Palestine, the joint chiefs of staff estimated that there would have to be a minimum of 104,000 troops to keep a truce between Arabs and Jews while such a trusteeship was set up. A few weeks before, they had estimated that the United States could not have sent abroad more than a division, about 15,000 men, without partial mobilization.[21]

It was an impossible situation, and the denouement, American recognition of Israel, was the only recourse after what had gone before. Recognition when it came was quick enough, in fact only eleven minutes after birth of the new state. Israel was to be born at 6:00 P.M. Washington time on May 14, 1948, and the United States gave *de facto* recognition at 6:11.[22] The administration had received word from Elihu Epstein as agent of the provisional government that it would establish itself at midnight in Palestine when the British mandate expired, but no official request for recognition came from the State of Israel until almost twenty-four hours after everything was over. The decision to recognize was entirely a presidential affair, the State Department hearing about it shortly before the event. At the

[20] Zionists in the United States worked feverishly in favor of partition. Undersecretary of State Robert Lovett told Secretary of Defense Forrestal that "he had never in his life been subject to as much pressure as he had been in the three days" prior to the vote. Walter Millis, ed., *The Forrestal Diaries* (New York, 1951), p. 346. Truman faced a "constant barrage" from Jewish leaders. "I do not think I ever had as much pressure and propaganda aimed at the White House as I had in this instance." *Memoirs,* II, 158.

[21] Walter Millis, ed., *The Forrestal Diaries,* p. 411.

[22] *De jure* recognition occurred on January 31, 1949.

moment of recognition, United States representatives at the United Nations were still proposing trusteeship for Palestine.[23]

The results of this decision in Washington soon made themselves known in the Middle East. Few postwar acts of the American government have proved more far-reaching in importance for the area for which they were made. Sometimes the formalities of diplomacy have little meaning, but the recognition of Israel on May 14, 1948, was no run-of-the-mill piece of diplomacy. Recognition secured the new state in the Middle East, at least for the foreseeable future. The United States thereafter was to support Israel, either through private funds from the pockets of American citizens or from public funds. The latter were by no means small, amounting ten years later to half a billion dollars, two or three times the sums contributed to all the Arab countries combined—which countries had populations about thirty times larger than Israel. Private American support for Israel, in terms of gifts through the United Jewish Appeal and other campaigns, had enjoyed the inestimable advantage of being made tax exempt. Israel also was receiving $715 million, payable in goods by 1965, as an indemnity from West Germany. Moreover, by 1960 about $425 million of Israeli bonds had been floated, mostly in the United States. The 1960 bond program looked forward to sales of an additional $75 million. It was, in sum, a marvelous sustenance for a small new country, made possible through American recognition.

Meanwhile there commenced a calamitous series of Middle Eastern tragedies. An Arab-Israeli war sputtered for months after proclamation of Israeli independence. Nearly a million Arab refugees left Palestine—as of June 30, 1959, the figures for refugees stood at 131,-732 temporarily sheltered in Lebanon; 111,429 in Syria; 248,742 in a small strip of territory administered by Egypt about the town of Gaza; 595,725 in Jordan.[24] The enormous influx to Jordan changed

[23] Walter Millis, ed., *The Forrestal Diaries*, p. 440. See also the excellent account of recognition in Alfred M. Lilienthal, *What Price Israel*, pp. 84-86. Lilienthal has written another good book, *There Goes the Middle East* (New York, 1957), in which he develops the theme of *What Price Israel*.

[24] United Nations, *Annual Report of the Director of the United Nations Relief and Works Agency for Palestine Refugees in the Near East: 1 July 1958–30 June 1959* (New York, 1959), p. 10. The United Nations General Assembly passed the following resolution on December 11, 1948: "That the refugees wishing to return to their homes and live at peace with their neighbors, should be permitted to do so at the earliest practicable date, and that compensation should be paid for the property of those choosing not to return,

completely the complexion of that penniless state, stirring it to near-revolution, bringing assassination of the able King Abdullah, the single Arab monarch with political sagacity and sophistication. Defeat in the Palestine war together with the corruption of the Farouk regime brought revolution to Egypt in 1952, and a new train of troubles between Egypt and Britain culminating in the Suez crisis of 1956. Syria and Lebanon, both insecure states, went into convulsions, with Syria passing uncertainly into partnership with Egypt, and Lebanon enjoying its own murderous revolution of 1958. Jordan in 1956-1958 came again within an ace of revolution, after the abrupt dismissal of the head of the Arab Legion, Lieutenant General Sir John Bagot Glubb, and his replacement by the pro-Nasser enthusiast, Major Aly Abu Nuwar. The inexperienced King Hussein kept control only by appealing to the loyalty of the Legion's Bedouin troops. The populace of Iraq, long restive under its pro-British Hashemite dynasty and its premier Nuri as Said, rose in a swirling melee in July, 1958, killed its rulers, and went over to a tottering regime headed by Brigadier Abdel Karim Kassem.

Nothing looked the same after the Zionist victory in Palestine, a coup made possible by an American political leader, acting without the advice of his State Department. President Truman, as we have seen, had favored the creation of Israel for several reasons. Among them was the element of domestic politics—"squalid political purposes" (so at least Secretary of Defense James Forrestal interpreted them at a meeting of the National Security Council), the aligning of New York State's large Jewish population behind the Democratic Party and President Truman during the extremely close presidential election of 1948.[25] But regardless of the American president's reason-

---

and for loss or damage to property." The Assembly reaffirmed the resolution in later sessions, to no avail. Meanwhile the UN Relief and Works Agency was feeding the refugees. Out of a total of $319,114,000 spent from 1948 to June, 1959, the United States contributed $220,349,000, the United Kingdom $59,635,000, France $12,856,000, and Canada $9,450,000. Driblets (a total of $16,824,000) came from the Arab countries and the rest of the world. UNRWA, *Statistical Summary: June 1959* (n.p., n.d.), p. 1. The Soviet Union freely criticized the wicked imperialist West for its action in the area, but not a ruble went toward upkeep of the Arab refugees.

[25] Walter Millis, ed., *The Forrestal Diaries*, p. 508. In the winter of 1947-1948 Forrestal conducted an unsuccessful personal campaign to keep the Palestine question out of politics. *Ibid.*, *passim*, and especially pp. 309-10, 344, 346-48, 357, 359, 361, 363. In regard to the argument that politics—the close presidential election of 1948—moved Truman to a pro-Israel policy, there is

ing—whether it was right or wrong or both—the creation of Israel helped inspire a series of diplomatic tragedies in the Middle East which has run on down to the present day. In the course of these difficulties there has developed a considerable hatred for America by many of the peoples of the area, especially evident when American foreign policy sought to make Israel a *fait accompli,* to persuade the Arabs to write Palestine off and forget it. "It was the same and one question and ever the same answer," so Totah discovered when he visited the refugee camps of the Gaza strip in 1952. " 'Why did America sell the Arabs so cheaply to the Jews? Was Truman a Jew himself? Is there not a sense of justice in the United States and where is American democracy and fair play? Is it not high time for the Arabs to make a deal with the Communists?' " [26]

Surely there was little American foresight in the years when the Truman administration hastened the creation of the State of Israel, but one must say in fairness that the events that flowed from this creation of an alien state in the Middle East would have been difficult to anticipate because they were parts of a larger series of crises, themselves unanticipated. The decision about Israel took place at a time of transition, before the power-political implications of the cold war and its alliances were generally understood.[27] It reached its conclusive stage at the time of the developing crisis over Berlin; the Arab-Israeli war of 1948-1949 covered roughly the same period as the Berlin blockade. Shortly thereafter came the Korean War, which turned American attention in earnest to the Far East. With the

the dissenting view offered in the interesting book by John M. ("Jack") Redding, *Inside the Democratic Party* (Indianapolis, 1958). Redding was director of public relations for the Democratic national committee in 1948. He shows in his volume that civil rights and Palestine were two extremely touchy issues during the campaign. Judging by the book, the Democratic henchmen had large difficulties over Palestine, especially with two pro-Israeli Democratic political leaders, Mayor William O'Dwyer of New York and the boss of Chicago, Jack Arvey. Truman however, according to Redding, would not let the Democrats make political capital on the issue. See pp. 104-105, 120, 127, 137, 146-47, 166, 215, and particularly 149: "The Palestine issue will be handled here," the president said. "And there'll be no politics involved."

[26] Khalil Totah, *Dynamite in the Middle East*, p. 38.

[27] M. A. Fitzsimons, "The Suez Crisis and the Containment Policy," *Review of Politics*, vol. 19 (1957), 429. This article is extremely well done. For an excellent analysis of American diplomacy toward the Middle East in recent years, see John C. Campbell, *Defense of the Middle East* (New York, 1958).

death of Stalin and the adjournment of the Korean imbroglio in 1953, there also occurred the Soviet explosion of a thermonuclear bomb. Then came the Geneva conferences of 1954 over Indochina and 1955 over the world in general, the outbreak of war in French North Africa, the Austrian peace treaty of 1955. The next year, 1956, was full of large events; beginning with Khrushchev's famous speech about Stalin to the Twentieth Party Congress, there followed the revolutions in Hungary and Poland and, in the Middle East, the crisis over Suez. Which is to say, again, that creation of Israel occurred before the tempo of postwar events had begun to accelerate. If a mistake was made in the Middle East, it was in the context of the times somewhat understandable.

Actually the clash of Soviet-American policies in the Middle East did not begin until ten years after the end of the Second World War, seven after the independence of Israel. The year 1955 marked the first major Russian move in the area, with sale of arms to Egypt, an open challenge to a Franco-British-American Declaration of 1950 that the three Western powers would maintain the rough territorial-armaments balance of the moment, Israel versus the Arab states. For ten years after the war both of the superpowers were engaged elsewhere, first in Europe, then in the Far East. Only after a rough stalemate in these two major areas did the Soviet Union make its appearance in the Eastern Mediterranean.

The initial American power move in the area had come in the year 1951, several years before Soviet entry into Middle Eastern politics. In October, 1951, the United States together with Great Britain, France, and Turkey had proposed a Middle Eastern counterpart of NATO which was to be known as the Allied Middle East Command, and later discussed a Middle Eastern Defense Organization (MEDO). The arrangement was intended especially to meet the interests of Great Britain—the British desired some kind of treaty arrangement in the Middle East whereby the Western powers, with Britain in the leading role, could continue the bases and other special positions Britain had maintained during and prior to the war, especially Suez. Another idea, advanced somewhat later, was that there existed a sort of northern tier of states, Turkey, Iraq, Iran, and Pakistan, the independence of which was threatened by the Soviet Union, the territory of which might conceivably be used, among other purposes, for American bomber bases against the USSR. A mutuality of interests seemed to dictate an organization of these states along the

NATO pattern. But the Egyptians, to whom a Middle East Command was first proposed, rejected it out of hand, and the idea languished, to be revived in abbreviated form as the Baghdad Pact four years later.

In this latter scheme concluded in 1955, the British became signatories and the United States stood aloof, though everyone presumed, and the presumption eventually proved correct, that the American government would give military and economic aid to the pact's Middle Eastern adherents. Prompted by the events of July, 1958, in Lebanon and Iraq, the United States in that month accepted the "same obligations" under the Baghdad Pact as did nations which were full members of the pact.

The Baghdad Pact, so slow in taking a clear form, contained advantages which were more apparent than real. One must question whether the pact represented a carefully thought-out action, or rather was an afterthought, an appendage to more serious diplomacy in other parts of the world. Secretary Dulles was a man of action; he believed that his predecessors at the State Department had been cautious and lacking in imagination; he liked large treaty schemes, and in 1954 established an Asian counterpart to NATO, the Southeast Asia Treaty Organization, SEATO. It is well known that many of Dulles's policies were virtually personal policies, which because of the secretary's influence with President Eisenhower received the ready support of the White House. In the case of the Baghdad Pact there was little calculation of the attitudes of such states as Egypt, which might regard the scheme as an attempted anti-Egyptian move by the Iraqi government of Nuri as Said. The Egyptians, under Nasser the leaders of Arab nationalism, could also argue that establishment or confirmation of Western bases in the Middle East was one more Western attempt to preserve colonialism and imperialism. Maintenance of Western power in the area also subtracted from Arab freedom of movement, thereby tending to present Israel to the Arabs as a *fait accompli.* As far as concerned any possible Western advantages, the pact soon showed itself of dubious value. American bomber bases were becoming less advantageous in the latter 1950s because of perfection of intermediate- and long-range ballistic missiles. Maintenance of the British bases proved impossible for local political reasons. All in all the decision to establish the pact was ill-timed and ill-considered.

Western difficulties in the Middle East in the years after 1955 centered on Egypt and the government of President Nasser. This revolutionary regime had come into power by a military coup in 1952, quite unexpectedly so far as the American government was concerned and perhaps other Western governments as well. Ambassador Stanton Griffis, accredited to King Farouk in 1948-1949, failed to mention the name of Nasser in his memoir published in 1952, and Griffis's preoccupation with the regime of Farouk was not merely a result of the American ambassador's own inabilities.[28] Once the officers' regime came into power, and the officers led by Nasser were able after a few months to depose their nominal leader, General Mohammed Naguib, a new force of great importance soon was in operation. Nasser was the first truly attractive Arab leader. If he talked roughly and at times irresponsibly to Western nations, he had an attractive personality, was honest in his affairs, was a good public speaker, and his successes in foreign policy obscured the nearly impossible economic situation of his country. Nasser was a benevolent dictator, and he managed to keep the forms of republican government. There was free speech only to a degree within Egypt, and censorship of incoming and outgoing mail as well as domestic letters—though there was probably no more

[28] Stanton Griffis, *Lying in State* (New York, 1952). Griffis was not the ordinary type of American ambassador in the Middle East, for most American envoys there have been career diplomats. He was an unfortunate exception to this rule. When as a foot-loose campaign-chest contributor he appeared in the Middle East for a few months in 1948 and 1949, the government of Farouk to whom he was accredited was in process of final dissolution or dissoluteness, and it is a pity that the United States at so difficult a moment was not better represented. The ambassador discovered that life in the Egyptian capital was "one continual round of cocktail parties, dinners and dances. I doubt if I have averaged more than one free night a week . . ." Griffis on one round of social exchanges alone, the initial visits to his Cairo colleagues, found that he consumed 479 cups of Turkish coffee, 84 cups of French coffee, 306 Coca-Colas, 4 cups of Arabian coffee, and 76 other national drinks from slivovitz to vodka and arak. *Lying in State*, p. 219. Perhaps he was joking; but he surely took little time to learn about the country to which he was assigned. He had desired Spain rather than Egypt, and accepted the Egyptian assignment as a way station to Madrid. His attitude toward things Egyptian appears clearly from his account of a plane flight which passed over Luxor, in which locality there is of course the greatest collection of antiquities in the entire Middle East. The ambassador told his pilot not to stop, dismissing the glories of Egypt with a wisecrack: "I have seen so much of archeology around Cairo that I had no great ambition to tramp around more ruins, and I see one every day at shaving time . . ." *Ibid.*, p. 235.

tampering with civil liberties in Egypt than had long obtained in several other Middle Eastern states. Certainly he was no Hitler, and the analogies to Munich which Prime Minister Sir Anthony Eden often drew when he spoke of Nasser were false (so far as they were intended to describe Nasser, apart from his actions; whether the Suez crisis was similar to Munich is, of course, another question).[29]

The advent of Nasser in Egypt in 1952-1953 and the consolidation of his regime by 1955, the year when Russian-American antagonisms began to spill over into the Middle East, boded ill for peace in the region. There followed the Suez crisis of October-November, 1956. The Egyptians had been raiding into Israeli territory from bases in the Gaza strip, and in February, 1955, the Israelis retaliated massively with a raid on the strip. The Egyptians thereupon asked the Western powers for arms, and met refusal or at least long delays that resembled refusal; the Western powers had determined to keep the armaments status quo, in accord with the Triple Declaration to that effect concluded in May, 1950. So the Egyptians bought arms from the Czechoslovaks and Russians. Meanwhile they had sought to obtain finances for building a higher dam at Aswan in Upper Egypt, and it appeared as if they might get the necessary money, by a combination of loans from the United States and Britain and from the World Bank. At this point their arms purchases began to affect their credit standing. The Western powers initially had been favorable to the loans if only because the World Bank would have tied up the Egyptian exchequer for ten to fifteen years—through pledges to the dam —and hence made impossible any large Egyptian maneuvering on the Middle Eastern stage that required money, and most Middle Eastern maneuvers required money. But the Egyptians began to play both sides of the street, and treated the Western loans as a kind of hush money, implying that they would take their allegiance elsewhere if they failed to get the loans. The United States became annoyed in the early summer of 1956—some evidence indicates that Secretary Dulles was personally peeved—and ostentatiously backed out of the

[29] See for example the comments in Sir Anthony Eden, *Full Circle* (Boston, 1960), p. 481: "Some say that Nasser is no Hitler or Mussolini. Allowing for a difference in scale, I am not so sure. He has followed Hitler's pattern, even to concentration camps and the propagation of *Mein Kampf* among his officers. He has understood and used the Goebbels pattern of propaganda in all its lying ruthlessness."

Aswan dam project.[30] Nasser then nationalized the Suez Canal Company, allegedly to obtain money to build the dam.

Events moved rapidly to a climax. The British fulminated, and the French fumed. Secretary Dulles projected a Suez Canal Users Association, which would have given the United States a legal part in the picture—it had not been a party to the Suez Canal treaty of 1888. The British and French lost confidence in Dulles's diplomacy.[31] While the Russians were embroiled in first-class rebellions in Poland and Hungary in October, 1956, the governments in London and Paris apparently connived with the Israelis and the Israeli army attacked Egypt.[32] The Anglo-French allies—without consulting the United States—sent an ultimatum to Egypt and failing of a satisfactory answer attacked and occupied Port Said, meanwhile bombing Al Maza airport at Cairo and other Egyptian installations.

[30] See John Robinson Beal, *John Foster Dulles* (rev. ed., New York, 1959), virtually an authorized biography. "Nasser was making it look as though the United States could be played for a sucker" (p. 257). The Egyptian president had given the impression that he did not want money from the United States, and could get it from Russia; he then changed his mind: "In effect, it was Nasser who created the dramatic spectacle. Until he sent [Egyptian Ambassador Ahmed] Hussein back to announce that Egypt wanted the money for the dam, after all, the United States had gradually reached the conclusion from Nasser's disinterest that he did not intend to pick up the offer. Since it appeared he did not want the money, it seemed unnecessary to announce he would not get it. Only after he raised the issue publicly did it seem appropriate to answer" (pp. 259-60).

[31] See Sir Anthony Eden, *Full Circle*, pp. 467-650; Randolph S. Churchill, *The Rise and Fall of Sir Anthony Eden* (New York, 1959), pp. 229-320; John Robinson Beal, *John Foster Dulles*, pp. 246-88. Relations between Washington and London deteriorated to almost zero. Moved by publication of Sir Anthony's memoirs, President Eisenhower told a press conference on January 26, 1960, that for two weeks before the Suez intervention not a single item of information was received in Washington from the British Foreign Office. He quoted the late Secretary Dulles as saying that there was "a blackout of news." *New York Times*, January 27, 1960.

[32] The exact arrangements between the French and British, on the one hand, and the Israelis on the other, remain a matter for speculation. Apparently the British left the Israelis to the French. The British government must have known what was going on, but there is little light on this *haute politique* in Sir Anthony Eden's *Full Circle* despite devotion of one third of his volume (pp. 467-650) to Suez. As for those individuals who believe in Britain's innocence, Randolph Churchill was reminded of the observation of the Duke of Wellington on a famous occasion: "If you can believe that, you can believe anything." *The Rise and Fall of Sir Anthony Eden*, p. 268.

The Americans and Russians found themselves joined together in the United Nations, entreating the Cabinets of London and Paris to stop fighting and make peace. The United Nations entered the scene, the French and British and Israelis agreed to an armistice, and beginning on November 15, 1956, the UN sent to the Israeli-Arab borders its newly raised armed forces, the United Nations Emergency Force, UNEF. By Christmas, 1956, they had replaced the British and French and Israelis, establishing bases in the Gaza strip and Sharm-el-Sheikh, the latter a locality controlling the entrance to the Gulf of Aqaba.

The Suez affair was a saddening episode for American diplomacy, for it openly estranged the United States from its NATO allies, Britain and France. The world was treated to the demoralizing spectacle of the United States and the Soviet Union acting together through the United Nations against London and Paris. The damage in the Middle East was reparable, and by the autumn of 1959 Egypt had prepared for resumption of relations, commercial and diplomatic, with the two European "aggressors" (as Egyptians liked to describe them). Replacement of Sir Anthony Eden with Harold Macmillan, who was dedicated to reforging the ties with America, eliminated the more obvious uncertainties of the Suez fiasco. It was probable that with Macmillan as prime minister there would be no further secret British arrangements with the French and (apparently) with the Israelis. But the damage to American prestige in Britain and France remained. The Western alliance was to that extent weakened.

The canal remained in Egyptian hands. Contrary to the predictions of Western specialists the Egyptians ran it with exemplary efficiency. They made a monetary settlement on June 11, 1958, with the Universal Suez Canal Company, a company organized in 1856 which had been managing the canal since its construction.

Initiative in the Middle East passed to the United States, what with the British and French humiliation at Suez, and the American government quickly enunciated the Eisenhower Doctrine which, it hoped, would bring peace to the disturbed area. The doctrine turned out to be unfortunate. Its principle was unexceptionable, a promise of American military assistance if requested by any nation threatened by "overt armed aggression from any nation controlled by international communism." To sugar-coat this principle there was a crash program of economic assistance, $200 million, and a retired congressman named James P. Richards went hurriedly out to the Middle

East as head of a special mission to advocate the doctrine and its coating to the governments of the region. Many people in the Middle Eastern nations were skeptical of this approach. The behavior of the United States was exactly as the communists and Arab nationalists had been claiming: that all the Americans wished to do was to enlist the Middle East in the cold war between America and Russia; that any economic largesse from America was devoted to that end, not the welfare of the Arabs. Besides, the Arabs were offered protection against a far-off enemy, while the doctrine did not provide any protection against the immediate danger of Israeli attacks.

The Richards mission was an ill-fated safari, if ever there was one. Richards knew little about the Middle East. A former chairman of the House Foreign Affairs Committee, he had quit Congress, he told his friends, so that he could retire on his South Carolina plantation. Recalled to duty as a special assistant to the secretary of state with the personal rank of ambassador, he gave his own explanation for his new job. "If you come right down to it," he said, "I guess they wanted a Democrat for the job. I've been a Democrat all my life." In several of the Middle Eastern capitals he met rebuff. The Eisenhower Doctrine alienated Syria and the government in Damascus continued to move away from Iraq and toward an understanding with Egypt and the USSR. In Beirut, Richards did find success, but there he so overplayed the doctrine to the receptive chief of the Lebanese state, President Chamoun (who thought he could use the economic and military assistance against his political and religious enemies), that the doctrine contributed to the outbreak of civil war, not preservation of peace, and brought deep embarrassment to the United States.

The events of Lebanon and Iraq in 1958, like those of Suez, were complicated.[33] In Lebanon there had long been a confused political situation, Muslims against Christians, Arab nationalists against Lebanese nationalists. The political balance of the country was ever so delicate, and when Chamoun, a Maronite Christian, took up the cause of the United States, many of his opponents espoused that of President Nasser's United Arab Republic (Nasser had united Egypt with Syria on February 1, 1958). Some people, of course, simply did not like Chamoun. He was the duly elected president of Lebanon, chosen through democratic process, but he was said to be seeking to

[33] For an excellent account, based on extensive conversation with American officials in Lebanon, see Charles W. Thayer, *Diplomat* (New York, 1959), pp. 1-37.

amend the Lebanese constitution so as to enjoy another term of office. He was busily gerrymandering electoral districts. For such reasons open warfare broke out in Lebanon, beginning on May 10, 1958. On July 14, when revolution erupted in Iraq, Chamoun said he needed the Marines of the American Sixth Fleet within forty-eight hours or he was a dead man and Lebanon would become a Nasser satellite.[34] President Eisenhower, deeply stirred by the recent murderous bloodshed in Baghdad (for which see below), sent in 14,300 troops. Undersecretary of State Robert Murphy went out to Beirut posthaste in an attempt to settle the situation, and helped to arrange for opposition representation in the government and for Chamoun to step down from the presidency in September. The new president was the Lebanese army commander, Fuad Chehab, a Christian, not an admirer of Chamoun. After Chehab took over there was a short private war between Chamoun's faction and the Muslims (the Christian counterrevolution), but the basic principle of a compromise political settlement was preserved.

Just before American military involvement in Lebanon came the explosion in Iraq, a bloody affair which, other than dethroning the Hashemite dynasty, seems not to have changed drastically the politics of that state. The British had dominated Iraq in the interwar period, but beginning with the rebellion of the pro-Nazi Rashid Ali al Gailani in 1941 the hold of Britain began to loosen, and in the postwar years the Western orientation of Iraq was always uncertain. Nuri Pasha manfully held the lid on, until the eventual explosion killed him in 1958. It also killed Iraq's young monarch, King Feisal. The crown prince Abdel Illah likewise was killed. Abdel Illah's headless body went up on public display in Baghdad. Another headless body, believed to be that of Nuri Pasha, was dragged through the streets. Hawkers afterward openly sold pieces of human flesh reported to be that of Nuri. After the revolution Iraq seemed to be moving toward an Egyptian alignment. Nasser eagerly saluted "the great victory of the people of Iraq under the leadership of their hero Abdel Karim Kassem." Even so, Brigadier Kassem turned anti-Egyptian, and a year after the revolt the politics of Iraq were settling down to about where they had been before. Iraq had left the Baghdad Pact, and that structure had taken a new name, the Central Treaty Organization, CENTO. Iraq's position in the pact had never been secure, and the pact without Baghdad was perhaps a more realistic structure.

[34] *Ibid.*, p. 28.

Mirabile dictu, after Kassem turned against Nasser the government of Egypt began once more to court the United States, welcoming a Point Four mission and other technical assistance.

Having become involved in the strife of the Middle East by gratuitously promoting and assisting the creation of Israel and thereby antagonizing the Arab world, the United States saw its diplomatic fortunes move up and down and up again. The Americans in the first years after the war became extraordinarily vulnerable diplomatically because of their support of Israeli independence. The Russians commenced maneuvering in the area in 1955. When British influence vanished after Suez in 1956 the American government felt the full weight of Arab displeasure and Russian intrigue. The Lebanon and Iraq revolutions of 1958 were deeply embarrassing. But Egypt then began to move toward something resembling friendship. Lebanon was friendly, although not altogether grateful for the intervention of 1958. Iraq floundered in a positive neutralism of its own understanding. The Israelis were of course friendly to the transatlantic nation which had ensured their independence.

Where American policy toward the Middle East would finally lead to, no one knew as the 1960s dawned on an area full of troubles at a crossroads of civilizations old and new. America could attempt to raise living standards, to educate the illiterate millions of the region to some intelligent regard for their own advantage. But perhaps education and the raising of standards were methods too slow and cumbersome to avail against communist subversion. Meanwhile Americans could look into the far future, to the remote possibility of American-Russian friendship, and to the maturity of Arab nationalism, for the Middle East's only permanent basis of peace and prosperity.

10: AMERICAN POLICY TOWARDS THE SATELLITES AND NATIONAL COMMUNISM

John C. Campbell

There has been no more frustrating field for American diplomacy in the past two decades than Eastern Europe. During the Second World War American leaders declared as two of the nation's war aims the restoration of national liberty to peoples forcibly deprived of it and fulfillment of their right to governments of their own choosing. American arms played a major part in the defeat of Germany, but American diplomacy could not bring about a postwar settlement based on the principles of freedom and self-determination in Eastern Europe, where the Soviet Union substituted its own domination for that of the Nazis. Ever since, the United States has deplored that situation as unjust, protested it as a violation of wartime pledges of the Soviet Union, attempted to negotiate about it and to change it, and declared that it cannot be accepted as permanent. Yet, except in the case of Yugoslavia, there has been no basic change in the situation for fifteen years.

Is this outcome a classic example of the futility of diplomacy to right wrongs imposed by force? Is it the result of miscalculations and unwise decisions on the part of American diplomats? Or does it merely illustrate a lack of realism in setting objectives impossible to reach? The record of American policy has already been discussed and debated, attacked and defended, by many persons expert and inexpert, by practitioners of the diplomatic art, candidates for public office, scholars, and interested onlookers. More recently silence has been the order of the day. After 1956 there has seemed to be little to say. Sober analysis, however, will continue to be needed both for an understanding of the past, with the perspective time has provided, and for the decisions of the future.

Some points seem particularly to lend themselves to further examination and cautious speculation: such questions as the relationship between policy and diplomacy, between principles and practical politics, the choice between a "hard" and a "soft" diplomacy in attacking this problem of Eastern Europe, and above all the real possibilities of negotiating any settlements with the Soviet Union on the basic political and territorial questions that lie at the heart of the East-West conflict.

Mindful of the fullness of the historical record which makes the task of generalization without oversimplification difficult, we can follow the course of American policy on Eastern Europe through a series of fairly well-defined periods, seeking the guiding threads and the basic considerations which have determined that policy. The exception mentioned above—Yugoslavia—is worth more attention than its size and resources might imply, for the very fact that it is an exception in an otherwise largely negative record illustrates some truths of more than local significance.

THE DIPLOMACY OF VAGUE OBJECTIVES

During the Second World War American official concern over the future of Eastern Europe took shape in studies prepared in the Department of State covering a great number of territorial, political, and other questions on which the United States, as a major allied power, could expect to have a good deal to say.[1] Unfortunately from that viewpoint, the planning was largely fruitless because of decisions taken or not taken during the war, and because of the course of the war itself. Among the decisions based strictly on military considerations were those which left Eastern Europe (except Greece) entirely within the sphere of operations of the Soviet armies, when another course might have saved part of it from Soviet control. Others were political in nature, such as the insistence of President Roosevelt and Secretary Hull that territorial questions should not be negotiated until after the conclusion of hostilities. Whether any of them could have been decided in wartime negotiations to American satisfaction is a debatable question. Whether such agreements, if made by the Soviets, would have been honored by them after their armies occupied Eastern Europe, is another. What the record clearly shows is a lack of correspondence between talk and action, between declared objec-

[1] Harley A. Notter, *Postwar Foreign Policy Preparation, 1939-1945* (Washington, 1949), especially pp. 117-23, 146-48, 173-83, 220-22.

tives and the means of attaining them, between military strategy and political purpose.[2]

Part of the explanation lies in the vagueness of the objectives. The main idea was to restore freedom, in Eastern Europe as in Western Europe, to nations overrun by the Germans. This aim was not, of course, a matter of idealism or morality alone, or of a sense of obligation to carry out wartime declarations. Concern over the danger to the West that a swollen Soviet empire would represent, although far from a determining factor, was not absent from the thinking of some American officials. It was not clear, however, whether these were any more than principles that America *would like* to see applied, or interests that were secondary to more important ones such as maintaining good relations with Russia. They were not calculated objectives, based on firm convictions concerning the postwar balance of power in Europe and matched by a choice of means for their attainment other than a vain reliance on Soviet good faith.

If there was any weighing of objectives, it was by the negative process of failing to assert a reasoned interest when the opportunity arose. Not only were political considerations cast aside when proposals for operations in the Balkans (except Greece) or in the Danube valley were rejected; the American attitude illustrated a deliberate disinclination to assert a positive political interest in the fate of Eastern Europe. Admiral Leahy expressed the view prevailing in the highest official circles when he spoke of Russia's military capacity to dominate postwar Europe as requiring for America a mediating role between Britain and Russia and a special effort to keep on good terms with the Russians. He discounted the possibility of doing anything to prevent their achieving such a position.[3] Again, when Churchill and Stalin made their famous "percentage deal" on the Balkans in 1944, Ambassador Harriman was present as an observer and stated no American position. As a government we

[2] Philip E. Mosely, "Hopes and Failures: American Policy Toward East Central Europe, 1941-1947," in Stephen D. Kertesz, ed., *The Fate of East Central Europe* (Notre Dame, Indiana, 1956), pp. 51-74; John C. Campbell, "Negotiations with the Soviets: Some Lessons of the War Period," *Foreign Affairs*, vol. 34 (January, 1956), 305-19.

[3] US Department of State, *The Conferences at Malta and Yalta, 1945* (Washington, 1955), pp. 106-108.

opposed spheres of influence. We opposed the idea of making political settlements before the peace negotiations. We chose to ignore the fact that spheres of influence were being established and political settlements were imposing themselves as the Soviet armies advanced into Eastern Europe, and that a peace conference, if there were one, would not have before it the map of Europe as a *tabula rasa*.

What was to be done, then, as Soviet forces pursued Hitler's legions westward and it became ever more obvious that their physical presence would weigh heavily in determining the postwar settlement? As a means of mitigating its effects the United States tried two tactics: (a) to internationalize Eastern European questions as much as possible through special agreements, armistice negotiations, allied control commissions and other devices which would place Western representatives, with international responsibilities, alongside the Russians in those countries, and (b) to obtain Soviet commitments to general Western objectives such as representative governments and free elections, as in the various agreements on Poland, on Yugoslavia, and on "liberated Europe," reached at Yalta. The results are well known. The Soviets agreed to American and British representation on allied control organs in the occupied former enemy states, and then made a mockery of it. They agreed to general principles on broadly representative governments and free elections, and then violated them with impunity.

THE DIPLOMACY OF PROTEST

It was true that circumstances—especially the military decisions, the facts of geography, the importance of the alliance with Russia at a time the war was still being fought, the desire of President Roosevelt to keep every avenue open to co-operation with the Russians in the new world organization, and the policy of keeping in Western hands the control of territories occupied by the Western armies—made it especially difficult to assert American interests in Eastern Europe against the Soviet Union. It would have required bold decisions which the United States did not really seriously consider making. It was clear by late 1944, if not earlier, that the Soviet Union intended to establish its domination over that area. And it was clear by the end of 1945, in its reaction to Soviet moves and to Winston Churchill's cries of alarm, that the United States did not consider it important enough for a showdown. This is not stated as a matter of right or wrong, but as a fact.

What complicated the picture was the divergence between the public posture taken by the United States and its actual conduct. The US Government took seriously the agreements made at Yalta. It made an issue of freedom in Eastern Europe at the Potsdam Conference and even allowed the first treaty-making session of the Council of Foreign Ministers at London in September, 1945, to break down largely on that issue. Yet when the Soviet Union, being almost everywhere in physical control of the area, went right ahead with its practice of helping to install communist governments and to rig elections, the United States, having ruled out resort to force, could find no remedy in diplomacy either. It tried persuasion, appeals to allied solidarity, and detailed bills of particulars on how the agreements were being violated, but had nothing to offer that was of sufficient interest to Stalin to induce him to change his policies in Eastern Europe. Consequently, it was reduced to a diplomacy of ineffective protest.

Until the end of 1946 the United States, although well aware that the cold war was already at hand, engaged in a series of retreats in search of arrangements that would save at least something of the Yalta principles and of Western influence in the area; so great was its concern with preserving the fabric of great-power solidarity. The compromise on Poland reached in June, 1945, under pressure of the desire to preserve Big Three unity at the critical moment of the launching of the new United Nations Organization, was a substantial retreat from Yalta in that it turned over power to a communist-dominated regime. The agreements on Rumania and Bulgaria reached at Moscow in December, 1945, when Secretary Byrnes was anxious to get on with the job of negotiating peace treaties, saved but a shadow of the right of those nations to governments of their own choosing. These were, in fact, more in the nature of face-saving devices than serious attempts to guarantee that right to them.

Having itself backed the local communists and helped them destroy their democratic opponents, while the latter looked vainly for support from the West, the Soviet government replied to Western protests by blandly invoking the doctrine of nonintervention. The United States, after protests and delays, ultimately recognized the communist governments despite their unrepresentative character, on the ground that it could not really accomplish anything by being absent from the scene. In the peace treaties concluded with Hungary, Rumania, and Bulgaria in 1947, clauses guaranteeing the exercise of human rights, including freedom of speech, assembly and political activity, provided a legal basis for further protests, discussions at the United Nations, and appeals for arbitration or judicial settlement, but they were unenforceable.

It was important that all these protests be made for the record, that the world continue to be told that the United States did not formally accept the violation of international agreements or Soviet domination of Eastern Europe. But there was little doubt of the *de facto* acceptance of both.

CONTAINMENT

The hardening of American policy toward the Soviet Union, already evident in Turkey and Iran and later finding expression in the Truman Doctrine, the Marshall Plan, and NATO, was a reaction against Soviet attempts to expand into Western Europe and the Mediterranean area. It reflected a determination to hold the line between the Soviet bloc and the free world where it then was. "This far and no farther" was the message of the policy which came to be known as containment. But what did it say or imply with respect to the countries east of the Lübeck–Trieste line where "armed minorities," to cite the language of the Truman Doctrine, had already seized power or were soon to seize it?

For a brief moment the peoples of Eastern Europe and those who could speak freely on their behalf looked hopefully for a stronger Western policy aimed at loosening the Soviet grip on them or preventing complete domination. Those hopes were dispelled by the weak American reaction to the communists' coup in Hungary in May, 1947, and to their seizure of power in Czechoslovakia the following February. It was still a diplomacy of protest despite President Truman's assertion with respect to Hungary that "we will not stand idly by" and the strong statement put out by the United States, British, and French governments on the subject of Czechoslovakia. Admittedly it would have been difficult to prevent what happened. Hungary was still occupied by Soviet troops; Czechoslovakia had long been following the Soviet lead in matters of foreign policy and did not ask for Western help. In any case, what happened made it clear where the line of containment ran. Eastern Europe was not vital to the survival of the West, as Western Europe was.

The concentration of American effort on the defensive task of preventing further expansion of the Soviet bloc did not imply an acceptance of the permanent division of Europe or of the world. It remained an aim of American policy, after 1948, to help bring about the reduction and eventual elimination of Soviet control over the nations of Eastern Europe. The aim was based on a series of concerns involving the balance of power (now more clearly understood), the need for a stable settlement in Europe, and the principles of national and individual freedom. The United States Government believed that domination of the satellites added substantially to Soviet strength and to the magnitude of the threat posed to Western Europe, and that their recovery of independence would represent a welcome shift in the world balance. It believed that no stable settlement could be made in Europe when one half of the continent was dominated by one great power. Finally, it continued to believe that the denial of self-determination to the Eastern European peoples was wrong in itself and a betrayal of pledges made to them.

This aim was not loudly proclaimed, before 1953, because the means of doing anything about it were so limited. Neither broadcasts nor economic measures nor covert operations were effective in bringing about any basic change in the situation. The peoples of Eastern Europe were in large majority opposed both to their communist regimes and to Soviet domination, but neither they nor the Western powers could find a way to make that opposition effective. If they could not do so during the relatively fluid situation of the 1945-1948 period, when the United States had its atomic monopoly, what ground was there for believing it possible to reverse the tide after Stalin had consolidated his hold on the area and the USSR had also become a nuclear power? For obvious reasons American diplomacy in Europe concentrated on Germany, where it still had bargaining power.

The power of decision lay with the Soviet leadership, as Secretary Acheson recognized in his speech at Berkeley, California, in 1950.[4]

[4] "Tensions between the United States and the Soviet Union," address by Secretary Acheson, March 16, 1950, Department of State Publication No. 3810 (Washington, 1950).

If the Soviet leaders wanted to contribute to peace and security, he said, they had only to recall their military forces from Eastern Europe and to refrain from "using the shadow of that force to keep in power persons or regimes which do not command the confidence of the respective peoples . . . Nothing would so alter the international climate as the holding of elections in the satellite states in which the true will of the people could be expressed." But American diplomacy could do little more than to put the question. Stalin did not feel impelled to withdraw either because of pressure from inside or outside the area or because of a desire for a broad political settlement with the West.

But already there was a new element in the picture that gave Stalin more to worry about in Eastern Europe than did speeches by an American secretary of state. This was Tito, and the idea of national communism.

NATIONAL COMMUNISM: AID TO TITO

The break between Tito and Stalin put a new complexion on American policy toward the communist bloc. Here was a communist government, which had come to power with the full support of the USSR and had seemed its most loyal satellite, insisting on its right to run its own country, proclaiming its own interpretations of Marxism-Leninism, and in due course charting an independent foreign policy. The United States was faced with a choice: should it support Tito, to help him maintain Yugoslavia's independence, or should it stand aside from the quarrel between communist regimes, both of them hostile to Western democracy?

Judgments had to be made on several points. Was the break genuine? If so, could Tito hold out? Was it right to give aid and comfort to a communist regime, which we had publicly branded as aggressive, in violation of its agreements, and unrepresentative of the people of its own country? The United States Government answered all three questions in the affirmative. To put it more specifically: the break in the "monolithic unity" of the communist world was real; whether Yugoslavia's independence could survive was likely to depend on whether Tito got help from the West; and it was in the interest of the United States and of the West to provide help regardless of the nature of the regime. The main reasons were strategic (pushing the frontier of the Soviet empire back from the Adriatic, except for isolated Albania, to the middle of the Balkan peninsula; easing the pressure on Italy and Greece; ensuring that Yugoslavia's armed forces would no longer be in the enemy camp) and political (exploiting a fissure in the communist world that could shake it to its foundations). That this reasoning was shared by the British and French governments does not detract from the importance of the American decision, which was taken independently, for it was known that Western help could not be adequate unless the United States carried the major burden.

It is not necessary here to give the detailed story of American aid to Tito's Yugoslavia, from the loosening of export controls (February, 1949) and the first Export-Import Bank loan (September, 1949) to the flood of grants, loans and military deliveries that came with the Yugoslav Emergency Relief Assistance Act (passed by Congress in special session in December, 1950) and the subsequent inclusion of Yugoslavia in the general mutual security programs of economic and military aid.[5] As an "operation" the extension of aid was carried through with reasonable speed and efficiency and with successful results. It helped Yugoslavia to withstand Soviet pressures and ward off economic disaster at critical times when its people were short of food, its factories lacked raw materials, its international credit was exhausted, and its army was in need of weapons. It enabled the Yugoslavs to face up to Stalin with confidence that they were not alone. But we are concerned here less with the details of the effectiveness of American assistance than with the policy which underlay it and the diplomacy which made it possible.

The United States was fortunate in its diplomatic representation in Belgrade in this critical period. At the time of the break the American ambassador was Cavendish W. Cannon, a career Foreign Service officer with a background of many years of experience in the Balkans and in handling Yugoslav affairs in the State Department. Late in 1949 he was succeeded by George V. Allen, also a professional

[5] In the period up to the Bulganin-Khrushchev visit to Yugoslavia in May-June, 1955, the totals were $390 million in grants, $55 million in loans, $74 million in the sale of surplus agricultural goods for local currency, and in the neighborhood of half a billion dollars in military equipment and training. (See US Department of Commerce, *Foreign Grants and Credits by the United States Government*, June 1955 Quarter, pp. 5, S-34, S-56.) Additional aid was provided by Great Britain and France (pursuant to a tripartite share-the-burden program in which they were associated with the United States) and through two loans of the World Bank totalling $58 million.

with a brilliant record of "crisis diplomacy" in Iran. It so happened that each was admirably suited to the task of the day: Cannon to analyze the significance of the break, to urge important changes of policy on Washington, and to manage the difficult transition in relations with the Tito regime; Allen to convince the Yugoslavs of the benefits of growing co-operation, to negotiate the basic agreements on economic and military aid, to translate new policies into action, and to help explain them to the Congress and the American people. Both were well served by a competent staff in Belgrade.

It is worth citing these facts because they illustrated the capacity of the United States to act promptly and realistically in Eastern Europe when the situation offered firm ground on which to stand. American diplomacy did not take refuge in declarations of principle as the answer to specific problems. Although the issue of aiding a communist regime raised political and moral questions that might have led to doubt and delay, the government consistently followed its main purpose of doing what could practically be done to support Yugoslavia's independence. It was a policy adopted under a Democratic administration and continued by a Republican one at the very time that the bitter controversies over "softness on communism" and "liberation" were at their height. The reason was that Tito had created conditions in which American policy could be effective, whereas in the rest of Eastern Europe similar conditions did not exist, nor could the United States itself create them.

NATIONAL COMMUNISM AND LIBERATION

The two salient political facts of the years immediately following the Tito-Stalin break were the former's success in maintaining "Titoism" in its country of origin and the latter's success in containing it there. A series of purges in the Soviet satellite states had the effect of removing potential Titoists from the party leadership in those countries. Their rapid trend toward Sovietization seemed to rule out any chance that the Yugoslav experience could be repeated elsewhere. It also set narrow limits to what American policy and diplomacy could accomplish.

The State Department had hopes that the germs of national communism would spread beyond Yugoslavia, but it could find no way to encourage the process except through the efforts to make Yugoslavia an example of the advantages of heresy. The great obstacles were the absence in the satellites of the combination of conditions which had made the Yugoslav break possible (such as full local control of army and police, and geographical access to the West), the ruthless countermeasures taken by Stalin, and the hesitancy of the United States itself to try to do more for Tito than to keep him "afloat."

The Democratic administration thus bequeathed to its Republican successor two separate approaches to Eastern Europe, neither of which, during the last years of the Stalin era, offered much scope for diplomacy. One was to look primarily to the anticommunist mass of the people of those nations: keeping up their morale, encouraging their opposition to the communist regimes and to Moscow, and keeping their cause before the world, so that eventually, by one means or another, conditions would be created permitting them governments of their own choosing and freedom to rejoin the European community. The other approach was to encourage antagonism between the satellite governments and the Soviet Union: continuing aid to Yugoslavia as an example, opening the doors to economic and cultural relations with the satellite regimes, and encouraging any tendencies they might show toward restiveness or independence, so that they might at least question Soviet domination and increase the measure of control over their own policies even if they could not break openly with Moscow as Tito had. This latter approach assumed a degree of common interest, actual or potential, between the regimes and the people in opposition to full-scale Soviet domination.

In many ways the two courses were mutually inconsistent. It was not easy to reconcile efforts to support peoples in opposition to communism with attempts to widen the gap between the local regimes and Moscow. Largely because it met with so little success in either course, American policy did not have to make the choice posed by their inconsistency. It was therefore quite natural that the Republican administration which took office in January, 1953, should place no great emphasis on Titoism (although prepared to continue aid to Yugoslavia) and should direct its policies primarily to the broader and obviously more popular goal of the liberation of the subjugated peoples of Eastern Europe from Soviet-communist rule.

Indeed, the leaders of the Republican party, in the election campaign of 1952, had made much of their intention to pursue the basic aim of freedom for Eastern Europe not merely by asking the Soviets to honor their commitments but by seizing the initiative on behalf of the United States. They wanted to denounce the "shameful" agreements such as those of Yalta under cover of which the Soviets had taken over Eastern Europe. They offered a "positive policy of liberation" in place of the "negative policy of containment." Although those propositions had a not inconsiderable impact on domestic politics, it would not be especially enlightening or useful to discuss that aspect here, for the reason that it was not really relevant to what could be achieved in the field of foreign policy.

The United States, after the new administration came into office, was in fact not able to seize the initiative or to be any more dynamic than before, as was soon apparent when it did nothing to take advantage of the revolt in East Germany in June, 1953. The study given to the possible detachment of one or more satellites from the Soviet bloc and the earnest efforts to use radio broadcasts and such devices as balloons to stir things up behind the curtain all foundered on the rock of the *de facto* division of Europe and the impotence of the West to challenge it without inacceptable risk. In fairness to the president and to Secretary Dulles it must be said that they never proposed to use force to bring about liberation, but the slogans and the oratory created the impression that they had in mind not merely a goal but also a means of getting there, and no great effort was made to correct that impression.

Not only was liberation a delusion as a practical alternative policy to containment. It also was injected into the picture at a time when the Soviet empire began to undergo changes, some rather obvious, some more subtle, which might have offered opportunities for American diplomacy had it not been mesmerized by the ideas and slogans of the recent electoral campaign. For Stalin left the political scene soon after Eisenhower came on it, and with him went the monolithic system which he had created and ruled.

THE EFFECTS OF THE THAW

The death of Stalin unloosed many forces in the Soviet empire, including some in the satellite states affecting both the stability of the regimes and their relationships with Moscow. Partly, the new atmosphere was the result of uncertainty and rivalry within the collective leadership in Moscow; partly, it stemmed from the moves of relaxation which were taken within the Soviet Union; even more, it reflected developments within the Eastern European states themselves. There was a growing feeling both inside the satellite communist parties and also among their subject peoples that the rigid Stalinist system could no longer be maintained without Stalin. Above all, there was recognition even in the Kremlin that some of Stalin's policies in the satellites, those that were driving them toward economic breakdown or popular revolt, could no longer be safely or sensibly maintained.

The rioting that broke out in East Germany and Czechoslovakia in June, 1953, was a warning. It could be, and was, met by repressive force in the first instance. It also confirmed the new Soviet leadership in the view that some easing of the reins was necessary. This fact was soon apparent in the "new course" adopted by one satellite government after another during 1953. Its most spectacular debut was in Hungary, where Imre Nagy, the new prime minister handpicked by Moscow, publicly discarded the Stalinist policies of his predecessor, Mátyás Rákosi, and announced a new program more suited to the country's economic possibilities and more attuned to the feelings of the people.

Looking back on the developments of the period from 1953 to 1956, one is struck by the uncertainty and the weakness of Soviet policy in Eastern Europe and by the change in atmosphere within the satellite countries. Once the rigid patterns of Stalinist conformity were broken, the road to experiment in new and more voluntary relationships was open, and the desire to question and to criticize made itself felt, especially within the communist ranks. Of course, Soviet force always remained in the background. In East Germany, Poland, Hungary and Rumania it was right at hand in the form of well-armed Soviet troops. But the apparatus of Soviet control that was omnipresent in Stalin's day—through the government structure, the secret police, the military, and the party—no longer operated with the same deadly efficiency and terror. There was still terror, but it was sporadic, no longer wrapped in a myth of invincibility or inspiring such fear that society, behind the fraudulent slogans of great common effort for the building of socialism, was reduced to an atomized collection of helpless individuals.

Amid their own rivalry and struggles for power the Soviet leaders seemed to be moving by zigs and zags toward a new conception of relations with the satellites, although it was not clear to them, or to the satellite regimes or peoples, just what that conception was. It seemed to involve a greater degree of latitude for the regimes in taking account of national conditions and in finding suitable policies within the over-all scheme of progress toward socialism and fraternal collaboration within the socialist camp.

Then Khrushchev, who was largely responsible for this trend, lifted the lid a little higher by the reversal of Soviet policy toward Yugoslavia, which reached its climax in the visit of the highest Soviet leaders to Belgrade in May, 1955. This extraordinary turn of events was not unrelated to the general trend in Soviet policy toward relaxation in relations with neighboring states and with the West, which included agreement on the Austrian treaty, withdrawal from the Soviet base at Porkkala-Udd in Finland, and preparations for a conference at the summit. It was surely intended also to draw Tito back from too close an association with the NATO powers.

Yet the main purposes probably were more closely tied to the future character of the Soviet bloc itself: to liquidate a policy which had obviously failed; to put an end to the annoying influence which an anti-Soviet Yugoslavia was exerting, or might exert, on the satellites or on Soviet-Chinese relations; and to make possible Yugoslavia's gradual return to the bloc on a basis both sides could accept. In this calculated risk there was a large element of miscalculation, for Tito was in fact unwilling to accept any limitations on his independence, and the legitimizing of his regime as a properly socialist one following its own road could not fail to encourage nationalist ideas among other communists, especially in Poland and Hungary. Furthermore, it exposed the Soviets to Tito's demands for the elimination of those satellite leaders (primarily Rákosi) who had taken the lead in the Stalinist campaigns to destroy him and who were still in many instances the most loyal to Moscow.

It is not possible to measure how much Yugoslavia's influence contributed to the growing unrest and freedom of expression in Hungary and Poland, but it undoubtedly had some part in it. The "revolt of the mind," which turned so many influential communist intellectuals and journalists against the Rákosis and the Bieruts, reflected not only the objective conditions in their respective countries but also the new atmosphere created by the Soviet reconciliation with Tito; not only the new insights and the courage of "revisionist" writers but also the apparent acceptance by the Soviet leadership itself, at the Belgrade meeting and again at the 20th Party Congress in February, 1956, of the principle of separate roads to socialism. Actually the Kremlin never did accept the full implications of that principle and never intended to. It sought a new order in which the satellite regimes would have a broader base on which to rest than Soviet bayonets, without endangering the basic unity of the bloc under Soviet leadership. Yet precisely what it did want, and how much diversity it would allow, was uncertain.[6]

The reaction of the United States to these developments was singularly leaden. At a time when changes in the satellite states, particularly within the communist parties, showed the first signs of the reality of national communism as a political force, American policy was still dominated by the idea that it could somehow find the means to restore full freedom to the captive peoples. The only change was that after the East German events had provided a salutary lesson that nothing concrete could be done even to help a people who had risen in revolt, and that to encourage such revolt was merely to increase the violence of its suppression, the adjective "peaceful" made its appearance before the word "liberation" in official pronouncements.

American officials tended to underestimate or to misread what was taking place within the satellite states. Admittedly, they were cut off from many sources of information. Their diplomatic missions lived in splendid isolation in the satellite capitals, except in Sofia and Tirana where the United States was not represented at all. So long as the governments were run by communists, the tendency was not to attach importance to the shifts in leadership. The advent to power of Imre Nagy in Hungary in 1953, for example, did not appear to have great significance, especially since Rákosi remained as first secretary of the communist party, whereas in fact it marked the beginning of a fierce struggle for power within the party which led in time to the upheaval of October, 1956. The Soviet-Yugoslav reconciliation in 1955 first provoked consternation in Washington and then relief on the receipt of assurances from Tito that Yugoslavia would not give up its independence or its ties with the West. Its potential contribution to the loosening or disintegration of the Soviet bloc tended to be lost from view.

What the United States could have done about Eastern Europe at this stage is another question. That would have depended, as before, chiefly on the Soviet government. Khrushchev never opened

[6] Zbigniew K. Brzezinski, *The Soviet Bloc: Unity and Conflict* (Cambridge, Mass., 1960), pp. 153-206, contains a documented and well-reasoned discussion of these issues.

these matters to discussion and negotiation with the West. Yet he was searching for new approaches both to Eastern Europe and to the West, and he was not in full control of developments. How much flexibility of diplomacy and political action the United States may have had, and whether the Soviets would have been receptive, are matters of mere speculation now. American views on disengagement were negative if only because of Germany: the Soviets were adamant in opposing Germany's reunification in freedom, and to weaken the Western position before the German Federal Republic had any real defensive strength of its own was considered far too risky. But it is still worth asking whether both sides may not have had an interest in averting a drift of events to the climax of October, 1956, which, as it turned out, was a searing experience for both. A disengagement reaching into Eastern Europe, surely a more real possibility in 1955-1956 than a year after the explosion when it became such a prominent subject of public discussion and diplomatic exchange, was never explored.

As it turned out, the American approach to Eastern Europe as a subject for negotiation remained on a *pro forma* basis and on the theme of liberation. The president told the Soviet leaders at Geneva in 1955 that the United States took the question of Eastern Europe seriously and that it could not put trust in Soviet protestations for peace so long as those nations were held captive against their will. This was no different than Secretary Acheson's public plea to Stalin in 1950. When Bulganin and Khrushchev indignantly rejected the argument and refused to put the question on the agenda of the summit conference, it was dropped.

Later in the same year Secretary Dulles visited Tito and there took the occasion to pay tribute to the Yugoslav leader's role in preserving his own country's independence and to speak out publicly to the effect that he and Tito were both in favor of independence for the satellite countries, noninterference from outside in their internal affairs, and their right to develop their own social and economic order in ways of their own choice.[7] The visit was a notable gesture of American good will toward Yugoslavia despite Tito's apparent reconciliation with Moscow. The secretary's statement seemed in some respects a throwback to earlier American hopes for national communism in Eastern Europe. Later Yugoslav comment, however,

[7] For the joint communiqué and the secretary's remarks see *Documents on American Foreign Relations, 1955* (New York, 1956), pp. 165-66.

made it clear that the two statesmen did not and probably would not agree on the process of Eastern Europe's "independent development" or on the social order which was the ultimate goal, for Yugoslavia would have no truck with a reversion to the "independence" of the "feudal and bourgeois" past.[8] This brief understanding, or misunderstanding, thus remained an isolated episode.

1956: THE DIPLOMACY OF IMPOTENCE

Partly because it had not occupied itself with thinking, probing, and negotiating on Eastern Europe during the period of the thaw, and even more because of the limitations inherent in the situation, the United States found itself with a very narrow range of action when the unrest and opposition in Poland and Hungary reached the point of explosion in the autumn of 1956.

The gains won by Poland in the "Polish October" were the result of the courage and resolve of Wladislaw Gomulka and his colleagues, the solidarity of the Polish people, and the decision of the Soviet leaders that half a loaf was better than a whole one gained by a blood bath. Poland won internal autonomy but remained within the Soviet bloc, with Soviet troops on its soil, and the basis for its future was a bilateral bargain between the Polish and the Soviet communist leadership, with the latter likely to exercise the greater weight as the bargain worked itself out in the long run.

The United States, as an interested spectator of these events, could find some comfort in the new situation. Whether it would last was another question, but at least it had been demonstrated that Polish communists had ideas on national rights and national interests that were not shared by Soviet communists. This was the biggest crack in the unity of the Soviet bloc since Tito's break in 1948. Gomulka was not a Tito—reasons of geography would not permit it, even if he wished to be—but he was obviously no mere puppet of Moscow. As in the Yugoslav case the West, having done nothing to bring about the rift, could perhaps help to widen it and to make it permanent.

Hungary was different. There the question of the role of the West was posed suddenly in a way that made it impossible to avoid immediate and hard decisions, if only in the negative sense of not making

[8] See, for example, J. Arnejc, "After the Brioni Talks," *Review of International Affairs* (Belgrade), VI (November 16, 1955), 9-10.

them. The revolt, long simmering in the form of demands for more freedom, for better conditions and for changes in the leadership, broke into open violence on October 23 and spun rapidly out of control. The Hungarian government, nominally headed by Imre Nagy from the second day of the revolution, was at no time master of the situation. The revolt, which began with modest demands on the part of students and writers, fed on its unexpected victories and soon became a national movement with aims that grew with each demonstration that the old system had no Hungarian defenders save the hated security police. The Soviet government, after intervening with its troops at the start, seemed anxious to stabilize the situation and reluctant to commit itself to all out repression. The United States lifted its official and unofficial voices in admiration and encouragement for the Hungarians. It watched the drama and hoped for the best. In the end the worst happened. The Nagy government finally asked for help in maintaining Hungary's independence and neutrality, but did not get it. The Soviets intervened again, this time in force, and the revolution was over.

Much has been written about whether the United States and other Western nations should or could have helped the Hungarians in their valiant effort for greater freedom. A judgment on that question depends on the answers to other questions: (1) What were the calculations and decisions of the Soviet leadership during the course of the crisis? (2) Could the government of Imre Nagy have stabilized the revolution at a point where some compromise with the Soviets was possible? (3) What means were available by which the United States could have helped to save some degree of freedom for Hungary?

American passivity has been explained on the ground that any intervention from the West would have precipitated the third World War, and this is very likely true if military intervention is meant. Effective military action on the spot would have been impossible anyway, Hungary being separated geographically from the NATO area by neutral Austria and Yugoslavia. The explicit threat of nuclear war to deter Soviet military action could scarcely have been effective either, for the Soviets would surely have taken it as the bluff it would have been. No other form of intervention, moreover, would have had any success if the Soviet leaders were determined from the start to crush the revolt and went through the stage of making reasonable and conciliatory noises only as cover for the necessary measures of military preparation. Nor would Western action have succeeded, even if we assume a more flexible Soviet policy, unless the demands of the Hungarian revolutionaries had been kept within limits that Moscow might conceivably accept, for example the terms it had already accepted for Poland.

Suppose that we make the most favorable assumptions: that the Soviet leaders, until the last days of October, were undecided whether to compromise with the revolution or to crush it—a theory for which there is some evidence[9]—and that the course of the revolution could have been controlled (which was improbable but not inconceivable, for it is worth noting that Nagy did not denounce the Warsaw Pact until after fresh Soviet troops began pouring across the Hungarian border). In that case there were, perhaps, a few brief days in which American initiative and action might have influenced Soviet and Hungarian behavior and affected the final outcome.

An essay intended as a description rather than as a critique of American policy cannot properly go into all the steps that might have been taken and the hypothetical results of each. Among the possibilities were an earlier and more positive effort to bring about specific action through the United Nations, such as the dispatch of a UN commission to Hungary (the Security Council met for inconclusive discussion on October 28 and then not until November 2 and 3, while the special session of the General Assembly was not convened until November 4 when it was too late); direct diplomatic initiatives to stay the Russian hand and bring the Hungarian question into a broader framework; or a serious attempt to mobilize world opinion as a means of pressure at a time when the Soviet leaders were suffering from shock and embarrassment over the Polish and Hungarian events.

It seems doubtful that such efforts would have changed the outcome of the affair, even under the favorable assumptions mentioned above. Even at moments of difficulty the Soviet leaders care little or nothing for the United Nations, diplomatic interventions, or world opinion when they feel the need to take action in their own interests.

[9] Khrushchev himself later stated that there was disagreement within the Soviet leadership at the time, and that some were against military intervention. (Speech at Budapest, December 2, 1959, *Pravda*, December 3, and *Current Digest of the Soviet Press*, XI, December 30, 1959, 9.)

It is easy to see, also, why the United States did not grasp every possible opportunity for bolder and more imaginative measures. Time was limited, and democracies function slowly. The factual situation, in the early period, was not clear. There seemed a chance that the Hungarians, like the Poles, could get more by themselves than if the Western powers injected themselves into the picture. Action by the West would have required a frame of mind which, despite all the talk of liberation, did not exist in the government or in the nation. It would have required planning and interallied agreement, which had not been prepared in advance and could hardly be improvised in the midst of the crisis, especially at a time when relations within the Western alliance were strained and about to break down completely over Suez. After the outbreak of war in the Near East, of course, there was no chance that the West would do anything about Hungary, and by that time the Soviet decision for reconquest may already have been taken.

Only in one public statement did the United States Government raise possibilities that might offer both Moscow and the Hungarians a way out of the impasse without war and without disaster to either. On October 27 Secretary Dulles made a speech in which he expressed the hope that the captive nations would have sovereignty restored to them and governments of their own free choosing, then added that we saw them as friends in a new and no longer divided Europe, not as potential military allies.[10] Whether these suggestions and disclaimers of ulterior motive had any effect on Soviet thinking we do not know. The Soviet statement on the proposed new order in the "socialist commonwealth," issued on October 30, seemed conciliatory and rather promising, encouraging President Eisenhower to hail "the dawning of a new day." But the clear indications that the United States would not use force in Eastern Europe no matter what happened, evident in several statements by Secretary Dulles and the president between October 21 and November 1, probably were more important in Soviet calculations. They provided the necessary reassurance, if any was needed, that Soviet troops could crush Hungary without fear of intervention from the West.

[10] Address to the Dallas Council of World Affairs, *Bulletin*, 35 (November 5, 1956), 695-99. Secretary Byrnes had made the same point eleven years earlier in a vain effort to persuade the Soviet Union that a free Eastern Europe would be compatible with its own security against any threat from the West (*ibid.*, 13, November 4, 1945, 709-11).

STATUS QUO AND WATCHFUL WAITING

The events of 1956 carried some sobering lessons for Moscow, for the Eastern European nations, and for the West. There could be no further doubt of the tremendous popular opposition in the satellite nations to Soviet domination and to the communist system as practiced by the local "Muscovites." It was the solid anti-Russian feelings of the Poles, communist and noncommunist, that made it possible for Gomulka to stand his ground against Khrushchev; and in Hungary the few days of free expression revealed the nearly unanimous revulsion against the Soviet occupation and against the Stalinism symbolized by Rákosi and Gerö. Ironically, this revelation of Soviet weakness was matched by the revelation of the inability of the West to take advantage of a situation in which a satellite nation, under its legal government, had succeeded momentarily in liberating itself.

Perhaps more important for the immediate future was the indication of the limits beyond which the Soviets would not be pushed by protest or revolt within their empire without using force. They would not allow any local leader, as they had allowed Tito in 1948, the time and the opportunity to consolidate his position and get significant help from the West. A satellite, apparently, would not be permitted to leave the Soviet security system. Nor could it destroy the system of communist party dictatorship. The Polish October stopped short of these changes. In Hungary the local communist leadership (Imre Nagy, who presumably spoke for what was left of the party) agreed to the free organization of noncommunist parties and sought an internationally guaranteed neutrality outside the Warsaw Pact. That made him a "counter-revolutionary" and sealed his doom.

As the Kremlin set about reconstituting the bloc on a basis that would better assure its control of Eastern Europe, the United States had to reappraise its own policies. Dulles, enlarging on the theme of his Dallas speech, expressed the view that it was up to the Soviet Union to make its own settlements with the Eastern European nations, and that eventually it would have to do so on the basis of the principle of freedom,[11] thus in effect handing over to the Kremlin the responsibility for carrying out the policy of liberation; but this did not sound so strange as it would have a few years before. The

[11] Statement at press conference, December 18, 1956 (*ibid.*, vol. 36, January 7, 1957, 8-9). See also his address to the Associated Press, April 22, 1957 (*ibid.*, 717-18).

secretary spoke of the possibility of neutralization of the satellites, on which the United States was "openminded"—but Khrushchev's reply to that suggestion had already been given in Hungary. He also mentioned Poland. Part of the reappraisal, apparently, was a new appreciation of the possibilities of national communism as a stage in "evolution to freedom." Poland's example showed that a satellite regime could win control of its domestic affairs and even make gestures in the field of foreign policy that were not 100 per cent along the Soviet line.

The United States, as Secretary Dulles put it, was prepared to respond to a situation like Poland's with "friendly acts." In other words, it was ready to treat Poland in a way that would help the Poles to consolidate and perhaps extend the gains they had won. It eased political relations, encouraged educational and cultural contacts, and extended economic aid at the Polish government's request. This aid was not comparable to the earlier American support of Tito. Yugoslavia after 1948 had left the Soviet bloc. Poland after 1956 was still in it. Aid to Poland brought the United States no strategic military advantage, no economic or obvious political gain. It promised nothing spectacular. It was merely a means of giving greater confidence to the new Polish regime, perhaps some greater bargaining power with the Russians through having ties with the West, and it was a means of helping the Polish people.

The first package of aid was modest ($97 million) and it came late, but it was followed by others in the ensuing years; the significant thing was that aid was provided at all to a communist government which loudly proclaimed its solidarity with the "socialist camp" and which, despite some surface differences, was in fact following Moscow on every important issue of international policy. By the time America's aid program began, the Soviet leadership had already had considerable success in reconstituting the unity of the bloc, including Poland.

The task before Khrushchev was to find sufficient means to hold the bloc together other than the ultimate recourse: force. Accepting the fact of national communism in China, he took account also of the diversity of conditions in the European satellites and pointedly refrained from trying to revert to the imposed uniformity of Stalinism. He showed in Poland that, for some time at least, he would bet on Gomulka rather than on the so-called Stalinists in the Polish Workers (communist) party. Even in Hungary he tried through

Kádár and Münnich to find the way to a new equilibrium that would have the toleration if not the support of the population.

In other words, the uncertainty and groping of the years from 1953 to 1956, which had done so much to encourage tendencies toward national communism, were being replaced with the new concept of a "socialist commonwealth" in which tendencies to diversity were to be recognized but contained by the common basic ideology, strong economic ties and general economic progress, and the Soviet-controlled arrangements for military security. Over time, Poland's position could well be reduced toward closer correspondence with those of the other satellites. There was, however, no room in such a commonwealth for Yugoslavia, which insisted on its own independent foreign policy and opposition to all blocs except those of neutralist states.

Khrushchev probably has little reason to fear another popular revolt, and he has gambled on keeping national communism within bounds. The United States, meanwhile, has confined itself to modest and long-term efforts, which include the increase of economic and cultural contacts with the countries of Eastern Europe. A dozen years after 1948, the year which saw both the completion of Stalin's conquest of Eastern Europe and Tito's break from the ranks, the United States still follows the two lines which grew out of those developments: nonacceptance of the justice or permanence of the Soviet denial of independence to the Eastern European nations, and encouragement to those forces at work within the communist structure toward the assertion of national as opposed to Soviet interests. But it follows them without fanfare and without expectation of rapid or spectacular results from either one. Events of the intervening years, as the line of division in Europe has taken on more and more aspects of permanence in a world living in the shadow of nuclear war, have shown how difficult it is to bring American and Western influence to bear on the destiny of Eastern Europe, how narrow are the limits of American policy.

If the Yugoslav regime should register dramatic successes, or if Poland should be able to consolidate beyond all question its own mixture of freedom and socialism, the idea of national communism may gain new force. Tying American policy exclusively to that idea, however, like tying it to the idea of free elections, has its drawbacks. Much depends on developments which cannot be foreseen. The very concept of national communism, indeed, is controversial and uncertain of definition. Even those who practice it, such as Tito, Gomulka, Mao Tse-tung, and Khrushchev himself (for Soviet Russia was the first national communist state), do not admit that they do so.

In one sense all communism is national communism as soon as it involves the exercise of state authority. From another viewpoint, some say national communism can have no future cut off from the great centers of power, Russia and China, and in any smaller state is bound in due time to be absorbed by the communist mass, as Poland's evolution since 1956 may suggest, or else cease to be communism at all. The experience of Hungary seemed to show that under the stress of a revolutionary situation the stage of national communism can be very temporary indeed. Perhaps Milovan Djilas was right in saying that national communism is just communism in decline.

The substantive idea behind American policy for the long run is still that the satellite communist states should cease to be satellites, whether or not they cease to be communist. Now no longer entrapped by slogans or driven by moral imperatives that call for action beyond available means, and taking account of the fact that Eastern Europe is not a vital factor in the military balance, American policy appears attuned to gradual change as the only way in which progress in the direction of independence can take place. President Kennedy, understandably cautious, has made no rash promises. Yet in his first State of the Union message he not only reaffirmed America's hope for the ultimate freedom and welfare of the Eastern European peoples, but spoke also of using economic tools in the interest of reestablishing historic ties of friendship with them. Whatever else this approach may mean, it seems to accept the idea of gradualism. Meanwhile, the fact is that the United States has to live with the status quo.

Unlimited sovereignty the Eastern European nations can never really have. Their past attempts to exercise it, chiefly in rivalry and conflict with each other, helped to bring them to the present pass. It is only in association with one another, and on the basis of some kind of equilibrium explicitly or implicitly accepted by the world's great powers, that these nations are likely to have governments which will respond primarily to national interests rather than to orders or pressures from an outside great power. If that is a possibility for the future, probably it can come about only through settlements that can be negotiated between the Soviet Union and the West.

It is the place of Eastern Europe in negotiations with the Soviet Union that has sharply posed questions of policy and of tactics to the United States ever since Khrushchev brought Europe back into the center of the cold war by raising the issue of Berlin. In part, Moscow's pressure on this Western outpost is a move to consolidate its position in East Germany and in the other satellites; in part, it is aimed at undermining the independence of the Federal Republic and the entire NATO position in Western Europe. The West has countered by relating the problem of Berlin to the problems of German reunification and European security. In this way Eastern Europe should remain on the agenda of East-West negotiation. If the Soviet leaders refuse to discuss it, as they did at Geneva in 1955, Western statesmen can discuss it nonetheless, not as an isolated item but as part of the unsettled problem of Europe and as an area to which proposals for arms limitation and control, disengagement, or neutral zones, should apply.

How to approach the question of negotiations has been a matter of debate in the United States. Among the different schools of thought, one holds to the belief that Soviet weaknesses in Eastern Europe can be successfully exploited, without concessions by the West, and therefore negotiations, if they need be undertaken at all, should be used as an adjunct to political warfare aimed at liberation. Another stresses the importance and inviolability of the NATO positions in Western Europe, sees nothing to be gained in negotiations which would call them into question whether Eastern Europe is brought into the picture or not, and therefore sees little that can be done save to hold the present line, including Berlin. A third argument, based on concern over the vulnerability of the Western position in Berlin and a willingness to experiment with disengagement, sees possibilities of mutual troop withdrawals and other measures which would promise, among other things, political gains in Eastern Europe without any net loss in the military balance. Finally, there are those who, while they may not accept the whole Soviet line on coexistence, regard relaxation of tension as in itself an urgent objective for which such a concession as formal acceptance of the status quo in Eastern Europe would be a reasonable price to pay; and that new atmosphere, presumably, would make it possible for the Soviet Union and the satellite regimes to work out relations based in greater degree on the consent of those regimes and of the peoples they govern.

These attitudes are based on varying estimates of Soviet intentions, of the risks involved in negotiation, and of the relative importance to the United States of numerous changing elements in the European equation. The official American position is not likely to be easily defined until it is clarified by the process of negotiation with our allies and with the Soviets. It does not seem likely to swing to the extreme of a return to the myths of the liberation policy or to that of concessions made under Soviet pressure or to gain Soviet good will. Nor do the prospects for serious exploration of mutual concessions seem favorable.

The United States Government has shown a consistent coolness to the idea of disengagement, although this is not a matter for generalization but for consideration in terms of specific propositions. It curtly rejected the Rapacki Plan for an "atom-free" zone on both sides of the dividing line and ignored the many unofficial proposals that have been put forward in the West. So long as the Soviet Union thwarts German reunification and rules out discussion of Eastern Europe, the American stand is to hold present positions, for any negotiated change can hardly be other than for the worse. This may be the situation for some time unless there is some fundamental turn in Soviet policy or a substantial shift in the balance of military and political strength between East and West.

The status quo, of course, is the result of the military stalemate. The United States accepts the line of the iron curtain as a political fact of today, ruling out, on both sides, any use of force or political moves which in the last analysis depend for success on the use of force. But the acceptance of the military stalemate cannot be based either on complacency or resignation. It does not rule out communication or political initiative or active diplomacy; at the very least it requires alert and watchful waiting. The political currents on both sides of the line, and across it, are not static. The Soviets are bending every effort to impart their own rhythm to the dynamic of events. If the West does not see this and act accordingly, it will open Western as well as Eastern Europe to Soviet domination.

This is the truth that puts the matter of an American policy for Eastern Europe in perspective: the problem is not just the satellite nations, it is the future of Europe. American policy, not always consciously or articulately, has recognized that truth. For that reason it has not accepted the legitimacy of Eastern Europe's absorption into the Soviet empire. To do so would be an unnecessary act of appeasement, a throwing away of bargaining power, a disservice to the future. If there is no room for serious negotiation now on a political settlement in Europe, this need not always be the case, unless the Soviet interpretation of history turns out to be the true one. The main task of the West is to strengthen itself, so that it never has to negotiate from weakness.

Over the long run Eastern Europe is for the Soviet Union a position of weakness, not of strength. The Soviet leaders have the problem of coming to terms with nationalism, just as the Western powers have it in the free world. Despite the semblance of stabilization achieved since 1956, they have not won the peoples or found the formula that will sublimate national differences in a higher synthesis, nor does Soviet history lead one to believe that they will find it. Communist ideology is certainly not that formula. The West, on the other hand, does have the capacity to build a community in which all nations of Europe, including those in its eastern half, can find a place.

There are periods in history when certain conditions have to be tolerated, even though they are most distasteful. For the peoples of Eastern Europe this is such a period; they have experienced others in the past. The United States and its Western allies know that they cannot expect to bring about any abrupt change in the status of those peoples. Knowing that change must be gradual and that the means at their disposal for exerting direct influence on Eastern Europe are limited, their task is to find policies which on the one hand do not exceed those limited means and, on the other, do not neglect or ignore them.

At the same time the United States must relentlessly pursue the goals of strength and unity of the Western world. That is indispensable to the ability of the West to hold its own. It is indispensable if opportunities for successful diplomacy are to be grasped when new Soviet policies or new crises bring the fate of Eastern Europe again to the fore.

11: VIRTUES AND SHORTCOMINGS OF AMERICAN DIPLOMACY*

J. B. Duroselle

It is relatively easy to decide what is an act of foreign policy: it consists of trying to modify a situation in a region where one does not exercise sovereign authority. It is however much more difficult to define what a foreign policy is. It is the resultant of all the acts of foreign policy. How can we see this result? One speaks of countries "which have a foreign policy" or "which do not have a foreign policy." Such expressions are taken to mean the existence or absence of a certain continuity in the formulation of objectives and in the efforts undertaken to achieve them. But that is a vague, empirical, or intuitive conception.

In order to speak of the virtues and shortcomings of American foreign policy we must first of all decide what a foreign policy is. Other chapters of this book try to do so by going into concrete details. Here I would like to try something else, namely, a global evaluation. This is perhaps easier for a foreign observer who examines the general picture from the outside.

This task calls for two series of initial observations. First of all, this global evaluation cannot be made from a moral point of view. It is not a question of judging American foreign policy according to moral criteria superior to it and hence outside it, but rather of analyzing its internal coherence in the name of a certain rationality. Secondly, we must try to set up criteria for this rationality. The choice of these involves arbitrariness and constitutes in a way the fundamental postulate of this study. But this postulate rests on certain observations which in the present state of history are made by most observers.

I propose therefore to use the four following criteria:

(1) Does American foreign policy have continuity or not? By this I mean, do the objectives sought by its leaders, either publicly

* This chapter was translated by Professor James A. Corbett, University of Notre Dame.

formulated or at least discernible, remain basically the same over a period of several years. On the scale of human societies this is sufficient because man can neither hope to work for eternity nor to build the indestructible.

(2) Is American foreign policy effective? Here we must compare the ends chosen with the partial attainments of these ends, for a state may set for itself specific objectives yet lack zeal, perseverance, skill, or luck in its efforts to achieve them.

(3) Is American foreign policy based on a certain internal support of public opinion? If we admit that over a long period of time in every modern state, especially in democratic ones, public opinion in all its forms is a decisive force, can we say that in the present state of things and over a period of years there exists a satisfactory relationship between public opinion and those who make and carry out foreign policy? This raises the problem of leadership. The leader is not the only one who makes the great decisions. Mussolini made a great decision on June 10, 1940, because he had the power to make it, not because he was an authentic leader. The leader is the one who makes decisions which public opinion will accept. If he simply follows public opinion, which is generally vague, he is not a leader. But if he guides it and sets his course according to what he believes desirable in itself and acceptable to public opinion then he is a leader.

(4) Does American foreign policy have a certain external support? This does not mean that this support should be universal. The countries in the communist group consider, doctrinally, that international relations are a dialectical movement. These countries are in the opposition; their aim is to extend their system over the whole world. Coexistence with them is possible for a while, their support never. But these countries represent only a part of the world. It is indispensable, however, to know the extent of the adhesion of the noncommunist countries to the specific policy followed by the United States. We have a very simple criterion for this. If we turn from the conflict between the communist and noncommunist worlds, which corresponds to the dialectical definition, we can see that there are other nondialectical conflicts or areas where minor differences exist between the United States and other countries. If such conflicts are numerous and important we can be sure that external support is very limited; if they are rare or insignificant then it is extensive.

The scientific analysis of these four criteria for determining the cohesion of American foreign policy would of course require extensive research, general and specific studies. The limitations of a chapter reduce my task to much more modest limits. I shall confine myself to confronting the most important facts with these criteria and to proposing an evaluation of the "virtues and shortcomings." This evaluation has no other purpose than to offer a basis for discussion and analysis.

THE CONTINUITY OF OBJECTIVES

Like every great country, and perhaps even more so because of its relative isolation in past centuries, the United States has established a tradition in its foreign policy. This tradition has been abundantly studied, commented upon, approved, or criticized. One has only to recall the books of Beard, Dexter Perkins, George Kennan, Morgenthau, Osgood, and Tannenbaum. But, like every great country, the United States has seen this tradition encounter a fundamentally new situation since the end of the Second World War. The bipolarization of power in the world from which it benefits—a benefit it tolerated rather than accepted enthusiastically—is combined with the ideological contradiction promoted by the other great power, Russia. It had to adapt itself to the new system.

This adaptation has not taken place without some hesitation. President Truman could choose between several solutions: make concessions to the Russians as Henry Wallace suggested in order to gain their confidence; refuse every concession while awaiting some "gesture" from the Russians as James F. Byrnes proposed; or again, accept the idea that the only way to live in the same world as the Russians consisted of preventing them from making new encroachments on the liberty of other people. This was the solution suggested by James Forrestal, George Kennan, and Dean Acheson. The nomination of General George Marshall as secretary of state in January, 1947, and the proclamation of the Truman Doctrine in March of the same year indicated the triumph of this last policy. This was the beginning of the policy of containment.

There was obviously a fourth possibility: liberate the oppressed peoples. Such a policy looked easy on paper and in campaign speeches. The Republicans in their 1952 campaign did not hesitate to advocate it. But how could one liberate communist-dominated peoples without war? Except for a handful of fanatical advocates of preventive war, no one could think seriously of it. The antiwar tradition of this country was irresistible. The Republicans, once in power, wisely abandoned the idea of rolling back communism and rallied to the containment policy of their predecessors. They, of course, gave this old policy new names: the "new look" of 1954, the "brinkmanship" of John Foster Dulles. The reality, however, was the same.

We can list therefore among the virtues of American foreign policy its continuity since it adopted the containment policy in 1947. It is one of those points settled beyond dispute in which the partners of a great country can trust. It is well known that the United States absolutely refuses, on the level of principle, to permit communism to make any further territorial advances. Examples abound but the principal one is obviously the decision of President Truman to intervene in the Korean War in June, 1950. The defense of Quemoy in July, 1958, fits into the same pattern.

The idea of containment has continued to develop in depth without changing its nature. It was never a question of linear containment. In the time of Dean Acheson one spoke of "situations of strength." An American shield was not enough. It had to rest on a solid arm. With foreign aid, as exemplified in the Marshall Plan of June, 1947, the United States offered to strengthen those nations exposed to internal subversion by communists. This, it should be noted, preceded by a year the declaration of Vandenberg which inaugurated the policy of alliances—a policy which went against the whole American tradition. Admiral Radford and John Foster Dulles went even further with the idea of linear defense: "no sanctuary," "massive retaliation," "instant retaliation." These expressions indicated that containment was a coherent plan, not a series of separate, local problems.

The constant determination to avoid any appeasement policy never led to the idea that reconquest was worth the risk of war. There were several crises even at the time when the United States still had a nuclear and thermonuclear monopoly. Each time there was a risk of seeing containment transformed into reconquest, a stop to it was called. The Republicans acted in exactly the same way as did the Democrats. The recall of General MacArthur in April, 1951, the refusal to risk a war with China in order to aid the French at Dien Bien Phu in April, 1954, fit into this same pattern of continuity. The risk of total war was accepted in order to contain, not to liberate. In the West Berlin crisis, even if President Eisenhower at

Camp David used an ambiguous expression, there is absolutely no sign that American policy would be disposed to make the slightest concession on basic policy.

The allies of the United States can, therefore, at least for the next few years, speculate with some certitude on the determination of their powerful partner to defend them at any price. The escape clause of Article 5 of the Atlantic Pact—that every signer of the pact (and therefore the United States) would, if any member were attacked, take "such action as it deems necessary, including the use of armed force"—was bitterly criticized in France in 1950 because it seemed to exclude the automatism of a real alliance. The moral certitude, however, is there; it is stronger than juridical certitude, and this is also a virtue.

Linked to the problem of East-West relations, and yet different from it by its nature, if not by its repercussions, is the problem of helping the independence movements in former colonies. Here the continuity of American policy is even greater since the new situation, far from interfering with the tradition of the United States, is perfectly adapted to it. American anti-colonialism has had its weak moments in the course of its history. In 1898 and afterward the United States acquired colonies and exercised an indirect imperialism in Central America and in the Caribbean. But, to use the expression of Dexter Perkins, Americans did it with a "bad conscience." The Clark Memorandum published in 1930, the Good Neighbor policy, the Tydings-McDuffie Act of 1934 put an end to it at a time when European colonization was unchallenged, at least on the international level, and when the last colonial conquest of history—that of Ethiopia by Mussolini—was taking place.

The rise of the United States and of Russia to first rank as powers coincided with the extreme weakening of the United Kingdom and especially of France, Italy, and Japan, and gave rise to a new world system. Instead of seven great powers, of which four were colonial and one, Germany, which wished to become a colonial power again, we now have at the head of the destinies of the universe two powers which are anti-colonial by doctrine and by sentiment. The policy of Roosevelt and of Cordell Hull as regards India as early as 1942, and the dream of international trusteeship which Roosevelt spoke of in a conversation with Stalin at Yalta when Churchill was not present, have developed since the war. In a few decisive cases such as Indonesia, the rejection of the Bevin-Sforza compromise on Italian colonies, the Suez Canal affair, the continuity of American policy was clear and consistent. It is well known that the United States will always encourage liberal solutions.

American policy, while foreseeable for a few years as regards East-West relations, is less so as regards the process of decolonialization. Here there has been an evolution. In the time of General Marshall it was above all necessary to save Western Europe. This required the greatest prudence as regards the nationalists in the European colonies. Today Europe is saved. It is prosperous if not strong. It can become strong. For sentimental anti-colonialism the United States can more freely substitute an anti-colonial policy based on self-interest. This means that containment must be carried on in depth. The uncommitted countries, often neutralist, always underdeveloped, must be won over to the free world and not to the communist world, the true or mythical image of which exercises a strong attraction on them. This implies a firm policy, which has not ceased to develop since 1956, of encouraging freedom for colonial peoples. It risks losing the alliance of European powers which consider that in certain cases—Algeria above all others—they have vital interests. The result is that the United States, unable to satisfy both, follows a hesitating and sometimes obscure policy.

This will serve as a transition to an evaluation of the shortcomings of American foreign policy, in so far as they concern the continuity of its objectives.

It seems that continuity, so praiseworthy in itself, contains a certain danger. It can easily become rigidity and lack of imagination. Rigidity is the rule as soon as containment is involved. Since the United States is on the defensive, the adversary has the initiative. American propaganda in the popular democracies consisted of awakening hopes—imprudently exaggerated by interested parties—of American support which events made impossible. When pushed to the wall in November, 1956, the United States could only watch with despair the repression in Hungary. Any action would have precipitated total war.

George Kennan proposed at the end of 1957 a policy of disengagement which many critics—including myself—deem impractical. But the initial argument Kennan made is unanswerable. We have never had the initiative. We must try to find solutions which give us this initiative.

Reduced to its simplest expression we can say that although the iron curtain is strongly established in Europe, there are many areas where the initiative can be taken. Here is a list of attitudes which have become rigid axioms of American foreign policy and which are, to say the least, very questionable:

(1) The productivity and standard of living in Russia, rising at a faster rate than in the United States, will have catastrophic effects, for such achievements will favor Soviet propaganda.

Would it not be wise to examine, on the contrary, whether growth of the Soviet standard of living to the level of that of the United States will not have such repercussions on the internal structure of Russia that a revolutionary attitude, favorable to a world upheaval, would become impossible? In this case, far from opposing covertly this growth, should not the United States encourage or even help it? Would not the effect of the "model" USSR on underdeveloped countries be lessened if the standard of living of the "model" surpassed even further that of its eventual imitators? Is it not desirable to see the disparity of living standards between Russia and China increase?

(2) American aid to underdeveloped countries is a means of propaganda, hence of containment which should be used against Russia.

Would it not, on the contrary, be much more effective to propose to all developed powers—including Russia—the transformation of unilateral aid into collective aid as evidence of the new East-West co-operation? If Russia accepted it this would first of all have the effect of ending the odious and immoral blackmail type of policy used by Nasser, for example, to play off the East against the West. This is a kind of deceit by threat which has been called "positive neutralism." It would be the only concrete evidence of a "peaceful coexistence" which today exists only in the form of smiles and toasts of vodka and may disappear overnight, as recent events have shown. If Russia refused, it would place her in a psychologically unfavorable position and would oblige her to give her reasons. Collective aid would also eliminate national tags that the aid given is charity, or that it is given out of self-interest, by those who have to those who are in need. Collective aid would create less irritation than the individual aid in which the beneficiary always sees imperialistic implications.

(3) We should limit as much as possible the sale of strategic

products to communist countries and especially to China, in order not to strengthen eventual enemies.

Would it not rather be necessary to envisage only the commercial aspect of the problem—it is a necessity, for example, for Japan to find markets in China—and to reduce to its just measure the strategic element? In any case Russia and China would like to build up their military power. The advantages of cutting off imports of strategic materials, a mere pinprick, are negligible by comparison with the economic inconveniences they involve.

(4) The United States—many Americans say—should encourage regional regroupings of newly independent countries: a united Maghreb, pan-Africanism, etc., in order to avoid the Balkanization of Asia and Africa.

Would it not be much more effective for containment to encourage only those groupings which are not based on xenophobia and on the most virulent forms of nationalism? Does the United States have a real interest in seeing a united Moslem empire directed by Nasser come into being? Should not the United States favor as much as possible every effort to maintain links compatible with the independence of European, African, and Asiatic countries (commonwealth, or community)? Certain signs seem to indicate that Americans are leaning in this direction.

THE EFFECTIVENESS OF AMERICAN FOREIGN POLICY

The continuity of objectives would make little sense if efforts undertaken to achieve them were insufficient or the methods used ineffective.

If we examine the results of American foreign policy since 1947 we can say that the objectives have been attained on certain essential points. First of all, world peace has been maintained. On several occasions there were serious alarms: in March, 1948, when General Lucius Clay warned the government that Soviet aggression could be unleashed within fifteen days; in the summer of 1950 when there was fear that the Korean War would become a general war or that a similar attack would be launched against West Germany or Yugoslavia; in the second half of 1958 the affair of Iraq, of Quemoy, and the sudden claims of Khrushchev on Berlin in November, 1959. But these alarms, often accompanied by brief moments of panic in public opinion, were always short. No doubt one can attribute the maintenance of peace to the peaceful intentions of Russia. But it should be noted that neither the president nor Congress ever backed down before costly decisions. The best example is that of the military budget. Reduced to $13 billion before the Korean War, it suddenly jumped, as soon as this war showed the extreme weakness of conventional forces, to a level of over $40 billion and has generally oscillated since then between $38 and 40 billions a year—or around ten per cent of the gross national product.

Americans have likewise never hesitated to adopt new methods if these seemed to promise results. Thus, the procedure of programs of military and economic aid to other countries, usually in the form of gifts, has been generalized and stabilized. This is a new diplomatic method whereby inequality of wealth and power is transformed into a one-way form of aid. There is no need to underline the brilliant success of this policy for Western Europe. No doubt Western Europe pulled itself together through the hard work of its people. But one may ask whether the "economic miracle" of the German economy, accompanied by miracles of nearly the same scope in France, Great Britain and Italy, could have occurred so quickly without the help of the Marshall Plan. Europe no longer needs economic aid. A recent French minister of finance, M. Pinay, was able to tell American journalists jokingly that France would soon be able to lend money to the United States. There is a wide difference between European and American living standards, but Europe has recovered hope and this is a great achievement of American foreign policy.

On the whole, the containment policy has worked. It succeeded in Greece where the civil war ended in 1949; it protected South Korea, Formosa, and the offshore islands. Communist revolts in Malaya, Burma, the Philippines, were put down. So far South Viet Nam has resisted communist infiltration. The situation in Laos, at this writing, is still uncertain. No doubt the armistice of July 20, 1954, in Indochina recognized a new communist state in North Viet Nam. This simply confirmed an already existing reality.

In the case of China one cannot blame American foreign policy for the fact that the country fell to the communists. The situation was already ripe in 1945, and General Marshall, who returned from there when he was named secretary of state, admitted that the corrupt Nationalist regime could not be saved.

Thus on the whole the dike has held. In only one place, Iraq, it appeared to be crumbling, since the communists controlled many key positions. But the most recent trend seems to indicate that Iraq has eliminated a part of the communist influence. The United Arab Republic, while doing 37.2 per cent of its trade with the Sino-Soviet bloc, has outlawed the communist party and its relations with Iraq are very poor. Guinea, called a popular democracy by General de Gaulle on November 10, 1959, no doubt deserves "neither this exaggerated honor nor this indignity." Still, its president, Sékou Touré, declared in April, 1960, that Africa cannot accept communism.

The American alliances have held except for the indirect one with Iraq. This network of alliances extends to nearly all developed countries (Western Europe, Canada, Australia, New Zealand, Japan) and also includes, directly or indirectly, the key positions all around the iron curtain: South Korea, Formosa, Pakistan, Iran, Turkey, and Greece.

On the Soviet side Yugoslavia has broken away—a phenomenon, incidentally, not attributable to any American action—but revolts or agitation in East Germany and Hungary have failed. The Polish revolt succeeded in a cautious, tentative way. The revolts have shown in a startling manner that the satellites are not trustworthy allies. Their youths have not been won over to communism, and in case of war Russia would have serious difficulties in those countries.

It seems, therefore, that on the whole there is every reason to be satisfied with the effectiveness of American foreign policy. Yet the general tone of Western commentators is pessimistic. In this pessimism one can see traces of the psychological warfare cleverly waged by Khrushchev. He repeats too often that his ideology will triumph in the long run for it not to have some effect.

It remains nonetheless true that the effectiveness of American foreign policy has had and still has serious limitations. It has not succeeded in preventing Russia from acquiring a nuclear and thermonuclear power equal to that of the United States. This was, no doubt, inevitable but until Russia launched the first Sputnik in November, 1957, there was a certain tendency in the United States to underestimate her. The panicky reaction was expressed by somber pessimism and minute analyses of the "missile gap" in the years to come. The rational reaction has consisted of a gigantic effort to close the gap. This effort has not yet been completed.

It is well known that Americans like to be loved by other peoples. If in a given year their economic aid in the form of gifts is greater than all the Soviet aid in the form of loans to foreign countries from 1950-1958, it is in part in order to be liked. Yet in fact anti-Americanism has continued to grow. The famous essay, *The Ugly American,* is in part exaggerated and in part true. American aid has not helped make America popular. Her relations with several Arab countries are bad. With Latin America they are, here and there, and especially with Cuba, openly hostile. In Japan events indicate the existence of effective hostile forces.

Is it necessary to be loved? Here we touch upon a sort of myth about which something should be said. Americans have a curious tendency to believe that there is such a thing as a world public opinion and that it has its seat in the United Nations. Instead of treating the United Nations as a center for discussions and therefore a political force it must rationally take into consideration, they have a tendency to consider the opinion of the United Nations as an expression of the opinion of the majority of mankind. Yet a simple summary study would prove that most of the delegates there come from authoritarian governments whose contacts with the masses of their peoples are at a minimum. Even more often, their governments use foreign policy to turn the minds of the masses away from the true problem: the incredibly low standards of living, the odious exploitation of the people by the dominant and corrupt feudal classes. One has the impression that the American government is often paralyzed by fear of the international "what will they say?" that is, the opinion expressed by representatives of other countries in the corridors of the United Nations building. Now a great part of this anti-Americanism stems from a lack of respect caused by the extraordinary timidity of a very great power when confronted with the blackmail of some forty delegations from poorly organized countries or states which are always supported in their anti-Americanism by the nine votes of the Soviet bloc. These delegations represent only a few dozen million persons, not world public opinion.

It is not a question of minimizing the value of the United Nations, as is too often done in France, but of eliminating all sentimentality from the conception people have of it.

Personally, I believe that American effectiveness would be stronger if the United States, instead of flattering this pseudo world public opinion, spoke up frankly and firmly more often. Were this the case, a certain number of international scandals, such as the closing of the Suez Canal to Israeli ships, would certainly have been avoided.

INTERNAL SUPPORT

All American writers insist, and rightly so, on the fact that American foreign policy is influenced more by public opinion than is that of any other country. All samplings of opinion, like the Gallup polls, prove that since 1947 there has been general agreement on the broad lines of the containment policy. Naturally, the election campaigns, especially that of 1952, brought out differences about details; the Korean War, "Truman's War," was unpopular more because it did not lead to a positive solution than because it existed. But the election campaign of 1956 and the preliminaries of that of 1960, apart from a few differences about details on the methods of foreign policy, manifested a deep agreement on general lines. Moreover, this policy is in principle and in most cases bipartisan. This general support is an "essential virtue" and few democratic countries can boast of having it to the same degree.

There is another side to it. The support of public opinion is easier to have, the less exacting and less energetic are the solutions offered. Now for effective policy one sometimes needs forceful and painful solutions. If the country has a strong leader he knows how to develop them and get them adopted.

Wilson was a leader, but in an imperfect way. He knew how to conceive solutions—the "new diplomacy"—and to take dramatic decisions. He did not succeed in his effort to impose adhesion to it. Roosevelt was a true leader. To be sure, on several occasions, especially in the spring of 1941, Henry L. Stimson complained of the president's hesitation over the problem of convoys; but in a revolutionary initiative of great historical importance—the lend-lease policy—Roosevelt was the perfect type of leader. He waited for the general elections to measure the character of public opinion, and then invented the lend-lease solution. By the famous comparison of the garden hose and his speech on the great arsenal of democracy, he convinced public opinion that the time for sacrifice had come. He was the creator, the courageous initiator, the educator.

President Truman also knew how to make great and courageous decisions: in June, 1950, on the Korean War, and in April, 1951, when he recalled General MacArthur. His successor did not give the same impression, at least up to the time of the death of John Foster Dulles.

When the president of the United States fails to exercise the leadership which the Constitution not only permits him but requires him to exercise, the disadvantages can be serious. Two examples come readily to mind.

Sometimes elementary and primitive emotions of a poorly informed public opinion can lead to excess. McCarthyism was an example of such excess. The internal logic of McCarthyism can be reduced to this: communism is bad in itself; the containment policy proves that this is the government's opinion; therefore, any infiltration of communism into the United States should be fought as if one were fighting an enemy. One does not allow the enemy freedom to invade one's territory. One must therefore deny communism any freedom of action. But this position endangers freedom itself, which is the supreme principle of the United States. It is the formula of St. Just: "No liberty for the enemies of liberty." This is a specious formula to which a democracy ought to prefer the formula of Lamennais: "The free combat of truth against error."

Every one knows that the reaction of the American people against McCarthyism was healthy, but for two years the atmosphere was poisoned by McCarthy's excesses, which certainly did not increase the prestige of the United States in the world.

The other serious consequence of the absence of leadership is proliferation of "anonymous" decisions, excessive recourse to committee decisions, too much confidence in the results of operational research. General Eisenhower in 1944 could not have prepared the great landing in Normandy but for the laborious work of committees of technicians. Modern governments can no longer have recourse to empiricism without the greatest danger, and we are in a world in which the Napoleonic type of general, who can master a battle by himself, has become an impossibility. But General Eisenhower himself during the war had to take some great decisions, the most formidable being that of delaying the Normandy landing for twenty-four hours. He listened to all possible opinions, but in the silence of his own soul he alone had to decide.

Politics cannot always be scientific. Ultimately it needs leadership. If the leader does not lead, if the president of the United States who has no prime minister dons the role of a constitutional king—to use a comparison of Hans Morgenthau—either someone like McCarthy tries to take his place, or politics ceases to be continuous and becomes a broken line. The several authorities act separately even against each other, or, as was the case in France under the Fourth Republic, there is avoidance of any innovation. The Fourth Republic did not dare to act, and its continuity became routine conservatism, a fear of adapting to evolution. Perhaps future historians will explain certain miscalculations such as the "missile gap" by the fact that during a certain period the United States lacked a decisive leader.

EXTERNAL SUPPORT

Outside the communist world what kind of support does American foreign policy have abroad? The problem is so complex and the situation so fluid that one can at best only risk a few estimates.

It is certain that no country in the world has so many allies as the United States. NATO, SEATO, ANZUS, the Rio Pact, bilateral alliances with South Korea, Japan, and Formosa bring much more than half the nations of the world into the American camp without even counting Iran, Spain, and South Viet Nam which are indirectly linked. But if one studies the votes in the United Nations in the recent period one realizes that only the Hungarian problem permits the United States to obtain a large majority (fifty-three votes in December, 1959).

This is because the United States considers her alliances as directed only against communism. This prevents her from supporting her allies as regards their own interests independently of the anticommunist struggle. This likewise prevents her allies from voting in principle with the United States, the leader of all the alliances of the "free world," in those cases where the communist problem is not clearly involved. The USSR has nine sure votes in the United Nations; the United States can count on more, but not an overwhelming majority—something it had at its disposal in practice prior to 1955.

Moreover, the very size of the alliance system seems to weaken it. In the Rio Pact, Cuba is more adversary than friend. The Declaration of Caracas in March, 1954, was voted by all the Latin-American republics except Guatemala—at the time suspect. But under the guise of avoiding the establishment of communism in America it seemed to re-establish the right of intervention that the Good

Neighbor policy had eliminated and was voted with the greatest reluctance.

In the other alliances, the conflicts of a given ally with the United States, or of allies amongst themselves, are innumerable. The complaints of Iceland, the Greco-Turkish conflict, quarrels with France, the conflicts between the common market countries and the outer seven are only a few examples among many. The American shepherd has therefore much to do—and often without success—in order to keep his flock together.

One wonders whether it would not be preferable to reduce the alliances to certain solid points: Western Europe, British dominions of the Pacific, and Japan. And one also wonders whether it would not be better to substitute a policy of guarantees for the reciprocal alliances. This formula exists for the three noncommunist states of Indochina. Would it not be preferable to alliances with countries like Thailand, Pakistan, South Korea, and Formosa?

An alliance should imply moral as well as military solidarity. There are sometimes conflicts between the United States and France, between the United States and the United Kingdom, but the moral solidarity is stronger than these conflicts, for the common democratic ideals, the old and deep friendships are essentially more fundamental than written treaties. One wonders what the great American democracy has in common morally with the military regime of Pakistan, with a Latin-American dictator, the repressive system of the now-deposed Syngman Rhee. By making such alliances the United States gives a moral guarantee to regimes of which its public opinion disapproves. It attaches more importance to a certain fear of communism than to the Wilsonian ideal of a world "made safe for democracy." It irritates India by allying with Pakistan, the liberals of Latin America by supporting Trujillo and others like him. The system would be much more coherent if an alliance was a rare privilege instead of something offered, even prostituted, to anyone willing to accept it.

When Soviet Russia was attacked by the Nazis in 1941 Churchill had a strong but not very courteous formula. He said that he would gladly make an alliance with the devil against Hitler. But the devil had to be a big and powerful one, not a nest of little devils. Moreover, alliances which do not rest on the support of peoples are fragile; the example of Iraq has shown this clearly. This "inflation" of alliances seems to be one of the most remarkable shortcomings of American policy.

One should add what Hans Morgenthau calls neo-isolationism. This is not the traditional isolationism which consisted of avoiding involvement in the affairs of the world. Neo-isolationism consists of becoming involved in the affairs of the whole world but without regularly consulting those in whom one is interested. There is in this procedure a dangerous reflex of excessive confidence in oneself. The feeling of being right because one has experts and a moral and material superiority leads to the conclusion that consultation with others will add nothing to the quasi-unilateral decision of Americans since it is good and righteous. Neo-isolationism exists everywhere, whether it involve aid to refugees, in regard to which the United States prefers to act alone, or economic aid, in regard to which Americans, contrary to the Russian method, do not take into consideration sufficiently the opinions of the experts of the country concerned. They insist rather that American experts alone judge whether or not the proposed project is rational.

Here is the principal source of this irritating, superficial, blameworthy but widespread anti-Americanism which exists throughout the whole world. It provokes a very human reaction from him who is humiliated in receiving and who detests his benefactor. The art of giving consists principally of inquiring about the desires of him who will receive the gift. The child who dreams of receiving an electric train will be disappointed if he receives a medicine ball, on the pretext that the giver wants him to strengthen his muscles.

There is reason to believe, however, that neo-isolationism appears to be a declining survival of the isolationism which involved the same superiority complex rather than a movement with a future. We were happy to see the effort of President Eisenhower to make contacts throughout the world, even if we wished at times that he had been more cautious. It is a matter for rejoicing to see so many eminent and ordinary citizens travelling throughout the world with a passionate curiosity and returning with a broader view. May my American readers forgive a French author for citing this conclusion of a book published in 1928 by two Americans, Dexter and Sedgwick, on war debts:

> In the meantime, while the voters are making up their minds, Americans will also do well to stop lecturing Europe and instruct-

> ing foreigners as to our moral superiority, the magnificence of our ideals and the excellence of our methods of dealing with all human affairs. English and French dislike for Americans is due far more to our attitude of superiority than to our exactions. If we are superior, let us keep it to ourselves, instead of telling the world about it. The Greeks may have been entitled to describe all other people as barbarians, but no nation of today has the right to behave as if its virtues were superior to those of any other.[1]

By way of conclusion to these reflections on foreign support, seen from the point of view of the allies, let us note that most of these allies adhere to American policy out of necessity because one has to find protection from the strongest when one cannot assure it oneself. This necessity is sometimes deeply resented. The more or less vain efforts of Great Britain to maintain its own deterrent at any price, and the rather unreasonable claims of France to do the same, stem from this. The fault is certainly that of Great Britain and of France, but is also due to the neo-isolationist policy—the McMahon Act is an example—of this powerful ally.

In brief, and despite the impression that one may draw from some of these reflections, the over-all balance is favorable and the pessimism which seems to characterize most American commentators since Sputnik seems to me somewhat exaggerated. What impresses the foreign observer is the admirable facility Americans have for adaptation. This country which never had, except occasionally, an active world foreign policy found itself in the necessity of creating one. It has felt its way along but without excesses. It has had the regret of being unable to restore the freedom of the "satellites," but it has on the whole conserved the rest of the nations of the world. It has known how to master crises courageously and has not really lost ground. It has succeeded in maintaining peace.

Moreover, the shortcomings—and what country doesn't have them—are perhaps less serious for great nations than for small ones. General de Gaulle in the second volume of his war memoirs drew a conclusion after his first meeting with President Roosevelt which shall be ours also: "The proposals of the American President confirm me in the conviction that in relations between states logic and sentiment do not weigh heavily in comparison with the realities of power.

[1] Philip Dexter and John Hunter Sedgwick, *The War Debts: An American View* (New York, 1928), p. 132.

What matters is what one gets and what one knows how to hold." [2] Despite all its shortcomings, the United States has known, knows, and—we would be wrong to doubt it—will know how to hold its own.

[2] Charles de Gaulle, *Mémoires de Guerre,* II (Paris, 1956), 240.

PART TWO

POLICY MAKING AND ORGANIZATIONAL PROBLEMS

12: WHO DETERMINES OUR FOREIGN POLICY?

Lindsay Rogers

Fifty years ago, a distinguished ornament of the Harvard Law School, John Chipman Gray, intrigued students of politics with an aphorism that has been much quoted: "The real rulers of a political society are undiscoverable." [1] Ten years later, Harold Laski elaborated: "The new Chancellor of the Exchequer may be dependent upon a permanent official whose very name is unknown to the vast majority whose destinies he may so largely shape; and, indeed, the position of the English civil servant has been defined as that of a man who has exchanged dignity for power." I add that the position of a Cabinet member has been defined as that of a man who puts restraints on his civil servants so that he and his colleagues will not be hanged to the nearest lamp posts. "Public opinion may be the ultimate controlling factor," Mr. Laski continued; "but not the least complex of our problems is, as Mr. Lowell has said, when it is public and when it is opinion." [2]

In October, 1957, the English monthly *The Twentieth Century* devoted an entire issue to a symposium under the title "Who Governs Britain?" Eminent contributors discussed whether a governing class could be isolated and defined; the authority of parliament; the influence of the press; and the occult leverage exerted by trade unions, lobbies, committeemen, technicians, university dons, and journalistic gadflies. In his contribution to the symposium, A. J. P. Taylor said that it had lately become the fashion to call these undiscoverable rulers "The Establishment" and that he had been charged with starting it. "I regret the idea, whoever had it. The very word, so plummy, so ponderous, so respectable, tempts us to acknowledge the moral

[1] John C. Gray, *The Nature and Sources of the Law* (New York, 1909), p. 77.

[2] Harold Laski, *Authority in the Modern State* (New Haven, 1919), p. 29; A. Lawrence Lowell, *Public Opinion and Popular Government* (New York, 1913).

superiority of 'the Establishment.' It conjures up benign, upholstered figures, calm, steady, reliable." Mr. Taylor preferred Cobbett's name: The Thing.[3]

Well, in the United States the business of choosing policies and carrying them out cannot be thought of in terms of an "Establishment" or "The Thing." Some of my academic colleagues have latterly been seeking "conceptual frameworks" for their writings. They sometimes propose, with an air of originality, a framework which, although not always explicitly stated, has preoccupied all historians: "Is power concentrated in the hands of a single power holder or state organ, or is it mutually shared and reciprocally controlled by several power holders or state organs?"

No modern academic adventurer dealing with the United States would dream of discussing "The Thing." Our politics have a variety made infinite by federalism, sectionalism, checks and balances, the separation of powers, and a press whose influence is local rather than national. Those who from day to day determine our foreign policy may escape definite identification save in periods of crisis government—war, for example. Even then we can not be sure and are always more unsure about the less important periods. We must wait until the executors of the dead disclose their secrets and the living write their memoirs; until the historians get to work; and since the first in the field will be contradicted by his successors, we must guard against hardening our beliefs prematurely. Hence my attempted answers to the question posed at the head of this essay will be little more than speculations and hints, and they will be bereft of any conceptual framework. Tie a man to a text, said Renan, and he will escape in the exegesis. When the question permits no definite answers, a writer is entitled to roam. That I now proceed to do.

For the period from the end of the Second World War to March, 1953, our foreign policy, if not determined, was greatly influenced by Iosif Vissarionovich Dzhugashvili, better known as Stalin ("man of steel"), whom Franklin Roosevelt called "Uncle Joe." For Stalin's role I have the authority of Nikita S. Khrushchev who, in December, 1955, said that the Soviets had inspired American aid to Europe, that we were frightened into offering it. If this is too extreme, certainly awareness of the Soviet threat stilled Congressional and press criticism

[3] Hugh Thomas has recently edited a collection of essays: *The Establishment* (London, 1959).

of the Marshall Plan—"the greatest peacetime offer in history," Dean Acheson recently called it.

Since 1953 the response to the challenge has not been so simple, but "Uncle Joe's" successors have continued to influence decisions reached in Foggy Bottom, and sometimes, I fear, have been responsible for an inability to reach decisions. To put the matter differently: since the cold war succeeded the hot war, we have successfully met crisis after crisis. Sometimes it may have seemed that we did nothing between emergencies—that dealing with a crisis had so exhausted the determiners of our foreign policy that they were lacking in energy to plan to postpone the next crisis. Nevertheless—and for this we can be thankful—each interim convalescence restored strength to our policy makers so that they could surmount the next difficulty. Propaganda-wise, policy makers now and then have made us recall the advice of Colonel Blimp, whom David Low made famous during the interwar period: "Gad, Sir, Garvin is right. There is only one way to stop these bullying aggressors—find out what they want us to do and do it." Sometimes it appears that the undiscoverable rulers in respect to foreign policy are not the same as those who rule our propaganda.

On several occasions Professor Edward S. Corwin has reminded us that our Constitution has parcelled out authority: to the president; the commander in chief; to the legislative branch; to the appropriating bodies; to the Senate which advises and consents to the ratification of treaties and confirms diplomatic appointments; and to either branch of Congress which can, at its own sweet will, pass a resolution and be irresponsibly hortatory. This parcelling-out is silent as to where the ultimate responsibility rests, and, as Mr. Corwin says, issues "an invitation to struggle for the privilege of directing American foreign policy." Moreover, we have now reached a situation where peacetime civil-military relationships are much more important than they used to be. Our machinery for determining them is sadly in need of an overhaul. As the Alsops have written, the National Security Council "has clearly become our most important non-policy making organ."

But, it may be asked, are not such difficulties inevitable because we live under a democracy, a form of government which is ill-equipped for living abroad? "I do not hesitate to say," wrote Tocqueville, "that it is especially in the conduct of their foreign relations that democracies appear to me decidedly inferior to other governments. Experience, instruction, and habit almost always succeed in creating in a democracy a homely species of practical wisdom, and that science of the petty occurrences of life which is called good sense. . . . Foreign politics demand scarcely any of those qualities which are peculiar to a democracy; they require, on the contrary, the perfect use of almost all those in which it is deficient. . . . But a democracy can only with great difficulty regulate the details of an important undertaking, persevere in a fixed design, and work out its execution in spite of serious obstacles. It cannot combine its measures with secrecy, or await their consequences with patience. These are qualities which more especially belong to an individual or an aristocracy and they are precisely the qualities by which a nation, like an individual, attains a dominant position."

A century before, Joseph Addison had told readers of *The Freeholder*: "If we may believe the Observation which is made of us by Foreigners, there is no Nation in Europe so much given to Change as the English. There are some who ascribe this to the Fickleness of our Climate; and Others to the Freedom of our Government." Napoleon III complained to Malmesbury of the British form of government "which changes the Queen's Ministers so often and so suddenly. It is such a risk to adopt a line of policy with you, as one may be left in the lurch by a new Administration."

On this score (methods and lack of tact apart), we have given foreign governments little to complain about. Indeed our citizens can complain on precisely the opposite ground. Our presidents, secretaries of state, and even senators too often seem anxious to commit the mistake that Lord Salisbury described as clinging to the carcass of a dead policy. They are unwilling to scrap a formula even when it has clearly become fantastic. The old that is failing seems preferable to the new that is untried. There is too often a tendency to follow what is thought to be public opinion; too rarely an attempt to direct it. One is sometimes reminded of the French revolutionary figure who, hearing the mob shouting outside his window, said: "I am their leader. Therefore I must go out and follow them."

In these respects dictators may seem to have an advantage. They can change courses whenever they want to, and hence it is frequently said that democratic decision makers who have to explain themselves confront greater difficulties than their opposite totalitarian numbers. Whether this matters a great deal is doubtful. What has transpired about the decisions of the Nazi and Nipponese leaders shows that their mistakes were many—irretrievable and fatal. To this the records of the Nuremberg and Tokyo trials bear eloquent testimony. If Hitler had not wanted war when he was fifty instead of when he was older, Germany could have been dominant in Europe. Without becoming incandescent, Japan could have been the overlord of the Far East; and if Stalin had played his cards more cautiously, he could have advantaged the Soviet Union and made us more nervous than we have been, and now are. There are benefits in a governmental system that cannot insure secrecy and must put up with a discussion of pros and cons.

We are sometimes told that every people has as good a government as it deserves, but the saying is even truer when turned around: "Every government has as good an electorate as it deserves." Those who seek to shape policy can muddle as well as clear the public mind; they can debauch as well as educate their electorates. No one in Washington goes in for debauchery but the official record of the last decade does not gibe with the facts. Intentions may have been good but there has been as much confusion as education. We listen to many voices and hear different things. Pronouncements glitter but sometimes do not throw much light. Reasoned criticism and illuminating debate are rare.

During the last two administrations "bipartisanship" has been greatly extolled. The late Senator Arthur H. Vandenberg's leadership in the Senate enabled the Charter of the United Nations to be accepted with only two dissenting votes, but the senatorial debate did little toward educating the nation. Senator Vandenberg himself thought that the Assembly of the United Nations would be a great town meeting of the world and there was hardly a senator who warned the country that the new international organization was no panacea, that it was simply a piece of intergovernmental machinery which it was hoped might work, and that the success of its workings depended on the good faith and the intentions of its members.

Since 1945 the principal if not the only real debate on foreign policy was when Congressional sensibilities were affected; when Mr. Truman, as commander in chief, wished to send four additional divisions to Europe. On foreign aid, debate has been sporadic but not very informing, and one reason I think is the fetish of "bipartisanship." Nevertheless, bipartisanship, if unfortunately lessening discussion and criticism of policies, did make some Republicans become less isolationist although, perhaps, not less "Asia-lationist." Even so the percentages of Republicans in Congress who favored Bretton Woods, aid to Greece and Turkey, and the European recovery program was noticeably less than the percentage of Democrats who approved.

Certainly there should not be partisanship in the sense that Democratic senators would criticize what they thought were the policies of a president and his secretary of state simply because these two gentlemen happened to be Republicans. Bipartisanship can be carried much too far, however, and it would be well if its sedative effects were understood. Is not the situation healthier in Great Britain where the Laborites do not hesitate to criticize the foreign policy of the Conservative government?

The two principal branches of our government sometimes seem more concerned about protocol than about substance. Woodrow Wilson was once very scrupulous in consulting the Congress; later he thought that only he had the key to unlock the door through which evangelicals should pass to make the world safe for democracy. Early in his first administration (1914) Mr. Wilson ordered the landing of the Marines in Tampico: Mexican soldiers had taken two American citizens ashore and had put them under arrest. The president appeared before Congress and reported: "I therefore come," he said, "to ask your approval that I should use the armed forces of the United States in such ways and to such extent as . . . may be necessary to obtain . . . the fullest recognition of the rights and dignity of the United States, even amidst the distressing conditions now unhappily obtaining." Both houses passed an approving resolution by large majorities. It was Wilson's view that the president of the United States should not be a "mere department of the government, hailing Congress from some isolated island of jealous power" but that he should be "a human being trying to cooperate with other human beings in a common service." This was sound doctrine which he ignored when he went to Paris and brought back the Treaty of Versailles.

President Truman failed to follow the good Wilson precedent when he ordered the intervention in South Korea (a message was drafted but for some reason remained undelivered) and the result was unfortunate. Mr. Truman's omission permitted the Republicans (even though they contributed heavily to the majorities voting the necessary appropriations) to maintain for campaign purposes that the "police action" had been ordered by a Democratic president without consulting Congress. Failure to consult Congress in advance also triggered the "great debate" of 1951 over whether the president could station four additional divisions in Germany. Nevertheless the Truman omissions may have been less important than two Eisenhower commissions: a request for prior Congressional approval to use armed force if the Chinese communists attacked Formosa, and the resolution of 1957 approving a Middle Eastern "Eisenhower Doctrine" which, happily, was not long-lived. Is it wise for presidents to get advance approval of decisions which, when the time comes, they may not wish to make? Our constitutional arrangements, to quote Mr. Corwin again, are "an invitation to struggle," and it may be added, to pass the buck.

Be silent as a politician
For talking may beget suspicion,

Dean Swift warned his generation. The advice was obsolete by Walter Bagehot's day. "An inability to keep quiet," he once wrote, "is one of the most conspicuous failings of mankind." Calvin Coolidge, agreeing with Swift (although he probably was unaware of it), thought "that four-fifths of all our troubles in this life would disappear if we would only sit down and keep still." If anyone now in Washington thinks that there is anything in the Swiftian-Coolidgian principle, his ghost writer would keep him from practicing it and make him preach. No other electorate in the world endures such a continuous stream of speeches and statements which seek to instruct us and to warn foreigners. "I don't know whether they will frighten the enemy," said the Duke of Wellington after reviewing some new recruits, "but by God they scare me."

"Man does not live by bread alone but by catch phrases," said Stevenson (Robert Louis, not Adlai); and this it seems to me is particularly true of the American man. "Give me liberty or give me death"; "I'd rather be right than president"; "No entangling alliances" (in recent years we have been able to say, "Give us this day our daily pact"); "Too proud to fight"; "The war to end war"; "Make the world safe for democracy"; "The outlawry of war"; "The only thing to fear is fear"; "Unconditional surrender." More recently we have been told of "the new look" which proved rather myopic, "a bigger bang for a buck," and other phrases which will be dealt with elsewhere. Most of them ignore the sound slogan that Theodore Roosevelt once gave the country: "Speak softly and carry a big stick."

Moreover, there is another respect in which we differ from other countries—save perhaps some in Latin America. We permit persons in uniform to queue up for the dais and the microphone. Not long ago a *New Yorker* cartoon showed a woman looking disgustedly at a much epauletted man. The caption: "A fine husband you are. Never make a speech; never wrote a book; no television appearances, and no political ambitions." There used to be a saying that generals fire guns while governments fire generals. The latter rarely happens no matter how reckless the verbal outbursts that come from the brass hats.[4] To them, ghost writers are now more important than their physicians or their confessors. The servicemen vie with the civilians in making work for wives who keep scrapbooks.

At the highest level there are press conferences—an American political invention—but one may doubt the usefulness of most as well as fear the consequences of some. In the era of Franklin Roosevelt much was off-the-record, some for indirect attribution, and a little that was thought out, for direct quotation. Now the conferences are held in a goldfish bowl and televised. The flowing voice flows on:

> nor all thy Piety nor Wit
> Shall lure it back to cancel half a Line
> Nor all thy Tears wash out a Word of it.

Mr. Eisenhower's voice comes from the summit, but the words pass through a cloud and sometimes sentences do not parse. Translations into foreign languages must often bewilder instead of inform. Secretary Dulles' prose was fluent and grammatical, but not infrequently he had to issue explanatory statements correcting extemporaneous indiscretions. Is it wise for those who are among the determiners of American foreign policy thus to appear in mental undress? It was an

[4] General Bradley once made a pronouncement to the effect that we would not allow "local wars to divert us unduly from our central task," and cited Turkey as an area where there might be a "local war." We had to send special emissaries to Turkey, a fellow member of NATO, to pay visits and give reassurances.

Admiral Felix B. Stump, on assuming the Pacific Command (July 1, 1957) burst forth as follows:

"If the communists start a war, they'll take an awful licking. We would use nuclear weapons in small wars as well as large wars, if necessary."

offhand remark of President Truman's about the possible use of the atomic bomb in Korea that made Prime Minister Attlee take the first plane available for Washington.

At the highest level the voices are sometimes discordant. When he was secretary of state, John Foster Dulles twice expressed views that were quite different from the views of the president. In December, 1957, President Eisenhower, attending a NATO conference in Paris, called for doing more than papering the cracks in the alliance; he believed that he could end what he described as a "crisis of confidence." Mr. Dulles thereupon summoned representatives of the press agencies and of the principal newspapers and gave them a "briefing." They were warned not to expect much, if anything, to result from the NATO meetings. All this was off-the-record and "in confidence," but within a week the reading public knew that the briefer had been the secretary of state; diplomatic representatives in Washington probably knew this within a few hours.

A second, even more remarkable performance, was in connection with Communist China's bombardment of the offshore islands in September, 1958. Mr. Eisenhower was at the summer White House in Newport; Mr. Dulles visited him, conferred at some length, and then issued a thousand-word statement that was confused and fuzzy. Newspapers were able to say that it represented a "weakening" of the American position. But within an hour after the statement was released, Mr. Dulles in "briefing" the correspondents was militant and threatening. Of the statement, the *New York Times* could say that "the President has not yet . . . determined" what response he would make, but carried the report of the "briefing" under this headline: "US Decides to Use Force if Reds Invade Quemoy." [5]

[5] During a single week in the Truman administration there were the following pronouncements: General Bradley declared that if events were not worse, "The accumulation of them makes the situation worse." The defense secretary (Louis Johnson) said "War is not on the horizon at the moment." The chairman of the National Security Resources Board (Mr. Symington) announced that "the nation must be ready for war at any time without warning or formal declaration." The Army chief of staff was still of the opinion that "we can prevent war." The secretary of the navy saw nothing "in the current international picture to justify the assumption that we shall not again be called upon to defend ourselves." Secretary Johnson assured the country that "Americans will find an army, navy, and air force in a healthy state of preparedness." The Air Force chief of staff maintained that "The strength of our air forces at the present time is not sufficient to continue an all-out war more than a few months." On the same day the head of the Office of Defense Mobilization announced that we

Historians tell us that Lord Palmerston was much franker with the House of Commons (and with the press) than Sir Edward Grey was sixty years later. We have as yet little means of determining whether Sir Edward Grey's measure of frankness revealed more than the apparent candor of, say, Sir Anthony Eden, or, in our own country, of Secretary Dulles. But one fact is indisputable: despite the tremendous flow of words—from press conferences and in many speeches by civilian and epauletted orators—we are no better informed than are the citizens of countries where the press conference is quite rare and where the inability to remain silent is less conspicuous than among us. Debates in foreign legislatures perform the informing function more effectively than debates in Congress plus the rain of words I have been discussing. Hearings before the Senate Committee on Foreign Relations are useful but not very influential. To be sure, responsible officials from the secretary of state down appear before the committee and make statements, but they frequently seem to make these statements so lengthy that there will be no time for any questions or, when the answers are not satisfactory, for supplementaries. In other words effective criticism of those who determine American foreign policy is confined for the most part to circles that are extragovernmental.

A century ago Walter Bagehot pointed out the absurdity of requiring the British Parliament to fix the details of a trivial statute and allowing the executive a free hand in respect to the negotiation and ratification of important treaties. The Founding Fathers willed differently. Thirty-four senators—that is, one sixteenth of the members of the federal legislature—may now prevent the Senate from giving advice and consent to the ratification of a treaty, and these thirty-four may conceivably come from the seventeen smallest states which contain not more than one twelfth of the population of the

were becoming strong so rapidly that no nation would dare to attack us, and the secretary of defense declared that the world situation was getting worse and we should not be complacent.

During the Eisenhower administration, at the time of the Indochina crisis, Admiral Carney thought that we should fight to keep any part of that country from going communist; otherwise we would find ourselves much weaker than "the coalition that is dedicated to our destruction." Admiral Radford believed and announced that since the Chinese military potential must be destroyed, we should attempt this sooner rather than later.

country. Or, as John Hay once put it: "Thirty-four per cent of the Senate may be on the blackguard side of the question." And John Hay again: "Give and take," an "axiom of diplomacy to the rest of the world, is positively forbidden to us, by both the Senate and public opinion. We must take what we can and give nothing, which greatly narrows our possibilities." Or the late John W. Davis: "Senatorial jealousy of senatorial prerogatives and senatorial difficulty in making up two thirds of the senatorial mind" may hamstring an intelligent executive branch that has real popular backing. Fortunately, in recent years, this constitutional provision has not really bothered us.

During the Franklin Roosevelt era, there was much talk about substituting for treaties executive agreements approved by Congressional joint resolutions, when only a majority instead of two thirds of the Senate would have to be on the "whiteguard" side of the question. There was some action as well: the United States entered the International Labor Organization by way of a joint resolution. This gun is still in the executive arsenal and, if the occasion arose, could be pulled out.[6]

Happily, even though a Democrat may have been in the White House and a Republican may have chaired the Senate Committee on Foreign Relations—or vice versa—there has been no recurrence of the antagonism between Woodrow Wilson and Henry Cabot Lodge that did such hurt to our country and to the world. Senator J. William Fulbright "with a wry smile" told an interviewer recently "that he has a pretty clear idea of the limits of his own power and doesn't expect any applause for not exploiting the nuisance value of his job." In the senator's view, the Foreign Relations Committee should "try to be the conscience of the executive—without in any way indulging in the frivolous delusion of co-equality."[7] On recent occasions the committee has attempted to contribute to the education of the executive, Congress, and the public in three important sectors of public policy: propaganda—that is, the Voice of America (1953); economic aid (1956); and "a full and complete study of US foreign policy" (1959-1960). For the last two inquiries the Committee in-

[6] See Lindsay Rogers, *Constitutional Aspects of Foreign Affairs* (Williamsburg, Va., 1944).

[7] Sidney Hyman, "The Advice and Consent of J. William Fulbright," *The Reporter*, September 17, 1959.

vited assistance from universities and research institutions and published their reports—one or two bad, two or three indifferent, but the rest good.

Under Senator Fulbright's chairmanship, the Committee has paid more attention than it previously had to the fitness of nominees for diplomatic posts. To be sure, when President Roosevelt wished to send Edward J. Flynn to Australia in 1943, the committee inquired about a "paving block" episode and was skeptical of Mr. Flynn's knowledge of or interest in Australia. The White House withdrew the nomination. A Senate subcommittee examined Mayor William O'Dwyer for two days and, without publishing the hearings, recommended his confirmation as ambassador to Mexico. But by and large the practice had been to recommend confirmation with no hearings at all, or after assurances of the nominee's fitness. The increased interest of the Senate committee antedates Mr. Fulbright's chairmanship and on occasion has seemed an attempt to see to it that American representatives abroad do not hold views contrary to those of certain senators.

On September 22, 1951, a subcommittee examined Chester Bowles, who had been nominated as ambassador to India. Mr. Bowles gave the committee an autobiographical sketch of himself and then answered questions concerning his views on India, the Soviet Union, and the possibility of a cease-fire settlement in Korea. A note to the published hearings states that they were held in executive session and "subsequently edited for security reasons." It might have been more accurate to say that the deletions were made in order not to give offense to the states and individuals who were discussed. The context of the deletions shows that there were interchanges on, in the phrase of Senator H. Alexander Smith (Rep., N.J.), "the attitude of India toward the admission of Communist China into the United Nations" or on what, in a larger context, some would-be wit has called "Nehrutrality." Mr. Bowles said that it would be "blackmail" to accept a cease-fire settlement on the basis of admitting Chinese communist representatives to the United Nations and turning over Formosa to the Peiping government. "I am glad you feel that way," Senator Smith told Mr. Bowles, "because I feel that very strongly." Mr. Bowles was confirmed. What other executive of a great state has to consider tailoring the representatives it wishes to send abroad in order to satisfy the whims of a branch of the legislature, a committee of that branch, or, perhaps, individual members of that committee?

But on the Ides of October, 1951, Senator Smith went a little further. He made public the fact that he had submitted a five-point questionnaire to the ten delegates and alternates to the United Nations Assembly and that the State Department had permitted its nominees to answer. All of them assured Senator Smith, although some made certain qualifications—"under present conditions," for example—that they agreed with his well-known views on not recognizing the People's Republic of China, on not seating a communist delegate on the Security Council, and on the desirability of retaining Formosa for the benefit of Chiang Kai-shek. The State Department did not tell the delegates that they should refuse to reply; that the official policy of the government was known to the Senate committee; that the persons who went to the United Nations would be given instructions; that they would have to follow these instructions; and that knowledge of their individual views on certain points was not germane to an efficient performance of the Senate's constitutional duty which, as Thomas Jefferson had said, was to do no more than to see that "no unfit person be employed." Whether the Jeffersonian view should prevail raises questions that range beyond my terms of reference. Suffice it to say that the American executive, in appointing instruments to carry out whatever foreign policy has been determined, faces hurdles that do not have to be jumped by the chief executives of other states.

International affairs now require far more legislation and more frequent and larger appropriations than ever before. The military assistance program; foreign aid; reciprocal trade agreements; the International Bank and International Monetary Fund; the Marshall Plan; agreements that deal with aviation and health; labor conditions; narcotics; displaced persons; human rights—foreign affairs are no longer the exclusive preserve of the State Department but cut across the interests of many other Washington departments and agencies. The Hoover Commission noted that 46 agencies of the federal government were interested in the conduct of foreign policy and that only five per cent of the appropriations that might be called nondomestic were under the control of the State Department. Different Congressional committees must have their say, but the danger is that

Congress will be demagogic and that the Senate will attempt the role of tutor or governess.

There are recent examples of Congressional assertiveness, and even demagogy. When the House of Representatives voted to withhold aid from the United Kingdom so long as the "partition" of Ireland was not corrected, that aberration was temporary. But in 1950, the Congress rewrote the Far Eastern Economic Assistance Act to include a grant to Nationalist China and in the Omnibus Appropriation Bill provided for a mandatory loan to Spain. Legislative riders have sought to deny financial assistance to the countries that permit trade with the Soviet Union and its satellites. When there was great resentment about the entry of the Chinese communist volunteers into the Korean War, the Senate called upon the United Nations to declare Red China an aggressor and resolved that the Chinese communist government should not be admitted to membership in the United Nations. When there seemed to be reluctance to take the succeeding steps that the aggression-calling resolution logically demanded, the House and Senate cut parliamentary red tape and, with no dissenting votes, demanded that members of the United Nations put an embargo on shipments of war materials to Communist China. The Senate unanimously called for an embargo on Czechoslovak trade in retaliation for that government's behavior in the case of an Associated Press correspondent, William N. Oatis. The administration accepted all these Congressional interventions with little protest; it allowed its hands to be manacled by Congressional instructions on the policies that should be followed in respect to Far Eastern questions, the countries that should receive economic assistance, East-West trade, and reprisals again certain governments.

Moreover, apart from formal action, senators informally let their opinions be known. The "Asia-lationists" are always to the fore. Fifty-six senatorial ones went on record against the recognition of Communist China. That was reminiscent of the Henry Cabot Lodge-Philander C. Knox "round robin" of October, 1919, when thirty-seven senators warned Woodrow Wilson that they did not approve of the draft of the League of Nations Covenant that was then being discussed. The House of Representatives once seriously considered withholding aid to Europe unless the European Defense Treaty was ratified.

No other legislature can behave this way in respect to the conduct of foreign relations. Where, other than in the United States, could a member of the legislature—in this case Senator McCarran—summon to his office representatives of a Department of State and of an Export-Import Bank who, when they arrived, were presented to a foreign ambassador (Don Jose Felix de Lequerica, from Spain)? The senator asked the officials to explain why American economic aid was not reaching Spain more swiftly. To be sure these are minor matters, but they strike our friends and enemies as vagaries which are largely unknown to governments other than ours when they endeavor to formulate a foreign policy and to carry it out.

There are few effective pressure groups in the field of international policy and many legislators share (with Dr. Johnson) a dislike of all foreigners save those with voting strength in their constituencies. By and large the country is still isolationist in the sense that we want to go it alone and the others can follow. We think there is still truth in the adage: "He who pays the piper can call the tunes." We are shocked when some pipers refuse to pipe, and we ignore the fact that a piper may well know more about the best tunes than does the one who pays him. We lecture our teammates when the members of the opposing team can overhear. We foolishly think (despite Woodrow Wilson's experience with Italy) that we can appeal to the opinions of the man in the street or the elected deputies of other countries.

While we were making an appraisal which did not prove to be agonizing, the headlines announced that the president was "Set to Cut Holiday if French Reject Arms Pact." What a return to Washington from the nineteenth hole at the Augusta golf course would have accomplished was not clear. Suppose Anthony Eden had told the United States that British policy would undergo an agonizing reappraisal if the American Senate did not act the way he desired on some matter. How many senators would have voted "No" just to spite the British prime minister? (Suppose Selwyn Lloyd were to visit Panama and give a revolver to its President as Dulles did to Naguib?) Washington apparently does not realize that public exhortations and objurgations may boomerang. "President Warns France to Reverse Bonn Vote." Who do we think we are? And in attempting to lead the free world we ignore the maxim of La Rochefoucauld: "It is a great folly to be wise all alone." One wonders whether the British have ever sent a note to us quoting what Cromwell wrote to the General Assembly of the Church of Scotland: "I beseech you, in the bowels of Christ, think it possible you may be mistaken." We said this, more positively, to the British (France and Israel, as well) in the autumn of 1956. According to Thucydides, the Corinthians told the Athenians, in answer to the arguments of the Corcyrian ambassadors: "Every power should have the right to control its own allies." General Charles de Gaulle may have thought of this in November, 1959, when he was controlling his allies in NATO.

A secretary of state is by no means as dependent as a chancellor of the exchequer may be on an unknown permanent official. The subject matter is more comprehensible to the layman than is the interest rate appropriate for a new bond issue, and there is no necessity for dealing with decimals—"those damned dots" which puzzled Lord Randolph Churchill. If an underling in our State Department determines policy it is only when the matter is trivial and does not interest his political chief. An underling's enthusiastic memoranda and minutes may have some influence, but the political chief is more likely to be pulled and pushed by what he thinks are the currents of opinion in Congress and the country. He may also have to see himself, the lord of Foggy Bottom, become a rubber stamp for the occupant of the White House.

Take Wilson's administrations: his secretaries, William Jennings Bryan, Robert Lansing, and Bainbridge Colby were ciphers in determining our foreign policy. Under Franklin Roosevelt, Sumner Welles (undersecretary) was more influential—or perhaps less uninfluential—than Cordell Hull (secretary). Edward Stettinius (a student of mine at the University of Virginia) owed his appointment to his willingness to be a titular rather than a real secretary, and the Yalta papers provide eloquent and distressing testimony that Mr. Roosevelt did not bother to learn how the State Department wished to brief him. President Truman fired James F. Byrnes, and while George Marshall and Dean Acheson were far from being rubber stamps, Mr. Truman always had his hand on the throttle.

But John Foster Dulles? My guess is that historians will describe him as a secretary of state who was allowed a freer hand than was vouchsafed to any of the previous occupants of his office. I qualify this by saying that in the days when Brussels was more important internationally than Washington, some of our secretaries of state may have paddled their own canoes, but who cared where they went on their excursions? During important periods—the formative days of the republic; European interests in our War between the States; the Spanish-American War; the first and second World Wars; the cold war—no president ever gave his secretary of state as free a hand as Dwight D. Eisenhower gave to his.

To the question "Who Determines American Foreign Policy?" I have suggested a tentative answer for the period ended by Stalin's death. For the years 1953-1959 one may say, "John Foster Dulles." He was the most itinerant secretary of state we have ever had and when he was off on his journeys there was a hiatus in the determination of policy in Washington. But even Mr. Dulles thought it politic to do obeisance toward Capital Hill. He attempted to appease Senator Joseph R. McCarthy by taking Scott McLeod into the State Department and making him responsible for security matters. He bowed to Senator William F. Knowland and the China Lobby in being so enamored of Chiang Kai-shek and so averse to speaking, even through intermediaries, to the rulers of Communist China.[8] Indeed, Mr. Dulles took out of his book *War or Peace* (published in 1950) the expression of his belief that "if the Communist government of China in fact proves its ability to govern China without serious domestic resistance, then it, too, should be admitted to the United Nations." This seems unnecessarily overcautious; but Mr. Dulles, as secretary, was compelled to eat a good many words that he had spoken incautiously and the astonishing thing was that he was able to survive so many verbal *gaffes*. Perhaps one explanation is that internationally things now happen so quickly that before criticism mounts there is something else that seems just as important to criticize or fear.

Mr. Dulles drafted the Republican Party's platform plank (1952) calling for the "liberation" of the communist satellites—a slogan that no one, save perhaps the enslaved peoples, took seriously.[9] He made a campaign speech viewing with alarm the treaty-making authority of the federal government, swallowed it manfully, and then valiantly

[8] A recent Brookings Institution volume, *United States Foreign Policy, 1945-1955* (by Reitzel, Kaplan, and Coblentz) accomplishes the remarkable feat of not mentioning Senator Knowland or the China Lobby, but this is no discrimination against them. The volume does not mention Hamlet, Dwight D. Eisenhower; his Polonius, John Foster Dulles; or the gravediggers, United States senators.

[9] Not referred to at the time of the Hungarian revolt of October, 1956, save by Vice President Nixon, who at first boasted of the success of the "liberation" policy.

opposed the Bricker Amendment. For the president's first State of the Union message he ghosted a passage which seemed to contemplate the "unleashing" of Chiang Kai-shek to invade the Chinese mainland. That, militarily speaking, was chimerical. His announcement before the Council on Foreign Relations in New York City of a policy of "massive retaliation" required him to issue many more words of "clarification" than had been required to phrase the original threat. He endeavored to make himself out more warlike than he was when he encouraged *Life* magazine to publish the article on his "brinkmanship" which on occasion President Eisenhower had held in check.

On a journey to Egypt he gave a silver-plated revolver to General Mohammed Naguib who was shrieking for the withdrawal of the British garrison from the Suez zone; later he infuriated Gamal Abdel Nasser (and the Egyptian people) by abruptly—almost insultingly—withdrawing from the negotiations over the Aswan Dam, and the Soviet Union accepted the invitation to step in. The *gaffes* invited gibes: Mr. Dulles "was born with a silver foot in his mouth"; he was our country's "unguided missile"; he was like the weather, "unpredictable; hence, when the blizzard comes unexpectedly, one must wait for its end and then try to dig out." But the most astounding thing was not that he survived all his indiscretions, but that his critics—abroad, where they were the more bitter, as well as at home—were fearsome when he became unable to continue as secretary.

His inflexibility might have been extreme, but at least we knew it was inflexible. Flexibility? How flexible? We did not know. Almost overnight President Eisenhower transformed himself from King Log into King Stork. Summitry—which Mr. Dulles had always opposed—became popular. Until his departure from office Mr. Dulles was certainly a principal determiner of our foreign policy. His successor or successors have been shadowy figures.

"Why can't we let it alone?" Lord Melbourne is reported to have asked while he was prime minister. But bureaucrats and ghost writers must keep busy and don't want to leave anything alone. They, I suspect, are responsible for letting other states sometimes conclude that we not only insist that we preach the funeral sermons, but provide the honorary pallbearers, drive the hearse, and dig the grave. We must have our way even in unimportant matters. We want the new presidents of the United Nations Assembly and the new members of the Security Council to be our favorite sons of the moment.

Our most juvenile performance of this kind was probably in August, 1953, when we were able to prevent India from being represented at the political conference on Korea. By putting on pressure we got the votes of seventeen Latin-American countries, and of Greece, Pakistan, and Nationalist China—a number sufficient to prevent the necessary two-thirds majority.[10] And in addressing the Assembly on the issue, Henry Cabot Lodge seemed to his fellow members to talk as if he were still a United States senator and anxious to placate irate constituents. In Molière's play, *Le Bourgeois Gentilhomme*, the count looked down on M. Jourdain who had just gone through the mummery of being made a gentleman. We became "Le Premier Gentilhomme" rather suddenly without any mummery and forgot the homely truth that a top dog is always unpopular, that the dogs below and looking up are bound to feel some kinship with each other. Our leaders have neglected to pause on Massachusetts Avenue in Washington and ponder the words carved on the base of Edmund Burke's statue: "Magnanimity in politics is not seldom the truest wisdom and a great empire and little minds go ill together." Instead our attitude has too often been reminiscent of Mr. Podsnap's famous remark: "This island is blessed, sir, by Providence, to the direct exclusion of such other countries as there may happen to be."

Again—and this is a large subject on which I can barely touch—our State Department has usually been in bondage to the lawyers. With less than a handful of exceptions, our secretaries have belonged to the profession which Edmund Burke said may quicken the intellect, but does not enlarge the understanding, save in those happily born. (One of the few lawyers in Downing Street was Sir John Simon, who, as foreign secretary, was far from a success. He had prevented so many convictions, a cruel wit said, that he had ceased to have any convictions of his own.) The lawyer, as Hans Morgenthau has noted, "is particularly averse to long-range planning that entails risks and requires daring because he has been conditioned in dealing with his clients—and is not the government just another client?—to chart a course that avoids trouble, minimizes risks, and

[10] When U.N.O. concord seems remote
Small nations must think twice
For every nation has a vote
And every vote its price. (F.P.A.)

is plainly calculable." Before a "case" arises there is nothing to be done; when the "case" presents itself, win it if possible, and wait for the next one. Mr. Morgenthau said this in the context of the Suez crisis of November, 1956.

Who then determined our policy is still unclear. Unfortunately Mr. Dulles was ill and even more unfortunately his undersecretary had been appointed because of his name and not by reason of his qualifications. Underlings in the State Department had divided opinions. There was no attempt to consult Congressional leaders; there was no time for newspaper comment. Is it unfair to say that in this crisis the United States abdicated and allowed the United Nations to determine US foreign policy? But the United Nations is not a world government or a court of justice; in the words of the Charter it is no more than "a center for harmonizing the actions of nations in the attainment of common ends." When there is no agreement on the ends or no will to attain them, the machinery doesn't work. Or, as the London *Economist* has aptly put it: [11] the United Nations may be "plausibly depicted as a kind of Vatican City built into a latter-day Rome, where temporal powers seek benisons for their rival policies." The Eisenhower administration asked this "Vatican City" to determine its policy. The English historian, Douglas Jerrold, once wrote of the "fateful and, as we believe, fatal decision to put the conscience and the moral and military authority of the great powers into commission at Geneva."

"Moral authority" in commission at Turtle Bay? President Eisenhower, who approved the determination to have our Suez policy determined by the United Nations, puts "moral and spiritual values" above other earthly considerations and defines them as meaning "honesty, decency, fairness, service—all that sort of thing." The president is on record as believing that the earthly revelation of moral rightness is to be found in "mankind in the mass." *Vox dei, vox populi.*

Mankind in the mass as represented in the United Nations? Some delegates represent the consciences of states headed by Khrushchev, Trujillo, Tito, and Franco. The statistical method applied to international politics enables us to see that one third of eighty-one (the members of the United Nations) is twenty-seven. There are ten communist countries and twenty-eight Arab-Asian-African countries

[11] "What Hope for UNO?" March 16, 1957.

with Israel being omitted. One third of eighty-one is twenty-seven and the United Nations must take many of its decisions by a two-thirds vote. Those who determine our foreign policy have failed to stress to the American "mankind in the mass" the vast transformation of the United Nations since it was set up in San Francisco. There is no birth control in respect to new members and this is as it should be; but in respect to some of the new members, one may mutilate Lovelace's famous lines and say: "I should not love thee, dear, so much, feared I not Russia more."

Foreign policy by itself—say the recognition of Communist China, whether Poland or Turkey should be a new member of the Security Council, or our position in respect to a United Nations resolution on Algeria—can presumably be settled by the president and the secretary of state. Both have an amount of "staffing" which must intrigue the author of "Parkinson's Law." While Mr. Dulles was secretary there were frequent complaints that he remained unaware of what the hierarchy he headed was thinking, or at least putting in "position papers," and that Mr. Eisenhower left too many things to his staff. But when it comes to matters that may require some measure of agreement between civil and military authorities the machinery is truly formidable.

There is the National Security Council, where the president chairs the vice president, the secretary of state, the secretary of defense, and the director of the Office of Civil and Defense Mobilization (what he can say about policy is unclear). The chairman of the joint chiefs of staff and the director of the Central Intelligence Agency attend as "advisors." The Council has a staff of eleven "think people" who, "scrupulously nonpolitical and non-policy making," give to the president's special assistant for national security affairs "an objective analysis of every policy paper." Since 1950 the Council has had "a second level group" which, under President Truman, was called the "Senior Staff," but under President Eisenhower came to be called "the Planning Board." Each member of the National Security Council is represented on the Planning Board by "an official of assistant secretary rank" but latterly these officials have relied on "Planning Board Assistants" to do the detailed drafting work.

Since 1953, in order to maximize "the psychological impact of United States policy" (on Congress, our allies, or our potential enemies?) the National Security Council has had an Operations Planning Board. Here the deputy undersecretary of state chairs the deputy secretary of defense, the director of the Central Intelligence Agency (now no humble "adviser"), and the directors of the United States Information Agency and the International Cooperation Administration. On this group the joint chiefs of staff are not represented, presumably because they do not think it would be worth their while. This Operations Coordinating Board has its own staff which is "somewhat separate from the staff of the National Security Council-Planning Board structure" and since 1957 the vice chairman of the Board has been a "Presidential Special Assistant for Security Operational Coordination." To inform the Board, "detailed [*sic*] scrutiny of policy execution in various geographical and functional areas is actually carried out by approximately fifty Operating Coordinating Board working groups." These are "interdepartmental committees of working level officials with one professional staff person from the Board's staff also sitting as a member." (The State Department, it is estimated, sends representatives to seven hundred interdepartmental committees.)

The preceding paragraphs carefully followed, and quoted from, a report on "The Formulation and Administration of United States Foreign Policy" that the Brookings Institution made to the Senate Committee on Foreign Relations (November, 1959). The authors of the Report themselves quote a good deal from Messrs. Robert Cutler and Gordon Gray, who have been presidential assistants, and some of my quotations are from them. The Brookings Report, as may be sound policy for an institution that wants to be employed to make more reports, deals with this overly complex administration structure in a dead-pan manner. So do I, save to ask the reader to remember John Chipman Gray and to quote Junius: "Masks, hatchets, racks and vipers dance through your letters in all the mazes of rhetorical confusion." So Junius wrote to Sir William Draper.

Officials, subofficials, presidential assistants, and committees dance in all the mazes of administrative confusion when foreign policy involves departments other than the State Department or interests the military and naval people. The decision-making bodies are then legislative rather than executive in character. The "frocks" and the "brass hats," to quote Admiral Fisher, represent constituents, engage in log rolling, and are worked on by pressure groups. Samuel P.

Huntington compares the process to the tariff making of yesteryear when Congress gave each industry the protection it wanted. "Over-all objectives get lost in the mechanism," Mr. Huntington remarks, and "a premium is put upon agreement rather than decision." [12] In comparison, the way in which the British joint chiefs of staff worked with Winston Churchill and the War Cabinet was quite simple and effective.[13] Moreover, the British relationships made it clear whether foreign policy decisions were made by the civilians or the military. Not so with us. Who, for example, determined in 1950 to press Germany to rearm? Foggy Bottom or the Pentagon? Whose decision was it to establish bases in Spain?

"Depend upon it, Sir," said Dr. Johnson. "When a man knows he is to be hanged in a fortnight it concentrates his mind wonderfully." Those of us who now face the shapelessness of things to come are not under such a compulsion to concentrate: the timetable is not definite. Moreover, as I have suggested above in another connection, so many things happen so rapidly that before we can have a calm informed judgment on one matter we are called upon to think about and judge another matter.

But there is one note of comfort and on this I close. Some years ago my friend Charles A. Beard wrote an essay published in *Harper's* magazine, and then reprinted as a little book, *Giddy Minds and Foreign Quarrels*. His target was Franklin Roosevelt's foreign policy; but Beard, I think, failed to establish his point. Our foreign policy, or as some would have said, our lack of policy (1939) was not intended to draw attention from our domestic problems. As I have said above, I think that on occasion we have too much bipartisanship or nonpartisanship and that this is a sedative on thinking. But of one thing we can be certain: those who determine our foreign policy —or who attempt to determine it—pay no heed to the advice that Henry IV on his deathbed gave to his son, Henry V:

> I . . . had a purpose now
> To lead out many to the Holy Land,
> Lest rest, and lying still, might make
> them look

[12] *Foreign Affairs*, January, 1960.
[13] See Sir Arthur Bryant's description in *Triumph in the West* (London, 1959).

Too near unto my state. Therefore, my Harry,
Be it thy course, to busy giddy minds
With foreign quarrels; that action, hence
borne out,
May waste the memory of the former days.

My friend Beard erred in maintaining that this was a Rooseveltian tactic.

Editor's note. A version of this essay was delivered at Notre Dame on May 7, 1956, and was updated in the spring of 1960.

Several aspects of United States government operations criticized in this chapter underwent profound changes in 1961. President Kennedy revoked the executive order which had created the Operations Coordinating Board (see below p. 440) and he abolished a large number of interdepartmental committees. These reforms aim at simplifying the Executive Branch and at placing responsibility for decisions on individuals in specific departments rather than on committees. Moreover, the Kennedy Administration has curbed the civil and military spokesmen whose oratory sometimes created the impression abroad that the United States is a divided country without continuity in policy, or reliable leadership.

13: CONGRESS AND THE MANAGEMENT OF AMERICAN FOREIGN POLICY

Ernest S. Griffith

The end of the Second World War found Congress with an outlook upon world affairs fundamentally different from that which followed the First World War. Prior to 1945, it had declared by resolution its intent to support America's entry into an international organization. During the first war, it is true, there had been a somewhat similar altruistic, or at least, responsible, motivation. On the surface it might have been expected that such motivation would again prove transient. New factors, however, were present. The difference between the two aftermaths was that in considerable measure the majority of the nation had learned certain lessons by 1945—especially the lesson of our inevitable involvement in the world, and that this involvement called for continuous, enlightened intervention—for the national interest as well as for altruistic reasons. This gave a much firmer foundation for international co-operation. A minor note was the presence of a curious sense of corporate guilt on the part of the Senate for its earlier behavior, a sense to some extent aided by a defensive uneasiness at the not inconsiderable calls for revision or removal of the constitutional requirement of a two-thirds vote for treaty ratification. Other factors were also operative. The executive, too, had learned its lesson. Continuous consultations with the Congressional leadership were held by the president and State Department officials. During the course of these a mutual confidence emerged. The issues clearly transcended party lines, and were so treated. Senators and representatives were freely used as participating delegates to conferences, the products of which they would be called upon to justify and ratify.

The level of education of the individual congressman was thus higher, as was that of the electorate as well. The United States ended the war in a position of clearly predominant power, and this fact brought a corresponding sense of responsibility. Moral lectures had been so clearly inadequate to preserve peace that the alternative of an exercise of power in the interest of international order no longer had to face militant isolationism. Ratification of the United Nations Charter in 1945 was by vote of 89 to 2, a measure of the changed climate.

The story of Congress and foreign policy in the years since 1944 could in large measure be written in terms of a series of climaxes or crises. Almost without exception, these crises have been met or resolved in what were clearly internationally-minded votes. Such outcomes were perhaps not too surprising in the earlier years after the war. What is more surprising is the persistence of such an attitude over the entire period to the present day. Only the occasional setbacks in the reciprocal trade program can properly be regarded as major exceptions.

Ratification of the United Nations Charter was a foregone conclusion. With great sophistication, the Marshall Plan was also carried by very large majorities, even though its anticommunist overtones were much less prominent, and hence, with Congress, less influential at that time than they became later. The Truman Doctrine under which the United States assumed guardianship of the safety of Greece and Turkey revealed a surprising degree of consensus. By the time of Truman's inaugural speech in 1949, Congress was ready for the Point Four program.

The collapse of our China policy in 1947 and 1948 strained Executive-Congressional relations, but not at the point of our international responsibilities. In the end it may well have strengthened the latter, as the magnitude of the communist threat was there for all to see. NATO appeared in 1949; and an aroused Congressional anticommunism joined with the realities of the power situation to achieve this widespread Congressional endorsement of the abandoning of our traditional nonalliance policy.

Then came the Korean War, and Red China's entry therein. For the war itself there was virtually unanimous Congressional support; but the entry of China, the recall of MacArthur, and the eventual stalemate exacerbated and extended the criticism of our earlier China policies. To this day, large sectors of Congress believe that the China policy of the mid-1940s was the greatest single foreign policy blunder in our history—and possibly worse than a blunder in some of its origins.

In spite of this belief, the hearings on the recall of MacArthur left as a by-product a much better understanding of the intimate relationships between military and foreign policy than Congress had possessed previously. Resolved also, and in traditional fashion, was the issue of military responsibility to the civilian authority.

The "great debate" of 1951 centered upon the power of the president to send troops abroad in time of peace. In a sense the central issue was bypassed for the time being by the president's promise to consult in advance of such an eventuality. The Formosa Resolution stirred the Congress of 1955; the Middle East crisis raised similar issues in 1958. On both occasions Congress endorsed a measure of freedom for the president; on both it accepted United States responsibility on a global scale.

Foreign aid was reappraised in 1957 and 1959. Its emphasis was altered, but in the end it emerged with substantial vindication, in spite of much extremely vocal criticism.

These crises reveal certain constants. Along with the internationally-minded majority, there was always some undercurrent of isolationism. There was also an undercurrent of suspicion of the executive and jealousy of Congressional prerogatives. Where this isolationism, suspicion, and jealousy combined forces, as in the proposed Bricker Amendment,[1] the challenge was formidable, but abortive. Never did any of these undercurrents win a substantial victory, except that the practice of annual appropriations with its attendant policy review was the rock on which for a time much would-be long-range planning foundered. It is interesting to note that in 1959, Congress, especially the Senate, seemed to be ahead of the president in this regard.

On the other hand, economic parochialism or particularism was occasionally successful, especially in limiting the reciprocal trade expansion program. Yet even here a notable victory for the international approach occurred in its most recent test.

Present also in all these crises was the expressed desire on the part of a number of congressmen for a "fresh start," a "new approach," a "reappraisal." Some of these expressions were merely political tactics, in that they made it unnecessary for members to reveal their stand on issues politically hot in their districts or states; in other instances the members would indicate in broad outline what they felt should be done by way of change.

Yet more constant than any of these minor strands was the com-

[1] Added support was forthcoming on account of its states' rights overtones, and its conformity to the Senate's idea of its own peculiar prerogatives.

bination of enlightened national interest and international-mindedness which had come to dominate the postwar years.

One turns naturally from this brief survey of the tide of events to a closer examination of the instruments through which Congress arrived at its policies.[2]

The Foreign Relations Committee of the Senate and the Foreign Affairs Committee of the House are the focus of special Congressional action in foreign policy. Only the Appropriations Committee of the House constitutes a formidable rival, though other committees play significant roles. Of these, more presently.

The two foreign policy committees are by no means as dissimilar in their jurisdictions as might be supposed from the Senate's special concern with treaties. The growth of the "program" and the increasing use of the executive agreement have been responsible for an erosion of the importance of the formal treaty. Programs such as foreign aid in all its ramifications, or extension of cultural relations, or reciprocal trade, are foreign policy moves of the first magnitude. They arouse widespread popular interest; they call for enabling acts and appropriations; they engage the House equally with the Senate. Then, too, it is not unfair to say that virtually every action that historically had been the subject of a treaty has likewise been taken by an executive agreement, and the implementation of these, where legislatively necessary, requires bicameral action.

Much has been made of the bipartisanship of these two committees. Such a characterization arose in part from the fact that the choice of participants in legislative-executive consultations and the use of congressmen as delegates to international bodies and conferences have usually followed two-party lines. This practice was tacit recognition that, organizationally speaking, Congress has been and is strictly partisan.

Actually in most policy matters, and certainly in foreign policy, Congress has been not so much bipartisan as nonpartisan or unpartisan. Such a characterization recognizes the frequent existence of differences; but it recognizes, also, that these differences have sprung from conviction, temperament, or local coloration, and not from party alignment or discipline.

Even here, the Senate committee for many years brought only

[2] See R. A. Dahl, *Congress and Foreign Policy* (New York, 1950), for an earlier study.

unanimous reports to its parent body after leaning over backward to find a basis for agreement. The House never went quite this far, but its spirit and composition were not dissimilar.

The Senate committee was almost unique among Congressional committees. Its prestige was and is very great. Its chairmen possessed national stature. Its leadership was respected and accepted among its peers. It has not hesitated to evolve and to press for changes in national policy, while at the same time it has maintained a posture of dignified co-operation with the executive as its equal. Its leadership during these years was always competent; and under Senators Vandenberg, George, and Fulbright it rose to heights of distinction. One of the major changes in the committee's functioning arose out of its acquisition of a competent and even brilliant staff. In 1945 the Legislative Reference Service was authorized to employ four "senior specialists" in as many fields. Apart from the professional staff of the Joint Committee on Internal Revenue Taxation, and a few exceedingly competent "clerks" of certain other committees, these were the first permanent experts of stature deliberately engaged to serve Congress. One of these was Francis O. Wilcox, and almost immediately he found himself occupied with research and analysis for Senator Connally, the Foreign Relations Committee's chairman, and for the committee itself. In 1946 the Legislative Reorganization Act was passed, and the Foreign Relations Committee, along with the other committees, was authorized to employ a professional staff. Dr. Wilcox was made its first director, to be followed later by his able associate, Carl M. Marcy. If the full and true history of these critical years is ever written—and that is, I believe, unlikely—the former might well be found to occupy a place of statesmanship and significance roughly comparable to that of Senator Vandenberg. Always keenly aware of the respect due the position, ability, and motivation of his senatorial masters, Wilcox (assisted by his staff and the Legislative Reference Service), was the one to whom the committee came more and more for analyses, critiques of executive proposals, and accurate and detached appraisals of the world situation. Wilcox's passion for anonymity allayed any suspicion of potential rivalry, and his integrity disarmed any thought of ulterior motives. These staff studies, together with the wise counsel always forthcoming from Wilcox and his associates, focused the committee's thought upon essentials, sharpening the issues, elevating the motives, and letting facts determine the answers.

Of late, the committee has favored larger-scale studies, usually under contract. Such studies are able to make recommendations, a facility which by the inherent nature of their positions both the committee's own staff and the Legislative Reference Service must almost necessarily forego. Such studies noticeably influenced or reinforced committee opinion in the direction of negotiated agreements for reduction of armaments, and longer-range planning for economic and technical assistance overseas. The upshot of this latter is still uncertain, but it is interesting to note that the lines of argument were drawn between a Foreign Relations Committee eager for longer periods of aid and greater emphasis on development; and an executive not yet ready to break with the traditional approach. On the side of the executive point of view were aligned many of the Appropriations Committees' members, unwilling to surrender the power of annual review. Kennedy, however, has shifted to the longer-range planning.

For its part, the House Foreign Affairs Committee has grown steadily in prestige and effectiveness. Even so, it is still a considerable distance from its illustrious opposite number. This has arisen chiefly from the fact that certain other committees in the Lower House, interested in one or another aspect of foreign policy, have been formidable centers of power in their own right, and also to the great prestige and weight of the House Appropriations Committee. Interlocking committee memberships, plus the long and distinguished story of the Senate committee, have dimmed potential rivals in the Upper House.[3]

While the House committee has conscientiously studied executive proposals, it has not itself been the generator of rival ideas to the extent of its Senate counterpart. Some of its membership did share with several Senators a skepticism with regard to our China policy, and this skepticism affected executive policy. Yet since the days of the Herter Committee (incidentally a special or select committee) the House has exhibited only a modest counterpart to the exhaustive and at times spectacular Senate committee inquiries into foreign aid, disarmament, the president's prerogative, the Korean War, our Latin-American relations, revision of the United Nations Charter—to mention those inquiries which have ranged most widely and revealed the most independence of thought.

[3] For an excellent study of the House and its committees in this regard, see Holbert N. Carroll, *The House of Representatives in Foreign Affairs* (Pittsburgh, 1958).

Time is on the side of an equalization of the responsibilities of the two Houses. The aforementioned shift from an emphasis on treaties to an emphasis on programs is only part of the picture. The economic and ideological have joined the political and military as centers of concern. Appropriations, laws, and joint resolutions are all necessary for action in these spheres, and all are bicameral. As the House committee gains in confidence, it too is likely to investigate widely as well as deeply; and man for man, its members have more time to give to such work than has the average Senator with his multiple committee assignments.

It is common knowledge that concern with and control of certain aspects of foreign policy rest with committees other than the two foreign relations committees. Second only to these in power and importance are the appropriations committees. Here, as in other functions, Congress brings to bear upon its wishes, as indicated in authorizations, the factor of fiscal policy. At its best this latter represents an over-all, programming, co-ordinating approach; though in this particular field, more often than not, other factors have also been operating. For a combination of reasons—including the accidental one of who the personalities assigned to the respective committees happen to be—substantial differences have arisen between the appropiations committees of the two houses. The House Subcommittee on Foreign Operations, and to a considerable extent its full Appropriations Committee, have fairly regularly imposed drastic cuts upon the authorized and requested amounts for mutual assistance.[4] Moreover, this committee and its subcommittees have at times been sharply critical of State Department policies and practices, and even more so of the executive's overseas information agencies. Some of this criticism has been highly specific, the committee members frequently serving as conduits for grievances or exposures. To some extent a censured episode has served as an excuse for a more general attack. In disputes between its Foreign Affairs Committee and its Appropriations Committee, the House as a whole has tended to side with the latter.

It has remained for the Senate to come to the rescue. Its Appropriations Committee has been much more friendly and its Foreign Relations Committee much more influential than their opposite

[4] See *ibid.*, pp. 139-93; also the illuminating study by H. Field Haviland, Jr., "Foreign Aid and the Policy Process, 1957," *American Political Science Review*, vol. LII (Sept. 1958), 689-724.

numbers in the House. Memberships in these two committees overlap. Then, too, the Senate Appropriations Committee has in many fields regarded itself as a board of appeals from House action, often concentrating on the few points that an agency desires especially to press. On the other hand, at least occasionally it operates in reverse, and itself imposes cuts, aiming thereby to divest itself of the tag of being "softer" than the House.

Both appropriations committees, and especially that of the House, have been extremely cautious of any legislative extension of executive powers of discretion that would lessen their powers of review. On this rock have foundered (or at least been deflected) many of the attempts to extend the time limits of authorized expenditures and to set up developmental loan funds financed by other than appropriated funds.

All in all, the appropriations committees have been not only part of the process of foreign policy formation, but at times they have been the decisive sector, especially in limitation of amount, of advance planning, and of freedom of allocation.

The knowledgeable members of both houses—and there are many—recognize that foreign policy and defense, in many of their major aspects, are a seamless web. In the Senate there is overlapping membership between the Foreign Relations and Armed Services Committees. In both houses, and especially in the Senate, special or select committees with memberships from these two "parent" committees are occasionally formed; and joint hearings (in the Senate) have been instituted on occasion. In defense and foreign policy alike, Congress regarded it as its role to review and criticize, though not usually to oppose, the programs of the executive. Disarmament, foreign aid, the conduct of the Korean War, control of outer space,[5] were the most noteworthy of the jointly-explored problems. In fact, it was the audit of the Korean War, especially in the hearings on MacArthur's recall, that probably did more than any other single thing to bring greater realization of the close relationships between these two great aspects of national policy. So what was decided about atomic and limited warfare, the nature of our overseas defense commitments, and many another item which at first glance appeared primarily military, bent or channeled foreign policy by the choices made.

The Select Committee on Foreign Aid (the Herter Committee)

[5] Representatives of other interested committees also appeared on this special committee.

served as the counterpart of the Senate Foreign Relations Committee in the considerations leading up to the adoption of the Marshall Plan in its final Congressional form. The issues were so important, and interest so widespread, that it was realized intuitively that a broader base of deliberation and support was needed than would have been afforded by the then Foreign Affairs Committee. Yet this was the committee which furnished the nucleus of membership and staff for the select committee. Added to it were members of other committees concerned with the problem.

In reality there were few committees in either house that in some fashion or other were not concerned with foreign affairs.[6] The Ways and Means and Finance Committees largely determined our tariff policy. House Merchant Marine and Senate Interstate and Foreign Commerce dealt with shipping. Judiciary was concerned with immigration and Banking and Currency with international finance. The Government Operations Committees concerned themselves with certain post-audits of the administration of foreign affairs. Numerous committees, such as Agriculture, Interior and Insular Affairs, Banking and Currency, dealt with sectors of our economic order which had widespread international implications. We have advanced enormously in stature and responsibility on a world scale. With this involvement has come an international dimension to most of our domestic policies that has brought foreign affairs issues into discussion in committees that two decades ago would have deemed such considerations irrelevant, had they ever been mentioned at all. Yet many of these committees, especially in the House, remained basically "clientele" committees, and as such found their loyalty toward the groups, strong in their districts, that elected them. Considerations of foreign policy at the most came off second best, with the Foreign Affairs Committee not possessed of the necessary strength and prestige to induce the House as a whole to overrule the domestically-favored groups, or even to obtain the initial assignment of responsibility for consideration of a problem.

The basic political reason for this situation was surely that foreign affairs in general and the State Department in particular had no such powerful clientele among the electorate as the clienteles that supported legislation and appropriations in connection with agriculture, the merchant marine, veterans' affairs and other interests. Yet

[6] Professor Carroll has brought this out sharply in his excellent study mentioned in footnote 3.

this argument can be pushed too far, for thousands of voters made their wishes known in behalf of an enlightened foreign policy, one which met ready response among scores of members of both houses. The result of the legislative process is more likely than not measurably better than the original clientele or appropriation subcommittee proposals.

It has been the action of these clientele committees, as well as the appropriations process, which has given the dispersive and unco-ordinated character to the Congressional expression of our foreign policy—especially in its economic aspects. Yet this dispersiveness was itself but the manifestation of the dispersiveness in an electorate and society whose interest groups remained the principal political factor. It extended to the executive branch as well, where the clientele departments and agencies were the counterpart of the Congressional committees and subcommittees. The interest groups and their agents, the departments and the interested congressmen, formed the "whirlpools" in our government within which policy of a limited and unco-ordinated application was normally generated. In contrast with this dispersiveness, the forces of integration were less fully developed.

The years since 1940 have witnessed a major change in legislative-executive relations involving foreign affairs. Early in the war the custom was instituted of frequent (at times regular) briefings of the Congressional leadership by the executive.[7] This was on a bipartisan basis, and there was obviously give as well as take. Of late these briefings have been more intermittent, but they are still a recognized "usage" on the occasion of any serious crisis. Occasionally one hears criticism based upon a feeling that the consultations have come too late for the Congressional leadership to exercise any influence. There was left only the alternative of support of the administrative position, or its serious embarrassment in the eyes of the world.

The White House and the departments and agencies continued their practice of "winning friends and influencing people" during the entire period. Breakfasts at the White House, visits and telephone calls by "liaison" men from the State Department and related agencies—these ebbed and flowed with the ebb and flow of the legislative and appropriation processes. For the most part these took into account the partisan hierarchical structure of the houses and committees,

[7] See Roland Young, *Congressional Politics in the Second World War* (New York, 1956).

but at times they reached into the rank and file at strategic points. Such contacts were by no means universally successful. At times they stirred such resentment as to defeat their own objectives. Nevertheless they remained a major element in informal and operative government.

Of almost equal importance has been the fairly frequent use of members of both parties as delegates or advisers at international conferences. Examples include Senators Connally and Vandenberg at San Francisco and London; and Gore, Humphrey, and Hickenlooper at the conference on suspension of nuclear tests. It is also now fair to say that it is customary to include alternately two from the Senate and two from the House among our delegates to the United Nations General Assembly. For practical purposes this practice has served to give such representatives a genuine authority among their colleagues in Congress regarding the actions and institutions involved. It has also provided respected spokesmen for the official point of view in these matters—a point of view toward which the members who served as delegates had doubtless themselves made a contribution.

This use of members as delegates to international bodies was by no means confined to the foreign relations committees. It extended to many other committees—the Atomic Energy Committee for its field;[8] the Interstate and Foreign Commerce for the World Health Organization; the Judiciary Committee for conferences on refugees and migration; the Labor Committees for the International Labor Organization. So frequent has been such usage that it has attained the status of custom, a device looking toward better legislative-executive co-operation.

Formal appearances before committees on the part of executive officials still constituted the chief instrument for mutual understanding. In 1950 the Senate Foreign Relations Committee went so far as to establish a number of subcommittees to foster consultative relations with the executive, each in its own field. Before the committees in both houses there came a stream of official witnesses, some to give an account of themselves, others to advocate passage of a bill or ratification of a treaty.

These then were some of the institutions set up to make the Constitution work at the point of its greatest controversy. To convince the other branch, to pool ideas, to compromise if need be—

[8] See Morgan Thomas, *Atomic Energy and Congress* (Ann Arbor, 1956).

these were and are elements in the living principle of separation of powers.

Looked at in perspective, it is possible to discover a number of important trends during these postwar years.

At least two have already been mentioned—the shift from treaty to executive agreement and program, and the concomitant rise in stature of the House of Representatives. Back of these lie basic considerations—the need for an instrument more flexible than the treaty, the rise of popular interest and concern, the growing costliness of an effective foreign policy.

There was also a "new" Congress, new in the sense that by comparison with the Congress of the 1920s it was more publicly oriented, less partisan, more able—though the problems with which it dealt were far more numerous and more complex. By comparison with the Congress of the 1930s it was more ready to strike out on its own, intelligently as well as independently, in its dealings with the executive. The reasons for these changes are many, and often obscure. Certainly the increased sense of the importance of the age had something to do with the change. So also had the higher level of education and the increased attention to religion, both among the members and in the electorate that chose them. The multiplication of issues made the binding of members to a single composite party "program" impossible without sacrifice of intellect or conscience or both. Finally the acquisition of a staff competent enough to give skilled analyses and numerous enough to meet quantitative demands has surely played its role in the change. The Legislative Reorganization Act of 1946 marked the turning point in this regard. It emancipated Congress from dependence for technical competence upon the executive and the special interests.[9]

All of these general trends were reflected in the special field of foreign affairs.

Bipartisanship, nonpartisanship, unpartisanship—call it what you will—has come to dominate foreign policy in almost all of its aspects.[10] This situation is likely to continue, for the forces that created it will be with the nation for the foreseeable future. A com-

[9] For an extended appraisal of Congress, see E. S. Griffith, *Congress: Its Contemporary Role,* 3d ed. (New York, 1961).

[10] See H. B. Westerfield, *Foreign Policy and Party Politics* (New Haven, 1955).

mon enemy unites; and so does a common cause great enough to transcend partisan boundaries. World communism is the former; a peaceful and prosperous and free world, the latter. These are the great concerns in the light of which the committees and, for the most part, Congress as a whole, approach international questions. Dissent on the China policy in the late 1940s; even the search for communists in the government and elsewhere in the middle years of the century; the sniping at the reciprocal trade program—all provoked heated differences, but the differences were not basically partisan. In the China and communist issues, the criticism was of softness or blindness on the part of the executive—not criticism as to its ultimate objectives. As to the tariff, it remained as it had always been, largely a local or regional issue; but no longer could either party claim a vested right to a monopoly of Congressional seats in any region. The parties were divided among themselves.

On foreign policy issues in particular there will continue to be differences of opinion, especially as limited success or even failure may result from policies adopted in the past. Defenders of earlier decisions will always find it difficult to change their minds in public, and instances similar to the criticism of the executive's China policy and Congressional insistence on a change are likely to recur. These too are not basically partisan, but rather a part of the dynamics of separation of powers in the modern age.

One must anticipate a continuation of executive initiative and responsibility in foreign affairs. The leadership of today's Congress has recognized this. It has also rightly insisted, in the words of Senator Vandenberg, that more and more it must be present at the "take-off" as well as at the "crash landing." This does not mean irresponsible and inhibiting interference, as certain of the bureaucracy have been wont to think. It does mean a reappraisal of the judgment of the Founding Fathers that advice as well as consent of the Senate is necessary. This dictum, so long regarded as decently interred with President Washington's unfortunate experience with the Senate, now deserves respectful re-examination. The arguments against it are well-known and need not be repeated. Obviously some decisions, such as resistance in Korea, must be quickly made—but how quickly is the question. Surely if ultimate support is desired, it is wise at least to inform responsible members in advance, if at all possible. If time allows, such members through committee and staff may wish to conduct parallel investigations prior to the presentation of a program. The Marshall Plan will serve as a classic example of such fruitful parallelism. Reappraisals of foreign aid, of the armaments problem, probably of attitudes toward Communist China, lie in the not too distant future. Omniscience does not lie in the executive, however much it may be possessed of allegedly full and confidential information. It is still made up of human beings with limitations and rivalries, who are often the prisoners of their earlier decisions. Fresh minds can usually with advantage be brought to bear upon complex and stubborn problems; and the role of His Majesty's Loyal Opposition may well be played by a Congressional committee, equipped with staff, whose hearing would also provide a forum for the informed and thoughtful who are outside the government.

Yet this should not be pressed too far. Teamwork is essential, and legislative-executive relations may well be, as Cheever and Haviland have written, the weakest link in our foreign policy chain.[11] It takes time, and is often annoying for those convinced of the rightness of their course, to have to take what seems an inordinate amount of time to convince the legislative branch. There are the temptations to try to "handle" rather than convince; or to present *faits accomplis*, which must be ratified lest the nation suffer a serious loss of prestige or worse. Instances of this sort are every bit as responsible for bad relations as are the "soundings off" of congressmen or their alleged obstructionism.

Of another nature is the problem presented by attempts of the executive to mollify certain Congressional opponents of its program. This often has had the psychological effect of leaving its supporters out on a limb. The latter, having taken their stand publicly for expanded foreign trade or enlightened and generous foreign aid, find later that the executive has changed its program materially in the hope that additional support will thereby be generated from among the uncommitted or opponents. The results have been two, both negative: not only have supporters grown discouraged; but gains have been negligible. If compromises were to be engineered, the Congressional leaders wanted to undertake the task themselves. Then too, the friends of the president's policy at times have seemed left in the lurch politically. The president's failure to intervene in Senator Wiley's primary fight or assist in his election campaign, did not greatly encourage supporters of an internationalist orientation to take

[11] Daniel S. Cheever and H. Field Haviland, Jr., *American Foreign Policy and the Separation of Powers* (Cambridge, 1952), p. 164.

a position unpopular among a substantial sector of their constituents.

On the other hand, Congress clearly has obligations in the matter. Its machinery for resolving differences between appropriations committees and the substantive policy committees was and is defective. Integration between the armed services committees and those in the field of foreign policy has been better handled, but here too there is room for improvement. In these matters the Senate has done better than the House. The very smallness of its numbers has made a virtue out of the necessity of multiple committee assignments. Partly by accident, partly by design, such dual or multiple memberships undoubtedly result in better co-ordination in policy matters, such as reciprocal trade, foreign aid, armaments, atomic energy—in all of which the Foreign Relations Committee has a substantial interest.

Moreover, there have been elements in the behavior of some congressmen that no rule could handle—only self-discipline and a sense of group disapproval. While the lecturing of distinguished witnesses, the parade of top-level executives from committee to committee, and the irresponsible criticism on the floor under the protection of immunity, were not as frequent as one might have supposed from the newspapers, they were frequent enough to be an important factor on the negative side of the ledger. The conduct of the late Senator McCarthy is an extreme example; but the danger of such behavior will be present as long as headlines go to those who act in such a fashion. Then too, far too many of the trips overseas of members and even of committees not only do not give them the competence they subsequently claim; the visits themselves reveal some members as indiscreet, overbearing, or worse.

A word must be said on the other side as to the achievements of individual members who have specialized in particular problems. Senator Cooper's experience as ambassador to India has made his a voice listened to when that nation is discussed. The specialization of Representative Judd on the China question has made him the most influential member of the House on the subject. There have been others also, but these examples will suffice.

Floor debate and public hearings will remain among the very best instruments for the illumination of the electorate, if not for the focusing of issues in Congress itself. For the latter purpose, staff analyses may be fully as valuable and far less time-consuming. Yet, as educational tools, these analyses can never take the place of the drama of public controversy. The price of such controversy at times is very high, in misunderstandings and resentments abroad, in harassed statesmen at home, in frustrations and delays. The process of a legislative body making up its mind in public is seldom orderly.

Debates and hearings on relatively minor questions involving racial and economic groups probably take up too much time and receive the attention only of the "converted." Also, what is more serious, this deference to such groups may result in a disproportionate amount of attention in legislation and appropriations. Organized emigré groups are usually articulate and insistent, perhaps on balance fortunately so, for otherwise our statesmen might be tempted into a modern Munich. The favored position of our merchant marine is probably an anachronism in an age of submarine warfare.

When one recounts the series of great debates and hearings in the foreign policy field, it is difficult to underrate their role in popular education. Not even the public addresses of the president can evoke such sustained attention, though nothing that Congress can do can equal the immediate impact of an aroused presidency.

The committees of Congress have now had almost a decade and a half of sustained and competent staff work. Reliance upon such work has grown rather than diminished. It has become accepted usage in the legislative process. The tradition of tenure and staff nonpartisanship has been consolidated in both houses as regards their foreign relations staffs, and only a degree less in most of the other committees having a concern for foreign affairs. Emergencies extend the range of staff service—to the Legislative Reference Service, to temporary additions for special inquiries, to a liberal use of contract research. Both House and Senate use the Legislative Reference Service for supplemental and overflow needs when the work load presses or when specialists on a subject or area are not included in their committees' own staffs. Fully as important also is the use of Legislative Reference by individual members who may question or differ with the main line of inquiry or policy followed by a committee. Here too is a fruitful source of debate and clarification of issues at an informed and responsible level. In expertise, if not in numbers, the Congressional staffs need not fear comparison with those specialists from the executive branch whose policies are presented or defended. This is a permanent element of the first magnitude in the enhanced role of Congress in foreign policy.

Frequent, though incidental, mention has been made of the effect of the electorate on Congress, of its economic regionalism, its nationality groups, the endemic isolationism of certain elements—also of its increasingly higher level of education, of its frequent acceptance of strong and intelligent leadership.

Alliances and world organizations, foreign aid, expanding imports —all have traditional forces and groups opposing them; and they have their spokesmen within Congress. Yet Congress has its own bag of tricks for dealing with these and other special interests, for "delousing" measures which have become infested with clauses making to a special group this concession or that, contrary to the general interest. In the Marshall Plan legislation, the conference committee served this purpose. At other times it may be a willingness to allow a president's veto to stand, or to accept a House Rules Committee refusal to report out a measure. Bicameralism is a great help in this regard, allowing one house to play politics while the other plays statesman. There are times in which such strategic or tactical obfuscation is an instrument in the public interest if it can fend off the importunities of special interests.

The general verdict of the postwar years is unmistakable, regardless of minor defections. Congress has supported programs in foreign policy that were imaginative, responsible, and far-reaching. It has not hesitated to criticize, to spur, to suggest alternatives. Almost without exception the product, if not the process, has been worthy of the times. Even the process has had its moments of public greatness; and when the executive sessions, the behind-the-scenes efforts, the research are taken into account, the verdict for representative government is strongly affirmative. Moreover, imaginative programs and high policy are likely to remain with us for many years to come; the habits within Congress of bipartisanship, of staff work, of a sense of responsibility are likely to prevail in the future as they have in the more recent past.

14: ORGANIZATIONAL REFORM IN THE DEPARTMENT OF STATE AND THE FOREIGN SERVICE

William Gerber

Any institution which is approaching its 200th birthday is unlikely to have escaped the attention of organizational reformers. The Department of State has not been neglected in this respect.

While the reformers applied their efforts only occasionally before the Second World War, they have been measurably more active in the period since then. Indeed, with uncanny regularity, approaching that of clockwork, the Department of State has been struck by a reorganization every four years since the war ended. The first occurred in 1945-1946; the second, in 1949-1950; the third, in 1953-1954; the fourth, less drastic than the others, in 1957-1958.

What cause or causes brought about these shakeups? Why did they occur when they did? By what general laws or categories may they be explained? Were all of them beneficial? If not, why not? What lessons may be derived from them for the future?

Indisputable answers to these questions will be difficult to formulate. But a careful scrutiny of what happened in each case will be instructive—both in our desire to understand the present scene through its evolution from the past, and in our concomitant desire to plan now for the future with greater wisdom than we possessed yesterday in planning for today.

The shape of the organizational struggles in the Department of State and the Foreign Service since 1945 was foreshadowed by earlier developments and problems. Among the issues which from time to time have demanded decision in the light of new situations are these:

Should responsibility for action on a problem involving, say, trade with France be assigned to functional authorities—the assistant secretary for economic affairs, or to regional authorities—the assistant secretary for European affairs?

Should administrative, technical, and advisory functions be centralized in strong autonomous bureaus, or should they be carried out in small units within the substantive bureaus?

Should liaison with Congress on appropriations be conducted by officers having substantive responsibilities or by the Department's budget officers—or by the staff on Congressional liaison?

Should overseas operations involving technical and financial aid, cultural exchange and propaganda, agricultural reporting, and the like be carried out by the regular Foreign Service or by overseas staffs of other government agencies?

Should functions not pertaining to a Foreign Office be retained in the Department of State or transferred to other arms of the government?

In the recruitment and development of personnel, should emphasis be placed on the creation of a corps of able generalists or on well-trained experts and specialists?

Should the personnel of the Department of State and the Foreign Service be separate or interchangeable?

These problems, or problems like them, emerged in the 170 years between 1775 and 1945.

The earliest body having organizational problems, to which the Department of State can trace its continuous existence, is the Committee of Secret Correspondence, with Benjamin Franklin as chairman, which was appointed by the Second Continental Congress on November 29, 1775. Its principal organizational problem was to stay alive, in view of the habit which the Congress displayed of dealing with problems of "secret correspondence" itself, without reference to the committee. This problem of relations with the people's chosen representatives is the greatgrandsire of today's problem of how best to manage relations with Congress.

Through organizational reforms in part, and in part through changes in nomenclature motivated by considerations of dignity (and the problem of staying alive), the Committee of Secret Correspondence became the Committee of Foreign Affairs in 1777 and the Department of Foreign Affairs, under a secretary of foreign affairs, in 1781. Since there was no executive branch, even the Department of Foreign Affairs was a part of the Congress, and its problem remained to establish its authority.

During the same pre-Constitution period, the Continental Congress appointed Franklin, John Jay, Thomas Jefferson, and others as agents, commissioners, ministers, and consuls, to serve abroad. These men were well-balanced, perceptive statesmen, rather than specialists trained expressly for diplomacy; but Franklin, it is true, had acquired quasi-diplomatic experience through serving in London as the agent of various colonies.

The first Congress under the Constitution, in 1789, took two successive actions based on opposite premises with reference to foreign office organization. First, in July, it created, in the executive branch, a Department of Foreign Affairs to conduct negotiations with foreign countries. Six weeks later, however, in September, it reversed itself by changing the name of the organization to "Department of State" and transforming it into an organization to conduct both foreign affairs and also affairs of "state," such as the publication of laws. The same issue, whether the Department of State should be exclusively a foreign office, agitated the Hoover Commission in 1949.

In mid-1790, soon after Thomas Jefferson had entered upon his duties as the first secretary of state of the United States, the staff of the Department, as planned for the coming year, consisted of Jefferson, five clerks (two of whom, at least, were of officer rank), an interpreter, and two messengers. Jefferson's first problem was whom to appoint as chief clerk, *i.e.*, which of the two top holdovers from the pre-Constitution Department should be appointed to this post. He solved it by giving to both the same title, chief clerk.

As a consequence of the increasing contacts of Americans with foreign countries, and the proliferation of domestic duties assigned to it, the Department was large enough in 1833 to be divided as follows:

(1) Two top-level offices, namely, that of the secretary, Louis McLane, and that of the chief clerk, Asbury Dickens, whose duties were those of an undersecretary.

(2) Two policy offices, namely, the Diplomatic Bureau and the Consular Bureau, exemplifying what would today be called a sharp functional breakdown (on the basis of the difference between diplomatic policy and consular affairs) as distinguished from a regional breakdown.

(3) Six bureaus concerned with domestic affairs, technical functions, administration, or a combination of these, namely, the Home Bureau, the Patent Office, a bureau concerned with the registration of copyrights and the operation of the library, one concerned with

publication of the laws and maintenance of the archives, one charged with translating, and one which maintained the accounts.

The regional emphasis came to the fore, however, in 1870, when Secretary of State Hamilton Fish established a First Diplomatic Bureau, in charge of diplomatic correspondence with Western Europe, China, and Japan; a Second Diplomatic Bureau, in charge of diplomatic correspondence with all other nations; and First and Second Consular Bureaus with regional jurisdictions corresponding to those of the First and Second Diplomatic Bureaus.

Some of the domestic duties of the Department of State—such as the registration of copyrights, the issue of patents, and the taking of the census—were sloughed off from time to time, in the middle decades of the century, to other departments of the government. This process reflected an increasing identification of the Department of State with the idea of a foreign office, but the question of a complete identification is still an issue.

The infrequency of major reorganizations in the Department of State during the 19th century was matched by correspondingly slow change in what may, for convenience, be called the Foreign Service, *i.e.*, the Diplomatic Service and the Consular Service.

Nineteenth-century reforms in organization of the Foreign Service included the gradual and almost imperceptible development of interchangeability of high-level personnel between the Foreign Service and the Department of State (an idea which rocked the Department as recently as 1954). The first secretary of state, Thomas Jefferson, was appointed on September 26, 1789, as he was returning from his post as minister to France. A number of his successors likewise had served as ministers abroad prior to their service in the Department, or became such afterward. In addition, some other high officers, and even a few clerks, were appointed in the Foreign Service before or after their employment in the Department.

Another notable step in the organization of the Foreign Service, with significance for today, was the Act of Congress signed by President Franklin Pierce on August 18, 1856, which prescribed grades and salaries in the diplomatic service and placed the position of consul—at certain large posts only—on a salary basis, requiring all consular fees collected at those posts (which fees had previously been legally pocketed by the consul, in lieu of a salary) to be turned over to the government. Exclusion of smaller posts from the salary basis meant that our consuls at those posts would continue to be noncareer people, usually individuals engaged in business and performing consular duties as a sideline. At various times Congress overruled the recommendation of at least three secretaries of state that all consular posts be put on a salary basis. The problem of the scope of the career service is still with us, as the Department grapples today with the problem of the relation of the Foreign Service Reserve and the Foreign Service Staff to the career Foreign Service officers.

Lastly, in 1893, in recognition of the growing importance of America's position in the world, Congress agreed to appropriate funds for some American embassies abroad, to be headed by ambassadors, our highest diplomatic missions theretofore having been legations, headed by ministers. In the same year American ambassadors were appointed to France, Germany, Great Britain, and Italy. By 1961 all the American legations had been advanced to the rank of embassy, except four: those at Budapest, Bucharest, Sofia, and Sana'a (Yemen).

In the Department of State the first few decades of the 20th century saw the regional channelization of the policy work of the Department, begun in 1870, intensified by the establishment in 1908-1909 of the divisions of Western European, Near Eastern, Far Eastern, and Latin-American Affairs. In 1915 and 1919 the divisions of Mexican and Russian Affairs were created, and in 1922 the name of the latter was changed to Division of Eastern European Affairs. During 1937 these six were reduced to four, the divisions of European, Near Eastern, and Far Eastern Affairs, and of the American Republics. The present setup is a fivefold grouping, Africa comprising a separate element.

Meanwhile, the functional offices (for legal affairs, commercial affairs, etc.), the technical offices (for international conferences, treaties, etc.), and the administrative offices (for press relations, personnel, etc.) underwent changes up to 1944 in which it is difficult to perceive any pattern other than one based on expansion of the Department's responsibilities and reflection of the personalities of division chiefs and other high officers. For example, the organizational preferences of Undersecretary of State Edward R. Stettinius, Jr., which were personal though not at all arbitrary, resulted in the grouping of the divisions of the Department of State in 1944 into twelve offices, each with an office director. The headaches encountered in this process of expansion and grouping were severe, but they were normal, and they present no special lesson for today and tomorrow.

In step with the expansion of the Department as a whole, the organizational structure of the Department's top level expanded also from 1900 to 1944. The positions of undersecretary of state and counselor were established; the numbering of the assistant secretaries as first assistant secretary of state, second assistant secretary of state, etc., was abandoned; and several additional positions of assistant secretary were created. This too was normal, and the accompanying problems were *ad hoc* problems. These experiences suggest that similar future problems should be solved on an *ad hoc* basis, taking account of the personalities, ranks, and other considerations regarding the human beings involved.

While the Department of State in Washington was thus expanding, the Foreign Service advanced organizationally from 1900 to 1944 through several stages.

On November 10, 1905, and June 27, 1906, President Theodore Roosevelt issued executive orders which inaugurated the merit system for appointments to the Diplomatic Service and the Consular Service and for promotions within each service. Entrance to either service was to be based on examinations, written and oral. These were forward steps in an area still in debate—the scope of the career Foreign Service.

The Act of Congress signed by President Roosevelt on April 5, 1906, was also a move toward a broader career service. It completed the steps begun in the Act of 1856 for remunerating all consuls by paying them standard salaries instead of permitting some of them to pocket fees collected for official services.

A further Act of Congress, which President Woodrow Wilson signed on February 5, 1915, provided for the appointment of officers of the Diplomatic Service and the Consular Service as such, instead of to specific posts. In other words, it provided for the transfer of officers from post to post as needed, another move which broadened the concept of the Foreign Service career.

From 1900 to 1924 a radical notion was taking form, namely, that the wall between the Diplomatic Service and the Consular Service should be broken through; and, at the same time, some agitation began toward greater ease of transfer between the Civil Service and the Foreign Service. Under executive orders of 1906 and 1909, employees of the Department of State could be transferred to the Diplomatic Service or the Consular Service under specified conditions, officers in the Diplomatic Service (but not the Consular Service) could be detailed to the Department of State, and an officer could even transfer from the Consular Service to the Diplomatic Service or vice versa but only on the basis of his taking the usual entrance examination for the other service. Agitation for amalgamating the Diplomatic Service and the Consular Service reached a high point in 1919, when the Civil Service Reform League published a report advocating merger.

The year 1924, however, is remembered in the annals of the Foreign Service as the year of the Rogers Act, which once for all merged the Diplomatic Service and the Consular Service into the Foreign Service, and strengthened the merit features of the service, with personnel completely interchangeable between diplomatic and consular assignments and with provision for the assignment of Foreign Service officers to the Department of State for limited periods. The Moses-Linthicum Act of 1931 resulted in part from an effort to rectify the disproportionate number of promotions, under the Rogers Act, among those assigned to diplomatic posts compared with those granted to officers acting as consuls. Thus it also served to broaden the concept of a genuine career service.

A further important amalgamation occurred in 1939, when the Foreign Commerce Service and the Foreign Agricultural Service, which had been administered respectively by the Department of Commerce and the Department of Agriculture, were made a part of the Foreign Service administered by the Department of State. The former of these two mergers has remained in effect, but the Department of Agriculture succeeded in persuading Congress in 1954 that the Foreign Agricultural Service should be returned to the administration of the Department of Agriculture.

America's role in the Second World War added important new elements to the overseas work of the government, including operation of the lend-lease program, procurement of strategic materials, obstruction of the sale of strategic materials to the Axis powers, dissemination of information about the United States calculated to win friends among foreign peoples, and maintenance of the Allied coalition. The usual dilemma arose at the outset: to integrate these functions into the framework of the Foreign Service or to set up special units for them?

The dilemma was solved by a compromise. On the one hand, Secretary of State Cordell Hull insisted that the role of the Department of State was to formulate policy and not to conduct operations. Therefore special agencies were set up outside the Department of State for overseas information, preclusive buying, and lend lease; and each such agency in Washington had its own overseas staff, theoretically (but not in practice) co-ordinated by the American diplomatic mission in the country of operation. On the other hand, the Department of State, grasping the second horn of the dilemma, added to its own overseas staff a unit called the Foreign Service Auxiliary, which conducted cultural relations in Latin America, supervised the blacklisting of foreign firms which dealt with the Axis, procured enemy publications through neutral countries, and even carried out some of the economic reporting traditionally done by the regular Foreign Service.

Thus evolved the problem-rich heritage which was handed down to the organizational planners of the period since 1945.

In the spring and summer of 1945, when Germany and Japan surrendered, the Department of State in Washington consisted of the following five organizational categories, totalling some 3,700 persons (four times what the total had been in 1939):

(1) The secretary of state and the undersecretary, each with immediate advisers and assistants; and a unit, called the Central Secretariat, which co-ordinated papers requiring action by the secretary or the undersecretary.

(2) Two assistant secretaries for regional affairs—one of them for the American republics, supervising one office, and the other for the rest of the world, in charge of three offices.

(3) Four additional assistant secretaries—one for economic affairs, in charge of three offices; one for public and cultural relations, in charge of one office; one for Congressional relations, with a small staff and no office; and one for administration, with three offices.

(4) A legal adviser, with a staff of international lawyers.

(5) A special assistant for international organization and security affairs, in charge of one office.

Each of the twelve offices mentioned had three to eight divisions. In an organizational chart of the Department dated May 1, 1945, the number of "boxes," representing mainly divisions, offices, and assistant secretaries, was eighty-two.

At the same time, the United States Government had the following main groups of civilian officers and employees overseas:

(1) Foreign Service of the United States, administered by the Department of State and consisting of four categories (with a total of about 10,000 positions), namely, chiefs of mission, some of whom had been promoted from the career Foreign Service; Foreign Service officers (career officers); noncareer American personnel (principally administrative specialists and clerks); and local employees (clerks, interpreters, custodians, etc.).

(2) Foreign Service Auxiliary, administered by the Department of State.

(3) Overseas personnel of the Office of War Information.

(4) Overseas personnel of the Foreign Economic Administration.

The end of the war, and the reshaping of the world in the decade and a half thereafter, led to profound organizational alterations in the Department and the Foreign Service. These alterations occurred in cyclical rhythmic sweeps, which in part were merely inevitable adaptations, and in part partook of the nature of planned reform.

FIRST WAVE, 1945 AND AFTER

The first wave of organizational changes began softly in the month of May, 1945, reached a loud, dramatic peak in the following year, and subsided to silence in 1947-1948.

On May 3, 1945, President Harry S. Truman signed an Act of Congress which sprang from motives purely of reform or improvement and not of adaptation to war conditions. The act contained the germ of two Foreign Service entities (the Staff corps and the Reserve corps) which were born officially and were christened in the following year.

The first main object of the Act of May 3, 1945, was to free the regular Foreign Service officers from responsibility for administrative tasks, so that they might concentrate on negotiation, the appraisal of conditions and developments, and other high-level activities. Giving recognition for the first time to the tedious administrative and fiscal work done in the Foreign Service, the act replaced the two categories of clerks (senior and junior) established by the Moses-Linthicum Act of 1931 with three new categories (administrative officers, administrative assistants, and clerks) which were later merged as the Foreign Service Staff.

The administrative functions performed by these noncareer officers and employees were broad. They included not only office management, disbursement, and accounting, but interpretation and application of laws and regulations on citizenship and immigration, in noncontroversial cases.

A second basic provision of the Act of May 3, 1945, similarly reform-inspired, was to bear fruit later in the Foreign Service Reserve. This provision authorized the designation of qualified personnel from the Department of State or other agencies of the government "for special duty as officers of the Foreign Service for nonconsecutive periods of not more than four years." The purpose of this clause was to enable the Department of State to fill the needs of, say, the Bureau of Mines for reporting about minerals from overseas in a period when such reporting was of special importance, through the appointment of men selected by the Bureau to the cadre of overseas officers supervised by the Department of State. The theory was that this authority would make possible the easy expansion and contraction of the Foreign Service.

The wheels of organizational reform, which had begun to whirl with the passage of the Act of May 3, 1945, were given an extra spin when James F. Byrnes was appointed to succeed Stettinius as secretary of state, on July 3, 1945, and immediately asked the Bureau of the Budget to prepare a report on the organization of the Department. The Bureau of the Budget, in its report of August 15, 1945, recommended a radical measure, which was sure to arouse controversy but was aimed at introducing a basic improvement in the foreign policy machine. It proposed that steps be taken toward the amalgamation of the Departmental Service and the Foreign Service. The Budget Bureau's historic recommendation was not made public, but in the process of consideration it became known to various Foreign Service officers, some of whom strongly opposed it.

Before a decision could be made on the weighty question of amalgamation, however, the Department of State was flooded with colossal new problems resulting from the transfer to it, by executive orders dated August 31 and September 20 and 27, 1945, of more than 10,000 employees from the foreign branch of the Office of War Information (OWI), the information and cultural units of the Office of Inter-American Affairs (OIAA), the lend-lease and other units of the Foreign Economic Administration (FEA), and the research units of the Office of Strategic Services (OSS).

In the process of digesting this immense mouthful—which doubled its size—the Department of State began by establishing on September 10, 1945, in Washington and overseas, an Interim International Information Service, consisting of the personnel, records, facilities, etc., of the transferred elements of the OWI and the OIAA. Soon thereafter the Department consolidated the analysis personnel inherited from the OSS with the library and other old-line departmental units into the Office of the Special Assistant to the Secretary of State for Intelligence. It also established an Office of the Foreign Liquidation Commissioner, to settle lend-lease matters, sell war surplus equipment located overseas, and administer United States participation in the United Nations Relief and Rehabilitation Administration (UNRRA).

Having thus disposed, temporarily at least, of these organizational headaches, the Department buckled down to a decision on the amalgamation proposal of the Bureau of the Budget. Shelden Chapin, director of the Office of the Foreign Service, who had been given the task of recommending action on the proposal, came up in October with a possible compromise aimed at mollifying those career officers who were horrified by the threatened diminution of the career officers' eliteness. The compromise: spread amalgamation over a period of ten years. Donald S. Russell, assistant secretary of state for administration, considered the pros and cons of the proposal and decided against it in December, 1945. Secretary Byrnes agreed with Russell's decision, and amalgamation remained a dead issue for almost a decade.

Switching back then swiftly to its half-digested new elements, the Department on the last day of 1945 replaced the Interim International Information Service with an Office of International Information and Cultural Affairs (OIC), which it organized partly in functional divisions, for broadcasting, publications, etc., and partly in area divisions, for the American republics, occupied areas, the Near East, etc.

This crescendo of organizational adaptation and reform rose to an even higher level in the year 1946. In April of that year the Department established the position of assistant secretary of state for occupied areas, for co-ordination of policy within the Department on occupation matters and for maintaining liaison at a high rank with the War and Navy Departments on those matters. This new assistant secretary had a Germany-Austria secretariat and a Japan-Korea secretariat as parts of his establishment. Creation of the establishment, one must admit, was necessitated by circumstances and had only a modicum of true reform flavor.

In the same month, however, the Department put into effect the short-lived Russell Plan, a reform move if ever there was one, under which the regional divisions of the Department's intelligence area (Division of Research for Europe, Division of Research for Near East and Africa, and others) were extracted from the jurisdiction of the special assistant to the secretary of state for intelligence and placed under the direct supervision of the respective policy offices (under the Office of European Affairs, the Office of Near Eastern and African Affairs, etc.). Left with the special assistant for intelligence, under this plan, were the Office of Intelligence Collection and Dissemination and the Office of Intelligence Co-ordination and Liaison. Loud criticisms of the change, on the ground that the intelligence analysts were less likely to be objective when working under the thumb of policy officers, led to its reversal ten months later, soon after the appointment of General George C. Marshall as secretary of state.

July and August, 1946, also marked the crest of the wave of organizational adaptation. On July 3, 1946, President Truman signed the Foreign Service Manpower Act, which was designed to fill the need for Foreign Service officers at the middle grades to staff the American embassies, legations, and consulates reopened as a result of the end of the war. It authorized the appointment of 250 career officers, within two years, in any grade for which their experience would fit them. This was the first substantial break, since the passage of the Rogers Act of 1924, in the rule that new officers *en masse* were to be recruited only at the bottom.

Early in August, 1946, Congress established, also for a two-year period, the position of undersecretary of state for economic affairs. William L. Clayton, however, who was appointed to the post in August, 1946, resigned in October, 1947, and was not replaced. The Department's highest policy officer in the economic field was thereafter once more an assistant secretary until 1956.

Still riding the top of the wave, Congress passed, and President Truman signed on August 13, 1946, the Foreign Service Act which is still the basic statute of the Department's foreign arm. The act was the outcome of two years of discussion within the Department of State and the Foreign Service and between the Department and members of the House Committee on Foreign Affairs. Its principal reforms were as follows:

(1) It set up five basic groups in the Foreign Service, namely, ambassadors and ministers, Foreign Service officers, Foreign Service Reserve officers, Foreign Service Staff officers and employees, and alien personnel.

(2) It reduced the number of classes of Foreign Service officers from eleven to seven, of which the highest was designated "class of career minister."

(3) By the establishment of the class of career minister, it enabled Foreign Service officers to become ambassadors and ministers without resigning from the career Foreign Service.

(4) It created the position of director general of the Foreign Service and assigned to that officer wide responsibilities for administration of the service.

(5) It established the Foreign Service Institute in the Department of State for training those who have passed the Foreign Service entrance examination and have been appointed to the service.

(6) It increased salaries.

(7) It added new forms of financial allowance (transfer allowance, allowance for extra housekeeping expenses of the principal officer at a post, and others) to the forms previously authorized (such as rent, cost-of-living differential, and representational allowances), and it improved the retirement system.

(8) It authorized home leave after two instead of three years of overseas service.

(9) It provided for the "selection out" of those career officers who are not promoted after reasonable periods.

In 1947 and 1948 the first wave of postwar organizational reform had spent its force. Among the few changes of 1947 were the appointment of the first permanent representative of the United States to the United Nations (Warren R. Austin), in January, and the establishment of the United States Mission to the United Nations, in April; the appointment, for the first time, in March, of an assistant secretary of state for transport and communications (a position which lapsed in 1949); the formal inauguration, in March, of the Foreign Service Institute authorized by the Act of the previous year; the creation, during May, of the Policy Planning Staff in the office of the undersecretary of state (with George Kennan as its director); and the appointment of a science attaché at London, for the first time, in December. That year also saw the physical move of the Department of State from the old Department of State Building and many annexes to the new Department of State Building (formerly the War Department Building) and several nearby annexes.

An abortive organizational move was made in March, 1947, when Secretary of State Marshall asked Congress to remove the overseas-information function from the Department of State and set it up as an independent agency. Instead, Congress passed the Smith-Mundt Act, signed on January 27, 1948, which squarely placed responsibility for international information and cultural exchange in the Department of State. In April, 1948, the Department rearranged its overseas public affairs units into an Office of International Information (OII) and an Office of Educational Exchange (OEX).

SECOND WAVE, 1949 AND AFTER

The second wave of postwar organizational reform in the Department of State and the Foreign Service was set in motion by the winds and tides of the Hoover Commission. It resembled the first wave in that it remained at a high peak for two years and then subsided. It also had an additional resemblance to the earlier wave: it was made up in part of adaptations to current needs and in part of reforms.

The Commission on Organization of the Executive Branch of the Government, headed by Herbert Hoover and known as the Hoover Commission, was appointed pursuant to an Act of Congress signed in July, 1947. The group worked quietly throughout 1948 in an atmosphere of no-holds-barred reform thinking.

In January, 1949, the commission's task force on foreign affairs submitted its report to the full commission. The task force consisted of Harvey H. Bundy and James Grafton Rogers (both former assistant secretaries of state), with former Secretary of State Henry L. Stimson as adviser. The reforms and general organizational principles recommended by the task force were as follows:

(1) The Department of State should concentrate on formulating the basic objectives of the United States, proposing policies for achievement of the objectives, and suggesting the choice and timing of "means and instruments" for carrying out the policies.

(2) The Department should not have responsibility for such operations as the dissemination of propaganda and specific programs

of economic aid, "except in very unusual instances," such as those in which "particularly sensitive situations exist."

(3) The Department should have four regional assistant secretaries of state, corresponding to the traditional areas of the world (Western Hemisphere, Europe, Near East and Africa, Far East) and one for United States participation in international organizations. The secretary should delegate day-to-day action responsibility to these assistant secretaries. Each of the five organizational units should, in determining its actions, consult with, but "never be required to secure the concurrence of," the other interested offices. (This was a blow aimed at the power of the "functional" offices—*e.g.*, those concerned with economic policy—to veto a policy proposal of the "regional" offices.)

(4) The undersecretary of state should have a deputy for policy and a deputy for administration.

(5) The "economic and other functional staffs," *i.e.*, the economic, intelligence, public affairs, and administrative offices of the Department, should be reduced to (a) a group of functional operatives attached to each of the five organizational units mentioned and (b) a few experts for advising the top level of the Department as well as for maintaining liaison with other agencies. In this process of diminution of the functional staffs, the regional intelligence divisons, functioning under the special assistant to the secretary for research and intelligence (some of which, the task force said, were engaging in "made work"), should be decentralized as provided in the Russell Plan of 1946; the overseas information program should be transferred to and operated by an outside public corporation; and educational exchange should be transferred to the Federal Security Agency (predecessor of the present Department of Health, Education, and Welfare). As an exception, Congressional relations should be placed under an assistant secretary devoting full time to that function.

(6) In view of the prevalence of "serious unrest in the relations between the Foreign Service and the State Department personnel of the civil service," the two groups, "above certain levels" (roughly, those paid more than $4,500 a year), should be "amalgamated over a short period of years" into a Foreign Affairs Corps. The new corps should consist of (a) generalists; (b) specialists, *i.e.*, those who have expert knowledge in agriculture, labor, minerals, administration, etc., but who "do not have the full general qualifications"; (c) staff employees, comprising the clerical and custodial elements of the

Foreign Service Staff; and (d) a corps corresponding to the Foreign Service Reserve.

(7) The chief of mission in a given country, although primarily responsible for diplomatic functions, should also have "ultimate authority overseas with respect to program operations" such as those of economic aid.

The historical antecedents of some of these proposals will be fresh in the mind of the reader.

One month later, in February, 1949, the full Hoover Commission, having appraised the proposals of its task force, presented its own more moderate conclusions. It formulated in classic terms the age-old pull between regional and functional authority:

> A . . . major impediment is the system whereby coordinate authority at the substantive policy action level is vested in two different types of units, geographic and economic . . . This coordinate authority arrangement necessitates an elaborate and time-consuming system of lateral clearance . . . , prevents the fixing of responsibility, and tends to foster undesirable duplication of work.

In its recommendations, the full commission agreed with the reforms and organizational principles proposed by the task force, with the following differences:

(1) Although, in principle, non-policy foreign operations should be carried on outside the Department of State, the overseas-information and educational-exchange functions should remain in the Department of State, under the assistant secretary of state for public affairs, who should, however, delegate the operational aspects (as distinguished from the policy aspects) to a "general manager."

(2) There should be an assistant secretary of state for economic and social affairs, with staff duties only, *i.e.*, without the power of decision.

(3) In the light of the heavy staffing at the top level—an undersecretary with two deputies, four regional assistant secretaries, four functional assistant secretaries (for multilateral affairs, public affairs, economic and social affairs, and Congressional relations), a legal adviser, a policy-planning adviser, and a special assistant for research and intelligence—the Department should abolish the positions of counselor, assistant secretary for occupied areas, assistant secretary for transport and communications, director general of the Foreign Service, and special assistant for press relations.

(4) Instead of reviving the Russell Plan for decentralizing the in-

telligence-research divisions, the Department should let them remain under the special assistant for research and intelligence but should, at the same time, (a) direct them to concentrate on current appraisals and to de-emphasize "academic research," and (b) appoint intelligence advisers to the four regional units.

The Department of State considered the reports of the task force and the full commission, agreed with some of the recommendations and not with others, and took corresponding reform action in the period from March to December, 1949.

It abolished two positions of assistant secretary of state—for occupied areas and for transport and communications. It then sought and obtained Congressional authority for a setup with ten assistant secretaries, of whom two would serve as deputy undersecretaries of state. The Act of Congress granting this authority (signed May 26, 1949) also vested generally in the secretary of state certain operational responsibilities which had been assigned by the Foreign Service Act of 1946 specifically to the assistant secretary of state for administration and the director general of the Foreign Service.

The Department appointed two assistant secretaries to serve as deputy undersecretaries of state, one for substantive matters and one for administration. It also appointed an assistant secretary for Congressional relations and retained its assistant secretaries for economic affairs and for public affairs. In addition to these five, it appointed four assistant secretaries to head regional bureaus for relations with the areas of the world and one to head a bureau for multilateral affairs, thus rounding out the ten authorized positions. Attached to each of the four regional bureaus were: (a) advisers on intelligence, economics, public affairs, and United Nations affairs; and (b) an executive director charged with administrative functions.

The Department did not abolish the position of counselor of the Department of State, and it retained for a few years that of special assistant to the secretary for press relations, until the incumbent accepted an ambassadorship, and his work was transferred partly upward (to the assistant secretary for public affairs) and partly downward (to the chief of the news division).

A temporary Bureau of German Affairs, headed by a director "with the rank of assistant secretary," was established in the Department in connection with the end of the Military Government of Germany (OMGUS) and the transfer to the Department of State of occupation responsibilities other than military. In Germany, the

Department set up an Office of the United States High Commissioner (HICOG). The transfer of occupation work to it once more doubled the size of the Department, as had been done in 1945.

In absolute figures, the total number of employees of the Department, including those overseas, expanded roughly as follows: from 13,000 at the beginning of 1945 to 26,000 at the end of that year, chiefly through transfer of elements of the OWI, the OSS, and other agencies; down to about 20,000 at the beginning of 1950, by attrition; up to about 40,000 at the end of 1950, including about 19,000 transferred in Germany and Austria.

With regard to the hottest potato handed over by the Hoover Commission—the recommended amalgamation of the Departmental and Foreign Service—the Department took three pertinent actions. First, in May it abolished the Office of the Foreign Service (but not the position of director general of the Foreign Service) and transferred the two main constituents of the office, the divisions of Foreign Service Personnel and Foreign Service Administration, to new co-ordinating, but not unifying, entities. The Division of Foreign Service Personnel was moved to an Office of Personnel, which included also a Division of Departmental Personnel; and the Division of Foreign Service Administration was merged in an Office of Operating Facilities, which was made responsible for facilities both at home and abroad.

Secondly, in August the Department inaugurated a program of individual two-year exchanges of personnel between the Department and the Foreign Service. In the first such exchange, Margaret Joy Tibbetts, a divisional assistant in the Office of British Commonwealth Affairs (Bureau of European Affairs), went to London, replacing David Linebaugh, of the Foreign Service Reserve, who returned to Washington.

Thirdly, on December 19, 1949, Secretary of State Dean Acheson wrote to James H. Rowe, Jr., who had served on the Hoover Commission, Robert Ramspeck, a former member of Congress, and William E. DeCourcy, a career Foreign Service officer who had served as ambassador, requesting recommendations from them as a committee of three regarding "any change you may feel is required in the existing classified personnel system of the Department or the career system of the Foreign Service" and "any action which you feel will bring about a closer integration of the two systems."

Meanwhile, apart from consideration of the Hoover Commission's recommendations, the Department appointed three new high-level officers: a special assistant to the secretary of state for the Mutual Assistance Program (later called "Director of Mutual Defense Assistance"), an ambassador-at-large (who pinch-hit for the secretary of state at important international conferences), and a consultant to the secretary on international scientific matters.

The year 1950 was also an active year in organizational adaptation and reform. During that year the administration of the Point Four Program of technical assistance and economic development in underdeveloped areas was assigned to the Department of State, which established first an Interim Office for Technical Co-operation and Development, in the Office of the Assistant Secretary for Economic Affairs, and later a semi-autonomous Technical Co-operation Administration (TCA) reporting directly to the secretary of state.

In keeping with the theory of the Hoover Commission that the Department of State should concentrate on foreign policy, the president transferred from the Department to the National Archives in 1950 the functions of publishing the Statutes at Large, certifying the adoption of constitutional amendments, and certifying the selection of presidential electors. This move left in the Department of State, as almost its sole remaining domestic duty, the affixing of the Great Seal to state papers.

Perhaps the major organizational development of 1950, seen in perspective, was the submission of the report of the Rowe-Ramspeck-DeCourcy Committee, which called itself the Secretary's Advisory Committee on Personnel. The report was based on interviews with officers of the Department, the Foreign Service, other government agencies, national organizations, and business firms; on the results of an employee-attitude questionnaire distributed to 2,200 officers and employees of the Department and the Foreign Service; and on the committee members' own background and judgment.

The committee stated, in its report, that the personnel arrangement in effect in the home service and the Foreign Service "tends to produce a certain amount of rivalry and misunderstanding between the two services and between personnel categories within the Foreign Service." The committee therefore recommended several improvements:

(1) That the Department of State, on its own authority and without awaiting legislative approval, identify those positions in the Department ("dual-service positions," estimated to number 1,500)

in which overseas experience is necessary for the best performance of the job, and step up at once the program of two-year exchanges of personnel between the Department and the Foreign Service.

(2) That the Department seek Congressional authorization for the establishment of a Foreign Affairs Service, covering personnel to be assigned at home or abroad.

(3) That, after enactment of the legislation, incumbents in the designated positions in the Department, and also members of the Foreign Service Reserve and the Foreign Service Staff, be admitted, if found suitable, to the appropriate grades of the new Foreign Affairs Service.

(4) That the new service be organized, by the secretary of state and not by legislation, into a foreign-affairs-officer group (including both generalists and functional specialists) and a foreign-affairs-clerical-and-technical group (including clerks, radio operators, couriers, procurement employees, etc.).

(5) That the Department's Office of Personnel be reorganized on functional lines instead of being broken down into a Division of Department Personnel and a Division of Foreign Service Personnel.

(6) That the Department's training programs, which "still fall far short of recognizable needs," be expanded, especially (as regards methods) through on-the-job learning in other government agencies and in business firms, and (as regards objectives) for greater ability in international negotiations and for service with international organizations.

The report was submitted to Secretary of State Acheson in July, 1950, but it did not receive an enthusiastic reception. It remained under consideration in various offices for months at a time, and such implementation as it was accorded came in 1951. Toward the end of 1950 the reform fever subsided. The two-year wave of 1949-1950 was descending from its peak.

The biennium 1951-1952 was a meager period in organizational reform.

The year 1951 saw the winding up of the Rowe-Ramspeck-DeCourcy affair with the issuance in April of the secretary's Personnel Improvement Plan (also called the Acheson Plan), which consisted of three main features:

(1) An increase in the program of two-year exchanges between the Department and the Foreign Service.

(2) Facilitation of the lateral entry of Department officers into

the Foreign Service. Such lateral entry, although authorized by the Foreign Service Act of 1946, had been stymied by highly restrictive regulations in 1948.

(3) Approval of the idea of designating jobs in which foreign experience was desirable, with a view to considering what further action should be taken after the task of designating the jobs was completed. But, the secretary said, "it is essential that departmental employees not be penalized for failure to accept the conditions of employment implicit in an integrated service."

Not one of the measures outlined in the Acheson Plan was energetically carried out.

In 1951, as the organizational fervor was decreasing, one more report was made on the problem of the best organization of the Department and the Foreign Service. The Bureau of the Budget, pursuant to a general suggestion of the Hoover Commission, had contracted with the Brookings Institution in 1950 to study the administration of foreign affairs and the overseas operations of the government. The Brookings report, issued in 1951, recommended (a) that the Department of State should retain the overseas information program; (b) that in general, reversing the Hoover Commission's emphasis, the Department should carry out all other overseas operations of the government unless there were special reasons against its doing so; and (c) that the Departmental Service and the Foreign Service be merged through the lateral entry of Department officers into the Foreign Service and perhaps with the assistance of new legislation. The report was noted and filed, but nothing came of it.

In 1952, near the end of the second wave of reform, only two notable organizational developments occurred. In January the Department established an International Information Administration (IIA) which reported directly to the secretary and not through the assistant secretary for public affairs. In April, President Truman issued an executive order in which, in pursuance of the views of the Hoover Commission, the United States chief of mission in a foreign country was once more declared to have "general direction and leadership" over economic missions, military-assistance-advisory groups, etc.

THIRD WAVE, 1953 AND AFTER

That organizational reform was to be the order of the day, was plain at the very beginning of the first Republican administration in twenty years.

Early in 1953 the administration requested, and Congress passed, a law authorizing the appointment of an undersecretary of state for administration, for a period of two years. Donold B. Lourie, president of the Quaker Oats Company, was appointed to this position in February, 1953. Undersecretary Lourie was not only in charge of administration for the whole Department, but was also given direct supervision over (a) the Department's two operating elements, namely, the Technical Co-operation Administration and the International Information Administration, and (b) the Department's technical-advisory units, namely, those headed by the assistant secretaries for public affairs and Congressional relations, the legal adviser, the special assistant to the secretary for research and intelligence, and the science adviser.

The officer who had served up to that time as deputy undersecretary for administration, Carlisle Humelsine, resigned, whereupon the Department appointed Edward T. Wailes, a career Foreign Service Officer, as assistant secretary for administration. Wailes' job was to supervise the budget and fiscal activities of the Department.

There was also established, on a par with Wailes' position, that of administrator of the Bureau of Security and Consular Affairs, to which Robert W. S. ("Scott") McLeod was appointed. This bureau contained a number of offices—for personnel, security, passports, visas, and munitions control—which had previously been part of Humelsine's bailiwick.

The spring of 1953 saw a gigantic reduction-in-force (RIF) program, aimed at economy in government, under which, for example, the IIA announced that it would drop from its rolls 371 people overseas, 399 in the Voice of America and supporting operations in New York, and 60 in Washington, and would also abolish 160 unfilled positions. One result was a drastic reduction in the broadcasts to the free world, including elimination of broadcasts in French, Spanish (to Latin America), Portuguese, Hebrew, Malayan, and Thai, and reduction of English-language broadcasts from 5¾ hours daily to half an hour daily. Broadcasts in Eastern European languages, however, were increased.

The RIF resulted in closing some twenty-five American consulates in 1953 and 1954, including those at these key cities: Gibraltar; Georgetown, British Guiana; Adelaide, Australia; Godthaab, Greenland; Hamilton, Canada; Malaga, Spain; and Tananarive, Madagascar. It later became necessary to reopen most of these.

On June 1, 1953, President Eisenhower—largely on the advice of Secretary of State John Foster Dulles—took four decisive organizational steps. First, by executive order, he transferred from the Department of State to the Mutual Security Agency the TCA, the function of providing aid to escapees from iron-curtain countries, and the work based on United States participation in the United Nations International Children's Emergency Fund (UNICEF), the United Nations Technical Assistance Program (UNTAP), the United Nations Korean Reconstruction Agency (UNKRA), and the Intergovernmental Committee for European Migration.

The second step taken on June 1, 1953, was the submission to Congress of a reorganization plan, effective August 1, 1953, unless Congress should object (Congress did not object). The plan provided for the establishment of the Foreign Operations Administration (FOA) to replace the Mutual Security Agency (MSA), with a broader range of responsibilities, including administration of the technical-assistance program and the other programs transferred on June 1 by executive order.

The third step was the submission to Congress of a reorganization plan (to which, likewise, Congress did not object) providing for the establishment of the United States Information Agency (USIA) as an independent agency and transfer to it of all the overseas information activities of the government, *i.e.*, the Voice of America and other elements of IIA in the Department of State, the overseas information work of MSA (*i.e.*, the new FOA), and the information work in occupied areas. The secretary of state, the plan said, was to provide the USIA with foreign policy guidance.

The fourth move was the transmission by President Eisenhower of a communication to the heads of all executive departments and the director of mutual security, emphasizing anew the co-ordinating responsibility of the Foreign Service: "The Chief of the United States diplomatic mission in each foreign country must provide effective coordination of, and foreign policy direction with respect to, all United States Government activities in the country."

The organizational philosophy behind these moves was expressed thus by the president on June 1, 1953: "We are taking the necessary steps to confirm the historic responsibility of the Department of State as the agency responsible under the President for the development and control of foreign policy and all relations with foreign governments." The Department of State, in an internal announcement of June 4, 1953, added: "One of the main results is to relieve the Secretary of State of supervising operational programs, freeing his time to concentrate on the important problems of foreign policy."

The transfers out of the Department, combined with the RIF, reduced the size of the Department by about one half, from approximately 42,000 to approximately 21,000.

As in the case of the previous periods of organizational activity, the third inundation continued into a second year.

The year 1954 will long be remembered as the year of the Wriston Report. Early in the year, Secretary of State Dulles asked the following eight individuals to serve as the secretary's Public Committee on Personnel:

Henry M. Wriston, president of Brown University, as chairman; John Hay Whitney, financier, as vice-chairman; Robert Murphy, deputy undersecretary of state, ex officio; three former assistant secretaries of state, namely, Norman Armour, a retired Foreign Service officer, who had served as ambassador, Donald Russell, president of the University of South Carolina, who had served as assistant secretary of state for administration, and Charles E. Saltzman, businessman, who had served briefly as deputy undersecretary for administration following his period as an assistant secretary; two businessmen, namely, John A. McCone, formerly undersecretary of the Air Force, later to become chairman of the Atomic Energy Commission, and Morehead Patterson, president of the American Machine and Foundry Company.

The committee's "terms of reference" were signed on March 5, 1954, by Acting Secretary of State Walter B. Smith. Under these terms, the committee was requested to make recommendations on the organization of "the Service" (which, from the context, could be taken to mean either the Foreign Service or the total personnel service of the Department and the Foreign Service), including recruitment, training, assignment, morale, and—here was the bombshell—"amalgamation and interchangeability."

The committee had the assistance of two consultants and a staff of thirteen professional officers, including several borrowed from the Department and the Foreign Service. Background papers were prepared for the committee; the committee considered the conclusions of previous bodies comparable to itself; and, on May 18, 1954, the eight members of the committee signed a formal letter to Secretary

Dulles transmitting their report, which was immediately dubbed the Wriston Report by the press and within the Department.

The report not only complied with the request for recommendations. It went further. It consisted of two distinct elements: (a) recommendations; (b) serious criticisms of the administration of the Foreign Service since the enactment of the Foreign Service Act of 1946. As the criticisms were, in part at least, the basis for the recommendations, it will be instructive to survey the main criticisms:

(1) The low state of morale in the Foreign Service, attributed by many to the attacks of Senator Joseph McCarthy on the loyalty of the corps, was, according to the committee, due only in part to the operation of the security program. "Perhaps the most serious single contributing cause has been the absence of strong administrative leadership within the Department of State and the Foreign Service —a void which has resulted in poor management of the Service."

(2) The committee criticized the Department for having recruited only 355 Foreign Service officers at the bottom since the passage of the Foreign Service Act of 1946, despite the fact that "expansion of the Foreign Service was one of the purposes of this Act." (It may be noted that Congress appropriated less each year than the Department had requested.)

(3) Prior to the Eisenhower administration, officers were retained on the rolls who were "not regarded as of the highest quality."

(4) "Even more significant, no new Class 6 officers have been taken into the Service for nearly two years. The halt in appointments occurred during the last administration." (Later in the report the committee admitted that seventy-five officers had been taken in at the bottom during 1952, but it emphasized that no appointments had been made "since August, 1952.")

(5) After the advent of the new administration, the size of the Foreign Service officer corps was reduced, through the RIF and through "accelerated retirement of Foreign Service officers not regarded as of the highest quality," from 1,427 to 1,285. "Whatever the justification, such impairment of the professional corps is deplorable when the Department is charged with executing a dynamic foreign policy in so many parts of the world."

(6) "Not only is the Service too small for the tasks devolving upon it; it is also critically deficient in various technical specialties—notably economic, labor, agriculture, commercial promotion, area-language, and administrative—that have become indispensable to

the successful practice of diplomacy in its vastly broadened, mid-twentieth century meaning."

(7) The maintenance of separate personnel provisions for the Department of State, for Foreign Service officers, for the Foreign Service Reserve, and for the Foreign Service Staff has resulted not only in injustice but also in maladministration. "The differences bespeak inequalities which inevitably have tended to make for inequities between the systems and subsystems as well as some jealousy and occasional ill feeling. They have given rise to a sense of separateness where there should be a pervading sense of oneness. And this separateness has indisputably hampered the State Department in the conduct of its business, most seriously in the restraints it has laid upon the free interchange of skills and experience between the home and foreign organizations."

(8) "Lateral Entry Has Been Too Slow." This was the title of Chapter 4 of the committee's report, which sternly rebuked the Department for selecting only 26 of the 228 candidates for lateral entry from the Civil Service into the Foreign Service from 1946 to 1951 and for appointing only 25 (and holding 108 "in process") of the 2,150 applicants for lateral entry under the relaxed rules of 1951.

(9) Summarizing, the report made these further serious charges: ". . . the most serious personnel problems stem from faulty organization, discontinuity of policy, and a lack of vigorous management leadership. . . . A personnel system, in the contemporary meaning of the term, simply does not exist in the Department. Its management of its human resources has been irresolute and unimaginative. . . . the simple tools for effective personnel operations either do not exist in the Department or are hopelessly outmoded. Personnel files and qualification records are scattered and clumsily organized."

Affirmatively, the committee made these recommendations:

(1) The personnel of the Department and the Foreign Service, "where their official functions converge," and "above a certain level," should be integrated into a single administrative system, the career Foreign Service. The number of positions in the Department to be designated as "Foreign Service positions" was estimated as 2,250.

(2) The incumbents in the Foreign Service positions in the Department of State, and eligible applicants from the Foreign Service Reserve and the Foreign Service Staff, should, "within the limits of feasibility," be incorporated into the career Foreign Service.

(3) "Where Departmental officers presently holding 'Foreign Serv-

ice' positions are unwilling or unqualified to transfer, the recommendation is that in due course they be moved either into non-Foreign Service posts or be assisted in finding other employment."

(4) The Foreign Service Reserve and the Foreign Service Staff should be retained, but the former should be used only for unique and temporary problems, and the latter should be used only for technical, clerical, and custodial personnel "of lower than officer rank."

(5) Recognition should be given, in the integrated service, not only to "generalists" (predominantly the kind of Foreign Service officer in the past) but also to specialists.

(6) The Department should institute a nationwide system of competitive scholarships, "so as to provide a steady and adequate flow of officer material into the integrated service."

(7) The Foreign Service Institute should be revitalized.

(8) A deputy undersecretary for administration should be appointed who is "suitably qualified" and "prepared to stay."

Six of these eight recommendations have been implemented. Numbers three and six have fallen by the wayside. The process of putting the chosen six into effect was not easy, nor was everyone affected entirely happy with the results.

The carrying out of recommendations one, two, and four may be briefly summarized. A total of 1,362 positions in the Department became Foreign Service positions in 1954, but in the next year 205 of these were removed from that category. Of the incumbents in the remaining 1,157 positions, about 650 were integrated into the Foreign Service over a period of three years, about 450 declined to be integrated or were overage or otherwise ineligible, and about 50 resigned, retired, or transferred voluntarily to other jobs. In the same three post-Wriston years, about 850 officers of the Foreign Service Reserve and the Foreign Service Staff became career Foreign Service officers.

The Wriston recommendation here numbered five, on recognition for specialists, is related to the problem of the reception accorded to the "Wristonees" (many of whom were specialists) by the "elite corps" of long-time Foreign Service officers, many of whom strongly opposed the integration program. It is noteworthy, in this connection, that in the first promotions after the mass integration (1956), the Wristonees fared badly—only two of them being promoted as against 718 old-line Foreign Service officers. The explanation given was that the performance records of former Department officers were not sufficiently full, as compared with those of the regular Foreign Service officers. Whether, indeed, the recommendation for adequate recognition to specialists will be implemented in the long run, remains a question, since the top jobs will inevitably tend to be given to able generalists.

In the 1959 promotion list, the Wristonees fared much better than before. For example, in 1959 they constituted only 52 per cent of the total number of Foreign Service officers of class 2, but they got 70 per cent of the promotions from class 2 to class 1; in class 3 they were 65 per cent of the total, and they got 59 per cent of the promotions; and in class 4, where they made up 57 per cent of the total, they were given 51 per cent of the promotions.

Recommendations seven and eight of the above enumeration were taken seriously. Loy W. Henderson was made deputy undersecretary of state for administration, and he continued to serve in that capacity until 1961. The work of the Foreign Service Institute has been expanded, especially in language and area specialization and in mid-career and senior-officer training.

In the same month in which the Wriston Committee was appointed (March, 1954), the Department on its own initiative modified its personnel setup. The Office of Personnel was transferred from the jurisdiction of "Scott" McLeod to that of Assistant Secretary Wailes, and their respective units were renamed: the name of McLeod's unit, from Bureau of Security, Consular Affairs, and Personnel to Bureau of Inspection, Security, and Consular Affairs; Wailes' title was changed from assistant secretary for administration to assistant secretary for personnel administration. Later in the year, Wailes' title was changed again to assistant secretary for personnel and administration, as his province covered personnel, budget, buildings occupied abroad, and related topics.

Another non-Wriston reform of 1954 (contrary, indeed, to the spirit of the Wriston amalgamation) was the removal from the regular Foreign Service, by Congress, of the agricultural attachés who had been merged with it in 1939, and assignment of responsibility for them to the secretary of agriculture. Apparently the unhappiness of the Department of Agriculture over the results of the 1939 merger was greater than that of the Department of Commerce, for commercial attachés (as well as the labor attachés appointed since the 1940s) remained in the regular Foreign Service.

As was true of the two previous periods of organizational reform, this one also was marked by fewer changes in the last two years of the quadrennium. Reforms of 1955 and 1956 included several of merely secondary importance and only one of primary importance (the return of the technical co-operation function to the Department).

Congress, at the request of the Department, passed an amendment, signed April 5, 1955, to the Foreign Service Act authorizing payment to Wristonees of salaries roughly equal to, or slightly higher than, their previous Civil Service salaries, instead of requiring them, under the Foreign Service Act of 1946, to be paid at the base rate of their corresponding Foreign Service grades, which were in some cases lower than their Civil Service salaries.

In the summer of 1955 the transfer of the technical-assistance operation out of the Department was reversed. FOA, except its military aspects, was transferred to the Department of State as the International Cooperation Administration (ICA), which however was to report directly to the secretary of state and was to retain its identity as a self-contained organization, with its own personnel and budget units in Washington and its own personnel operating overseas. Although Secretary Dulles preferred in principle to confine the work of the Department to the field of policy, he agreed to receive the ICA, and he explained the retention of its own organizational integrity, which he strongly favored, by telling a subcommittee of the Senate Committee on Foreign Relations in January, 1956, that (a) the functions of the ICA were different from those of the Department, (b) it was important to keep mutual security funds separate from funds appropriated for diplomatic and consular work, and (c) the number of employees engaged in budget, personnel, security, and related work would not be reduced if the ICA units for budget, personnel, etc., were merged with those of the Department.

Separation of the ICA from the rest of the Department was broken down in one respect in March, 1956, when by executive order the Escapee Program (for assistance to those who had fled from behind the iron curtain) was transferred from the ICA to the Department's Bureau of Security and Consular Affairs.

FOURTH WAVE, 1957 AND AFTER

The most recent wave of organizational alteration has been modest, in comparison with its predecessors.

Vice-President Richard M. Nixon in 1957 made three recommendations on administration of foreign affairs, two of which have been implemented. Following a visit to Africa he proposed that greater emphasis be given to that continent in American foreign policy. Accordingly the Department of State requested that the position of assistant secretary of state for African affairs be established. Congress agreed, and the new assistant secretary became head of a separate Bureau of African Affairs in the Department. This purely procedural or organizational development was, of course, only the outer sign of greater inner or substantive emphasis on Africa.

After Vice-President Nixon's visit to Latin America and the submission of his report on that area, emphasis was also given to it. This was manifested organizationally as well as in essence. The Bureau of Inter-American Affairs, which previously had had two regional offices (Office of Regional Political Affairs and Office of Regional Economic Affairs) and two country offices (Office of Middle American Affairs and Office of South American Affairs), broke the latter two into four (offices of Caribbean and Mexican Affairs, of Central American and Panamanian Affairs, of East Coast Affairs, and of West Coast Affairs) to make possible high-level attention to each segment of the area.

Speaking at San Francisco late in 1957, Vice-President Nixon said: "The economic sections of our embassies abroad should be upgraded and strengthened both in quantity and quality. Every American embassy should be staffed with qualified personnel who can devote an adequate amount of their time and energy to the active promotion of policies which encourage private investment." Putting this suggestion into effect will depend in part on increased Congressional appropriations.

The organizational reformers may have been expecting a field day when President Eisenhower by an executive order in November, 1957, authorized the secretary of state to merge particular functions of the ICA with the regular setup of the Department of State. But Secretary Dulles did not contemplate any extensive mergers. He announced promptly that the ICA would remain intact within the framework of the Department of State. Nevertheless, three steps have been taken to integrate the ICA in the Department: the deputy undersecretary of state for economic affairs, appointed in 1956, was given responsibility for co-ordinating the work of the ICA in administering the new Development Loan Fund established by Congress; the press and public information activities of the ICA were transferred to the Bureau of Public Affairs of the Department of State; and the export-control work of the ICA, aimed under the Battle Act at restricting the sale of strategic materials by the United States and its allies to the Soviet bloc, was transferred to the Bureau of Economic Affairs of the Department of State.

At the beginning of 1958, while the fourth wave, though a little one, was at its height, the Department reactivated the position of Science Adviser with the appointment to it of Wallace R. Brode, who had been associate director of the National Bureau of Standards and was president of the American Association for the Advancement of Science. At the end of the year the Department sent science attachés to France, the German Federal Republic, Great Britain, Italy, Japan, and Sweden. These steps were in part the outcome of a heightened feeling of the importance of science in national survival, resulting from the exploration of outer space.

The year 1958 saw three additional reforms which may have lasting significance: first, the Foreign Service Institute inaugurated its advanced course for senior officers, pursuant to the recommendation of the Wriston Committee that the Institute provide training comparable to that of the National War College.

Secondly, the Mutual Security Act of June 30, 1958, established the position of undersecretary of state for economic affairs as the third-ranking position in the Department, to "give further emphasis to Congressional insistence that the mutual security program is an integral part of United States foreign policy and, as such, is under the immediate direction of the Department of State" (quoted from the Senate-House conference committee's report on the bill). On the day after signing the bill, President Eisenhower appointed Douglas Dillon, who had been serving as deputy undersecretary of state for economic affairs, to the new position.

Thirdly, President Eisenhower issued an executive order establishing the succession to the post of acting secretary of state. He ordered that after the secretary and the undersecretary, the sequence should proceed from the undersecretary for economic affairs to the deputy undersecretary for political affairs and then to the deputy undersecretary for administration.

In 1959 the Department's Bureau of Intelligence and Research achieved an upgrading of some of its parts, by which the divisions of research for the major areas of the world became offices. When

Undersecretary of State Christian A. Herter became secretary of state, Douglas Dillon became undersecretary of state rather than undersecretary for economic affairs, and the top three posts became those of secretary, undersecretary (Dillon), and undersecretary for political affairs (Livingston T. Merchant). Whether, after those developments and a few other changes of 1959 and 1960, the fourth postwar wave of organizational reform will, like its predecessors, peter out, remains to be seen.

How best to organize the Department of State and the Foreign Service is a problem that is still open. It will come to the fore from time to time, for one or more reasons, such as these: developments or increased complexities in international relations will make it necessary to streamline the current organization; new programs will necessitate a decision as to how they shall be administered; and new brooms arriving in the Department will find ways of sweeping corners which have previously suffered neglect.

As to the present and the immediate future, one may reasonably ask: Is the present organization the best that can be devised in the light of circumstances? Apart from changes in the world situation or in the substance of American foreign policy (which would reopen the organizational problem), are there elements in the present organization which should be reviewed now?

There are aspects of the current organizational pattern which naturally—from the standpoint of logic—lend themselves to question. This is not to say that the questioning would in all cases be answered with a prescription for a change. Some of the present peculiarities are undoubtedly warranted by special circumstances.

Here, however, are some of the situations, in question form, that appear on the surface to be subject to examination:

(1) Should there be co-ordination of the offices charged with long-range thinking, such as the Policy Planning Council, elements of the Bureau of Intelligence and Research, and the Historical Office in the Bureau of Public Affairs?

(2) Can the new techniques of operations research be applied to problems of foreign policy? If so, how should the operations research staff be related to the Department?

(3) What should be the long-term relation between the deputy undersecretary for administration (an officer appointed pursuant to a recommendation of the Hoover Commission) and the assistant secretary for administration?

(4) As to the educational-exchange staff, which is fully integrated in the Department of State, the overseas information staff, which is fully outside the Department, and the technical co-operation staff, which is inside the Department but not fully integrated with it in administrative functions, what criteria should prevail in determining whether a foreign program should be fully in, or partly in, or wholly outside of, the Department?

(5) How much integration is desirable between technical, administrative, and other positions in the Department, on the one hand, and positions in the Foreign Service, on the other; should those hired to do—in the Department of State—editing, or personnel classification, or supply purchasing, be required to serve at home and abroad? Also, how much integration is desirable between the segments of the Foreign Service—between, say, the present Foreign Service Staff and the career Foreign Service?

(6) Is it reasonable for the Foreign Agricultural Service to be independent while our commercial and labor attachés are parts of the regular Foreign Service?

(7) Should there be a high-level officer whose duty it would be to test day-to-day policies against the basic long-term objectives of the United States and of mankind; that is, to weigh the arguments for expediency against those for basic principle—to weigh the arguments for winning a diplomatic victory against winning the more basic war on human ills?

Reflection on these and similar questions, in the light of the postwar organizational structuring of the Department of State and the Foreign Service, may serve a practical purpose. Such reflection could provoke the emergence of far-reaching, creative ideas for a more effective organization of our Foreign Office and its overseas establishments. Through better organization, perhaps we can more intelligently carry out the task of achieving a better world society.

15: THE FOREIGN SERVICE INSTITUTE

Harold B. Hoskins

Formally established on March 13, 1947, upon the authority given by Congress in the Foreign Service Act of 1946, the Foreign Service Institute is the product of experience plus several years of intensive planning during and immediately after the Second World War. It had its origin in the widespread realization, both inside and outside the government, that the new and unaccustomed role the United States was playing in world affairs required a professional competence of the highest order on the part of the public services engaged in the conduct of foreign relations. Supplementing a more exacting recruitment process and improved administrative policies, an effective in-service training program was regarded as necessary to ensure an organization adequate to the complex tasks ahead. Such a program, it was felt, could best be provided by an institution in the Department of State operating at the graduate school level.

A few members of Congress and others in public life have from time to time advocated a Foreign Service Academy, which would prepare persons for Departmental and Foreign Service careers in the same manner that West Point and Annapolis serve the Army and Navy. Against such an undergraduate preparatory institution, and in favor of the present form of the Foreign Service Institute, it was argued that the best foundation for a career officer position lay in a general liberal arts type of undergraduate education obtainable in representative American colleges and universities where there would be maximum contacts with the main currents of American life. With this broad foundation, successful applicants for Departmental and Foreign Service positions in any given year should be furnished at government expense advanced professional and technical instruction as required.

During the period immediately following the Second World War the views of leading educators in the foreign affairs field were sought and obtained. DeWitt C. Poole, formerly director of the School of Public and International Affairs at Princeton University, drafted in

1945 "Some Preliminary Observations and Recommendations on Foreign Service Training." A brochure prepared by the Division of Foreign Service Planning (in the Department of State), entitled "Tentative Plans for a Foreign Service Institute," provided the basis for a fruitful discussion with a committee of the Council on Foreign Relations especially appointed to advise the Department in the matter. Both of these memoranda served at the time to sketch, in broad, imaginative terms, the outlines of a leading educational institution for government officers charged with the administration of foreign affairs. They have continued to guide and stimulate the staff of the Institute.

Meanwhile in April, 1945, the Department of State had established by departmental order the Division of Training Services which set up experimentally a pattern of organization and programming that was later inherited by the Institute. Prior to the Division of Training Services, experience in the Department of State with in-service training had been limited to programs for select groups of new employees. New consular officers were given a brief period of training after the year 1907, and a similar course was established for new diplomatic officers in 1909. Upon the consolidation of the two corps into the Foreign Service in 1924, a Foreign Service Officer Training School (for new officers) was established and operated, with some interruptions, for two decades. The only advanced training given consisted in the assignment of a dozen officers over the period from 1936 to 1941 to university graduate schools of economics, and of a detail of officers to study Far Eastern languages. The Department of State established some training courses for clerical and other employees during the war.

Under the stimulus of fresh, creative thinking, and the growing conviction that the training devices of an earlier day would be wholly inadequate to equip Foreign Service and Departmental officers for their greatly expanded responsibilities of the postwar world, Congress included Title VII in the Foreign Service Act of 1946, authorizing a Foreign Service Institute. This act was made law by the president on August 13, 1946. It became effective ninety days later, paving the way for the Department regulation formally establishing the Institute.

The Institute holds a unique position in the framework of national government. The special authorities conferred upon it by statute, and the range and extent of its instructional responsibilities, lift it out of the pattern of the usual departmental in-service training agency. And although the House Committee Report described the Institute as "comparable to the Army and Navy command schools and staff colleges," it would correspond more properly to all the training establishments of any armed service rolled into one.

The Institute has to train both officers and clerks. It has to set up programs for personnel going overseas and personnel employed in Washington. It must equip employees for service in approximately 100 countries. It must offer facilities not to one department but to all government agencies concerned with the conduct of foreign relations. It must deal, on the one hand, with administrative, procedural, and technical training, and, on the other hand, with graduate-level education in professional and substantive fields. The Institute must provide not only for young officers entering upon government service, but for older men at progressive stages during their careers, concluding with a carefully tailored program for senior officers prior to their assumption of positions of the highest responsibility.

The range of training services that the Institute provides these categories of government personnel is rendered even more extensive by the complexity of the duties of the Foreign Service and the Department of State in the conduct of foreign relations. Science and technology, expansion of our commercial and financial interests, obligations under the United Nations, and our vital concern with the advancement of freedom and democracy, have radically altered traditional diplomacy. The modern Department of State and Foreign Service require the trained political analyst and negotiator, but they also need officers thoroughly versed in industry, agriculture, banking, labor, and engineering. There must be officers to deal with political and economic aspects of international civil aviation, shipping, radio communications, mining, and oil production; to operate world-wide information and education programs; and to participate in international conferences as well as perform the traditional tasks of administering visas, immigration regulations, citizenship cases, and services to American citizens abroad. Moreover, the services must have personnel who have specialized in acquiring an understanding of and therefore a capacity to treat effectively with, peoples of half-a-hundred diverse cultures—each with their own language, customs, and "peculiar" ways.

Overriding all of these activities is the paramount responsibility of the Department of State and the Foreign Service for promoting the security of the United States in a troubled, divided world. We have had thrust upon us problems of unprecedented complexity and gravity, and, consequently, responsibilities in every quarter of the globe. The semi-isolationist American of prewar years has become a world leader of today.

Of importance is the Institute's responsibility for personnel development. Obviously, in-service training does not bear this responsibility alone. Recruitment procedures for the selection of men and women possessing ability to grow, wise and sympathetic direction by supervisors, and judicious personnel administration are as necessary as in-service training in a program productive of high individual proficiency. Moreover, both in the Department of State and in the Foreign Service (the reserve and staff corps), recruitment is utilized to bring specialists and technicians into the organizations at advanced levels. This continuous infusion of specialized talent results from the necessity to provide training in many professional, scientific, and technical fields.

At the same time, the Institute's potential contribution to the creation of a corps of personnel uniquely competent to conduct American foreign relations today is almost limitless. Granted the possession by an officer of rich native endowment, brought to fruition through academic and official experience, he cannot fail to benefit measurably from educational programs progressively adapted to the stages of his career. The only exception would be one whose mind had lost its capacity to grow, in which case he has outlived his usefulness to the public service. In addition to providing stimulation to the perceptions and imagination, and deepening understanding of the human world we inhabit in all its intricate design, systematic instruction can assist the officer in bringing into a conscious, articulate, and ordered form (therefore translatable to new environments and assignments) the insights and intuitions he has gained through experience. Proof of the value of formal higher education to officers even in their forties (and a few in their fifties) is furnished by the testimony of those who have attended the War Colleges and the Senior Officer Course.

In the years 1947 to 1952 the Institute endeavored to promote new approaches by universities to which officers were assigned for advanced area studies. It sought to round out the emphasis of schools of international relations on international law, organization, politics, economics, and diplomatic history with further study of human personality and human behavior in different cultures. This approach involved work in cultural anthropology, psychology, and social psychology, and the integration of these with traditional social studies in such a manner as to illumine the social totality of a given foreign people rather than just the economic and political segments thereof. Emphasis was given to seminar courses such as "Cultural and Psychological Factors in International Relations." Because human behavior and institutions vary greatly with the social and cultural environments of which they are manifestations, stress was laid on this approach also in the preparation of Foreign Service specialists for particular areas of the world.

In language studies, conceived as part of area studies, the Institute, along with a few major universities in the country, blazed a new trail. Scholars who played leading roles in the development of language training methods for the armed forces in the Second World War joined the staff and have undertaken to refine, improve and expand descriptive linguistic materials that they and others originally developed under the auspices of the American Council of Learned Societies. The intensive method and materials used are based on a careful description of the language as it is spoken and written. While initial concentration is placed on developing a control of the spoken language under the close supervision of a linguistic scientist working with tutors who are native speakers, the ultimate objective is to develop speaking and reading proficiency. At each level of language study officers are presented with appropriate grammatical explanations and drills, and audio-visual aids are extensively used to supplement classroom work.

During the period from 1946 to early 1949 the Institute was under the organizational authority of the Office of Foreign Service. When this office was abolished in May, 1949, as part of a reorganization undertaken following studies made by the Hoover Commission,[1] the decision was taken not to make the Institute autonomous under the deputy undersecretary for administration but to place it under the director of personnel where it was to operate as one of the three major units of the Office of Personnel. The then deputy undersecretary on that occasion reaffirmed the educational role of the organization in these terms:

> . . . The program and future plans of the Institute continue to receive my complete endorsement and support, and arrangements will be made to permit the Institute to operate with the freedom necessary for it to maintain its relationships with the academic

[1] See Dr. Gerber's essay above, pp. 399ff.

world, and to fulfill the ambitions we have for making the Institute into a genuine graduate school of foreign affairs for our Departmental and Foreign Service Officers.

Despite these intentions the prominence and influence achieved by the Institute in its initial program rapidly diminished. Operational requirements were given priority over training assignments because a budgetary restriction in 1952 and 1953 resulted in staff slashes without commensurate reductions in the responsibilities confronting the Foreign Service. Under these circumstances the few officers remaining in the Service were assigned to functional and statutory duties, and training was relegated to a token status.

The national budgetary decisions that compelled the Department of State to absorb a reduction in-force of more than 22 per cent of its strength created severe dislocations, and in March, 1954, the Secretary of State's Public Committee on Personnel was created to recommend needed corrections. The Public Committee found the Institute dying of neglect. It was critical of the Department of State for not supplying the Institute with the kind of director stipulated by Congress; it said that the Institute was not staffed with the sort of faculty that had been expected, and that the students assigned to the Institute were not of a grade capable of taking full advantage of the facilities Congress intended to supply. The committee stated that until the director of the Institute reported to the highest levels of the Department, just as the president of the National War College reports directly to the joint chiefs of staff, and until much more imagination and energy were poured into its work, it would never meet the expectation of Congress or the urgent needs of the Foreign Service. The committee strongly recommended that the Institute be given a status equal to that of the war colleges; and that the faculty be re-created at once, the curriculum revised, and the direction be committed to a man of first-class ability.

Recognizing the validity of these criticisms, the Department took prompt steps to revitalize the Institute. Its renaissance dates from March, 1955, when the Institute was transferred to the office of the deputy undersecretary for administration and a new director was selected. The staff was increased in March, 1954, from twenty-two to sixty-three, and a full curriculum of courses designed to meet the ever expanding requirements of the Department of State was reinstituted. At the same time a new Public Advisory Committee to the Institute was appointed. A member of Congress, academic leaders, scholars active in the foreign affairs field, and men prominent in public affairs were selected to provide the Institute with the benefits of their rich experience by advising as to the general character and scope of the training programs, and by periodically reviewing the activities of the Institute.

As of 1960 the Institute provides career and language training to meet the minimal needs of the Department of State, the Foreign Service, and some personnel from other agencies dealing with foreign affairs, particularly the International Cooperation Administration and the United States Information Agency. Personnel from twenty-five other government agencies are enrolled as compared with representatives of three or four government agencies which used the Institute's facilities five or six years ago.

Career training is provided in pyramidal form. At the base, all officers newly entering the Foreign Service, 8 per cent of whom are women, are enrolled for initial training which is divided into three parts.

The first part is the basic foreign service officer course, an eight-week introduction given to officers upon appointment to Class 8, the beginning class in the Foreign Service officer corps from among those who have passed the highly competitive entrance examination. For most officers it is an introduction to employment with the Department of State. It therefore seeks to familiarize them with the organization and functions of the Department of State and Foreign Service and the interests and activities of other agencies of the US government participating in foreign affairs. It acquaints the new officers with the roles they may expect to play in their newly acquired professional status, particularly in the years immediately ahead of them, and is intended to imbue them with a sense of professional pride which will be of assistance throughout their careers.

The second stage of initial training is intensive language instruction. Upon completing the basic Foreign Service officer course, those officers who do not possess a minimum professional proficiency in speaking French, German, Spanish, Italian or Portuguese (which is still the case of the majority of junior officers) undertake sixteen weeks of full-time training in one of these languages. In this period of intensive instruction officers who have some background in the languages usually find it possible to achieve the desired proficiency. Those with little or no speaking knowledge in their language at the beginning of instruction will frequently require additional part-time work on language tape recordings and home study.

The third and final part of the initial training consists of the consular operations course. This course is scheduled to immediately precede the first assignment to a field post in the Foreign Service. Officers whose initial work assignments are to field posts receive consular training immediately after their intensive language training, if such instruction had been required, or after the basic Foreign Service officer course. On the other hand, the officer whose initial work assignment is to the Department of State in Washington returns to the Foreign Service Institute for consular training a year or so later, shortly before being assigned to the field. This in-training is designed to teach what consular functions are and how to perform them. It equips an officer with the necessary skills to discharge the technical, statutory responsibilities of the Foreign Service. In the period from 1955 through 1959 there have been 34 classes of introductory training from which have graduated almost 900 students now in the Foreign Service.

At the second level in the pyramidal structure of career training is the mid-career course to which approximately 35 per cent of the officers in the middle grades of the Service are assigned between their sixth and twelfth year in the Service. This twelve-week training period is designed to broaden the outlook and increase the awareness of these officers of basic factors in inter-cultural relations, international affairs, and good management. Generally speaking, an officer reaches mid-career rank on the basis of demonstrated ability in a job or area specialty. If he is to shoulder the responsibilities demanded of a senior officer, he must acquire a more comprehensive understanding of the ingredients of foreign policy formulation and of the operations of the Foreign Service, and must learn to approach these problems in a general perspective rather than within the limits of a specialized focus. The plan of the mid-career course has been designed to permit officers to concentrate on stimulating intellectual matters in an atmosphere that could not be duplicated under the pressures of day-to-day involvements.

The most important objectives of the course are:

(1) To draw the attention of officers to several concepts for the interpretation of man's social behavior which may assist them in systematizing their foreign service reporting and analysis.

(2) To acquaint students with the most significant of the other

agencies and branches of government, and with certain private interests, that are concerned with influencing foreign policy.

(3) To provide officers with the opportunity for a fresh look at the basic American values and attitudes that underlie our foreign policy.

(4) To develop in students a better understanding of the managerial task in the Foreign Service, and of the interdependence of the substantive and administrative functions.

(5) To utilize training techniques that involve a maximum degree of student participation as well as the broadest basis for realistic evaluation of the executive potential of each student.

From 1955 through 1959 approximately three hundred officers were graduated from the eighteen classes of the mid-career course.

At the apex of the pyramid, senior training is offered through assignment to the several service war colleges, the National War College or the senior officer course conducted at the Foreign Service Institute. The first session of the latter, which lasts nine months, was inaugurated in the fall of 1958. The senior officer course is the most advanced training program in international relations and foreign policy offered by the Department of State. It completes a cycle of specialized career training provided for officers beginning at junior grade through mid-career on to the senior policy-making level. It prepares officers for the highest positions of responsibility in policy recommendation and execution, co-ordination, planning and administration in the Department, in diplomatic posts abroad, and in interagency and international organizations.

The senior officer course participants are a small group of Department and Foreign Service officers of Classes 1, 2, and 3, and similarly ranked representatives from other departments and agencies of the government, including the Department of Agriculture, the US Information Agency, the International Cooperation Administration, the Central Intelligence Agency, and an officer of colonel rank from each of the Army, the Air Force and the Marine corps, and a captain from the Navy.

Owing to their academic and professional attainments and the prospect that many of the participants will ultimately assume positions of highest importance in the policy-making organism of the US Government, the course seeks to provide mainly the intellectual framework for a free and vigorous spirit of inquiry into the complexities of foreign policy.

Career training is supplemented by numerous seminars designed to keep officers concerned with the conduct of foreign relations informed of recent developments in the shifting international scene, and to provide a meeting place for discussion of how such developments affect US foreign affairs. The seminars fall into two groups.

The first group considers topics that provide a background of factors permanently affecting US foreign relations. Included are such subjects as communist strategy, the current American scene, international labor affairs, regional organizations in Europe, and political stability and development. A second group of seminars considers current topics selected from the many fields of international interest; these are operated as field trips and are often combined with instruction at educational institutions in the area being studied. The Near East Seminar for example utilizes the American University of Beirut, and students in the African seminar were enrolled in special programs at three university colleges in Africa.

Courses at the Institute are also offered in the specialized functions of the Foreign Service, such as administrative operations and budget, and fiscal management. In addition, general orientation is provided for the officers of agencies of the government other than the Department of State going overseas and also for wives and dependents on a "space available" basis pending legal authority to expand this activity.

Effective representation of the US abroad requires that members of the Foreign Service know and understand the peoples and cultures with whom they work. Thus area training is offered to acquaint the officers with the manifold political, economic, and social aspects of the various important areas of the world. Intensive area training is provided usually in connection with language specialization for periods lasting up to ten months, at facilities selected from American and foreign universities, the Institute, and at branch schools in Taiwan, Japan, and Lebanon.

To supplement the needs of the Department for officers with a specialized knowledge of international economics and international labor affairs, approximately forty officers are assigned each year for full-time study on the graduate level at prominent American universities.

The language policy of the Department of State is rooted in two ideas: first, that there is no substitute for knowing the language of the area that an officer, particularly a "substantive" officer, has to work in, second, each officer is primarily responsible for acquiring the skill that he needs in the languages of the areas in which he serves. There are corollaries to both of these postulates, for it must be recognized that if the Department is to require every officer who has need of a language in his work to acquire skill in that language, it must provide all possible assistance to him, both in the way of language classes and materials and in granting him necessary time to study. The Department supplies the know-how and for the most part bears the expense of training in languages, particularly in hard languages,[2] but the individual officer is given every incentive through career development policies to have the proper motivation without which training in languages becomes unrewarding for both the Department and the officer.

To supplement these career incentives, the Department has established a combination program for part and full-time language training that is recognized as a sophisticated and mature attempt to teach adults a foreign language. Full-time instruction is provided for upwards of 250 officers from almost a dozen different agencies in Washington alone, and more than 50 officers are studying abroad in the three "hard language" schools at Beirut, Tokyo, and Taichung, Taiwan (Formosa). Twenty-six languages are, on the average day, taught at the Institute, and over fifty different languages are taught in part-time language programs at posts abroad. There is hardly a Foreign Service post where officers are not studying, in classes or on their own, either one of the five widely-used "world languages" [3] or the particular language of the area. Nearly five thousand officers, staff employees, and their dependents are enrolled in these formal Institute programs abroad, which are supplied with a steady flow of new and advanced language materials, the product of the twenty-six scientific linguists employed by the Institute. More such highly trained language scientists are on the staff of the Foreign Service Institute than at any other institution of learning, government or private, in the United States today. Thousands of tape recordings and hundreds and even thousands of pages of language

[2] Merely for purposes of internal administration the Department of State divides foreign languages broadly into two kinds: "world languages," those languages of widest use in Foreign Service posts as native or second languages (French, Italian, Spanish, German, Portuguese and sometimes Russian); and "hard languages," a category that includes all other languages.

[3] See preceding footnote.

lesson materials are produced for use in the classes at the Institute and in the part-time programs abroad.

What about the incoming young officers recruited from college campuses through the Foreign Service examination? How well prepared are they in languages? Many, perhaps a majority, voluntarily offer a language on the written examination, but seventy-five per cent of the new Foreign Service officers entering on duty with the Department of State require some training to bring them up to the professional speaking level of proficiency in a widely used language that is demanded before they remove their probationary status. Such training for junior officers either immediately follows the initial basic officers training course and is keyed to the requirements of their first assignment abroad or is given later in a four-month program immediately preceding their departure from the United States. Although more and more junior officers are entering the Service with ability to speak a widely used language, American universities still appear to be lagging in offering modern courses of language training to undergraduates. Until effective training in spoken languages is given by American universities, there will continue to be a need for training in both world and hard languages. During the fiscal year 1958-1959, 491 Foreign Service officers entered on full-time language training in Institute programs in Washington and abroad. Most of these were assigned to four-month intensive training in world languages—French, Italian, Spanish, German, or Portuguese—but about one hundred were in training in the hard languages. In less than ten years, the Institute's language training effort has increased ten to fifteenfold.

Today the language program begins with the new junior officers, who attend four-month intensive courses in the world languages most commonly in use at their first post of assignment, if they do not already have a professional speaking and reading knowledge of the language. After several tours they are encouraged to volunteer for training or "specializing" in one hard language, such as Chinese, Arabic, Hindi, Hebrew or any one of dozens of others. Following a nine to twenty-four-month course in language, supplemented by part-time or even full-time training in area studies at one of the American universities or, in some cases, at the Institute, the officer serves in his area of choice for one, two, or three tours.

Tours of duty for Foreign Service officers are now usually four years in length, broken by home leave at the end of the first two years. This break permits the officer time to acquire some facility in the language of the area through the part-time post programs. If he is already a language specialist in the area, he almost inevitably continues his training by two, three, or even five hours of tutoring or classes a week.

At any one time almost 40 per cent of the 3,500 American Foreign Service officers are serving in Washington, filling political, functional, and even administrative and intelligence positions in the Department of State and its related agencies. While in Washington on a four-year tour, an officer's speaking knowledge of a language may decline markedly or he may wish to acquire facility in a second or third world language. Part-time (usually early morning) classes are available to him nine months out of the year, and before returning abroad he may be given an opportunity to attend short, intensive, and even full-time language refresher classes, although this depends naturally on the availability of tutors and class time.

Practically speaking, the Department of State has been seeking to provide high quality language instruction for all Foreign Service officers while giving them the specific career incentive which may eventually include additional pay for officers acquiring language skills, though this will require legislative changes which are now being sought. To check on the progress being made, a mandatory language-testing program standardized through use of native speakers working under precepts laid down by scientific linguists, was placed in operation in the summer of 1958. All Foreign Service officers are required to take medical examinations upon their return to the United States on home leave. Similarly, all officers are now being required to offer themselves for language testing at the Institute before travel orders are released. Over 40 per cent of the officers have so far been tested under the extremely high standards set by the Institute, based on a ranking system from S-0 (no speaking knowledge) to S-5 (bilingual). Similar marks are given for reading knowledge of the language. The tests require about half an hour, are given individually, and sometimes, though not always, are recorded.

The results achieved by the 40 per cent tested in the first 15 months of operation of the formal testing program indicated that nearly one fourth had a specialist (S-4) or bilingual (S-5) knowledge of at least one foreign language. One officer was tested in seven different languages and several hundred other officers offered themselves for testing in more than one language. Sixty per cent of those tested up to the fall of 1959 achieved a professional level of proficiency or better in one or more languages. Only 16.5 per cent had less than a working knowledge of any foreign language. This includes, it should be pointed out, all types of officers in the service—administrative and technically or functionally trained—many of whom have a minimal need to know languages even while working abroad.

More important than any over-all testing figures are the growing numbers of graduates of the Foreign Service Institute program in hard or difficult languages, ranging from Korean through Indonesian and Hindi to Bulgarian, Polish and the languages of the Middle East. More than one hundred officers a year have been scheduled to enter training in these languages during the years from 1961-1965. From mid-1956 until mid-1960, 296 Foreign Service officers entered training in these hard languages. The pipeline of training in hard languages was, by the beginning of 1960, almost filled to capacity both in terms of the Institute's capability to train in Washington and at its three special schools in Tokyo, Taichung, and Beirut, and also in terms of need in some of these languages, notably those of Eastern Europe. Certain languages, notably those of Africa, still were projected for training purposes into the future, but the development of specialists in other areas had progressed remarkably from the mid-1950s.

For the future, there will be a further rationalization of the basic principle adopted by the Department of State that all Foreign Service officers should have a high level of skill in one world language, seek to acquire such skill in a second widely used language, and study and achieve some measure of ability in the language of each post of assignment, either as an intensively trained area specialist or as a student of the language while working in the area. The basic framework to carry out this policy has already been built, and further progress in it will depend only on continuing support both from universities preparing candidates for a Foreign Service career and from Congress for the Institute's programs in language, language and area, and functional training. The direction of the tide for Foreign Service officers and for other Americans serving the United States abroad is definitely toward higher and higher standards of professional skills in recruitment and programs of training.

16: THE ROLE OF SPECIALISTS IN THE POLICY-MAKING PROCESS

Robert E. Elder

THE CHALLENGE OF OUR TIME

The generalist is dead! Long live the specialist! Through the years, emphasis has been on the role of the generalist in the policy-making process.[1] True, some Foreign Service officers or civil servants have successfully hurdled a variety of assignments, acquired a broader background of experience than others, and are sometimes called generalists. Even so, at a given time, working in any position, these "old hands" are really serving as specialists. At the highest level in the Department of State, even the secretary on occasion defers judgment, refers to the undersecretary or undersecretary for economic affairs questions within their fields of specialization and responsibility. The deputy undersecretary for political affairs spends most of his time on politico-military matters. The deputy undersecretary for administration, as his title implies, rules over a broad yet limited domain. The assistant secretaries are regional or functional specialists. The lower one goes on the policy totem pole, the greater the specialization. One finds country desk officers, intelligence analysts, policy planners, legislative liaison specialists, public information officers, and public opinion analysts, plus economic, legal, mutual security, international organization, communication, training, personnel, budget, and finance specialists—and a host of subspecialists too numerous to mention. All of these specialists perform functions necessary to the operation of the policy-making machine. For better or worse, the secretary of state may be the one remaining generalist in the Depart-

[1] For a more thorough discussion of the role of the Department of State in the government policy-making structure, see Robert E. Elder, *The Policy Machine: The Department of State and American Foreign Policy* (Syracuse, 1960). Alternative means of establishing a proper balance to meet "generalist" and "specialist" requirements of the Foreign Service are explored at some length in Chapter 9, "Personnel Management: Matching People and Jobs," of *The Policy Machine.*

ment of State. He alone among the Department's 6,500 employees in Washington and New York, or its 6,100 American personnel (and 9,400 aliens) at 277 posts overseas, has general responsibility for American foreign policy. As a matter of fact, viewed in the broader context of the government-wide structure grinding out national security policy for the president's consideration and approval, the secretary of state becomes a specialist on politico-economic affairs. The dichotomy suggested by the terms generalist and specialist is unreal and the distinction less meaningful at most levels in the Department than in "the good old days" before "Wristonization." It is still easier to argue that Department employees become specialists when assigned to a job than to claim they remain generalists. But it must be admitted that there are certain specialties that require a degree of expertise beyond the capacity of the typical generalist to learn by on-the-job training alone. Furthermore, the Department has not yet been able to meet adequately its personnel needs in certain specialties after more than a half decade of "Wristonization."

In our dynamic, confused, contemporary world, adequate co-ordination of Department specialists, and those of other departments or agencies participating in the formulation of national security policy, to produce some kind of unified and consistent policy to guide American foreign relations becomes a requirement for national survival. If policy making and co-ordination of specialists were taking place in the relatively stable world society of yesteryear, the problem of constructing a satisfactory mechanism to agree on assumptions concerning the nature of man and the world in which we live, to determine broad policy goals, and to establish political, economic, military, and informational implementing policies would be difficult enough. For we currently have eighty-six tools of American foreign policy at our disposal in any given country overseas and a budget process which makes it practically impossible to obtain an efficient combination of these tools on an individual country basis.

Whether we like it or not, the environment of international relations is rapidly changing. Although policy makers have discovered to their dismay that leadership is a tremendous and thankless task when America possesses a favorable power position, specialists within the policy machine can already project conditions in foreign areas to a time when the balance of power is likely to be much less favorable, when additional states will be strong enough to demand participation in shaping world affairs. Within the next forty years, populations of other continents and nations will multiply far beyond our own, the productive capacities of some of these areas may equal or outstrip American industry, the potential intellectual capabilities of less developed peoples may be more fully realized. Policy making must be conducted in an unsteady situation evolving toward an uncertain future, the outlines of which are yet dimly perceived.

The problem is far more than carrying on daily operations. It is to project the nature of the world in two, five, ten, twenty-five, and forty years, to provide realistic long-range policies which will enable America to emerge from the evolutionary changes through which society must pass as a respected and influential partner among nations. This involves understanding the present organization of the specialists who participate in the policy-making process, and providing for adaptation of the policy machine to insure that specialists will always make policy to meet an onrushing tide of events which cannot be held back, to insure that long-term considerations are not crushed by daily operations. The test of leadership and national greatness does not lie in resolving current problems as though the world were static and American pre-eminence indefinitely guaranteed. Today's actions must be measured against world society and the American role in world affairs at the close of the 20th century.

A correspondent who has covered the Department of State with distinction for more than a decade believes that John Foster Dulles as secretary of state was more often right than wrong in dealing with specific or limited problems of foreign policy, such as sending American troops to Lebanon or holding his ground against Communist Chinese pressure on Quemoy and Matsu. If the Dulles stewardship of foreign affairs is criticized, according to this well-informed source, it must be for failure to provide alternate assumptions or new principles to replace the containment policy inherited from the regime of Secretary of State Dean Acheson. Containment has caused policy to be formulated as a counter to communist action, it is said, reducing American flexibility and leaving initiative to the Soviet Union. If one accepts this analysis, Dulles may have failed to reorient his attitude on containment because the policy machine was not organized to develop and present ideas which could create such change. The machinery of policy making had become so massive that the flaws in the performance of a secretary of state might stem from, or be exaggerated by, shortcomings in the machine itself. Department leaders have difficult work loads. They have little time for thinking or looking beyond the current crisis.

Department specialists at staff levels may have to provide challenging ideas and look to the future before perception and new decisions can result in redirection of policy from the top. Even specialists are almost buried under a daily avalanche of words and paper. Department policy makers at all levels have been under increasingly mounting pressure in postwar years as American policy became more positive, as American commitments to world affairs developed breadth and permanence. But adaptation of the policy machine may—indeed, ought to—come. By analyzing the role of six major types of specialists in the policy-making process, we may discover the factor which will enable America to meet the challenge of our time and give hope of fruitful American participation in world affairs for centuries into the future. A quick look at the Department's country desk officers, intelligence analysts, policy planners, legislative liaison specialists, public information officers, and public opinion analysts may indicate the strength and weakness of the policy machine today.

1. Country Desk Officers

Country desk officers good-naturedly refer to themselves as "the lowest form of life" in the policy-making process.[2] This modesty is deceptive. They are generally able and alert young men. Although a country desk officer in one of the Department's five regional bureaus is "low man on the totem pole" so far as seniority is concerned, he wields significant power in the formulation of foreign policy. Essentially he is an operator, concerned with day-to-day relations with his assigned country. He usually gets first crack at a solution for problems which demand Department attention. He is "the wheelhorse and sparkplug" of the policy-making process.

In the comfortable days before the Second World War, when the Department had less than 1,000 employes, policy making centered in small regional divisions which maintained close contact through desk officers with American embassies and legations in their areas of responsibility. Desk officers were in close contact with the single assistant secretary of state who headed the regional divisions, and

[2] Much of the material in this section is drawn from the author's "Country Desk Officer: Low Man on the Totem Pole," *Foreign Service Journal*, May and June, 1958.

often consulted directly with the secretary of state. They were sometimes referred to as "little despots" who "made policy on the cables." As the recognized Department experts on particular countries, their tenure was practically endless, or so it seemed to Foreign Service officers in the field. They were men to be reckoned with, to be feared and courted.

The growing work load of the Department during and after the Second World War, with increase in personnel and almost continuous reorganization, changed the divisions to offices and then to bureaus. The country desk officer worked at the same old last, but the hierarchy above him became more complex. The office director separated him from regular contact with his assistant secretary, now one among five assistant secretaries heading regional bureaus. A deputy undersecretary for political affairs—at one time even an undersecretary for political affairs—lessened the need for consultation with the secretary of state, who had become much too busy to see desk officers anyway. Coupled with Wristonization in the mid-1950s, which ended permanent tenure of an expert on a country desk and initiated the system of three or four-year rotation of Foreign Service officers through country desks (often with several years of special training and experience before assignment), the Department's country desk officers have suffered a shattering devolution which markedly changed their status in the policy-making process.

In spite of this, almost every young man entering the Foreign Service dreams of being able to hold down a country desk in the Department of State at some point in his career. The desk is viewed both as an end in itself and as a steppingstone toward further preferment in the Foreign Service. The Department's 114 country desk officers are still "the eyes and ears, the brain and voice, of America in a troubled world." They keep constant watch over developments in 179 political entities from Aden through Zanzibar, including such danger spots as Algeria, Iraq, Korea, and Poland. Almost every bit of information which government agencies collect on an area, and many policy papers from other agencies proposing action in the area, cross the country desk, at a rate of 250 to 350 documents per day. The desk man learns to scan a document in ten seconds, to know whether he must read it in detail or not. The desk remains the key point of contact in the Department for the diplomatic post abroad and the foreign embassy in Washington.

The country desk man is a drafting officer. When a despatch or telegram arrives in the Department from a post in his assigned country, the desk man usually receives the yellow action copy. It is his job to work out a reply. Sometimes, on simple routine matters, he can reach a decision by himself and forward it to the field over the secretary of state's signature. In cases a little out of the ordinary, before final action, he must clear his draft with superiors—his office director and assistant secretary—or with desk officers in other interested offices or bureaus of the department, sometimes holding conferences with representatives of other agencies. Experience is his teacher on when and where to seek review and guidance. There is no forgetting the anguish of a Department officer who with an information copy of an incoming dispatch, and an interest in the action, expected to be consulted and was overlooked. Many times the telegrams, memoranda, or even more formal policy papers drafted by a country desk officer are modified slightly if at all by reviewing officers. The "tyranny of the written word" works in his favor. If the desk officer is not too far out of step, it is easier for those above him to concur or make minor revisions in his draft than to come up with something different. This does not mean that the desk officer has a free hand in policy making. He is usually well aware of the views of his superiors. He does not make policy in a vacuum. The basic assumptions and goals of American policy already considered by the National Security Council and approved by the president, as well as implementing policies formulated by the Operations Co-ordinating Board between 1953 and 1961, are inherent to his thinking. These decisions are of a relatively stable nature and often antedate his coming to the desk. They tend to set the limits within which he must operate. His knowledge of public, legislative, and executive opinion in America and abroad further limits his alternatives. Reviewing officers can and do disapprove his recommendations; broader regional and functional considerations may override his views. In time of major crisis, higher-ranking officers in the Department—the assistant secretaries, deputy undersecretaries, undersecretaries, and the secretary of state—step into the foreground of policy making. The more narrow country interests of the desk officer are buried under this parade of high brass. Nonetheless, a country desk officer's duties are important, numerous, and varied. His day has no routine. He is more a man of action than a philosopher, more an extrovert than an introvert. He operates in the land of quick-think, although conferences to achieve interagency agreement on policy questions sometimes force more thorough consideration of problems upon him.

An active country desk like Indonesia demands fifty to fifty-five hours of hard work during a five-day week. The desk man may come in almost an hour before the Department's regular 8:45 A.M. opening to read incoming correspondence or telegrams and to draft replies before the day's hustle and bustle descends upon him with its steady stream of telephone calls for information, briefings of visitors with overseas problems, staff meetings or interagency conferences, and the never-ending clearance of papers drafted by officers in other bureaus or departments. If the ambassador of his assigned country visits the Department on business, the desk officer accompanies him to the meeting with the assistant secretary or undersecretary. Ahead of time he has prepared a briefing memorandum for the assistant or undersecretary, outlining an American position on points which may be raised for discussion. After the meeting he will draft a memorandum of the conversation for his superior. He may be drawn into preparation of a position paper to guide American negotiators at the United Nations or at an international conference. He participates in discussions and drafting of legislation to be proposed to Congress by the Department. He may testify before Congressional committees, usually in executive session. He is often called upon to answer letters from members of the House of Representatives or Senate. He gets away from the office at 6 P.M. more often than at the scheduled 5:30 P.M. and sometimes attends evening social engagements at the embassy for business reasons.

Of particular significance to the effective adaptation of American foreign policy to changing world conditions is his participation within the National Security Council structure on questions involving his assigned country. He may prepare drafts of policy papers as the Department works out a position on matters scheduled to come before the National Security Council. Because a consistent body of NSC policy has been accumulating since the National Security Council was created in 1947, his paper is usually a recommendation for amendment of an already approved NSC policy whose implementation was co-ordinated through OCB from 1953 to 1961. During this period he served on Operations Co-ordinating Board interagency working groups to draft specific policies to carry out the intent of the broad National Security Council policies approved by the president. Later he participated in drafting OCB reports on how implementation of policies was progressing in the field, which were forwarded by the OCB to the NSC annually—or on a "spot" basis if trouble arose. On February 18, 1961, President John F. Kennedy revoked the executive order which had created the Operations Coordinating Board. Responsibility for much of the Board's work was assigned to the secretary of state, and to his subordinates, including the desk officer. If the formal organization to co-ordinate implementation of NSC policies disappeared, the function will continue to be performed more informally and the desk officer will still be involved. The desk man's influence at all these points in the policy-making process is the result of his detailed knowledge of an area and his role as a drafting officer. It is well to recall that he is a busy individual, functioning in his daily tasks within the accumulating and accepted framework of NSC policy, from a point low on the totem pole. His close association with the amendment and appraisal of NSC policy may raise a problem, for "agonizing reappraisal" of such policy seems more likely to come from above than from below.

2. Intelligence Analysts

Over three hundred intelligence specialists (including sixty-four on country research desks) in the Bureau of Intelligence and Research (INR) of the Department of State perform tasks essential to the policy-making process, although they are not directly involved in policy making in the same fashion as the country desk officers in the Department's regional bureaus. These intelligence analysts are "the Department's memory and long range weather forecaster." They provide background material relevant to daily operations in the regional bureaus, report and analyze current conditions, interpret trends, and consider future developments in every country of the world except the United States. The intelligence research specialist in the Department of State, a far cry from the sinister black-cloaked operative or the seductive siren sometimes pictured in the public mind, is more Walter Mitty than Herbert Philbrick. He has access to whatever covert information may be available, but he functions at the coffee rather than the cocktail level of intelligence operations. If modern Mata Haris exist, the relation of research analysts to them is too indirect to be of interest. The sad truth of the matter is, although the point is sometimes argued, that the intelligence analysts spend more time reviewing information from overt sources than from any other.

For the first decade after the Second World War, personnel turnover was low, for there was no determined length of tenure. Analysts tended to be college professor types, with research ability and a desire to write, less interested in their personal appearance than in documents and reports. Within the past four years, Wristonization has replaced almost half of the Civil Service intelligence analysts with young Foreign Service officers, mostly FSO 8's. Within the same period, Foreign Service officers have also taken over leadership of the bureau. The bureau director, his deputy, and the directors of the regional and functional offices are now all FSO's. Advancement of civil servants to top intelligence positions has been curtailed if not eliminated. These changes are important. Some observers believe they have led to an upgrading of operational intelligence as opposed to basic intelligence reports and estimates, with unfortunate implications for long-range policy planning. If the old-style intelligence research specialist seemed to belong in an ivory tower, he did not function in one. Neither does the new-style analyst. Intelligence analysts are in touch with world developments on an hour-to-hour basis. They might like to escape the insistence of the pace but are forced by circumstances to meet deadlines.

Intelligence materials flow into the Bureau of Intelligence and Research all day and through the night. Analysts serving as briefing officers participate in a race against time each morning as they summarize the preceding twenty-four hours' take for a 9:15 A.M. deadline, the daily intelligence briefing sessions for the secretary of state and his chief advisers. Ten or twelve analysts assigned briefing duty come into the Department about dawn to draft reports on the areas for which they are responsible. Between 8:20 and 9:00 A.M., they brief the director of Intelligence and Research. He in turn briefs the secretary and other top-level officials at 9:15 A.M. Of course, not all intelligence activities of the bureau proceed at the rapid pace of the briefing operation.

Knowledge of current events is necessary, but vision or foresight is just as important in the formulation of foreign policy. The Department intelligence estimate is prepared with less haste, adds a forward-looking dimension to the thinking of policy makers. Intelligence analysts often work on rough drafts of estimates looking two, five, even ten years ahead. One estimate attempted to envision population and economic conditions of a particular continent in the year 2,000 A.D. Estimates project but do not predict. An estimates group has hammered out more than eighty-seven intelligence estimates for the Department from rough drafts submitted by research specialists. Members of the group include the directors of the bureau's regional and functional offices. Copies of the estimates go to the director of Intelligence and Research, to leading Department policy makers, to members of the Policy Planning Staff, and are forwarded to the Central Intelligence Agency.

The day-to-day work of the bureau for the Department is in the form of intelligence reports and intelligence briefs, covering either regional or functional topics. Reports are five pages or more in length, and may run to several hundred. Briefs are four pages or less. Both bear some resemblance to intelligence estimates but are less rigid in form and are cleared at the office level. They go to officers in the Department or other government agencies. Two periodicals are prepared for Department policy makers and other government officials: *Soviet Affairs* and *International Communism*. These journals are classified and, thus, not available to the public. Some of the most useful information for daily operations in the Department is provided by the Biographic Information Division. Its biographic reports are seldom dull, and contain information on political, economic, and cultural leaders of every country in the world, except the United States. A negotiator at an international conference can be more effective if he knows the people sitting across from him, their fundamental beliefs, their most personal likes and dislikes. If new faces appear in the Cabinet of a foreign government, the country desk officer in the regional bureau may know better how to adapt American policy when he has detailed knowledge of the Cabinet members' backgrounds and attitudes. Intelligence information is in daily use by policy makers throughout the Department, from the country desk officer to the secretary himself. A big user of bureau reports and estimates is the Department's Policy Planning Staff.

The intelligence analysts in the Bureau of Intelligence and Research actually face two ways, serving the internal needs of the Department of State and co-operating with the Washington intelligence community to serve the Central Intelligence Agency and the National Security Council. Department intelligence analysts contribute elements of two Central Intelligence Agency products used extensively by the National Security Council and other government agencies: the national intelligence estimate, and the national intelligence survey. National estimates, parts of which are drafted by the

Department estimates group in the Bureau of Intelligence and Research, are blended through interagency discussion into a finished product which is approved by the United States Intelligence Board, chaired by the director of Central Intelligence, whose members are the heads of the agencies in the Washington intelligence community—that is, the director of Intelligence and Research represents the Department of State. The factual nature of national intelligence surveys requires less interagency discussion of the finished product, and places considerable responsibility upon each participating agency for the substantive detail in its chapters. State's analysts do chapters on political and sociological conditions, and a considerable portion of the material on economic affairs. Each intelligence survey is a comprehensive analysis of information about a foreign country which may be needed for future deliberations of the National Security Council or operations of other government agencies. They afford insight to the formal and informal structure of foreign governments, economies, and social systems.

Stated simply, the function of intelligence research specialists in the Bureau of Intelligence and Research (INR) is to present background, facts, and trends on geographic areas and functional topics so that the formulation and conduct of American foreign and national security policy may rest on a realistic analysis of world conditions. To achieve the effective performance of this function, good relations must be established between intelligence research specialists, action officers in the regional bureaus, and the policy planners. Relations between research, action, and planning officers are fostered at a variety of levels. Intelligence analysts participate in meetings of interagency working groups, alongside country desk officers from the regional bureaus, engaged in implementation of National Security Council policy and in preparing progress reports for the NSC on operations in the field. The INR division chiefs attend office directors' staff and policy meetings in the regional bureaus; INR office directors, the assistant secretaries' staff and policy meetings. A special assistant to the director of Intelligence and Research participates regularly in discussions of the Policy Planning Staff.

Policy makers may become emotionally bound up in their decisions and defend policies long after they have served their purpose. Intelligence analysts should have no interest in defending a policy because it exists, and should pull no punches if they feel it runs counter to fundamental needs or trends. There is a fine line between policy making and analysis of the effect of policy; the latter may influence the former to such an extent that analysis—to all intents and purposes—becomes policy making. To the young Foreign Service officer serving as an intelligence analyst on policy committees with fellow Foreign Service officers from the regional bureaus, this will be a provocative line, over which he is likely to step on occasion with peril to the proper performance of the intelligence function.

3. Policy Planners

Country desk officers and their superiors—office directors and assistant secretaries—in the regional bureaus of the Department of State are hounded by the nagging duties of daily operations. Intelligence research specialists are "objective collectors and projectors of facts" on foreign areas, pledged to abstain from partisan intervention in the policy-making process—but sometimes falling off the wagon. In establishing the Policy Planning Staff on May 7, 1947, Secretary of State George C. Marshall asked that it be staffed by "highly qualified thinkers" who were not to be "deluged with small stuff" by daily operations or time-consuming research. Its ten members were to integrate future needs with present realities, and lead the nation toward its long-term goals and interests. Disengaged from routine policy making and research, they were to help the secretary of state chart a course between the passing shoals without losing sight of strategy for the years ahead. This was a big order, and not all secretaries have asked that it be filled.

The first director of the Policy Planning Staff was George F. Kennan, a man of ideas, adept as a discussion leader. His successors have been Paul Nitze, Robert Bowie, and Gerard Smith. Kennan's containment thesis, first expressed in despatches from Moscow during 1946, later delivered as a lecture at the National War College, and finally given public expression in the Mr. X article, "The Sources of Soviet Conduct," *Foreign Affairs*, July, 1947, was the accepted frame of reference for the policy planners in their early discussions. But the static concept of "containment" was not considered sacrosanct. By 1949, in a preparatory paper for the Council of Foreign Ministers' meeting scheduled for Paris in late May and June, Kennan was proposing carefully phased disengagement of East and West as a resolution of the German problem. This was the same thesis he was to advance publicly over the facilities of the British Broadcasting Corporation in 1957. As a policy planner who served with Kennan on the Policy Planning Staff in 1949 has observed, "The only startling thing about Kennan's 1957 proposals was their familiarity." Rightly or wrongly, Secretary of State Dean Acheson must have overruled Kennan's "disengagement" thesis in 1949, although Kennan was a top expert on the Soviet Union. There is no question of the right of a secretary of state to rule against a recommendation of his chief policy planner. The point is that in 1949 the Policy Planning Staff discussions were still freewheeling affairs which challenged the assumptions and goals of American foreign policy.

Secretary Acheson said on April 25, 1949, in testifying on the role of the Policy Planning Staff before the House Committee on Foreign Affairs:

> There are many plans which were formulated and on which the operating people are going ahead. With the passage of time, such plans become no longer useful. However, an operating fellow is not likely to see that. He just drives in every morning at quarter to nine and carries on policy. He may seem to be getting into hot water, but that just calls for more courage and determination. Mr. Kennan is sitting back there and says: 'This thing is outmoded. We shouldn't be doing this anymore. This is a waste of time. Do it differently, or scrap it, or change the whole thing.' He is both forewarner and foreplanner on problems, and he is the critic. He says: 'What we are doing was fine when we started, but it is no longer a proper answer to the thing we are dealing with.'

Two and one-half months after the creation of the Policy Planning Staff, the 80th Congress by Public Law 253 established the National Security Council (July 26, 1947). The broader and more intricate NSC machinery was clumsy compared to the tightly-knit Policy Planning Staff. The historic primacy of the Department of State in foreign affairs buttressed the influence of the policy planners and tended to inhibit development of the National Security Council system. During the first Eisenhower administration the National Security Council gathered momentum and emerged as the dominant factor in government-wide policy making. The role of the Policy Planning Staff as a sort of grand adviser and trouble shooter for the secretary of state gradually shifted toward the more routine procedures of monitoring preparation of Department position papers for consideration by the NSC Planning Board and briefing the secretary for meetings of the National Security Council. The secretary called for fewer "think pieces" on long-range requirements.

Through the years since 1947 a sizable body of NSC policy has accumulated, stating the basic assumptions and goals of American policy for more than thirty areas—individual nations, blocs, or continents—and on some twelve functional topics. Of necessity the assumptions and goals of these policy papers possessed an internal consistency so that the assorted NSC policies did not work at cross-purposes. For the sake of practicality, any alternatives proposed on individual problems coming before the National Security Council for discussion tended to be conceived within the approved framework of NSC policy. As one participant has pointed out, "Today, NSC papers spend much time in saying expand this program, better that one, do more in this field. Attention is diverted from what we are really trying to accomplish. Agencies try to get statements in NSC papers to justify adding on to programs. The papers are a means of furthering little plans." Any serious challenge to assumptions or goals would threaten the policy structure so patiently constructed over a thirteen-year period. These developments have reduced the flexibility of thinking on the Policy Planning Staff and affected the maneuverability possible in the formulation of either American foreign policy or national security policy. The process has taken place so slowly and naturally that some present policy planners may hardly be aware of any significant difference in the scope of their functions—or they are good enough soldiers not to admit it.

Department Order No. 393 of May 7, 1947, which established the Policy Planning Staff, stated its major functions as follows:

1. Formulating and developing, for the consideration and approval of appropriate officials of the Department, long-term programs for the achievement of US foreign policy objectives.
2. Anticipating problems which the Department may encounter in the discharge of its mission.
3. Undertaking studies and preparing reports on broad politico-military problems.
4. Examining problems and developments affecting US foreign policy in order to evaluate the adequacy of current policy and making advisory recommendations on them.
5. Co-ordinating planning activities within the Department of State.

This was said to constitute as good a statement of Policy Planning Staff functions in 1960 as it did in 1947.

Questions may be placed on the agenda of the Policy Planning Staff at the request of the secretary of state to resolve a purely Departmental problem or they may stem from matters discussed at some level within the National Security Council structure. Consideration of questions may be initiated by the director or one of the policy planners. The policy planners have dealt with every major problem confronting American foreign policy in the post-Second World War era: the Marshall Plan, NATO, Point Four, the Berlin airlift, Korea, SEATO, the first summit conference, peaceful use of atomic energy, Suez, the Hungarian revolt, proposed additional summit conferences, and the German problem. Staff members meet regularly for policy discussion. They often consult top Department officials or American ambassadors home on leave; occasionally, former staff directors or outside experts. Drafts of Policy Planning Staff papers are discussed with country desk officers and intelligence analysts, and circulated around the Department for review. As suggestions and criticisms are received, the papers are redrafted, finally submitted to the secretary or thrown into the National Security Council hopper. Of the staff's membership in 1959, four were Foreign Service officers, four had served for years in the Department or related agencies, only two were "outsiders." Were fresh ideas harder to come by in 1960 than in 1950? The planners were renamed the Policy Planning Council early in 1961. There is little doubt that the policy planners continue to perform a function important to formulation of policy and to the conduct of American foreign relations. Whether their plans are leading policy makers toward an effective adjustment to a brave new world—in which the United States will continue to play a secure and prosperous part—only the future can tell.

4. Legislative Liaison Specialists

One of the harsh facts of life to which policy makers in the executive branch of government have had to resign themselves after the Second World War is an increasing legislative interest in the nature of American foreign policy. The power of the purse, in an age when conduct of foreign relations seems to require more than occasional quiet conversations between professional diplomats, has enabled the legislative camel to get its nose well within the executive tent. If the checks and balances written into the Constitution by the Founding Fathers are an invitation for conflict between the executive and legislative branches, the role of the legislative liaison specialists of the Department of State is—at least—to civilize the struggle by fostering accommodation between contending parties on matters affecting foreign policy. If legislative liaison specialists serve as one of many channels through which Congressional ideas on current questions of foreign policy can flow into the Department, they are not dedicated to seeing that these ideas, often in conflict and reflecting differences of opinion within the legislative branch, are incorporated into foreign policy formulated in the Department or in the government-wide machinery of the National Security Council. Rather, such information tends to set limits upon Department policy makers and indicates problems they will face in legislative implementation of the executive machine's foreign policy program. One could hardly expect more. The legislative branch is not organized, nor could it easily be organized, in such a way as to sustain initiative in the international field, to pay constant attention to foreign policy questions, or to contribute integrated and balanced directives to the policy machine. This statement is not to imply that committee reports, special studies by Congressional consultants, and speeches by members of the House or Senate do not from time to time exert influence upon executive-branch policy makers.

Congress has traditionally discouraged large Congressional-relations staffs in government departments or agencies. The legislative branch does not want to increase its problem of competing with the executive branch in the field of foreign policy by appropriations with which the Department of State could influence Congressional voting patterns. The Congressional Relations Area in the Department is modest in size, with only twenty-three employees, over half of whom perform secretarial duties. Headed by an assistant secretary who spends most of his time "on the Hill," the legislative liaison staff includes a deputy assistant secretary, a deputy assistant secretary for mutual security affairs, four regional or functional legislative management officers, and two or three additional members who serve in the legislative reports and non-legislative requests sections.

As one assistant secretary of state for Congressional relations has explained, the legislative liaison specialists perform four functions, two of which are internal, two, external. Within the executive branch of government, they participate in the formulation of the administration's foreign affairs legislative program. In carrying out this function they co-operate with bureaus and areas of the Department, with other departments and agencies, and with the Bureau of the Budget in the Executive Office of the President. Also within the executive branch, the legislative specialists participate in conferences on non-legislative policy decisions important enough to be of interest to members of

Congress. In performing both internal functions, they are in part the representatives of the legislative interest, in greater measure the advisers on how Department interests can be accommodated with Congressional views, enough anyway to insure passage of a program. There are times, certainly, when the Congressional factor is weighed less heavily than other considerations by Department policy makers, and one can sometimes be thankful for their courage at these moments; but even in this situation policy makers have some understanding of the Congressional position—although they may believe their own decision to be more in the national interest. In external relations with Congress, the legislative specialists serve as a funnel into the Department for Congressional requests which are fanned out to experts for reply, and serve as a funnel out of the Department for information to members of Congress and their constituents concerning either legislative or non-legislative questions related to the Department or foreign policy. Also in their external relations with Congress, the legislative specialists encourage Department leaders to consult with members of the legislative branch on foreign policy questions. The proper execution of the information and consultation functions is as important to the Department as to Congress; for no policy can exist for long unless both parties understand and accept it, rather than having it imposed by either one upon the other.

Several variables establish the Department's relations with Congress at any given time, for example the personality and past experience of the secretary of state or his assistant secretary for Congressional relations, the political parties in control of the executive or legislative branches, the centralization or dispersion of power on foreign policy matters in the House and Senate, and the increase and decrease of world tensions. Since 1949 there have been assistant secretaries of at least four types, each representing a different climate of executive-legislative relations. There was the substantive expert type, exemplified by Ernest Gross, the first assistant secretary for Congressional relations; the legislative professional staff type, represented by Jack McFall, who had long years of experience on the staff of a Congressional committee before appointment as assistant secretary; the Congressional type, represented by Thruston Morton and Robert Hill, both of whom had served in the House of Representatives before appointment; and the personal representative type, of whom William B. Macomber, Jr., may be considered characteristic, with experience as a legislative assistant to a senator but assuming his post as assistant secretary after several years' service as a special assistant to the secretary of state. The number of general briefing sessions for interested members of Congress, special breakfast meetings with new members of the House or Senate, or discussions with consultative subcommittees of the House Foreign Affairs or Senate Foreign Relations committees may vary according to the political complexion of the Congress and the temper of the times. A gradual dispersion of power among and within Congressional committees has led the legislative liaison specialists to work increasingly through the top leadership of the Senate and House. The ability and vigor of Senator J. William Fulbright, who assumed chairmanship of the still powerful Senate Foreign Relations Committee at the age of fifty-three, may retard further decentralization of power; but even he may find the process impossible to reverse.

The legislative liaison specialists in the Department of State, whatever variables may alter the specific approaches, devices, or techniques they employ, interpret Congress to the Department, and the Department to Congress. They have shown little disposition and perhaps are in no position to introduce fundamental alterations in the relations or roles of the legislative and executive branches in the policy-making process. One might wish that some progress could be made toward development of regular consultative procedures—honest-to-goodness exchanges of opinions and ideas—between the Department and bipartisan foreign affairs leaders in Congress, without infringing in any way upon executive responsibility for policy making. Such progress would involve growth in self-restraint among legislators. It would necessitate willingness by the Department to explore undecided questions with legislators rather than conducting briefings on decisions already made.

The assistant secretary, his deputies, and the regional and functional legislative management officers serve as a reasonably efficient two-way conduit between the Congress and the Department. Without such a staff of legislative specialists, serving to communicate and co-ordinate between the executive and legislative branches of government, implementation of a legislative program and a general foreign policy with public support would be difficult to achieve.

5. Public Information Officers

The Department of State conducts foreign relations in a fish bowl, both by intent and necessity. American action and policy positions can be explained directly to the peoples of the world, bypassing their governments in some instances, through news coverage of the Department by global press services and correspondents for foreign news outlets, including *Le Monde*, the London *Times*, and even Tass. The secretary of state's "weekly" press conference is a dramatic adventure in public diplomacy overseas, however one judges the results.[3] His words are analyzed by diplomats in foreign ministries, by the world's editorial writers and commentators, and by intellectuals of every nation in their easy or uneasy chairs. The secretary's press conference comments also have domestic importance. Under a democratic system of government, there is need for public information. The Department of State has no built-in interest group supporting its policies, no rubber-stamp Congress to back its legislative policies or appropriate funds for its programs. Approval of the secretary's conduct of foreign policy must be secured from the public and the Congress in the "market place of ideas." The president's weekly press conference is, of course, a supplemental plea for public support, for almost half of the president's remarks are in response to foreign policy questions. If the press conferences are attention getters, providing the glamor for telling the American foreign policy story to the people of the world and to the domestic public, including ordinary members of Congress who concentrate in fields other than foreign affairs, a variety of types of Department information specialists backstop the press conference and disseminate additional information. They initiated a follow-through in greater depth to explain the issues that come to the fore in the public mind, resulting from the flurry of discussion in the fast media—press, radio, and television—kicked off by the press conferences.

Key figures in preparing the secretary of state for the press conference, which, when held, packs some 225 correspondents into the Department's auditorium, are the assistant secretary for public affairs and the director of the Office of News. Assisted by their staffs and public information advisers attached to regional and functional bureaus, these two men attempt to foresee the major questions the secretary will be asked at the press conference. Substantive policy officers, from the desk through the assistant secretary level, are drawn into the process of drafting or clearing statements in answer to the projected questions. These statements are individually reviewed by

[3] Some of the material in this section is based upon the author's "Thank You, Mr. Secretary," *Foreign Service Journal*, August, 1957.

the secretary the night before the press conference. The assistant secretary for public affairs and the director of the Office of News also check the proposed statements. The following morning, just before meeting the reporters, the three spend an hour discussing the most likely questions and tentative answers. During the forty-minute news conference that follows, the secretary, subjected to a withering cross fire of examination by the press, is on his own, and uses no notes unless he makes a brief introductory statement. Newsmen who cover the Department regularly, who have received background briefings through the years from policy experts on every conceivable problem, are able to make quick assessments of the secretary's statements, note shifts in emphasis or policy, and report to the American public and the world in a matter of minutes after the conference closes.

Plodding along at a quieter pace, reaching a narrower segment of the public, are the public information officers attached to the Department's Office of Public Services, also part of the domain of the assistant secretary of state for public affairs. These specialists maintain relations with major national nongovernmental organizations, like Rotary International or the League of Women Voters. They provide speakers for groups desiring to schedule foreign policy discussions, answer letters from thousands of citizens requesting information or giving advice on foreign affairs, and publish a wide range of pamphlets for public distribution to groups or individuals interested in contemporary foreign policy. Four organization liaison specialists deal on a daily basis with representatives of national organizations or interest groups in an exchange of information and ideas that sometimes leads to an accommodation between the views of the Department and the organizations concerned. Two other public liaison specialists handle over sixteen hundred requests made to the Department each year for speakers, and manage to find officers in the Department who are willing to fill over a thousand speaking engagements in addition to the performance of their regular duties. Three young Foreign Service officers and some four Civil Service specialists handle over a hundred thousand letters per year from individual citizens, asking questions or wishing to express opinions on foreign policy, addressed to congressmen, the secretary of state, and the president, which are channeled through the public correspondence section of the Office of Public Services. A weekly analysis of this mail is forwarded to public affairs advisers in regional and functional bureaus, and included in the secretary of state's weekend reading folder. Other information specialists write or edit pamphlets and publications for public distribution. About three hundred current titles are available. Some ten thousand individuals and organizations have asked to receive one or more of the Department publications regularly. This is a small number out of 180 million Americans.

Servicing an even more special clientele are the historians and researchers in the Bureau of Public Affairs' Historical Office. This staff prepares historical narratives that set contemporary policies in perspective, publishes diplomatic documents, and assists private researchers or those of other government agencies analyzing past or present policies of the United States. Collections of documents on international conferences are released for ready reference by organization discussion leaders, newsmen, and students of foreign policy. Invaluable source material for research by lawyers, courts, professors, and Department officers is contained in the Historical Office's *Foreign Relations of the United States*, published from 1861 through the early 1940s. State Department files are generally open for study of detailed aspects of policy through 1929. More than a thousand individuals request information or access to Department records each year, and specialists review over eighteen thousand typewritten pages per year based on such research.

The primary function of the Department's public information specialists is to tell what American policies are and why they have been adopted. Such information is important and provides the basis for discussion. National organizations such as the Foreign Policy Association, the American Association for the United Nations, and the Council on Foreign Relations also perform an informational function. These organizations have an additional obligation to raise issues and stimulate discussion by presenting alternative policies and justifications. This is a function the Department's information officers cannot perform. In view of this limit upon the role of the public information specialists, government information programs must be kept in balance with those of private agencies. When government funds are too small, the Department finds it difficult to keep the public adequately informed as to what our foreign policies are. If they are too large, public opinion might be overwhelmed and consideration of policy alternatives cease. There is a delicate balance between too much and too little.

6. Public Opinion Analysts

In the "model T days" of American diplomacy, whose closing date can be argued by historians, Department of State policy makers rattled over the bumpy roads of foreign relations more as sight-seers than men of action, lost in the dust of the British Rolls-Royce which set the pace in foreign affairs. They didn't travel far—mostly to Latin America—or do much after they arrived there, but they got good gas mileage and the cost of upkeep was low. The machine they drove was simple, without much horsepower, but the load was light. The roads sometimes were muddy, the visibility restricted by rain seeping through the side curtains, but members of the small, expert elite driving the car putted along at a sedate pace, pointing out an occasional accident along the route but seldom giving more than a bit of first aid to the injured. They rarely excited the attention of the broad membership of Congress or the general public. If restless outlanders threw stones from time to time, they usually aimed at the powerful Rolls-Royce rather than the old model T.

Those days are long since gone. The sleek black Cadillac that symbolizes contemporary American diplomacy, with its highly complex policy-making mechanism, draws critical attention at home and abroad. The idea of total diplomacy evolved after the Second World War, involving heavy expenditure for overseas military and economic assistance and a combat-ready defense force in time of peace, has made foreign policy every American's business, whether he be well informed concerning the facts of international life or not. As Secretary of State George Catlett Marshall once said, "No policy—foreign or domestic—can succeed without public support." Today there is no department or agency in government more sensitive to American public opinion than the Department of State. Public opinion analysts—eight professionals and four secretarial assistants, all civil servants—on the Public Opinion Studies Staff of the Bureau of Public Affairs provide daily reports on the state of that opinion to decision makers and policy planners, from the country desk level to the secretary of state, as well as to American Foreign Service officers and United States Information Agency representatives serving at posts overseas.[4]

[4] Much of the material in this section first appeared in the author's "The Public Studies Division of the Department of State: Public Opinion Analysts in the Formulation and Conduct of American Foreign Policy," *The Western Political Quarterly*, December, 1957.

Public opinion specialists do not manufacture public opinion; they measure it, with information gathered from many sources. They seek out public expressions on foreign policy questions by members of Congress, leaders of national organizations, or pressure groups. They review opinions expressed in letters from the general public processed by the public correspondence section of the Office of Public Services. No one of these three sources is an accurate reflection of general public opinion, of what the common garden variety of citizen, old John Q. Public himself, is thinking. The most useful indicators of "attentive public" opinion on a day-to-day basis are representative editorial writers, columnists, and commentators in the press and periodicals, and on radio and television. Specialists on the Public Opinion Studies Staff have found that major schools of thought are represented in a press sample that includes the *New York Times, New York Herald Tribune, New York Journal-American* (Hearst), *Philadelphia Inquirer, Baltimore Sun, Chicago Tribune, Washington Post and Times Herald, Washington Star,* and *Washington News* (Scripps-Howard). Further analysis shows that material from ninety-one other newspapers, forty-eight periodicals, and twenty-four radio and television broadcasts may be "a little stronger here and there one way or another" but is essentially the same.

Probably the most accurate means for periodically measuring the thinking of the general public remains the oft-maligned nationwide opinion poll. Such polls have shown that daily analyses of representative news sources do reflect public opinion on most issues. The results of Dr. George Gallup's polls are released to the Public Opinion Studies Staff at the same time as to the press. The public opinion specialists have discovered that the Minnesota Poll, sponsored by Cowles Publications and appearing each Sunday in the *Minneapolis Tribune,* comes close to indicating public opinion throughout the nation on questions it covers. Analysis of polls indicates that sectional differences of opinion on foreign policy are less significant than sometimes imagined. From 1943 to 1957 the Public Studies Division contracted with leading university public opinion centers for a half-dozen polls per year on some twelve to twenty questions of interest to policy makers. An inadvertent leak of poll figures to the press through public information officers in the International Cooperation Administration aroused Congressional discontent. The polling contract with the National Opinion Research Center at the University of Chicago was cancelled by the Department. Knowledge of the relationship of polling results to other sources of public opinion acquired over a fourteen-year period will enable specialists to project what polling results might be, even though polls are not conducted for a brief time. There is no current interest among top Department officials in restoring the poll as a device for sampling public opinion, but its loss will be felt as issues change and projection becomes more difficult (the polls contracted by the Department were costing no more than $43,200 per year at the time of cancellation). Congressional opposition to the polls stemmed from fear that the executive branch would use poll figures to influence opinion so that public pressure would be brought on Congress for appropriations to implement programs with strong public support, a strange problem in the world's leading democracy.

Public opinion specialists are more interested in what ordinary citizens think for determining the broad limits of policy than for obtaining new ideas to guide policy makers. They are more interested in reactions to present policies than in suggestions for new ones. Within the policy machine, even this limited interest in public opinion is more likely to be displayed at the assistant secretary level and up than at lower levels on the policy-making ladder. As one busy country desk officer phrased it, commenting on his use of the daily opinion summary, "I'd rather ask my wife what she thinks." On the other hand, these summaries reach the secretary of state's office—are prepared for him in even greater detail when he travels abroad—and go to top advisers of the president on the White House staff. The daily opinion summary, as well as weekly, monthly, and area summaries, are valuable to the executive branch for comprehending the public mind. They can hardly be considered channels through which broad forward-looking ideas might cause redirection of foreign policy assumptions or goals. The endless flow of paper across Department desks, and a host of conflicting considerations that influence decision makers, minimizes the impact of Public Opinion Studies Staff reports upon American foreign policy.

7. The Missing Specialists

This rapid survey of the role of six types of specialists in the policy-making process, from among whom ideas challenging the assumptions or goals of American policy seemed most likely to come, suggests absence of specialists in the government capable of performing this critical function today. The National Security Council structure, with its accumulating body of consistent policy, makes penetration of challenging ideas from the Congress, or from a private citizen like George Kennan, difficult indeed. Specialists within the machine, all of whom are busily carrying out important tasks, seem to be trapped by the machine's inflexibility, and to have lost room for maneuver in considering policy questions. All the specialists and their superiors are working under pressure. Thinking-time is at a premium, if it can be said to exist at all. New ideas are few and far between. In a changing world, failure to provide a continuing challenge to all aspects of American foreign or national security policy, or failure to look ahead adaptively, is to court catastrophe. The old techniques of diplomacy, our basic assumptions about the conduct of human relations at the international level, may not be adequate to confront the needs of the present; almost certainly, not the imperatives of the future. Lacking from the present machinery, excellent as it is in some respects, are specialists in new and challenging ideas, men with an interest in and time for intelligent and practical forward planning.

The government is pouring millions of dollars into theoretical research in the physical sciences, billions into the application of such research findings to practical projects as Vanguard, Thor, Polaris, Jupiter, and Pioneer. There is missing from the government and among its leaders comparable recognition of the value of theoretical and applied research in the social and behavioral fields as related to the formulation and conduct of American foreign policy, to the proper blending of present necessities and long-range needs. If America is to survive the changes wrought in the world by developments in the physical sciences, if American democracy is to be adapted and defended in parlous times of social readjustment, the president may find it necessary to develop a program for the stimulation of theoretical and applied research on social and behavioral problems. He may need to authorize application in limited areas and to limited functional problems of foreign policy some of the best working-hypotheses that researchers can evolve.

In a world hurtling toward destruction or salvation, or struggling in a morass of confusion, America will do well to draw on its best resources—in social disciplines as well as physical—looking to the far reaches of the various subject-matter fields to the men in the front of the search for knowledge. Their ideas could be channeled to specialists in the fields of international relations, foreign policy, and government, employed, probably on a rotation basis, within the policy machine. These specialists, possessing both academic and government experience, could discuss, integrate, and supervise the experimental application of basic principles of social and behavioral knowledge in a forward-looking way from within the National Security Council framework. They could search for ideas from any source that would enable them to recommend to the president and lower-level policy makers the "calculated risks" worth taking, in light of knowledge available, to assure an American way of life and participation of America as a partner among nations in the centuries that lie ahead.

The problem is to find means of injecting challenging ideas into the policy machine, to escape the treadmill approach to foreign policy problems, to relate the present to the future. A practical government official overstated the case in 1959 when he said, "There is *no* long-range thinking on policy questions in Washington at the present time." But the long-range thinking that does occur—even in 1961—may not be the best that could be done. What the present author recommends as a partial remedy to this situation is the establishment of a Social and Behavioral Research Board within the National Security Council structure. Such a Research Board would add a much needed dimension to policy making. Subsidiary Social and Behavioral Research Planning Staffs would function within the five principal agencies already participating in the National Security Council structure (the Department of State, the Department of Defense, the United States Information Agency, the International Cooperation Administration, and the Central Intelligence Agency). Each such planning staff would be backstopped within its agency by an Office of Social and Behavioral Research. This particular organizational structure may not be the best that can be designed, but the idea it represents is vital. It is possible that survival of our way of life and a useful role for America at the turn of the century depend not only on what we now know but do not fully comprehend and are not using, but also on what we can learn to know—if we show determination to stimulate imaginative social and behavioral research, and have an efficient mechanism for relating its findings to the formulation and conduct of American foreign policy.

17: UNITED STATES PARTICIPATION IN THE UNITED NATIONS

Lincoln P. Bloomfield

In its more than fifteen years of participation in the United Nations the United States has constructed what is without question the most elaborate policy-making and policy-executing structure of any of the members of the organization. In fact, the administrative procedure which results in the co-ordinated assertion of US policy in the hundreds of UN meetings each year is in many ways unique even within the framework of our own government's "arrangement-making" process, as one observer has called it.

Only the result of American diplomacy in the United Nations is visible to the naked eye. Like an iceberg, seven eighths of its bulk is beneath the surface. To comprehend the place of UN diplomacy in the larger scheme of American foreign policy, a twofold approach is necessary.

In the first place what are the facts about the way in which the US Government is organized and staffed to participate in the UN system? For students of the diplomatic process and of public administration alike, this constitutes the "bone structure" of the subject. But as students of both subjects well know, formal organization reflects only a part of the story. An understanding of the formal organization needs to be enriched with insights into the substratum of informal operations and relationships. In much the same relationship, formal assertions of public policy acquire meaning for the student of diplomacy only when it is possible to set the words in a realistic historical and political perspective. Normally this is the task of the diplomatic historian. But even this close to the events, some useful things can be said.

This chapter therefore consists of an examination of the formal structure of US participation, followed by some more impressionistic observations about what might be called the institutional or bureaucratic background for such participation during the postwar years.[1]

THE ORGANIZATION OF THE US GOVERNMENT FOR PARTICIPATION IN THE UN SYSTEM

The United Nations, under its Charter, to which the United States and, in 1961, ninety-eight other nations were signatories, is a center for harmonizing the acts of nations in the maintenance of international peace and security, and for the development of friendly relations among nations, and the achievement of international co-operation in the economic and social fields.

The United Nations deals in the first instance with a wide range of international political problems involving security, regulation of armaments, peaceful settlement of disputes, and peaceful change of the international status of territories, all of which are of major concern to the United States as a leading world power. In addition to political and security problems, there is a host of complex functional problems which cut across national boundaries. The self-interest of nations, including our own, requires international co-operation in order to deal with them constructively. Economic, social, educational, human rights, and related international problems are dealt with by the United Nations and the specialized agencies that together make up what is here referred to as the UN system.

In practice, the United Nations has acquired major significance as an agency for influencing world opinion and for openly combating the political warfare and propaganda of world communism. At the same time, it was proved an important center for diplomatic negotiation.

Multilateral diplomacy is complementary to bilateral diplomacy, not a rival to it. The United Nations is an important means to achieve broad foreign policy ends to which the United States is committed. The American national interest is served by a proper use of this instrument and by our effectiveness in preventing its misuse by others.

For these reasons, the Congress has provided a body of legislation under which the executive branch develops and carries out policies

[1] For a detailed exposition of the content of United States policy toward the United Nations, see Lincoln P. Bloomfield, *The United Nations and US Foreign Policy* (Boston, 1960).

and programs through international organizations to further the interests of the United States.

THE UNITED NATIONS SYSTEM

In the United Nations proper, the representative organ is the General Assembly, which meets annually for approximately three months and may hold special sessions. All member nations participate with equal voice and vote.

The Security Council has eleven members including the five permanent members, who have the right to veto important matters. The Economic and Social Council consists of eighteen nations, the great powers always having been re-elected. Until 1961 the Trusteeship Council has had fourteen members among whom the five permanent members of the Security Council were always represented. The Disarmament Commission has the same membership as the General Assembly, by decision of the 1958 Assembly Session. The Military Staff Committee consists of military representatives of the "big five" chiefs of staff, including our own. All members are entitled to sit on the Interim Committee. Temporary UN bodies include the Collective Measures Committee and Peace Observation Commission (fourteen members each), and the Committee on the Peaceful Uses of Outer Space (twenty-four members).

UN operating programs include the Technical Assistance Administration, Korean Reconstruction Agency, Relief and Works Agency for Palestine Refugees in the Near East, the Children's Fund, the United Nations High Commission for Refugees, and the United Nations Special Fund.

Under the Economic and Social Council are eight functional commissions—Transport and Communication, Statistical, Population, Social, Human Rights, Status of Women, Narcotics, and International Commodity Trade—plus four regional economic commissions (Europe, Asia, Latin America, and Africa). The United States has been elected to membership in all but the Economic Commission for Africa.

The International Court of Justice, sitting at The Hague, consists of fifteen judges elected by the General Assembly and Security Council. It has jurisdiction in cases brought by agreement of states and renders advisory legal opinions at the request of the Assembly or Security Council.

The UN Secretariat, with personnel drawn from member nations, serves all organs of the United Nations.

Outside the United Nations but considered part of the UN system are the twelve specialized agencies—intergovernmental bodies in technical fields where what might be called functional problems cross national and regional boundaries and require co-operative efforts. These are the Food and Agriculture Organization (FAO), World Health Organization (WHO), International Monetary Fund (IMF), International Bank for Reconstruction and Development (IBRD), International Finance Corporation (IFC), Universal Postal Union (UPU), International Civil Aviation Organization (ICAO), International Labor Organization (ILO), World Meteorological Organization (WMO), International Telecommunication Union (ITU), Intergovernmental Maritime Consultative Organization (IMCO), and the United Nations Educational, Scientific and Cultural Organization (UNESCO).

The specialized agencies are autonomous and directed by their governing bodies, on which the United States and other member governments sit. Through agreements between these agencies and the Economic and Social Council, as prescribed in the UN Charter, their programs and administration are reviewed and co-ordinated by the United Nations.

The International Atomic Energy Agency (IAEA) is also an autonomous intergovernmental organization, but it is related to the United Nations through an agreement with the General Assembly.

Outside the UN system but performing functions of concern to the United Nations are such *ad hoc* intergovernmental consultative arrangements as those under the General Agreement on Tariffs and Trade (GATT) and the Intergovernmental Committee on European Migration (ICEM), as well as the ten-nation disarmament commission established by the big four Foreign Ministers in August, 1959.

United States Chain of Command

The president is responsible for the formulation, execution, and co-ordination of foreign policies. As chief executive, as commander in chief, and as chairman of the National Security Council, he presides over the process of defining US objectives in the world and coordinating activities to achieve those objects.

In directing US participation in international organizations the president under his constitutional authority determines policy and designates representatives and agencies for its execution.

The National Security Council advises the president as prescribed by statute and acts on major policy problems arising in the United Nations in the same way as with other foreign policy issues.

The secretary of state is principal adviser to the president in the determination and execution of US foreign policy and is charged with the responsibility for all the activities of the State Department. In directing US relations with international organizations, the secretary performs his functions in the same fashion as he does in all fields of international relations.

The assistant secretary for international organization affairs is one of the seven assistant secretaries with action responsibilities[2] who, in the words of the Hoover Commission, have "responsibility for decisions within clearly defined limits" and "serve as focal points of contact between the Department and the overseas and international organization missions in both substantive and administrative matters." The Hoover Commission described the assistant secretary for international organization affairs as "in charge of relationships with international organizations, including the United Nations and its affiliated organizations" and as "the channel for instructions to and from United States representatives and delegations at the United Nations" as well as to certain other international organizations and conferences. We shall see in the next section that this plan has been somewhat modified in practice.

The assistant secretary for international organization affairs acts as the headquarters office, so to speak, for the US representative to the United Nations and US delegates to other UN agencies (and some non-UN bodies). He insures that these representatives of the United States follow national policy.

To furnish this staff support, the assistant secretary supervises the Bureau of International Organization Affairs, which provides three services:

(1) It co-ordinates the policy views and technical requirements originating in other parts of the Department and other agencies, so that US representatives in international organizations can be sure they are always stating consistent and unified US positions.

(2) It develops US policy on questions that are peculiarly mul-

[2] The five regional bureaus, the Bureau of International Organization Affairs, and the Bureau of Economic Affairs.

tilateral in nature, that cut across the bilateral functions of the geographic units and the specialized subject units in other agencies, and that no other office is staffed to handle.

(3) It assembles in one unit the knowledge and experience the United States has built up in the field of multilateral diplomacy so that the government can most efficiently prepare itself to uphold its interests in international organizations.

Thus, in the first category, where another part of the Department of State or another government agency is responsible for relations with one area or subject, the Bureau furnishes policy guidance for use in international organizations in terms of precedents, relation to UN matters, parliamentary problems, UN personalities, etc.

In the second category, the Bureau of International Organization Affairs has the primary policy responsibility for specialized multilateral questions. Examples of these are political matters of an interregional nature (which in the United Nations has meant such items as admission of new members and counterstrategy to Soviet propaganda charges), collective security preparations, review of the UN Charter, parliamentary tactics that have been proved best by experience in specific UN agencies, international secretariat problems, operations of the UN trusteeship system and problems of non-self-governing territories, world health, social welfare, narcotics, human rights, interpretation of articles of the UN Charter, international budgets, and the UN aspects of arms regulation and control.

In the third category, the Bureau of International Organization Affairs contributes to the process of policy-making technical knowledge in the field of multilateral diplomacy. This means chiefly the political and organizational work of UN bodies—questions of credentials, elections (balancing of interests, blocs, and geographic distribution in the membership and officers of multilateral bodies), budgets, secretariat organization and practices, agenda and procedural problems, and the relation of other multilateral bodies to the United Nations.

The US representative to the United Nations is, as prescribed by Executive Order 10108,[3] the Chief of the United States Mission to the United Nations (USUN). In addition, President Eisenhower in 1953 appointed Henry Cabot Lodge, the US representative to the United Nations, to be a member of his Cabinet. This was the first

[3] 15 Fed. Reg. 757.

time such a designation had been made, and President Kennedy continued this practice.

The mission includes other US representatives and deputy representatives (*i.e.*, those serving in the United Nations Economic and Social Council and its commissions, the Trusteeship Council, Disarmament Commission, Military Staff Committee, etc.) and the deputy representative to the United Nations, who is also deputy chief of mission and deputy representative on the Security Council. There is also a second deputy for the Security Council.

The US representative co-ordinates "the activities of the Mission in carrying out the instructions of the President transmitted either by the Secretary of State or by other means of transmission as directed by the President." Thus he is responsible for directing US activities at UN headquarters, administers the US Mission, is the chief US representative in the UN Security Council, chairman or acting chairman of the US delegation to the General Assembly, representative *ex officio* and principal US spokesman in any UN body at the UN headquarters, and principal negotiator with the UN Secretariat and representatives in New York of other member governments.

The US Mission to the United Nations, while unique in many ways, is comparable to a major American embassy abroad in terms of its normal working relation with the State Department. Just as the Bureau of European Affairs is the home desk for our London embassy, so the Bureau of International Organization Affairs is the home desk for the United States Mission to the United Nations. American ambassadors in both cases are appointed by and responsible to the president. The appropriate assistant secretary of state, acting for the secretary, is in both cases responsible for insuring that they are instructed and advised, that such instructions and advice represent the co-ordinated views of the government (including where necessary the decisions of the secretary, the National Security Council, and the president), and for receiving the information they report and seeing that it is used in Washington. Under special circumstances, the head of the US Mission, like other ambassadors, occasionally receives his instructions directly from the secretary of state or the president. The head of the US Mission takes an active part in the formulation of US policy and tactics both prior to and during UN meetings and recommends changes in policies if in his opinion conditions require them.

Participating Agencies

Multilateral diplomacy involves a wide variety of subjects, only some of which are purely political. The Department of State, in collaboration with military and other agencies, directly manages US interests in problems which are primarily of a political or security nature, such as disputes between states, organization of collective defense against aggression, problems involving colonial areas of the world, and world trade.

The political and territorial problems that arise in the UN General Assembly, Security Council, and Trusteeship Council are basically the responsibility of the Department of State. The Department of Defense has a major interest in these issues and in the military and security aspects of the disarmament proposals, as has the Atomic Energy Commission. The international political aspects of disarmament are a continuing responsibility of the Department of State. In the case of the Trusteeship Council, the Departments of the Navy and Interior administer certain overseas territories and possessions of the United States, and their assistance is required periodically in reporting on the stewardship and administration of US territories.

Since the Second World War the United States has greatly increased its collaboration with many nations on such essentially technical questions of mutual interest as epidemic control, famine relief, currency stabilization, flight safety, labor conditions, narcotics smuggling, radio frequency allocations, and comparative statistical methods. This collaboration has meant that other agencies of the US Government must be looked to by the Department of State in order that it may define this country's interests in these technical matters. In addition, the Department of State often consults with business, farm, professional, and labor organizations to secure their views on such subjects. Because of the diversity of subjects dealt with internationally, the sources for technical advice range across much of the government, from the Atomic Energy Commission to the Tariff Commission, from the Narcotics Bureau to the Department of Agriculture, from the Budget Bureau to the Civil Aeronautics Board. In addition to the Department of State at least twenty-four other executive agencies are concerned with UN activities, and frequently the success of the domestic programs they undertake is materially affected by what happens in the UN body dealing with the same subject.

Co-ordination of Policy

The objective of US participation in the UN system is to realize this nation's role and forward its interests in multilateral diplomatic bodies. In organizing and disciplining government machinery to participate in this process, there are two objectives: (1), to insure that the United States speaks with one voice on issues arising in the international forums; and (2), to insure that this voice represents the best judgment and skill that can be brought to bear on problems of foreign policy. At all meetings of the UN organs, subsidiary bodies, and specialized agencies a US representative must be prepared to speak for his government on the matter at issue.

The structure must be pyramidal—a broad base to secure as many points of view as possible, to exchange ideas and information, and to develop policy recommendations; a system of screening and reviewing to secure responsible approval of policies and, where necessary, to reconcile them with positions on other matters; and, finally, a point of departure at which the official sanction of the government can be granted so that the US representative in the international body may be assured that he speaks with complete authority. This process involves not only the preparation of official positions before a meeting but also adjustment of those positions during the meeting, as circumstances require.

The stage at which the co-ordination process comes to light is the instruction of American delegates and representatives, and the expression by them of the official policies and views of the United States at meetings of international organizations. The United States has permanent missions at the United Nations in New York, at the International Civil Aviation Organization in Montreal, at the International Atomic Energy Agency in Vienna, and in Geneva for liaison with the UN European office and the several specialized agencies located there (in Geneva this function is handled within the framework of the American consulate by an augmented staff). There are also liaison officers for FAO at Rome, for UNESCO at Paris, for the Economic Commission for Latin America (ECLA) at Santiago, and for the Economic Commission for Asia and the Far East (ECAFE) at Bangkok. US delegations are assembled, instructed, and sent by the State Department to conferences of international bodies throughout the world, including those held at the seats of permanent organizations.

Between sessions of major UN organs, there is continuous consultation and exchange of views and information with other governments on UN problems. This consultation takes place among the permanent delegations to the United Nations in New York. Other exchanges are carried on by US missions abroad with the various foreign offices. Other talks are held by the Department of State with the foreign missions in Washington. The use of these diplomatic channels is intensified prior to major conferences and reaches its peak in the months immediately preceding the annual session of the UN General Assembly.

The final step in the process is the implementation of decisions and recommendations produced by the international organizations. When an adopted resolution of one of the organs of the United Nations or one of the special agencies is transmitted to the secretary of state by the secretary general or director general concerned, the machinery of the executive branch must insure that proper action is taken by this country. Reponsibility for action must be assigned; there must be mechanisms to insure action; and a report must generally be made to the organization. In addition, there is a stream of questionnaires and requests for information that require co-ordinated replies.

US participation in international organizations thus works like a funnel. At one end, experts in government agencies recommend policies for the United States to adopt in the United Nations on a wide variety of topics. At the other end US spokesmen in international forums are expected to state these policies with clarity and authority. This process presents the government with a formidable task of co-ordination.

When conflicts of views exist in the executive branch, they must be resolved before an American position can be confidently presented in an international forum. Even when no substantive conflict exists, varying approaches are often suggested by the interested agencies. These must be brought into harmony.

The ultimate purpose of co-ordination is to insure that when the United States speaks to the world it speaks with one voice and with knowledge that in the next room, the next city, or the next continent other US spokesmen are, so one might say, on the same wave length. US policies must fit into a program to advance US interests throughout the UN system.

The process within the government of funneling to a point of action all necessary views and interests on a host of political and nonpolitical subjects requires machinery of co-ordination. The central point for this co-ordination is the Bureau of International Organization Affairs in the State Department.

Under the assistant secretary for international organization affairs, the bureau's five offices—UN Political and Security Affairs, International Economic and Social Affairs, Dependent Area Affairs, International Administration, and International Conferences—pull together the many threads within the executive branch to insure that throughout the system of international organizations and conferences the representatives of this government are equipped with agreed policies on all topics of concern to the United States.

The Hoover Commission recommended that the assistant secretary for international organization affairs "while participating in the formulation of foreign policy . . . should, so far as possible, obtain his policy guidance from the various regional units, the Planning [Staff], and from other staff advisers." Consequently, as indicated earlier, the bureau acts in the first instance as the co-ordinator of Department and government policy formulating operations.

A considerable part of this co-ordination is done through informal day-to-day contacts between the bureau's desk officers and "subject specialists" elsewhere in the Department or other government agencies. Often this is the only way in which deadlines can be met at UN meetings or prompt action taken to deal with imminent votes or sudden shifts in position by other countries. In this way also the countless routine matters that arise in international organization operations can be resolved with a minimum of formal clearances.

In the political field, for example, when there are indications that a political problem will come before the United Nations, a team is formed. The representative of the Office of UN Political and Security Affairs usually chairs the group, prepares papers for its consideration, and drafts instructions for the US representative. His responsibility is to insure that the views of all interested offices are secured and that any information required is obtained from Department and overseas files. He furnishes the knowledge of UN Charter considerations, precedents in UN bodies, past performances of delegations and delegates, voting probabilities, and the operation of regional and special-interest blocs in the United Nations. He frequently acts as principal adviser to the US representative during UN meetings when a political problem is considered.

Also on the team are representatives of the affected geographic areas, who provide the general US policies toward the countries in question. These policies, however, must be reconciled where, for example, one desk officer is speaking of American interests with respect to Portugal and another regarding our interests in Africa, as in the Angolan case in the United Nations. In addition, they furnish knowledge of geographic factors, national idiosyncrasies, and official personalities; and often they participate in General Assembly or Security Council sessions as political liaison officers with delegates from countries in their areas. To harmonize the work of the geographic and economic bureaus with that of the Bureau of International Organization Affairs, each normally has a full-time adviser on UN affairs, who collaborates with officers of the bureau on international organization problems affecting the region.

These teams frequently include representatives of the legal adviser's office and, when necessary, of the public affairs, economic, and research areas. The member from the Office of UN Political and Security Affairs often consults informally on military aspects of the cases with officers in the Defense Department. The team members turn to their respective assistant secretaries for major decisions, and these in turn consult higher echelons, as required, before approving US positions. Many political issues in the United Nations require decisions by the secretary of state, and in some cases the president. Either the Bureau of International Organization Affairs or the geographic offices undertake consultation with appropriate US missions abroad and foreign envoys in Washington.

A similar process takes place within the Department on economic and social questions before the United Nations and specialized agencies. Here the clearance process involves not only many different units within the State Department but other government agencies as well.

A group of interdepartmental committees furnishes the chief means of co-ordination in the economic and social field. There are also a few committees which make recommendations on special political and security questions, such as colonial problems and regulation of armaments. Unless another agency clearly has a predominant interest (*e.g.*, the Department of Agriculture, for FAO), the State Department furnishes the chairman or secretary of the committees. Within the State Department, the bureau usually provides either or both. In the technical economic committees the economic area of the State Department generally leads the Department's participating group, which usually includes the bureau. Papers on multilateral economic subjects often require approval by several Cabinet officers before the normal process of clearance through the interdepartmental committees can be completed.

The same process also operates for dealing with problems of dependent and colonial areas, where issues of the greatest complexity arise which affect US relations with both its principal allies and the strategically important regions of Asia, the Middle East, and Africa, where most dependent areas are located. Conflicts between these two groups on colonial questions come to a head in the United Nations, both in the Trusteeship Council and in the General Assembly. The Office of Dependent Area Affairs teams up with the geographic desk officers concerned and with Defense and Interior Department officers for the task of harmonizing both within the US Government and in the United Nations the traditional US attitudes toward colonial peoples on the one hand and the special problems of the administering authorities, which include close allies of this country, on the other.

In the process of developing US policies the Department of State, through the Bureau of International Organization Affairs, consults the representative to the United Nations and members of his staff. The US representative consults his diplomatic colleagues in New York and carries the burden of top-level negotiation on behalf of the United States on all matters under discussion in the United Nations. As a source of political intelligence, the United Nations is an important diplomatic listening post for all member governments. US representatives are constantly in contact with high officials from ninety-eight other countries. This flow of information, combined with the recommendations of our representatives, significantly influences policy and tactics.

The Bureau of International Organization Affairs, like other areas of the Department, is responsible for providing the US Information Agency (USIA) with policy information on important aspects of United States participation in the United Nations. This is accomplished by formal communications through the public affairs area, by daily briefing conferences, and by informal contacts. An important purpose of this liaison with USIA is to insure that US positions and policies advanced through the United Nations, the specialized agencies, and other international organizations are given full and prompt dissemination abroad through facilities of USIA. The bureau also arranges for USIA officers to be represented on the US delegations to the General Assembly and to other important conferences.

Conference Operations

In the UN system most meetings are regularly scheduled and can be planned systematically. Other international bodies frequently issue invitations for conferences. The Office of International Conferences screens such invitations, recommends as to US participation, negotiates throughout the government the make-up of the US delegations, assists when appropriate with preparations of US positions, allocates funds, makes travel and housing arrangements, and, in meetings away from UN headquarters, furnishes the service staff of the delegation. After the meeting this office makes sure that responsibilities for official reports, documents, and other items are properly discharged.

Formal steps in the process of administrative preparations are:

Staff Study. The Office of International Conferences, with concurrences of all units affected, secures the written approval of the assistant secretary for international organization affairs or, if necessary, the secretary of state or the president, for US participation in each international meeting.

Naming of United States Delegations. Public Law 341, in addition to requiring presidential appointment of permanent representatives to UN organs, makes the president responsible for naming US delegates to the annual UN General Assembly. Presidential appointments are also required by statute for certain other US delegations, such as those to the WHO Assembly. To ease the burden on the White House for the appointment of delegates to numerous lesser meetings, the president on February 26, 1948, approved a delegation of authority to the secretary of state "to designate all . . . representatives and delegates as well as advisory and secretarial staff for all groups" other than those assigned by law to the president, or in special cases, such as the naming of Congressional consultants.

On March 6, 1953, the secretary of state redelegated his authority to the assistant secretary for international organization affairs. All delegation members are named subject to security clearance. The Bureau of International Organization Affairs, in addition to co-ordinating policy preparation, administers the funds for conference participation, and decides on the staffs of US delegations after weighing recommendations from interested offices and agencies. The basic factors are the scope of the agenda and availability of funds. The specific criteria are: (1), delegation members must be, to the greatest extent possible, working members responsible for agenda items; (2), they must be able to handle several items each; (3), they must, generally, represent the government as a whole; and (4), maximum use should be made of qualified US personnel at the conference site.

SOME REFLECTIONS ON POLICY AND ORGANIZATION

The brief survey we have just completed carries some implicit assumptions about American diplomacy, bearing on both the place of UN policy in its grand scheme and the institutional arrangements for managing this sector. As with all human endeavors and political institutions, nothing is ever black and white. The reality has subtleties of shading. This final section reflects on the participation process as a phenomenon of institutional and bureaucratic behavior, in a less formal vein.

There is danger in looking at this problem of national policy from such a point of view, for one of the first things such an examination reveals is a seemingly sharp element of conflict between principles and practice. This conflict is sometimes noticeable on the surface of policy, but is mostly beneath the surface.

One reason for confusion may lie in our tendency to oversimplify a highly complex history and set of circumstances. We often assume a continuity, a consistency, a purposeful US policy program regarding the United Nations that gives too much credit to the planning and directing capacities of a succession of leaders, and far too little to the contingent qualities of history and human nature. Certainly such sweeping depictions presuppose a control on our part over many international situations that is altogether lacking.

Like every other sector of foreign policy, our UN policy has taken its day-to-day configuration from the stresses and strains, the insights, the changing power alignments of the world around us. It has also been shaped by the stresses and strains of the bureaucracy, the traits of leaders, the qualities, good and bad, of US constitutional government, and the changeable complexion of public opinion. Throughout this process there has existed a strong sense of national responsibility to the transcendent idea symbolized by the United Nations. The effect is that, in general, US policies have been related to the standards of the United Nations producing a record that stands comparison with that of other members of the United Nations, and of which no American need feel ashamed.

Out of many facets of the institutional or bureaucratic background for US policy making and participation during the postwar years, eight angles of vision, so to speak, have been selected. They are not all of the same order of significance or type. But for convenience they are considered comparable. They do have in common their relevance to the mundane level of daily decisions and their contribution to the tone and mode of official action.

The Extravagant Quality of Public Pronouncements

Perhaps the most striking feature of the US-UN policy process is the literal impossibility of implementing without qualification the unqualified "cornerstone" theory of the United Nations asserted by our senior leaders.

This failure to realize grand principles has long characterized the diplomatic scene. It would not be worth commenting upon save that official proclamations of US adherence to the purposes and principles of the United Nations have over the years taken on a liturgical quality, proclamations whose characteristic repetitiousness and frequent lack of content dulls our perception and ability to use the United Nations with imagination and discrimination.

A few quotations from pronouncements by presidents and those speaking for them will illustrate the primacy our verbal national policy has assigned to the United Nations: "we have pinned our hopes to the banner of the United Nations" (Secretary of State James F. Byrnes, February 28, 1946);[4] "The United States will support the United Nations with all the resources that we possess" (President Truman, October 23, 1946);[5] "support for the United Nations is the cornerstone of our foreign policy" (Secretary of State George C. Marshall, September 14, 1947);[6] "The foreign policy of the United States is based squarely upon the United Nations," and "We are pledged to unfaltering support of the United Nations" (Secretary of State Dean Acheson, April 7 and 28, 1949);[7] "The United States supports the United Nations in all respects" (President Truman, May

[4] *Bulletin*, 14 (March 10, 1946), 355.
[5] *Ibid.*, 15 (November 3, 1946), 812.
[6] *Ibid.*, 17 (September 21, 1947), 541.
[7] *Ibid.*, 20 (April 24, 1949, and May 8, 1949), 532 and 603 respectively.

12, 1949);[8] we are "a government that is committed irrevocably to the support of the United Nations" (President Eisenhower, September 23, 1953);[9] "the architect of . . . peace must be the United Nations, fully supported by this Nation" (Vice-President Nixon, December 6, 1956);[10] "The American people are right in regarding the principles of the United Nations Charter as a cornerstone of their foreign policy" (Eisenhower, July, 1959).[11] Mr. Kennedy has followed suit.

In contrast with such pronouncements, policy regarding particular issues has generally been pragmatic, episodic, and quite often, in the best sense of the word, expedient. Policies have had to be worked out in the fires of domestic political pressures and conflicting international claims upon American support.

This process has often produced an impression of lack of fidelity to broad principle. One of the most common examples of this impression has been in the colonial field, where the United States is caught between Europe and the anti-colonial world. The United States initially voted against placing on the agenda the cases of Tunisia, Algeria, and Cyprus before recalling its own tradition of free debate. While it eventually was glad to have UN action help to disengage it, the United States in the summer of 1958 sent its troops into Lebanon in disregard of the findings of the UN body on the scene that the problem was primarily internal, not external. The recommendations made to South Africa regarding treatment of Indians, Negroes, and Southwest Africans so far have not aroused the same kind of US pressure for compliance as was registered with respect to Soviet brutality in Hungary. The difference between the two is, of course, tremendous. But another influential factor in the US position on these cases was the urgent extra-UN policy considerations that animated the United States in the case of Hungary, certainly far more than in the case of South Africa. Domestic pressure plays an important role in determining which Assembly recommendations the United States takes as directive (for example, the Palestine partition action of 1947). And, of course, it will be remembered

[8] *United States Participation in the United Nations,* Report by the President, 1948, Department of State Publication 3437, p. iv.

[9] *Bulletin,* 29 (October 5, 1953), 457.

[10] *Bulletin,* 35 (December 17, 1956), 948.

[11] *United States Participation in the United Nations,* Report by the President, 1958, Department of State Publication 6852, p. ix.

that this country takes Assembly recommendations far more seriously than perhaps most other countries.

It may be argued that avowed long-term American goals have been more faithfully and consistently adhered to in nonpolitical fields. But here we confront other apparent anomalies. Broad policy goals have been asserted regarding an international civil service, elimination of the veto on nonsecurity matters, economic assistance for underdeveloped countries, and human rights, but these goals have not always been measured up to in the positions adopted on the concrete issues, *i.e.*, US secretariat personnel, election of the secretary general, financing of economic development, and the drafting of international covenants in the human rights field, not to mention such an anomaly as continued nonratification by the host country of the General Convention on Privileges and Immunities.

There have probably been many more instances where immediate and obvious US interests seemed in harmony with assertions of broad principle—Korea, Iran, Indonesia, Palestine, Greece, the earlier (but not the later) stages of human rights debate, declarations regarding self-determination (but not when self-determination came to imply the right to nationalize), technical assistance, Suez and subsequent Middle East actions, Hungary, and, increasingly, disarmament. But the introduction of international disputes in the United Nations has by no means always been welcomed. In the Congo, of course, it was.

Many reasons may be assigned to this uneven record. One is that sometimes ideas and programs advanced in the United Nations seem unwise or poorly timed. Another is that the "cornerstone" of US policy tends to shift. At various times in the postwar period the cornerstone has been, respectively, the United Nations, co-operation with the Soviet Union, development of a defensive anti-Soviet coalition, rearmament, a balanced budget, and the rebuilding of arms and alliances.

Another reason is that some ideals, including several sponsored by the United States, may be seen in the light of history and with the benefit of afterthought as of doubtful validity. Examples might be found in the human rights field where the faulty premise of a world social consensus might be read into some early American efforts, or in the persistent American notion that somehow all states can be brought to commit themselves in advance to fight an unknown adversary at any time in the future.

Perhaps the greatest difficulty is that a correct interpretation of national interests changes with the world situation, while democratic governments reflect a tendency to remain prisoners of outmoded categories of policy. A prime lack has been the absence of a satisfactory measurement in meaningful detail of both short-term and long-term American goals as against UN actions and trends. As a consequence we are frequently witnesses to what appears a basic clash between principles and interests. We need to understand better the harmonies and tensions within a policy that comprehends both national and multinational values.[12]

The Practical Tests for Official Action

One of the questions that attracts students of this subject is whether national governments can and should apply to UN problems the standards of national interest that they apply to policies outside the United Nations. The long-range objectives of the United Nations are in the main perceived and acted upon by the United States as synonymous with its own interests. Nevertheless, as suggested, the decision-making process must look in several directions to find guides for action. The criticism of nongovernmental groups assigns a rather low score to the US Government for fidelity to what they believe are the interests of the United Nations. The reason for this lies in the difference between short- and long-range policies. For it is in the individual, detailed problem demanding action in the face of a seemingly rigid set of limits that the policy maker confronts what seem to be unremitting collisions between stated principle and practical necessity.

While a nongovernmental American organization can legitimately test US actions in the United Nations against the standards of the UN Charter, asking only if our actions benefit the United Nations as an institution, other tests are necessarily applied by the government. The State Department's approach to a problem in the United Nations is dominated not by the question "What is good for the United Nations?" but by "What is good for the United States?" Frequently such tests amount to asking the same question. But sometimes they do not. This circumstance is true not only of the United States. It is true of all nations.

It is thus natural that United States initiatives in the United Nations have been justified within government circles primarily on grounds of self-interest, just as they are in chancelleries the world

[12] See the author's *The United Nations and US Foreign Policy*, *op. cit.*, Part I.

over. Arguments resting exclusively on an altruistic or a "UN-improvement" basis have generally had short shrift in competition with arguments about national security and short-term national interest. Action in the United Nations has not by any means become natural or logical for national policy makers in dealing with difficult problems involving important national interests.

The effect within the bureaucracy has been that proponents of UN action, as opposed to bilateral or regional action, or perhaps inaction, have increasingly been on the defensive, despite the continuing high-level expressions of support. The burden of proof has been on them to justify UN involvement, with its attendant complications and unpredictability, over the presumably more desirable status quo or more manageable devices of bilateral and coalition diplomacy.

Perhaps the most egregious example of this internal tension was provided during the period from President Gamal Abdul Nasser's edict of July 26, 1956, announcing nationalization of the Suez Canal Company, through the tense and, as it turned out, futile period of limited diplomacy, to the last days of October when the United Kingdom and France verified the bankruptcy of that diplomacy with their effort to resolve the question forcibly.

During this period staff proposals were continually advanced within the Department for serious UN involvement in resolving or stabilizing the Suez Canal question by broadening the international framework then being urged on Egypt to make it more acceptable. These proposals were rejected, and when the matter went before the Security Council in early October it was in a different and, it must be said, unconstructive context. It will remain forever moot whether constructive measures through the United Nations during the summer of 1956 would have been feasible or promising. All one can say is that they might have improved what eventually took place.

The same might be said of the lost possibility of coming to terms with the Arab-Israeli dispute and the refugee problem during the Suez crisis. The United States never followed through, during that rare moment of fluidity, with action through the United Nations on these root matters, preferring to concentrate on the abortive "Eisenhower Doctrine" for the Middle East.

But national decisions are not always made on entirely rational grounds, and there is not always an objective weighing of national interest against common interest in deciding whether to use the United Nations.

Another factor in deciding whether to link national policy with the United Nations is the sheer size and weight of the government structure.

When the United Nations is already seized of a question there is of course no option for the United States other than to formulate policy. Even when the issue is repugnant to the United States and would never have been voluntarily pursued, it must be faced. Some examples of such issues are the more expensive proposals for UN financing of economic development, for draft covenants on economic rights, increased budgets, or self-determination definitions that Woodrow Wilson would never have recognized. Here the United States must decide not only what policy it wishes to follow; but also what image of this country such a policy will create in the highly symbol-conscious setting of the United Nations. Action of some sort is called for.

Therefore it has been necessary to devise much less drastic alternatives to a UN program for financing economic development, to offer a substitute "action" program on human rights, to go along temporarily with budget quotas that Congress never really accepted, and to suggest committee devices to make sense of the contemporary definitions of self-determination. In the political field, Algeria and Kashmir are examples of unwelcome UN issues between friends that periodically strain our diplomatic resources.

When, however, a question involves a clear option as to whether the United Nations should take an initiative, the internal process is more complicated. The task the United States faces in going into action on any new issue, winning its internal battles with itself, and producing decisions, is sometimes underestimated. A primary complication for what may fairly be described as a status quo nation is the problem of inertia, *i.e.*, the preference for letting sleeping dogs lie. In addition, there is the difficulty of preparing and seeing through a government decision. Finally, there is the preoccupation of the top command with the crushing and paramount problems of national policy, which, for reasons both good and bad, customarily relegates the United Nations to a secondary category except at moments of crisis. Again, the Congo crisis of 1960-1961 illustrates the point.

Except at such moments, it is difficult to divert the attention of top policy levels of government from other preoccupations to the potentialities of UN initiatives. And in some cases, even when seriously considered, UN action seems to the troubled and harassed policy maker only to enhance the difficulties of this country's diplomacy, particularly where it would bring a sensitive matter into an unmanageably large forum, or where it appears to substitute rigid formulas for flexible diplomacy, or where it seems to promise endless forensics and moral exhortations instead of effective action.

Still another criterion for turning to or from the United Nations is the increasing role of the Congress in foreign policy. Congressional weight on the policy scales ranges from insistence on writing the United Nations into the Greek-Turkish Aid Program, despite initial administration opposition, to resolutions advising the president of the unanimous sense of the Congress that Communist China should not be seated in the United Nations.

The fundamental dilemma remains how best to use the United Nations more constructively without departing from other large national and free world purposes and from the strategies that must be followed to achieve those purposes.

Stature and Status of the UN Operation in the State Department

The position of UN affairs within the State Department has shifted in a number of ways since 1945. The first postwar unit of the Department devoted to the preparation and execution of US policy in the United Nations was the Office of Special Political Affairs (SPA), established on January 15, 1944. Parallel to and technically equal with the geographic offices, it reported to a special assistant to the secretary of state, Leo Pasvolsky. With Pasvolsky's departure in March, 1946, the Office of Special Political Affairs remained technically on a par with the then four geographic offices, but without representation at the assistant secretary level.

When the geographic offices became bureaus, on October 3, 1949, so did the former SPA (which on January 21, 1948, had been rechristened the Office of United Nations Affairs). The Hoover Commission report of February, 1949, recommended endowing all five bureaus with assistant secretaries—the five assistant secretaries "at the action level." [13] References were to "five operating vice-presidents." The only distinction was reflected in the injunction that UN affairs

[13] Hoover Commission *Report on Organization of the Executive Branch of the Government* (New York, 1950), p. 161. The Bureau of African Affairs has since been added.

should secure substantive area policy guidance from appropriate regional bureaus.

When the position of deputy undersecretary for political affairs was established in 1949, pursuant to the Hoover Commission's recommendations, his task of assisting the secretary in the management of political policy making was applied to all five bureaus, which as a group had come to be regarded as the political bureaus, in distinction to economic affairs, intelligence, administration, etc. This attitude has continued through the period of the present Bureau of International Organization Affairs.

Beneath this façade, however, the institutional position of the UN affairs unit was undergoing a more subtle process of assimilation, in many ways far less conclusive than the landmarks referred to above would indicate. Unquestionably the revelations concerning Alger Hiss' conduct some years before his connection with UN affairs set back the process of internal acceptance of the unit by several years, an early and extraordinarily persistent example of taint by association on an organization chart, so to speak.

Yet the process of assimilation was going on. Functions were added to the bureau from elsewhere in the Department, as for example narcotics control, international health, and social welfare from the disbanded Division of International Labor, Health, and Social Affairs in 1948 and 1949. The Division of International Conferences was acquired on April 1, 1949, from the administrative area of the Department. The chief of the bureau has been a member of the secretary's staff, meeting from the time of Secretary Byrnes (although for a time a limited group began to meet regularly with the secretary at a different time of day from the staff meeting, and early in the Eisenhower administration the assistant secretary for international organization affairs was not invited to the more select meetings).

In the winter of 1945-1946 a distinguished military figure who had surveyed the Department was heard to predict that the geographic offices would resent, oppose, encroach upon, and soon absorb the new UN unit, much as they, like the Chinese, had always absorbed rivals. This has not happened, and it probably will not. Ostensibly, acceptance of UN affairs within the diplomatic machine is complete.

But the organization façade bulges and the seams occasionally split because of pressures within. One interesting example is the change in name from "UN Affairs" to "International Organization

Affairs" on August 25, 1954. There were sound reasons for the change, including the bureau's responsibility for many aspects of US participation in the specialized agencies, as well as the Caribbean and South Pacific commissions. But the change was made with the tacit acknowledgment that the new label would not inflame quite so many members of Congress who had become disenchanted with the United Nations. In June, 1957, again for administratively logical reasons, some of the personnel working on disarmament problems were transferred from international organization affairs to the Office of the Special Assistant to the Secretary for Atomic Energy Affairs. This event still merits an entry on the lower half of a graph depicting the standing of UN affairs in the Department. The pendulum is not necessarily swinging back. Rather, it has never passed the midpoint of equilibrium. (Disarmament personnel are now concentrated in the United States Disarmament Administration.)

A pamphlet entitled "How Foreign Policy Is Made," issued by the State Department in October, 1957, speaks only of four "operating vice-presidents"—not the picture painted in 1949.[14] International organization affairs, like economics, intelligence, public affairs, and administration, is again seen as occupying a staff rather than line category. Since it partakes of both staff and line characteristics, it is not surprising that its place is hard to describe.

On balance, the UN operation within the Department has occupied a generally minority position, lying athwart, but not in, the traditional mainstream of foreign policy. Often, as suggested, the operations of the United Nations are in harmony with major US policy objectives, as are a succession of pacific settlement cases starting with Iran in 1946, the UN program for peaceful uses of atomic energy, and many other cases. But only in two ways has the UN position within the US Government ever achieved what might fairly be called pre-eminence: in terms of the abstract verbal support in our public pronouncements, which is predictable and constant; and at the historic moments when a massive coincidence of factors has set the UN standard alongside the American, as with the decision to oppose the communist invasion of South Korea in 1950, the near unanimous opposition to the Israeli, British, and French action in Egypt in 1956, and the Congo operations of 1960-1961.

[14] Department of State Publication 6519. See footnote 13.

Washington and New York

The relation between the US Mission to the United Nations in New York and the Department in Washington has been of particular interest to American students of the United Nations.

The basic functions of the US representative to the United Nations were stated by the so-called UN Participation Act of 1945 as amended in 1949[15] and by President Truman's executive orders of 1947 and 1950.[16] Warren R. Austin was the US representative at the time. Henry Cabot Lodge succeeded him in 1953. Both men had been influential Republican senators. But there was one important difference. Lodge was also made a member of the president's Cabinet.

The formal responsibilities of the representative did not change, but his domestic political stature had been sharply upgraded, particularly by contrast with his nominal "home desk" in the person of the assistant secretary for international organization affairs.

There was one immediate effect in the General Assembly delegation. The Department's practice during the years 1946-1953 had been to furnish the US representative with what was in effect a ready-made Assembly delegation each fall, co-operatively planned, to be sure, but characteristically "chief-of-staffed" by senior officers of the bureau. All this changed in 1953, and the directing staff positions in the Assembly delegation became fixed to the permanent mission. This practice remains, but with passage of time and the renewed realization of the benefits from harmonious relation between the field and Washington, the procedure of selecting and briefing delegations was once again co-operative. It remains so under Adlai Stevenson.

Undoubtedly many policy initiatives have been pressed on Washington by the US Mission in recent years, although it is not generally appreciated how often these are, for public relations reasons, inspired by Washington. An instance is the unanimous declaration of the US delegates to the Tenth Assembly on foreign economic aid,[17] which could only mean support for a more positive US attitude toward economic development programs through the United Nations.

[15] Respectively, Public Laws 264, 79th Congress, and 341, 81st Congress.

[16] Executive Order 9844 of April 28, 1947, amended by Executive Order 10108 of February 19, 1950.

[17] Announced by Secretary Dulles in *Department of State Press Release* No. 14, January 11, 1956.

Dramatic as this declaration was, it has had little perceptible effect on US policy. Despite all that happened, the shifts of prestige to New York have not much affected national policy. The US delegation to the United Nations is, as always, an instructed delegation in the technical sense and, more often than not, in the real sense. Perhaps the sharpest reminder of where the levers of power are in the US Government was furnished during the major crises of Korea, Suez, Hungary, Lebanon, and other comparable round-the-clock situations, during which the permanent staff of the US Mission in New York functioned tirelessly and skillfully as servants and executors of policy made by the hour, as it were, at Washington. It could not be any other way, nor is it any other way in US missions elsewhere in the world, where the lines of authority and responsibility are perhaps in better equilibrium than in New York.

The Assistant Secretary and the Pre-eminence of Political Problems

In the policy-making echelons of the US Government the key figure regarding UN participation is the assistant secretary of state for international organization affairs. This presidential appointee must be able to maintain relations of mutual confidence and respect with two personages central in our government who both outrank him: the secretary of state and the US representative to the United Nations. If these relations break down, the assistant secretary's usefulness is, of course, critically impaired.

Protocol places a handicap on the assistant secretary of state in carrying out his duties. The US representative, particularly when he sits as a member of the president's Cabinet, outranks the assistant secretary through whom he normally receives his instructions. (A problem that some anticipated but that does not appear to have arisen concerns the ambiguity of the United States representative's role vis-a-vis his superior, the secretary of state, both cabinet-level officials.) All US ambassadors, of course, enjoy nominal relations with the president that transcend, again nominally, their obligations to the secretary of state's deputies. These deputies, however, are clearly in a command position, both over the cables and in such settings as regional chiefs-of-missions meetings, over which the regional assistant secretary generally presides.

In the New York setting, where protocol governs to a heavy degree if only because of the sheer number of functionaries and dignitaries present, the assistant secretary tends to remain far more of a background figure vis-a-vis the mission chief. The primary responsibility of the Department UN affairs chief is, of course, to advise the secretary of state in Washington. Nonetheless, unlike some of their counterparts in foreign governments, the US assistant secretary or deputy has not often been designated even an alternate representative on a US General Assembly delegation,[18] and, up to 1960 when Francis O. Wilcox was named a representative on the US General Assembly delegation, he has never been a full representative. In the first six years or so, with only a few exceptions, the "home-desk chief" or his deputy did usually sit at the right hand of the delegation chairman at Assembly sessions, and functioned as *éminence grise* as well as a source of government policy. There was a shift in this relation in 1953, as indicated.

The relation between the assistant secretary and his principal, the secretary of state, has in the past had its episodes of friction, of apparent lack of confidence, even of what can only be described as neglect. But in the main it has been harmonious.

One consequence of the secretary's confidence in the United Nations assistant secretary has been the preoccupation of the latter with political, as opposed to economic, social, trusteeship, technical, and other facets, of his responsibilities.

The reasons for this preoccupation are several. The most obvious one is that great political crises have dominated the foreign policy scene over the last decade—Soviet relations in general, the Berlin Blockade, the Korean War, Indochina, Suez, Hungary, Quemoy, summitry, and the renewed threats to Berlin—all issues where the stakes were extraordinarily high.

Another basic institutional factor resided in the dominantly political interests and proclivities of secretaries Byrnes, Marshall, Acheson, and Dulles, whose attention to UN affairs was characteristically limited to the more acute political aspects. To the extent that the UN affairs chief came to participate in the high command, he became caught up in the current crises, regardless of whether they involved the United Nations or not. Secretary Marshall's use of Dean Rusk, then director of UN affairs, in the Berlin Blockade crisis is a case in point, and there are others.

[18] The cases of record are: Dean Rusk, Second Special Session on Palestine, 1948, and Third Session, both parts, 1948-1949; John D. Hickerson, Fourth Session, 1949; and William Sanders, Seventh Session, second part, 1953.

Thus, in the very nature of the job it has been natural for this officer to devote the bulk of his overburdened time and energies to the political aspects of the work, despite the other heavy responsibilities he carries, and the considerable amount of time he must somehow find for, as one example, problems involving the specialized agencies. After the Korean War broke out, the then assistant secretary, John D. Hickerson, took part in daily meetings with the joint chiefs of staff, and for a long period could be concerned with little else. Suez and Hungary posed much the same problem for a subsequent assistant secretary, Francis O. Wilcox.

Nonetheless, other problems claimed their attention and had somehow to be dealt with. The utilization of two deputy assistant secretaries has from time to time taken the form of a fairly sharp division of responsibility. At one time one of them followed the economic and social work of the bureau, and the other oversaw the administrative decisions and often certain specialized interests, such as inter-American organization matters and, more recently, refugee problems. Later the division was between economic, social, budgetary, refugee, and other international administrative matters on the one hand, and assistance on political, atomic energy, disarmament and related problems on the other.

On balance it can be said that political affairs have consistently dominated the economic and social components within the Department's UN structure, and which it may not be accurate to postulate a one-to-one relation between this situation and the generally secondary role of economic and social policy in the American UN effort, it is a factor.

The Fate of the UN Affairs Specialist

The staff personnel engaged in UN affairs in the Department for a long time represented a sort of enclave within the foreign service-dominated system. Many of the bureau's officers were recruited to assist in the preparations for postwar organization, preparations largely of a research nature. The roster of officers on this staff prior to 1946 reveals some names now familiar outside the Department as professors, college presidents, and research directors.[19] Others stayed in after coming from the academic world or from other than the foreign service, and for some years were keenly aware that as a group

[19] See *Postwar Foreign Policy Preparation 1939-1945* (Washington, 1950), pp. 566-75.

they were often regarded, particularly by the more traditional-minded in the geographic bureaus, as dilettantes of diplomacy, intellectuals, even visionaries—at any rate, not quite members of the "in-group."

Such distinctions were increased because the vast majority of officers in UN affairs were members of the Department's civil service, while at the same time most of the key officers of the geographic bureaus were Foreign Service officers.

Prior to the Wriston program for integrating Department officers into the Foreign Service some tentative steps had been taken toward integration of the two services. But only twenty-six lateral appointments were made under section 517 of the Foreign Service Act of 1946, and as of the year 1954 only twenty-five under the March, 1951, directive liberalizing section 517.[20]

New legislation, signed by the president in August, 1954, changed all this. Replacements began to stream into the bureau from field duty, and many key positions were taken over by Foreign Service officers.

The long-term effect of this change can be salutary both in terms of the diversity of experience it offers former civil service personnel and career Foreign Service officers and in terms of the needful institutional amalgamation and acceptance of the UN segment of our foreign affairs machinery.

Nevertheless, a heavy short-term price was exacted in the name of a theory. The group of UN specialists had over the years developed skills that could be relied upon in times of need, and which by no stretch of the imagination could be acquired overnight. When the dual crises of Egypt and Hungary struck in October-November, 1956, the bureau was sorely handicapped by lack of trained and experienced personnel. A handful of officers who remained "un-integrated" bore a disproportionate burden over many days and nights.

Money and the Congress

I have suggested that political problems in the UN affairs operation have enjoyed a priority over other features of US participation, a priority that results from such factors as the world situation, intensity of political crises, and the natural proclivities of secretaries of state.

Nevertheless, no understanding of the internal process of policy

[20] *Toward a Stronger Foreign Service*, Department of State Publication 5458 (Washington, 1954), pp. 15-19.

making is possible without an awareness that budgetary and other financial issues have invariably occupied a prominence out of all proportion to other factors. Perhaps no other UN issue has preoccupied the Congress and, consequently, the Department to a greater extent over the years than the matter of percentage contributions by the United States to the United Nations and specialized agency budgets.

In 1946 at the first Assembly session, the United States asserted the view that no member should normally pay more than one third of the budget. The US share was nonetheless fixed at 39.89 per cent, and even though the principle of a one-third ceiling was adopted in an Assembly resolution in 1948, by 1950 the US share had only been reduced by a token one tenth of one per cent.

Meanwhile pressure was mounting from Congress, which adopted the practice of attaching a rider to appropriations affirming the one third principle (and ultimately framing it in such a way that no funds could be expended where the US share was greater than one third, a move that the Department strenuously resisted on the ground that, while it would work energetically toward the goal, it did not wish to see the United States in default of its obligations if it came to be outvoted).

As a result of such pressures the US share of the WHO and UNESCO budgets was modestly reduced in 1949, although at the same time our share in the ILO, ICAO, and FAO was increased, since it was well below one third.

Further reductions took place in 1950 and 1951 in our United Nations, UNESCO, and WHO quotas, and again in 1952 in the United Nations. In 1953 the one third ceiling was finally reached in the United Nations, WHO, and UNESCO, and was below one third in all other assessed budgets in the UN system. Based on the increase in membership, pressure grew for a further drop in the US percentage contribution. On October 14, 1957, the General Assembly voted in principle that the US quota should be gradually reduced to 30 per cent.[21]

It would be difficult to estimate the hours of labor that went into the seemingly simple achievement of bringing the US quota down to one third. The importance this government attached to the assessment question is signified by the fact that its spokesman in the Budgetary and Administrative Committee at the 1946 and 1947

[21] General Assembly Resolution 1137 (XII), October 14, 1957.

Assembly sessions was the architect of bipartisan foreign policy and the senior foreign policy spokesman for the Republican party, Senator Arthur H. Vandenberg. The practice has since been followed of assigning one of the two Congressional members of the United States Assembly delegation to the Budgetary and Administrative Committee.

Even this procedure has not eased the task of the Department in mediating between its Congressional purse strings and its international negotiations. The Technical Assistance Program has been placed in recurring jeopardy by Congress, and more than one assistant secretary has devoted long days to persuading one Congressional committee or another that the United States would stand convicted of parsimony, bad faith, and sheer political blindness if it had to appear empty-handed at a pledging conference to support an international program such as technical assistance that this country had itself initiated.

The capacity of budgetary questions to share the stage with substantive issues was well illustrated in the fall of 1956 with regard to the financing of the UN Emergency Force and the clearing of the Suez Canal. It may be too much to say that both these politically imperative ends became for a time almost totally dependent on the ability of the United States to provide funds without assurance that they would be either returned or shared under the regular UN budget, or that they were in any way authorized by the secretary general. That these questions were temporarily finessed, the money provided, and the jobs done, is a tribute to the ability of American officials to overcome the seemingly endless set of barriers that their government arrangements have thrown up to prevent a more flexible and purposeful use of public funds for the international political purposes of the United States. The point was brought home once again with the Congo crisis and its financing in the fall of 1960 and into 1961.

The Diplomacy of Policy Making

The final category is in a sense an extension of the previous ones. If there is any feature that stands out in the task of formulating and implementing multilateral diplomatic policy, it is the multilateral nature, as it were, of that very process within the government. The process is described in detail in the first part of this chapter, particularly the multiplicity of elements and agencies within the US Government that play a role in the formulation of our UN policy. What can be said about it in the context of "informal organization" is that the International Organization Bureau is above all a servant of policy directives not its own and that it yet must find ways of effectuating these directives in a diplomatic setting that includes virtually all the nations of the world. The multiplicity of subject matters combines with this internal mediation to yield a complicated and sometimes unwieldy task within the US Government of conference, negotiation, compromise, and other intrafamiliar dealings.

It is therefore quite natural that such a process should result in what might be termed the cross-sterilization of ideas. In a period when even ordinary government decisions about foreign policy must undergo the curiously debilitating process of agreement up the line to the National Security Council, often losing their punch, their purpose, even their literacy in the process, the addition of the UN element to such problems brings in further competing interests and neutralizing factors.

This situation points to perhaps the greatest internal difficulty the American government experiences as an active member of the UN system. What Paul Appleby once called "Big Democracy" is also a species of big bureaucracy, with built-in controls that are necessary for successful democratic policy but that sometimes obstruct, inhibit, and embarrass desirable international action.

Yet this condition is tempered by many factors, not the least of which is the constructive co-operation and support often received by the Department from Congress. The creation of special subcommittees on international organization affairs under the Foreign Relations and Foreign Affairs committees has helpfully channeled a portion of the necessary liaison between the two branches. Perhaps the most significant set of informal relations between the Department and the Congress on UN problems is a direct result of the practice of including members of Congress on US delegations to the General Assembly. The Congressional "alumni club" started in the first session with Senators Connally and Vandenberg and Representatives Bloom, Eaton, and Helen Douglas. Resumed in 1950 with Senators Lodge and Sparkman, the roster of "graduates" now includes such Senate names as Mansfield, Green, Wiley, Alexander Smith, Pastore, Humphrey, Knowland, and Hickenlooper,[22] and members of the House Vorys, Frances Bolton, Richards, Hays, Merrow, Carnahan, Judd, Zablocki,

[22] The two Congressional delegates to the 1960 General Assembly were Senators Aiken and Morse.

and Fulton. As a two-way educational process, this practice has been enough of a success to outweigh the disadvantages, remarked by foreign and domestic observers, of the US practice of appointing nonprofessional delegations.

Another tempering element is that the National Security Council at least in theory provides a tailor-made channel for securing presidential decisions, and avoids both the necessity for frequent interventions with the White House (although these are not uncommon with regard to such matters as presidential plans, patronage, or other domestic political matters), as well as the necessity to involve the Cabinet. Only the historian will be able to decide whether, after all, foreign policy was more successfully conducted in the day of the virtuoso president or of the staff-minded official. Each process has its pitfalls and implications for the quality and utilization of the ideas generated from below.

18: DEVELOPMENT OF INFORMATIONAL ACTIVITIES

H. Rowland Ludden

Experiment and controversy have dominated the international informational activities of the United States during the decade and a half since the Second World War. The government has been engaged continuously in using an information and cultural relations program in support of its foreign policy, while simultaneously trying to learn methods and devise machinery for such a program. This process has been subjected to more controversy and less understanding per budget dollar than probably any other aspect of American diplomacy.

Dilemmas facing our free society as it conducts an active foreign policy in the dangerous 20th century have caused some of the controversy. Without differentiating between those problems which are eternal and those to which solutions are possible this side of infinity, we can list some major questions. How actively should the United States strive to promote its interests through foreign policy, and by what balance among economic, military, political, and psychological means? How can conflicting domestic political interests be reconciled with foreign policy in the interest of the country? How can we protect policy formulation and execution from communist influence while simultaneously conducting policy and preserving our heritage of human liberty? How can government, the people's servant, disseminate information promoting its foreign policy without interfering with the delicate machinery by which the people control their democracy? Should our society speak with a single voice for maximum effect in the international field? If so, how can we do it and preserve the individual's freedom of expression?

While these problems excited the body politic or lay beneath the surface of immediate events, more specific and technical questions about the role, methods, and structure of the international informational function were considered. How can information policy and general foreign policy be co-ordinated? At what level should co-ordination take place? Is information merely a tool of policy? To what extent and how should informational factors enter the making of policy as distinguished from the implementation of policy? How can central, top-level direction of information policy be maintained to provide consistency and co-ordination with policy while at the same time making adequate provision for meeting the infinite variations in the field? What is the necessary and proper division between private and public international communication with people of other countries? Is there a valid and necessary distinction between "informational" and "cultural" activities?

These more specific problems and others of an even more technical nature were not considered in a vacuum free from the more fundamental and political dilemmas. Indeed, they should not have been considered separately since the answers to the more specific questions provided, in large part, the temporary answers to the broader problems. (There may well be a line beyond which political and philosophical considerations should abdicate to technical, even engineering, factors. The burden of proof of such a line rests, however, with him who claims its existence.)

The complexities of international informational activities by the United States will be more understandable following a brief explanation of the hypothetical role of informational factors in foreign policy. The explanation involves assuming some answers to questions raised above, answers sometimes the same as those reached pragmatically in recent years as well as some answers that have at times been repudiated in the structure and operation of the program.

Feeding into the complex machinery engaged in foreign policy are many factors, including public opinion both domestic and foreign. Decisions are made and issue forth as policies to be carried out by such methods as international information activities and domestic public relations operations. To implement decisions, these activities, designed for direct effect on public opinion, foreign or domestic, must at all times be co-ordinated with activities of other types, economic, political, and military.

Public opinion in foreign countries and within the United States is affected not only by the informational activities explicitly directed toward it but also by American foreign policy as conducted via other methods. In addition, the opinions of foreign and domestic publics are affected by other factors, most of which are not under the control of the government of the United States. Public opinion thus affected feeds back into the policy-formulation process through a multiplicity of direct and indirect channels including formal measurement processes when and where available.

This concept of informational activities is, of course, greatly oversimplified. Within the central complex of foreign policy formulation processes and machinery is the whole of the legislative and executive establishment touching foreign affairs, as well as the interest group and political party aspects of our society that impinge on foreign policy decision making. Distinctions must be made between foreign publics and foreign governments. Also, there are many relations, such as contact between the publics of different countries, that may play a role in the whole international information field. Likewise, this explanation overlooks the manifold internal and operational patterns of output measurement, evaluation of impact, target analysis, and so on.

This explanation includes some assumptions not always acceptable in recent years. Tendencies still exist to use international informational activities only after policy formulation, instead of taking foreign public opinion factors into consideration throughout the formulation process. Serious problems remain in achieving maximum coordination between international information policy and aspects of foreign policy within the control of other departments of the government. One battle centers on the distinction between "information" and "cultural relations." The two have been kept partly separate, organizationally at least, though this author's explanation combines the two as essentially inseparable.

1. Historical Background

The conduct of international informational activities by the government of the United States may be divided into six periods. First, developments from the time of the Revolutionary War to the end of the Second World War provide the historical background for establishment of a peacetime international information program. Second, the transition from the Second World War to peacetime operations within the State Department, though formally taking place during the last few months of 1945, lasted until the beginning of 1948. Third, the ultimately successful 1946-1948 fight for legislative authorization took place during this transition from war time and also overlapped the beginnings of the East-West cold war. Fourth, following authorization by Congress, the information program went through a period of slow growth from 1948 to 1950. Fifth, in the 1950-1953 period the program expanded rapidly in the face of international crisis, and towards the end of the period was endangered by domestic political developments. Sixth, the period from 1953 to the present (1960) started with the birth of the United States Information Agency (USIA), thus removing the "informational" program from the State Department and putting it into an independent agency. In spite of problems, this last period has developed as one of relative stability and maturation in international information activities.

The United States engaged in international information activities prior to the Second World War, but these earlier efforts, usually extemporized during wartime, did not provide a pattern of effort to which our present activities could trace their lineage. No pattern developed from the international informational activities carried on overseas by the United States during the Revolutionary War, the Civil War, and the First World War. Indeed, there are no definitive scholarly studies of the operations prior to those of the First World War, and the fragmentary reports from the participants in the early ventures provided no foundation on which to build in subsequent operations. Much material of a scholarly nature has been available on the First World War operations and fairly extensive records and personal accounts were left by participants in the activities of George Creel's Committee on Public Information. But international informational activities ended with that war, and it was not until the late 1930s and the mushrooming of Nazi and Fascist propaganda activities that the United States started "cultural relations" activities in the Western Hemisphere. Our present program can trace its ancestry no further than to the Second World War period and the temporary agencies of the Office of War Information (OWI) and the Office of Coordinator of Inter-American Affairs (CIAA), though there had been modest beginnings of public information activities within the State Department during the 1920s and 1930s.[1]

[1] Research on 18th and 19th-century information activities of the United States has given little more than fragments of the story. For examples see Philip G. Davidson's excellent book, *Propaganda and the American Revolution: 1763-1783* (Chapel Hill, N.C., 1941); John Herbert Kiger, "Federal Government Propaganda in Great Britain during the American Civil War," *Historical Outlook*, XIX (May, 1928), 204-209. For the latter there was apparently no exhaustive search of official records, memoirs, or other biographical materials.

Standard works on propaganda in the First World War are Harold D. Lasswell, *Propaganda Technique in the World War* (New York, 1927), and

A public relations consciousness crept over almost the entire executive branch of the government of the United States in the first half of the 20th century, especially during the years between the two world wars.[2] In the State Department this was evidenced in several ways: (1), under pressure from scholarly groups such as the American Society of International Law, the American Political Science Association, and the American Historical Association, the State Department's modest publication program, dating from 1861, was expanded in 1929 with the publication of current materials; this "new" publications program developed gradually during the 1930s but never approached mass distribution until after the outbreak of the Second World War;[3] (2), State Department press conferences by the secre-

James R. Mock and Cedric Larson, *Words that Won the War* (Princeton, 1939). For the story of the Creel Committee by its chairman, see George Creel, *How We Advertised America* (New York, 1920). A German account of Allied propaganda against Germany is given in Hans Thimme, *Weltkrieg ohne Waffen: Die Propaganda der Westmaechte gegen Deutschland, ihre Wirkung und ihre Abwehr* (Stuttgart, 1932).

The considerable research on propaganda by the United States in the Second World War has produced no definitive history of the Office of War Information (OWI). However, see Charles A. H. Thomson, *Overseas Information Service of the United States Government* (Washington, 1948), chs. 2-6; Wallace Carroll, *Persuade or Perish* (Boston, 1948); *The Public Opinion Quarterly's* special issue, "Office of War Information," VII (Spring, 1943), 1-138, ed. by Harwood L. Childs; US Bureau of the Budget, War Records Section, *The United States at War* (Washington, 1946), chs. 4, 8, 13. The final report by Elmer Davis to the president on OWI has never been released, and the files of the OWI in the United States archives appear to have had much of the important material removed at some time in the past.

Detailed coverage of the Office of the Coordinator of Inter-American Affairs (CIAA) is contained in US Bureau of the Budget, War Records Section, *History of the Office of the Coordinator of Inter-American Affairs* (Washington, 1947). See also Thomson, *op. cit.*, ch. 7.

Complete histories of the Office of Strategic Services (OSS) and military psychological warfare activities will not be available for some time, since much of the material that would have to be consulted remains classified for security reasons. Some analyses have been made. For example see William E. Daugherty and Morris Janowitz, *A Psychological Warfare Casebook* (Baltimore, 1958), *passim.*

[2] See James L. McCamy, *Government Publicity* (Chicago, 1939).

[3] Pressures leading to expansion of the publications program can be seen in the State Department appropriations hearings before the House and Senate appropriations committees for the years 1923 through 1941 and in the American Society of International Law, *Proceedings* (published annually by the Society, Washington, D. C.) for the years 1928 through 1944, but see especially "Re-

tary began under John Hay (1898-1905) but became regular only under William Jennings Bryan (1913-1915) and Robert Lansing (1915-1920); they have continued as part of the pattern of the Department and serve as a most important method of reaching publics both domestic and foreign;[4] (3), dating from at least the early 19th century, the function of providing current information to Department officers overseas was performed at one place or another within the State Department. During the First World War the Division of Information (soon renamed the Division of Foreign Intelligence), then responsible for that function, was given added authority to prepare and distribute materials through local channels, "for publication in the foreign press in explanation of American policies and activities." [5]

---

port of Special Committee on Enlargement of the Scope of the Publications of the Department of State," in the *Proceedings,* 1929, pp. 63-70; 1943, pp. 84, 149-50; and 1944, p. 160.

For announcement of changes in the publication program see Department of State, *Press Releases,* I (October 5, 1929), 1, and *Bulletin,* 1 (July 1, 1939), 3. For a brief history of some phases of the publications program see E. R. Perkins, "Foreign Relations of the United States," *Bulletin,* 27 (December 22, 1952), 1002-1006.

See also Department of State, Departmental Orders 210 (May 28, 1921), 309 (August 11, 1924), 377 (June 15, 1926), 468 (February 15, 1929), 769 (August 1, 1938), 751 (April 5, 1938, but not released until November 29, 1938), and 796 (June 19, 1939). These orders trace the evolution of Department policy regarding access to its files and records by nonofficial researchers and indicate a growing awareness of public relations needs. (From February 27, 1908, Departmental Orders have been numbered serially. Bound volumes of the orders may be consulted in the Department of State library, though the most complete set in temporary bindings may be consulted in the Office of the Chief, Advisory and Review Branch, Historical Division, Department of State.)

[4] Bertram D. Hulen, *Inside the Department of State* (New York, 1939), pp. 130-50; Graham H. Stuart, *The Department of State, A History of Its Organization, Procedure, and Personnel* (New York, 1949), p. 201.

[5] Quotation from Department of State, Departmental Order 82 (May 7, 1917). See also Departmental Orders 15 (July 28, 1909), 18 (August 31, 1909), 62 (October 20, 1915), 64 (November 11, 1915), 72 (July 7, 1916), 78 (January 30, 1917), 83 (May 7, 1917), 85 (October 1, 1917), 201 (May 5, 1921), 203 (May 13, 1921), 206 (May 24, 1921), 985 (October 9, 1941), 1064 (June 25, 1942), 1218 (January 15, 1944), and 1229 (February 22, 1944).

See also *Outline of the Functions of the Offices of the Department of State 1789-1943* (prepared in the Division of State Department Archives, National Archives, by Natalia Summers, 1943; mimeo.; may be consulted in Office of the Chief, Advisory and Review Branch, Historical Division, Department of State), p. 96 for 19th-century activities; Stuart, *op. cit.,* pp. 217, 261; Thomson, *op. cit.,* pp. 171-72, 177 n38.

This function continued and was ultimately merged into the Second World War information effort through liaison with OWI and other information agencies of that period.

The major "informational activity" reaction to the penetration of the Axis powers in Latin America was the establishment in May, 1938, of the Interdepartmental Committee on Co-operation with the American Republics (renamed the Interdepartmental Committee on Cultural and Scientific Co-operation in December, 1944).[6] Through this committee co-operative projects and exchanges were conducted to promote understanding and solidarity in the Western Hemisphere. A Division of Cultural Relations, established within the State Department at this time (July, 1938), had its geographic and functional authority broadened during the Second World War but remained within the cultural field as distinguished from fast media information activities. In 1943 it received a portion of the activities of the Coordinator of Inter-American Affairs, and in January, 1944, its activities were placed in the newly established Office of Public Information (renamed Office of Public Affairs in December, 1944) within the Department of State.[7]

The course of these developments (here greatly condensed) up to the wholesale transfer of OWI and CIAA information activities to the State Department in August, 1945, included three elements of importance for the international information function as part of the country's diplomatic effort. First, the State Department had gradually become aware of the possibility of using current information to conduct diplomatic relations. However, secondly, the wartime pattern of crisis establishment of emergency agencies to do the bulk of the job of disseminating information established a pattern of separateness between information activities and traditional diplomatic meth-

[6] US Department of State, *Press Releases*, XVIII (January-June, 1938), 609-610, and XIX (July-December, 1938), 385-98. For international agreements providing basis for the Interdepartmental Committee see "Convention for the Promotion of Inter-American Cultural Relations, Buenos Aires, December 23, 1936," 51 *U.S. Statutes* 178 (1937), and *Final Act of the Eighth International Conference of American States, December*, 1938 (Lima, Peru, n.d.), p. 81. For statutory authority see 53 (*Part* 2) *U.S. Statutes* 1290 (1939).

[7] Department of State, Departmental Orders 768 (July 28, 1938), 1047 (April 15, 1942), 1218 (January 15, 1944), and 1229 (February 22, 1944). For statutory authorization see 52 *U.S. Statutes* 442 (1938) and 53 (*Part* 2) *U.S. Statutes* 652 (1939). See also *History of CIAA*, pp. 91-103, and Thomson, *op. cit.*, pp. 159-71.

ods. This gulf was increased by the successful resistance of State Department Press Officer Michael McDermott against incorporation of his office into the Office of Public Information in January and February, 1944.[8] Thus the closeness, administrative intimacy, and trust from personal contact between the secretary of state and the office that handled his press relations day in and day out were denied to the separate office that was engaged in the task of disseminating information through all media to the rest of the world. Thirdly, there was the impact of the early (1939) development within the Department of a "cultural relations" operation and its receipt of expanded cultural functions from the emergency operations of the Second World War (the 1943 transfer from CIAA) two years before the transfer of the Second World War information activities. The noncontroversial cultural program had the advantage of earlier administrative identity with the State Department as well as the unifying influence of the mutual State Department and CIAA memories of friction with OWI. The informational activities, more controversial and arriving later in the Department, were never as well accepted as were the cultural activities. These things have helped to create and perpetuate the separateness that continues to this day between "cultural" activities and "informational" activities.

2. Transition from the Second World War

Transfer of informational activities of the wartime agencies by Executive Order 9608 of August 31, 1945, found the State Department with the beginnings of a philosophy of the role of such operations in foreign policy. Archibald MacLeish as Assistant Secretary of State for Public and Cultural Relations had stated the previous December that

> the foreign relations of a modern state are conducted quite as much through the instruments of public international communications as through the diplomatic representatives and missions.[9]

Dr. Arthur W. Macmahon, Consultant on Administration to the Department of State, had echoed this view, though in more moderate form, and had gone on to state the objectives of international information activities as

[8] Department of State, Departmental Orders 1218 (January 15, 1944) and 1229 (February 22, 1944).

[9] *Bulletin*, 11 (December 10, 1944), 692.

first, to see that the context of knowledge among other peoples about the United States is full and fair . . . and, second, to see that the policies which directly affect other peoples are presented abroad with enough detail as well as background to make them understandable.[10]

The activities of government in this field should be "facilitative" of the "normal currents of private interchange" and "supplementary" to them where necessary. This view was laid down in Executive Order 9608 which gave the secretary of state four months, until December 31, 1945, to "study our foreign informational needs, and to formulate . . . the program which he considers should be conducted on a continuing basis." [11]

With the newly transferred functions lumped together within an Interim International Information Service (IIIS) for the balance of 1945, William Benton, replacing MacLeish as assistant secretary of state, faced a most complex set of tasks. While cutting down far-flung wartime operations of great magnitude but continuing to operate them, decisions had to be reached about peacetime operations, their levels and locations and integration into the State Department. In addition, the next year's budget had to be readied, and, a matter of basic importance, Congress had to be convinced that legislation should be passed to continue the function on something other than a temporary, crisis basis. (At this time only a portion of the cultural activities were being conducted on the basis of Congressional statutory authorization, all the rest having been established by executive action only.)[12]

Though the IIIS was succeeded by the OIC (Office of International Information and Cultural Affairs) at the beginning of 1946, the transitional status continued for another two years. The monumental task of integrating operations, administrative procedures, and personnel from the emergency agencies with the previously existing State Department operations in the information field, while at the same time reaching decisions on the nature and level of activities in

[10] Arthur W. Macmahon, *Memorandum on the Postwar International Information Program of the United States* (Washington, 1945), p. xi.

[11] *10 Federal Register 11223*. Text of the order and covering statement by the president are in *Bulletin*, 13 (September 2, 1945), 306-307. On the background of the decision see Thomson, *op. cit.*, pp. 185-86; and especially pp. 195-96, nn 11, 14, 16.

[12] *Bulletin*, 13 (September 16, 1945), 417, and (September 23, 1945), 430; Thomson, *op. cit.*, pp. 186-90.

peacetime, was carried on during 1946 and 1947 under serious handicaps. These handicaps, which at times threatened the whole program, consisted of: (1), an inadequate but developing philosophy of the nature and purpose of government international information activities held by persons in charge of the program within the State Department; (2), indifference and even hostility towards the program by other parts of the Department of State, most importantly the secretary himself at times; (3), Congressional antipathy towards all or parts of the program and objection to some of its personnel; (4), objections from commercial news-gathering and disseminating concerns to competition or interference from government information activities; and (5), a general public that lacked interest in and knowledge about government operations in this field.[13]

The drastic reduction of operations during the transition is indicated by the cut in personnel from the 11,000 wartime level of mid-1945 to approximately 3,000 by mid-1946. Appropriations show a similar picture of reduction from the over $60 million level in 1945 to $31 million in 1946 and about $20 million in 1947. During this same period appropriations for the cultural co-operation program were: $3,850,000 in 1945; $4,148,379 in 1946; and $5,555,900 in 1947. The appropriations pattern indicates not only the postwar reduction of expenditure to a peacetime level but also reflects a strong opposition to the basic information activity. The greater strength and stability of the cultural activities contrast sharply with the insecurity of the controversial information program.[14]

The pattern of informational activities at the end of 1946, a year and a half after the transfer of wartime activities to the State Department and a year before the basic legislation of 1948, consisted of the following features: (1), information staffs attached to seventy-six United States missions in foreign countries—a typical staff in a larger European country consisted of four Americans in the responsible positions of chief public affairs officer, an information officer doubling as press attaché to the embassy, a cultural relations

[13] Thomson, *op cit.*, pp. 199-240.

[14] *Bulletin*, 13 (December 30, 1945), 1045-47; Thomson, *op. cit.*, pp. 54-75; *History of CIAA*, pp. 41-103 and 263; US House, 79th Cong., 1st sess., *Hearings . . . on the Department of State Appropriation Bill for* 1946, p. 220 and *passim*; *ibid.*, 79th Cong., 2nd sess., for 1947, pp. 19, 527, and *passim*; *ibid.*, 80th Cong., 1st sess., for 1948, pp. 373, 1020, and *passim*; and US House, 79th Cong., 1st sess., *Hearings . . . on the National War Agencies Appropriation Bill for* 1946, pp. 882 and 1130.

officer, and a librarian, with these persons supervising a dozen or more local employees; (2), a daily 7,000-word wireless bulletin (reduced from the 100,000-word OWI daily bulletin) containing texts of documents and speeches, press conference reports, editorial excerpts, and news highlights sent to forty missions and made available in translation, except for the news highlights, to editors, writers, radio commentators, and government officials in the foreign countries; (3), background information on America sent from Washington in feature stories and pictures to the press of other lands; (4), exhibition pictures and film strips for schools and other groups abroad; (5), the Russian-language magazine, *Amerika,* with a 50,000-circulation permitted by the Soviet government; (6), a documentary and informative motion picture service made available to foreign groups in twenty-four languages using films made on commission from the State Department, adapted from documentary films made by other government departments, contributed by private organizations or businesses in the United States, or inherited from OWI and CIAA; (7), sixty-seven information libraries and twenty-seven cultural centers with forty-five branches, the latter being operated as co-operative enterprises in the twenty American republics, serving readers and arranging photographic, book, and art exhibits; and (8), the Voice of America broadcasts beamed over thirty-six transmitters in twenty-five languages to a listening audience of unknown size, though there were known to be about 20 million radio sets outside the United States capable of receiving short-wave signals and the Department had received over sixty thousand letters from listeners all over the world during 1946.[15]

The scientific and cultural exchange program, at this time authorized by statute only in the Western Hemisphere, provided travel or subsistence grants to a modest number of students and professors from Latin America to come to the United States. Financial assistance was also given to a few American students and professors for visits to Latin America. In addition, the program under the Interdepartmental Committee on Scientific and Cultural Co-operation had developed by the beginning of 1947 into exceedingly complex activities carried on co-operatively with all twenty of the Latin-American countries by agencies of the United States Government. These activities could be described as consisting of scientific and

[15] US House, *Hearings on 1948 State Department Appropriation,* pp. 373-85.

technical co-operation, exchange of special information, and exchange of persons.[16]

3. 1946-1948: Fight for Legislative Authorization

The years 1946 and 1947 were years of trial, tribulation, and near despair for supporters of the international information program. Congressional antipathy reached a new high when the House Appropriations Committee eliminated all funds for the program on the ground that it lacked legislative authorization. (Ultimately some $23 million, including liquidation funds, were provided for the fiscal year 1948 in the regular and supplemental appropriations.) Congressional authorization of cultural activities had expanded since the initial action in the latter 1930s, notably in the 1946 Fulbright Act providing for a large educational exchange program, but no such foundation had been provided for informational operations.[17]

Threats to the international information operations came for other reasons as well. Adverse Congressional and public reaction to parts of art exhibits, inclusion of "objectionable" books in overseas libraries, and one or two radio broadcasts threatened the whole operation. Support for and understanding of the information activities within the Department of State was increasing but was still at an extremely low level. In early 1946 the Associated Press and the United Press refused to continue their wartime arrangements for government use of their news services. Though commercially profitable short-wave broadcasts to the rest of the world were admittedly not possible, there were objections to the State Department's continued monopolization, through lease arrangements maintained after the war, of all the commercially owned facilities. Station WRUL, operating on a nonprofit, foundation basis, wanted to resume some use of its facilities

[16] *Ibid.*, pp. 1019-61.

[17] Extensions of authorization took place in Public Laws 370, 79th Cong. (April 30, 1946), and 882, 80th Cong. (July 2, 1948) for the Philippine citizens training program; 701, 79th Cong. (August 9, 1946) for the Merchant Marine Academy program; 369, 80th Cong. (August 5, 1947), and 283, 81st Cong. (September 3, 1949) for the Institute of Inter-American Affairs program; 584, 79th Cong. (August 1, 1946), and 400, 82nd Cong. (June 20, 1952), for the Fulbright program. Other related and/or subsequent extensions of authorization included provision for US participation in UNESCO, an exchange program with Finland making use of payments on the Finnish First World War debt, and use of counterpart funds received from sale of surplus agricultural commodities.

for international broadcasting. The American Society of Newspaper Editors feared that government bias in spot news presentation was inevitable as long as spot news was written or broadcast by government employees. Educational circles feared that the cultural activities would be used for propaganda, and thereby destroyed, through too close an association with informational activities. Directors of the information program could give strong arguments as to the need for information activities but were unable to meet Congressional demands for proof of the success of past operations. (Proof of the effect of international propaganda is not possible in present social science method, and it is possible that satisfactory solutions to the problem will never be found.)[18]

In the face of these adverse conditions, the path of legislative authorization proved both long and tortuous. A bill authorizing world-wide informational activities as well as cultural relations passed the House of Representatives in 1946 but died without Senate action. Again in 1947, but after much more detailed hearings and floor consideration, legislation was approved in the House by a roll call vote of 273 to 97 on June 24, 1947.[19] Though Senate passage before adjournment was again impossible, a key decision was made to send committees from both House and Senate to study the information program overseas during the fall of 1947.[20]

This group of touring senators and representatives, known as the Smith-Mundt group from the chairmen of the respective Senate and House groups, gained firsthand knowledge and experienced some of the "horrors" of the developing cold war. The group witnessed Soviet liquidation of opposition groups in Eastern Europe and Soviet propaganda against the United States. The committee reported

[18] See House and Senate *Hearings* on State Department appropriations for 1947, 1948, and 1949; US House, 79th Cong., 1st sess., *Interchange of Knowledge and Skills between People of the United States and Peoples of Other Countries*, Hearings before the Committee on Foreign Affairs. . . . on H.R. 4368 . . . and on H.R. 4982. . . . (Washington, 1946).

On methodological problems involved in measuring propaganda effectiveness see Daugherty and Janowitz, *op. cit.*, pp. 681-775.

[19] US Congress, *Congressional Record*, 79th Cong., 2nd sess., vol. 92, part 8, July 20, 1946, pp. 9591-95; 80th Cong., 1st sess., vol. 93, part 5, pp. 6490 ff., 6537 ff., and part 6, p. 7617. See also Thomson, *op. cit.*, pp. 234-35, nn 9, 11.

[20] *Congressional Record*, 80th Cong., 1st sess., vol. 93, parts 7, 8, and 9, pp. 8996, 9764-65, 9931, 10128-34, 10310, and 10403.

that the Soviets and the Communists are today conducting aggressive psychological warfare against us in order thoroughly to discredit us and drive us out of Europe. In order to prevent this, to safeguard our national security, to promote world peace and implement our own foreign policy . . . a strong and effective information and educational exchange program is essential.[21]

The task of an information program was seen essentially as getting others to know and understand us so that they would believe us. This could be done by the information service serving as

the voice of America and the means of clarifying the opinion of the world concerning us. To be effective it must (1) tell the truth; (2) explain United States motives; (3) bolster morale and extend hope; (4) give a true and convincing picture of American life, methods, and ideals; (5) combat misrepresentation and distortion, and (6) aggressively interpret and support our foreign policy.[22]

Congress continued to see the role of government as supplementing and facilitating private international communications, though the committee recognized that private efforts were not always of service to the country. While recognizing the need for counterpropaganda, Congress provided that the information service "disseminate abroad information about the United States, its people, and [its] policies." (Though strict interpretation of this language would appear to be a serious limit which would prevent giving information about other countries and their policies, it was apparently not so considered by the State Department in 1948. In fact it has not operated as a limit except possibly during the height of the McCarthy period when quotation of communists, even in programs citing Stalin against himself, was not permitted.) The philosophy of the committee saw an information program primarily to sell American policy to others. To some extent this need was seen as temporary—necessitated by the extraordinary conditions of the time—and short-run, as contrasted with the long-term cultural operations from which they felt it should be kept separate.[23]

[21] US Senate, 80th Cong., 2nd sess., *Report No.* 855 (January 30, 1948), part 1, pp. 2-5, quotation from p. 4. See also Edward W. Barrett, *Truth Is Our Weapon* (New York, 1953), pp. 61-62, and Oren Stephens, *Facts to a Candid World* (Stanford, Calif., 1955), p. 37.

[22] Senate *Report No.* 855, p. 3.

[23] Quotation from Public Law 402, 80th Cong., 2nd sess. (January 27, 1948), section 2 (1). See also Senate *Report No.* 855, and US Senate, 80th Cong., 2nd sess., *Report No.* 811 (January 7, 1948).

The bill that was to become Public Law 402 of the 80th Congress was presented to the Senate in January, 1948, after a brief return to committee for amendments reflecting the experience of the Smith-Mundt touring group. In the context of the pressures and fears of that time safeguards against communist infiltration and subversion were included as were provisions to protect private enterprise in the international information field. There were separate advisory commissions for the information and cultural relations programs. (Cultural relations had come to be referred to as educational exchange by that time.) Semiannual reports to Congress were called for, both from the advisory commissions and from the State Department.[24]

Thus safeguarded, and under the impetus of the cold war, the bill passed both House and Senate and was shortly thereafter, on January 27, 1948, signed into law by President Truman. A "full and fair" picture of America was to be given to the world, with the government "supplementing and facilitating" the international communications carried on by private individuals and groups. A new foreign policy tool had been provided for the government of the United States.

4. 1948-1950: Slow Growth

At the time of passage of the Smith-Mundt Act, however, the level of international information operations was lower than at any time since the beginning of the Second World War. Under the appropriations cut of the previous year, most operations were being carried on at little more than holding levels.[25] Though the fight for legislative authorization had finally been won under William Benton, thereafter George V. Allen, a respected career diplomat, took over

[24] Senate *Report No. 811*, *passim; Congressional Record,* 80th Cong., 1st sess., vol. 93, part 9, p. 11118; 80th Cong., 2nd sess., vol. 94, part 1, pp. 29, 153, 247-71. For House action in 1948 see *Congressional Record,* 80th Cong., 2nd sess., vol. 94, part 1, pp. 314-16, and for the record of presidential action see *ibid.*, pp. 370, 373, 458, and 679.

[25] US Department of State, *Report to the Congress, First Semiannual Report of Expenditures Made and Activities Carried on Under Authority of Public Law 402—United States Information and Educational Exchange Act of 1948, January 1-June 30, 1948, passim.* (The first three of these semiannual reports by the secretary of state covering 1948 and the first six months of 1949 were mimeographed and may be consulted in the National Archives, Legislative Records Branch, SEN 81A-F6, Committee on Foreign Relations, Communication from the Secretary of State: *First Semiannual Report.* Hereinafter cited as *Secretary's (First,* etc.) *Semiannual Report.*)

direction of the program. This change helped integrate information activities with the State Department and seemed to improve relations with Congress as well. The years from 1948 to 1950 brought gradual increases in appropriations, expansion of operations, modification of the structure of the State Department in the information field especially, and a general professionalization of informational activities.

Quantitative expansion of operations took place gradually from 1948 to 1950. Appropriation increases after passage of the Smith-Mundt Act added $3 million for fiscal year 1948, bringing the total for the year to approximately $24 million. In 1949 $33 million was provided, and for the fiscal year 1950 the amount rose to $47 million, including $11.5 million in a supplemental appropriation for radio facilities. Personnel in the program at home and overseas rose from a low of about 2,500 in 1948 to an authorized 6,030 in 1950. Actually, at the end of fiscal year 1950 only 4,370 persons were on duty due to the difficulties of attracting people to a program whose status had been so insecure and due to the lag involved in FBI investigation of persons to be employed—such investigation being another safeguard required by Public Law 402.[26]

Production and levels of operation generally increased throughout this period, though there were some notable exceptions. Radio broadcasting decreased temporarily in late 1948 when, under a Congressional reversal of an earlier mandate, origin of broadcasts was returned to the State Department. More than two thirds of broadcast output had been contracted to CBS and NBC under Congressional pressure to have as much of the information work as possible conducted by private enterprise. Lack of government control allowed some "objectionable" material to go out from the Voice of America, and Congressional insistence that the State Department take respon-

[26] For details of expansion of operations see: *Secretary's First, Second,* and *Third Semiannual Reports, passim;* US Department of State, *United States International Information and Educational Exchange Program, Fourth Semi-Annual Report of the Secretary . . . July 1, to December 31, 1949 . . .* (Washington, 1950), *passim;* US Department of State, Office of Public Affairs, Division of Publications, *International Information and Educational Exchange Program: Fifth Semiannual Report of the Secretary . . . , January 1 to June 30, 1950* (Washington, 1951), *passim.* For summary of budgetary and personnel information, differing in details from material in semiannual reports, see Howland H. Sargeant, "The Overt International Information and Educational Exchange Programs of the United States," *Bulletin,* 26 (March 31, 1952), 483-89.

sibility for broadcast content brought withdrawal of the commercial concerns. Following a temporary reduction when the State Department took over production, broadcasting expanded both as to number of hours on the air and languages used.[27]

Other changes in media or area concentration saw a shift of energy from the less critical Latin-American area to the more rapid political development in Europe, Asia, and the Middle East. In China the use of motion pictures and publications fell as the communists overran the country. As Soviet jamming increased sharply in 1949 after a small beginning in 1948, short-wave and medium-wave facilities were concentrated to get through to iron curtain areas. These and other similar operating shifts took place within the increase in program output in the period 1948-1950.[28]

This expansion took place within a modified structure in the State Department. Heedful of the Congressional demand, resulting from educational pressures and from cultural aspects of the program, the Office of International Information and Educational Exchange split into two separate offices early in 1948. Within the Office of International Information (OII) were the "fast" media dealing with information—radio broadcasting, publications, and motion pictures—while the "slow" media—exchange of persons, and libraries and institutes—were under the Office of Educational Exchange (OEX).[29]

The respective advisory commissions were established later in 1948 and, filled with exceptionally capable presidential appointees, began their study, advice, and reporting. Through the years these commissions have proved valuable to the program. Their profound and sympathetic analyses helped the program's structure and operation, and, in addition, their reports to Congress brought legislative appreciation for the international information program.[30]

[27] *Ibid.* See also US House, 80th Cong., 2nd sess., *House Report No. 2350*, June 15, 1948 (the Fourteenth Intermediate Report of the Committee on Expenditures in the Executive Department).

[28] *Ibid.*

[29] *Ibid.*

[30] *Ibid.* See also US Department of State, Division of Publications, Office of Public Affairs, United States Advisory Commission on Information, (First) *Semiannual Report to the Congress, March* 1949 (Washington, 1949), and US Advisory Commission on Educational Exchange, *First Semiannual Report of all Educational Exchange Activities Carried on from July 1 to December 31, 1948* (Washington, 1949). Subsequent reports of the advisory commissions were published in various formats and at irregular intervals.

The years 1948-1950 saw operational modifications that ultimately led to vast improvement in the program. Though during this period emphasis lay on quantitative output through the media divisions located in the United States and thus dangerously separated content-control decisions from contact with recipients in other countries, there was awareness of the need to tailor output to the requirements of local areas. More thinking began about specific groups. Closer liaison was established with area and country desks within the Department. This seemed to work more effectively in making the information operatives more aware of country and policy implications than in injecting informational factors into the formulation of foreign policy.[31]

The assistant secretary of state in charge of the information activities at this time had a difficult position. He was not only the secretary's adviser on opinion factors both foreign and domestic, but he also had to direct the somewhat heterogeneous elements of the informational and educational exchange programs. This difficult situation was noted in the Hoover Commission report of 1949 which also felt it would be desirable to have the program separated from the State Department but could see no alternative to its continuation within the Department. In the interest of allowing the program operating flexibility, improving its internal co-ordination, and allowing the assistant secretary to free himself from administrative burdens, the post of General Manager of the International Information and Educational Exchange Program was established within the Department in 1949. All media, including the "cultural," were combined under this single, high-level manager recommended in the Hoover Commission report.[32]

Additional major administrative and co-ordinative problems continued in international information. Radio broadcasting concentrated

[31] See the *Secretary's Semiannual Reports* during the period for details on the structural and operating changes. The clearest statements of the desirability of more consideration of informational factors in policy and for more funds for program appear in the *Semiannual Reports* of the Advisory Commission on Information.

[32] *Secretary's Fourth Semiannual Report*, pp. 1-3; US Commission on Organization of the Executive Branch of the Government, *Foreign Affairs, A Report to the Congress . . .* , February, 1949 (Washington, 1949), pp. 15-19, 32-35, and 54-55; US Commission on Organization of the Executive Branch of the Government, *Task Force Report on Foreign Affairs*, appendix H (Washington, 1948), pp. 2-3, 8, 18-19, 80-81, and 97-99.

in New York City, but this geographic separation from the other parts of the program was not to be eliminated for several years. And this problem was minor compared with that caused by several other international information operations by other branches and departments of the government. Information programs in the occupied areas of Germany, Austria, Korea, and Japan were operated by the military government in "liaison" with the State Department. Army radio broadcasts for armed forces overseas were achieving audiences among the local inhabitants. Separate information programs were conducted by and on behalf of both the new Point Four technical assistance program and the larger and older economic and military aid operations of the government. These separate operations made it impossible for the government of the United States to speak abroad with a single voice.[33]

Some of these problems were eliminated later with the end of military occupation or transfer to the State Department of responsibility for the information programs. Attempts to establish interdepartment information liaison through an Interdepartmental Foreign Information Staff in the State Department, however, were not successful. Though co-operation and co-ordination were achieved in the field, there was no substitute for central policy formation and direction.[34]

5. 1950-1953: Crises and Expansion

The year 1950 marked a turning point in the international program, as had passage in 1948 of the Smith-Mundt Act. The frightening international situation in early 1950 was recognized by the National Security Council (NSC) as requiring national rearmament and a major change of the country's security plans. Included was a massive development and expansion of the international information program.[35]

[33] See especially the *Secretary's Fourth* and *Fifth Semiannual Reports* and both House and Senate appropriations hearings for the State Department and Foreign Aid appropriations for fiscal 1950 and 1951.

[34] *Ibid.* See also Barrett, *op. cit.*, pp. 64, 91, and *passim;* and Stephens, *op. cit.*, pp. 39-41.

[35] US Department of State, Office of Public Affairs, Division of Publications, *Launching the Campaign of Truth, Sixth Semiannual Report of the Secretary . . . , July 1 to December* 31, 1950 (Washington, 1951), p. 1; Barrett, *op. cit.*, p. 72; Stephens, *op. cit.*, p. 39.

Outbreak of communist aggression in Korea impressed Congress with the need for action, and resulted in a tremendous increase in appropriations to support the recently announced Campaign of Truth. (President Truman, calling for implementation of the NSC recommendations, urged rearmament of the country for the psychological warfare waged against us by the Soviet Union. His use of the phrase "campaign of truth" in his speech when referring to our expanded operations led to adoption of the slogan as a popular title.) [36] Over $41 million was appropriated for radio facilities by Public Law 843 of the 81st Congress. All in all, supplemental appropriations of nearly $90 million during fiscal year 1951 added to the regular appropriation of $32.7 million made over $120 million available during the first year after the start of the Korean war.[37]

The immediate result of the appropriations transfusion was a modest increase in output and preparations for a vast expansion of personnel and equipment during succeeding months. And more than a mere quantitative expansion of the program was called for. Qualitative modifications and a general refocusing of the program took place to meet the desperate state of international relations. Radio broadcasting aimed more at the danger points of Soviet-Western conflict. New languages and dialects were put into use to reach populations in the Soviet Union and on its borders. Program content was changed by cutting time on music and drama and increasing news and analysis. As new equipment came into use stronger signals and special techniques were used to break through Russian jamming.[38]

The development or expansion of regional publication centers at Manila, London, and Beirut not only saved transportation time and costs but permitted production more closely tuned to the needs of specific countries and audiences. Eventually a system was established in which each publication was approved before production by the ambassador to the country in which it was to be used. Even the exchange of persons program shifted to the short-run situation by expanding exchange operations among leaders and others who could

[36] Barrett, *op. cit.*, pp. 73-74.

[37] For a summary of funds available see US Department of State, *Launching the Campaign of Truth, Second Phase, Seventh Semiannual Report of the Secretary . . . , January 1 to June 30, 1951* (Washington, 1952), p. 46.

[38] *Secretary's Sixth* and *Seventh Semiannual Reports, passim.*

have a more immediate impact on public opinion.[39] In fact, before the end of the 1950-1953 period there was a general reorientation of all operations. The needs of the field received recognition with establishment of country plans through consultation with operating personnel in each country. The media operations in the United States came to be seen as units serving the field rather than vice versa as had been the case until then.[40]

Increased co-operation with American private enterprise also took place during this period. Begun on a modest scale shortly after passage of the Smith-Mundt Act in 1948, the practice of bringing private groups and businesses into the international information operation was expanded during the Campaign of Truth period. By the middle of 1952 over six hundred arrangements had been made to stimulate such activities as use of American themes in export advertising and sales materials by large commercial organizations, private publication and distribution of orientation booklets for American tourists, and letter writing by Americans to friends and relatives in other countries. The Informational Media Guaranty Program, conducted earlier through MSA and ECA, was transferred to the State Department in 1952. This program provided guarantees of the convertibility into dollars of foreign currencies received by private American publishers and motion picture producers from sale of their approved products abroad, thus stimulating the export of books and movies.[41]

Differing from these activities was the technique of action by private groups in other countries. Attention to these channels helped create activities and projects supplemental and parallel to the regular information operations, which the official agency was not equipped to handle or which were more effective if not identified with the government of the United States.[42]

[39] *Ibid.*; US Department of State, *Waging the Truth Campaign, Eighth Semiannual Report of the Secretary . . . July 1 to December 31, 1951* (Washington, 1952), pp. 10-15, and 21-25; *Ninth Semiannual Report of the Secretary . . . , January 1952 to June 1952* (Washington, 1953), p. 2 and *passim*. See also Barrett, *op. cit.*, p. 91.

[40] The pattern can be seen in the *Secretary's Semiannual Reports* for these years. See especially US Department of State, *Tenth Semiannual Report of the Secretary . . . , July 1952-December 1952* (Washington, 1953), p. 4.

[41] *Secretary's Ninth Semiannual Report*, pp. 25-26.

[42] Barrett, *op. cit.*, pp. 91-93.

Informational activities within the State Department, including the "cultural" programs, were more tightly integrated with each other and given semiautonomous status within the Department by establishment of the International Information Administration in January, 1952.[43] This move put information operations under a single administrator responsible to the secretary of state. At the same time that it provided more freedom and flexibility for the information program it further freed the assistant secretary from administrative duties so that he could better advise the secretary on informational factors. Thus, by going beyond just the establishment of a general manager for the program, this change furthered the Hoover Commission recommendations and, though without precise anticipation, helped prepare for the establishment of the separate United States Information Agency some eighteen months later.

Though most of these 1950-1953 developments proved of continuing and permanent importance in the international information program of the United States, there were other aspects of the operation during this period that have come to be looked upon as of doubtful value. There was an understandable emphasis on counterpropaganda activities under the conditions of warfare in Korea and the vituperation of Soviet propaganda of the late Stalin period. Even so, there developed a shrillness of tone and a dogmatic anticommunism in content that was disturbing to those who recognized the need for subtlety. Audience receptivity for our information, and the reputation for truthfulness and objectivity in the information activities of the United States, appeared endangered by the blatant anticommunism of informational output in these years.[44] (It is impossible to determine how much of this was caused by the activities of McCarthy and how much was due to the operational enthusiasm engendered by the higher level of appropriations and the dangerous international situation.)

A most enthusiastic and overambitious statement of the objectives of the information program had been developed upon inauguration

[43] *Secretary's Ninth Semiannual Report*, pp. 2, 6, and *passim*.

[44] Careful reading of the media and region reports in the *Secretary's Semiannual Reports* for these years will disclose the build-up of ebullient anticommunism. Samples of materials disseminated are described in these reports. The atmosphere of the period is clearly shown in Barrett, *op. cit.* Compare with Stephens, *op. cit.*

of the Campaign of Truth. These objectives included the establishment of a healthy international community, deterring the Soviets from further encroachments and "helping to roll back Soviet influence." The operators of the information program had concluded "that most, if not all, of these objectives can be achieved with the correct deployment of America's psychological resources." [45]

Military psychological warfare in Korea emphasized the need for closer co-ordination among agencies engaged in international information activities for the government of the United States. A compromise among the views of the military and civilian agencies involved resulted in establishment of the Psychological Strategy Board (PSB) by Executive Order in 1951. The Board, consisting of the undersecretary of state, the deputy secretary of defense, and the director of the Central Intelligence Agency, attempted to co-ordinate psychological strategy and operations. During the few years that PSB and its lower-level, predecessor namesake within the State Department attempted to co-ordinate psychological strategy, however, the function never developed as hoped. Two causes of this failure have been noted. Edward W. Barrett states that the distance from Washington to the fields of operations made it difficult for PSB to handle complex problems in an operational near-vacuum. Oren Stephens emphasizes the fundamental proposition that psychological strategy does not exist apart from the political, economic, and military aspects of grand strategy. Since PSB had practically no influence in these other fields or upon the great executive departments of government involved, it could never operate satisfactorily.[46] A more workable system was to develop after the 1953 reorganization that established the separate USIA.

6. 1953-1960: Birth and Development of USIA

The international information program of the United States became a subject for political oratory during the 1952 presidential campaign. Political bitterness fed popular fear and distrust with charges of mismanagement and worse in the State Department and the International Information Administration. General Dwight D. Eisenhower, the Republican presidential nominee, promised that if elected he would see to the improvement of the country's psychological weapon.

[45] Barrett, *op. cit.*, pp. 78-79; Stephens, *op. cit.*, pp. 82-83.
[46] Barrett, *op. cit.*, p. 301; Stephens, *op. cit.*, pp. 39-40.

Following the election, Eisenhower and his advisers surveyed the whole organization and operation of the government. A committee under Nelson Rockefeller studying the executive branch agreed with John Foster Dulles that operational programs, including the international information operations, should be removed from the State Department. Since the middle of 1952 a subcommittee of the Senate Foreign Relations Committee had been studying the information program. Congressional study continued on into 1953 in a searching look at the problem at the same time as the Jackson Committee (appointed by Eisenhower following his inauguration, with William H. Jackson as chairman and including, among others, the special assistant to the president in psychological matters, C. D. Jackson) was studying foreign information activities in preparation for making recommendations to the president. Simultaneously the Advisory Commission on International Information Activities, established under the 1948 Smith-Mundt Act, was surveying the same ground in preparation for its seventh semiannual report.[47]

Out of all of these studies came the decision to establish a separate agency to conduct the international information program. Though the committee and commission reports differed on many points, some of them substantial, agreement was reached on Reorganization Plan No. 8, presented to Congress on June 1, 1953. Thus a separate and independent agency, the United States Information Agency, was established to conduct the international information program. The secretary of state was to provide policy guidance to the new agency. Educational exchange activities were retained in the State Department, thus protecting them from identification with "propaganda" activities as feared by the Congressional advocates, Senators J. William Fulbright and Karl Mundt. Doubts were expressed both inside

[47] The Rockefeller and Jackson committee reports have never been released though much of their content has appeared in the press and various Congressional hearings. See Stephens, *op. cit.*, pp. 42-44, and 71-78; Barrett, *op. cit.*, p. 113.

US Senate, 82nd Cong., 2nd sess., Committee on Foreign Relations, *Overseas Information Programs of the United States, Hearings . . .*, part 1, November 20 and 21, 1952; 83rd Cong. 1st sess., part 2, March, April, and May, 1953; 83rd Cong., 2nd sess., part 3, January 15, 1954. The interim report of the committee appeared as 83rd Cong., 1st sess., Senate *Report No.* 30, January 30, 1953.

The Seventh Semiannual Report of the US Advisory Commission on Information was published as 83rd Cong., 1st sess., *House Document No.* 94, February 23, 1953.

and outside Congress as to having the State Department establish policy while separate agencies engaged in operations in such fields as information and foreign aid. But the solution appeared to meet the demands of the professional information operators in the program for autonomy to allow "fast-moving" and "hard-hitting" operations.[48]

Before the new agency could have a test of its usefulness, certain temporary problems had to be overcome. During the first half of 1953, morale within the IIA had dropped to a record low and operations proceeded timidly amidst confusion and even chaos. The death of Joseph Stalin in early 1953 found the agency's responsible, expert, policy-making Russian desks empty while the key personnel waited for hours to appear before the McCarthy investigations. In the spring a hasty order from the secretary of state had forbidden use of materials written by Russians, thus preventing the technique of quoting communist against communist and Stalin against himself. The order was superseded by a more reasonable directive, but action had been started that led to charges that the new administration was engaging in book-burning. In addition to the McCarthy charges and the zealous investigative practices of his staff, operations in 1953-1954 were affected by the major reorganization and relocation of the function, the change of politics in the White House, and the reductions in force that were the answer to demands for economy in government and for "cleaning up the mess" in Washington.[49]

The middle of 1954 saw the end, for the most part, to these conditions of crisis. The new, separate administrative structure was stabilized and drastic personnel changes were a matter of history. McCarthy's star had waned if not set. In general, bureaucratic stability returned and morale was on the rise.

The half decade of the USIA era, since the first transitional year, can be considered as a substantially homogeneous period. The developments of these years can be organized in four categories: (1), interagency policy and operations co-ordination; (2), intra-agency administration and co-ordination; (3), changes in emphasis in content and methods; and (4), expansion of facilities and of the geographic scope of operations.

[48] *Ibid.* See also US House, 83rd Cong., 1st sess., *Reorganization Plans Nos. 7 and 8 of 1953, Hearings before the Committee on Government Operations,* June 22, 23, and 24, 1953; Stephens, *op. cit.*, pp. 78-79.

[49] See Barrett, *op. cit.*, pp. 101-114, and 124-25; Stephens, *op. cit.*, p. 43; United States Information Agency, *First Review of Operations, August-December, 1953* (Washington, 1954), *passim.*

The major developments in interagency co-ordination stemmed from the same 1953 reorganization that led to the birth of the USIA. The recognition, contained in the Jackson Committee report, that psychological strategy could not be separate from total national strategy, led to abandonment of the old Psychological Strategy Board and establishment of the Operations Co-ordinating Board (OCB) under the National Security Council. With the undersecretary of state as chairman, OCB includes a representative of the president, the deputy secretary of defense, and the directors of the Central Intelligence Agency, USIA, and the International Co-operation Administration (formerly the Foreign Operations Administration). The staff of OCB, and as of recently the National Security Council staff, provides a communications channel or interagency forum for co-ordination of operations of all agencies involved.[50]

This establishment of improved interagency forums did not immediately lead to greater recognition of the role of informational activities in policy nor to increased consideration of opinion factors in the formulation and enunciation of policy. These changes took place gradually during succeeding years as USIA gained, maintained, and used its separate agency identification. This separate institutional existence of the information agency was in sharp contrast with the period when the function was within the State Department. From being a section of that Department, and a somewhat unloved section at that, the information agency became independent with a budget of its own and access to the President. With its prestige and recognized separateness growing, as in any institutional development, the USIA has come to have an important impact in OCB, NSC, and through the channels of direct interagency liaison.[51]

The 1960 level of interagency co-ordination and consideration of informational and opinion factors in policy was probably higher than that of any previous period. This was due not only to the pattern of institutional development but also to the personality and experience of the then director of USIA, George V. Allen. He brought to this position his experience with the information program and his lengthy career and detailed knowledge in the traditional diplomatic field.

[50] US Congress, 85th Cong., 2nd sess., *Congressional Directory*, p. 393. For early membership see Stephens, *op. cit.*, p. 73. Information on most recent developments is from interviews with USIA personnel of the OCB and NSC staffs in Washington, June, 1959.

[51] Interviews with USIA personnel in Washington, June, 1959.

The trust and respect accorded him by the State Department and President Eisenhower increased the receptivity of the State Department and other agencies in OCB and NSC towards USIA participation in policy councils. (It is not known at this writing whether this interagency co-ordination pattern has become institutionalized sufficiently to carry over into Edward R. Murrow's directorship of USIA.)

With the State Department having responsibility for foreign policy and giving policy guidance to the USIA, the relations between these two agencies are of utmost importance. Within the State Department the assistant secretary for public affairs, divorced from contact with the international information operations, serves as the secretary's adviser on information and public opinion. Daily policy meetings between USIA personnel and the geographic and functional divisions of the State Department provide valuable briefings. In addition, contact by phone takes place between the Washington desks of the two agencies. In the field missions, the information officer from USIA serves, as do other personnel in overseas missions, under the chief of mission from the State Department. The information officer, however, can now participate on equal terms in staff meetings—something that was nearly impossible before the increase in stature attendant upon establishment of the independent USIA.

Within USIA the movement initiated in the 1950-1953 period for increased discretion in the field and more field control over media operations has continued. The upgrading of regional organization and the subordination of media divisions have helped the media serve the field. In addition, since 1953 a system of roving area directors has given new force to the concept. Such area directors serve half the time in Washington and half the time in the field surveying operations and keeping informed of operational needs and problems.[52]

A move was made in 1954 to bring radio broadcasting into closer co-ordination with the rest of the information program. The Voice of America operations were moved to Washington from New York, increasing opportunities for contact with area desks and other media desks.[53]

[52] USIA, *First Review of Operations*, p. 4.

[53] *Ibid.*, p. 10; USIA, *2nd Review of Operations, January-June, 1954* (Washington, 1954), pp. 9-10; *3rd Review of Operations, July-December, 1954* (Washington, 1955), p. 6.

In contrast to development of intra-agency co-ordination patterns which were largely continuations and perfections of patterns begun prior to establishment of USIA, some of the directions of development of content and operating method have differed from those of the 1950-1953 State Department days of the Campaign of Truth. Instead of the fast-moving, frequently shrill, anticommunist counter-propaganda of the earlier period, the USIA under Streibert, Larson, and especially Allen has concentrated on the positive, the objective, and the long-range. More attention has been paid to the broad picture of American life, culture, and commerce. Stress has been placed on objectivity of tone and factual news presentation instead of propagandistic approaches. While daily handling of short-run problems has not decreased, emphasis is on the long-range, cultural impact. These changes appear in increased teaching of English in other countries, book translation and publication, increases in the information media guarantee program, an increase in the VOA world-wide English broadcasts, more music on VOA, increases in feature presentation by private experts and professionals, and increased participation in international trade fairs.[54]

Private co-operation, in existence for several years when the information program was in the State Department, received emphasis in 1956 with President Eisenhower's "People to People" program. In addition to the many earlier methods of private co-operation, new methods of city-to-city contact and salutes were begun while older operations expanded. New groups participated in the program; the Advertising Council contributed ideas and assistance. Consultation and co-operation increased between USIA and private groups.[55]

International exchanges of persons and films with the Soviet Union, unthinkable in the days of Stalin and McCarthy, were inaugurated in 1957 and 1958. In addition, another method of breaching the iron curtain was renewed with the distribution within the Soviet orbit of *America Illustrated*, the successor to the earlier magazine, *Amerika*.

[54] The change of emphasis can be seen in the semiannual USIA *Review of Operations*, both House and Senate *Hearings on USIA Appropriations*, and in the Advisory Commission on Information, *Semiannual Reports*. See especially US Advisory Commission on Information, *Fourteenth Report, March,* 1959 (Washington, 1959), *passim;* USIA, *11th Review of Operations, July 1-December 31,* 1958 (Washington, 1959), *passim.*

[55] *Ibid.*

(Publication of *Amerika* had ended during the Korean war when restrictions on distribution within Russia had increased so much as to make the whole operation of doubtful value.) These contacts with the USSR were of great importance, but they also formed part of the shift from counterpropaganda to more long-range, cultural operations.[56]

Associated with these new directions, and to a great extent underlying them, has been a marked redefinition of objectives since the ambitious days of 1950-1953. A far more modest and realistic listing of objectives has taken place in recent years. The Advisory Commission on Information now sees the proper functions of the Agency: (1), as a counselor on international public opinion; (2), as an expositor of US foreign policy; (3), as a special and noncompetitive overseas information service; (4), as a portrayer of the United States to peoples abroad.[57]

Expansion of facilities and geographic extension of operations under USIA have not been as great as during the 1950-1953 period. Following the large appropriations for radio facilities in 1950 and 1951, no large amounts for capital outlays were provided for several years. In 1958 and 1959 funds were made available for much new equipment for radio broadcasting. These funds allow construction of new equipment in the United States to provide a stronger signal to relay bases overseas or for direct short-wave broadcast to listeners in the rest of the world.[58] (The 1950-1951 appropriations allowed the construction of part of the then contemplated Ring Plan of overseas relay bases for reaching Europe and Asia with a signal strong enough to overcome Soviet jamming. Funds were never forthcoming to complete the facilities nor to provide new equipment in the United States. Facilities in the United States have been primarily the pre-Second World War facilities of private broadcasting companies leased to the government.)

Modifications have taken place in broadcasting operations over the

[56] USIA, *5th Review of Operations, July 1-December 31, 1955* (Washington, 1956), p. 8; *6th Review of Operations, January 1-June 30, 1956* (Washington, 1956), p. 12. On the exchanges with the USSR see US House, 85th Cong., 2nd sess., *Report No. 2712, Government Programs in International Education: A Survey and Handbook*, Forty-Second Report by the Committee on Government Operations, January 3, 1959 (Washington, 1959), pp. 65-66, 210-11, and 223-33.

[57] Advisory Commission on Information, *Fourteenth Report*, p. 13.

[58] USIA, *11th Review of Operations*, pp. 3 and 26.

last several years. In addition to the development of program materials for television facilities in friendly countries, there has been emphasis on packaged programs and materials for broadcasting over national and commercial radio facilities abroad. Such programs and VOA originations rebroadcast or relayed over the long-wave and medium-wave facilities of other countries reach much larger audiences than short-wave broadcasts to the same areas. Expansion of these activities has allowed a decrease in the hours of VOA broadcasts to many areas while at the same time increasing the effect of the informational material presented via radio.[59]

The speed and efficiency of the news and press program increased with completion in 1958 of a teleprinter network to seventy-five missions overseas. This improved both the speed and accuracy of distribution of the news bulletin as compared with the earlier wireless or courier transmission.[60]

In recent years an expansion of operations in Africa has been taking place. With the increased importance of this awakening continent, new posts have been established and services expanded. Though African operations are but a small part of the total USIA activities, they will increase as more areas gain independence and a more important role in world affairs.[61]

Though a higher degree of institutional and operational stability has been achieved under USIA than before its establishment, there are problems of long standing that affect the international information activities of the United States. Even under USIA appropriations for salaries and expenses have fluctuated widely. Appropriations for fiscal years 1954 through 1959 were, in millions of dollars: 84.2, 77.3, 87.3, 113.0, 96.5, 101.9.[62] Such fluctuation makes it difficult if not impossible to maintain efficient and stable operating levels. The effect on personnel can be disastrous.

The personnel problem is intensified by lack of a career civil service. Employees need protection of such a system for optimum performance. Hiring of specialists and administrators in an international information program will probably become easier and personnel turnover decrease when Congress enacts a career service for USIA.

[59] See USIA, *First* through *11th Review of Operations, passim.*

[60] USIA, *11th Review of Operations*, p. 2.

[61] See USIA, *8th* through *11th Review of Operations, passim.*

[62] USIA, *11th Review of Operations*, p. 26.

The administratively-established career service and entrance examination system, which became operational in 1960, only partially meets the need.

The problem of program and output evaluation has never been solved though various techniques have been tried. Mere quantitative measures of audiences and of media output, when and where these are possible, do not give satisfactory measure of the returns from time and money spent. Evaluation teams, tried in three or four countries, were discarded. The present inspection staff engages in more than a mere administrative efficiency study. It looks at broad problems and makes suggestions for meeting them.[63] In this field of international information programs there is no objective technique available for evaluation of operations. About the best substitute is evaluation by trusted, experienced individuals, plus faith in the nature of the operations.

Another continuing problem, at least to the theoretical mind, is separation of cultural activities from the bulk of the information program. Probably no complete separation or amalgamation of these overlapping and interlocking aspects of international relations would ever prove satisfactory. The latest development was establishment in July, 1959, of a Bureau of Cultural Affairs in the State Department. This is an attempt to pull together in one place under an assistant to the secretary of state such cultural activities as the UNESCO staff, international exchange of persons, and cultural presentations by performing artists.

Another problem, again one to which there will probably never be a solution satisfactory to the agencies and interests involved, is consideration of information and opinion factors in the formulation, enunciation, and implementation of policy. Persons more aware of one set of factors than of others will almost inevitably feel that their factors are not receiving sufficient consideration. The United States Advisory Commission on Information stated in March, 1959 that

> USIA too often is expected to perform after policies have been determined rather than to advise during the formulation of policies. . . . there is some lack of acceptance both in Washington and abroad of the importance of the public relations aspects of foreign policy. Often advice in this area is not even sought by the relevant departments or agencies.[64]

[63] Interviews with USIA personnel in Washington, June, 1959. See Advisory Commission on Information, *Fourteenth Report*, pp. 18, 29-30.

[64] Advisory Commission on Information, *Fourteenth Report*, p. 4.

During the winter of 1960-1961 considerable attention began to be paid to the "P" (for psychological) factors in foreign policy making. The probable reactions of overseas populations were supposed to be considered by policy makers at all levels in all departments of the government. However, no institutional changes or increased consultation of USIA by other agencies to facilitate consideration of the "P" factor took place during the last weeks of the Eisenhower administration.[65] President Eisenhower's Committee on Information Activities Abroad (Mansfield D. Sprague, Chairman) called for great expansion in the information program and emphasized its interrelationship with diplomatic, economic, and military activities.[66] However, the action that the Kennedy administration might take had not been announced at the time of this writing (February, 1961).

While these and many other minor and not so minor problems will come and go, it is clear that since the end of the Second World War some answers have been provided to questions raised at the beginning of this essay. The United States will continue an international information program in the conduct of foreign policy. In spite of the deservedly higher reputation of the operation in recent years, the psychological method has not yet been accepted on an equal footing with the economic, military, and political. Frequently it is consulted or informed after policy formulation rather than before, though actions are not usually taken these days without clearance through OCB.

Fears that a government international information program would impinge upon the internal politics of our society have proved largely groundless. Though members of Congress still pass judgment on the artistic merits of selections for overseas art shows, and even presidents exhibit their artistic knowledge and taste at times, there is no longer the widespread inclination to see sinister communist influences at work in the information program.

More and more the government speaks with one voice in foreign affairs, though this may be a temporary by-product of internal political stability. Citizens of foreign countries will probably always be puzzled or alarmed by Congressional exercise of free speech. The only solution to this problem is being attempted through our international information program in explanations to the rest of the world about our democratic system. Likewise, the problem raised by citizen exer-

[65] Interviews with USIA personnel in early January, 1961.

[66] *The Washington Post*, January 12, 1961.

cise of free speech is being solved through increased understanding abroad. Co-ordination of private expressions of opinion with official foreign information policy is being promoted through the "People to People" program.

Our government has developed the machinery and skills to answer its critics, exhibit and explain our values, indicate areas of interest between us and others, and in general to promote the achievement of foreign policy through international informational activities.

19: THE IMPACT OF MILITARY FACTORS ON AMERICAN FOREIGN POLICY

Fred Greene

In the bitterness of the cold war, military considerations have gained a prominent place in our foreign policy. The rise in importance of national security is ample evidence of the key role played by issues involving war and defense. Budgetary expenses, technical efforts, contacts and interests abroad are devoted to the relief of our precarious position.

But this does not mean that foreign policy has become the handmaiden of new security requirements. For one thing, security is essentially negative, a condition for the pursuit of other interests and objects which are so important that they demand attention even under trying military conditions. Secondly, military factors and security needs may have a profound effect on the environment in which a nation conducts its foreign policy, but they do not of themselves determine or dominate the policies adopted.[1] The choices open to us are many and the selection remains a political act, involving considerations beyond the military-security realm.

Military factors do not control all defense problems, and security considerations are not the essence of foreign policy. Nevertheless, they do change the conditions under which diplomacy operates, requiring at times new rules, often reducing the trustworthiness of traditional approaches.[2] Our concern, therefore, is both with the extent and the limit of the military impact on foreign policy.

[1] For an excellent analysis of security in this context see Arnold Wolfers, "National Security as an Ambiguous Symbol," *Political Science Quarterly*, LXVII (December, 1952), 481-502.

[2] For a convenient brief summary of American military policy since 1945, including bibliography, see Charles Donnelly, *United States Defense Policies Since World War Two*, 85th Cong., 1st Sess., House Doc. 100 (Washington, 1957), and *United States Defense Policies in 1957*, 85th Cong., 2nd Sess., House Doc. 436 (Washington, 1958).

MILITARY INEQUALITY AND ALLIANCE RELATIONS

In recent years, the notion that we are living in a bipolar world has lost currency. The reconstruction of Europe, the birth of a free India, the rise of China, and the appearance of outspoken neutralists are cited as evidence that a new political order is in the making. There is also an effort to shift the struggle from its military orientation and make it a political-economic competition. With this stress on nonmilitary factors, the argument goes, the weaker Afro-Asian states can use their position as neutrals to help redress slight shifts in the balance of power. Finally, many see a military stalemate in which the very destructiveness of the weapons has restricted our use of them and so has reduced the power of both America and Russia.[3]

This writer holds the opposite view—that bipolarity will be with us for a long time, and that its citadel is the military force required today of a great power. It is true that Soviet-American equality and the emergence of the world from the numbing experiences of the 1940s have permitted other states more freedom of maneuver. But this is not a reversion to normal times; diplomacy is still operating in a different context.

The strategic and military considerations which underlay bipolarity also affect foreign policy. Of fundamental importance is the strategic position of the competitors, at opposite sides of the globe and possessing vast continental homelands. The new technology has brought them within each other's range, but has also made the in-between states more vulnerable. Only the two superpowers are able to mount the peacetime forces required to provide *couverture* and some strategic capability at the start of a war. In the past, the British navy and continental armies, with their elaborate mobilization plans, sufficed. Today the problem is so vast and complex that only the US and the USSR have any hope of withstanding or striking back against a sudden, massive attack.

The forces needed today are staggering beyond imagination—long-range and tactical aircraft, air transport, war missiles of various sizes, complex electronic communication systems, air and sea continental defense networks, a ground army that must constantly be retrained and re-equipped, and vast supply programs. In addition,

[3] See, for example, Charles Lerche, *Foreign Policy of the American People* (New York, 1958), pp. 361-72, and W. W. Rostow, "Rostow on Growth," *The Economist*, CXCII (August 22, 1959), 525-26.

their priorities must be determined with two possibly unrelated considerations in mind—danger and probability. The breathtaking rate of change produces new combat doctrines for the army, the transformation of our great surface fleet into a versatile but expensive submersible force, pressures to build new aircraft as the combat plane threatens to disappear, and missile generations which literally tumble upon one another. By any standards, America and Russia possess formidable forces which cannot be matched by third powers even if they develop a nuclear capability.

To the requirements of a great power must be added ability and willingness to assist allies and other friendly powers in a vast effort at military modernization. The steady streams of fresh equipment and new combat doctrine and training methods comprise an enormously expensive aid program which would have seemed revolutionary a generation ago. Today its size is not appreciated because the entire operation consumes but a fraction of our military budget. Yet even the industrialized Western allies needed financial and technical aid just for conventional rearmament.[4] To sustain them in a nuclear capability, we would have to double the cost of the program.

There is finally the open future of research and development and the creation of new weapons systems. The expense and technological capacity required for such efforts also explain why the two superpowers are in a class of their own.[5] Just recently, we have had to develop multiple approaches (Jupiter and Thor), undertake expensive feasibility studies (chemically-powered aircraft), and scrap a workable item outdated at birth (Regulus II). A new anti-ICBM missile may prove superior to its current intended victims but inferior to weapons on the drawing board, and even this limited success is uncertain. The anti-ICBM missile could cost $3 billion in 1961-1964, or 50 per cent more than the wartime Manhattan project.[6] And its realization would spawn still more programs.

[4] Summary tabulations of military aid are in the Draper Report. *Composite Report of the President's Committee to Study the United States Military Assistance Program* (Washington, 1959). See especially I, pp. 142, 144.

[5] Britain's difficulties in sustaining research are discussed in Andrew Shonfield, "A Deadlock on the Left," *Encounter*, XII (September, 1959), 11-19.

[6] This estimate is deduced from testimony of General Maxwell Taylor and Major General R. J. Wood in *Department of Defense Appropriations for 1960. Hearings, Subcommittee of the Committee on Appropriations*, House, 86th Cong., 1st Sess. (Washington, 1959), Part 1, pp. 324-25.

Here then are the military factors that distinguish America from its friends—vast differences in security, allied dependence upon American treaty commitments and military aid, and a clear American superiority in research and development. An alliance system characterized by such inequalities is subject to strain, which becomes the more damaging if the built-in causes are not understood when their effects are most pronounced. This diplomatic situation is made more tense by the knowledge that a lesser state without security links to one superpower is severely restricted in its freedom to act. Our European allies feel acutely the weight of bipolarity, for they are major industrial powers unexpectedly placed in a weakened, dependent position.

Frequently in an alliance one signatory's survival hinges upon the treaty, whereas another partner derives some important but less vital benefit (*e.g.*, France and Russia, 1891-1894). The psychological pressure on the more vulnerable ally is enormous and may give rise to reactions that are irrational. Thus, the appearance of a Soviet thermonuclear missile capability in the late 1950s, making the United States highly vulnerable, brought a first reaction of relief and even jubilation in Europe at this more even distribution of danger. There was even a desire for a while to drive a harder bargain with America over bases, as though Europe's diplomatic position could be improved thereby. This situation righted itself somewhat with the appearance of an American missile program, and the alliance paradoxically benefitted from the realization that America had slipped toward Europe's level of vulnerability.

Difficulties rooted in military inequality also crop up when the United States seeks to fulfil its self-interpreted global responsibilities.[7] Our involvement in the Far or even Near East is a source of dismay to Europe as much as Russia's actions were to France a half century earlier. This dismay stems partly from doubts of the wisdom of American policy, but also reflects a lack of national interest in those distant areas, certainly not worth the price of draining off military power. When American and British forces entered Lebanon and Jordan in 1958, one German critic suggested the invocation of Article 51—by which he meant the West German sanity code rather than the UN Charter on collective self-defense.[8] In all, we

[7] H. F. Armstrong stressed the global nature of our problem in "The World is Round," *Foreign Affairs,* XXXI (January, 1953), 175-99.

[8] See *New York Times,* July 19, 1958. Criticism of this operation was universal, but the nature of the arguments reflected a marked insularity of outlook.

are subject to unequal pressure from Europe and Asia. Europe contains our close allies, traditional friends, and centers of industrial power. On the other side are a doggedly neutralist India, and a Japan that resists serious rearmament. It is difficult for the strongest power, though centrally located, to give attention to the military problem in Asia when Europeans oppose a "global balance of effort" and the key nations in Asia are hostile or indifferent.

Heavy dependence upon the United States, coupled with concern over America's inexperience in world politics, gave rise to allied anxiety about the basic nature of Soviet-American relations. Hypersensitivity in this instance takes the form of contradictory fears—that we will not negotiate with the Russians or that we will make a private deal. Fear of American recourse to atomic warfare preys on European thoughts, and it brought a hurried visit from Prime Minister Clement Attlee during the Korean War. But matching it is a suspicion that we would not use the ultimate weapon to protect others if it meant endangering ourselves. The fear that Russia might move on Europe, warning America to stay out for fear of reprisal, is strengthened by the inadequacy of European retaliatory and field forces. Hence, American leadership at SHAPE must brandish the threat of nuclear retaliation in case of aggression, because any logical application of graduated deterrence will cause our allies to fear that we are hedging on our commitments. However, this position means that any war will be a nuclear one, signifying the destruction of Europe.[9]

To restrict nuclear weapons to field operations does not reduce the problem if combat zones are several hundred miles deep. To renounce nuclear power at the tactical or longer-range level is to give up the ghost of defensibility,[10] for it is impossible to imagine that so grave a move as a Soviet thrust at Western Europe would be made without nuclear weapons in the attacking arsenal. An attacker will not muffle his firepower, ignore years of training in the employment of such devices, and obligingly concentrate his forces so as to get the required intensity of conventional firepower. He

[9] Two valuable discussions of NATO problems are Malcolm Hoag, "NATO: Deterrent or Shield?" *Foreign Affairs*, XXXVI (January, 1958), 278-92; and Roger Hilsman "On NATO Strategy," in Arnold Wolfers, ed., *Alliance Policy in the Cold War* (Baltimore, 1959), pp. 140-83.

[10] For an opposite viewpoint, see James E. King, "The Berlin Controversy," *The New Republic*, CXL (April 13 and 20, 1959), 10-15 and 9-13.

would be too easy a mark for defensive nuclear air strikes and ground counterblows.

Hence it is very difficult to imagine SHAPE defenses which are not nuclear-armed able to oppose or deter a Soviet attack. Political leaders in Europe who want to limit the nuclear club or withdraw from it must take into account the existing NATO decision to resist aggression with nuclear weapons, implemented by a joint allied decision. The allies cannot escape the burden of responsibility whether they own the weapons or not.

This problem weighs less heavily in the Far East because Communist China still lacks a nuclear capability and, as far as we know, does not have access to such weapons. The United States, having struck once against Asians, would find the ill effects of further nuclear attack outweighing advantages in all but an extreme situation. The attitude of India and the vulnerability of Japan point emphatically against an initial American employment. Finally the noncommunist states of Asia would be totally dependent upon America for the development and maintenance of nuclear forces.

The difference in military power between America and the Far Eastern states is so great that the nuclear problem can hardly have an impact. In Europe, however, the new military technology has widened a narrow gap, and given it an appearance of definitiveness which tends to set the two continents apart. Despite Western Europe's industrial advances during the past decade, it has not demonstrated the political cohesion, technical capacity, and financial ability to keep up with the pace of modernization. It therefore became an American interest to give Europe an atomic capability in intermediate range missiles, with our continued production dependent on European demand.[11]

This move was to place the IRBMs on effective launching sites. It was also designed to give Europeans a sense of dignity and control over their own destiny, and put teeth in the retaliatory threat by making it a means of immediate defense against attack. To our surprise, the response was very cautious, with only Britain, Italy, and Turkey accepting IRBM bases. Much opposition stems from a fear of involvement in what otherwise might be a direct American-Soviet confrontation, adding to America's defense at no benefit to Europe.

[11] Testimony of Secretary of Defense Neil McElroy and General Nathan Twining in *Department of Defense Appropriations for 1960, Hearings, op. cit.*, pp. 142, 157-58, 160.

Despite this disappointment, it is to our credit and advantage that we bring such problems as the location of weapons, equipment for troops, and use of weapons in crisis before our allies. Otherwise suspicion of an atom-brandishing American directorate might have undermined the NATO alliance.

We must conclude that the advent of nuclear power has added to our difficulties in dealing with Europe by creating a terrifying choice regarding operational employment and increasing European reliance on America for its security. Europeans with a deep sense of vulnerability liken nuclear missile dispositions on the Continent to magnets that would attract an irresistible Soviet counterblow. There is no confidence that such efforts will enhance Europe's protection, or contribute to a global effort of deterrence through dispersal of power. We are left with a European self-portrait as an isolated region, confronting the Russians with the mixed blessings of American backing.

As the senior military partner, the United States has had to avoid a domineering or imperial attitude toward its allies. It has responded to this challenge with considerable success in treating all treaty partners as sovereign equals. But we have now learned that the task begins with this relationship of mutual respect, for equality also signifies considerable freedom of maneuver for our friends. They would seek to pursue their lines of interest under any event, but the protective mantle of alliance gives them greater freedom for action, and it is here that complications set in. A balance must be drawn between a superpower and its allies, measuring the contribution signatories make toward furthering their mutual interests against their use of alliance benefits to satisfy particular interests that may be irrelevant or even harmful to the common cause.

The stark fact that he cannot protect his very existence can lead an ally to assume that this problem is no longer primarily his own but ours, and that he should not be required to devote his major effort in this direction. In fact one of the values of the alliance, making an important contribution to its durability, is that it affords him an opportunity to pursue more cherished objectives. These may be a struggle to preserve an empire (France in Algeria), security against a neutral (Pakistan and India), a wrangle over *irredenta* (Greece and Britain and Turkey over Cyprus, Italy and Yugoslavia over Trieste), a struggle against a traditional oppressor (South Korea against Japan), avoidance of military burdens (Japan), or exacting a higher price for defense efforts (West Germany after 1950). Disputants seek American support in their quarrels, but if it is not forthcoming they demand neutrality, at least. A changed technological situation may induce an ally to raise the "monetary tax" for the use of his territory, though the additional benefit (*e.g.*, a missile base) is mutual. Treatment of allies on a basis of reciprocity has therefore proved to be a point of departure, since no political relationship is simply static, not even one of allies in the presence of an awesome danger.

Since the major American national interest is to preserve the general balance, we are prone to self-righteousness in claiming to be truer to the alliance than those who use its protection for other purposes. Moreover, we have the military power to spare for such side excursions without reducing the power available for the common task.

A further complication is the desire of some allies to be "more equal than others." There is a widespread belief that the key to a preferred position is enhanced military power. This makes the new weapons a prestige item within the allied camp, the price of admission to some imagined directorate. The consequences for the group's security are not thought out, and very often the benefits do not match the large-scale expenses entailed.[12]

We have also found it difficult to restrain a weaker ally from moving against the common enemy in a reckless and, to us, unrewarding manner. Thus, Nationalist China's reinforcement of the offshore islands in the mid-1950s was undertaken against American wishes and led to two serious military incidents within five years. It is not true that the weaker power in an alliance can use this lack of strength to compel support for his actions. This argument was originally based on the German experience with Austria-Hungary in 1914, which is in a class of its own. Our treaty arrangements with South Korea and Nationalist China reflect a determination to keep the initiative and decision for action in our own hands.[13] If the stronger partner holds firm, the other will have difficulty finding another source of help and can do so only at great cost. Basically, the allies remain too weak to stand by themselves militarily, and their attitude toward the com-

[12] This point is discussed further, pp. 542ff.

[13] See *Mutual Defense Treaty with the Republic of China. Report of the Committee on Foreign Relations,* Senate, 84th Cong., 1st Sess., on Executive A, Feb. 8, 1955 (Washington, 1955).

munist bloc is one of hostility rooted in fear of aggression and subversion. We have not yet, of course, had to face the test of a thrust against the communists by a more powerful ally like West Germany.

A "leader of equals" therefore can use his military superiority mainly to keep an alliance system within general bounds. It cannot forbid Chiang's efforts but can mitigate their consequences; it cannot compel Japanese and German rearmament but can indicate that the price is continued vulnerability; it cannot avert clandestine operations like the Suez affair but it can thwart them; it cannot induce French co-operation in NATO military arrangements but need not succumb to blackmail threats of non-co-operation and loss of friendship.

We wish to keep our allies from precipitating conflicts, taxing us excessively for mutually beneficial military efforts, or squandering on some irrelevant purpose the strength gathered for the common cause. For lesser states some maneuverability in these matters is essential if sovereign independence is to be more than a hollow shell.[14] In fact, the more successful the common mission, the more likely we are to encounter all sorts of disruptive activities. Hence it is a great test of American statesmanship to distinguish between leadership and imperial dominance, in finding and demanding a reasonable level of allied military performance in the common cause.

BASES AND FORCES OVERSEAS

The intricate network of overseas bases and the sizable American forces-in-being are manifestations of our policy of collective defense. Both their size and location affect our foreign policy in routine operations and pursuit of long-range objectives. The composition of the forces mustered seriously influence our freedom of choice and may determine that choice in a crisis. A change in deployment or technological developments may invalidate an earlier decision, in which case a lag in responding to this new situation may prove dangerous.

The need for ready forces and bases reflects the explosive capacity and speed of the new weapons. Since we may be unable to mobilize protection for other vital interests as well as our homeland, we must fashion a military potential in advance, and keep it properly deployed and serviced. Reserve formations must be ready in case a crisis arises

[14] For a classic statement of the "independent ally" position, see the press conference of President Charles de Gaulle, March 25, 1959.

suddenly and does not rapidly evolve into a thermonuclear exchange. This discussion therefore assumes the existence of places abroad that we wish to defend under priorities of importance, an evaluation of types and sizes of forces required to satisfy these needs, plans for mustering them in sequence if time allows, and a method and place for their overseas deployment.

American forces overseas are deployed to perform these missions and serve as evidence of our intentions. Their presence often acts as a catalyst for mustering local defense forces which might otherwise have disintegrated. Britain's Army of the Rhine (at 45,000 men), the moderate conscription laws in Western Europe, and the evolutionary growth of a West German army stem in great part from the location of an American field army in Europe.[15]

Our deployments and military aid programs are supposed to sustain major foreign policy objectives. Yet these military commitments are subject to erosion by contrary policies or nationalist currents abroad, and require American diplomatic efforts to protect them. Even when matters proceed smoothly, such military considerations remain major points at issue with our allies.

We have noted certain unfortunate concomitants of the projection of American power abroad, such as Japan's failure to rearm and France's deployment of massive forces in colonial wars. Possession of a base may be a cause of difficulty with an ally, as in the case of the Philippines. Admittedly nationalist sentiment is on the rise anyway, but our base arrangement has been a potent irritant, especially since it came as a price for Filipino independence and was not freely negotiated. The arrangement is constantly in dispute, accords became subject to drawn-out negotiations, and the issue becomes woven with insistent requests for American aid.

The "mortgage of a birthright" is an even stronger issue in Morocco where our bases, in contrast to nearby Libya, were negotiated during the unlamented French rule. Here the desire to assert independence is mingled with a belief in neutralism. Consequently, we came under pressure to heed Morocco's complaints on other issues, such as the

[15] The decision to send four divisions to Europe in 1951, during the Korean War, underlined the importance of western security in the government's strategic thinking. See *Assignment of Ground Forces of the United States to Duty in the European Area. Hearings, Committee on Armed Services and Committee on Foreign Relations*, Senate, 82nd Cong., 1st Sess. (Washington, 1951), especially testimony of Secretary of Defense George Marshall and Secretary of State Dean Acheson, pp. 77-125.

situation in Algeria, and eventually decided to yield our base rights in 1959. Any citation of how valuable a base or a country is to the common military cause does not bring a glow of camaraderie in the underdeveloped states. Instead, in weak states like Libya, or exposed states like South Viet Nam, such American declarations encourage a search for better terms in negotiating a base agreement or an assistance program.[16]

Bases may cause friction because of the disturbing physical impact of the establishment itself. In Japan, the need for more airfields, the expansion of old ones, and the requirements for large gunnery ranges present a problem of space which adds substance to the long-standing dispute over bases between the two Japanese political parties. Or, as in Spain, the presence of American troops and the influx of American funds may cause some dislocation. Since we favor political and economic liberalism, we may justify this activity, but cruel experience has shown that a shaken traditional order can evolve into an extremist regime hostile to our ideals and foreign policy.

Our desire for Pacific naval bases in 1945 led to the establishment of strategic trust territories not amenable to UN control. This was a backward step from our historic position of advancing self-rule and international authority through a mandate system in colonies disgorged by defeated empires.[17] The smallness of these old Japanese mandates may be a mitigating factor, but our exercise of sovereign control is a source of political vulnerability. The strategically related situation of Okinawa is much more explosive. We have returned to Japan only partial control over the island in order to guarantee American control of a military base. This is the only instance in which we enjoy such power without the express consent of the sovereign foreign power concerned. Okinawa has become a center of virulent anti-American agitation and a source of contention in Japanese-American relations. If the situation worsens, it may become difficult to reach a new accord in line with our normal base agreements.

Among the most publicized complications are the status-of-forces

[16] On Vietnamese attitudes, see John D. Montgomery, "'Gilded Missiles:' Reflections on the Politics of Foreign Aid," *Far Eastern Survey*, XXVIII (June, 1959), 86-87.

[17] "Arrangements for International Trusteeship," Additional Chapter proposed by the United States, *United Nations Conference on International Organization* (1945) *Documents*, III, 607-608 (Doc. 2, G/26 (c)).

agreements under which American troops abroad are subject to local justice when involved with the law for acts not committed in the line of duty.[18] In this instance it has been American nationalist nerves that have been jangled. The notion of American troops coming under foreign control, when they are serving the national interest and helping protect a foreign land, is difficult to accept. There is the additional fear of encountering a different system of justice when other states gain equal treatment with our Western European allies. The argument that Americans are treated more leniently by foreign civilians than by our courts-martial does not eradicate the ill feeling. Emotions quickly became aroused in the Girard case of 1957 when local jurisdiction in Japan was interpreted to include derelict behavior while on duty. Though quiescent, nationalist sentiment may not be appeased on this score; the government might later feel obliged to make a concession on another, unrelated issue in order to square this account.

In general, there has been a considerable political expense incurred in backstopping the military bases and deployments undertaken in the national interest. As long as the original rationale holds, the gains generally are found to outweigh the costs. Political or technological changes, however, may rob the arrangement of its validity. A specific mission may no longer be essential or realizable; local opposition may reduce the reliability of a base in an emergency; changed enemy capabilities may make a staging area vulnerable; more flexible and mobile missile systems may reduce our dependence on airplane or missile installations; a submersible, nuclear-powered, "long-legged" navy may not need as many overseas port and supply facilities as the navy does now. One can make a powerful argument for retaining bases whose original value is gone, because of other benefits they bring to our foreign policy position.[19] But their high political cost and absorption of valuable military dollars indicate that we will seldom choose to maintain a base in these circumstances.

In a sense, overseas bases have two missions, to protect the area in question and to enhance the deterrent-protective capacity of the United States. Though these are difficult to separate in practice, the differences may become sufficiently marked to serve as policy guides.

[18] See Joseph M. Snee and A. Kenneth Pye, *Status of Forces Agreements and Criminal Jurisdiction* (New York, 1957).

[19] This point is made by Townshend Hoopes, "Overseas Bases in American Strategy," *Foreign Affairs,* XXXVII (October, 1958), 69-82.

When our homeland is involved, we may well be willing to pay a high political and monetary price. We might not find this worth our while if the overseas military effort is designed primarily to show the flag, protect a foreign target, or sustain an alliance connection. In Japan, for example, if the bases remain a major political issue, give rise repeatedly to fundamental constitutional issues which may harm the new democratic order, and keep the country in a fantasy world regarding its security problem, the value of the bases and the alliance may be properly questioned. We can probably benefit from a more relaxed view of our foreign military relations and not consider them as necessary arrangements. By treating them as more expendable instruments of foreign policy, we can reduce their political and monetary cost. This might induce others to be careful of using an American offer or commitment as a bargaining counter, as Iran did with Russia in 1959, in negotiating with third powers for terms that might not be in our common interest.

Though there is an intimate relationship between alliances and installations, the two are not inseparable. We have air bases in several Arab states without any formal alliance. By contrast, Norway and Denmark are in the complex NATO alliance-planning network, yet neither state has permitted the entry of foreign air units prior to a crisis. This latter attitude, if it becomes widespread, weakens a defense arrangement, especially in an area so important that the availability of forces becomes vital to the survival of the alliance. The position taken by France—an army in Algeria, withdrawal of Mediterranean naval forces from NATO, and refusal to tolerate nuclear-equipped bomber or missile forces on its soil under standard NATO arrangements—has seriously compromised NATO's capability.

At the other extreme, we have been unwilling to back SEATO with a military force allocation, despite the area's vulnerability to military pressure from the north. It is natural to inquire whether SEATO is an overcommitment.[20] The utility of this alliance hinges on our answer to these questions: are the required peacetime forces available, is it politic to place forces there, are we willing to fight in this region, and can we apply effectively the threat of retaliation against sources of aggression?

[20] For a critique of SEATO see W. McMahon Ball, "An Australian View of Southeast Asian Security," *Far Eastern Survey*, XXIII (November, 1954), 165-69, and M. L. Thomas, "A Critical Appraisal of SEATO," *Western Political Quarterly*, X (December, 1957), 926-36.

In the Korean situation we moved in an opposite direction from that implied in negative answers to these questions, from a peacetime plan for noninvolvement to military commitment in a crisis. The military calculations of the joint chiefs of staff guided our policy between 1945 and 1950: the peninsula was not considered vital to our security and the Asian mainland was not the place to engage field forces against the communist powers.[21] Despite the valid and triumphant arguments favoring action against the aggression of 1950, this original negative evaluation persisted, albeit in modified form. Comparing American and Soviet power and fearing that the Korean War was a feint to draw us away from the major European theater, the joint chiefs successfully insisted on a limited effort in this sector.[22] They were worried that the entire venture was an overcommitment, just as our diplomats before the war were "carrying on a twenty-division foreign policy with a fourteen-division army." [23]

Forces available today may again be below the level needed to fulfill our military obligations. Political disadvantages to using nuclear weapons in Asia, a reduced rate of modernization of our forces, and an inadequate number of combat units may have policy effects similar to those experienced before and during the Korean War. Annual struggles at the margins of our huge military budget may appear inconsequential in the face of such high and stable expenditures but they determine the availability of one or two more STRAC (Strategic Army Corps) divisions, the relation of Polaris to anti-submarine-warfare (ASW) submarines, the relative strength of tactical and strategic aircraft, and the availability of air transport. These considerations, in turn, guide the joint chiefs in their judgment of our capability to act in a crisis, with due attention to the sustained protection of other vital interests. From this they may again derive, despite the Korean experience, a set of cautious peacetime evaluations which can go up in smoke in a crisis. But the lesson of Korea may have different consequences—to follow a military evaluation against fight-

[21] Memorandum to the Secretary of State from Secretary of Defense James Forrestal, September 26, 1947, expressing the opinion of the joint chiefs of staff in favor of a withdrawal of American forces from South Korea. *New York Times*, November 3, 1952.

[22] *Military Situation in the Far East, Hearings, Committee on Armed Services and Committee on Foreign Relations*, Senate. 82nd Cong., 1st Sess. (Washington, 1951). See especially the testimony of General Omar Bradley, Part 2, p. 729ff.

[23] Comment of Charles B. Marshall to the writer.

ing, as we may have done regarding Indochina in 1954 or, to cite one possible variation, to fight with atomic weapons or not at all in a specific circumstance.[24]

A purely military calculation would lead us to raise our forces to levels required to satisfy our commitments, though this could touch off a greater arms race with explosive consequences. Or we might carefully reduce our commitments, according to priorities of importance, to a level more compatible with our annual budgets. The latter approach, however, is neither technically nor politically feasible. Some counts against it are: the highly volatile rate of military invention, the rapid fluctuation in the importance of certain areas (*e.g.*, control of the equatorial belt may become necessary for space travel), and a crisis which, itself, may change the importance of an area. Then, too, a reduced force can be a strategic reserve for the protection of several pressure points. After all, no other attacks occurred during the Korean War and the dreaded possibility of multiple limited aggressions has not transpired, possibly because the Soviet government feels that we would see in this situation a "total" threat.[25] The disjointed correlation of alliance obligations, forces available, and bases will be with us for some time, with the advantages as well as the dangerous ambiguities and strains they provide for the conduct of our foreign policy.

THE EFFECTS OF MILITARY TECHNOLOGY

One of the most revolutionary developments in our time has been the ascendancy of the technological and scientific aspects of military affairs. Not only does national security hinge on the rapid, open-end development of new weapons, but civilian industrial progress is now intimately linked to military advances in electronics, fuels, nuclear power, aircraft engines, and the like.

[24] On the Indochina crisis of 1954, see Chalmers Roberts, "The Day We Didn't Go to War," *The Reporter*, XI (September 14, 1954), 31-35, and Robert J. Donovan, *Eisenhower: The Inside Story* (New York, 1956), Chap. 19.

[25] See testimony of General Twining in *Department of Defense Appropriations for 1960. Hearings, op. cit.*, pp. 113-14, and a Department of Defense statement stressing our capability for limited war. *Ibid.*, pp. 254-55. However, for weaknesses in light of the Berlin crisis, see *Major Defense Matters. Hearings, Preparedness Investigating Subcommittee of the Committee on Armed Services*, Senate, 86th Cong., 1st Sess. (Washington, 1959), testimony of General Taylor, p. 5ff.

The United States shifted into high gear in atomic production about five years after the cold war began, under the twin incentives of an unmistakable communist threat and technological progress. Though this effort won considerable publicity as the "new look" at the start of the Eisenhower administration in 1953, it had already begun in the last years of the Truman period. The basic military decision was to stress strategic over tactical weapons. This was a variation of a similar problem we faced with regard to aircraft and conventional weapons generally in the late 1940s. In both instances the decision was to favor a strategic retaliatory capacity, to safeguard the American homeland.[26]

There was no intention of omitting tactical weapons from the arsenal, but there was a lag in supply of the smaller elements of the "atomic mix" for a few years. Despite an ultimate quest for balanced capabilities, however, during the mid-1950s we were strongest in strategic weapons and lacked other types. The absence of an equivalent Soviet striking power and the decade-old American worry about a brusque attack contributed to excessive concentration on strategic weapons and their use. A most significant case was the doctrine of massive retaliation employed by Secretary of State John Foster Dulles at that time.[27] He sought to use our advantage in strategic weapons to deter acts of aggression which could not yet be efficiently countered by modern field forces. As a result we placed a double burden on a weapon, selected basically for defensive purposes against major threats (to ourselves, Western Europe, and perhaps Japan), to cover

[26] The most dramatic confrontation of views came in 1949. See *Investigation of the B-36 Bomber Program*, House. 81st Cong., 1st Sess. (Washington, 1949), and *The National Defense Program—Unification and Strategy. Hearings, Committee on Armed Services*, House. 81st Cong., 1st Sess. (Washington, 1949). See especially the statements of General Hoyt Vandenberg, Chief of Staff, USAF, *Investigation of B-36*, pp. 165-73, and the critical comments of Admiral W. H. P. Blandy, *National Defense Program*, pp. 201-209. See also the Committee's *Report, Investigation of the B-36 Bomber Program*, House. 81st Cong., 2nd Sess. (Washington, 1950). For the 1950s, see *Study of Airpower. Hearings, Subcommittee on the Air Force, Committee on Armed Services*, Senate. 84th Cong., 2nd Sess. (Washington, 1956).

[27] The position of Secretary Dulles and its later modifications are found in his address "The Evolution of Foreign Policy," of January 12, 1954, in *Bulletin*, 30 (January 25, 1954), 107-110; "Policy for Security and Peace," *Foreign Affairs*, XXXII (April, 1954), 353-64; and "Challenge and Response in United States Foreign Policy," *Foreign Affairs*, XXXVI (October, 1957), 25-43.

our military weakness regarding another requirement, namely the protection of lesser areas.

This diplomatic overcommitment of a military capability led to a series of great debates over what appeared to be a doctrine of despair, lacking in feasibility or credibility.[28] It was not realized that massive retaliation was a short-term policy, an attempt to turn temporary conditions, created by military priorities for weapons, to our political advantage. Ironically, these disputes gave rise to a new and vast literature on the value of a limited war just as the new tactical weapons became plentiful and planning turned more fruitfully in that direction.[29]

The basic military problem faced in the late 1940s and early 1950s recurs with every turn of the wheel of invention. What is the proper balance between tactical and strategic power, between new research and production of the soon-to-be obsolete? When and in what proportions should adjustments be made in the components of a weapons mixture? In the late 1950s the appearance of Soviet missile power increased our own vulnerability.[30] But it muffled the threat of our retaliation in case of a Russian attack upon our allies, making an effective on-the-spot field force more essential than ever.[31] Our trying experiences with efforts to get extra political mileage from military decisions should give us pause in deciding upon our next major production efforts and in what manner they can enhance our diplomatic as well as security position.

The unbelievable rate of technological change in military affairs also has a more direct and profound impact on our foreign relations,

[28] The problem of credibility was raised by William Kaufmann in Kaufmann, ed., *Military Policy and National Security* (Princeton, 1956), Chap. 1. A vigorous European critic of the new look was F. O. Miksche, *Atomic Weapons and Armies* (New York, 1955).

[29] The major American studies of limited warfare were Henry Kissinger, *Nuclear Weapons and Foreign Policy* (New York, 1957) and Robert Osgood, *Limited War* (Chicago, 1957).

[30] Albert Wohlstetter, "The Delicate Balance of Terror," *Foreign Affairs,* XXXVII (January, 1959), 211-34. See also William Kaufmann's strenuous critique of Kissinger's study "The Crisis in Military Affairs," *World Politics,* X (July, 1958), 579-603.

[31] The strongest recent presentation of this position was made by the Advisory Council of the United States Democratic National Committee, "The Military Forces We Need and How to Get Them," *Democratic Program for Action* (Washington, 1959).

even with our nearest allies. The problem facing Canada in the field of air defense is a good example, because technical change is placing it perilously close to total dependence upon the United States. Such dependence makes matters extremely difficult for the Conservative government, which seeks to assert Canadian interests in economic as well as political-military affairs and yet remain a loyal ally.

Joint defense arrangements, planned less than a decade ago, were to use Canadian territory to provide installations for the protection of both Canada and the United States. Today, with new attack and defense systems, the buffer role remains, but Canadian territory cannot be safeguarded against physical assault. Only the fact that it helps protect America and that country's striking power can be used as an argument for continued Canadian co-operation. Furthermore, Canada shoulders one third of the cost, which at first took the form of supplying that share of the equipment on a basis of technical equality. Now costs are mounting, Canada still pays one third, but can no longer keep pace in producing the new and complex mechanisms required.[32] The best it can do is subcontract for parts; it could drop the financial burden entirely but this would lose Canada its close contact with industrial developments. By accepting an industrially subordinate position, it can keep abreast of technical military developments, which have so often led to civilian application within a few years. Thus Canadian economic development and physical security can be guaranteed only through arrangements which must tax national pride severely. United States foreign policy has another problem requiring tactful handling, perhaps by concesssions in sensitive areas of economic relations. At least we should recognize why Canada may adopt a more adamant nationalist position in other, apparently unrelated diplomatic issues.

Technological considerations have strained the Western alliance system in the realm of rational military planning as well as diplomatic relations. A position in the second rank has gained in prestige as the gap between the superpowers and the others increases. And it appears most readily attainable through a modern military capability. It avails little to argue that the United States is covering the strategic requirement and that specialization of effort makes for better mili-

[32] "Dief and the Two Uncles," *The Economist*, CLXXXIX (December 27, 1958), 1165; "The Avro Nettle Patch," and "Canada's Defense Perplexities," *ibid.*, CXC (February 28 and March 28, 1959), 790-91 and 1186-87.

tary efficiency and greater economy. Nor does it help to point out that massive capability, rather than the weapon of the moment, is the true source of today's bipolarity. In recent years Great Britain and France have sought independent nuclear capabilities, and the attitudes displayed by our closest allies will undoubtedly prevail when less friendly powers are able to pursue atomic missile production.

The famous British White Paper of 1957 on the defense establishment is important, for it carried to a logical conclusion the arguments and policies which dominated the mid-1950s.[33] The British held that only with a strategic capability could they be fully insured against being left in the lurch by the United States in a crisis, be certain that their military efforts would serve their own national interests, and be assured of a full voice in decisions. They also maintained that by meshing strategic and tactical forces they could hold down the cost of defense.

Experience has brought a change of heart on all counts. Britain's strategic striking power is not secure or strong enough to insure its defense, so that it is dependent upon American protection. Hence it was not just a gratuitous avowal to admit, as Britons did in their 1959 discussions with the French, that suspicion of the United States was unjustified. The notions of curtailed expenses and flexibility to bolster conventional forces have also proved wrong. The expensive "V" bomber group, now outdated, costs less than the second-generation Blue Streak missile, and future developments will cost even more.[34] To those Americans who accept the counterforce theory of sustaining a maximum retaliatory capacity, the more allied strategic power the better. To others, who see a widening in the gap between strategic and conventional operations, and note the sharp reduction in the effectiveness and size of Britain's combat batallions, the price seems too high. In any event, the program has lost its original justification and the British have had to jettison the Blue Streak in their quest for a rational defense policy. The stress on strategic power

[33] *Outline of Future Policy on Defense*, Cmnd. 124. See also the critique by Air Marshall Sir John Slessor, "British Defense Policy," *Foreign Affairs*, XXXV (July, 1957), 551-63. For his essays on deterrence, see *The Great Deterrent* (London, 1957).

[34] The moderate British 1959 White Paper is summarized along with comments in "Progress of the Five-year British Defense Plan," *Survival*, I (March-April, 1959), 18-20.

leaves too many national interests without proper military support.

Britain always claimed pride of place in its alliance relationship with the United States, and had emphasized this point as a justification for its strategic program. The French believe this favored relationship exists; they see Britain's thermonuclear capability, and insist that there is a direct cause-effect relationship here. British admissions of earlier faulty reasoning fell on deaf ears, and any rational exposition of other reasons for close Anglo-American ties—such as cultural affinity, the experience of 1941-1945, the stability of democratic institutions—simply exasperate the French, the more so if these arguments are valid. If France's political instability and difficult colonial policies are handicaps to intimacy, then, since the French obtained a nuclear capability, they will minimize all other factors and see in the new technology the solvent to their difficulties within the alliance system.

The new weaponry, then, can be a source of friction. It presents difficulties which are hard to master through diplomacy. One consequence may be military inefficiency and greater political strain in the NATO alliance. From a larger perspective it is difficult to see how the nuclear club can be restricted in membership under present international organization, since the national desire for a nuclear capability seems so powerful and can be clothed in many conveniently available political and military justifications.[35] It is unlikely that other lesser states can threaten the security of the superpowers any more than Britain or France could by 1960, but the explosive potential behind each crisis will mount and what might otherwise be a minor blow-up may take a nuclear form. These crises will be much more difficult to contain in comparison with the first fifteen years of the cold war.

An alternative would be some form of arms control, but the history of disarmament efforts has not been encouraging. In addition to the traditional problem of limiting conventional forces, we face today many novel issues: restricting the nuclear club, curtailing tests of weapons, regulating tests of missiles and space vehicles, controlling the use of space, providing safeguards against surprise attacks of an-

[35] See, however, A. L. Burns, *Power Politics and the Growing Nuclear Club* (Princeton, 1959); and William C. Davidon, Marvin I. Kalkstein and Christopher Hohenemser, *The Nth Country Problem and Arms Control* (Washington, 1960).

nihilation, and regulating the production of fissionable materials.[36] Moreover, national security is endangered if we fall behind in our capability in research and development, so that weaponry has three central aspects—present capacity, immediate (five-year) potential, and ability for the long haul. Even if workable restrictions can be agreed upon concerning the first two categories, as long as there is a nation-state system, technical and theoretical scientific potential will be a source of power, quickly applicable to the military arts and therefore difficult to control and impossible to ignore.

For Americans, current efforts at disarmament differ from all earlier attempts because now the United States is imperilled, its security involved. Other major powers were in similar positions in the past but they never reached an accord. The only significant arms-limitation agreement on record is the Anglo-American-Japanese naval treaty system of 1921-1936, wherein Japan was accorded dominance in its home waters. Apart from a loss of the strategic initiative in the western Pacific and the military exposure of the Philippines, the accord affected no major American interests.[37] We were willing to run these risks to reduce tensions and avoid an arms race. One can argue that the treaty proved its worth in underpinning the status quo in the Pacific, and was respected until legally denounced. Even within its self-imposed limits, however, we must be concerned with two points: it was unilaterally dissolved by a contracting party and it did not involve or mortgage what the American government and people considered vital interests.

There is the additional discouraging argument that armaments are symptoms of conflict, effects rather than causes of whatever difficulties dominate the international scene at the moment. We can break the present stalemate only if the world political society determines that modern armaments, because of their great power, are a cause as well as a symptom of tension. This was the philosophy underlying the ill-fated American plan for atomic controls presented

[36] Brief chonological surveys of disarmament negotiations are *Control and Reduction of Armaments,* Staff Study No. 3, Subcommittee on Disarmament, Committee on Foreign Relations, Senate. 84th Cong., 2nd Sess. (Washington, 1956), and Anthony Nutting, *Disarmament* (London, 1959).

[37] On the strategic problem of the western Pacific, see Louis Morton, "War Plan ORANGE: Evolution of a Strategy," *World Politics,* XI (January, 1959), 221-50.

after 1945. The question now is whether the ensuing years, which brought equality and tremendous power to America and Russia, have created the emotional and strategic environment for the development of controls.

It is difficult to maintain parity when technical change is so rapid and when more intense efforts by one side can create an imbalance which might be turned to permanent advantage. There is also the great pressure of other states to improve their power position; an agreement to curtail nuclear tests could founder on the determined opposition of France or some other Western aspirant, or Communist China's efforts to obtain or develop a nuclear weapon. At stake is some type of functional international government, for only a substantial and sophisticated arrangement of this nature can police an arms control agreement. However narrowly defined at first, an agreement must involve important mutual concessions, requiring workable safeguards. And an even more important justification for a sturdy agency will be its task of handling unexpected problems. No matter how limited its original frame of reference, it will face new technological problems and political challenges, especially from states lacking an atomic capability. There is always the possibility of expanding the agency's authority if results of the first experiment prove successful.

There may be something basically unrealistic about efforts to control or limit armaments. We have listed past failures, accords which avoided conflicts of vital interests, the unscrupulous nature of the foe, and the need for a substantial international agency.[38] Yet the terrible power of the new weapons, proved equality between the two camps, and the success of a short-term experiment, might bring a control system to pass. The effect upon international organization, and so upon national policy, would be more profound than we now realize. There would be a marked shift toward universal membership, more efficient functioning of UN political bodies, a more realistic relation between power and political strength in international institutions, and a swift rise in the importance of such institutional channels of decision making. This would not mean the arrival of a golden age even if disarmament progressed beyond some cautiously defined limit. Money saved would not all be poured into foreign development

[38] It is exceedingly difficult to get communist states to honor agreements, even with inspection. See Jacques Freymond, "Supervising Agreements: The Korean Experience," *Foreign Affairs*, XXXVII (April, 1959), 496-503.

projects as one might conclude from repeated proposals to link economic aid projects to disarmament. Not only would Americans tax themselves less, but Russia would undoubtedly step up the satisfaction of consumer wants. Nor would the cold war end, since the political features which are its essence would become even more important. An arms control agreement would have to develop a momentum of its own, and afford improved security benefits, to survive temptations to renounce it because of some provocation or opportunity too important or tempting to let pass.

We are in danger of becoming paralyzed by the pull of contrasting fears: the image a future war invokes in us and the evident dangers in any agreement to disarm while the political struggle with Russia continues. The loss of specific and comforting benefits is measured against hypothetical gains and so, as in other aspects of our foreign policy, our efforts develop cautiously. In general, military considerations and responsibilities have reinforced a tendency in American foreign policy toward rigidity and reliance on the status quo, noted even by our closest allies.

Nor have we been able to neutralize the many harmful effects our military policy has had upon political relations with the Afro-Asian world. In many of these states, military power is considered basically evil, more so perhaps in Western hands than when possessed by the Soviet Union or neutralists. Our military aid has not enhanced the cause of democracy in those lands where our assistance has been accepted; in some cases, like Iraq, it has not even sustained a pro-Western regime. Still, the effort to help the weaker states around the communist periphery must continue for want of a better alternative. Our own uneasiness over such heavy reliance on military assistance programs perhaps reflects an American moral repugnance to this type of assistance and realization of the value of a more balanced effort. Our policy in the 1960s may therefore stress civilian aid, as was the case before the Korean War.[39]

Finally, the most profound influence of military factors upon our foreign policy occurs through the efficiency displayed by our military experts and planners. The way in which military power is organized to meet our defense and alliance requirements—in missions, proportion of forces, and size—is of paramount importance. The skill in

[39] For a strong argument in favor of continued military aid to underdeveloped states see The Draper Report, *op. cit.*, II, Annex C, 45-90.

selecting projects for development, and their priority and speed of execution, are of historic significance. Budgetary considerations and the skill with which foreign and military policies are co-ordinated often play determining roles. But competence in military affairs remains more than ever, in the nation-state system, an essential condition for greater freedom of choice in foreign policy and flexibility in its execution. Our military achievement affords us the opportunity; how well we do with this opportunity is a question of political competence.

PART THREE

FUTURE POLICIES AND EXPECTATIONS

20: AMERICAN POLICY: DANGERS AND PROSPECTS

Philip E. Mosely

It is not easy or comfortable for a democratic society to pursue its goals of freedom and plenty at home while at the same time bearing world-wide responsibilities for helping a great many other nations work toward their own security and progress. It is especially difficult for it to reconcile the domestic requirements of satisfying a broad and diverse electorate, absorbed in its personal, group and regional interests, with the strategic, political and economic efforts and sacrifices that are necessary if that same society, continental in scope and traditionally devoted to putting its own expanding opportunities to full use, is to contribute effectively to building an international environment in which it and its cherished values can survive and prosper.

Even after the experience gained in winning, together with strong allies, a two-front war fought in Europe and Asia, and in carrying on a multifront resistance to a new menace of totalitarian and hostile expansionism, it is hard for Americans to believe that their future security and prosperity may be affected profoundly by a leap-ahead in Soviet military technology, by India's success or failure in creating new economic resources, by the ability of Brazilians to overcome the growing pains of modernization, or even by the outcome of struggles among obscure military cliques in Laos. Yet these and many other chains of events, fully reported and often dimly understood, influence in one degree or another the direction and the prospects of American foreign policy.

The timely understanding of multiple and varied dangers, and the mustering of resolution to meet them with will power and resources, is complicated by widespread illusions of omniscience and omnipotence. The unwieldy American electorate, informed and at the same time distracted by an omnipresent network of modern communications, believes or almost believes that its government is somehow able to direct events everywhere and is therefore responsible for whatever happens anywhere. When American hopes for a genuine freedom of choice by the peoples of Poland or Hungary are destroyed by Soviet intransigence, backed by armed might, when India and Pakistan pursue an unresolved and debilitating quarrel over the future of Kashmir, when the Congo, suddenly released from the corseting of Belgian paternalism, places in jeopardy the hopes for an orderly evolution of Africa toward freedom and progress, or when a revolutionary Cuba eagerly invites Soviet intervention in the Western Hemisphere, Americans typically blame, not uncontrollable outside forces, but their own leaders.

Even if the level of information and foresight is substantially higher in the executive than in the legislative branch, and considerably higher in the Congress than in the electorate, the assumption of omniscience is, on closer examination, seen for what it is, an illusion. The fact of the matter is that, under any human system, the individuals and groups that act, and act often in unforeseen ways, usually do not know what they are going to do next or what further steps will follow from a first one.

This same assumption of omniscience also plagues United States policy abroad. Because America is powerful and has confronted and surmounted great dangers, and because it has made great and generous sacrifices to help allies, friends and even neutrals achieve their national purposes, many people in many parts of the world assume that the only reason why all their conflicting claims have not been settled to their full satisfaction, the only reason why many economic and social ills remain uncured, is because the United States has not chosen to wave its magic wand.

If the illusions, at home and abroad, of American omnicompetence ever had any substance, they must be decisively discarded if we are to perceive clearly the nature of the new challenges to our hopes. In retrospect, the first decade and a half of the cold war may then seem to have been comfortably simple and old-fashioned both in the nature of the risks and the means for containing them. In the onrush of missile-nuclear technology, power and purpose are perhaps coming unhinged. It is apparently becoming more difficult to master unlimited power and make it the servant of limited purposes, whether those of an elusive stability or a hoped-for orderly advance of mankind.

The Changing Definition of Deterrence

In the age of monarchical rivalries, deterrence was provided in the main by regiments of trained mercenaries and by the accumulated weight of bullion in the king's treasury. As Europe moved into the democratic age, the ability to train great reserves of manpower in peacetime, and to mobilize them in war for national rather than dynastic purposes, became the decisive factor of strategic arithmetic. In the 20th century, the need to harness all resources, human and material, to the quest for victory has twice led logically to total war. And total war in turn, has given rise to totalitarian systems of power whose rulers seek total domination in the name of all-encompassing ideologies. No wonder that nations which are democratic in structure and in purposes or aspirations, which desire, above all, to live for their people's own self-fulfillment, are confused and anxious as they dispute among themselves the nature of the threat and the means of assuring their survival in this new, undesired, and dangerous kind of world.

Within a few years, the ability to deter any large-scale aggression, at least for a few strongest powers, will again rest, as it did in the age of monarchies, on the possession of forces-in-being, manned by highly trained technicians, armed now with missiles rather than muskets. Within a few years, the only strongest powers will be those that possess the means of swift and relatively invulnerable retaliation, even against an adversary's surprise attack. The stage of mutual nuclear deterrence has not yet been achieved. Neither of the two strongest powers can now turn back from this race for the protected deterrent. Neither of them can afford to lag behind in arming itself with any of its essential components.

The Soviet Union appears to be ahead in the number and weight of its intercontinental missiles. It also has the advantage of being able, in substantial measure, to conceal the numbers and locations of its weapons. The United States may be ahead in the sophistication of its power systems and its instrumentation. But, after the experience of past miscalculations, neither American public opinion nor American policy makers can afford to rely on unfavorable estimates of Soviet scientific ingenuity or Soviet technical competence in missilry. Nor is it safe to underestimate the willingness of Soviet leaders to accept substantial damage to their country if they could be mathematically certain of winning a decisive victory through launching a surprise attack against the only barrier to their world-wide domination. The temptation to seek a short cut to the definitive triumph of their system of power, re-enforced by the Bolshevik sense of revolutionary duty, would make the political decision a relatively easy one for the Soviet leaders of today, if only they felt they could rely on the technical calculations of their scientists and strategists. Unfortunately, neither ethical scruples, nor domestic limitations on their power, nor a respect for "the decent opinion of mankind," can have any real effect on their decisions, based as they are on complex calculations of power.

Even when a stable deterrent has been achieved—and present US programs may or may not be adequate to achieve it and to achieve it rapidly enough—the new status of strategic equilibrium, pursued at breathless strain and great cost, may in turn prove illusory. If, for example, one side should develop an effective anti-missile missile first, it could then press its advantage, perhaps a temporary one, to achieve supremacy through either blackmail or direct attack. Likewise, the greater material and political readiness of one side or the other to resist nuclear blackmail may be decisive. This may depend on whether it has systematically prepared the protection of its civilian population and economy against the consequences of the threat of a nuclear exchange.

The creation of these several interdependent capabilities cannot wait on budgetary conveniences or preferences. The strengthening of the armature of the civil society against blackmail and attack must proceed simultaneously with the development of a protected and relatively invulnerable missile-nuclear deterrent. Any other approach is a standing invitation to the Soviet leadership to press the art of brinkmanship right up to the brink and beyond.

After the noncommunist world had pulled its wits together following the cataclysm of the Second World War, and had recognized the meaning of Stalin's pressure to expand the communist sphere in several directions, it was still able, in its response, to resort to a familiar political recipe. In Europe it set about organizing the will and the forces to resist Soviet expansion. Behind moderately strong NATO forces there stood for some years a US monopoly of nuclear power and of the means of its delivery. Elsewhere, except in Korea, the throwing up of far feebler dikes, in the Middle East and Southeast Asia, served for the same reason to deter all except probing attacks. The resulting impression that a new equilibrium had already been assured was due more to the absence of any American ambition to move back the boundary stones than to any genuine abandonment by Moscow and Peking of their plans and preparations for further expansion. Nevertheless, precarious as it may now seem in the harsh light of the missile-nuclear revolution, that temporary stability won valuable time for the remarkable recovery of Western Europe and Japan as well as for the strengthening of new governments in much of noncommunist Asia.

The strategic deterrence of central war, difficult and costly though it will be, may well be within our reach if we exert our full efforts. But if this purpose becomes the be-all of American policy, it can also become the end-all of American influence in world affairs. An exclusive concentration on deterring a Soviet surprise attack against North America may for a time preserve intact the material equipment of Canada and the United States. But unless our strength and resources can be so rationed and used as to serve the security and progress of the entire world, a "Fortress North America" would eventually be reduced to a beleaguered and isolated garrison, dazedly wondering from what direction the next attack will come.

Obviously, the ability to stand up to the threat or the reality of a central war of surprise attack is essential to the survival of the United States and of the noncommunist world; there is nothing preordained or automatic about our acquiring or retaining that minimal assurance. Beyond that, however, the ability both to deter local forays from the communist bloc and to develop the political, economic and cultural strength of the free-world countries requires a great many other policies. Central to them are the will and the resources to make them effective over a long span of time.

Alliances and Security in a Bipolar Stalemate

As one consequence of a persistent but now outdated belief in an American monopoly of nuclear power, US thinking, both official and popular, has clung to a policy of restricting the spread of nuclear-missile technology. Only Britain, as a reward for lengthy and costly efforts of its own, has been admitted partially within the sanctum of US nuclear secrecy. This attempted monopoly, while useful at first, did not prevent the Soviet Union from independently achieving a missile-nuclear capability of its own. Today the automatic continuation of this policy seems less and less adapted to the new risks of the emerging stage of nuclear stalemate.

Many of our allies now harbor growing doubts as to whether the United States will be willing to face the devastation of its cities and industries in response to any except a direct nuclear attack on North America. Those fears can be overcome at present only by continuously persuading ourselves and our adversaries, as well as our friends, of the irrational and automatic character of our future decision to come to their defense and even to the aid of neutrals.

A different and, in the long pull, a more effective approach would be to organize the planned diffusion of nuclear-missile power by setting up several partially decentralized, preferably regional, strategic deterrents. Once in place, this system of deterrence would make it necessary for the Soviet bloc to destroy a number of strong centers of resistance, rather than a single one, and to do this in a single co-ordinated blow. The alternative, it seems, is for us to sit by and watch while one after another of our European partners achieves, at great cost to other vital programs, a small and inadequate deterrent of its own. It would be better for the security of the West to plan, systematically and with strong political safeguards, an orderly spread and control of the new technology.

It would, I believe, be far better, for both Western Europe and the United States, for the European members of NATO to be equipped with a partially independent West European deterrent. This would preferably include the nuclear resources presently possessed by Britain and France, to be supplemented as rapidly as possible by American equipment. The collective and regional character of such a deterrent, as distinguished from single-power ownership, would assure its use for retaliatory purposes only. With a West European deterrent in place, the Soviet leadership would find it difficult, and even useless, to continue its present rapid succession of threats. Both it and the West Europeans would know that, if that threat were ever carried out, the consequence would be a European retaliation, based on a European decision, against the Soviet Union. Equipped with its own "sword" as well as its "shield," Western Europe would be released from the gnawing doubts which now arise from its growing dependence on the US strategic guarantee.

Against this concept the argument is often raised that somehow Europeans would be more rash than Americans, or, for that matter, than Russians, in resorting to missile-nuclear weapons to settle minor quarrels. Among an informed public, on the contrary, the actual possession of nuclear power seems regularly to lead to very serious second thoughts. The United States has not resorted to the use of nuclear weapons since 1945. British defense policy has veered sharply away from the decision of 1956 to build its "independent" deterrent. And substantial French progress toward the same goal has recently given rise to many doubts as to its feasibility. Placing the control of the weapons under a West European command controlled by a regional political council, such as the dormant West European Union, would probably be the best means to make sure that the regional deterrent would be used only for its basic purpose, that of deterring a Soviet attack and undercutting Soviet blackmail.

With the coming into operational status of long-range missiles of proven accuracy, the West European deterrent could conceivably be located outside Europe, perhaps in the Sahara, in areas remote from Soviet observation. Even if it were located in Western Europe, it could be dispersed over many thinly populated areas, for example, in central France or Spain. In any case we do not yet know the full advantages and hazards of underground and mobile launching sites.

It has been argued that the spread of US nuclear technology, even to stable and trusted allies, will force the Soviet Union to transfer its own technology to Communist China and even to its European satellites. The parallel assumption is that by preventing or delaying the spread of this technology, the United States somehow encourages or persuades the Kremlin to exercise a similar restraint. There is no evidence that this reasoning rests upon anything stronger than the all-too-familiar mirror type of reasoning. If the Kremlin should decide that the transfer of nuclear-missile technology to China is to its advantage, it would act accordingly, regardless of US hopes and fears. If it has intra-bloc reasons of its own for withholding these new weapons from Peking, it is not likely to disregard them merely because the United States may be equipping Western Europe with a deterrent of its own.

If free Europe could rely on a deterrent of its own, its re-enforced self-confidence would presumably free the American deterrent to make its weight felt elsewhere, more especially to strengthen the wavering lines of defense in Asia and the Middle East. It is doubtful at present whether the United States would be able, even if it felt obliged to do so, to use or threaten to use its nuclear power against any attack that might occur along the thinly defended periphery which stretches from the Turkish straits to the Korean Sea. At the first hint of such a possibility, its European allies would surely rush to dissuade the United States, for fear of being exposed to Soviet retaliation.

On the other hand, a Europe that could rely on its own deterrent could also dissociate itself politically, if it so chose, from any new crisis in Asia without denying to the United States the political advantage of the right to use its most powerful strategic weapon as a final resort. This is not to imply, as I hope to make clear shortly, that it is presently sensible, or will long be feasible, for the United States to rely primarily on nuclear power to hold the line in Asia. But since that is just what we are doing now, as we made plain in the Taiwan Strait crisis of 1958, is it not sensible to make sure in advance that a threat, if we should be forced to make one, is not rendered unconvincing and therefore ineffective by the natural fears of our allies in Western Europe?

Apart from NATO, none of the US-sponsored alliances has so far developed into a genuinely regional defense organization, with a truly regional strategy. Within both CENTO and SEATO, the key to their efficacy is, whether we like it or not, the bilateral nexus that they have created between their individual members and the United States. This is said, not to belittle the political importance of regional co-operation, but to point out that, except in Western Europe, it is not feasible to set up regional deterrents within the US alliance system. On the other hand, if India and Pakistan should decide that their common safety required the re-establishment of a shared defense of the subcontinent, the United States should be prepared to help them create a deterrent of their own, even without entering into an alliance with them. Similarly, if the growing efficiency and, hopefully, the declining costs of missile-nuclear strategy should make it possible, several years from now, for a nonaligned Japan to maintain a deterrent of its own against communist-bloc attacks or threats, it would probably be to the US advantage to facilitate that change by Japan to a position of a greater strategic independence.

Probably the basic strategic change by the mid-1960s will prove to be the weakening or abandonment of the peripheral concept of defense which seemed firmly anchored in the political thinking of the mid-1950s. By the time of Stalin's death the reaction to the repeated challenges of Soviet-bloc expansionism had hardened into a bipolar confrontation along a more or less clearly defined periphery. This strategy had presented the noncommunist world, or at least its strongest powers, with the more or less traditional problem of bolstering exposed states and building up a credible threat of collective resistance backed by the prospect of US retaliation against any new Soviet aggression.

In the new situation which has been crystallizing since 1956, Soviet power has been partially successful in projecting its political influence and its strategic threats beyond the laboriously erected peripheral barriers. Since the Suez crisis Khrushchev has been uttering frequent threats to destroy any point on the globe. Skillfully combined with the political support of many varieties of militant, especially anti-Western, nationalism, and implemented by an extensive program of Soviet "trade-and-aid," Khrushchev's new global strategy has broadened out of all recognition Stalin's more modest ambitions of patient and peripheral expansion.

Deterrence of Local Aggressions

A defending power will soon be able to use its retaliatory force to deter a direct attack by an adversary. At the same time an aggressor will likewise be able to use his retaliatory power to deter the defender, or his friends, from using his own missile-nuclear strength to oppose any aggression short of a direct attack on the defender's homeland. This unwelcome by-product of an emerging two-way nuclear stalemate can be extremely dangerous to any alliance system. It creates special dangers for the free-world coalitions, for their cohesion rests upon free decisions adopted by each of its members. Soviet spokesmen have not been backward in pointing out to members of the opposing alliances the new dangers which they incur in the missile age through remaining allied with the United States.

One way to stiffen resistance to Soviet blackmail and thus to re-enforce the alliance system is to make clear to our free-world allies that the US response to a Soviet attack will be both defensive and automatic, and that its counterthreat will be adequate to deter the Soviet leadership from carrying out its threats. Another possible and important stiffener is to make clear to our allies that any non-nuclear attack can be met or deterred by means of retaliation short of global war. Is this second form of guarantee in our hands today?

Under the influence of "massive retaliation," US strategic planning has assumed that one weapon can do the job of two, that air-nuclear power (soon, missile-nuclear power) can either deter or win local as well as central wars. As we move into the age of missilry, it is now becoming clear that this is no longer the case. The problem of deterring a central war and the different one of deterring a wide variety of possible local aggressions are increasingly seen as two more and more distinct responsibilities. And what if local aggression should take the extreme form—which happens to be that which is preferred by communist doctrine and strategy—of local subversion or coups d'état? In this type of situation, in which the principal adversary may refrain from moving a single uniformed soldier across a more or less well-defined border, the inapplicability of the central deterrent is even clearer.

The problem of preparing a convincing deterrent against local on-the-ground or below-ground aggressions presumes a wide range of situations and presents an even wider variety of complexities. Both are too numerous to treat in detail. In some respects, however, despite recurrent panics over the future of NATO, the problem of the local defense of Western Europe is more manageable than any other. If it is equipped with its own nuclear deterrent, Western Europe can likewise deter a Soviet ground invasion by building its strength substantially above its present level. It has the skilled manpower and national cohesion to do so, and its economic strength is at an all-time peak. On the other hand, no solid regional deterrent on the ground seems feasible at this time in the Middle East. India and Pakistan could provide strong resistance to an invasion by ground forces, but Southeast Asia seems incapable, in the foreseeable future, of providing much more than a token defense through its own efforts.

In several crucial sectors where regional defenses are weak, the United States, with some support from its allies, will have to do more than it is now doing to raise the threshold of risk for Soviet-bloc aggression. This means setting up a kind of hedgehog system of forward mobile forces, able to move on very short notice to bolster any threatened point. The Philippines, for example, might be willing to shelter such a force for re-enforcing the defense of Southeast Asia, and to contribute to it. A major decision of this kind would, of course, involve a considerable shift in present allocations of military and economic aid and political support.

In effect, planning for a hedgehog strategy would involve cutting back defense investment in some areas and stepping it up decisively in others. To this extent it would place a greater political strain on our alliance system in Asia than the present somewhat blunderbuss system of allocating our resources. Yet, insofar as it demonstrated our serious preparation to raise the cost of local aggression to Communist China and its allies, it would also provide new and convincing evidence that our political interest in the survival of free Asian countries is being backed up by serious and concrete planning.

Of course, much of the planning has doubtless been done, and well done. What is uncertain at present is whether a sudden incursion from without, or an unexpected flare-up of internal subversion, can be dealt with resolutely in a matter of several days by forces that are not now battle-ready or which would have to be moved across the Pacific. Whatever specific programs may be most effective, it is, in any case, important to recognize that, as we move into the stage of bipolar deterrence of central war, the dangers of local and even camouflaged aggression are likely to increase.

Beyond Deterrence, What?

So far, this brief survey of the new challenges to American policy has dealt with the risks of mutual destruction and the problems of mutual deterrence. For better or for worse, the national ability to pursue more attractive and constructive purposes depends, first of all, on our being demonstrably prepared to defend ourselves, our allies, and, for that matter, all peoples not now a part of the communist bloc against the sudden or gradual extinction of their national independence and their identities. The problem, economically, is how to pay a large but equitable share of the defense of the noncommunist world. The problem, politically, is how to assure a broad base of shared purposes, backed by an agreed minimum of voluntarily shared policies. The problem, psychologically, is to define and advance a broad range of shared goals, which can be summed up, at the risk of stating a truism, as encouraging and assisting all free-world nations to advance their political, economic and cultural welfare to the maximum of their capacities.

One welcome alternative to this program, which demands strong nerves, wisdom, and continuing sacrifices, would, of course, be for the Soviet and Chinese communist leadership to abandon their ambition to reshape the entire world in their image, cease stirring up new tensions and conflicts, and agree to a genuinely inspected and controlled limitation of armaments. This would allow both parties to the struggle to devote a far greater share of their growing resources to economic competition, and it would allow people everywhere to judge for themselves which system can do more for the welfare of its own people. It would also imply a willingness on the part of the communist powers to open their own bloc to a free flow of ideas and a genuine competition of values. Certain hopes for an inevitable and early evolution of the Soviet system in this beneficent direction were widely held by Western statesmen after 1953, and especially after the summit conference of 1955; sometimes they even became an axiom of policy. The problem for the Soviet leadership was, to some extent, to hold out the possibility or prospect of this development, without actually allowing it to happen.

Whatever the long-range prospects of maintaining Bolshevik tension of will in Soviet society, Khrushchev has made it clear over and over that "relaxation of tensions" is, for him, an article of export. "Coexistence" of ideas is to be practiced abroad, in the free world; at home in the Soviet Union Khrushchev is determined to suppress "rotten bourgeois notions." Though his methods are milder than Stalin's, the determination is as strong.

The growing arrogance with which the Soviet leadership brandishes its missile-nuclear threats against nations near and far hardly indicates a willingness to follow a policy of "live-and-let-live." Khrushchev's travels and smiles seem designed to relax vigilance abroad rather than to help remove the real sources of tension in this dangerous period of world politics. Even in the somewhat marginal question of an inspected ban on nuclear testing, the Soviet leadership insists that all concessions of substance be made by the West. Otherwise, it is hard to understand why, after negotiating for almost two years over the various modalities for enforcing inspection, the Soviet government then flung at its negotiating partners the contemptuous offer of three inspections a year!

Since making a few genuine concessions in 1953-1955, the Soviet leadership—and even more its Chinese partner—have clearly sought to impose one-sided retreats, rather than arrange two-sided accommodations. In effect, Khrushchev says to those who resist his demands, "You must relax your nerves (and your wills) while I continue those acts and those threats that have caused the tension in the first place." Coexistence, in its present Soviet version, means that the non-communist world must respect the gains, however achieved, of the Soviet bloc and must refrain from strengthening its ability to resist present or future Soviet demands. It is to be "forced," as Khrushchev puts it, to accept far-reaching limitations on its armed strength without any effective means of knowing whether similar or equivalent limitations are actually being carried out within the Soviet sphere.

In the meantime, both the fears and the hopes of the noncommunist countries are being played upon by swiftly alternating changes in outward Soviet moods and tactics. This course of treatment is apparently designed to concentrate its opponents' responses upon each new crisis, meanwhile denying them the breathing spell which democratic societies need if they are to take stock of the changing situation and formulate and rally support around their own positive goals.

The basic purposes of American foreign policy are, of course, not merely to assure the survival, prosperity, and strength of the United States, but equally to assure to all nations of the world a similar opportunity to strengthen their security, their institutions, and their livelihood through decisions freely made, preferably in co-operation with their neighbors and friends in the noncommunist world. It wants also to reduce the danger of war and leave the way open for new generations of communist societies to adopt a genuinely relaxed attitude, one which connotes their acceptance of the indefinite survival and prosperity of noncommunist systems. Thus, American thinking rejects instinctively both the concept of the inevitability of a fateful and definitive clash and the possibility of resorting to a preventive war.

The real problem is to define the applications of this attitude and to outline the policies through which it can be made effective. Since the values which this attitude reflects are those of the greater part of mankind—just as the purposes spelled out in the Charter of the United Nations basically mirror American and democratic beliefs—the wide sharing of this attitude is in itself a fundamental asset of the free world as it seeks not only to survive (a dull but essential purpose!) but to grow in political, economic, and cultural strength.

The Decline of Bipolarity?

Under present conditions imposed by strategic technology, the opportunity for escaping or reversing the polarization of power would seem slight. Yet the same years that see the emergence of missilry may also witness, paradoxically, a decline of bipolarity. One line of escape from the confrontation between the two towering giants may, as briefly suggested above, be found in the development of several regional deterrents. Another line of relaxation may be marked out through the growing strength of international institutions and the interposition of their moral weight between the strongest contestants.

When one of the two greatest powers, even on slight pretext, threatens to rain destruction upon many other nations, the non-nuclear powers have an obvious and urgent interest in disarming this threat and averting a holocaust. If the two giants remain indefinitely locked in unending conflict, in which each new crisis seems more difficult to resolve, the other powers may be driven to take the initiative in finding some way to hold the bipolar struggle within the bounds of a common interest in survival. Perhaps the way to an effective limitation and inspection of armaments will, eventually, be found by powers other than the two, three or four strongest. The big question mark would then be whether those powers that do not possess missile-nuclear power will have the knowledge and the determination to define and enforce truly effective controls. In a question of this crucial nature it is tempting to seek the form rather than the substance of enforcement, or to tip the balance of compromise against those countries and governments which are more respectful of the hopes and good opinion of other peoples.

As the bipolar deadlock tends to become more and more a fixed feature of the international landscape, the urge has grown to interpose the fragile presence of the United Nations more boldly. As problems grow in range and intensity and cannot be solved either by agreements between the two greatest powers or by the measuring of their strength, too vast to be employed in any day-to-day struggle, the organized community of world opinion is coming to be viewed increasingly as the only available channel through which adjustments can be worked out short of a bipolar confrontation. Since 1956, instead of merely registering the degree of agreement that the great powers are able to reach, the United Nations has shown definite signs of developing powers which may enable it to slow down or turn aside crises and to devise positive solutions of its own.

As survival becomes too important to be left in the hands of the missile-nuclear powers alone, the "opinion of mankind," which has always seemed so nebulous and ineffective a concept, may assert itself as an effective "third force." If this trend continues and if it makes of the United Nations a political instrument of real strength, American purposes will be well served, and Soviet goals will not. For this reason, within the prudent safeguarding of its retaliatory power, the United States should do everything it can to help the international community grow in its ability to formulate and enforce its will.

For the same reasons American purposes would be served if a variety of defensive regional groupings should grow up under the umbrella of a nuclear stalemate. If Western Europe can be strengthened and unified to the point of pursuing its own aims even at some cost to direct American interests, this will still be, in the large, an advantage to the broader purposes of the United States. Provided they offer the basis for a more orderly movement by the peoples of Africa from a tribal existence to a modern society and for limiting the risks of outside interference in their affairs, the emergence of several federations or confederations in tropical Africa would, from a general as well as an American point of view, be preferable to a long period of internecine warfare, disunity, and outside intervention.

Economic, educational and cultural ambitions may provide a better cement of regional co-operation than direct political aims. US policy has hardly begun to develop the many channels through which the educational and social experience of the more advanced countries can be offered to the many newly independent peoples. Millions of people, equipped with thousands of new skills, are needed; and these same people will also provide the leadership of new nations. The opportunities to train farm experts, homemaking experts, technicians of many specialties, physicians, educators, administrators, have hardly been touched.

In this effort both bilateral and international programs have their place, and countries that have moved part way along the road of modernization are often better equipped than the most advanced ones to provide simple and sympathetic help to those that are taking the first steps. A vast educational, technical and cultural effort is needed. It cannot be postponed, as has often been suggested, until such time as an agreement on arms limitation has "freed" sufficient funds for this purpose. It is needed now, and it offers the most fruitful testing ground of "competitive coexistence."

In the absence of adequate programs of cultural and educational assistance, an excessive stress on economic and military assistance may well lead new nations away rather than toward the goals sought by their peoples. The overambitious building of steel mills and other large plants may intensify inherited social contradictions, or add new ones. Military programs have more than once overstrained the resources of the recipients, making the donor-nation a focus of resentments rather than a respected ally.

To achieve its broader purposes, American policy needs to visualize its individual programs and efforts, more than at present, as parts of a larger process of building or strengthening national and regional capabilities and self-confidence. This means planning economic and technical programs on a longer than year-to-year basis. It means giving a larger place, as in the new program of 1960 for Latin America, to basic social needs, such as housing and health. It means admitting more frankly than in the past that military and economic assistance do carry with them many political overtones. This wider responsibility has been recognized, perhaps belatedly, in US policy toward Latin America, with the shift since 1958 toward avoiding the embraces of dictators and by showing a special warmth for those regimes which are striving to strengthen the ability of their people to choose or check their own rulers. Fortunately, the image of America as a friend of freedom and a relatively unselfish partner has survived many turns and twists of policy. The political crises of 1960 in South Korea and Turkey showed, for example, that a basic confidence in American purposes can outlast the overthrow of oppressive and unpopular regimes.

The policies of successive US administrations have demonstrated the permanence of America's interest in and contributions to the development of many unindustrialized or underindustrialized nations. Perhaps it is no longer necessary at home to deny this sympathetic concern by a constant harping on the primacy of "military assistance" and on the argument of "mutual defense." As shown by the major US aid to India's development, American influence gains when the label of "mutual security" and "anticommunism" can be removed from what is, after all, an unprecedentedly generous and farsighted program for helping less developed countries in their advance into the modern world.

The growing recognition of the scientific and educational achievements of the Soviet Union has had the benefit of shocking other industrial nations into a realization that there is nothing automatic or preordained about their present advantages. They have discovered that a high level of technical and scientific achievement is possible under a system of political and ideological dictatorship. They have seen more clearly that the competition between freedom and dictatorship must be waged, not only on the level of strategy and politics, but through the scientific and educational opportunities that each can offer to the uncommitted one third of mankind which is seeking in its various ways to build modern societies.

Whether more aspiring scholars and technicians from Asia, Africa and Latin America should be invited to the United States and other advanced countries for further education, or whether much more should be done to help build strong systems of training in the home countries—these and many other specific questions of program and methods may now take on a new urgency with the establishment in Moscow of a pompously styled "University of the Friendship of the Peoples." The real challenge is to help aspiring nations achieve excellent standards in the light of our own best accomplishments, not to waste much time on wondering whether Soviet institutions and educators are doing a better or worse job.

Cultural and economic assistance to the ambitions of the underprivileged and largely uncommitted one third of mankind may influence their basic choices in profound ways. Naturally, we hope that their developing institutions and political habits will prove compatible, even if not identical, with the liberal traditions and aspirations of the West. It is easy, however, to forget how recent these democratic traditions are, even in the West, how many trials and errors are necessary before a society and its economy and its educational system are able to support both the demands for wider opportunities and the habits of tolerance and self-restraint that underlie the practice of freedom.

Remembering how few Americans, relatively, enjoyed the franchise in 1789, and how many Americans are still denied their full birthright of active citizenship and equal opportunity, we may learn to be more tolerant of nations where so much remains to be done in order to develop and sustain democratic institutions and practices. Among the often unheeded prerequisites are an efficient and impartial system of public order, equitable and prompt justice, an alert administration, responsive to new needs of its people, a fairly numerous, educated body of citizens, sufficiently assured in their livelihood and occupations to advise and criticize their government. To these must be added the absence of extremes of wealth and want, a workable balance between resources and livelihood, the presence of sufficiently widespread part-time leisure to allow the informed judgment of public issues, and access to a continuing flow of independent and diverse information. In the light of these many requirements, it is not surprising that many countries, old or new, fall short of the ideal they set themselves.

The important thing in the process of democratic institution-building is not whether a full-fledged state of democratic bliss has been or will soon be achieved. The crucial question is whether the choices that are made leave open the opportunity for further growth and new decisions, rather than forcing human aspirations into a rigid totalitarian pattern which, by definition, tells its people not only what to do but what to think, now and for the future.

The strength, and the weakness, of American policy, like that of democracy itself, lies in its open-endedness. Unlike communist dogmatism, which claims to offer a precise pattern to explain everything in the present and to predict the future, democracy assumes that no one can set a single goal forever and for all mankind. It expects its own and other peoples of today, and new generations of tomorrow, to define their own goals. That is the source of its great resilience.

The promise of the opportunity for people to think and decide and act for themselves nourishes the staying power of the democratic ideal and continuously re-enforces its power of attraction, even within the sphere of totalitarianism. It provides the resources of inventiveness and devotion by which democratic or democratically inclined countries can meet the multiple challenges of the new decade—the challenge of collective survival in the missile age, the challenge of organizing effective action through the community of nations, the challenge of helping newly independent peoples measure up to their new opportunities, the challenge of strengthening man's freedom to learn by trial and error. In taking its share in meeting these multiple challenges, the American people, which has been thrust, almost despite itself, into the forefront of a world-wide struggle for democratic self-fulfillment, faces grave dangers and greater opportunities to serve mankind.

GENERAL INDEX

D

E

H

I

Q

R

S

V

W

Y

Z

INDEX OF NAMES

L

M